The Complete Book of Who's Who in the Bible

THE COMPLETE BOOK OF

WHO'S WHO

IN THE BIBLE

PHILIP COMFORT
WALTER A. ELWELL

Tyndale House Publishers, Inc.
CAROL STREAM, ILLINOIS

Visit Tyndale's exciting Web site at www.tyndale.com.

The Complete Book of Who's Who in the Bible

Compiled by Jason Driesbach

Designed by Ron Kaufmann

The articles in this dictionary have been adapted from other works published by Tyndale House Publishers, including *The Tyndale Bible Dictionary* and *iLumna Gold* (a Bible software product).

Library of Congress Cataloging-in-Publication Data

Comfort, Philip Wesley.
   The complete book of who's who in the Bible / Philip Comfort, Walter A. Elwell.
     p. cm.
   Includes index.
   ISBN 978-0-8423-8369-1 (sc)
   1. Bible—Biography—Dictionaries. I. Elwell, Walter A. II. Title
   BS570.C643 2004
   220.9′2—dc22   2004020184

Printed in the United States of America

15   14   13   12   11   10   09
10   9   8   7   6   5   4

INTRODUCTION

Ever wondered how many names in the Bible start with "W"? You've come to the right place! (We'll give you a hint: the Hebrew and Greek alphabets don't contain any letters that English Bibles translate as "w.") Ever wondered how many people in the Bible were named Zechariah? Again, we can help. Here, in alphabetical order, we give you *The Complete Book of Who's Who in the Bible.*

This book is a comprehensive guide to all the proper names attributed to individual people in the Bible. As such it generally does not list entries for titles (such as "Centurion," "Son of God," or "Almighty") or nicknames (such as "Didymus"). The people listed here are historical human beings, with the entry "God" being the only instance of an entry for a non-human subject. Additionally, the size of this work did not permit us to include Deuterocanonical entries (such as "Cleopatra" or "Tobit") or entries pertaining to idols (such as "Baal" or "Asherah").

BIBLE VERSIONS AND ALTERNATE SPELLINGS
Although the New Living Translation was used as the base for the names listed here, this dictionary can be used with any of the major Bible translations, including King James Version, Revised Standard Version, New International Version, New American Standard Bible, New Jerusalem Bible, and Today's English Version. Names with alternate spellings (i.e. spellings not found in the NLT, many of which are found only in the King James Version) are listed in the Alternate Spellings appendix at the back of this book. There the reader will be referred to the relevant entry in the main text or given a brief explanation as to the absence of a relevant entry.

CROSS-REFERENCES
Two types of cross-references are utilized in this dictionary:

- **"See" references** point to one or more articles that contain information considered necessary for a complete understanding of the topic in question.
- **"See also" references** point to one or more articles that contain information considered interesting but not essential.

ABBREVIATIONS
Apocryphal Books

1 Esd	1 Esdras	Jdt	Judith
2 Esd	2 Esdras	1 Macc	1 Maccabees
Ecclus	Sirach (Ecclesiasticus)	2 Macc	2 Maccabees

Other Writings

Antiquities	Josephus, *Antiquities of the Jews*
Apion	Josephus, *Against Apion*
Eusebius	Eusebius, *Historia Ecclesiastica*
War	Josephus, *The Jewish War*

Books of the Bible

Gn	Genesis	Na	Nahum
Ex	Exodus	Hab	Habbakkuk
Lv	Leviticus	Zep	Zephaniah
Nm	Numbers	Hg	Haggai
Dt	Deuteronomy	Zec	Zechariah
Jos	Joshua	Mal	Malachi
Jgs	Judges	Mt	Matthew
Ru	Ruth	Mk	Mark
1 Sm	1 Samuel	Lk	Luke
2 Sm	2 Samuel	Jn	John
1 Kgs	1 Kings	Acts	Acts
2 Kgs	2 Kings	Rom	Romans
1 Chr	1 Chronicles	1 Cor	1 Corinthians
2 Chr	2 Chronicles	2 Cor	2 Corinthians
Ezr	Ezra	Gal	Galatians
Neh	Nehemiah	Eph	Ephesians
Est	Esther	Phil	Philippians
Jb	Job	Col	Colossians
Ps(s)	Psalms	1 Thes	1 Thessalonians
Prv	Proverbs	2 Thes	2 Thessalonians
Eccl	Ecclesiastes	1 Tm	1 Timothy
Song	Song of Songs	2 Tm	2 Timothy
Is	Isaiah	Ti	Titus
Jer	Jeremiah	Phlm	Philemon
Lam	Lamentations	Heb	Hebrews
Ez	Ezekiel	Jas	James
Dn	Daniel	1 Pt	1 Peter
Hos	Hosea	2 Pt	2 Peter
Jl	Joel	1 Jn	1 John
Am	Amos	2 Jn	2 John
Ob	Obadiah	3 Jn	3 John
Jon	Jonah	Jude	Jude
Mi	Micah	Rv	Revelation

Bible Versions

KJV	King James Version
NASB	New American Standard Bible
NEB	New English Bible
NIV	New International Version
NLT	New Living Translation
NRSV	New Revised Standard Version
RSV	Revised Standard Version
TLB	The Living Bible

Other Abbreviations

approx.	approximately
c.	circa—approximately
cf.	compare
ch, chs	chapter, chapters
d.	died
ed	edition, editions; editor, editors
e.g.,	for example,
et al.	and others
etc.	and so forth
ff.	following (verses, pages)
i.e.,	that is,
lit.	literal, literally
LXX	Septuagint
mg	a variant reading noted in the margin or footnote of a translation
MS, MSS	manuscript, manuscripts
Mt	Mountain, Mount
MT	Masoretic Text
NT	New Testament
OT	Old Testament
p, pp	page, pages
St	Saint
TR	Textus Receptus
v, vv	verse, verses
vid	Latin for "it appears [to read as such]"
vol, vols	volume, volumes
yr., yrs.	year, years

AUTHORSHIP OF ARTICLES

Many writers contributed to this volume, either by writing articles or editing and rewriting articles substantially. Because so many articles were worked on by so many different hands in the editorial process, it is impossible to assign authorship to each article. Furthermore, if we noted authorship for some articles while excluding others, our acknowledgments would be uneven and therefore unfair. Consequently, we have listed all of the contributors beginning on page ix.

We pray that this volume will help you, the reader, in your study of God's Word, and that such study will enrich your appreciation for the inspired Scriptures.

Philip Comfort, Ph.D.
Walter A. Elwell, Ph.D.

CONTRIBUTORS

GENERAL EDITORS
Philip Comfort
Walter A. Elwell

COORDINATING EDITOR
Jason Driesbach

PHOTOGRAPHY
Barry Beitzel

WRITERS

Wallace Alcorn
Robert L. Alden
L. C. Allen
Ronald Allen
James F. Babcock
Clarence B. Bass
Barry Beitzel
W. Wilson Benton, Jr.
Gilbert Bilezikian
E. M. Blaiklock
George Blankenbaker
Gerald L. Borchert
Manfred T. Brauch
Kenneth J. Bryer
H. Douglas Buckwalter
George E. Cannon
J. Knox Chamblin
Philip Comfort
Roger Douglass Congdon
Mark T. Coppenger
David Cornell
John Crandall
Robert D. Culver
Peter H. Davids
Bruce A. Demarest

Carl E. DeVries
Paul H. DeVries
James C. DeYoung
Raymond B. Dillard
J. D. Douglas
J. Driesbach
James D.G. Dunn
J. J. Edwards
John Elliott
Walter A. Elwell
H. K. Farrell
Paul F. Feiler
David A. Fields
Charles L. Feinberg
Harvey E. Finley
John Fischer
Francis Foulkes
Louis Goldberg
Wesley L. Gerig
Robert Guelich
D. L. Hall
J. Gordon Harris
R. K. Harrison
Ginnie Hearn
Walter Hearn

Paul Helm
Carl Wayne Hensley
Andrew E. Hill
Harold W. Hoehner
James M. Houston
E. Margaret Howe
F. B. Huey, Jr.
Philip Edgcumbe Hughes
David K. Huttar
Edgar C. James
Jakob Jocz
Paul Kaufman
Donald Kenney
William Nigel Kerr
Eugene F. Klug
George E. Ladd
William Lane
William Sanford LaSor
F. Duane Lindsey
Robert W. Lyon
W. Harold Mare
James L. Mason
Gerald L. Mattingly
Paul K. McAlister
Jim McClanahan

AARON

Moses' brother and Israel's first high priest. In the books of Exodus, Leviticus, and Numbers, Aaron was Moses' spokesman and assistant during the Israelites' Exodus from Egypt. Aaron was three years older than Moses and was 83 when they first confronted the pharaoh (Ex 7:7). Their sister, Miriam (Nm 26:59), must have been the eldest child, old enough to carry messages when the infant Moses was found by the pharaoh's daughter (Ex 2:1-9). Aaron's mother was Jochebed and his father was Amram, a descendant of the Kohath family of Levi's tribe (Ex 6:18-20).

Aaron and his wife, Elisheba, had four sons (Ex 6:23), who were to follsow him in the priesthood (Lv 1:5). Two of them, Nadab and Abihu, violated God's instructions by performing a sacrilegious act while burning incense and were burned to death as a result (Lv 10:1-5). The priesthood was then passed on through the other two sons, Eleazar and Ithamar, who also sometimes failed to carry out God's instructions precisely (10:6-20).

Aaron's prominence in the events of the Exodus arose partly from the fact that he was Moses' brother. When Moses tried to avoid becoming Israel's leader on the grounds of having a speech impediment, Aaron's ability as a speaker was recognized and used by God (Ex 4:10-16).

Events of Aaron's Life

The Hebrew people were slaves in Egypt at the beginning of Aaron's life. Raised as an Egyptian by one of the pharaoh's daughters, Moses had fled into the Midian Desert after killing a cruel Egyptian taskmaster (Ex 1–2). When God sent Moses back as a liberator (chs 3–4), he also sent Aaron out to meet Moses in the desert (4:27). Moses was a stranger to his people after so many years of exile, so Aaron made contact with Israel's elders for him (4:29-31). When Moses and Aaron went to see the pharaoh, God told the Egyptian monarch through the two of them to let the Israelites go (Ex 5:1). When the pharaoh made life even more miserable for the Hebrew slaves, God began to show his power to the Egyptian ruler through a series of miracles (chs 5–12). God performed the first three miracles through Aaron, using a rod (probably a shepherd's staff). The pharaoh had his palace sorcerers do similar tricks. After God brought a plague of gnats (KJV "lice") over all Egypt, the Egyptian magicians admitted defeat and said, "This is the finger of God!" (Ex 8:19, NLT). Then God brought on more plagues through Moses, culminating in the deaths of all the Egyptians' firstborn sons. Aaron was with Moses (12:1-28) when God revealed how he would "pass over" the properly marked homes of the Israelites, sparing their children on the night the Egyptian children died. That event was the origin of the Passover feast still observed by Jews today (13:1-16).

After God led the Israelites to safety and destroyed the pursuing Egyptians, Aaron participated with Moses in governing the people on their long wilderness journey to the Promised Land (Ex 16:1-6). Later, battling against Amalek's army, Aaron helped hold up Moses' weary arms in prayer to maintain God's blessing (17:8-16). Although always subordinate to Moses, Aaron seems to have been recognized as an important leader (18:12). God summoned him to be with Moses when God gave the law on Mt Sinai (19:24). Aaron

QUICKTAKE

AARON

STRENGTHS AND ACCOMPLISHMENTS
- First high priest of God in Israel
- Effective communicator; Moses' mouthpiece

WEAKNESSES AND MISTAKES
- Pliable personality; gave in to people's demands for a gold calf
- Joined with Moses in disobeying God's orders about the water-giving rock
- Joined sister Miriam in complaining against Moses

LESSONS FROM HIS LIFE
- God gives individuals special abilities, which he weaves together for his use
- The very skills that make a good team player sometimes also make a poor leader

VITAL STATISTICS
Where: Egypt, wilderness of Sinai
Occupations: Priest; Moses' second in command
Relatives: Brother: Moses. Sister: Miriam. Sons: Nadab, Abihu, Eleazar, and Ithamar

KEY VERSES
"Then the LORD became angry with Moses.'All right,' he said.'What about your brother, Aaron the Levite? I know he speaks well. And look! He is on his way to meet you now. He will be delighted to see you.... Aaron will be your spokesman to the people. He will be your mouthpiece, and you will stand in the place of God for him, telling him what to say'" (Exodus 4:14, 16).

Aaron's story is told in Exodus—Deuteronomy 10:6. He is also mentioned in Hebrews 7:11.

was among the representatives of the people who ratified God's statutes in the Book of the Covenant (24:1-8). Aaron went with those leaders partway up the holy mountain and saw the vision of the God of Israel (24:9-10). With Hur, he was left in charge when Moses was with God on the mountaintop (vv 13-14).

Moses was gone for over a month, and in a moment of weakness, Aaron gave in to the people's request for an idol to worship. He melted down their gold ornaments to make a golden image of a calf (Ex 32:1-4). (The Israelites had probably been influenced in Egypt by the cult of Apis, a fertility god in the form of a bull.) At first, Aaron seemed to think he might be doing something acceptable to God (v 5), but things got out of hand and a drunken sex orgy took place around the idol (v 6). God was angry enough to destroy the people, but Moses interceded, reminding God of his promise to multiply Abraham's descendants (Ex 32:7-14). Moses furiously confronted Aaron about the immorality and idolatry, which Aaron blamed on the people without admitting any guilt of his own (vv 21-24). Although the idolators were punished by death (Ex 32:25-28) and the whole camp by a plague (v 35), Aaron was evidently not punished. In a retelling of the events, Moses said that Aaron was in great danger but was spared because he had prayed for him (Dt 9:20).

In their second year of nomadic wilderness life, Aaron helped Moses carry out a census (Nm 1:1-3, 17-18). Eventually, Aaron may have become jealous of Moses' position of leadership, for Miriam and Aaron began to slander their brother, even though the elderly Moses was by then more humble than any man on earth (Nm 12:1-4). God's anger toward the two was averted by Moses' prayer, although Miriam did suffer for her sin (12:5-15). Aaron again seems to have escaped punishment entirely. With Moses, Aaron opposed a rebellion at Kadesh (14:1-5). He stood with Moses against a later revolt (ch 16). After a final incident at Meribah, where the Israelites almost revolted again, God accused Moses and Aaron of having failed to take him at his word and denied them entry into the Promised Land (20:1-12). Aaron died at the age of 123 on Mt Hor, after Moses had removed his elaborate priestly garments and put them on Aaron's son Eleazar (Nm 20:23-29; 33:38-39).

See also Levi.

DIGGING DEEPER

AARON THE PRIEST

Because it marked the beginning of the priesthood in Israel, the consecration of Aaron to his office was both instructive and solemn. Nothing was left to human ingenuity; all was precisely commanded by God. There were three ceremonies: washing, clothing, and anointing. When the Tabernacle was finished, Aaron and his sons were set apart to the priesthood by washing (to signify purification), clothing with official garments (for beauty and glory), and anointing with oil (to picture the need of empowering by the Spirit; cf. Ex 28; 40:12-15; Lv 8). Aaron thus became the first high priest, serving nearly 40 years. The character of his office was hereditary; this is attested to by his sons' wearing his garments when they succeeded to the office of high priest (Ex 29:29-30; Nm 20:25-28). Although all priests were anointed with oil, the anointing of Aaron and his successors was distinct from that of the ordinary priests (Ex 29:7; 40:12-15; Lv 8:12). Because the priesthood was inherited, all subsequent priests had to trace their ancestry back to Aaron (Ezr 7:1-5; Lk 1:5). Also, a sharp distinction was always drawn between the family of Aaron and the rest of the Levites (cf. Nm 3:5). Thus, the high priest was designated as the anointed priest in a special sense (Lv 4:3-4; 6:20-22; 21:10).

Because of Aaron's priestly role, the NT looks upon him as prefiguring the Messiah of Israel. Jesus Christ was appointed High Priest (Heb 3:1-2) in the same way God chose Aaron (Heb 5:1-5), but he was described as a greater high priest than Aaron (Heb 7:11-28).

●　●　●

ABAGTHA
One of the seven eunuchs commanded by King Ahasuerus to bring Queen Vashti to his drunken party (Est 1:10)

ABDA
1. Adoniram's father. Adoniram was superintendent of public works under King Solomon (1 Kgs 4:6).

2. Shammua's son, who was a Levite leader in Jerusalem after the Exile (Neh 11:17). The same father and son are elsewhere identified as Shemaiah and Obadiah (1 Chr 9:16).

ABDEEL
Shelemiah's father. Shelemiah was an officer sent by King Jehoiakim of Judah to arrest Jeremiah and Baruch after the king had read and burned their prophetic scroll (Jer 36:26).

ABDI
1. Member of the Merari clan of Levites. Abdi's grandson Ethan was a musician in David's time (1 Chr 6:44; 15:17).

2. Levite whose son Kish served in Hezekiah's time (2 Chr 29:12). This Abdi has sometimes been confused with Abdi #1.

3. Member of the Elam clan in Ezra's time. This Abdi is listed as one of the Israelites who married a foreign woman after the Exile (Ezr 10:26).

ABDIEL
Guni's son and father of Ahi (1 Chr 5:15). Ahi was a clan leader in Gad's tribe during the reigns of King Jotham of Judah and King Jeroboam II of Israel (1 Chr 5:15-17).

ABDON
1. Hillel's son who judged Israel for eight years (Jgs 12:13-15). Abdon was a very wealthy man, as indicated by reference to the 70 donkeys he owned.

2. Shashak's son from Benjamin's tribe who lived in Jerusalem (1 Chr 8:23, 28).

3. Jeiel's oldest son from Benjamin's tribe who lived in Gibeon. This Abdon is mentioned in Saul's genealogy (1 Chr 8:30; 9:36).
4. Micah's son (2 Chr 34:20), also called Acbor, son of Micaiah. *See* Acbor #2.

ABEDNEGO
One of Daniel's three friends who was sentenced to death by Nebuchadnezzar but was protected in the fiery furnace by an angel (Dn 1:7; 3:12-30). *See* Shadrach, Meshach, and Abednego; Daniel.

ABEL
Second male child of Adam and Eve (Gn 4:2). The name is probably related to Sumerian and Akkadian words meaning "son" and was thus used as a generic term for the human race.

Abel's older brother, Cain, was engaged in agriculture, but Abel himself was a shepherd. When both brothers brought offerings, God accepted Abel's animal sacrifice but rejected Cain's vegetable offering. As a result, Cain became jealous of Abel and killed him.

The narrative indicates that Abel's character was more worthy of God's blessing; hence his offering was accepted and Cain's was not (Gn 4:7). There is no scriptural evidence that cereal or vegetable offerings were less effective as either sin offerings or fellowship meals than offerings involving the shedding of blood, since in later Mosaic law both were prescribed. In the NT Abel is regarded as the first martyr (Mt 23:35; Lk 11:51; Heb 11:4).

ABI-ALBON
Alternate name of Abiel in 2 Samuel 23:31. *See* Abiel #2.

ABIASAPH
Kohathite Levite, a descendant of Korah, Elkanah's son and the father of Assir (1 Chr 6:23, 37; 9:19; Exodus 6:24). Alternate form of Ebiasaph.

ABIATHAR
One of two high priests during the reign of King David. The other high priest was Zadok, who evidently was appointed by David after his conquest of Jerusalem.

Only Abiathar escaped when the priestly families at Nob were massacred at the instigation of King Saul. The priests of Nob had given food and Goliath's sword to David during his escape from the wrath of Saul, thus earning Saul's hatred (1 Sm 21–22). When Abiathar joined David he brought the ephod, which David then used in determining the will of God (1 Sm 23:6, 9-11; 30:7-8). Abiathar was one of the first persons from Saul's administration to support David. His support was formidable because he represented the priesthood of the old tribal league of the line of Eli.

During the last days of David's kingship, his sons struggled for the throne. The two major rivals were Adonijah and Solomon. Abiathar the high priest supported Adonijah's claim to the throne, probably because Adonijah was David's oldest living heir and because David's general Joab, one of the strongest men in the kingdom, supported Adonijah (1 Kgs 1:5-7). Zadok supported Solomon, who actually succeeded David on the throne. Having fallen out of favor with the new king, Abiathar was banished to his estate in Anathoth (1 Kgs 2:26-27), a village about four miles (6.4 kilometers) northeast of Jerusalem.

The relationship of Abiathar to Ahimelech is confusing. Ahimelech could have been the name of both Abiathar's father (1 Sm 22:20; 23:6) and son (2 Sm 8:17; 1 Chr 18:16; 24:6). If each of the references was to the same Ahimelech, then the names were reversed in the later passages. In the NT, Abiathar is mentioned as the high priest when David came to Nob needing food and weapons (Mk 2:26). The OT account says that Ahimelech was the priest at that time (1 Sm 21:1-2). The apparent discrepancy may have resulted from a copyist's error or from the fact that Abiathar as high priest was more prominent than Ahimelech.

ABIDA

One of Midian's sons. Midian was Abraham's son by his concubine Keturah (Gn 25:2, 4; 1 Chr 1:33).

ABIDAN

Gideoni's son and leader of Benjamin's tribe when the Israelites were wandering in the Sinai wilderness after their escape from Egypt (Nm 1:11; 2:22). As leader, he presented his tribe's offering at the consecration of the Tabernacle (Nm 7:60-65).

ABIEL

1. Father of Kish and Ner and grandfather of King Saul, according to 1 Samuel 9:1 and 14:51. Other genealogies in 1 Chronicles list Ner, instead of Abiel, as Kish's father and Saul's grandfather (1 Chr 8:33; 9:39). This confusion is due either to a copyist's error or to the possibility that Saul had two relatives named Ner, a great-grandfather and an uncle.

2. Warrior among David's mighty men who were known as "the thirty" (1 Chr 11:32), also called Abi-albon the Arbathite (2 Sm 23:31).

ABIEZER

1. Descendant of Manasseh (Jos 17:1-2). Although Abiezer's father is not named, Abiezer is listed with the descendants of his mother's brother, Gilead (1 Chr 7:18). In Numbers 26:30, Abiezer's name is shortened to Iezer (KJV "Jeezer"), and the family is called Iezerites (KJV "Jeezerites"). Abiezer's family, to which Gideon belonged, was the first clan to respond to Gideon's call to fight the Midianites (Jgs 6:34). Abiezer's descendants were referred to as Abiezrites (Jgs 6:11, 24, 34; 8:32).

2. Member of Benjamin's tribe from Anathoth and warrior among David's mighty men, known as "the thirty" (2 Sm 23:27; 1 Chr 11:28). This Abiezer was commander of the ninth division of the army in the rotation system established by David (1 Chr 27:12).

ABIGAIL

1. Nabal's wife, who later became the wife of David (1 Sm 25:2-42). Nabal was a wealthy sheep owner whose holdings had been protected by David's men. When David requested provisions in return for that protection, Nabal refused. Enraged, David set out with 400 armed men to destroy Nabal and his house. Abigail had been informed of her husband's behavior and met David with many provisions, taking the blame for her foolish husband. David thanked God for using Abigail to restrain his anger.

   When Nabal woke from a drunken stupor the next morning and learned what had happened, he had a stroke from which he died 10 days later. Abigail then married David and shared his adventurous life among the Philistines (1 Sm 27:3). She was captured by the Amalekites and rescued by David (1 Sm 30:1-19). Abigail went with David to Hebron when he became king of Judah (2 Sm 2:2), and she bore his second son, Chileab (2 Sm 3:3), also called Daniel (1 Chr 3:1).

2. David's sister, who married Jether and gave birth to Amasa (1 Chr 2:16-17). There appears to be confusion as to the ancestry of this Abigail. In 1 Chronicles 2:13-17 she is listed as a daughter of Jesse. However, in 2 Samuel 17:25, her father is identified as Nahash. The discrepancy could be due to scribal error, or Nahash may be another name for Jesse, or the widow of Nahash could have married Jesse.

ABIHAIL

Name used for both men and women in the OT.

1. Zuriel's father and a leader of the Merari family of Levites in Israel's wilderness community (Nm 3:35).

2. Abishur's wife, and mother of Ahban and Molid (1 Chr 2:29).

3. Huri's son, a descendant of Gad, living in Gilead and Bashan (1 Chr 5:14).

4. Woman named in 2 Chronicles 11:18 whose relationship to King Rehoboam is not clear from the Hebrew text. In some translations, Abihail seems to be the second wife of Rehoboam. However, only one wife is mentioned at first, so Abihail was probably the mother of Rehoboam's first wife, Mahalath. This Abihail was thus a daughter of Eliab, David's eldest brother. She married her cousin Jerimoth, one of David's sons.

5. Esther's father, and uncle of Mordecai (Est 2:15; 9:29).

ABIHU

Second son of Aaron and Elisheba (Ex 6:23; Nm 26:60; 1 Chr 6:3). Abihu and his brother Nadab joined Moses, Aaron, and the 70 elders of Israel in worshiping the glory of God on Mt Sinai (Ex 24:1-11). The four sons of Aaron were made priests along with their father (Ex 28:1), but later Abihu and Nadab were burned to death for offering "the wrong kind of fire" before the Lord (Lv 10:1, NLT; see also Nm 3:2-4; 26:61; 1 Chr 24:1-2).

ABIHUD

One of Bela's nine sons (1 Chr 8:3). Abihud should not be confused with the Abiud of Matthew's genealogy of Christ in the NT.

ABIJAH

1. Samuel's second son who, with his older brother, Joel, was a corrupt judge in Beersheba. Because of the corruption, Israel's leaders demanded to be ruled instead by a king (1 Sm 8:2; 1 Chr 6:28).

2. Son of Jeroboam I of the northern kingdom of Israel. The boy's illness impelled his family to seek guidance from the prophet Ahijah at Shiloh (1 Kgs 14:1-2).

3. Alternate name for Abijam, king of Judah, in 2 Chronicles 12:16–14:1 and Matthew 1:7. *See* Abijam.

4. Ahaz's wife, and mother of King Hezekiah (2 Kgs 18:2, short form "Abi"; 2 Chr 29:1). This Abijah was Zechariah's daughter.

5. Becher's son from Benjamin's tribe (1 Chr 7:8).

6. Levite who headed the eighth of 24 priestly divisions established in David's time (1 Chr 24:10; Lk 1:5).

7. Head of a priestly family who signed Ezra's covenant of faithfulness to God with Nehemiah and others after the Exile (Neh 10:7).

8. Head of a priestly family who returned to Jerusalem with Zerubbabel after the Exile (Neh 12:4). Perhaps of the same family as #7.

ABIJAM

Rehoboam's son and successor as king of Judah, 913–910 BC (1 Chr 3:10; alternately called "Abijah" in 2 Chr 11:18-22; 12:16; 13:1-22; 14:1). A major focus of Abijam's reign was his war with King Jeroboam I of Israel (2 Chr 13:1-3). Before a decisive battle, Abijam stood on Mt Zemaraim and shouted condemnation of Jeroboam's political divisiveness and religious idolatry (2 Chr 13:4-12). Abijam and his army then prayed for God's help in their precarious military position. Against two-to-one odds, they fought their way out of an ambush and won a stunning victory over Jeroboam (2 Chr 13:13-19). Abijam's reign in the southern kingdom of Judah was summed up rather unfavorably in 1 Kings 15:1-8: "He committed the same sins as his father before him, and he was not faithful to the LORD his God, as the heart of his ancestor David had been" (v 3, NLT). But God had promised to keep David's descendants on the throne in Jerusalem (1 Kgs 11:36), so Abijam's son Asa succeeded him. Being of David's line, Abijam was an ancestor of Jesus, the Christ (Mt 1:7, "Abijah").

ABIMAEL

One of the many sons or descendants of Joktan, and thus a descendant of Shem (Gn 10:28; 1 Chr 1:22).

ABIMELECH

Royal title for Philistine rulers, similar to the designation "pharaoh" among the Egyptians and "agag" among the Amalekites.

1. King of Gerar in Abraham's time. At Gerar, a city a few miles south of Gaza, Abraham presented his wife as his sister out of fear for his life (Gn 20:1-18), as he had once done in Egypt (Gn 12:10-20). Because of this, Sarah was taken into Abimelech's harem. But Abimelech was warned by God in a dream not to come near her on pain of death because she was a married woman, so she was restored to her husband. The same Abimelech and Abraham later entered into a treaty to clarify water rights in the Negev Desert at Beersheba (Gn 21:22-34).

2. King of Gerar in Isaac's time. Isaac, too, passed off his wife, Rebekah, as his sister at Gerar. Abimelech, perhaps remembering the near judgment on his predecessor, acted decisively to protect Rebekah's integrity. He proclaimed a death penalty on any who touched her or her husband (Gn 26:1-11). Abimelech asked Isaac to leave Philistine territory because of overcrowding and continuing dispute over water (Gn 26:12-22). Eventually, at Beersheba, Isaac and Abimelech ended their hostility by renewing the treaty made by Abraham and the earlier Abimelech (Gn 26:26-33).

3. Gideon's son by a concubine in Shechem (Jgs 8:31). After his father's death, Abimelech conspired with his mother's family to assassinate his 70 half brothers. Only one of them, Jotham, escaped (Jgs 9:1-5). In Abimelech's third year of rule, he cruelly suppressed a rebellion (Jgs 9:22-49). Eventually his skull was crushed by a millstone thrown down by a woman on a tower. Abimelech ordered his armor bearer to kill him with a sword so that no one could say he had been killed by a woman (Jgs 9:53-57).

4. Achish, king of the Philistine city of Gath (Ps 34:title; 1 Sm 21:10-15).

5. Abiathar's son, a priest associated with Zadok in David's time (1 Chr 18:16).

ABINADAB

1. Resident of Kiriath-jearim to whose home the Ark of God was brought on its return by the Philistines (1 Sm 6:21–7:2).

2. Jesse's second son, and brother of David (1 Sm 16:8; 17:13; 1 Chr 2:13). This Abinadab served in Saul's army for part of the Philistine war.

3. One of Saul's sons (1 Chr 8:33; 10:2).

4. KJV form of Ben-abinadab, one of King Solomon's administrative officers in 1 Kings 4:11. See Ben-abinadab.

ABINOAM

Barak's father. Barak was the companion of Deborah, an Israelite judge, in the war against the Canaanites (Jgs 4:6, 12; 5:1, 12).

ABIRAM

1. One of Eliab's two sons. Abiram and his brother Dathan joined in an uprising against Moses and Aaron. At Moses' word, the ground split open beneath the two rebellious brothers and everything associated with them was swallowed up in a massive earthquake (Nm 16:1-33).

2. Hiel's oldest son, who died prematurely when his father presumptuously rebuilt Jericho (1 Kgs 16:34). Joshua's prophetic curse was thereby fulfilled (Jos 6:26).

ABISHAG

Beautiful young woman from Shunem who was appointed to care for David during his last days (1 Kgs 1:1-4). After David's death, Adonijah asked permission from his half brother King Solomon to marry Abishag. In the ancient Near East, to claim the concubine of a deceased king was to claim the throne. Enraged, Solomon ordered Adonijah to be killed (1 Kgs 2:13-25).

ABISHAI

David's nephew, son of Zeruiah (by an unnamed father) and brother of Joab and Asahel (1 Chr 2:16). Abishai volunteered to accompany David to Saul's camp one night and would have killed the sleeping Saul if David had not restrained him (1 Sm 26:6-12). He also helped Joab kill Abner, Saul's general, in revenge for the death of another brother (2 Sm 3:30). Later Abishai won a victory over the Edomites (1 Chr 18:12-13) and was second in command in a decisive battle against the Ammonites (1 Chr 19:10-15). Often vengeful and cruel, Abishai wanted to behead the spiteful Shimei during Absalom's rebellion, but again David intervened (2 Sm 16:5-12; 19:21-23). When King David fled beyond the Jordan, Abishai was given command of one of David's three divisions that crushed the rebellion (2 Sm 18:1-15).

In a later battle with the Philistines, Abishai saved David's life by killing the giant Ishbi-benob (2 Sm 21:15-17). He ranked among David's bravest warriors (2 Sm 23:18-19; 1 Chr 11:20-21).

ABISHUA

1. Aaron's great-grandson, son of Phinehas and ancestor of Ezra (1 Chr 6:4-5, 50; Ezr 7:5). Abishua's name also appears in the apocryphal genealogy of Ezra (1 Esd 8:2; 2 Esd 1:2).

2. Bela's son, and grandson of Benjamin (1 Chr 8:4).

ABISHUR

Shammai's son and the father of Ahban and Molid from Judah's tribe. Abishur's wife was Abihail (1 Chr 2:28-29).

ABITAL

Mother of King David's fifth son, Shephatiah (2 Sm 3:4; 1 Chr 3:3).

ABITUB

Son of Shaharaim and Hushim from Benjamin's tribe (1 Chr 8:11).

ABIUD

Individual listed in Matthew's genealogy of Christ in the NT as Eliakim's father (Mt 1:13).

ABNER

Ner's son and Saul's cousin. Abner was commander of Saul's army (1 Sm 14:50; 17:55). Highly respected by Saul, he even ate at the king's table together with David and Jonathan (1 Sm 20:25).

Five years after Saul's death, Abner made Ishbosheth, Saul's son, king over Israel (2 Sm 2:8-9). War between Ishbosheth and David, who then was king over Judah, lasted for two years. Abner was in command of Ish-bosheth's army, Joab of David's, in a series of skirmishes. David's position was generally stronger, but Abner became a powerful figure among Saul's followers.

Although only the king had a right to sexual relationships with the previous king's concubines, Abner slept with Saul's concubine Rizpah, perhaps planning to take over the kingdom himself at the first opportunity. When Ishbosheth rebuked him, Abner became so angry that he broke with Ishbosheth and came to terms with David. David showed him great respect, and in return, Abner promised to bring the whole of Israel over to David. Joab, however, feared Abner's influence with the king and killed him, claiming revenge for the death of his brother at Abner's hand in battle. Abner was honored with a public funeral and mourning, an honor given only to a ruler or great leader. King David wept aloud at the tomb, and even the people wept with him (2 Sm 3:7-34). David condemned Joab for murdering Abner.

See also David.

ABRAHAM

One of the Bible's most significant personalities, whom God called from the city of Ur to become patriarch of God's own people.

Abraham's name was originally Abram, meaning "[the] father is exalted." When he was given that name by his parents, they were probably participants in the moon cult of Ur, so the father deity suggested in his old name could have been the moon god or another pagan deity. God changed Abram's name to Abraham (Gn 17:5), partly, no doubt, to indicate a clear-cut separation from pagan roots. The new name, interpreted by the biblical text as meaning "father of a multitude," was also a statement of God's promise to Abraham that he would have many descendants, as well as a significant test of his faith in God—since he was 99 years old at the time and his childless wife was 90 (Gn 11:30; 17:1-4, 17).

Abraham's Life

The story of Abram begins in Genesis 11, where his family relationships are recorded (Gn 11:26-32). Terah, Abram's father, was named after the moon deity worshiped at Ur. Terah had three sons, Abram, Nahor, and Haran. Haran, the father of Lot, died before the

QUICKTAKE

ABRAHAM

STRENGTHS AND ACCOMPLISHMENTS
- His faith pleased God
- Became the founder of the Jewish nation
- Was respected by others and was courageous in defending his family at any cost
- Was not only a caring father to his own family, but practiced hospitality to others
- Was a successful and wealthy rancher
- Usually avoided conflicts, but when they were unavoidable, he allowed his opponent to set the rules for settling the dispute

WEAKNESS AND MISTAKE
- Under direct pressure, he distorted the truth

LESSONS FROM HIS LIFE
- God desires dependence, trust, and faith in him—not faith in our ability to please him
- God's plan from the beginning has been to make himself known to all people

VITAL STATISTICS
Where: Born in Ur of the Chaldeans; spent most of his life in the land of Canaan
Occupation: Wealthy livestock owner
Relatives: Brothers: Nahor and Haran. Father: Terah. Wife: Sarah. Nephew: Lot.
   Sons: Ishmael and Isaac
Contemporaries: Abimelech, Melchizedek

KEY VERSE
"And Abram believed the LORD, and the LORD counted him as righteous because of his faith" (Genesis 15:6).

Abraham's story is told in Genesis 11–25. He is also mentioned in Exodus 2:24; Matthew 1:1, 2; Luke 3:34; Acts 7:2-8; Romans 4; Galatians 3; Hebrews 2; 6–7; 11.

family left Ur. Terah took Lot, Abram, and Abram's wife, Sarai, from Ur to go to Canaan but settled at the city of Haran (v 31). It is stated in Acts 7:2-4 that Abraham heard the call of God to leave for a new land while he was still in Ur.

A note of major importance to the course of Abram's life is found in Genesis 11:30: "Sarai was unable to become pregnant and had no children" (NLT). The problem of Sarai's barrenness provided the basis for great crises of faith, promise, and fulfillment in the lives of Abram and Sarai.

After Terah's death, God told Abram, "Leave your native country, your relatives, and your father's family, and go to the land that I will show you." This command was the basis of a "covenant" in which God promised to make Abram the founder of a new nation in that new land (Gn 12:1-3, NLT). Abram, trusting God's promise, left Haran at the age of 74. Entering Canaan, he went first to Shechem, an important Canaanite royal city between Mt Gerizim and Mt Ebal. Near the oak of Moreh, a Canaanite shrine, God appeared to him (12:7). Abram built an altar at Shechem, then moved to the vicinity of Bethel and again built an altar to the Lord (12:8).

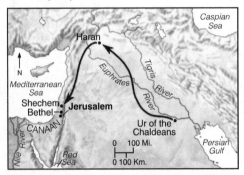

Abram's Journey to Canaan: Abram, Sarai, and Lot traveled from Ur of the Chaldeans to Canaan by way of Haran.

The expression "to call on the name of the LORD" (RSV) means more than just to pray. Rather, Abram made a proclamation, declaring the reality of God to the Canaanites in their centers of false worship. Later Abram moved to Hebron by the oaks of Mamre, where again he built an altar to worship God. Another blessing given in a vision (15:1) led Abram to exclaim that he was still childless and that Eliezer of Damascus was his heir (15:2). Discovery of the Nuzi documents has helped to clarify that otherwise obscure statement. According to Hurrian custom, a childless couple of station and substance would adopt an heir. Often a slave, the heir would be responsible for the burial and mourning of his adoptive parents. If a son should be born after the adoption of a slave-heir, the natural

DIGGING DEEPER

ABRAHAM, THE FRIEND OF GOD

Referred to as the "friend of God" (2 Chr 20:7; Jas 2:23, NLT), Abraham played an important role in Hebrew history. Through Abraham's life, God revealed a program of "election" and "covenant," which culminated in the work of Jesus Christ. God said to Abraham, "All the families of the earth will be blessed through you" (Gn 12:3, NLT). Centuries later, the apostle Paul explained that the full import of God's promise was seen in the preaching of the gospel to all nations and the response of faith in Christ, which signifies believers from all families of the earth as sons of Abraham (Gal 3:6-9).

● ● ●

son would of course supplant him. Thus God's response to Abram's question is directly to the point: "No, your servant will not be your heir, for you will have a son of your own who will be your heir" (Gn 15:4, NLT). God then made a covenant with Abram insuring an heir, a nation, and the land. Abram was 86 years old when Ishmael was born. When Abram was 99, the Lord appeared to the aged patriarch and again reaffirmed his covenant promise of a son and blessing (Gn 17). Circumcision was added as the seal of covenantal relationship (17:9-14), and at that point the names Abram and Sarai were changed to Abraham and Sarah (17:5, 15). Abraham's response to the promise of another son was to laugh: "Then Abraham bowed down to the ground, but he laughed to himself in disbelief. 'How could I become a father at the age of 100?' he thought. 'And how can Sarah have a baby when she is ninety years old?'" (Gn 17:17, NLT).

Genesis 18 and 19 recount the total destruction of two cities of the Jordan plain, Sodom and Gomorrah. Chapter 18 begins with three individuals seeking comfort in the heat of the day. Abraham offered refreshment and a meal to his guests. They turned out to be no ordinary travelers, however, but the Angel of the Lord along with two other angels (18:1-2; 19:1). There is reason to believe that the Angel of the Lord was God himself (18:17, 33). Another announcement of a promised son made Sarah laugh in unbelief and then deny having laughed (18:12-15).

Genesis 21 to 23 form the climax of the story of Abraham. At long last, when Abraham was 100 years old and his wife 90, "the LORD kept his word and did for Sarah exactly what he had promised" (Gn 21:1, NLT). The joy of the aged couple on the birth of their long-promised son could not be contained. Both Abraham and Sarah had laughed in unbelief in the days of promise; now they laughed in joy as God had "the last laugh." The baby, born at the time God promised, was named Isaac ("he laughs!"). Sarah said, "God has brought me laughter! All who hear about this will laugh with me" (Gn 21:6, NLT).

The laughter over Isaac's birth subsided entirely in the test of Abraham's faith described in chapter 22, God's command to sacrifice Isaac. Only when one has experienced vicariously with Abraham the long 25 years of God's

ABRAHAM
The Times of Abraham and Sarah

C. 2166 BC
Abraham (originally named Abram) is born in Ur (Genesis 11:26).

C. 2157 BC
Sarah (originally named Sarai) is born.

C. 2120 BC?
Abraham moves with his father Terah, wife Sarah, and nephew Lot to Haran (Genesis 11:31).

C. 2091 BC
God calls Abraham move to Canaan (Genesis 12:1-6).

C. 2083 BC
God makes a covenant with Abraham, promising him the land of Canaan and many descendants (Genesis 15:1-21).

C. 2081 BC
Childless, Sarah gives her servant Hagar to Abraham to produce an heir. The following year, Ishmael is born to Hagar (Genesis 16).

C. 2067 BC
Sodom, where Lot lives, is destroyed by God, despite Abraham's appeals (Genesis 18–19).

C. 2066 BC
Isaac is miraculously born to Abraham and Sarah (Genesis 21:2-3).

C. 2064 BC?
Hagar and Ishmael are sent away by a jealous Sarah, but God protects them (Genesis 21:9-20).

C. 2054 BC?
At God's command, Abraham nearly sacrifices Isaac (Genesis 22).

C. 2030 BC
Sarah dies (Genesis 23:1-2).

C. 1991 BC
Abraham dies (Genesis 25:7-8).

DIGGING DEEPER

ABRAHAM'S BOSOM

This figure of speech probably derived from the Roman custom of reclining on one's left side at meals with the guest of honor at the bosom of his host (cf. Jn 13:23-25). It was used by Jesus in the story of Lazarus as a description of paradise (Lk 16:22-23). In rabbinical writings, as well as 4 Maccabees 13:17, righteous people were thought to be welcomed at death by Abraham, Isaac, and Jacob. Jesus, probably aware of this, was also alluding to the "messianic banquet," an image he used a number of times. Thus, in the world to come, the godly poor like Lazarus would not only be welcomed by Abraham but would occupy the place of honor next to him at the banquet.

● ● ●

promise of a son can one imagine the trauma of such a supreme test. Just as the knife was about to fall, and only then, did the angel of God break the silence of heaven with the call, "Abraham!" (22:11). The name of promise, "father of a multitude," took on its most significant meaning when Abraham's son was spared and the test was explained: "I know that you truly fear God. You have not withheld from me even your son, your only son" (Gn 22:12, NLT).

Those words were coupled with a promise implicit in the discovery of a ram caught in the thicket. The Lord provided an alternative sacrifice, a substitute. The place was named "the Lord will provide." Christian believers generally see the whole episode as looking ahead to God's provision of his only Son, Jesus Christ, as a sacrifice for the sins of the world.

See also Sarah #1.

ABRAM

Original name of Abraham (Gn 11:26). *See* Abraham.

ABSALOM

Son of King David and his wife Maacah (2 Sm 3:3). The name is also spelled Abishalom (1 Kgs 15:2, 10). Absalom was a handsome young prince who was noted for his long, full hair (2 Sm 14:25-26). He had a beautiful sister, Tamar, who was raped by their half brother Amnon. After dishonoring Tamar, Amnon refused to marry her (2 Sm 13:1-20).

Absalom took his dejected sister into his own house, expecting his father, David, to punish Amnon for his incestuous act. After two years of suppressed rage and hatred, Absalom plotted his own revenge. He gave a feast for King David and his princes at his country estate.

Although David did not attend, Amnon did and was murdered by Absalom's servants after Absalom got him drunk. Then, afraid of King David's anger, Absalom fled across the Jordan River to King Talmai of Geshur, his mother's father (2 Sm 13:21-39).

After three years in exile, Absalom was called back to Jerusalem through the efforts of David's general, Joab, and a wise woman from Tekoa. After two years he was back in full favor with the king (2 Sm 14), and in that position he began to maneuver himself to gain the throne. He put on an impressive public relations campaign, in the process undermining confidence in his father, the king (2 Sm 15:1-6).

Eventually, Absalom plotted a rebellion against David, gathering supporters in Hebron from all over Israel. After Ahithophel, one of David's wisest counselors, joined Absalom, the prince announced his own kingship. By the time news of Absalom's conspiracy reached him, David was unable to do anything but flee from Jerusalem (2 Sm 15; Ps 3).

Absalom arrived in Jerusalem without a struggle, and Ahithophel asked permission to attack David immediately with 12,000 troops. But Hushai, David's secret agent in Absalom's court, advised Absalom instead to take the time to mobilize the entire nation against David. He also used flattery, suggesting that Absalom himself should lead the attack. Absalom preferred Hushai's advice, and Ahithophel out of desperation committed suicide. Meanwhile, Hushai sent word of Absalom's plans to David by two priests, Zadok and Abiathar. With this information, David crossed the Jordan and camped at Mahanaim (2 Sm 16–17).

Absalom led his forces across the Jordan to do battle in the forest of Ephraim. David's loyal forces were under the able generalship of Joab, Abishai, and Ittai the Gittite, who routed Absalom's forces. Absalom himself fled on a mule, but his long hair got caught in the branches of an oak tree, and he was left dangling helplessly. Joab, leading his men in pursuit, came upon Absalom and killed him. Joab's men threw the body in a pit and piled stones on it (2 Sm 18:1-18). Absalom's death stunned David, who had given explicit orders to keep Absalom from harm. David moaned: "O my son Absalom! My son, my son Absalom! If only I had died instead of you! O Absalom, my son, my son" (2 Sm 18:33, NLT). In his excessive grief, David took no notice that a serious rebellion had been crushed until Joab reminded him that David's followers had risked their lives for him (2 Sm 19:1-8). *See* David.

ACBOR

1. Father of the Edomite king Baal-hanan before the establishment of Israel's monarchy (Gn 36:38-39; 1 Chr 1:49).

2. Micaiah's son, courtier of King Josiah of the southern kingdom of Judah. Josiah sent Acbor in a delegation to ask Huldah the prophetess about the newly found Book of the Law (2 Kgs 22:12-14). Acbor was also referred to as Abdon, son of Micah (2 Chr 34:20). He was the father of Elnathan (Jer 26:22; 36:12).

ACHAICUS

Early Christian convert in Corinth. Achaicus, Stephanas, and Fortunatus were visiting Paul in Ephesus when he wrote 1 Corinthians (1 Cor 16:17). It was probably Achaicus and his companions who brought Paul a letter from the Corinthian church (1 Cor 7:1) and returned with Paul's reply.

ACHAN

Member of Judah's tribe who kept some of the spoils from the Israelite victory at Jericho in violation of Joshua's order and God's command (Jos 6:1–7:1). A subsequent Israelite defeat at Ai, a weaker city than Jericho, revealed God's anger to Joshua. With God's help, Joshua determined which of the Israelites had been guilty of disobedience. Achan confessed that he had buried a robe and some gold and silver from Jericho in his tent (Jos 7:20-22). The recovered loot was taken to the valley of Achor (meaning "trouble," "calamity"), where Achan and his family were stoned. In the Hebrew text, 1 Chronicles 2:7 gives Achan's name as Achar ("disaster") because he "brought disaster on Israel by taking plunder that had been set apart for the LORD" (NLT).

ACHISH

King of the Philistine city of Gath. Although David had killed Goliath, Gath's champion (1 Sm 17), David later fled from Saul to Achish's court. Realizing his mistake, David pretended to be crazy in order to preserve his life. His feigned madness caused Achish to throw him out (1 Sm 21:10-15), but later when David came back to Gath with a band of 600 guerrilla fighters, Achish gave him the city of Ziklag as a base of operations (1 Sm 27:1-7). Achish thought David's men were raiding the Israelites, not realizing they were actually wiping out Philistine towns (1 Sm 27:8-12).

ACSAH

Caleb's daughter (1 Chr 2:49). Othniel, Caleb's nephew, accepted his uncle's challenge to capture Kiriath-sepher in order to marry Acsah. She persuaded Othniel to ask her father, Caleb, for a field, and she herself asked Caleb for two springs of water, a necessity for life in the desert (Jos 15:16-19; Jgs 1:12-15).

ADAH

1. One of Lamech's two wives, and mother of two sons, Jabal and Jubal (Gn 4:19-21, 23).

2. Esau's first wife, daughter of Elon the Hittite and mother of Eliphaz (Gn 36:2-16).

ADAIAH

1. Josiah's maternal grandfather. Josiah's mother, Jedidah, was Adaiah's daughter (2 Kgs 22:1).

2. Ethan's son, a Levite of the Gershon clan and an ancestor of Asaph the psalmist (1 Chr 6:41). He is sometimes identified with the Iddo of 1 Chronicles 6:21. *See* Iddo #2.

3. Shimei's son, a minor member of Benjamin's tribe (1 Chr 8:21).

4. Jeroham's son, a priest who returned to Jerusalem after the Exile (1 Chr 9:12; Neh 11:12).
5. Maaseiah's father. Maaseiah was a captain under Jehoiada the priest (2 Chr 23:1).
6. Bani's son, who obeyed Ezra's exhortation to divorce his pagan wife after the Exile (Ezr 10:29).
7. Son of a different Bani, who also obeyed that exhortation (Ezr 10:39).
8. Joiarib's son, descended from Perez, and an ancestor of Maaseiah (Neh 11:5).

ADALIA

Fifth of Haman's ten sons, all of whom were killed with their father when his plot to destroy the Jews was foiled (Est 9:8).

ADAM

First man and father of the human race. Adam's role in biblical history is important not only in OT considerations but also in understanding the meaning of salvation and the person and work of Jesus Christ.

The creation of Adam and the first woman, Eve, is recited in two accounts in the book of Genesis (1:26-31 and 2:4–3:24). Adam and Eve were created in God's image and entrusted with the care of a garden in Eden. From the beginning they enjoyed perfection in the world and in their relationship with God. Their story does not end on such a positive note, however. It moves on to record the great deception Satan played upon Eve through the serpent. By clever insinuations and distortion of God's original commandment (cf. 3:1 with 2:16-17), the serpent tricked Eve into eating the forbidden fruit and sharing it with Adam. Eve seems to have eaten because she was deceived (1 Tm 2:14), Adam out of a willful and conscious rebellion. Ironically, the two beings originally created in God's image and likeness believed that they could become "like" God by disobeying him (Gn 3:5).

The effects of their disobedience were immediate, though not at all what Adam had expected. For the first time a barrier of shame disrupted the unity of man and woman (3:7). More important, a barrier of real moral guilt was erected between the first couple and God. The story relates that when God came looking for Adam after his rebellion, he was hiding among the trees, already aware of his separation from God (3:8). When God questioned him, Adam threw the blame on Eve and, by implication, back on God: "It was the woman you gave me who gave me the fruit" (3:12, NLT). Eve in turn blamed the serpent (3:13).

According to the story in Genesis, God held all three responsible and informed each one of the calamitous consequences of their rebellion (3:14-19). The two great mandates, originally signs of pure blessing, became mixed with curse and pain—the earth could now be populated only through the woman's birth pangs and could be subdued only by the man's labor and perspiration (3:16-18). Further, the unity of man and woman would be strained by man's subjugation of her, or possibly by the beginning of a struggle for dominance between them (3:16b can be taken both ways). Finally, God pronounced the ultimate consequence: as he had originally warned, Adam and Eve were to die. Someday the breath of life would be taken from them, and their bodies would return to the dust from which they were made (3:19). That very day they also experienced a "spiritual" death; they were separated from God, the giver of life, and from the tree of life, the symbol of eternal life (3:22). God sent them out of Eden, and there was no way back. The entrance to paradise was blocked by the cherubim and flaming sword (3:23-24). Only God could restore what they had lost.

The story is not devoid of hope. God was merciful even then. He made them garments of skin to cover their bodies and promised that someday the power of Satan behind the serpent would be crushed by the woman's "seed" (Gn 3:15; cf. Rom 16:20). Many scholars consider that promise to be the first biblical mention of redemption.

The Significance of Adam

Adam's significance is based upon several assumptions, the first being that he was a historical individual. That assumption was made by many OT writers (Gn 4:25; 5:1-5; 1 Chr 1:1; Hos 6:7). The NT writers agreed (Lk 3:38; Rom 5:14; 1 Cor 15:22, 45; 1 Tm 2:13-14; Jude 1:14). Equally essential to Adam's significance is a second assumption, that he was more than an individual. To begin with, the Hebrew word *adam* (more correctly *'a–dha–m)* is not merely a proper name. Even in the Genesis story it is not used as a name until Genesis 4:25. The word is one of several Hebrew words meaning "man" and is the generic term for "human race." In the vast majority of cases it refers either to a male individual (Lv 1:2; Jos 14:15; Neh 9:29; Is 56:2) or to humanity in general (Ex 4:11; Nm 12:3; 16:29; Dt 4:28; 1 Kgs 4:31; Jb 7:20; 14:1). The generic, collective sense of the word *adam* is also behind the phrase "children (or sons) of men" (2 Sm 7:14; Pss 11:4; 12:1; 14:2; 53:2; 90:3; Eccl 1:13; 2:3). That phrase, literally "sons of *adam*," simply means "men" or "human beings," and when it is used the entire human race is in view. Indeed, the universalistic human connotation of the word *adam* indicates a concern in the OT going far beyond Israel's nationalistic hopes and its God—to all the earth's people and the Lord of all nations (Gn 9:5-7; Dt 5:24; 8:3; 1 Kgs 8:38-39; Pss 8:4; 89:48; 107:8-31; Prv 12:14; Mi 6:8).

It is no accident, then, that the first man was named "Adam" or "Man." The name intimates that to speak about Adam is somehow also to speak about the entire human race. Such usage can perhaps best be understood through the ancient concept of corporate personality and representation familiar to the Hebrews and other Near Eastern peoples. Modern thinking emphasizes the individual; existence of the social group and all social relationships has been seen as secondary to, and dependent upon, the existence and desire of the individual. The Hebrew understanding was quite different. Though the separate personality of the individual was appreciated (Jer 31:29-30; Ez 18:4), there was a strong tendency to see the social group (family, tribe, nation) as a single organism with a corporate identity of its own. Likewise the group representative was seen as the embodiment or personification of the corporate personality of the group. Within the representative the essential qualities and characteristics of the social group resided in such a way that the actions and decisions of

QUICKTAKE

ADAM

STRENGTHS AND ACCOMPLISHMENTS
- The first zoologist—namer of animals
- The first landscape architect, placed in the garden to care for it
- Father of the human race
- The first person made in the image of God, and the first human to share an intimate personal relationship with God

WEAKNESSES AND MISTAKES
- Avoided responsibility and blamed others; chose to hide rather than to confront; made excuses rather than admitting the truth
- Greatest mistake: teamed up with Eve to bring sin into the world

LESSONS FROM HIS LIFE
- As Adam's descendants, we all reflect to some degree the image of God
- God wants people who, though free to do wrong, choose instead to love him
- We should not blame others for our faults
- We cannot hide from God

VITAL STATISTICS
Where: Garden of Eden
Occupation: Caretaker, gardener, farmer
Relatives: Wife: Eve. Sons: Cain, Abel, Seth. Numerous other children. The only man who never had an earthly mother or father

KEY VERSES
"The man replied, 'It was the woman you gave me who gave me the fruit, and I ate it'" (Genesis 3:12).

"Just as everyone dies because we all belong to Adam, everyone who belongs to Christ will be given new life" (1 Corinthians 15:22).

Adam's story is told in Genesis 1:26–5:5. He is also mentioned in 1 Chronicles 1:1; Luke 3:38; Romans 5:14; 1 Corinthians 15:22, 45; 1 Timothy 2:13-14.

the representative were binding on the entire group. If the group was a family, the father was usually considered the corporate representative; for good or for ill his family, and sometimes his descendants, received the results of his actions (Gn 17:1-8; cf. Gn 20:1-9, 18; Ex 20:5-6; Jos 7:24-25; Rom 11:28; Heb 7:1-10).

As the original man and father of humankind, in whose image all succeeding generations would be born (Gn 5:3), Adam was the corporate representative of humanity. The creation accounts themselves give the impression that the mandates of Genesis 1:26-30 (cf. Gn 9:1, 7; Pss 8:5-7; 104:14) as well as the curses of Genesis 3:16-19 (cf. Ps 90:3; Eccl 12:7; Is 13:8; 21:3) were meant not only for Adam (and Eve) but, through him, for the entire race.

In Romans 5:12-21 the apostle Paul contrasted the death and condemnation brought upon humanity by Adam's disobedience with the life and justification given to humanity through Christ's obedience. More explicitly, in 1 Corinthians 15:22, 45-50 (RSV), Paul called Christ the "last Adam," "second man," and the "man of heaven" in juxtaposition to the "first Adam," the "first man," and the "man of dust." Thus, Christ is sometimes refered to as the "Second Adam."

For Paul, the human race was divided into two groups in the persons of Adam and Christ. Those who remain "incorporated" in Adam are the "old" humanity, bearing the image of the "man of dust" and partaking of his sin and alienation from God and Creation (Rom 5:12-19; 8:20-22). But those who are incorporated into Christ by faith become Christ's "body" (Rom 12:4-5; 1 Cor 12:12-13, 27; Eph 1:22-23; Col 1:18); they are recreated in Christ's image (Rom 8:29; 1 Cor 15:49; 2 Cor 3:18); they become one "new man" (Eph 2:15; 4:24; Col 3:9-10, KJV); and they partake of the new creation (2 Cor 5:17; Gal 6:15). The old barriers raised by Adam are removed by Christ (Rom 5:1; 2 Cor 5:19; Gal 3:27-28; Eph 2:14-16). For Paul, the functional similarity of Adam and Christ as representatives meant that Christ had restored what Adam had lost.

See also Eve.

ADDAR

Alternate name for Ard, one of Benjamin's descendants, in 1 Chronicles 8:3. *See* Ard.

ADDI

1. One whose descendants obeyed Ezra's exhortation to divorce their pagan wives after the Exile (1 Esd 9:31). The parallel list of Ezra has Pahath-moab in place of Addi (Ezr 10:30).

2. Ancestor of Jesus, mentioned in Luke's genealogy (3:28).

ADIEL

1. Prince of Simeon's tribe who led some Simeonites to the entrance of Gedor to find pasture for their flocks (1 Chr 4:36-39).

2. Ancestor of Maasai, a priest of Israel who was among the first to return to Palestine following the Babylonian captivity (1 Chr 9:12).

3. Ancestor of Azmaveth. Azmaveth was in charge of King David's treasuries (1 Chr 27:25).

ADIN

1. Ancestor of a group of people who returned to Judah with Zerubbabel after the Babylonian exile. Comparison of various lists (Ezr 2:15; 8:6; Neh 7:20; 1 Esd 5:14; 8:32) shows that groups of Adin's descendants returned at different times.

2. Political leader who signed Ezra's covenant of faithfulness to God with Nehemiah and others after the Exile (Neh 10:16).

ADINA

Shiza's son and a warrior among David's mighty men who were known as "the thirty" (1 Chr 11:42).

ADLAI

Father of Shaphat, the chief herdsman of the king's cattle in the valleys during David's reign (1 Chr 27:29).

ADMATHA

One of seven counselors of King Ahasuerus (Est 1:14). The king's counselors advised him to banish Queen Vashti for refusing his summons to appear at a drunken party.

ADMIN

Ancestor of Jesus mentioned in Luke's genealogy (3:33).

ADNA

1. Descendant of Pahath-moab who obeyed Ezra's exhortation to divorce his pagan wife after the Exile (Ezr 10:30).

2. Priest under the high priest Joiakim who returned to Jerusalem with Zerubbabel after the Exile (Neh 12:15).

ADNAH

1. Captain from Manasseh's tribe who left Saul to join David's army at Ziklag (1 Chr 12:20).

2. General under King Jehoshaphat of Judah (2 Chr 17:14).

ADONI-BEZEK

Title of the Canaanite king of Bezek, a city in northern Palestine. Soon after Joshua's death, the tribes of Judah and Simeon defeated Adoni-bezek and amputated his thumbs and big toes. Adoni-bezek himself had treated many captured kings that way, so he regarded his fate as divine retribution (Jgs 1:5-7). Some have suggested that he and Adoni-zedek (Jos 10:1) were the same person.

ADONIJAH

1. David's fourth son, born to Haggith at Hebron (2 Sm 3:4). After the deaths of his three older brothers (Amnon, Chileab, and Absalom), Adonijah was next in line for the throne. According to 1 Kings, David had promised his wife Bathsheba that their son Solomon would be the one to succeed him (1:17). When his elderly father seemed to be dying, Adonijah began preparations to crown himself king (1:1-10). Before the ceremonies could take place, David appointed Solomon as his successor (1:11-40). Adonijah kept out of Solomon's way at first (1:41-53) but eventually worked up enough courage to ask King Solomon for permission to marry Abishag, the woman from Shunem who was appointed to care for David during his last days. In the ancient Near East, to claim the concubine of a deceased king was to claim the throne. Enraged, Solomon ordered Adonijah to be killed (2:13-25).

2. Levite sent out by King Jehoshaphat of the southern kingdom of Judah to teach the people the law of the Lord (2 Chr 17:8).

3. Political leader who signed Ezra's covenant of faithfulness to God with Nehemiah and others after the Exile (Neh 10:16).

ADONIKAM

Head of a family whose descendants returned to Jerusalem with Zerubbabel after the Babylonian exile (Ezr 2:13; Neh 7:18). Ezra states the number of Adonikam's family returning as 666; Nehemiah gives the number as 667 (as does 1 Esd 5:14), probably a scribal variation.

ADONIRAM

Important official in Israel during the reigns of David, Solomon, and Rehoboam (1 Kgs 4:6; 5:14). Adoniram is also referred to as Adoram, possibly a contraction of his name (2 Sm 20:24; 1 Kgs 12:18), and as Hadoram (2 Chr 10:18). While Solomon's Temple was under construction, Adoniram was overseer of a labor force of 30,000 men (1 Kgs 5:13-14). Evidently David had instituted a system of forced Israelite labor that Solomon continued, not only for building the Temple, but for many other projects.

When Rehoboam became king the people asked for relief, but Rehoboam announced that instead, he would increase the labor requirements (1 Kgs 12:1-15). When Adoniram was sent to enforce the king's orders, he was stoned to death by the rebellious people (12:16-19).

ADONI-ZEDEK

Amorite king of Jerusalem at the time of the Israelite conquest of the Promised Land (Jos 10:1-5). A battle between the Amorites and Israelites for control of Gibeon was the occasion on which Joshua prayed for the sun to stand still (Jos 10:6-15). The Israelites won a decisive victory. Adoni-zedek and four other enemy kings were discovered hiding in a cave and were executed by Joshua (Jos 10:16-27).

ADRAMMELECH

1. Son of the Assyrian monarch Sennacherib. This Adrammelech and his brother Sharezer killed their father in the temple of Nisroch in Nineveh (2 Kgs 19:37; Is 37:38). The nonbiblical *Babylonian Chronicles* also refers to this assassination but does not name the sons.

    See also Sennacherib.

2. Deity worshiped by the Syrians from Sepharvaim whom the Assyrians resettled in Samaria. Adrammelech was a god to whom children were sacrificed by the Sepharvites (2 Kgs 17:31).

ADRIEL

Barzillai's son, to whom Saul gave his daughter Merab in marriage, although she had been promised to David (1 Sm 18:19). King David later handed over Adriel's five sons to the Gibeonites to execute in vengeance against Saul's family (2 Sm 21:1-9).

AENEAS

Bedridden paralytic in Lydda who was miraculously healed by the apostle Peter (Acts 9:33-35).

AGABUS

Prophet of NT times who made two predictions referred to in the book of Acts. His prophecy of a severe famine was fulfilled in the time of Claudius (Acts 11:27-28). He also predicted that Paul would be turned over to the Gentiles by the Jews in Jerusalem if he went there (Acts 21:10-11).

AGAG

1. Name of an Amalekite king, or perhaps a general title for their kings (like the Egyptian "pharaoh"). Balaam prophesied that Israel's king would be greater than Agag (Nm 24:7).

2. Name of another Amalekite king. God told Samuel to send King Saul to wipe out the Amalekite nation down to the last sheep. Saul conquered them but spared Agag's life and the Amalekites' best sheep and oxen. Samuel then executed Agag and told Saul that, because of his disobedience, he could no longer be Israel's king (1 Sm 15).

AGEE

Father of Shammah, one of the warriors among David's mighty men who were known as "the thirty" (2 Sm 23:11).

AGRIPPA

Name of two Roman rulers of Judea from the Herodian family line. *See* Herod.

AGUR

Jakeh's son. Although not an Israelite, he wrote or collected the sayings in Proverbs 30. Agur was from Massa (Prv 30:1), an area of northern Arabia evidently settled by a son of Ishmael (Gn 25:14; 1 Chr 1:30).

AHAB

1. Eighth king of the northern kingdom of Israel, who reigned about 874–853 BC. His father, Omri, founded a dynasty that lasted 40 years, through the reigns of Ahab and his two sons, Ahaziah and Jehoram. Omri's dynasty had an impact beyond biblical history, being mentioned on the famous Moabite Stone and in several Assyrian inscriptions. According to 1 Kings, Omri was a general in the army of King Elah, son of Baasha. When Elah was assassinated, Omri was acclaimed king by his own forces in the field (16:8-16). He prevailed in the resulting civil war and occupied Tirzah, the capital city (16:17-23). Soon he moved his capital to Samaria and built fortifications in the region (16:24). Omri also made an alliance with the Phoenicians, as David and Solomon had done, but was condemned for it by later generations. When Ahab succeeded his father (16:28), he pursued this alliance by marrying the Phoenician king's daughter, Jezebel (16:29-31).

Ahab's marriage to Jezebel, an immoral and fanatical pagan, strongly affected Israel (21:21-26) and had consequences even in the southern kingdom of Judah. Athaliah, their daughter, married Jehoram of Judah and the results of this marriage were disastrous (2 Kgs 8:17-18, 26-27; 11:1-20). Under Jezebel's influence Ahab gave up the worship of God and took up Baal worship. Ahab's new religion was a fertility cult that featured sexual unions between priests and temple "virgins," practices explicitly contrary to the laws of God. Even in marrying Jezebel, Ahab had violated the biblical prohibition of marriage to pagans (Dt 7:1-5).

The biblical narrative mentions that Ahab built many cities (1 Kgs 22:39) and fought a number of wars, but for the most part it centers on the great prophetic figure, Elijah (1 Kgs 17:1; 18:1; 19:1). Early in Ahab's reign, God sent Elijah to predict years of drought and famine as punishment for the king's sin (1 Kgs 17:1; 18:16-18). The drought lasted three and a half years and was such a remarkable period in Israel's history that it was remembered into NT times (Lk 4:25; Jas 5:17). It was a time of great suffering for both people and animals (1 Kgs 18:5). At the end of the three and a half years Elijah challenged Ahab to gather all the pagan prophets for a final confrontation between God and Baal. Elijah taunted the 450 prophets of Baal for not being able to attract the attention of their false god. Then he prayed to God, and fire fell from heaven on God's altar. The people shouted their belief in God and helped Elijah execute the pagan prophets (1 Kgs 18:16-40). The drought ended immediately (18:41-46).

When she heard what had happened to her prophets, Jezebel swore revenge. Elijah fled, and on Mt Horeb, God told him to anoint Jehu to become king of Israel in place of Ahab (1 Kgs 19:1-16). This assignment was carried out by the prophet's successor, Elisha (1 Kgs 19:19-21; 2 Kgs 9:1-10). Elijah then challenged Ahab's acquisition of a vineyard owned by a man named Naboth (1 Kgs 21:1-16). When Naboth refused to sell his land to the king, Jezebel had false witnesses swear that Naboth had cursed God and the king. Naboth was stoned to death for blasphemy. Elijah denounced Ahab, saying that as a judgment God would bring a bloody end to his family (1 Kgs 21:17-24). Ahab's repentance caused God to postpone the judgment until after Ahab's death (1 Kgs 21:27-29; 2 Kgs 10:1-14).

During his reign Ahab had military encounters with King Ben-hadad II of Syria (Aram), largely provoked by the Syrians. In the first encounter Ben-hadad besieged Samaria, Israel's capital, and demanded heavy tribute. Ahab refused the demands and called a council of elders. As the Syrians were preparing to attack, a prophet advised Ahab to attack first (1 Kgs 20:1-14). The Syrians were routed and Ben-hadad barely escaped with his life (1 Kgs 20:15-22). The following year Ben-hadad mounted another attack on Ahab's forces, was again defeated, and eventually surrendered to Ahab (1 Kgs 20:23-33). Ben-hadad gave up some Israelite cities that had been overrun by his father and granted Israel trading posts in Damascus (20:34). God rebuked Ahab through a prophet for forming such an alliance with a pagan power (1 Kgs 20:35-43).

In Ahab's last war with Syria, he had the advantage of an alliance with the king of Judah, Jehoshaphat (1 Kgs 22:2-4; 2 Chr 18:1-3). That alliance had been fortified by the marriage of Ahab's daughter Athaliah to Jehoram, son of Jehoshaphat. Ahab proposed a campaign for the recovery of Ramoth-gilead in the northeast corner of Israel. When Jehoshaphat refused to believe the optimistic predictions of Ahab's 400 prophets, a prophet of God named Micaiah was called, who foretold Ahab's death (1 Kgs 22:5-28; 2 Chr 18:4-27).

For the battle with Syria, Jehoshaphat put on his royal robes. Ahab tried to disguise himself as an ordinary soldier, but a Syrian archer hit him between the joints of his armor. Ahab died that evening, and his troops gave up the battle. His chariot and armor were washed beside the pool of Samaria, where, as Elijah had prophesied, dogs licked Ahab's blood. The fallen king was succeeded by his son Ahaziah (1 Kgs 22:29-40; 2 Chr 18:28-34).

See also Elijah #1; Jezebel.

2. Kolaiah's son, a notorious false prophet in the closing days of Judah. He was among the Jews taken to Babylon in the deportation of Jehoiachin (598–597 BC). This Ahab and his colleague Zedekiah were denounced by the prophet Jeremiah for lying in God's name and for their sexual immorality (Jer 29:21-23).

AHARAH
Alternate name for Ahiram, Benjamin's third son, in 1 Chronicles 8:1. *See* Ahiram.

AHARHEL
Harum's son from Judah's tribe (1 Chr 4:8).

AHASBAI
Eliphelet's father. Eliphelet, from the city of Maacah, was a warrior among David's mighty men who were known as "the thirty" (2 Sm 23:34).

AHASUERUS
1. Persian king better known to Western readers as Xerxes I (486–465 BC); the son and successor of Darius I (Hystaspis). In Ezra 4:6 Ahasuerus is mentioned as receiving letters of accusation from enemies of the Jews about their rebuilding the Temple.

   Ahasuerus played a role in biblical history in the book of Esther. According to the Greek historian Herodotus, in the third year of his reign Xerxes (Ahasuerus) convoked an assembly of his leaders to plan an invasion of Greece. The book of Esther begins with a banquet scene probably reflecting that situation. The Greek campaign, begun in 480 BC, was unsuccessful. Afterward, Xerxes turned to private matters, such as the events recorded in Esther. The Jewish heroine of that book was the second wife of Xerxes (Ahasuerus). She and her cousin Mordecai influenced the king to reverse an edict condemning all Jews to death. Ahasuerus hanged Haman, his chief minister, who had asked for the edict.

   Ahasuerus, who controlled an immense area "from India to Ethiopia" (Est 1:1), was celebrated for massive building projects at Susa and Persepolis. His rule ended in 465 BC when he was assassinated in his bedchamber. He is called the conqueror of Nineveh in Tobit 14:15, but this is manifestly impossible: Nineveh was destroyed in 612 BC, over a century before Ahasuerus was born. See Esther.

2. Father of Darius the Mede (Dn 9:1). The identity of this father and son in secular history is uncertain.

AHAZ
1. King of Judah (735–715 BC) who was especially remembered for his apostasy. The name Ahaz (Mt 1:9) is a shortened form of Ahaziah or Jehoahaz. The three main accounts of Ahaz (2 Kgs 16; 2 Chr 28; Is 7) treat him as one of the most evil rulers of the southern kingdom of Judah. Consequently, his burial was relatively dishonorable (2 Chr 28:27). He was succeeded by his son Hezekiah (2 Kgs 18:1).

   There is little agreement on the chronology of this section of the OT. The chronological system that seems to have the fewest problems would place Ahaz's accession in 735 BC. If he first came to the throne as co-regent with his father, Jotham, from 735 to 732 BC, his entire reign covered a span of approximately 20 years, ending in 715 BC.

   Ahaz reigned over Judah during a critical time in the history of the ancient Near East. The Assyrians were pushing westward, threatening the Syro-Palestinian area.

Pekah, king of Israel, and Rezin, king of Syria, adopted a policy of resistance against the Assyrians and invaded Judah in order to effect a solid coalition by deposing Ahaz. Blatantly revealing a lack of trust in God, Ahaz appealed to Tiglath-pileser III, the Assyrian king, for help. That appeal brought the wrath of the prophet Isaiah upon Ahaz. The ensuing encounter (Is 7) led to Isaiah's prediction of the birth of Immanuel as a sign of the dissolution of the countries of Israel and Syria. Those two kingdoms were ultimately destroyed by Tiglath-pileser in a campaign that lasted about two years (734–732 BC).

Before the two kingdoms to the north were conquered by Assyria, their invasion of Judah caused great turmoil (2 Chr 28:8). The invaders not only carried off much spoil but also attempted to depopulate portions of Judah by taking 200,000 people captive to Samaria. That attempt was protested by a prophet in Samaria named Obed, who condemned the act of slavery and ordered the captives returned (v 9). He was joined by several leaders of Israel (v 12), who succeeded in having the captives returned to Jericho with provisions from the spoil that had been taken.

During that time, the kingdom of Judah may have been threatened from the south as well. The Edomites, who had long been under the domination of Judah, may have taken advantage of Judah's growing internal weakness to assert their independence. The Masoretic Text of the OT refers to an invasion of the seaport town of Elath on the Red Sea by Aram, the Hebrew name for Syria (2 Kgs 16:6). The name Aram is quite similar to the name Edom in Hebrew, however, so many scholars think that invasion was actually by Edomites.

By virtue of the alliance he had made, Ahaz placed his country in a dangerous position of dependence on Assyria. The kingdom of Judah became essentially a vassal state under the tacit control of Tiglath-pileser. Ahaz went to Damascus, the capital of fallen Syria, to appear before Tiglath-pileser, possibly to assure his allegiance to the king to whom his nation had become tributary (2 Kgs 16:10).

While in Damascus, Ahaz saw an Assyrian altar, a model of which he sent back to Judah. Under the direction of Uriah the priest, a similar altar was built in Jerusalem, replacing the original bronze altar. Several other alterations were made in the Temple by Ahaz, all indicating his turning away from Jewish religion.

The "dial of Ahaz" (2 Kgs 20:11; Is 38:8) later figured in a sign given to his son Hezekiah; the Hebrew word actually refers to a flight of stairs, no doubt built by Ahaz and used to tell time by the movement of a shadow across it.

2. Micah's son and Jehoaddah's father, a descendant of Saul, otherwise unknown (1 Chr 8:35-36).

AHAZIAH

1. Ahab's son, who ruled the northern kingdom of Israel for two years as its ninth king· (853–852 BC). He came to the throne when Ahab was killed while trying to recover Ramoth-gilead from Syrian control. Ahaziah was a contemporary of King Jehoshaphat

of Judah and of Jehoshaphat's son Jehoram. Politically, his short reign was characterized by peace with Judah, in contrast with the days of Asa and Baasha (2 Chr 20:37; cf. 1 Kgs 22:48-49). No sooner had he become king than he was compelled to launch an expedition against Mesha of Moab, who had ceased paying tribute to Israel.

Evidently Ahaziah followed not only the corrupt religion of Jeroboam I but also the overt Baal worship of his parents, Ahab and Jezebel (1 Kgs 22:51-53). The first chapter of 2 Kings is devoted to Ahaziah's terminal illness. He fell from the second story of his palace and was seriously injured. Instead of turning to the Lord for aid, he turned to the god of Jezebel, "Baal-zebub, the god of Ekron." When the prophet Elijah condemned the king for his actions, Ahaziah, enraged, tried to arrest him. Two groups of soldiers were consumed by fire from God, a sign of victory over Baal since Baal was worshiped as the god of fire and lightning by his followers. Ahaziah died as predicted in Elijah's pronouncement from God (2 Kgs 1:2-18). He was succeeded by his younger brother, Jehoram, at a time when Ahaziah's brother-in-law, also named Jehoram, was king of Judah.

2. The son of Jehoram of Judah, grandson of Jehoshaphat and nephew of the Ahaziah just described. He ruled as the sixth king of Judah for only one year (841 BC) at the age of 22 (2 Kgs 8:25-26). The apostasy of the northern kingdom of Israel reached into the southern kingdom of Judah partly because this Ahaziah was a grandson of Ahab and Jezebel (his mother, Athaliah, was their daughter).

Ahaziah joined his uncle Jehoram of Israel (sometimes abbreviated Joram) in a campaign against King Hazael of Syria. In the battle Jehoram was wounded and went to Jezreel to recover. When Ahaziah went to visit his fallen kinsman at the royal residence at Jezreel (2 Chr 22:7-9), the visit proved to be a fatal mistake. Jehu, the army commander, anointed by Elisha to destroy Ahab's descendants (2 Kgs 9:1-13), seized this opportunity to kill both Joram and Ahaziah together (9:14-29).

When Ahaziah's mother, Athaliah, learned of his death, she seized the throne for herself and tried to kill all of his children. One child, Joash, escaped death and eventually became king (2 Kgs 11:1-21). Ahaziah's name is sometimes given as Jehoahaz (2 Chr 21:17) or Azariah (2 Chr 22:6, KJV; cf. NLT mg).

AHBAN
Son of Abishur and Abihail from Judah's tribe (1 Chr 2:29).

AHER
Alternate name for Ahiram, Benjamin's third son, in 1 Chronicles 7:12. See Ahiram.

AHI
1. Abdiel's son, a clan leader in Gad's tribe (1 Chr 5:15).
2. Shemer's brother and therefore a member of Asher's tribe (1 Chr 7:34). The word "Ahi"

in this verse, however, is probably not a name and should be translated "brother," as in most modern translations.

AHIAH

1. Political leader who signed Ezra's covenant of faithfulness to God with Nehemiah and others after the Exile (Neh 10:26).
2. KJV form of Ahijah. See Ahijah #1, #2, and #6.

AHIAM

Sharar's son and a warrior among David's mighty men who were known as "the thirty" (2 Sm 23:33).

AHIAN

One of Shemida's four sons from Naphtali's tribe (1 Chr 7:19).

AHIEZER

1. Ammishaddai's son, a leader of Dan's tribe when the Israelites were roaming in the Sinai wilderness after their escape from Egypt. As leader he presented his tribe's offering at the consecration of the Tabernacle (Nm 1:12; 2:25; 7:66, 71; 10:25).
2. Shemaah's son, a leader of the warriors from Benjamin's tribe who joined David at Ziklag in his refuge from King Saul. Like his men, Ahiezer was an ambidextrous archer and slinger (1 Chr 12:2-3).

AHIHUD

1. Shelomi's son, a leader of Asher's tribe. Ahihud was appointed to help Eleazar and Joshua divide the territory of Canaan among the Israelites (Nm 34:17, 27).
2. According to some English versions (KJV, RSV), a leader in Benjamin's tribe whose father, Gera (also called Heglam), was exiled to Manahath (1 Chr 8:7). But according to the Hebrew Masoretic Text, this Ahihud's father was Ehud (1 Chr 8:6), while Gera was the one who exiled Ahihud and his mother to Manahath.

AHIJAH

1. Ahitub's son who served as priest at Shiloh and had charge of the Ark of the Covenant at Gibeah during Saul's last campaign (1 Sm 14:3, 18). This Ahijah was evidently either the same person as Ahimelech or closely associated with him (1 Sm 21:1-9; 22:9-20).
2. One of King Solomon's secretaries (1 Kgs 4:3).
3. Prophet of Shiloh who informed King Solomon's official, Jeroboam, of the approaching revolt of the 10 northern tribes. Before Solomon died, Ahijah acted out a prophecy before Jeroboam, giving him 10 pieces of his robe, which he had torn into 12 segments,

saying that God would tear 10 tribes from Solomon and give them to Jeroboam (1 Kgs 11:29-39; 2 Chr 10:15). Later, when Jeroboam had been unfaithful to Israel's religion, he sent his wife to ask the prophet about their son Abijah's illness (1 Kgs 14:1-5). Aware of her identity although he was now old and blind, Ahijah predicted both the child's death and the fall of Jeroboam and his family (1 Kgs 14:6-17; 15:28-30). "The Prophecy of Ahijah from Shiloh" was evidently a written source for Solomon's biography (2 Chr 9:29).

4. Father of King Baasha of the northern kingdom of Israel (1 Kgs 15:27-28, 33; 21:22; 2 Kgs 9:9).

5. Jerahmeel's son from Judah's tribe (1 Chr 2:25).

6. Ehud's son (1 Chr 8:7). The Hebrew is difficult to translate; therefore, some English versions make Ahijah one of Ehud's sons, while others make Ahijah the one who carried Ehud's sons, Uzza and Ahihud, into exile.

7. Warrior among David's mighty men who were known as "the thirty" (1 Chr 11:36); also called Eliam the son of Ahithophel (2 Sm 23:34).

8. Levite who oversaw King David's Temple treasury (1 Chr 26:20).

9. Ancestor of the prophet Ezra (2 Esd 1:2).

AHIKAM

Shaphan's son, an officer of the court of King Josiah of Judah (2 Kgs 22:12). Ahikam was among the group sent to the prophetess Huldah to ask about the Book of the Law (2 Kgs 22:14-20). Later, under King Jehoiakim, Ahikam was able to prevent the prophet Jeremiah from being killed (Jer 26:24). Ahikam's son Gedaliah was left as governor of Judah after Nebuchadnezzar destroyed Jerusalem and took most of its citizens to Babylon in 586 BC (2 Kgs 25:22; Jer 39:14; 40:5-16; 41:1-18; 43:6).

AHILUD

Father of the court historian Jehoshaphat. Jehoshaphat served under both David and Solomon (2 Sm 8:16; 20:24; 1 Kgs 4:3; 1 Chr 18:15). Probably Ahilud was also the father of Baana, one of Solomon's tax officials (1 Kgs 4:12).

AHIMAAZ

1. Father of Ahinoam, who was King Saul's wife (1 Sm 14:50).

2. Son of the high priest Zadok and father of Azariah (1 Chr 6:8-9, 53). Ahimaaz remained loyal to King David at the time of Absalom's rebellion. He and Jonathan, son of the priest Abiathar, served as couriers. News of Absalom's movements was sent from Zadok and Abiathar in Jerusalem to Ahimaaz and Jonathan in En-rogel and then communicated by them to David (2 Sm 15:27-29; 17:15-23). Ahimaaz was probably well known as a fast runner. He outran the official messenger bearing news to David of Absalom's defeat (2 Sm 18:19-33).

3. One of 12 officers appointed to requisition food for Solomon's household. This Ahimaaz, of Naphtali's tribe, married Basemath, one of Solomon's daughters (1 Kgs 4:15).

AHIMAN

1. One of Anak's three sons. The Ahimanites were one of the Anakim clans living in Hebron when the 12 Israelite spies scouted the land of Canaan (Nm 13:22; Jos 15:13-14; Jgs 1:10).

2. Levite gatekeeper in postexilic Jerusalem (1 Chr 9:17).

AHIMELECH

1. A priest at Nob who aided David in his flight from Saul (1 Sm 21:1-9). When he was asked for food, all he could provide was the holy bread in the Tabernacle (Jesus referred to this incident in Mt 12:1-8). Doeg the Edomite subsequently reported this action to Saul, who ordered Ahimelech put to death. Saul's guards were unwilling to execute a priest, but the informer Doeg had no such inhibitions. He killed Ahimelech and 84 other priests, plus their families and livestock (1 Sm 22:9-19). Only Abiathar, Ahimelech's son, escaped and fled to David's protection (22:20-23). Psalm 52 was written by David as an indictment of Doeg's treachery.

2. Hittite who joined David's guerrilla force during his flight from Saul (1 Sm 26:6).

3. Son of Abiathar and grandson of #1 above. This Ahimelech aided his father in the priesthood under King David (2 Sm 8:17; 1 Chr 24:3, 5, 31; cf. 1 Chr 18:16, where some versions have Abimelech instead).

AHIMOTH

Elkanah's son, a Levite in the family of Kohath (1 Chr 6:25).

AHINADAB

Iddo's son and one of 12 officers appointed to requisition food for King Solomon's household. Ahinadab's headquarters were in Mahanaim (1 Kgs 4:14).

AHINOAM

1. Daughter of Ahimaaz and wife of King Saul (1 Sm 14:50).

2. Jezreelite woman who became David's wife after Saul took back his daughter Michal and gave her to Palti (1 Sm 25:43-44). In Hebron, Ahinoam became the mother of David's oldest son, Amnon (2 Sm 3:2; 1 Chr 3:1).

AHIO

1. Abinadab's son. With his brother Uzzah, Ahio drove the ox cart carrying the Ark of the Covenant to its new home at Jerusalem (2 Sm 6:3-4; 1 Chr 13:7).

2. Elpaal's son from Benjamin's tribe (1 Chr 8:14).

3. Son of Jeiel and his wife Maacah. This Ahio was a brother or an uncle of Kish, Saul's father (1 Chr 8:31; 9:36-37).

AHIRA
Enan's son and the leader of Naphtali's tribe when the Israelites were roaming in the Sinai wilderness after their escape from Egypt. As leader he presented his tribe's offering at the consecration of the Tabernacle (Nm 1:15; 2:29; 7:78, 83; 10:27).

AHIRAM
Benjamin's third son and the ancestral head of the Ahiramite clan (Nm 26:38; 1 Chr 8:1, "Aharah"). Two abbreviated forms of the name Ahiram in genealogies may be Ehi (Gn 46:21) and Aher (1 Chr 7:12).

AHISAMACH
Father of the craftsman Oholiab, of Dan's tribe. Oholiab helped construct the Tabernacle and its furnishings (Ex 31:6; 35:34; 38:23).

AHISHAHAR
Bilhan's son and chief of the subclan of Jediael, of Benjamin's tribe, in the time of King David (1 Chr 7:10).

AHISHAR
Overseer in charge of Solomon's palace affairs (1 Kgs 4:6).

AHITHOPHEL
King David's trusted counselor who turned traitor and joined Absalom's conspiracy. Ahithophel's counsel was highly regarded, almost as though it were an oracle of God (2 Sm 16:23). On hearing about Ahithophel's defection to Absalom, David prayed, "O LORD, let Ahithophel give Absalom foolish advice!" (2 Sm 15:31, NLT). Ahithophel advised Absalom to take over the royal harem (2 Sm 16:20-22). Taking possession of the harem was a public act declaring a former king to be deceased and replaced. Since David was still alive, the act was meant to bring about a final cleavage between David and Absalom. It also fulfilled Nathan's prophecy to David that because David had taken another man's wife in secret, his own wives would be taken from him in public (2 Sm 12:7-12).

Ahithophel's second stratagem was to attack David quickly with 12,000 elite troops (2 Sm 17:1-3). Absalom rejected this advice, however, and accepted a counter suggestion by Hushai, David's spy in Absalom's palace. In a speech designed to inflate Absalom's ego and gain time for David, Hushai advised a full campaign (2 Sm 17:4-14). When Ahithophel saw that his counsel was not followed, he went to his hometown and hanged himself (2 Sm 17:23).

AHITUB

1. Member of the priestly line of Aaron's youngest son, Ithamar. Ahitub was a descendant of Eli through Eli's son Phinehas and father of Ahijah and Ahimelech, who were priests during Saul's reign (1 Sm 14:3; 22:9-12, 20).

2. Member of the priestly line of Aaron's third son, Eleazar. Ahitub was Meraioth's grandson, Amariah's son, and father of Zadok (1 Chr 6:4-7). Zadok was a chief priest during David's reign (2 Sm 8:17).

3. Possibly the same as #2 above (the scribes sometimes mistakenly copied names twice), but more likely another member of the priestly line of Eleazar, seven generations after #2 (1 Chr 6:11-12). This Ahitub's father was also named Amariah and his son or grandson Zadok (1 Chr 9:11; Neh 11:11), but his grandfather was Azariah. Ahitub is listed as an ancestor of Ezra (Ezr 7:2; 1 Esd 8:2; 2 Esd 1:1).

AHLAI

1. Sheshan's daughter, a member of Judah's tribe (1 Chr 2:31, 34). In verse 31 some translations refer to Ahlai as a son.

2. Zabad's father or ancestor. Zabad was one of David's mighty men who were known as "the thirty" (1 Chr 11:41).

AHOAH

One of Bela's nine sons, a member of Benjamin's tribe (1 Chr 8:4). Ahoah's descendants were called Ahohites, and two of them were among King David's most effective warriors: Dodo ("son of Ahohi," 2 Sm 23:9; spelled "Dodai" in 1 Chr 27:4) and Zalmon the Ahohite (2 Sm 23:28; called "Ilai" in 1 Chr 11:29).

AHUMAI

Jahath's descendant from Judah's tribe (1 Chr 4:2).

AHUZZAM

Son of Ashur and Naarah and a member of Judah's tribe (1 Chr 4:6).

AHUZZATH

Royal advisor to Abimelech of Gerar. Ahuzzath accompanied Abimelech to Beersheba to make a treaty with Isaac (Gn 26:26).

AHZAI

Priest of the order of Immer. Ahzai's descendant, Amashsai, was a leading priest in Jerusalem in Ezra's day (Neh 11:13). In all probability Ahzai and Jahzerah were the same person (1 Chr 9:12). *See* Jahzerah.

AIAH

1. Zibeon's son, a Horite descended from Seir. Aiah is listed in Esau's genealogies (Gn 36:24; 1 Chr 1:35-40).

2. Father (or mother?) of Saul's concubine Rizpah (2 Sm 3:7; 21:8-11).

AKAN

Alternate name for Jaakan, Ezer's son, in Genesis 36:27. *See* Jaakan.

AKIM

Descendant of Zerubbabel, listed in the NT as an ancestor of Jesus (Mt 1:14).

AKKUB

1. One of Elioenai's seven sons and a distant descendant of David (1 Chr 3:24).

2. Ancestor of a family of Levite gatekeepers who returned to Jerusalem with Zerubbabel after the Exile (Ezr 2:42; Neh 7:45). This family name was borne by two of his descendants (#3 and #6 below).

3. Descendant of #2 and head of a family of Levite gatekeepers who were among the first to return to Jerusalem after the Babylonian exile (1 Chr 9:17).

4. Ancestor of a group of Temple assistants who returned to Jerusalem with Zerubbabel after the Exile (Ezr 2:45).

5. Ezra's assistant who explained to the people passages from the law read by Ezra (Neh 8:7).

6. Descendant of #2 above and head of a family of Levite gatekeepers who lived in Jerusalem during the time of Ezra and Nehemiah (Neh 11:19; 12:25-26). He is perhaps the same as #5 above.

ALEMETH

1. Becher's son from Benjamin's tribe (1 Chr 7:8).

2. Son of Jehoaddah (1 Chr 8:36) or Jarah (1 Chr 9:42) and a descendant of King Saul.

ALEXANDER

1. Brother of Rufus and son of Simon of Cyrene, the man who was passing by at the time Jesus was being led to Golgotha and whom the Roman soldiers compelled to carry the cross (Mk 15:21).

2. A member of the high-priestly family along with Caiaphas, Annas the high priest, and John (Acts 4:6). It was this group who summoned Peter and John to appear before them to account for the healing of the lame man at the Beautiful Gate of the Temple (Acts 3).

3. Ephesian who was put forward by the Jews to serve as their spokesman when the silversmith Demetrius roused the Ephesians to riot (Acts 19:33). The preaching of the gospel by Paul and his companions had resulted in the conversion of many people, who left the worship of the goddess Artemis (Diana) and thus reduced the income of the silversmiths, whose revenue derived from the manufacture of images of this deity (Acts 19:23-41).

4. One who, with Hymenaeus, was mentioned as having shipwrecked his faith because of his rejection of conscience (1 Tm 1:20). Paul states that he had "turned them over to Satan so they would learn not to blaspheme God."

5. Coppersmith (2 Tm 4:14). Paul warns Timothy to beware of this man, who had done much harm to Paul and had strongly opposed the message of the gospel. Some scholars think this Alexander is the same as the Alexander of 1 Timothy 1:20 (#4 above).

ALLON
Ziza's ancestor from Simeon's tribe (1 Chr 4:37).

ALMODAD
Son or descendant of Joktan in the family of Noah's son Shem (Gn 10:26; 1 Chr 1:20).

ALPHAEUS
1. Father of James, one of the 12 apostles (Mt 10:3; Mk 3:18; Lk 6:15; Acts 1:13), thought by some to be the same as Clopas of John 19:25.

2. Father of Levi, the tax collector (Mk 2:14) who is also known in the Gospels as Matthew (Mt 9:9).

ALVAH
Esau's descendant and a chief of Edom (Gn 36:40); alternately called Aliah in 1 Chronicles 1:51.

ALVAN
Shobal's son and a descendant of Esau (Gn 36:23); alternately spelled Alian in 1 Chronicles 1:40.

AMAL
Helem's son and a descendant of Asher (1 Chr 7:35).

AMALEK
Amalek was the son of Eliphaz (Esau's son) by his concubine, Timna (Gn 36:12; 1 Chr 1:36). Descendants of this tribal chief of Edom were known as Amalekites. They settled in the Negev Desert and became allies of the Edomites, Ammonites, Moabites, Ishmaelites, and

Midianites. The Amalekites were notable enemies of Israel. Amalek inherited the fraternal feud that had begun with his grandfather Esau's antagonism toward Jacob. Since Jacob was one of the progenitors of Israel, the conflict between Amalek and Israel had both a theological and political basis.

The territory of the nomadic Amalekites in the Negev ranged at times from south of Beersheba to the southeast as far as Elath and Ezion-geber. They undoubtedly raided westward into the coastal plain, eastward into the Arabah wastelands, and possibly over into Arabia. In the Negev they blocked the path of the Israelites during the Exodus (Ex 17:8-16). Israel would fight numerous battles and skirmishes with the warriors of Amalek (Ex 17:1, 8-16; Dt 25:17-18; Nm 14:39-45; Jgs 6:3, 33; 7:12; 1 Sm 14:47-48).

AMARIAH
Common OT name, meaning "the Lord has spoken" or "the Lord has promised."
1. Son of Meraioth in the line of Aaron's son Eleazer (1 Chr 6:7, 52).
2. High priest, Azariah's son and Ahitub's father (1 Chr 6:11; Ezr 7:3).
3. Hebron's second son and Kohath's grandson from Levi's tribe (1 Chr 23:19; 24:23).
4. Chief priest during the reign of Jehoshaphat of the southern kingdom of Judah (2 Chr 19:11).
5. Levite who served faithfully under King Hezekiah of Judah (2 Chr 31:14-15).
6. One of Binnui's sons, who obeyed Ezra's exhortation to divorce his pagan wife after the Exile (Ezr 10:42).
7. Priest who returned from Babylon with Zerubbabel (Neh 12:2, 13) and who, with Nehemiah and others, signed Ezra's covenant of faithfulness to God after the Exile (Neh 10:3).
8. Shephatiah's son, a descendant of Judah and ancestor of Athaiah. Amariah lived in Jerusalem after the Exile (Neh 11:4).
9. Hezekiah's son and ancestor of the prophet Zephaniah (Zep 1:1).
10. Person mentioned in the Ezra genealogies of 1 Esdras 8:2 and 2 Esdras 1:2. In the first list he is Uzzi's son and Ahitub's father. In the second he is Azariah's son and Eli's father. He may be the same as Amariah #1 or #2 above, since both sources list him as Ahitub's father.

AMASA
1. Son of Ithra (Jether) and David's sister Abigail (2 Sm 17:25; 1 Chr 2:17), and therefore David's nephew. Amasa was a captain who supported Absalom in his rebellion against his father, David. After Absalom was killed by David's general Joab, David pardoned Amasa and replaced Joab with him (2 Sm 19:13). Greatly offended, Joab awaited his revenge and, as soon as he had opportunity, treacherously assassinated his unsuspecting rival (2 Sm 20:4-13). David was unable to punish Joab but instructed his son

Solomon to see that Joab was executed for murdering Amasa and another of David's generals (1 Kgs 2:5-6, 28-34).

2. Hadlai's son from Ephraim's tribe. Amasa supported the prophet Oded's opposition to making slaves of women and children captured from the southern kingdom of Judah in the time of King Ahaz (2 Chr 28:8-13).

AMASAI

1. Elkanah's son (1 Chr 6:25) and Mahath's father (1 Chr 6:35), listed in the genealogy of Heman the singer.

2. Leader of 30 warriors who joined David at Ziklag after deserting King Saul (1 Chr 12:18).

3. Trumpeter priest in the procession when David brought the Ark of God to Jerusalem (1 Chr 15:24).

4. Father of another Mahath. This Mahath was Hezekiah's contemporary and a participant in his revival (2 Chr 29:12).

AMASHSAI

Azarel's son and one of the leading priests who returned to Jerusalem after the Babylonian exile (Neh 11:13). Amashsai may possibly be identical with Maasai (1 Chr 9:12).

AMASIAH

Military leader in the time of Jehoshaphat, in charge of 200,000 men. Amasiah was Zichri's son and a man of unusual piety (2 Chr 17:16).

AMAZIAH

1. Ninth king of Judah (796–767 BC), who at age 25 succeeded his father, King Joash, when Joash was assassinated after a 40-year reign (2 Kgs 12:19-21). Amaziah's mother was Jehoaddin. He ruled Judah for 29 years before he too was killed by assassins (14:18-20). When Amaziah began his reign, another Joash was ruling the northern kingdom of Israel (14:1-2).

Amaziah was not like his ancestor David (2 Kgs 14:3). Like his father, Amaziah did things that pleased God, but he failed to remove the pagan shrines that were corrupting the nation's religious life. He himself was respectful of the law of Moses, at least at the beginning (14:4-6).

Amaziah was unwise in his dealings with the rival kingdom of Israel. To go to war against the Edomites, he hired 100,000 mercenaries from Israel. Warned by a prophet not to use them in battle, Amaziah discharged them. On their way out of Judah the angry soldiers raided cities and killed 3,000 people. Nevertheless, Amaziah's troops were victorious against the Edomites. At the Valley of Salt they killed 10,000 of the enemy in battle and executed another 10,000 prisoners (2 Chr 25:5-13).

Foolishly, Amaziah brought Edomite idols back with him after his conquest and was soon worshiping them. The Lord sent a prophet to announce Amaziah's doom for such spiritual rebellion (2 Chr 25:14-16). Proud of his conquest of Edom, Amaziah soon declared war on King Joash of Israel. Joash warned him in a parable that Judah would be crushed like a thistle. Amaziah refused to back down, and the two armies met at Beth-shemesh in Judah. Amaziah's army was routed. Jerusalem was captured and the Temple and palace looted. Amaziah was taken prisoner but was evidently left in Jerusalem. He outlived Joash of Israel by 15 years (2 Chr 25:17-26). Amaziah was murdered in Lachish, to which he had fled when he heard about a plot against him in Jerusalem. His body was brought back to the capital city and buried in the royal cemetery (2 Chr 25:27-28).

2. Father of Joshah, a member of Simeon's tribe (1 Chr 4:34).

3. Hilkiah's son, a Levite of Merari's clan (1 Chr 6:45).

4. Priest of Bethel in the days of Jeroboam II and an opponent of the prophet Amos (Am 7:10-17).

AMI

Official in Solomon's court whose descendants returned to Jerusalem after the Exile (Ezr 2:57). Also spelled Amon in Nehemiah 7:59. *See* Amon #3.

AMITTAI

Father of the prophet Jonah from Zebulun's tribe. Amittai came from the small village of Gath-hepher northeast of Nazareth (2 Kgs 14:25; Jon 1:1).

AMMIEL

1. Gemalli's son, one of 12 men sent by Moses to spy out the land of Canaan. Ammiel represented Dan's tribe (Nm 13:12) and later died because of a plague (Nm 14:37).

2. Father of Machir of Lo-debar. Mephibosheth, Jonathan's son, was hidden from David in Machir's house (2 Sm 9:4-5). Machir later helped supply David in his war with Absalom (2 Sm 17:27-29).

3. Father of David's wife, Bath-shua (or Bathsheba, 1 Chr 3:5). Ammiel is also called Eliam (2 Sm 11:3).

4. Sixth son of Obed-edom, who, along with his family, served as gatekeeper in the Temple during David's reign (1 Chr 26:5, 15).

AMMIHUD

1. Father of a leader of Ephraim's tribe, Elishama (Nm 1:10). Ammihud was Joshua's great-grandfather (1 Chr 7:26).

2. Father of Shemuel from Simeon's tribe. Shemuel helped Moses apportion the Promised Land (Nm 34:20).

A

3. Father of Pedahel from Naphtali's tribe. Pedahel also helped Moses apportion the Promised Land (Nm 34:28).

4. Father of King Talmai of Geshur. Talmai gave refuge to Absalom when he fled after murdering Amnon (2 Sm 13:37).

5. Omri's son and father of Uthai from Judah's tribe (1 Chr 9:4).

AMMINADAB

1. Father of Elisheba, who was Aaron's wife (Ex 6:23). Amminadab was also the father of Nahshon, Judah's tribal leader in the wilderness (Nm 1:7; 2:3; 7:12, 17; 10:14; 1 Chr 2:10). Amminadab is listed in the genealogy of David (Ru 4:18-22) and later in the genealogy of Jesus Christ (Mt 1:4; Lk 3:33).

2. Alternate name for Izhar, one of Kohath's sons (1 Chr 6:22). See Izhar #1.

3. Levite contemporary of King David who helped bring the Ark of the Lord to Jerusalem (1 Chr 15:1-4, 10-11).

AMMISHADDAI

Ahiezer's father. Ahiezer was leader of Dan's tribe when the Israelites were wandering in the Sinai wilderness after their escape from Egypt (Nm 1:12; 2:25; 10:25). As leader he presented his tribe's offering at the consecration of the Tabernacle (Nm 7:66, 71).

AMMIZABAD

Benaiah's son. Both Benaiah and Ammizabad were high-ranking officers in King David's army (1 Chr 27:5-6).

AMNON

1. David's oldest son by his wife Ahinoam, born in Hebron (2 Sm 3:2; 1 Chr 3:1). Amnon deceived and violated Tamar, his beautiful half sister, and was killed in revenge by Tamar's brother Absalom (2 Sm 13:1-33).

2. First son of Shimon from Judah's tribe (1 Chr 4:20).

AMOK

Priest who returned to Jerusalem with Zerubbabel after the Exile. Amok was the ancestor of Eber, a priest under Joiakim (Neh 12:7, 20).

AMON

1. Governor of the city of Samaria during the reign of Ahab in Israel (1 Kgs 22:26; 2 Chr 18:25). Amon imprisoned the prophet Micaiah while Ahab defied Micaiah's warning against attacking Ramoth-gilead.

2. King Manasseh's son, the 15th king of Judah (642–640 BC). Amon was 22 years old

when he became king. He indulged in idolatry like his father and after a two-year reign was assassinated in a palace coup (2 Kgs 21:19-26; 2 Chr 33:20-25).

3. Official of Solomon; his descendants returned to Jerusalem after the Exile (Neh 7:59). The spelling Ami (Ezr 2:57) is a variant of this name.

4. Egyptian god, probably a fertility deity (Jer 46:25).

AMOS

Hebrew prophet of the eighth century BC. Nothing is known about Amos apart from the book that bears his name. He was a shepherd living in Tekoa, a village about 10 miles (16 kilometers) south of Jerusalem, when God spoke to him in a vision (Am 1:1-2). The kingdom was then divided, with Uzziah king of Judah in the south and Jeroboam II king of Israel in the north. In Amos's vision, the Lord was like a lion roaring out judgment on injustice and idolatry, especially among God's own people. The short biographical section of his writings shows Amos preaching only at Bethel, in Israel, about 12 miles (19 kilometers) north of Jerusalem and just over the border. Bethel had been made the royal religious sanctuary of Israel by Jeroboam I to rival Jerusalem in Judah. Amos prophesied that Israel would be overrun and its king killed. The priest of Bethel, Amaziah, called Amos a traitor and told him to go back to Judah and do his prophesying there. Amos replied, "I'm not a professional prophet, and I was never trained to be one. I'm just a shepherd, and I take care of sycamore-fig trees." But the Lord told him, "Go and prophesy to my people in Israel" (Am 7:10-15, NLT). Amos was evidently a God-fearing man who deeply felt the mistreatment of the poor by the privileged classes. He did not want to be identified with an elite group of professional prophets, who may have lost their original fervor. His writings reflect the earthy background of a shepherd (3:12). But he spoke with authority the message given him by the Lord God of Hosts: "I want to see a mighty flood of justice, an endless river of righteous living" (5:24, NLT). The message of Amos was a call to repentance of personal and social sins and a return to the worship of the one true God and to the covenantal standards that made the Jewish people a nation.

AMOZ

Isaiah's father (2 Kgs 19:2; Is 1:1), not to be confused with the prophet Amos.

AMPLIATUS

Name of a Christian to whom the apostle Paul sent greetings at the end of his Letter to the Romans (16:8). Called "my beloved in the Lord" (RSV) by Paul, nothing further is known of this Christian who bore a common Roman name.

AMRAM

1. Kohath's son, a member of Levi's tribe. Amram married Jochebed and had three famous children: Aaron, Moses, and Miriam (Ex 6:16-20; Nm 26:58-59). During the

Israelites' wilderness journey, the responsibility of the Amramites was to care for the Ark and the table, lampstand, altars, and other furnishings used in the Tabernacle (Nm 3:27, 31). Later, the Amramites were one of the groups in charge of offerings placed in the Temple treasury (1 Chr 26:23-24).

2. Priest from Bani's family, who obeyed Ezra's exhortation to divorce his pagan wife after the Exile (Ezr 10:34).

3. KJV form of Hamran, Dishon's son, in 1 Chronicles 1:41. Hamran itself is an alternate form of Hemdan (cf. Gn 36:26). *See* Hemdan.

AMRAPHEL

King of Shinar (Babylonia), who helped King Chedorlaomer of Elam quell a revolt of five vassal cities in Palestine (Gn 14:1-11).

AMZI

1. Merarite Levite and an ancestor of Ethan the musician (1 Chr 6:46).

2. Forefather of Adaiah and a priest of Malchijah's division (Neh 11:12).

ANAH

1. Son of Zibeon the Hivite and father of Oholibamah. Oholibamah was one of Esau's wives (Gn 36:2, 18).

2. Fourth son of Seir the Horite. Anah was a chief among the Horites who also had a daughter named Oholibamah (Gn 36:20, 25; 1 Chr 1:38, 41).

3. Son of Zibeon who found hot springs in the wasteland (Gn 36:24). This Zibeon was a brother to #2 above. *See* Zibeon.

ANAIAH

1. Priest and assistant of Ezra who explained to the people passages from the law read by Ezra (Neh 8:4).

2. Political leader who signed Ezra's covenant of faithfulness to God with Nehemiah and others after the Exile (Neh 10:22). He is perhaps identical with #1 above.

ANAMMELECH

Deity associated with Adrammelech, who was worshiped by the people of Sepharvaim, whom the Assyrians relocated in Samaria after 722 BC. Anammelech is evidently the Hebrew rendering of the designation for a Mesopotamian deity, Anu-melek, meaning "Anu is King." Anu was the name of the chief god of Assyria, the sky god. The worship of this deity by the Sepharvites in Samaria included child sacrifice (2 Kgs 17:31). It is not certain whether the burning of children in the Anu cult was brought from Sepharvaim or was an innovation when the Sepharvites came to Canaan.

ANAN

One of the chiefs of the people who set his seal on Ezra's covenant to keep God's law during the postexilic era (Neh 10:26).

ANANI

One of seven sons of Elioenai, a descendant of David (1 Chr 3:24).

ANANIAH

Azariah's grandfather. Azariah was one of three men who repaired the Jerusalem wall near their homes after the Exile (Neh 3:23).

ANANIAS

1. Member of the early church in Jerusalem. Along with his wife, Sapphira, he was struck dead for attempted deception with regard to some money (Acts 5:1-5).

2. Early convert to Christianity who was living in Damascus when Saul of Tarsus (Paul) arrived there supposedly to arrest Christians. Ananias knew that Paul was a deadly enemy of Christians, but the Lord reassured him, explaining that Paul had been chosen as a special messenger of the gospel (Acts 9:13-16). The Lord sent Ananias to the newly converted Paul to restore his eyesight (Acts 9:17-19). Ananias told Paul the meaning of his unusual encounter with Christ on the road to Damascus (Acts 22:12-16) and probably introduced him to the church there as a new Christian brother rather than a persecutor. Various traditions say that Ananias later became one of the 70 disciples of Jerusalem, a bishop of Damascus, and a martyr.

3. High priest who presided over the Sanhedrin when the apostle Paul was arrested and questioned by that council in Jerusalem at the end of Paul's third missionary journey (Acts 22:30–23:10). Ananias was one of the witnesses who testified against Paul in Caesarea when he was on trial before Felix, the Roman governor (Acts 24:1). This Ananias was appointed high priest by Herod Agrippa II in AD 48 and served until AD 59. The Jewish historian Josephus wrote that he was wealthy, haughty, and unscrupulous. He was known for his collaboration with the Romans and for his severity and cruelty. Hated by nationalistic Jews, he was killed by them when war with Rome broke out in AD 66.

ANATH

1. Parent of Shamgar, one of the judges of Israel (Jgs 3:31; 5:6). Since the name Anath is feminine, it is likely that Anath was Shamgar's mother.

2. Canaanite goddess of fertility.

ANATHOTH

1. Becher's son from Benjamin's tribe (1 Chr 7:8).

2. Political leader who signed Ezra's covenant of faithfulness to God with Nehemiah and others after the Exile (Neh 10:19).

ANDREW, THE APOSTLE

One of Christ's 12 apostles. Andrew first appears in the NT as a disciple of John the Baptist (Jn 1:35, 40). After hearing John say, "Look, there is the Lamb of God!" (Jn 1:36), referring to Jesus, Andrew and another unnamed disciple followed Jesus and stayed with him for a day (Jn 1:36-39). Andrew then told his brother, Simon Peter, that he had found the Messiah and brought Peter to Jesus (Jn 1:40-42). From then on Andrew faded into the background, and his brother came into prominence. Whenever the relationship of the two is mentioned, Andrew is always described as the brother of Simon Peter and never the other way around (Mt 4:18; Mk 1:16; Jn 1:40; 6:8), although Andrew is also mentioned without reference to his relationship to Peter (Mk 1:29; 3:18; 13:3; Jn 12:22). Andrew's father was John (Mt 16:17; Jn 1:42; 21:15-17), and his hometown was Bethsaida (Jn 1:44), a village on the north shore of the Sea of Galilee.

The Gospel of John mentions disciples being with Jesus (2:2; 4:2), and it is likely that Andrew was one of that early group. Evidently, however, he returned to his activity as a fisherman on the Sea of Galilee, where he shared a house with Peter and his family in Capernaum (Mt 4:18-20; Mk 1:16-18, 29-33). While they were fishing, Andrew and Peter received a definite call to follow Jesus and become those who fish for people. From among the disciples of Jesus a group of 12 were later specially chosen as apostles. Andrew is always listed among the first four named, along with Peter and two other brothers, John and James (Mt 10:2-4; Lk 6:13-16; Acts 1:13).

Andrew is named in only three other contexts in the Gospels. At the feeding of the 5,000 he called attention to the boy who had five barley loaves and two fish (Jn 6:8-9). When certain Greeks came to Philip, asking to see Jesus, Philip told Andrew and then the two of them told Jesus (Jn 12:20-22). Finally, Andrew is listed among those who were questioning Jesus privately on the Mt of Olives (Mk 13:3-4). The last NT mention of Andrew is in the list of apostles waiting in the upper room in Jerusalem for the promised outpouring of the Holy Spirit (Acts 1:12-14).

Various documents associated with Andrew, such as the Acts of Andrew mentioned by the early church historian Eusebius, are of doubtful value. Some traditions indicate that Andrew ministered in Scythia. According to the Muratorian Canon, Andrew received a revelation at night that the apostle John should write the fourth Gospel. Tradition is rather uniform that Andrew died at Patrae in Achaia. A story developed that he was martyred on an X-shaped cross (a "decussate" or "saltire" cross), which has become known as St Andrew's Cross. Another tradition is that an arm of the dead Andrew was taken into Scotland as a relic by Regulus, and thus Andrew became known as a patron saint of Scotland. On the calendar of saints of the Roman and Greek churches, Andrew's date is set as November 30.

ANDRONICUS
Christian greeted by the apostle Paul in his Letter to the Romans (16:7) but not mentioned elsewhere. Paul called Andronicus his kinsman. The word could mean fellow countryman, fellow Jew, member of Paul's own family, or other relative. Andronicus may also have been a fellow prisoner for the cause of Christ, perhaps even in the same prison with Paul (2 Cor 6:4-5; 11:23). Paul described him as a man of note among the apostles and recognized him respectfully as an "older" Christian.

ANER
Amorite ally of Abram and brother of Mamre and Eshcol (Gn 14:13). With his brothers, Aner helped Abram defeat a confederation of four kings who had plundered Sodom and Gomorrah and had captured Abram's nephew Lot (Gn 14:14-16, 21-24).

ANIAM
Shemida's son from Naphtali's tribe (1 Chr 7:19).

ANNA
Phanuel's daughter from Asher's tribe and a prophetess in Jerusalem when Jesus was a young child. Advanced in years, she worshiped with prayer and fasting day and night in the Temple. When Jesus was brought by his parents and presented to the Lord in the Temple, she came up, thanking God and speaking of him to all who were looking for the redemption of Jerusalem (Lk 2:36-38).

ANNAS
Jewish high priest from AD 7 to 15. Appointed by Quirinius, Roman governor of Syria, Annas was put out of office by Valerius Gratus, procurator of Judea. Annas was succeeded by three minor figures before the post was assumed by his son-in-law Caiaphas (Jn 18:13, 24). The tenure of Caiaphas extended from AD 18 to 36; thus, he was high priest at the time of Jesus' public ministry.

Evidently Annas's power and influence remained considerable even after his removal from that office. Like an American Supreme Court justice, the high priest held a lifetime appointment. Deposition of a high priest by the pagan Romans would have been strongly resented by the Jews. Consequently, Annas may still have been referred to as high priest among the populace, as a sort of high priest emeritus. Such a practice, evidenced in the writings of the Jewish historian Josephus, tends to clear up those references in the NT to Annas as high priest during the same chronological period as Caiaphas (Lk 3:2; Jn 18:19, 22-24; Acts 4:6). The fact that Annas conducted a private inquiry of Jesus after he was arrested (Jn 18:13, 19-24) but before he was taken to Caiaphas, is a strong indication that Annas was still a person of considerable stature among the Jewish religious leaders.

Annas is also mentioned in the NT account of an investigation of the apostles Peter and

John. Interestingly, the penalty imposed on the apostles was far less severe than the one Jesus suffered (Acts 4:6-21).

ANTHOTHIJAH
Benjaminite and Shashak's son (1 Chr 8:24).

ANTIPAS
1. Early martyr in the church at Pergamum (Rv 2:13).
2. Son of Herod the Great. *See* Herod.

ANUB
Koz's son from Judah's tribe (1 Chr 4:8).

APELLES
Roman Christian who received special greetings from the apostle Paul and the complimentary assessment of being one who is "approved in Christ" (Rom 16:10, RSV).

APHIAH
Ancestor of King Saul in Benjamin's tribe (1 Sm 9:1).

APOLLOS
Native of Alexandria (Egypt), a Christian Jew who was an eloquent preacher at the time of the apostle Paul's missionary journeys. The chief biblical passage about Apollos is Acts 18:24–19:1. From Alexandria, Apollos went to Ephesus in Asia Minor. Enthusiastic in spirit, learned and cultured in his ways, well versed in the OT Scriptures, and instructed in the way of the Lord, he began to speak boldly and openly in the synagogue there. Apollos knew and preached accurately about the coming of Jesus but knew of it only from the message of Jesus' forerunner, John the Baptist. Priscilla and Aquila, Paul's friends and former associates, heard Apollos speak in Ephesus and realized that he had not heard what had happened to Jesus. They took him aside privately and explained the way of God to him more accurately. Before that, he had been convinced of the value of John's baptism and John's message that Jesus was the Messiah. He was evidently uninformed, however, about such teachings as justification by faith in Christ or the work of the Holy Spirit in salvation. At such points, Priscilla and Aquila, having lived and worked with Paul, were able to help Apollos.

Soon after this instruction, Apollos left Ephesus for the Roman province of Achaia in Greece with letters from the Ephesian Christians, urging the disciples in Achaia to welcome him as a Christian brother. On arrival, he vigorously and publicly refuted the Jews, using his great knowledge of the OT Scriptures to prove that Jesus was the Messiah. Paul considered Apollos's work in Corinth, capital of Achaia, so valuable that he described him as waterer of the seed that Paul had planted as the founder of the church (1 Cor 3:5-11). From 1 Corinthians it is also clear that one of the factions dividing the Corinthian church was a clique centered around Apollos, although he was not directly responsible for it (1 Cor 1:12; 3:1-4). Paul had difficulty convincing Apollos that he should return to Corinth, perhaps because Apollos did not want to encourage the continuance of that little group (1 Cor 16:12).

APPAIM
Nadab's son, and the father of Ishi in Judah's tribe (1 Chr 2:30-31).

APPHIA
Christian woman in Colosse, possibly the wife or sister of Philemon. The apostle Paul greeted her in his letter to Philemon (v 2). According to tradition, she was martyred during Nero's persecution. On the saints' calendar of the Greek Orthodox Church, she is honored on November 22.

AQUILA
See Priscilla and Aquila.

ARA
Son of Jether, a chief among Asher's tribe (1 Chr 7:38).

ARAD
Beriah's son, of Benjamin's tribe (1 Chr 8:15).

ARAH
1. Ulla's son from Asher's tribe (1 Chr 7:39).

2. Ancestor of a group of people that returned to Jerusalem with Zerubbabel after the Exile (Ezr 2:5; Neh 7:10).

ARAM
1. Shem's son and Noah's grandson (Gn 10:22-23; 1 Chr 1:17). Ancestor of the Arameans.

2. Kemuel's son, grandson of Abraham's brother Nahor (Gn 22:21).

3. Shemer's son from Asher's tribe (1 Chr 7:34).

4. The Aram occurring in the genealogy of Jesus Christ (Mt 1:3-4, KJV) is a mistranslation of the Greek word *Aram,* meaning "Ram"—an entirely different name (Ru 4:19). *See* Ram #1.

ARAN
Dishan's son, grandson of Seir the Horite, and a descendant of Esau (Gn 36:28; 1 Chr 1:42).

ARAUNAH

Jebusite whose threshing floor was the scene of some significant events in biblical history. (Jebus was the ancient Canaanite city that later became Jerusalem.) Araunah's threshing floor marked the place where the Lord stopped an angel from further inflicting Israel with a pestilence after the death of 70,000 Israelites (2 Sm 24:15-16). The plague from the Lord had come upon Israel as a result of King David's prideful census. At the instruction of the prophet Gad, the repentant David purchased the floor and built an altar to the Lord (2 Sm 24:17-25). Araunah offered oxen and everything needed for the altar as a gift, but David insisted on paying him, saying, "I will not present burnt offerings to the LORD my God that have cost me nothing" (2 Sm 24:24, NLT). A parallel account (1 Chr 21:15-16) uses the Hebrew form Ornan for the Jebusite's foreign name. David was in too much of a hurry to go to the Tabernacle to make his sacrifice, the Tabernacle and altar being farther away on the hill of Gibeon (1 Chr 21:27-30). David chose the threshing floor as the site for the Temple (1 Chr 22:1), and Solomon built it there on Mt Moriah (2 Chr 3:1). It was the same area to which God commanded Abraham to go for the sacrifice of Isaac (Gn 22:2). Tradition locates the present-day Muslim mosque, the Dome of the Rock, on the site of Araunah's threshing floor.

ARBA

Ancestor of the giant Anakim and a great hero among them (Jos 15:13; 21:11). Arba was the founder of Kiriath-arba (city of Arba), later known as Hebron (Jos 14:15).

ARCHELAUS

Son of Herod the Great who followed his father in governing Idumea, Samaria, and Judea (Mt 2:22). *See* Herod.

ARCHIPPUS

Contemporary of Paul whom the apostle encouraged to fulfill his ministry (Col 4:17) and referred to as a "fellow soldier" (Phlm 1:2).

ARD

One of the nine sons of Bela (Nm 26:40), Benjamin's firstborn son (1 Chr 8:1). Ard is called Benjamin's son in the Hebrew sense, meaning descendant (Gn 46:21). He was the founder of the Ardite family, a subclan of Benjamin's tribe. The Ard/Addar transposition in 1 Chronicles 8:3 is probably a result of scribal error.

ARDON

Caleb's third son by Azubah; a descendant of Judah (1 Chr 2:18).

ARELI

One of Gad's seven sons (Gn 46:16). After the plague of Baal-peor, Areli's descendants, the Arelites, were numbered in Moses' census in preparation for war with the Midianites (Nm 25:6-18; 26:17).

ARETAS

A king over Damascus mentioned in the NT. The apostle Paul had to escape from Damascus by being let down in a basket through a window in the wall because the governor there under King Aretas was guarding the city in order to seize him (2 Cor 11:32-33). This king has been identified as Eneas, who took the title Aretas IV and ruled from 9 BC to AD 40. He attacked and defeated Herod Antipas over a boundary dispute and also as revenge. (Antipas had divorced Aretas's daughter in order to marry Herodias.)

ARGOB

Individual supposedly killed with King Pekahiah of Israel in Pekah's revolt (2 Kgs 15:25). The early church father Jerome thought the name Argob (along with Arieh) referred to a place. Today some scholars think that Argob and Arieh may have been accidentally misplaced from a list of place names (2 Kgs 15:29) through scribal error.

ARIDAI

One of Haman's ten sons, who was killed with his father when Haman's plot to destroy the Jews was foiled (Est 9:7-10).

ARIDATHA

One of Haman's ten sons, who was killed with his father when Haman's plot to destroy the Jews was foiled (Est 9:7-10).

ARIEH

Person mentioned along with Argob in 2 Kings 15:25 (KJV, NIV, NLT).

ARIEL

1. Person or thing overcome in a heroic deed by Benaiah, chief of David's bodyguard (2 Sm 23:20; 1 Chr 11:22). It is not clear that the Hebrew word *ariel* is a proper name in these passages. Benaiah may have killed two "lionlike men" of Moab (KJV) or destroyed two Moabite altar hearths.
2. One of the men sent by Ezra to ask Iddo for Levitical priests to accompany the Jewish exiles returning to Jerusalem from Babylon (Ezr 8:16).

ARIOCH

1. King of Ellasar, who with three other kings captured five cities and took a number of prisoners, including Abraham's nephew Lot (Gn 14:1-16).
2. Nebuchadnezzar's captain of the guard (KJV) or chief executioner, who took Daniel to the Babylonian king to interpret his dream (Dn 2:14-25).

ARISAI

One of Haman's ten sons, who was killed with his father when Haman's plot to destroy the Jews was foiled (Est 9:7-10).

ARISTARCHUS

Companion of the apostle Paul; Macedonian from Thessalonica, possibly of Jewish ancestry. He is first mentioned as one of those seized by an angry mob in Ephesus (Acts 19:29). Later he accompanied Paul on the return from his third missionary journey (Acts 20:4) as well as to Rome to face Caesar (Acts 27:1-2). Paul described him as a coworker (Phlm 1:24) and fellow prisoner from whom he received great comfort (Col 4:10-11). Tradition says that Aristarchus was martyred in Rome under Nero.

ARISTOBULUS

Person whose family or household was greeted by the apostle Paul (Rom 16:10). The name (of Greek origin, meaning "best advising") was used in intertestamental times by ruling families in Palestine and mentioned once in the NT.

ARMONI

One of Saul's two sons by his concubine Rizpah. Seven of Saul's sons, including Armoni, were handed over to the Gibeonites by David to be killed to avenge Saul's slaughter of the Gibeonites (2 Sm 21:1, 8-9).

ARNAN

Rephaiah's son and Obadiah's father, a descendant of David through Zerubbabel (1 Chr 3:21).

ARNI

Ancestor of Jesus according to Luke's genealogy (3:33); also called Ram in Ruth 4:19 and 1 Chronicles 2:9-10.

ARODI

Gad's sixth son, founder of the Arodite family (Nm 26:17). He is called Arodi in the list of those who went to Egypt with Jacob (Gn 46:16).

ARPHAXAD

Shem's son and Noah's grandson, born two years after the Flood. Arphaxad's descendants were probably the Chaldeans (Gn 10:22-24; 11:10-13; 1 Chr 1:17-18, 24; Lk 3:36). Arphaxad was born two years after the Flood when his father was one hundred years old (Gn 11:10) and was the grandfather of Eber, whom some believe was ancestor of the Hebrews (1 Chr 1:17-25; Lk 3:35-36).

ARTAXERXES

Name of three kings of the Persian Empire.
1. Artaxerxes I (465–424 BC), known as Macrocheir or Longimanus, son and successor of Xerxes I (486–465 BC). Xerxes I was the Ahasuerus of the book of Esther and of Ezra 4:6. A few years after the succession of Artaxerxes I, the Greeks urged Egypt to

revolt against Persia. Only in 454 BC was that movement crushed along with other dissension in the Persian Empire. By 449 BC, when peace was made between the Greeks and Persians by the treaty of Callias, Artaxerxes had gained full control over his empire, and a period of peace resulted.

Artaxerxes I was the ruler who brought the rebuilding of Jerusalem to a temporary standstill (Ezr 4:7-23), and who commissioned Ezra to visit the city in the capacity of secretary of state of Jewish affairs in 458 BC (Ezr 7:8, 11-26). In 445 BC Nehemiah went to Jerusalem as civil governor in the 20th year of Artaxerxes I (Neh 1:1; 2:1). By altering the text of Ezra 7:7 to read "thirty-seventh" instead of "seventh," some scholars have tried to show that Artaxerxes II was the Persian king under whom Nehemiah worked. The Elephantine papyri, however, indicate that Sanballat, governor of Samaria, was quite advanced in years in 408 BC, shortly before the death of Darius II (423–405 BC); hence Sanballat's opposition to Nehemiah must have occurred years earlier under Artaxerxes I. The dates of Ezra and Nehemiah thus fall within the lifetime of this monarch.

Artaxerxes I was notable for his kindness toward the Jews in Persia, once matters of procedure had been established clearly; his support for the work of Ezra and Nehemiah is evident from their writings.

See also Ahasuerus.

2. Artaxerxes II Mnemon (404–359 BC), grandson of Artaxerxes I and son of Darius II. His reign was a time of unrest in the Persian Empire, one result of which was the loss of Egypt about 401 BC. He constructed several splendid buildings and seems to have enlarged the palace at Susa.

3. Artaxerxes III Ochus (358–338 BC), son and successor of Artaxerxes II. He brought peace to the empire by shrewd diplomacy, but he was assassinated. Neither he nor his father is mentioned in the OT.

ARTEMAS

Christian coworker with Paul, whom the apostle considered as a replacement for Titus on the island of Crete (Ti 3:12). Later tradition describes Artemas as bishop of Lystra.

ARZA

Superintendent of the palace at Tirzah belonging to King Elah of the northern kingdom of Israel. The drunken king was murdered in Arza's home by Zimri, who then declared himself king (1 Kgs 16:9-10).

ASA

1. Third king of the southern kingdom of Judah (910–869 BC) after the split of Solomon's Empire into independent kingdoms. Solomon's son Rehoboam, Asa's grandfather, had neither Solomon's wisdom nor his tact. Rehoboam failed to use diplomacy to avoid

an approaching explosion of popular resentment against Solomon's oppressive policies; in fact, Rehoboam actively precipitated the explosion. Asa came to the throne just after his father, Abijam (or Abijah), who reigned only briefly (913–910 BC). Asa thus inherited a shrunken, vulnerable kingdom. Moreover, he was thrust into a suddenly unstable political arena shaken by collapse of the great world empires of old Babylonia to the north and east in Mesopotamia, and of Egypt to the southwest. Hence, until the emerging might of Assyria was firmly established (mid-ninth century BC), the small Palestinian states (Israel, Judah, Syria, the Arameans, and Phoenicians, and to some degree the peoples of Moab and Edom) were free to push and shove among themselves.

The rival states had superficial similarities, especially Judah and Israel, but were divided by deep differences and intense self-interest. Borders were in perpetual dispute—never fully settled but seldom contested in all-out bloody conflict. Threats, expedience, bribes, payment of tribute, marriages purchased for power, and other cunning arts in the catalog of political kingcraft were employed to shift alliances. Since all were playing the same game, a kind of fluid balance resulted.

At the beginning of King Asa's reign there was an initial decade of peace and prosperity. Then, however, he was called upon to face enemy threats and invasion. In those crises he trusted God and forced out or defeated all who attempted to conquer, divide, or destroy Judah (2 Chr 14:1-8). Further, he cleansed the land of pagan shrines and places of worship and even took away the royal prerogatives and standing of Maacah, his mother. She had erected an image of the fertility goddess Asherah (1 Kgs 15:10; 2 Chr 15:16).

Nonetheless, later in his reign Asa abruptly abandoned his trust in God. By means of a huge gift that stripped the Temple treasures, he entered an alliance with Ben-hadad, king of Damascus (Syria) in order to force Baasha, ruler of the northern kingdom of Israel, to withdraw from newly conquered territory in Judah. Asa had become heedless of God's faithful protection when Israel, Judah's mortal enemy, stood triumphant and strategically poised to strike, only five miles (8 kilometers) from Jerusalem. Asa's power play worked. Israel had to retire from the field in the south to meet Ben-hadad's threat from the north. When Hanani spoke plainly to Asa about his disbelief in God, Asa was infuriated and had Hanani thrown into prison (2 Chr 16:7-10).

For the last years of his long 41-year reign, Asa was ill: "Even with the severity of his disease, he did not seek the LORD's help but turned only to his physicians" (2 Chr 16:12, NLT). He died and was buried with honor in the royal tombs (1 Kgs 15:24; 2 Chr 16:14).

2. A Levite and Berechiah's father. Berechiah lived in one of the villages of the Netophathites after the Exile (1 Chr 9:16).

ASAHEL

1. Warrior among David's mighty men known as "the thirty" (2 Sm 23:24; 1 Chr 11:26). Asahel was the son of David's half sister Zeruiah and the brother of Joab and Abishai (2 Sm 2:18; 1 Chr 2:16). In the battle of Gibeon, David's general Joab engaged the forces of Abner, leader of Ishbosheth's army. Asahel, who "could run like a deer," pursued Abner, but in the ensuing encounter Abner killed Asahel (2 Sm 2:18-23, 32).

2. One of the Levites sent out by King Jehoshaphat of Judah to teach the people the law of the Lord (2 Chr 17:8).

3. Temple aide appointed by King Hezekiah to take care of the tithed offerings given to support the Levites (2 Chr 31:13).

4. Father of Jonathan. Jonathan (not to be confused with Saul's son) opposed the appointment of a commission to take action concerning the foreign (pagan) wives of some of the Jews after the Babylonian exile (Ezr 10:15).

ASAIAH

1. Royal servant sent by King Josiah of Judah to ask the prophetess Huldah about the meaning of the Book of the Law found in the renovation of the Temple (2 Kgs 22:12, 14; 2 Chr 34:20).

2. Clan leader of Simeon's tribe who settled in Gedor (Gerar?) during Hezekiah's reign (1 Chr 4:36).

3. Levitical leader in the time of King David. Asaiah helped bring the Ark to Jerusalem (1 Chr 6:30; 15:6, 11).

4. Shiloni's oldest son. Asaiah's family was among the first to resettle in Jerusalem after the Exile (1 Chr 9:5). Perhaps the same as Maaseiah of Nehemiah 11:5. *See* Maaseiah #14.

ASAPH

1. Berechiah's son, an important Tabernacle musician during King David's reign (1 Chr 6:31-32, 39). Along with Heman, the head singer, and Ethan, Asaph was appointed to sound bronze cymbals during the ceremony when the Ark was brought to the new Tabernacle (1 Chr 15:1-19). David appointed Asaph to serve "by giving constant praise and thanks to the Lord God of Israel" (1 Chr 16:4-5, TLB) and to lead Israel in a special psalm of praise (1 Chr 16:7-36). Along with his relatives he ministered daily before the Ark (1 Chr 16:37; 25:6, 9; 1 Esd 1:15; 5:27, 59). He was also described as David's private prophet (1 Chr 25:1-2). Asaph's name appears in the superscriptions of Psalms 50 and 73–83 and in the guild he established, "the sons of Asaph" (1 Chr 25:1; 2 Chr 35:15; Ezr 2:41; Neh 7:44; 11:22).

2. Joah's father. Joah was the recorder (court historian or royal scribe) in King Hezekiah's administration (2 Kgs 18:18, 27; Is 36:33).

3. Temple guard or gatekeeper, seemingly the same person as Ebiasaph (1 Chr 9:18).

4. Keeper of the king's forest in Palestine under Artaxerxes I Longimanus (Neh 2:8). Nehemiah asked this Asaph for timber to rebuild the wall, gates, and structures of Jerusalem.

ASAREL
Jehallelel's son from Judah's tribe (1 Chr 4:16).

ASARELAH
One of Asaph's four sons appointed by David to assist with prophecy and music in the sanctuary (1 Chr 25:2); alternately called Jesharelah in verse 14.

ASENATH
Joseph's Egyptian wife who became the mother of Manasseh and Ephraim. Asenath was the daughter of the priest Potiphera (Gn 41:45, 50-52; 46:20).

ASHBEL
Benjamin's son who emigrated to Egypt with his grandfather Jacob (Gn 46:21; 1 Chr 8:1). The Ashbelites, his descendants, were included in Moses' census in the wilderness (Nm 26:38). Ashbel is elsewhere called Jediael (1 Chr 7:6).

ASHER
Jacob's son born to Leah's maid Zilpah (Gn 30:12-13). The name Asher, probably meaning "happy," was given to the child by Leah in her delight at his birth. Asher had four sons, Imnah, Ishvah, Ishvi, and Beriah, and a daughter, Serah (Gn 46:17; 1 Chr 7:30). Some have speculated that the tribe of Asher took its name from a locality mentioned in Egyptian texts of the 13th century BC. It is more likely that the tribe bore the name of its ancestor. Asher and his brothers received a special blessing and prediction from Jacob as he was dying (Gn 49:20; cf. Dt 33:24-25, where the dying Moses blessed Asher and the other tribes).

ASHHUR
Caleb's son and Tekoa's father (1 Chr 2:24; 4:5), or perhaps the founder of a village named Tekoa (2 Sm 14:1-3; Am 1:1).

ASHKENAZ
Gomer's son and Noah's great-grandson in Japheth's line (Gn 10:1-3; 1 Chr 1:6). Mention of the kingdom of Ashkenaz along with Ararat and Minni (Jer 51:27) suggests that he was the ancestor of the Scythians, a people who resided in the Ararat region in Jeremiah's time. An active, warlike people, the Scythians contributed to the unrest of the Assyrian Empire

and to its eventual collapse. The plural term "Ashkenazim" is now used for the Jews who settled in middle and eastern Europe after the Dispersion, in contrast with the Sephardim, those who settled in the Iberian Peninsula (Spain and Portugal).

ASHPENAZ

Official under Nebuchadnezzar in charge of palace personnel (Dn 1:3). Ashpenaz was reluctant to grant the captives from Judah, Daniel and his friends, a reprieve from eating the king's food, but eventually he did so (Dn 1:8-16). (Eating food from the table of Gentiles would have forced Daniel and his friends to violate the law of God.) Three years later, Ashpenaz presented the young men before the king. Nebuchadnezzar found them outstanding in wisdom and good judgment in spite of their vegetarian diet and abstemious lifestyle (Dn 1:18-20).

ASHURBANIPAL

Esarhaddon's son and the Assyrian ruler (669–633 BC) who reigned in the years during which kings Manasseh, Amon, and Josiah governed the southern kingdom of Judah. The northern kingdom of Israel, whose capital was Samaria, had fallen in 722 BC to another powerful Assyrian ruler, Sargon II.

Throughout his life, Ashurbanipal (also spelled Assurbanipal) had to fight continually to retain, regain, and defend his empire, which included Babylonia, Persia, Syria, and Egypt. Though his chief interests were evidently cultural, he was required to spend most of his time, and almost all the resources of his empire, maintaining the submission of conquered peoples, putting down a civil war fomented under the leadership of his brother, and coping with constant border skirmishes.

Much of what we know about the culture of ancient Mesopotamia—historical facts, religion, legends, and lore—comes from the cuneiform literature collected by Ashurbanipal and deposited in a large library he built in Nineveh, his capital. The remains of this library, discovered about a century ago and now in the British Museum, continue to have impact on biblical knowledge. Without doubt his library has been his most significant memorial.

Ashurbanipal was evidently the Assyrian monarch who sent alien people into Samaria (Ezr 4:10). Deportation of conquered peoples was standard Assyrian policy, which accounts for the assimilation and disappearance of the ten tribes of Israel after its fall to Sargon II. In Ezra 4:10 the Assyrian king is called Osnappar, a transliteration of the Hebrew spelling. The consonantal similarity of the Hebrew word to the Assyrian name Ashurbanipal, plus the list of conquered peoples mentioned in the text, point to Ashurbanipal as the most likely identification.

By 630 BC the Assyrian Empire was experiencing difficulty in maintaining its cohesiveness, and after Ashurbanipal's death it could no longer sustain itself. Innumerable Assyrian soldiers had died on faraway battlefields; mercenaries and captives pressed into the military did not serve well. Moreover, hordes of barbarians from the steppes of Asia battered Assyria from the outside. Vassal Babylon successfully revolted. Though a mere shadow of its former glory, Egypt also slipped from its Assyrian yoke. Ashurbanipal's sons were not equal to the task. Probably no one could have been. In less than 20 years a relatively weak coalition of enemies surrounded Nineveh and in 612 BC razed the city. A spark of resistance continued at nearby Haran, but within months it was snuffed out by Median troops. By the same ruthless, unrestrained cruelty with which it ruled its empire, Assyria perished.

The demise of Assyria gave a new lease on life to the tiny kingdom of Judah. Some scholars place Ashurbanipal's death in King Josiah's eighth year of reign (cf. 2 Chr 34:3-7). As Assyria lost its grip, the resulting vacuum brought back independence by default. Young King Josiah was able to begin and to consummate the most sweeping spiritual revival and political reforms in Judah's history.

ASHVATH
Japhlet's son, a great warrior and head of a clan in Asher's tribe (1 Chr 7:33).

ASIEL
Jehu's great-grandfather. Jehu was a prince of Simeon's tribe (1 Chr 4:35, 38).

ASPATHA
One of Haman's ten sons, who was killed with his father when Haman's plot to destroy the Jews was foiled (Est 9:7).

ASRIEL
Manasseh's son (1 Chr 7:14). His descendants, the Asrielites, were included in Moses' census in the wilderness (Nm 26:31) and were later given a portion of the land allotted to Manasseh's tribe (Jos 17:2).

ASSHUR
Uncertain translation of a Hebrew word, appearing in English translations of the Bible as Assyria, Assyrian, Assyrians, or merely "Asshur." These variants come from the Assyrian word *asshur*.

1. Shem's son (Gn 10:22; 1 Chr 1:17). The reference may be merely a personification of the whole Assyrian people; however, since other names in the account (e.g., Arpach-shad, Gn 10:24; 11:12) seem to indicate individual persons, perhaps Asshur should be taken in the same way. If so, this individual may have been the founder of the city Asshur to which he gave his name, the names of a god and nation being further derived from the city.

2. KJV translation of the word for Assyria in Genesis 10:11. It is improperly translated as a person and should be understood as in the NLT: "He [Nimrod] expanded his reign to Assyria." In that country, east of the Tigris River, Nimrod built four cities: Nineveh, Rehoboth-ir, Calah, and Resen.

ASSIR

1. Korah's son and a descendant of Levi through Kohath (Ex 6:24; 1 Chr 6:22).
2. Ebiasaph's son and a descendant of #1 above (1 Chr 6:23, 37).
3. Son of Jeconiah (Jehoiachin), king of Judah (1 Chr 3:17, KJV). It has been suggested that the Hebrew word *assir* may here be an adjective (as in NLT) describing Jeconiah and meaning "while captive" (cf. 2 Kgs 24:15). If so, his children were born while he was a captive.

ASYNCRITUS

One of the Christians in Rome to whom Paul sent greetings (Rom 16:14).

ATARAH

Onam's mother and second wife of Jerahmeel (1 Chr 2:26).

ATER

1. Ancestor of a group of people who returned to Judah with Zerubbabel after the Exile (Ezr 2:16; Neh 7:21).
2. Ancestor of a family of gatekeepers who also returned to Judah with Zerubbabel (Ezr 2:42; Neh 7:45).
3. Political leader who signed Ezra's covenant of faithfulness to God with Nehemiah and others after the Exile (Neh 10:17).

ATHAIAH

Uzziah's son from Judah's tribe, a resident of Jerusalem after the Exile (Neh 11:4).

ATHALIAH

1. Wife of King Jehoram of Judah, and daughter of King Ahab of Israel and his wife, Jezebel. Athaliah, Judah's only queen, ruled 841–835 BC (2 Kgs 11; 2 Chr 22–23).

   Like her mother, Jezebel, Athaliah worshiped the Canaanite god Baal and encouraged her husband to do the same. Evidently she had considerable influence over Jehoram. After his death their son Ahaziah was made king (2 Kgs 8:25-27; 2 Chr 22:1). Like Jehoram, Ahaziah was influenced by Athaliah and did "what was evil in the LORD's sight" (2 Kgs 8:27).

   Because the kings of Israel and Judah disobeyed the Lord, Jehu was anointed by God to be the true king of Israel (2 Kgs 9:2-3). Jehu then killed Joram, king of Israel (2 Kgs 9:24), and Ahaziah, king of Judah (2 Kgs 9:27; 2 Chr 22:9). After the death of her son, Athaliah seized the throne of Judah by destroying (so she thought) all the males in the royal family (2 Kgs 11:1; 2 Chr 22:10). But Jehoshabeath, Jehoram's daughter and the wife of Jehoiada the priest, rescued Ahaziah's son Joash and hid him away (2 Kgs 11:2-3, 2 Chr 22:11-12).

After six years Jehoiada "took courage" and resolved to reveal the young prince Joash to the people, making an agreement with some mercenary army officers who summoned to Jerusalem "the Levites ... and the heads of fathers' houses of Israel" (2 Chr 23:1-3, RSV). In a secret ceremony in the Temple Joash was crowned king. Athaliah heard people rejoicing and blowing trumpets and tried to halt the proceedings by tearing her clothes and yelling, "Treason!" She was immediately taken from the Temple area and executed (2 Kgs 11:13-16; 2 Chr 23:12-15).

2. One of the sons of Jehoram from Benjamin's tribe (1 Chr 8:26).

3. Father of Jeshaiah, the head of the sons of Elam who returned from Babylon with Ezra (Ezr 8:7).

ATHLAI
Bebai's descendant, who obeyed Ezra's exhortation to divorce his pagan wife after the Exile (Ezr 10:28).

ATTAI
1. Son of Sheshan's daughter and of Jarha, Sheshan's Egyptian slave. Attai was from Judah's tribe (1 Chr 2:35-36).

2. Warrior from Gad's tribe who joined David at Ziklag in his struggle against King Saul (1 Chr 12:11).

3. Son of King Rehoboam of Judah by Maachah, and Solomon's grandson (2 Chr 11:20).

AUGUSTUS CAESAR
Roman emperor from 31 BC to AD 14. See Caesars, The.

AZALIAH
Meshullam's son and the father of Josiah's scribe, Shaphan (2 Kgs 22:3; 2 Chr 34:8).

AZANIAH
Jeshua's father. Jeshua was a Levite who signed Ezra's covenant of faithfulness to God with Nehemiah and others after the Exile (Neh 10:9).

AZAREL
1. Warrior from Benjamin's tribe who joined David at Ziklag in his struggle against King Saul. Azarel was one of David's ambidextrous archers and slingers (1 Chr 12:2, 6).

2. Levite selected by David to assist in the music of the sanctuary (1 Chr 25:18, NLT "Uzziel").

3. Chief of Dan's tribe appointed by David to be tribal leader during David's ill-fated census (1 Chr 27:22).

4. Israelite of the family of Binnui who obeyed Ezra's exhortation to divorce his pagan wife after the Exile (Ezr 10:41).

5. Amashsai's father. Amashsai was a priest of Immer's family who lived in Jerusalem after the Exile (Neh 11:13).

6. Priest who blew a trumpet at the dedication of the wall of Jerusalem after the Exile (Neh 12:36).

AZARIAH

Very common Jewish name. Its numerous occurrences in the priestly genealogies has caused much confusion. The following is one of several possible arrangements:

1. Zadok's son or grandson. According to most translations, Azariah was high priest during Solomon's reign (1 Kgs 4:2). It is possible, however, that his position should be understood as that of a special counselor or keeper of the royal calendar.

2. Nathan's son, a high official in King Solomon's court. He was chief officer over the 12 regional administrators (1 Kgs 4:5).

3. Amaziah's son, king of Judah (2 Kgs 14:21; 15:1-7), more frequently known as Uzziah. *See* Uzziah #1.

4. Ethan's son, a descendant of Judah (1 Chr 2:8).

5. Jehu's son, another descendant of Judah (1 Chr 2:38).

6. Ahimaaz's son and Zadok's grandson (1 Chr 6:9). If Azariah #1 was indeed a high priest, this Azariah could be identified with him.

7. Johanan's son and Amariah's father (1 Chr 6:10-11). He is identical with the Azariah of Ezra 7:3 and 2 Esdras 1:2, whose father (meaning "ancestor") was Meraioth. The parenthetical note about Solomon's Temple (1 Chr 6:10) is generally held to go with the Azariah of verse 9 (see #6 above). It is possible, however, that this Azariah served in the Temple (built by Solomon) during the reign of Uzziah and is therefore identical with #17 below.

8. Hilkiah's son and Seriah's father (1 Chr 6:13-14; Ezr 7:1; 2 Esd 1:1). Some have identified this Azariah with #10 or #11 below.

9. Zephaniah's son, an ancestor of the singer Heman. Heman sang in the worship ritual instituted by King David (1 Chr 6:36).

10. Hilkiah's son or descendant, one of the first priests to settle in Jerusalem after the Exile (1 Chr 9:11; "Seraiah," Neh 11:11).

11. Oded's son, a prophet in the days of King Asa of Judah. He encouraged Asa to initiate badly needed reforms in the king's 15th year (2 Chr 15:1-15).

12, 13. Two sons of King Jehoshaphat of Judah. Along with four of their brothers, they were killed for political reasons by Jehoram, heir to the throne (2 Chr 21:1-4).

14. Alternate name of Ahaziah, king of Judah (2 Chr 22:6, KJV). *See* Ahaziah #2.

15. Jehoram's son, one of Judah's military commanders. This Azariah followed Jehoiada the priest in a rebellion that resulted in the execution of Queen Athaliah and the crowning of Joash as king (2 Chr 23:1).

16. Obed's son, another of the five commanders in league with Jehoiada against Athaliah (2 Chr 23:1).

17. High priest in Jerusalem during the reign of King Uzziah (2 Chr 26:16-21). He opposed Uzziah's arrogant attempt to burn incense on the altar. Perhaps the same as #7 above.

18. Johanan's son, a leader of Ephraim's tribe. Azariah and other leaders of the tribe joined the prophet Obed in protesting the capture of Judean prisoners by King Pekah of Israel and in effecting their release (2 Chr 28:12).

19. Descendant of Kohath and the father of a Levite named Joel. Joel participated in the temple cleansing instituted by King Hezekiah of Judah (2 Chr 29:12).

20. Jehallelel's son. This Azariah, a descendant of Merari, also participated in Hezekiah's cleansing of the Temple (2 Chr 29:12).

21. Zadok's descendant and high priest during the reign of Hezekiah of Judah (2 Chr 31:10, 13). He participated in Hezekiah's massive religious reforms.

22. Maaseiah's son, a householder in Jerusalem who participated in Nehemiah's rebuilding of the wall (Neh 3:23).

23. Leader who returned to Judah with Zerubbabel after the Babylonian exile (Neh 7:7; "Seraiah," Ezr 2:2).

24. Levitical assistant of Ezra who explained to the people passages from the law read by Ezra (Neh 8:7).

25. Priest who signed Ezra's covenant of faithfulness to God with Nehemiah and others after the Exile (Neh 10:2).

26. Participant in the dedication of the rebuilt wall of Jerusalem (Neh 12:33).

27. Alternate form of Jaazaniah, the name of Hoshaiah's son, in Jeremiah 42:1 and 43:2. *See* Jaazaniah #1.

28. One of the three young Jews taken into captivity with Daniel. In Babylon he was renamed Abednego (Dn 1:6-7, 11, 19; 2:17). *See* Shadrach, Meshach, and Abednego.

AZAZ
Shema's son and Bela's father from Reuben's tribe (1 Chr 5:8).

AZAZIAH
1. Levitical musician who played the lyre when King David brought the Ark of the Covenant into Jerusalem (1 Chr 15:21).

2. Hoshea's father. Hoshea was chief officer over the Ephraimites during King David's rule (1 Chr 27:20).

3. Levite appointed by King Hezekiah of Judah to help oversee the offerings stored in the Temple (2 Chr 31:13).

AZBUK
Father of the Nehemiah who was ruler of half the Beth-zur district (Neh 3:16). Azbuk's son assisted the more famous Nehemiah, the governor (Neh 10:1), in rebuilding the wall of Jerusalem.

AZEL
Descendant of Benjamin, Saul, and Jonathan. Azel was the son of Eleasah and the father of six sons (1 Chr 8:37-38; 9:43-44).

AZGAD
1. Ancestor of a group that returned to Judah with Zerubbabel after the Exile (Ezr 2:12; Neh 7:17).

2. Political leader who signed Ezra's covenant of faithfulness to God with Nehemiah and others after the Exile (Neh 10:15).

AZIEL
Alternative name for Jaaziel, a Levitical musician, in 1 Chronicles 15:20. See Jaaziel.

AZIZA
Zattu's descendant who obeyed Ezra's exhortation to divorce his pagan wife (Ezr 10:27).

AZMAVETH
1. Warrior among David's mighty men who were known as "the thirty." Bahurim was his hometown (2 Sm 23:31; 1 Chr 11:33).

2. Jehoaddah's son, a descendant of King Saul through Jonathan (1 Chr 8:36; cf. 9:42, "Jadah's son").

3. Father of Jeziel and Pelet from Benjamin's tribe (1 Chr 12:3). Possibly the same as #1 above.

4. Adiel's son, whom King David put in charge of the palace treasuries (1 Chr 27:25).

AZOR
Descendant of Zerubbabel and an ancestor of Jesus (Mt 1:1, 13-14).

AZRIEL
1. Family chief in the half-tribe of Manasseh that settled east of the Jordan River. Azriel was taken captive along with others by the king of Assyria (1 Chr 5:23-26).

2. Jeremoth's father. Jeremoth was an official over Naphtali's tribe under King David (1 Chr 27:19).

3. Seraiah's father in the reign of King Jehoiakim. Seraiah was sent by the king to arrest Jeremiah and Baruch for prophesying against the evil ways of Israel and Judah (Jer 36:26).

AZRIKAM

1. One of three sons of Neariah, a descendant of David through Zerubbabel (1 Chr 3:23).

2. One of six sons of Azel, a descendant of Saul (1 Chr 8:38; 9:44).

3. Ancestor of Shemaiah, a Levite who returned to Jerusalem after the Exile (1 Chr 9:14; Neh 11:15).

4. Palace officer under King Ahaz of Judah who was killed by Zichri (2 Chr 28:7), possibly the same as #2 above.

AZUBAH

1. Shilhi's daughter and mother of King Jehoshaphat of Judah (1 Kgs 22:42; 2 Chr 20:31).

2. First wife of Caleb and mother of three of his sons (1 Chr 2:18-19).

AZZAN

Paltiel's father and a member of Issachar's tribe. Paltiel was appointed to help Eleazar and Joshua in apportioning the Promised Land (Nm 34:26).

AZZUR

1. Political leader who signed Ezra's covenant of faithfulness to God with Nehemiah and others after the Exile (Neh 10:17).

2. Father of the false prophet Hananiah (Jer 28:1).

3. Father of Jaazaniah, one of the prominent men of Jerusalem whom Ezekiel saw in a vision (Ez 11:1).

BAAL

1. Reubenite, the son of Reaiah and the father of Beerah (1 Chr 5:5).
2. Benjaminite and one of the ten sons born to Jeiel, the father of Gibeon, by Maacah his wife. His brother was Kish, the father of Saul (1 Chr 8:30; 9:36).

BAAL-HANAN

1. Acbor's son, a king of Edom (Gn 36:38-39; 1 Chr 1:49-50).
2. Official appointed by King David to be in charge of the royal olive groves and orchards of sycamore-figs in the lowlands bordering Philistine territory (1 Chr 27:28). He came from Geder, a town in the area.

BAALIS

Ammonite king who arranged for the murder of Gedaliah, governor of the "remnant" left behind after Nebuchadnezzar's capture of Jerusalem and deportation of its inhabitants (Jer 40:14). Although warned by Johanan, a guerrilla leader, Gedaliah refused to take heed and was killed (Jer 41:1-3).

BAANA

1. Ahilud's son, one of 12 officers appointed to requisition food for King Solomon's household. He served in the district of Taanach and Megiddo (1 Kgs 4:12).
2. Hushai's son, another of King Solomon's supply officers; his district was Asher and Aloth (1 Kgs 4:16).
3. Zadok's father. Zadok helped Nehemiah rebuild the Jerusalem wall (Neh 3:4). He is possibly the same as Baanah (Neh 10:27).

BAANAH

1. Rimmon's son, a member of Benjamin's tribe. Baanah and his brother Rechab were captains under Ishbosheth after Ishbosheth's father, King Saul, died in battle. Ishbosheth, crowned king by Saul's general, Abner, was David's rival to the throne of Israel. Baanah and Rechab murdered Ishbosheth in his sleep and cut off his head (2 Sm 4:2-7). They took the head to David, thinking he would be pleased that they had killed the son of his enemy. But David, who had wept at the death of Saul, God's chosen king (ch 1), was angry instead. He ordered Baanah and Rechab executed. Their hands and feet were cut off and their bodies hanged (4:8-12).
2. Baanah's son, Heled, from the town of Netophah near Bethlehem in Judah's territory, was one of David's mighty men known as "the thirty" (2 Sm 23:29; 1 Chr 11:30).
3. KJV form of Baana, Hushai's son, in 1 Kings 4:16. See Baana #2.
4. Leader who returned to Jerusalem with Zerubbabel after the Exile (Ezr 2:2; Neh 7:7).
5. Political leader who signed Ezra's covenant of faithfulness to God with Nehemiah and others after the Exile (Neh 10:27). He is possibly the same as Baana (Neh 3:4).

BAARA
Divorced wife of Shaharaim from Benjamin's tribe (1 Chr 8:8).

BAASEIAH
Malchijah's son and ancestor of the Temple musician Asaph (1 Chr 6:40). Baaseiah may be a copyist's error for the common name Maaseiah (1 Chr 15:18).

BAASHA
Third ruler of the northern kingdom of Israel from 908 to 886 BC and violent founder of the second of its nine dynasties. Baasha was the son of Ahijah of Issachar's tribe, an unknown whom the Lord lifted "out of the dust" to leadership in the army (1 Kgs 16:2). While the Israelite army was besieging Gibbethon (inhabited by Philistines), Baasha assassinated King Nadab and then destroyed all other heirs of the former king, Nadab's father, Jeroboam (15:27-29). For much of his 24-year reign, Baasha warred with Asa, king of Judah (vv 16, 32), over control of the north-south traffic between Israel and Judah. Baasha threatened to cut off trade with Jerusalem and blockaded the northern frontier of Judah by building a fortress at Ramah, just north of Jerusalem (vv 17, 21). Fearing the new encroachment, Asa took all the silver and gold from the Temple and his palace treasuries and bribed King Ben-hadad of Syria to break alliance with Baasha (vv 18-20). When Ben-hadad battered several of Israel's northern storage cities and captured land at the headwaters of the Jordan, Baasha lost confidence and withdrew from Judah's borders (vv 20-21).

BAKBAKKAR
Levite who returned to Jerusalem from the Babylonian exile (1 Chr 9:15). His name is missing in a parallel list (Neh 11:17), unless it is the same as Bakbukiah.

BAKBUK
Ancestor of a group of Temple assistants who returned to Jerusalem with Zerubbabel after the Babylonian exile (Ezr 2:51; Neh 7:53).

BAKBUKIAH
It is not clear whether these three references refer to one, two, or three persons.

1. Shammua's son, a Levite who assisted Mattaniah at the thanksgiving services in the Temple (Neh 11:17).

2. Levite who returned to Jerusalem with Zerubbabel after the Exile (Neh 12:9).

3. One of the gatekeepers who had charge of collection centers at the Temple gates (Neh 12:25).

BALAAM
Beor's son, a prophet or soothsayer from northern Mesopotamia who was hired by a Moabite king, Balak, to curse the Israelites who had arrived at the Jordan Valley opposite

QUICKTAKE

BALAAM

STRENGTHS AND ACCOMPLISHMENTS
• Widely known for his effective curses and blessings
• Obeyed God and blessed Israel, in spite of Balak's bribe

WEAKNESSES AND MISTAKES
• Encouraged the Israelites to worship idols (Numbers 31:16)
• Returned to Moab and was killed in war

LESSONS FROM HIS LIFE
• Motives are just as important as actions
• Your treasure is where your heart is

VITAL STATISTICS
Where: Lived near the Euphrates River, traveled to Moab
Occupations: Sorcerer, prophet
Relative: Father: Beor
Contemporaries: Balak (king of Moab), Moses, Aaron

KEY VERSES
"They have wandered off the right road and followed the footsteps of Balaam son of Beor, who loved to earn money by doing wrong. But Balaam was stopped from his mad course when his donkey rebuked him with a human voice" (2 Peter 2:15-16).

Balaam's story is told in Numbers 22:1–24:25. He is also mentioned in Numbers 31:7-8, 16; Deuteronomy 23:4-5; Joshua 24:9-10; Nehemiah 13:2; Micah 6:5; 2 Peter 2:15-16; Jude 1:11; Revelation 2:14.

Jericho after 40 years of wandering in the wilderness. Israel's defeat of the Amorites (Nm 21:21-25) had instilled fear in the heart of the Moabite king (22:3). Because curses and blessings were considered irrevocable (Gn 27:34-38), Balak reasoned that if he could hire a prophet to curse the Israelites in the name of their own God, Yahweh, he could easily defeat them in battle and drive them away from his borders. Balak sent messengers to Pethor, where Balaam lived. The town is believed to be located near Haran along the Habur River, a tributary of the Euphrates. Balak offered Balaam an impressive sum to come down and curse the Israelites.

Balaam, however, was warned by the Lord that he should not go to Moab. The king of Moab would not accept Balaam's refusal and sent his royal messengers back with offers of greater wealth and honor. Balaam revealed an inner lust for wealth and position by returning to the Lord to ask whether he should go. His words to the messengers, however, were very pious: "Though Balak were to give me his house full of silver and gold, I could not go beyond the command of the LORD my God, to do less or more" (Nm 22:18, RSV). Although Balaam would do only what the Lord allowed, he became a prime example of someone who does the right thing for the wrong reason.

Balak had sent along with his messengers "the fees for divination" (Nm 22:7, RSV), which shows that he considered Balaam a diviner of the type pagan nations commonly used. The Israelites were forbidden by the Lord to consult diviners or practice divination (Dt 18:10-11). A true prophet would not have even considered the possibility that serving Balak might be right. God's final permission to let Balaam go, with the stipulation that he say only what God told him, was the Lord's way of frustrating Balak's cause and showing God's care for his chosen people.

Although he gave his permission, God was angry that Balaam went (Nm 22:22). So the Lord placed an angel with a drawn sword in Balaam's path. His donkey could see the angel but Balaam could not. Not knowing why the donkey balked, Balaam beat her, and she was then miraculously given a voice to complain against his cruelty (vv 28-30).

On the surface the story in Numbers 22 presents Balaam as a man who simply did what the Lord allowed him to do. But Deuteronomy 23:5 states that the Lord would not listen to Balaam and turned his intended curse into a blessing. When the Lord opened Balaam's eyes, he saw the angel and fell flat on his face (Nm 22:31). Then he acknowledged his sin and proceeded to say only what the Lord put in his mouth. Balaam's poems in Numbers 23 and 24 are in an archaic form of Hebrew that witnesses to their authenticity. They sometimes describe God's past blessing on his people, and at other points predict his future blessing of Israel in a unique way.

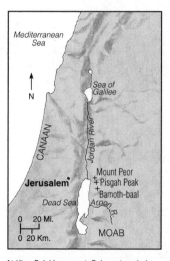

At King Balak's request, Balaam traveled nearly 400 miles (643.6 kilometers) to curse Israel. Balak took Balaam to Bamoth-baal ("the high places of Baal"), then to Pisgah Peak, and finally to Mt Peor. Each place looked over the plains of Moab, where the Israelites were camped. But to the king's dismay, Balaam blessed, not cursed, Israel.

Only blessings on Israel and never a single word of a curse were spoken by Balaam. The infuriated Moabite king took Balaam from one vantage point to another where they could look out over the Jordan Valley and see the Israelite encampment. When Balaam still did not curse them, Balak slapped his hands together in anger and packed the prophet off without any reward at all. But that was by no means the end of Balak's attempt to weaken Israel.

DIGGING DEEPER

BLIND BALAAM REBUKED BY A DONKEY

The purpose of this story is to show how spiritually blind Balaam was—no doubt because he had his mind set on the reward he would have if only the Lord would let him curse Israel. In other places in the Bible, Balaam is characterized as a man who "loved to earn money by doing wrong. But Balaam was stopped from his mad course when his donkey rebuked him with a human voice" (2 Pt 2:15-16, NLT). Jude said of certain persons that "like Balaam, they will do anything for money" (Jude 1:11).

Numbers 25 tells how the Moabite king almost succeeded in turning the Israelites against the Lord. It describes a scene at Peor where Israelite men engaged in debauchery with Moabite women. That may have meant participation in the common heathen practice of temple prostitution, for according to Numbers 31:14-16, that had been Balaam's advice to Balak and the Moabites on how to weaken Israel. Later Balaam was killed by the Israelites in their campaign against Midian (Nm 31:8; Jos 13:22).

See also Balak.

BALADAN

King of Babylon and father of Merodach-baladan. Baladan's son sent letters and a gift to King Hezekiah of Judah after Hezekiah's recovery from a serious illness (2 Kgs 20:12; Is 39:1).

BALAK

Zippor's son, king of Moab. Balak became fearful after the Israelites defeated the Amorites, so he attempted to hire a soothsayer named Balaam to pronounce a curse against Israel (Nm 22:1-7). Balak escorted Balaam to three different mountains and offered three different sacrifices, only to have Balaam each time deliver a blessing to the Israelites (chs 22–24). Enraged, Balak sent Balaam away. That event was later remembered as an example of God's special blessing on the Israelites and of the futility of trying to alter God's will (Jos 24:9-10; Jgs 11:25; Mi 6:5; Rv 2:14).

See also Balaam.

BANI

1. Member of Gad's tribe and warrior among David's mighty men who were known as "the thirty" (2 Sm 23:36).

2. Shemer's son and ancestor of Ethan. Ethan was the Levite of Merari's line in charge of the music in the Tabernacle during King David's reign (1 Chr 6:46).

3. Member of Judah's tribe and ancestor of Uthai (1 Chr 9:4). Uthai was one of the first to settle again in Jerusalem after the Exile. Possibly the same as #4 below.

4. Ancestor of a family that returned to Judah with Zerubbabel after the Exile (Ezr 2:10), alternately spelled Binnui in Nehemiah 7:15.

5. Ancestor of a family that returned to Judah with Ezra after the Exile (Ezr 8:10; 1 Esd 8:36). Possibly the same as #4 above.

6. Ancestor of some Israelites who were found guilty of marrying foreign women (Ezr 10:29).

7. Ancestor of another group of Israelites who were found guilty of marrying foreign women (Ezr 10:34).

8. Son (descendant) of Bani (#7 above). This Bani was among those found guilty of marrying foreign women (Ezr 10:38, KJV). Because Bani is spelled almost the same as "sons of" in Hebrew, most modern translations render verse 38 "of the sons of Binnui."

9. Rehum's father and a Levite. Rehum repaired a section of the Jerusalem wall after the Exile (Neh 3:17).

10. Levitical assistant of Ezra who explained to the people passages from the law read by Ezra (Neh 8:7). He was among those who offered praises to God on the steps of the Temple (Neh 9:4-5). He is probably the same as Binnui (Ezr 10:38) and Anniuth (1 Esd 9:48).

11. Another Levitical assistant who explained passages from the law read by Ezra (Neh 9:4b).

12. Levite who signed Ezra's covenant of faithfulness to God after the Exile (Neh 10:13). He was a leader of the people representing the Bani family mentioned under #4 above.

13. Uzzi's father. Uzzi was the head of the Levites in Jerusalem after the Exile (Neh 11:22). Possibly the same as #9 or #10 above.

The popularity of this name and its similarity to other Jewish names (e.g., Binnui) has caused much confusion in the genealogical lists. The list above is one of several possible arrangements.

BARABBAS

Criminal who was released instead of Jesus. All four Gospel writers took note of that event (Mt 27:15-26; Mk 15:6-15; Lk 23:18-25; Jn 18:39-40), as did the apostle Peter in his temple sermon (Acts 3:14).

Barabbas was a bandit and/or revolutionary (Jn 18:40) who had been imprisoned for committing murder during an insurrection (Mk 15:7; Lk 23:19). (The word translated "robber" in John 18:40 can denote either a bandit or revolutionary.) He was regarded as a notorious prisoner (Mt 27:16). His insurrection may have been an unusually violent act of robbery or an internal struggle among the Jews, but many scholars view it as a political insurrection against the Roman forces in Jerusalem. It is not unlikely that Barabbas was a member of the Zealots, a Jewish political group that sought to throw off the yoke of Rome by violence.

After examining Jesus, the vacillating Roman procurator, Pilate, recognized that Jesus was innocent and wanted to free him. Yet Pilate also had an interest in pleasing the Jewish leaders in order to protect his own political position. In the face of his dilemma he offered to release a prisoner to the Jews at their Passover feast (Jn 18:39). Given the option of Jesus or Barabbas, Pilate thought that the Jewish crowd would choose to have Jesus set free. Pilate underestimated either the mood of the mob or the influence of the Jewish leaders, or both. Whatever the reason, the throng shouted for Barabbas to be released and for Jesus to be crucified (Mt 27:21-22). Consequently, Jesus was crucified and Barabbas, after being released, disappeared from biblical and secular history.

BARACHIAH
Name attributed in the NT to Zechariah's father (Mt 23:35). Zechariah, executed in the temple by order of King Joash, was said to be the son of Jehoiada (2 Chr 24:20-22). "Son of Barachiah" could be a copyist's addition, since in the parallel passage in Luke's Gospel (Lk 11:51) the name does not appear in the most reliable manuscripts. A copyist may have confused the martyred Zechariah with the postexilic prophet Zechariah, whose father was Berechiah (Zec 1:1, 7).

BARAK
Son of Abinoam of Kedesh in Naphtali (Jgs 4:6; 5:1) and an associate of the prophetess Deborah. Barak led an army of Israel that defeated the forces of Jabin, king of the Canaanites (Jgs 4). Barak is one of the heroes of faith listed in the NT (Heb 11:32). *See* Deborah #2.

BARAKEL
Elihu's father, described as a Buzite (Jb 32:2, 6; cf. Gn 22:21; Jer 25:23). Elihu tried to counsel Job after the failed attempts by Job's three older friends.

BARIAH
Shemaiah's son, a descendant of King David (1 Chr 3:22).

BAR-JESUS
Jewish sorcerer, a "false prophet" who worked with the governor of Paphos on the island of Cyprus (Acts 13:6). When the governor, Sergius Paulus, took an interest in the message of Paul and Barnabas, Bar-Jesus tried to influence him against their teachings. Paul confronted Bar-Jesus, denounced him as a "son of the devil," and predicted that a temporary blindness would come upon him as a punishment from God. Bar-Jesus was instantly blinded (Acts 13:7-12), and the governor apparently became a Christian.

The many superstitious people of that day were easy prey for wonder-workers like Bar-Jesus (cf. Acts 8:9-11). The term "sorcerer" applied to him, however, connoted more than just a magician. It often referred to a wise man whose scientific understanding supposedly exceeded that of most others in that society.

Bar-Jesus was also called Elymas, which was his Greek name (Acts 13:8). It was common practice for Jews with contacts in both cultures to adopt a Greek name. According to one view, Elymas is based on an Aramaic word for "strong" and an Arabic word for "wise," which actually means "magician."

BARKOS

Ancestor of a group of Temple servants who returned to Jerusalem with Zerubbabel after the Exile (Ezr 2:53; Neh 7:55).

BARNABAS

Name given by the apostles to an early convert to Christianity in Jerusalem. Formerly called Joseph, Barnabas probably earned his new name through effective preaching and teaching.

Sources for the life of Barnabas are limited to passages in the book of Acts and Paul's letters. The apocryphal Epistle of Barnabas is almost certainly a mid-second-century composition and therefore not from the hand of Barnabas. The apocryphal Acts of Barnabas is from the fifth century and not useful in establishing reliable information on the person of Barnabas. Tertullian assigned to him the authorship of Hebrews, but internal evidence speaks against this view.

A native of Cyprus, Barnabas was a Jew of the Diaspora. His priestly family background gave him a special interest in Jerusalem. He probably came to live in the Holy City. It is possible that he may even have become acquainted with Jesus in Jerusalem, but his conversion to Christianity probably resulted from the apostles' preaching soon after the resurrection of Christ.

Barnabas first appears as a property owner named Joseph (KJV Joses) in the book of Acts who sold a field and gave the money to the Christian community (Acts 4:36-37). When persecution of Hellenistic Christians broke out in Jerusalem, Barnabas remained in the city though others of similar background fled (8:1-8; 11:19-22). His good reputation in Jerusalem may have influenced the apostles to select him as Paul's companion for missionary work.

As many of the scattered Christians gravitated to Antioch of Syria, the Jerusalem church sent Barnabas to help in the growing work (Acts 11:19-26). The writer of Acts said of Barnabas, "He was a good man, full of the Holy Spirit and of faith" (11:24, RSV). Barnabas recruited Paul, now a Christian, to help in Antioch, and the two men worked in the church for a year, teaching a large company of Christians (11:26). When famine hit Jerusalem, Barnabas and Paul were sent with relief funds. On their return to Antioch, John Mark went with them (12:25).

Barnabas was commissioned with Paul to preach beyond the boundaries of Antioch (Acts 13:2-3). The placing of Barnabas's name before Saul (Paul) may indicate the priority

QUICKTAKE

BARNABAS

STRENGTHS AND ACCOMPLISHMENTS
- One of the first to sell possessions to help the Christians in Jerusalem
- First to travel with Paul as a missionary team
- Was an encourager, as his nickname shows, and thus one of the most quietly influential people in the early days of Christianity
- Called an apostle, although not one of the original 12

WEAKNESS AND MISTAKE
- With Peter, temporarily stayed aloof from Gentile believers until Paul corrected him

LESSONS FROM HIS LIFE
- Encouragement is one of the most effective ways to help
- Sooner or later, true obedience to God will involve risk
- There is always someone who needs encouragement

VITAL STATISTICS
Where: Cyprus, Jerusalem, Antioch
Occupations: Missionary, teacher
Relatives: Aunt: Mary. Cousin: John Mark
Contemporaries: Peter, Silas, Paul, Herod Agrippa I

KEY VERSES
"When he arrived and saw this evidence of God's blessing, he was filled with joy, and he encouraged the believers to stay true to the Lord. Barnabas was a good man, full of the Holy Spirit and strong in faith. And many people were brought to the Lord" (Acts 11:23-24).

Barnabas's story is told in Acts 4:36-37; 9:27–15:39. He is also mentioned in 1 Corinthians 9:6; Galatians 2:1, 9, 13; Colossians 4:10.

of Barnabas at this time. They went to Cyprus and to several key centers in Asia Minor. At Lystra the citizens identified Barnabas with the mythical god Zeus, and Paul with Hermes (14:8-12).

At a Jerusalem council, Barnabas and Paul reported on their mission to the Gentiles (Acts 15). Following that council, as the two men planned another mission, a serious disagreement arose that led to their separating (vv 36-41). Barnabas wanted to take his cousin John Mark (Col 4:10), but Paul refused on the grounds that Mark had deserted them on the earlier mission (Acts 13:13). Barnabas left for Cyprus with John Mark, and Paul went to Syria and Cilicia with Silas. After that separation the focus shifted from Barnabas to Paul.

BARSABBAS

Biblical surname. Barsabas (KJV) means "son of Saba" in Aramaic. Barsabbas, "son of the Sabbath," is the preferred spelling in modern translations. Two people in the NT have this surname: Joseph Barsabbas and Judas Barsabbas (Acts 1:23; 15:22). *See* Joseph #12; Judas #6.

BARTHOLOMEW, THE APOSTLE

Disciple of Jesus included in all four lists of the 12 apostles (Mt 10:2-4; Mk 3:16-19; Lk 6:14-16; Acts 1:13), though not otherwise mentioned in the NT. Nothing is told about him in any of the lists. Because the name means "son of Tolmai," it has been speculated that he was known by another name in addition to his "patronymic" name. In the lists in Matthew, Mark, and Luke (the synoptic Gospels), Bartholomew is named immediately after Philip, suggesting the possibility that the Nathanael brought by Philip to Jesus (Jn 1:45-50)—who seems to be linked with some of the disciples (Jn 21:2)—was Bartholomew. It thus seems possible that the apostle Bartholomew is referred to in the fourth Gospel by another name; it is not certain, however, that John's references to Nathanael were intended to identify him as one of the Twelve.

Eusebius, an early church historian, recorded an early tradition that Pantaenus, the first head of the catechetical school in Alexandria (AD 180), went to India and there found Christians who knew of the Gospel of Matthew in Hebrew letters. According to Eusebius, Bartholomew had preached to them and had left the Gospel of Matthew with them. In other traditions, Bartholomew was an evangelistic partner of Philip and Thomas and suffered martyrdom in Armenia.

A number of spurious and apocryphal writings have been ascribed to Bartholomew; none of them is genuine. In the fourth century Jerome mentioned a Gospel of Bartholomew, which is also noted by a few other writers. There are also references to the so-called Questions of Bartholomew (extant in Greek, Latin, and Slavonic fragments) and to a Book of the Resurrection of Jesus Christ by Bartholomew (extant in Coptic). Other references were made to Acts of Bartholomew and Apocalypse of Bartholomew, both otherwise unknown.

BARTIMAEUS

Timaeus's son, a blind beggar who called out to Jesus as he left Jericho on his final journey to Jerusalem (Mk 10:46-52). Seeing Bartimaeus's faith, Jesus healed his blindness.

BARUCH

1. Neriah's son, secretary of the prophet Jeremiah. In the fourth year of King Jehoiakim of Judah (605/604 BC), Baruch wrote down Jeremiah's prophecy of the evil that God was going to bring upon Judah unless the nation repented (Jer 36:4). God also gave Baruch a special personal message through Jeremiah about humility in service (ch 45).

Baruch read the words of Jeremiah's prophecy to the people and to the princes (Jer 36:9-19). The message finally reached Jehoiakim, who destroyed the scroll and called for Baruch's and Jeremiah's arrest (vv 21-26). In hiding, Baruch again wrote down Jeremiah's prediction of Judah's destruction (vv 27-32). Baruch was the brother of Seraiah, a close associate of the later King Zedekiah. Seraiah was eventually deported to Babylon with the king by Nebuchadnezzar. With Nebuchadnezzar laying siege to Jerusalem in 587 BC, a year before its final destruction, the imprisoned Jeremiah purchased a field. His act symbolized the eventual restoration of Israel to the land. Baruch was ordered by Jeremiah to keep the evidence of the purchase safe (Jer 32:12-15).

Two months after the destruction of Jerusalem in 586 BC, rebellious Jews murdered Gedaliah, puppet governor of Judah under the Babylonians, and sought to flee to Egypt. Jeremiah advised them to remain in Jerusalem. The rebels blamed Baruch for influencing Jeremiah to give such advice and forced both Baruch and the prophet to accompany them into Egypt (43:1-7). Scripture does not refer to the final events in Baruch's life. The Jewish historian Josephus recorded that when Nebuchadnezzar invaded Egypt, Baruch was taken to Babylon. The apocryphal book of Baruch begins by noting that the author was in Babylon (1:1-3). Both accounts, however, are historically questionable.

2. Zabbai's son, mentioned in connection with the events surrounding the rebuilding of the Jerusalem wall (about 445 BC) under the supervision of Nehemiah (Neh 3:20).

3. Individual who signed Ezra's covenant of faithfulness to God with Nehemiah and others after the Exile (Neh 10:6); perhaps the same as #2 above.

4. Col-hozeh's son, and father of Maaseiah (Neh 11:5).

BARZILLAI

1. One of three men who offered hospitality to David and his supporters at Mahanaim during the dangerous time of Absalom's rebellion (2 Sm 17:27). After Absalom was defeated, Barzillai, a Gileadite, came to the Jordan River as David prepared to cross it in a triumphant return to Jerusalem. The 80-year-old Barzillai declined King David's invitation to be his permanent guest in Jerusalem but sent his son Chimham in his place (19:31-40; cf. 1 Kgs 2:7).

2. Adriel's father. Adriel married Saul's daughter Merab (2 Sm 21:8; cf. 1 Sm 18:19). Barzillai was thus the paternal grandfather of five of the seven men hanged in Gibeon in recompense for Saul's guilt in trying to wipe out all Gibeonites (2 Sm 21:1-9).

3. Priest who married the daughter (or descendant) of #1 above and adopted the family name. His descendants returned to Jerusalem in 538 BC with Zerubbabel after the Exile. They were refused priestly status because they had lost the genealogies establishing their heritage and priestly descent (Ezr 2:61; Neh 7:63).

BASEMATH

1. Daughter of Elon the Hittite. Basemath was a Canaanite woman whom Esau married against his parents' wishes (Gn 26:34). Basemath may be the same as Elon's daughter Adah, or perhaps was her sister (36:2).

2. Ishmael's daughter, who married Esau (Gn 36:3) and bore Reuel to him (vv 4, 10). This Basemath is probably the same as Ishmael's daughter Mahalath (28:9). Since Ishmael was the son of the patriarch Abraham, this marriage would have been more acceptable to Isaac and Rebekah (36:6-8). *See also* Mahalath #1.

   Identifications of #1 and #2 above are somewhat confused. Most scholars suspect that Esau married Elon's daughter Adah (Gn 36:2-4), who was also called Basemath (26:34). Later, Esau married Ishmael's daughter Mahalath (28:9), who was likewise called Basemath (36:3-4). That two of Esau's wives should be named Basemath could be because Esau chose to give both the same affectionate name, which means "fragrant."

3. King Solomon's daughter who married Ahimaaz, the king's administrator in Naphtali (1 Kgs 4:15).

BATHSHEBA

Uriah's wife, with whom David committed adultery and whom he later married. Bathsheba, also spelled Bathshua (1 Chr 3:5), was the daughter of Ammiel or Eliam (2 Sm 11:3) and possibly the granddaughter of Ahithophel, the king's adviser (2 Sm 15:12; 23:34). Her Hittite husband was one of David's top military heroes (2 Sm 23:39).

While Uriah was off fighting under Joab, King David saw a beautiful woman taking her evening bath. Discovering her name and that her husband was away on duty, he sent for Bathsheba and had sexual intercourse with her (2 Sm 11:1-4). When Bathsheba later informed him that she was pregnant, the king ordered Uriah back to Jerusalem, hoping that the husband's return would make Bathsheba's pregnancy appear legitimate. But Uriah considered himself still on active duty and stayed with the palace guard, refusing to go home (vv 5-13). Frustrated, David sent him back to the front and ordered Joab to put Uriah in the front lines and then pull back. Consequently, Uriah was killed (vv 14-25).

After Bathsheba's period of mourning, David installed her in the palace as his seventh wife, and she bore the child. The Lord sent the prophet Nathan to pronounce judgment on David's sin through a parable. Nathan prophesied a series of tragedies in David's household, beginning with the death of Bathsheba's infant son (2 Sm 11:26–12:14). David confessed his sin and repented, but the infant became sick and died. The prologue (or superscription) of Psalm 51 describes it as the psalm of repentance David wrote when confronted by Nathan over his adultery with Bathsheba and his murder of Uriah. David comforted Bathsheba, and eventually they had other children (2 Sm 12:15-25).

Of David's 19 sons by his seven wives (1 Chr 3:1-9), the sons born to Bathsheba were Shimea (also spelled Shammua, 2 Sm 5:14; 1 Chr 14:4), Shobab, Nathan, and Solomon.

Nathan (Lk 3:31) and Solomon (Mt 1:6) appear in NT genealogies of Jesus Christ. Bathsheba also appears in Matthew's genealogy under the description "she who had been the wife of Uriah." At the very end of David's life, the prophet Nathan told Bathsheba that David's son Adonijah (by his wife Haggith) was conspiring to usurp the throne. Bathsheba and Nathan persuaded David to make Solomon king as he had promised (1 Kgs 1).

See also David.

BATHSHUA

1. Canaanite wife of Judah who bore him three sons: Er, Onan, and Shelah (Gn 38:2-5; 1 Chr 2:3).
2. Alternate spelling of Bathsheba in 1 Chronicles 3:5. See Bathsheba.

BAZLUTH

Ancestor of a group of Temple assistants returning to Jerusalem with Zerubbabel after the Exile (Ezr 2:52, "Bazluth"; Neh 7:54).

BEALIAH

Warrior from Benjamin's tribe who joined David at Ziklag in his struggle against King Saul. Bealiah was one of David's ambidextrous archers and slingers (1 Chr 12:5).

BEBAI

1. Ancestor of a family that returned to Jerusalem with Zerubbabel after the Exile (Ezr 2:11; 8:11; Neh 7:16). Some of the members of that family were guilty of marrying foreign women (Ezr 10:28).
2. Levitical leader of Israel who signed Ezra's covenant of faithfulness to God with Nehemiah and others after the Exile (Neh 10:15). This individual was perhaps a member of the family of #1 above.

BECORATH

Zeror's father, a member of Benjamin's tribe and an ancestor of King Saul (1 Sm 9:1).

BEDAD

Father of Hadad, one of the kings of Edom before the Israelite monarchy (Gn 36:35; 1 Chr 1:46).

BEDAN

1. One of Israel's deliverers, along with Gideon, Jephthah, and Samuel, during the time of the judges (1 Sm 12:11, KJV; RSV mg). The name Bedan may be either a shortened form of Abdon (Jgs 12:13) or a scribal error for Barak (Jgs 4:6).
2. Ulam's son, a descendant of Manasseh (1 Chr 7:17).

BEDEIAH

Bani's son, who obeyed Ezra's exhortation to divorce his pagan wife after the Exile (Ezr 10:35).

BEERA

Zophah's son, a warrior in Asher's tribe (1 Chr 7:37).

BEERAH

Chief of Reuben's tribe (1 Chr 5:6, 26) taken captive by the Assyrian king Tilgath-pilneser (a later spelling of Tiglath-pileser).

BEERI

1. Judith's Hittite (Hethite) father. Judith was one of the wives of Esau (Gn 26:34).
2. Father of Hosea the prophet (Hos 1:1).

BEKER

1. Benjamin's second son, who migrated to Egypt with his grandfather Jacob (Gn 46:21; 1 Chr 7:6).
2. Ephraim's second son, from whom the family of Bekerites originated (Nm 26:35). He is also called Bered (1 Chr 7:20).

BELA

1. Beor's son, a king of Edom who ruled before Israel had a king (Gn 36:31-33). Because Balaam, the pagan prophet from north Syria, also had a father named Beor (Nm 22:5), some ancients and a number of modern critical scholars have confused the Edomite Bela with Balaam.
2. Benjamin's oldest son (Gn 46:21; 1 Chr 8:1), whose descendants were called Belaites (Nm 26:38).
3. Azaz's son, a descendant of Reuben who lived in Gilead in Transjordan. So vast were his family's holdings that they pastured their cattle as far east as the Euphrates River (1 Chr 5:8-9). In the reign of Saul, his family successfully held their land against Hagrite opposition.

BELSHAZZAR

Babylonian king who was co-regent with Nabonidus in the final days of the Babylonian Empire. His name means "Bel protect the king." Daniel identifies him as the son of Nebuchadnezzar (Dn 5:2, 11, 13, 18), though in fact he was the natural son of Nabunaid (Nabonidus). The seeming discrepancy arises from the fact that in Hebrew literature "father" may signify "ancestor" or "predecessor," and "son" may designate "descendant" or "successor in office." Some have concluded that Belshazzar's mother was a daughter of Nebuchadnezzar and that Belshazzar was therefore the grandson of the great Babylonian. Clearly his father, Nabunaid, was the son of a nobleman and the high priestess of the moon god at Haran. Nabunaid had usurped the throne in 555 BC.

A greater difficulty in the biblical text is the fact that Daniel presents Belshazzar as the king of Babylon when it fell to the Persians, whereas secular historical records picture Nabunaid as the last king of the Babylonian Empire. Critical scholars have therefore questioned Daniel's accuracy. Inscriptions have now been found, however, which make it clear that Belshazzar's father entrusted the rule of the capital to him and was out of the city for over 10 years campaigning in Arabia. Religious concerns also took Nabunaid out of Babylon during part of his reign. When Cyrus invaded the Babylonian Empire, Nabunaid marched east to meet him but fled before Cyrus's advancing armies. Later he returned to Babylon and surrendered to the Persians after the city had already fallen to Cyrus. Thus he was out of the city when the Persians overcame the royal forces there under the command of Belshazzar, the crown prince and co-regent.

While Nabunaid's armies were being routed by the Persians, Belshazzar was giving a sensual feast for the leaders of Babylonian society. Half drunk, he called for the gold and silver vessels from the Jerusalem Temple to be brought in for use in a deliberate act of sacrilege. Immediately handwriting appeared on the wall, his doom was announced, and Persian armies entered the city without a fight (October 12, 539 BC). They did so by diverting the waters of the Euphrates so the river would no longer serve as a moat around the city and its defenses could be easily breached. *See* Daniel.

BELTESHAZZAR

Daniel's Babylonian name (Dn 1:7). Daniel was one of the young men taken captive to Babylon to be trained as counselors for King Nebuchadnezzar (ch 1). *See* Daniel #3.

BEN-ABINADAB

One of 12 officers appointed to requisition food for King Solomon's household. His administrative district comprised the area around Naphath-dor, the coastal city south of Mt Carmel (1 Kgs 4:11). The name means "son of Abinadab" and probably indicates that Ben-abinadab was the son of Solomon's uncle Abinadab (1 Sm 16:8; 1 Chr 2:13).

BENAIAH

Popular name meaning "the Lord has built," used primarily by Levites.

1. Son of Jehoiada the priest, from the south Judean town of Kabzeel. Benaiah was engaged in military service, and his loyalty gained for him the rank of commander in chief of the army during the reign of Solomon (1 Kgs 2:35; 4:4). Before David became king, Benaiah distinguished himself in a number of daring military and protective feats to become one of the mighty men (2 Sm 23:20-22) during David's flight from King Saul. He attained command of "the thirty" (1 Chr 27:6), a group second only to "the three" of

highest valor (2 Sm 23:23). He later had a high place in the armed forces when Joab was commander in chief and was placed over King David's elite troops, the Cherethites and Pelethites (8:18). He was also made third commander by David, with 24,000 men under him, and with annual responsibility for priestly service in the Temple during the third month of the year (1 Chr 27:5-6). Benaiah stayed loyal to David during the rebellion of Absalom (2 Sm 20:23; see 15:18) as well as during the attempt by Adonijah to seize David's throne (1 Kgs 1:8), and therefore had the privilege of assisting in Solomon's coronation at Gihon (vv 32-40). As army commander and chief bodyguard to Solomon he was responsible for executing Adonijah (2:25), Joab (v 34), and Shimei (v 46) by orders of the new king.

2. Warrior from the town of Pirathon who was among David's mighty men known as "the thirty" (2 Sm 23:30; 1 Chr 11:31). Benaiah commanded the 11th division of the army in the rotation system established by David (1 Chr 27:14).

3. Prince in Simeon's tribe who participated in the conquest of Gedor during Hezekiah's reign (1 Chr 4:36).

4. Levitical musician who played the harp when King David brought the Ark to Jerusalem (1 Chr 15:18, 20; 16:5, RSV). Afterward, he was appointed to minister daily before the Ark under the direction of Asaph (16:5).

5. Priestly musician who blew the trumpet before the Ark when King David brought it to Jerusalem (1 Chr 15:24). Afterward he was appointed to play regularly before the Ark (16:6).

6. Father of Jehoiada, King David's counselor after the death of Ahithophel (1 Chr 27:34; see also 2 Sm 17:1-14).

7. Levite Asaph's descendant and grandfather of Jahaziel (2 Chr 20:14). Jahaziel delivered an encouraging prophecy to King Jehoshaphat of Judah before his battle against the Moabites and Ammonites (vv 1-29).

8. Levite appointed by King Hezekiah to help oversee the tithes and contributions brought to the Temple (2 Chr 31:13).

9. Parosh's son (or descendant), who obeyed Ezra's exhortation to divorce his pagan wife after the Babylonian exile (Ezr 10:25).

10. Pahath-moab's son (or descendant), who also obeyed Ezra's exhortation to divorce his pagan wife after the Exile (Ezr 10:30).

11. Bani's son (or descendant), another who divorced his pagan wife after the Exile (Ezr 10:35).

12. Nebo's son (or descendant), who also divorced his pagan wife after the Exile (Ezr 10:43).

13. Pelatiah's father (Ez 11:1, 13). Pelatiah was a prince of the people of Israel during the time of the prophet Ezekiel.

BEN-AMMI

Son born to Lot and his younger daughter. A similar incestuous liaison between Lot and his older daughter produced a son named Moab. The two sons are identified as the ancestral heads of the Ammonite and Moabite peoples (Gn 19:38).

Although the promise made to Abraham could have been enjoyed by Lot (Gn 11:31; 12:1-4), Lot went his own way (13:2-12) and failed to trust the Lord (19:15-23). Lot's relationship to Abraham, however, evoked deferential treatment by the Israelites (Dt 2:8-19) toward these occasionally powerful enemies (2 Chr 20:1-12).

BEN-DEKER

One of 12 officers appointed to requisition food for King Solomon's household (1 Kgs 4:9, KJV "son of Dekar"). Ben-deker's administrative district comprised an area along the southern border of Dan's tribe near Beth-shemesh.

BEN-GEBER

Literally, "Geber's son," an official in King Solomon's court who administered the sixth of 12 districts. Ben-geber's area of responsibility began at Ramoth-gilead in northern Transjordan and extended north as far as Argob in Bashan (1 Kgs 4:13). His identification with Geber, son of Uri (v 19), is debatable.

BEN-HADAD

Title of two or possibly three kings of Syria, meaning "son of Hadad." Hadad was the Syrian storm god probably identical with Rimmon (2 Kgs 5:18).

1. Ben-hadad I, son of Tabrimmon and grandson of Hezion. In spite of a history of Syrian hostility to Israel, Ben-hadad I entered into an alliance with King Baasha (908–886 BC) of the northern kingdom of Israel (1 Kgs 15:18-20). The pact was broken, however, when continuing hostilities between Israel and the southern kingdom of Judah erupted into a major encounter. Baasha conducted a major campaign against King Asa (910–869 BC) of Judah. In order to cut off infiltration into his kingdom and defection to the southern kingdom, Baasha fortified the city of Ramah, situated north of Jerusalem but uncomfortably close to it. His action extended Israel's territory into Judah. In the face of that threat, Asa sent his remaining wealth to Ben-hadad I, asking him to break his pact with Baasha (vv 18-19). The Syrian king took advantage of the offer and sent his armies against Israel. He conquered the cities of Ijon, Dan, and Abel-beth-maacah plus the territory of Naphtali (v 20), thus ensuring Syrian control of the main caravan routes through Galilee. Baasha was forced to abandon Ramah and move to Tirzah. Asa then conscripted the population of Judah to dismantle and carry off the fortifications erected by Baasha. Materials taken from Ramah were used to help build Geba in the territory of Benjamin. Asa's victory became the subject of a prophetic protest by Hanani, who berated Asa for his reliance on the king of Syria (16:7).

2. Ben-hadad II. The biblical accounts in 1 Kings and 2 Chronicles do not make a clear differentiation between Ben-hadad I and II. Some scholars have therefore identified them as a single person. This view finds apparent support in the "Melqart Stele," which mentions Ben-hadad and to which a date of about 850 BC has been assigned. It seems better, however, to posit a Ben-hadad II who was the son of Ben-hadad I. If one does not distinguish between the two, Ben-hadad's activity must overlap both the reign of Ahab (874–853 BC) and that of Baasha. In each, a military encounter with Ben-hadad was recorded; one must posit an interval of up to four decades between the encounters if no distinction is made.

Ben-hadad II led a coalition of armies against Samaria during the reign of King Ahab of Israel. In the course of the siege, Ben-hadad demanded that Ahab surrender his wealth, wives, and children to him. Ahab agreed to that demand, but when Ben-hadad added the condition that he be given anything that his aides laid their hands on, Ahab refused on advice of his counselors. His refusal enraged Ben-hadad.

An anonymous prophet predicted that Ahab would defeat the armies of Ben-hadad (1 Kgs 20:13). Ahab's victory came when aides of the district governors killed the soldiers who had come out of the Syrian camp to take them captive. The Syrian forces fled. Ben-hadad was again defeated by the Israelites the next year when he attempted to engage them in battle on the plain rather than in the hill country. His reason was his belief that the "gods" of the Israelites were gods of the hills (v 23). That Syrian defeat was also predicted by a prophet, who declared its cause to be Ben-hadad's misconception of the nature of Israel's God (v 28).

Ben-hadad pleaded for his life, promising to restore all the cities his father had taken from Israel. Ahab agreed, but his action met with prophetic protest (vv 35-43). The pact established by the two kings brought about a cessation of hostilities that lasted only three years. The peace was broken by Ahab, who, at the instigation of King Jehoshaphat of Judah, sought to regain the city of Ramoth-gilead. Guidance was first sought from a group of prophets who predicted victory. Micaiah, however, a true prophet, predicted defeat (22:5-28). Ahab's forces were defeated, and Ahab died in battle (vv 29-36).

Ben-hadad also figured in the life of the prophet Elisha, whom he sought to capture (2 Kgs 6:11-19). The attempt was thwarted when the Syrian army was stricken with blindness.

3. Ben-hadad III, son of King Hazael of Syria. This Ben-hadad was not related to Ben-hadad I or II but adopted the name. Because Jehoahaz (814–798 BC), king of Israel, did not follow the Lord, God allowed Israel to come under the control of Ben-hadad III. Release from the oppression of Ben-hadad III was accomplished by a "savior" (2 Kgs 13:5), probably a reference to Assyrian incursions into Syria.

BEN-HAIL

One of five officials sent out by King Jehoshaphat of the southern kingdom of Judah to teach the people the law of the Lord (2 Chr 17:7).

BEN-HANAN

Shimon's son of Judah's tribe (1 Chr 4:20).

BEN-HESED

One of the 12 officers appointed to requisition food for King Solomon's household (1 Kgs 4:10, KJV "son of Hesed"). His administrative district comprised an area south and west of Arubboth in the western part of Manasseh's tribe.

BEN-HUR

One of 12 officers appointed to requisition food for King Solomon's household (1 Kgs 4:8, KJV "son of Hur"). His district was the hill country of Ephraim.

BENINU

Levite who signed Ezra's covenant of faithfulness to God with Nehemiah and others after the Exile (Neh 10:13).

BENJAMIN

1. Youngest of Jacob's 12 sons and full brother to Joseph. Jacob named him Benjamin ("son of my right hand") after his dying mother Rachel had called him Ben-oni ("son of my sorrow," Gn 35:18). After Joseph had been sold into Egypt by his half brothers, their father, Jacob, assumed that Joseph was dead and became very protective of Benjamin. Later, with Joseph controlling the plot, Benjamin was used in the reunion in Egypt of Jacob and his 12 sons (Gn 42–45). When prophesying concerning each of his sons, Jacob spoke of Benjamin's skill as a warrior or prophesied of the military fame of his descendants by saying, "Benjamin is a ravenous wolf, devouring his enemies in the morning, and dividing his plunder in the evening" (49:27, NLT).

2. Bilhan's son and Jacob's great-grandson (1 Chr 7:10).

3. Member of Harim's clan of the postexilic community who married a pagan wife (Ezr 10:32).

4. One who repaired a section of the wall next to his own house (Neh 3:23).

5. One of the company of Jews who participated in the dedication of the wall at Jerusalem (Neh 12:34). He may be the same as #4 above.

BENO

Jaaziah's son in a list of Levites assigned to Temple duty (1 Chr 24:26-27). It is possible that the Hebrew word is not a proper name; it has sometimes been translated "his son."

BEN-ONI
Name Rachel gave to her last son as she died in childbirth (Gn 35:18). His father, Jacob, changed his name from Ben-oni ("son of my sorrow") to Benjamin ("son of my right hand"). *See* Benjamin #1.

BEN-ZOHETH
Ishi's son from Judah's tribe (1 Chr 4:20).

BEOR
1. Bela's father (Gn 36:32). Bela was a king of Edom.

2. Balaam's father (Nm 22:5; 2 Pt 2:15, KJV "Bosor"). Balaam was asked by Balak, king of Moab, to curse Israel.

BERA
Ruler of Sodom in the days of Abraham and Lot. Bera was one of five Canaanite city kings who unsuccessfully rebelled against King Chedorlaomer of Elam and his three allies (Gn 14:2).

BERACAH
Warrior from Benjamin's tribe who joined David at Ziklag in his struggle against King Saul. Beracah was one of David's ambidextrous archers and slingers (1 Chr 12:3).

BERAIAH
One of Shimei's sons from Benjamin's tribe (1 Chr 8:21).

BERED
Alternate name for Beker, one of Ephraim's sons, in 1 Chronicles 7:20. *See* Beker.

BEREKIAH
1. Son of Zerubbabel and descendant of King David (1 Chr 3:20).

2. Levite, Gershon's descendant and father of Asaph (1 Chr 6:39; 15:17). Asaph was a famous musician of Israel.

3. Asa's son and head of a family of Levites who returned to Judah after the Babylonian exile (1 Chr 9:16).

4. Levite appointed by King David as gatekeeper for the Ark of the Covenant (1 Chr 15:23).

5. Meshillemoth's son, a leader of Ephraim's tribe. He was one of three men in Samaria who supported the prophet Obed in sending prisoners of war back to their homes in Judah (2 Chr 28:12).

6. Meshullam's father. Meshullam assisted Nehemiah, the governor, in rebuilding the wall of Jerusalem (Neh 3:4, 30; 6:18).

7. Iddo's son and father of Zechariah the prophet (Zec 1:1, 7).
    See also Barachiah.

BERI
Zophah's son, head of a subclan. Beri was a skilled warrior (1 Chr 7:36, 40) listed with Asher's descendants.

BERIAH
1. Asher's son, who migrated to Egypt with his family, relatives, and grandfather Jacob (Gn 46:17; 1 Chr 7:30). His descendants were called Beriites (Nm 26:44).

2. Ephraim's youngest son, born after several of his brothers were killed at Gath for cattle rustling (1 Chr 7:20-23).

3. Elpaal's son, head of a family in Benjamin's tribe. This Beriah lived at Aijalon and helped repel invaders from Gath (1 Chr 8:13).

4. Shimei's son, a Levite of Gershon's clan who served in the Temple at Jerusalem. Because neither Beriah nor his brother Jeush had many sons, their families were counted as a single subclan in the Levitical system (1 Chr 23:10-11).

BERNICE
Eldest daughter of Herod Agrippa I. Bernice was present during the apostle Paul's speech before her brother King Agrippa II (Acts 25:13, 23; 26:30). Bernice (also spelled Berenice) was born around AD 28. At 13 she married Marcus, son of the Jewish official Alexander. After her husband's death, her father betrothed her to his elder brother, Herod of Chalcis. Two sons, Bernicianus and Hyrcanus, were born to them before her second husband's death in AD 48. When the young widow's relationship with her brother, Agrippa II, deepened, there were rumors of incest. In defense, Bernice persuaded Polemo, king of Cilicia, to marry her. But she left him shortly afterward.

In AD 66 Bernice bravely but unsuccessfully appealed to the mad Roman procurator Gessius Florus not to ransack the Temple in Jerusalem. She was at her brother's side when he warned the people against war. When war broke out that year, Jewish rebels set fire to her palace as well as to her brother's.

BESAI
Ancestor of a group of Temple assistants who returned to Jerusalem with Zerubbabel after the Babylonian exile (Ezr 2:49; Neh 7:52).

BESODEIAH
Meshullam's father. Along with Joiada, Meshullam helped rebuild a portion of the Jerusalem wall after the Exile in Babylonia (Neh 3:6).

BETHUEL

Youngest son of Abraham's brother Nahor and his wife, Milcah. Bethuel was thus Abraham's nephew (Gn 22:23). He was the father of Rebekah (24:15, 24) and was referred to as an Aramean of Paddan-aram (25:20; 28:5).

BEZAI

1. Ancestor of a group of people who returned to Jerusalem with Zerubbabel after the Babylonian exile (Ezr 2:17; Neh 7:23).

2. Political leader who signed Ezra's covenant of faithfulness to God with Nehemiah and others after the Exile (Neh 10:18).

BEZALEL

1. Uri's son and the master craftsman from Judah's tribe who was specially equipped by God to be in charge of the construction and furnishing of the Tabernacle (Ex 31:2; 35:30-31; 36:1-2; 37:1; 38:22; 1 Chr 2:20; 2 Chr 1:5) In the KJV the name is Bezaleel.

2. Pahath-moab's son, who obeyed Ezra's exhortation to divorce his pagan wife after the Exile (Ezr 10:30). In the KJV the name is Bezaleel.

BEZER

Zophah's son in Asher's tribe (1 Chr 7:37).

BICRI

Sheba's father in Benjamin's tribe. Sheba led a revolt against King David (2 Sm 20:1-22). Bicri's descendants were known as Bicrites (2 Sm 20:14).

BIDKAR

Aide of King Jehu of the northern kingdom of Israel. Bidkar fulfilled a prophecy about the fate of Ahab's family by throwing the body of Joram, Ahab's son, into Naboth's field after Jehu had killed Joram (2 Kgs 9:24-26).

BIGTHA

Eunuch who served King Ahasuerus of Persia. He and six others were in charge of the royal household (Est 1:10). He is perhaps the same person as Bigthana in Esther 2:21; 6:2. *See also* Bigthana.

BIGTHANA

Eunuch who served King Ahasuerus of Persia as a palace guard. He and a fellow guard named Teresh planned an assassination attempt on the king's life. When their plot was overheard by Queen Esther's uncle Mordecai, the two conspirators were executed (Est 2:21-23; 6:2, "Bigthana"). *See also* Bigtha.

BIGVAI

1. Ancestor of a group of people who returned to Jerusalem with Zerubbabel after the Babylonian exile (Ezr 2:2, 14; Neh 7:7, 19). Since his name is Persian, Bigvai may have been born or renamed during the Exile.

2. Political leader who signed Ezra's covenant of faithfulness to God with Nehemiah and others after the Exile (Neh 10:16); possibly a representative for the family descended from #1 above.

BILDAD

One of three friends who came to comfort Job in his anguish, identified as a Shuhite (Jb 2:11). That term suggests that he was a descendant of Shuah, son of Abraham and his second wife Keturah (Gn 25:1-2). Bildad spoke to Job on three occasions. In his first speech he asserted that God upholds the just and punishes the wicked (Jb 8). Job must therefore be a hypocrite to say that he is right with God. In his second speech Bildad emphasized the immediate punishment of the wicked in this life (ch 18). Job must therefore be wicked because of his intense suffering. In his third speech Bildad proclaimed the majesty of God and called man a worm by comparison (ch 25). He implied that Job was foolish to claim to be righteous before such a holy God.

BILGAH

1. Head of the 15th of 24 divisions of priests whom King David assigned to official duties in the Temple (1 Chr 24:14).

2. Priest who returned to Jerusalem under Zerubbabel's leadership after the Exile (Neh 12:18). He is perhaps identifiable with Bilgai in Nehemiah 10:8. *See* Bilgai.

BILGAI

Priest who signed Ezra's covenant of faithfulness to God with Nehemiah and others after the Exile (Neh 10:8); possibly the same person as Bilgah in Nehemiah 12:18. *See* Bilgah #2.

BILHAH

Servant given by Laban to his daughter Rachel when she married Jacob (Gn 29:29). Realizing her own childlessness, Rachel gave Bilhah to her husband as a concubine and accepted their two sons as her own, naming them Dan and Naphtali (30:3-8; 35:25; 46:25). Archaeological investigation has confirmed the custom of a barren wife's providing a concubine to guarantee children to her husband. Such an arrangement is mentioned in marriage contract documents dug up at Nuzi and dated from about the same time as the Genesis 29 events. Jacob's son Reuben was later guilty of incest with Bilhah (35:22).

BILHAN

1. Ezer's firstborn son and a descendant of Seir (Gn 36:27; 1 Chr 1:42).

2. Jediael's son from Benjamin's tribe (1 Chr 7:10).

BILSHAN

One, who with Nehemiah and Zerubbabel, led a group of Jews to Jerusalem following the Exile (Ezr 2:2; Neh 7:7).

BIMHAL

Japhlet's son, a great warrior and head of a clan in Asher's tribe (1 Chr 7:33, 40).

BINEA

Moza's son from Benjamin's tribe and a descendant of King Saul through Jonathan's line (1 Chr 8:37; 9:43).

BINNUI

1. Noadiah's father. Noadiah was a Levite in charge of weighing Temple valuables after the Exile (Ezr 8:33). Possibly the same as #4 below.

2. Pahath-moab's son or descendant. He obeyed Ezra's exhortation to divorce his pagan wife after the Exile (Ezr 10:30).

3. According to the Apocrypha and the KJV, one of Bani's sons (descendants) who also obeyed Ezra's exhortation to divorce his pagan wife (Ezr 10:38; 1 Esd 9:34). Because the list of Bani's descendants is proportionally very long and because verse 38 in Hebrew can easily be construed "of the sons of Binnui," most modern translations make Binnui an ancestor of a new group rather than a descendant of Bani.

4. Henadad's son who repaired part of Jerusalem's wall after the Exile (Neh 3:24). He was among the Levites who signed Ezra's covenant of faithfulness to God (Neh 10:9).

5. Alternate spelling for Bani in Nehemiah 7:15. See Bani #4.

6. Levite who returned to Judah with Zerubbabel after the Exile. He was one of several in charge of songs of thanksgiving (Neh 12:8).

The popularity of this name and its similarity to other Jewish names (e.g., Bani and Bavvai) has caused much confusion in the genealogical lists. The above is one of several possible arrangements.

BIRSHA

Ruler of Gomorrah in the days of Abraham and Lot. Birsha was one of five Canaanite city-kings who unsuccessfully rebelled against King Chedorlaomer of Elam and his three allies (Gn 14:2).

BIRZAITH

Malchiel's son of Asher's tribe (1 Chr 7:31). Since parallel lists fail to mention him (Gn 46:17; Nm 26:44-47), it is possible that Birzaith (KJV "Birzavith") was the name of a city Malchiel founded. If so, the city may have been northwest of Bethel, near Tyre, and is now called Birzeit.

QUICKTAKE

BOAZ

STRENGTHS AND ACCOMPLISHMENTS
- A man of his word
- Sensitive to those in need, caring for his workers
- A keen sense of responsibility, integrity
- A successful and shrewd businessman

LESSONS FROM HIS LIFE
- It can be heroic to do what must be done and to do it right
- God often uses little decisions to carry out his big plan

VITAL STATISTICS
Where: Bethlehem
Occupation: Wealthy farmer
Relatives: Elimelech, Naomi, Ruth

KEY VERSE:
"And with the land I have acquired Ruth, the Moabite widow of Mahlon, to be my wife. This way she can have a son to carry on the family name of her dead husband and to inherit the family property here in his hometown. You are all witnesses today" (Ruth 4:10).

His story is told in the book of Ruth. He is also mentioned in Matthew 1:5.

BISHLAM

Resident of the vicinity of Jerusalem who opposed the rebuilding of the city after the Exile. He and his associates wrote a letter complaining about the rebuilding to the Persian king Artaxerxes (Ezr 4:7).

BITHIAH

Mered's wife. Bithiah may have been a princess, or the phrase "daughter of Pharaoh" (KJV) may merely indicate that she was Egyptian (1 Chr 4:17-18). Her name (meaning "daughter of Yah") seems to indicate that she was a Jewish convert.

BIZTHA

One of the seven eunuchs King Ahasuerus commanded to bring Queen Vashti to his drunken party (Est 1:10).

BLASTUS

Royal secretary to Herod Agrippa I (Acts 12:20). The cities of Tyre and Sidon were looked down upon by Herod, so when their delegates wanted an appointment with the king when he was in nearby Caesarea, they approached him through Blastus. Herod addressed them and was struck by a fatal illness for accepting their worship (vv 21-23).

BOAZ

Salmon's son of Judah's tribe (Ru 4:18-22). Boaz lived in Bethlehem in the days of the judges and married Ruth, a Moabite woman. Boaz was an ancestor of Christ (Mt 1:5; Lk 3:32) and a wealthy relative of Ruth's father-in-law, Elimelech. Ruth attracted the attention of Boaz when she was gleaning in one of his fields (Ru 2). His kindness to Ruth convinced Naomi, Ruth's mother-in-law, that he might be willing to redeem some land her husband had owned and at the same time accept the levirate marriage with Ruth that such a transaction required.

See also Ruth.

BOKERU

Azel's son, a descendant of King Saul (1 Chr 8:38; 9:44).

BUKKI

1. Leader of Dan's tribe who assisted Joshua in dividing up the land of Canaan (Nm 34:22).

2. Ezra's ancestor (1 Chr 6:5, 51; Ezr 7:1, 4-5).

BUKKIAH

Heman's eldest son, who served with his father and 13 brothers as a Temple musician (1 Chr 25:4, 13).

BUNAH

Jerahmeel's son from Judah's tribe (1 Chr 2:25).

BUNNI

1. Levite who sang praise to God after Ezra's public reading of the law (Neh 9:4).

2. Political leader who signed Ezra's covenant of faithfulness to God with Nehemiah and others after the Exile (Neh 10:15).

3. Hashabiah's father (Neh 11:15), a Levite descended from Merari (1 Chr 9:14). Possibly the same as #1 above.

BUZ

1. Abraham's nephew, and one of Nahor's eight sons (Gn 22:21).

2. Member of Gad's tribe (1 Chr 5:14).

BUZI

Father of the prophet Ezekiel (Ez 1:1-3).

CAESARS, THE

Succession of Roman emperors. The name Caesar, which has derivatives in the German Kaiser, Dutch Keizer, and Russian Czar, goes back to the family name of Julius Caesar (100–44 BC), which his successors took to themselves. Luke's Gospel mentions Caesar Augustus (Lk 2:1) and Tiberius Caesar (Lk 3:1). In the book of Acts the title "Caesar" is used to refer to Nero (Acts 25:11-12, 21; 26:32; 27:24; 28:19). During NT times, 12 Caesars reigned, 6 of them actually of the Caesarean lineage. Here only Caesars from the NT period will be discussed.

Augustus (63 BC–AD 14, reigned 31 BC–AD 14)

Gaius Octavianus (Octavian) was the grandson of Julia, Julius Caesar's sister. He was 18 and studying in Greece when his great-uncle was assassinated. Caesar's will, which adopted him as son and made him heir, brought him into the resulting power struggle.

Within a year and a half, a trio consisting of Antony, Lepidus, and Octavian was confirmed in power. The following year, in a battle at Philippi (in Macedonia, now Greece), Octavian defeated both Cassius and Brutus, the chief conspirators against Caesar. Antony took command of the eastern provinces (which included Greece and Egypt), Octavian led his forces back to Italy, and Lepidus assumed jurisdiction over Gaul and western North Africa. Lepidus, however, was forced into retirement, and the area he controlled fell to Octavian. Thus Octavian and Antony, who had clashed even before their alliance, became rivals again. In the battle of Actium (31 BC), Octavian defeated Antony to become sole ruler of the Roman world and its first emperor.

Octavian did not possess the military brilliance of his great-uncle, but he had a talent for ending strife and maintaining peace, which immediately gained him the support of the people. During his reign Roman culture enjoyed a golden age, particularly in architecture and literature. Augustus founded the Praetorian Guard, the emperor's private honor corps of 9,000 soldiers. Originally intended to secure the emperor's position, it later became so influential that it could independently depose an emperor or elect a new one without Senate confirmation.

The title Augustus *(Augoustos)*, meaning "exalted one," was given to Octavian in 27 BC. The title reflects the practice of emperor worship that had been partly initiated in the reign of Julius Caesar, who declared himself to be "the unconquered god" and "the father of the fatherland." Augustus continued the cult, although at first he declared that he should be worshiped only in association with the goddess Roma. Later, however, Augustus's name became equated with Rome, and the emperor was regarded as the savior of the world. A temple to Augustus was built in Athens, and even Herod the Great built temples in his honor.

When Augustus became emperor, he devoted himself to reorganizing his empire. Because of the chaos that had prevailed in the provinces, he took it upon himself to restructure economic and financial policies.

Though Caesar Augustus is mentioned only once in the NT, he nevertheless is known to every reader of the Bible because of the census he decreed in all the provinces just before the birth of Jesus (Lk 2:1). Little information is available about that census, but Luke wrote that the first census was held when Jesus was born. The second was conducted in AD 6 and resulted in an uprising instigated by Judas of Galilee (Acts 5:37).

During the time of Augustus's reign, Herod the Great gained the emperor's trust and was allowed to rule the Jews without Roman interference. In appreciation Herod rebuilt the old city of Samaria and renamed it Sebaste to honor Augustus. Caesarea on the Mediterranean coast of Palestine was also named in his honor.

Conflicts between Herod and his sons were settled by Augustus in 12 BC. When dispute between father and sons arose again, however, Augustus ordered that it be settled in a Roman court, which ruled in 7 BC that two of them, Alexander and Aristobulus, be executed. In 4 BC, Augustus permitted the execution of Herod's son Antipater.

In Herod's last will and testament, three of his sons (Archelaus, Antipas, and Philip) were appointed to rule his kingdom. Augustus's approval of those appointments was necessary. Archelaus made a personal visit to Rome immediately after the death of his father to request possible changes in his status. Likewise, Antipas journeyed to Rome to see whether Augustus might be willing to grant him royal status as well. While the two of them sought separate audiences with the emperor, a delegation representing the people of Judea appeared before Augustus with the request that the Herodian rule—which was never very popular—be terminated. At the same time riots in Judea had to be suppressed by Roman legions sent from Syria.

Augustus compromised. He converted Herod's old kingdom to a Roman province and refused kingship to all of Herod's sons. Otherwise he kept to the provisions of Herod's testament: Archelaus became ethnarch (overlord) of Judea, Samaria, and Idumea (half of the new province); Antipas became tetrarch of Galilee and Perea (one quarter of the province); Philip became tetrarch of Iturea and Trachonitis (Lk 3:1; an area east of Galilee—the final quarter of the province). Because Archelaus was unable to rule effectively, he was deposed by the emperor in AD 6 and banished to Vienne in southern France.

Augustus died in AD 14 after a brief illness, leaving the empire to his appointed successor, Tiberius.

Tiberius (42 BC–AD 37, reigned AD 14–37)

Tiberius Claudius Nero became Octavian's stepson at the age of four, when his mother, Livia, divorced his father to marry the future emperor. Tiberius was made Augustus's co-regent in AD 13 and succeeded him the following year. When he became emperor, he changed his name to Tiberius Caesar Augustus.

Tiberius did not have an easy life. His stepfather had forced an unhappy marriage upon him. The Roman Senate often opposed him. In AD 27 Tiberius left Rome for the island of Capri, leaving the task of governing the empire in the hands of Sejanus, a Roman prefect (high-ranking official). During the next five years, Sejanus secretly tried to depose the emperor and seize power for himself. His conspiracy almost succeeded, but Tiberius eventually had him executed. Despite this, Tiberius's administration was characterized by wisdom, intelligence, prudence, and duty. He continued his predecessor's policy of striving for peace and security.

In AD 26, presumably before going into semiretirement, Tiberius appointed Pontius Pilate as governor of Judea. Directly responsible to the emperor, Pilate could be immediately removed from office if word of Jewish disturbances or complaints reached Tiberius. Pilate's capitulation to the Jewish authorities during the trial of Jesus can be best understood in view of this. The Jews accused Jesus of claiming to be king, implying a rivalry with the emperor. When Pilate judged Christ innocent of the charge and sought to release him (Jn 18:33-38), the Jews insisted he could not do so and still be a friend of Caesar (19:12). If he released Jesus, they insinuated, he would risk losing the emperor's favor. Because of crimes committed at his command against the Jews, Pilate knew they might carry out their threat, resulting in his banishment. So, surrendering to their demands, he condemned Jesus to death by crucifixion.

Tiberius Caesar is mentioned only once in the NT. The Gospel of Luke states that John the Baptist began his ministry in the 15th year of Tiberius Caesar's reign, when Pontius Pilate was governor of Judea (Lk 3:1). Whether that date was calculated from Tiberius's actual accession or from the time of his co-regency is difficult to determine.

Tiberius was a strangely humble emperor. At his own request he was never officially recognized as a god (a sort of honorary title that the Senate had given to his predecessors). Interest in emperor worship had waned, and Tiberius intended to confine deity to his two predecessors. He also stopped the practice of naming months of the year after emperors; thus there is a July for Julius, an August for Augustus, but no Tiber for Tiberius. Plagued by domestic and political problems all his life, Tiberius died a tired and dejected old man. In fact, he was an excellent administrator.

Caligula (AD 12–41, reigned AD 37–41)

At the death of Tiberius, Gaius Julius Caesar became emperor at the age of 25. He was the son of an influential general, Germanicus; Augustus had forced Tiberius to adopt Gaius and make him his heir. As a child, Gaius had accompanied Germanicus on his military duties along the Rhine River in Germany. The soldiers nicknamed him Caligula ("Little Boot") for his military attire. The name stuck.

To gain popularity with the Romans, Caligula began his reign by pardoning people and recalling exiles. He squandered the money of the Roman treasury, however, and was forced to levy new taxes. His popularity was short-lived.

Six months after assuming office, Caligula suffered a serious illness that left him insane. On one occasion, for example, he appointed his horse as consul (chief magistrate). He insulted many people, banished others on whim, and had others murdered without provocation. When he felt that he had been insulted by the Jews in Jamnia, a Judean town near the Mediterranean coast, he ordered a statue of himself placed in the Temple at Jerusalem in revenge. The Jews were outraged, and a full-scale revolt was avoided only by the prudence of the governor of Syria, Petronius, who delayed carrying out the order. Not long afterward the emperor was assassinated by one of the many men he had insulted.

It was Caligula who appointed Herod Agrippa I (Herod in Acts 12) king over a tetrarchy northeast of Galilee—one of the first acts he performed as emperor, according to the Jewish historian Josephus. The two had become close friends before either had come to power, while Agrippa was living in Rome, where even as king he later spent much of his time. But unlike Caligula, Agrippa was a capable and popular ruler. Both king and emperor, in the tradition of many eastern monarchs, fancied themselves gods. Caligula, in fact, revived the notion in Rome of the emperor's deity and madly proclaimed himself equal to Jupiter. The Senate, however, refrained from officially recognizing that status.

Claudius (10 BC–AD 54, reigned AD 41–54)

Tiberius Claudius Germanicus was born in Lyon (France). He was Tiberius's nephew and a grandson of Livia, the wife of Augustus. In AD 37 he was appointed consul by Caligula. After Caligula's death Claudius was proclaimed emperor by the Praetorian Guard, and the Senate approved the choice.

When Claudius became emperor, he faced the task of healing the broken relationships caused by Caligula's madness. He ended the persecution of Jews in the city of Alexandria. Josephus recorded an edict that Claudius sent to Egypt, which read, in part: "Tiberius Claudius Caesar Augustus Germanicus, high priest and tribune of the people, ordains thus.... I will, therefore, that the nation of the Jews be not deprived of their rights and privileges on account of the madness of Gaius; but that those rights and privileges that they formerly enjoyed, be preserved to them, and that they may continue in their own customs."

That change of policy reflected the emperor's friendship with Herod Agrippa, who had played an influential role in Claudius's succession as emperor. Claudius, in turn, added Judea and Samaria to Agrippa's kingdom, giving him the dominion that once belonged to his grandfather, Herod the Great. He also promoted him to consular rank. Further, having complete trust in Agrippa's abilities, Claudius removed Judea from Roman provincial rule.

Agrippa's rule, however, was of short duration. In order to please the Jews, he had the apostle James, Zebedee's son, killed. He also had the apostle Peter imprisoned, planning to have him executed after the Passover feast in the spring of AD 44 (Acts 12:1-5). Peter escaped. During the summer of that year, Agrippa, who was wearing a glistening garment made of silver thread, gave a speech from his throne. The people acclaimed him as a god (v 22), and immediately he was struck down by an angel of the Lord. Five days later he died.

The emperor wished to stay on the right side of the Jewish people, yet five years after the death of Agrippa, Claudius issued an edict expelling all Jews from Rome. Luke related that Aquila and Priscilla were among those who had been ordered to leave the imperial city (Acts 18:2). The Roman biographer and historian Suetonius wrote that "because the Jews of Rome were indulging in constant riots at the instigation of Chrestus he [Claudius] expelled them from the city." The writer could easily have been uncertain of the spelling, because Chrestus, a common slave name, was pronounced virtually the same as Christus. It appears that Suetonius sought to convey to his readers that Chrestus was the founder of a movement (presumably Christianity).

Because of mismanagement by Caligula, the supply of grain for food was at an all-time low when Claudius began his reign (cf. Acts 11:28). Josephus related that during Claudius's administration, famine plagued Judea, Samaria, and Galilee. To alleviate the famine in Jerusalem, Helena, mother of the king of Adiabene, bought grain from Egypt and dried figs from Cyprus. That must have taken place in AD 45–46. Various ancient historians, including Tacitus, Suetonius, and Eusebius, reported that on frequent occasions famines prevailed in Rome and elsewhere. Repeatedly, harvests were minimal and distribution of food supplies was poor.

Claudius's family life and reputation were marred by intrigue. His immoral third wife, Messalina, was eventually put to death. Causing a slight scandal, he married his niece Agrippina, who had a son by a former marriage. She wanted her son Nero to be emperor, but Britannicus, Messalina's son, stood first in line. In AD 54, when Claudius decided that Britannicus should succeed him, Agrippina poisoned her husband and made Nero emperor. The Senate officially deified Claudius, making him the third emperor to receive that honor.

Nero (AD 37–68, reigned AD 54–68)

Nero was born Lucius Domitius Ahenobarbus. His father was a senator and consul who died when Nero was still a boy. His mother, Agrippina, Germanicus's daughter, was reputed to be one of the wealthiest and most beautiful women in Rome. When she married the emperor, her son received the name Nero Claudius Caesar Germanicus at his adoption by Claudius.

Nero was at first dominated by his proud mother, who wished to reign alongside her son. In those years Rome was a hotbed of political intrigue, murder plots, and assassinations. During the first five years of his reign, Nero had Britannicus and Agrippina eliminated in quick succession. A few years later he banished his wife, Octavia, and had her killed.

Ironically, the church at Rome flourished at that same time. The last chapter of the apostle Paul's Letter to the Romans, written from Corinth in AD 57, contains a long and impressive list of names of personal acquaintances—especially impressive because Paul had never been in Rome.

Nero had reigned more than five years when Paul, imprisoned at Caesarea, appealed to Caesar (Acts 25:11). Motives for the appeal may have been a prison release for Paul and an opportunity to seek legal recognition of Christianity. Paul's appeal to Caesar, however, does not necessarily mean that he was judged by Nero. The emperor had made it known at the beginning of his reign that he would not be a judge. Instead, he appointed prefects of the Praetorian Guard to judge cases for him. In the early part of AD 62, Nero changed that rule and judged a case himself. Therefore, whether Paul stood before Nero or before one of the prefects is difficult to determine. If prosecutors failed to appear, Paul's case may not have come before the judge at all. According to Philippians 1:7-14, Paul was still expecting a trial at the time of his writing that letter.

In AD 62 Nero's adviser Afranius Burrus died. Burrus had been a prefect of the Praetorian Guard and, together with an able senator, Seneca, had ruled the empire effectively while Nero spent his time on pleasure. After Burrus's death (Seneca was forced to commit suicide three years later), Nero began to indulge his whims unchecked. His greedy advisers, who sought self-advancement at the expense of the state, caused a severe financial crisis. Nero was also unbalanced in regarding himself the savior of the world.

In AD 64 a fire broke out at the Circus Maximus in Rome. It spread quickly, devouring everything in its path. Fanned by the wind, it raged for more than five days and devastated a large area of the city before being brought under control. At the time, Nero was at Antium, his birthplace, some 33 miles (53 kilometers) to the south. He rushed to Rome to organize relief work. Because of his evil record, however, people put stock in the rumor that Nero had set the fire himself.

Nero, in turn, found a scapegoat in the Christians, whom he charged with the crime. Many were persecuted. Perhaps the apostle Peter in his first letter was referring to the sufferings of Christians during the last few years of Nero's reign (1 Pt 4:12). Nero may have been influenced by his second wife, Poppaea, to blame the Christians for the devastation of Rome. The church had increased in numbers and had become a movement. Tacitus alluded to the size of the church when he wrote that "a huge crowd was convicted not so much of arson as of hatred of the human race."

It is likely that Peter and Paul were executed during the Neronian persecution. Clement of Rome, an early church father, in his letter to the church at Corinth (written presumably in AD 95), referred to the heroes of faith "who lived nearest to our time," namely Peter and Paul, who suffered martyrdom.

In AD 66 a Jewish revolt broke out in Caesarea. Nero dispatched his general Vespasian to squelch the revolt, taking no interest himself in the affairs of state. He left Rome for a journey to Greece, leaving the responsibility of governing the empire to a Roman prefect, Helius. Because of the inescapable opposition he encountered from leading governors in France, Spain, and Africa on his return, Nero committed suicide in AD 68. He was the last emperor of the Caesarean line by blood or marriage.

Galba (3 BC–AD 69, reigned AD 68–69)

After Nero's death, the Praetorian Guard selected Serius Sulpicius Galba to become emperor. Galba was a popular and capable governor at various times in the provinces of France, Germany, Spain, and Africa. He was a less successful emperor and became increasingly unpopular with the army and the people for his frugality and dislike of ceremony. The German legions of the Roman army, who had only reluctantly recognized him as their commander-in-chief, withdrew their support in AD 69, proclaiming Aulus Vitellius emperor.

When Galba failed to appoint one of his chief supporters, Marcus Salvius Otho, as his successor, he in essence signed his own death warrant. Otho gained the support of the Praetorian Guard, was proclaimed emperor, had Galba killed, and was confirmed by the Senate.

Vespasian (AD 9–79, reigned AD 69–79)

In the fall of AD 69, Vespasian found Rome ready for a period of stability, peace, and order. The son of a tax collector, he lived frugally, reestablished Rome's finances, reorganized the armies, and reemphasized the outward forms of the old republic. According to Suetonius, no innocent party was ever punished while Vespasian was emperor. He grieved when convicted criminals were executed.

Because of Nero's financial mismanagement, Vespasian had to levy new taxes and increase existing taxes in order to meet his fiscal obligations. As a result he was slandered as avaricious, although he was generous in aiding underprivileged senators and impoverished ex-consuls. Vespasian improved a number of cities in the empire that had been devastated by fire or earthquake, and he promoted the arts and sciences. In Rome he built the Temple of Peace after the destruction of Jerusalem and the defeat of the Jews, erected a forum, restored the Capitol, and began construction of the Colosseum.

During his 10-year reign, Vespasian established peace throughout the empire. His son Titus ended the war in Palestine, and other Roman generals suppressed a revolt in Germany. Public confidence was largely restored with the return to earlier standards of morality. Vespasian appointed his sons Titus and Domitian to succeed him.

Titus (AD 39–81, reigned AD 79–81)

Titus Flavius Vespasianus had served efficiently as a colonel in Germany and Britain. When the Jewish revolt broke out, he accompanied his father to Palestine. When Vespasian left for Rome five years later, Titus was appointed general of the Roman forces in Palestine. On September 26, AD 70, the Temple in Jerusalem was destroyed by fire, the citadel fell into the hands of the Romans, and countless Jews were killed. Titus returned to Rome with Jewish captives and spoils from the Temple to celebrate his victory with his father. The Arch of Titus was erected in Rome, depicting his conquest of Jerusalem.

Until Vespasian's death, Titus was almost a co-ruler with his father. He served as Vespasian's secretary, drafted edicts, and addressed the Senate in session. Titus was a talented person, especially in politics and music. He had fallen in love with Queen Bernice, King Agrippa II's sister (see Acts 25–26) and allegedly had promised to marry her, but moral integrity prevented him when rumor reached him of an incestuous relationship with her brother.

During Titus's brief reign as emperor (AD 79–81), a series of catastrophes occurred: Mt Vesuvius in southern Italy erupted and buried the towns of Pompeii, Stabiae, and Herculaneum (August, AD 79); a fire raged for three days and nights in Rome (AD 80); and a plague spread throughout the imperial city. Suetonius wrote that during those disasters Titus cared for the people with a love resembling the deep love of a father for his children.

When Titus died unexpectedly, his death caused universal mourning; he was eulogized by senators and common people alike.

Domitian (AD 51–96, reigned AD 81–96)

During Titus's rule, his brother Domitian expressed bitterness at having to take second place, openly coveted power, and conspired to seize command of the armed forces. He secretly rejoiced over Titus's sudden death and tried to slight his older brother's reputation. As it turned out, Domitian proved to be a capable administrator: he restored the fire-gutted Capitol and built a temple to Jupiter, the Flavian Temple, a forum, a stadium, a concert hall, and an artificial lake for sea battles. He instituted the Capitoline Festival, promoted the arts and sciences, and maintained the public libraries.

After the custom of earlier emperors Domitian proclaimed himself divine and had his subjects call him "Lord God." The Senate, however, never officially deified him. Throughout his reign they resented and often opposed the power he exercised by prerogative. Domitian did not hesitate to persecute senators who made their objections known. In order to protect himself, he sought the army's support by periodically increasing their pay. He collected additional taxes and often resorted to extortion. Jewish people were especially affected by his taxation. In the last years of Domitian's reign, religious persecution was revived.

The early Christian writers Irenaeus, Tertullian, and Eusebius mention the persecution of Christians during Domitian's administration. Domitian appears to have been a relentless persecutor, second only to Nero. He even put members of his own family to death; his wife, Domitia, feared for her life because of her alleged affiliation with Christianity. With friends and freedmen, she plotted her husband's assassination.

After ruling the empire for 15 years, Domitian was murdered. Mourned by none, except perhaps his well-paid army, he left in the wake of his reign a bitter memory of oppression.

Trajan (AD 53–117, reigned AD 98–117)

Trajan was born Marcus Trajanus of Roman parents in Italica, Spain. His father was a soldier who was promoted to governor of an eastern province in Spain. Trajan, trained to be a military commander, proved himself in campaigns in Spain, Syria, and Germany. In AD 97, Emperor Nerva adopted him as his son and heir. Upon Nerva's death the following year, Trajan was named emperor.

A powerful military leader, Trajan expanded the Roman Empire by many conquests in Dacia (now part of Romania and Hungary), Arabia, and Parthia (now part of Iran). He established new cities, including Thamugadi in what is now Algeria. He also oversaw many building programs, including bridges across the Danube River in Dacia and Tagus River in Spain, and a harbor at the port of Rome. According to the writings of Pliny (see *Letters* 10.96), we know that Trajan instigated persecutions against Christians because their worship of Jesus threatened to exterminate the traditional forms of Roman worship. The Christians' refusal to invoke the Roman gods and make offerings to the emperor's statue was considered a treasonous act because it undermined the empire's security.

CAIAPHAS

High priest during the life and ministry of Jesus. As official head of the Jewish state, Caiaphas presided over the council, or Sanhedrin—its highest court. Next to the Roman governor, he was the most powerful man in Judea and was responsible to the Romans for the conduct of the nation. Caiaphas was, therefore, especially concerned about the popular enthusiasm and political unrest centering on the ministry of Jesus and about its implications for the revolutionary sentiment of the time. The activities of the Zealots were increasing and were destined to break out soon into open revolt.

A huge stir among the people, caused by the raising of Lazarus (Jn 11), brought matters to a head. Alarmed lest the activities of those seeking a political messiah should lead the Romans to intervene with armed force, Caiaphas advised that Jesus should be put to death (Jn 11:48-50). The Gospel writer John pointed out that, in so doing, Caiaphas unwittingly prophesied concerning the atoning nature of Jesus' death (Jn 11:51-52).

Caiaphas played a chief role in Jesus' arrest and trial. The leaders laid their plans in his palace (Mt 26:3-5); it was there also that part of Jesus' preliminary trial took place with Caiaphas presiding (vv 57-68). That was after Jesus had first been taken before Annas, Caiaphas's father-in-law (Jn 18:13). Matthew, Mark, and Luke omit the visit to Annas, and Mark and Luke do not refer to Caiaphas by name. Upon Jesus' admission that he was "the Christ, the Son of God," Caiaphas tore his robes and charged him with blasphemy (Mt 26:63-66). After Pentecost, he, along with other Jewish leaders, presided over the trial of Peter and John when the council attempted to stop the preaching of the apostles (Acts 4:5-6).

Annas, who had held the office of high priest before Caiaphas, remained influential in the affairs of the nation. That explains why Luke, in his Gospel, set the ministry of John the Baptist "in the high-priesthood of Annas and Caiaphas" (Lk 3:2), and in Acts called Annas the high priest (Acts 4:6). John's account of Jesus' visit to Annas makes plain that Annas was still popularly referred to as "high priest" (Jn 18:22).

The historian Josephus records that Caiaphas was appointed to his office about AD 18 and ruled until he was deposed about AD 36. The high priest held office at the whim of the Romans, so Caiaphas's unusually long term indicates that he was a man of considerable political skill. Caiaphas was removed from his position by the proconsul Vitellus, and nothing more is known of him.

CAIN

First son of Adam and Eve, who became a tiller of the soil while his brother, Abel, was a keeper of sheep. Cain's murder of Abel became proverbial of similarly violent and destructive sins (Jude 1:11). Each of the two brothers had brought a sacrifice to the Lord (Gn 4:3-4). According to Hebrews 11:4, Abel had acted in faith by bringing a more acceptable sacrifice than that of Cain. The latter's anger had flared against the divine rejection. In retaliation, he killed his brother, whose offering had been accepted (Gn 4:5-8). In seeking a reason for Cain's inappropriate violent reaction, biblical commentary simply says that he belonged to the evil one (1 Jn 3:12). The Lord confronted Cain with his guilt, judged him, and pronounced a curse upon him, driving him out to the land of Nod, east of Eden (Gn 4:9-16). When he complained that his punishment was greater than he could bear and that someone would find him and kill him, the Lord placed a mark on Cain and promised to take sevenfold vengeance on anyone who dared to kill him.

In the land of Nod, Cain built a city and named it after his son Enoch (Gn 4:17). Through Enoch, Cain became the progenitor of a large family that during its early generations became tent-dwelling herdsmen, musicians, and fashioners of metal objects and implements (vv 18-22).

CAINAN

1. A son of Arphaxad (Lk 3:36; Gn 10:24, LXX; 11:12-13).
2. Adam's great-grandson, also called Kenan (Gn 5:9-14; 1 Chr 1:2; Lk 3:37). *See* Kenan.

CALCOL

One of Mahol's three sons and a member of Judah's tribe (1 Kgs 4:31, KJV "Chalcol"; 1 Chr 2:6). He and his brothers were noted for their wisdom and musical abilities.

CALEB

1. Son of Jephunneh the Kenizzite (Nm 32:12; Jos 14:6) and older brother of Kenaz (Jgs 1:13). Caleb was one of the 12 spies sent to scout out the land of Canaan. Although he and Joshua, another spy, recommended an immediate attack, their suggestion was rejected by the Israelite tribes because of other reports of heavily defended fortresses. Consequently, entrance into Canaan, the Promised Land, was delayed for some years as a divine judgment (Nm 14:21-23, 34-35).

When Israel under Joshua's leadership finally occupied Canaan, Caleb, at age 85 (Jos 14:6-7, 10), was assigned Hebron, which he conquered by overcoming its Anakim inhabitants (vv 13-14). Caleb offered his daughter Achsah to whomever would overthrow nearby Debir (Kiriath-sepher). Othniel, Kenaz's son and Achsah's cousin, was able to claim her as his wife by conquering the town (15:16-17).

Hebron later became a Levitical city of refuge (Jos 21:13; 1 Chr 6:55-57). In some portion of Caleb's territory David spent time as an outlaw and met his future wife Abigail, then the wife of Nabal, a Calebite (1 Sm 25:3). Here also his wives were captured by Amalekite marauders who had raided southern Judah and "the Negev of Caleb" (1 Sm 30:14).

2. Hezron's son and brother of Jerahmeel (1 Chr 2:18, 42), also called Chelubai (v 9). Many scholars, however, believe that this Caleb is the same as #1 above because (1) Achsah is mentioned as the daughter of both (v 49); and (2) the prominent place of an otherwise unknown Caleb in the genealogy would be hard to account for. According to these scholars, Caleb was listed as a son of Hezron (the grandson of Judah) in order to establish his position and inheritance in Judah's tribe. In reality, however, Caleb was a foreigner, son of Jephunneh, a Kenizzite, who had joined himself

QUICKTAKE

CALEB

STRENGTHS AND ACCOMPLISHMENTS
- One of the scouts sent by Moses to survey the land of Canaan
- One of the only two adults who left Egypt and entered the Promised Land
- Voiced the minority opinion in favor of conquering the land
- Expressed faith in God's promises, in spite of apparent obstacles

LESSONS FROM HIS LIFE
- Majority opinion is not an accurate measurement of right and wrong
- Boldness based on God's faithfulness is appropriate
- For courage and faith to be effective, they must combine words and actions

VITAL STATISTICS
Where: From Egypt to the Sinai peninsula to the Promised Land, specifically Hebron
Occupations: Scout, soldier, shepherd

KEY VERSE
"But my servant Caleb has a different attitude than the others have. He has remained loyal to me, so I will bring him into the land he explored. His descendants will possess their full share of that land" (Numbers 14:24).

Caleb's story is told in Numbers 13–14 and Joshua 14–15. He is also mentioned in Judges 1 and 1 Chronicles 4:15.

and his clan to Judah's tribe. Some support this view by arguing that Caleb is a Horite rather than Israelite name.

3. Hur's son, according to the KJV (1 Chr 2:50). Most likely, however, the KJV joins what should be two separate phrases. The NLT correctly renders it, "These were all descendants of Caleb. The sons of Hur . . ."

CALEB-EPHRATHAH
Possibly a Hebrew place-name (1 Chr 2:24, KJV, NLT). A number of modern translations follow the Septuagint (early Greek translation of the OT) in treating Ephrathah as the name of one of Caleb's wives instead of a place.

CARCAS
One of King Ahasuerus's seven counselors, in Esther 1:10.

CARMI
1. One of Reuben's sons; he accompanied his grandfather Jacob into Egypt (Gn 46:9; Ex 6:14; 1 Chr 5:3) and founded the family of Carmites (Nm 26:5-7).
2. Achan's father and a member of Judah's tribe (Jos 7:1, 18; 1 Chr 2:7; 4:1).

CARPUS
Man with whom the apostle Paul left his cloak at Troas. Paul instructed Timothy to bring it when he came to see him in prison (2 Tm 4:13). Carpus was possibly one of Paul's converts. According to tradition, Carpus became bishop of Berytus at Thrace.

CARSHENA
One of seven princes who were wise men of Persia and Media, and whom King Ahasuerus (Xerxes) consulted for legal advice (Est 1:14).

CASIPHIA
Place to which Ezra sent for Levites when he realized that his company of returnees from the Exile lacked persons qualified for Temple service (Ezr 8:17). Casiphia was perhaps Ctesiphon on the Tigris River near modern Baghdad.

CEPHAS
Aramaic name of Simon Peter the apostle in John 1:42; 1 Corinthians 1:12; and Galatians 1:18. *See* Simon Peter.

CHLOE
Woman whose household members (possibly slaves) informed Paul in Ephesus of arguments in the Corinthian church (1 Cor 1:11). It is not known whether Chloe lived in Corinth or Ephesus, or even whether she herself was a believer.

CHUZA
Steward of Herod Antipas, either a manager of Herod's property or a political appointee; a man of influence and prestige. He was married to Joanna, who was healed by Jesus and subsequently accompanied Jesus and his disciples on their travels (Lk 8:3).

CLAUDIA
Christian woman known to the apostle Paul and to Timothy (2 Tm 4:21).

CLAUDIUS
Roman emperor from AD 41 to 54, mentioned twice in the NT (Acts 11:28; 18:2). *See* Caesars, The.

CLAUDIUS LYSIAS
Commander of the Roman garrison in Jerusalem who wrote a letter to the Roman procurator Felix concerning the apostle Paul (Acts 23:26). His title in Greek *(chiliarch)* identifies him as a

commander of 1,000 troops. Although Claudius Lysias is unknown outside the NT, some information about him is supplied by the book of Acts. His surname Lysias is Greek. The Roman name Claudius was evidently taken at the time he purchased his Roman citizenship (22:28).

Stationed in the Antonia fortress overlooking the northern sector of the Temple area in Jerusalem, he rescued Paul from a Jewish mob that was about to kill him there. He allowed Paul to speak to the Jews from one of the two staircases that led from the Court of the Gentiles in the Temple up to the Antonia (Acts 21:40) and prevented Paul from being scourged when he learned of Paul's Roman citizenship (22:22-29). Claudius Lysias sent Paul secretly to Caesarea under heavy guard when Paul's nephew informed the tribune of a Jewish plot to murder the apostle in Jerusalem (23:16-35).

How Luke, the writer of Acts, obtained a copy of the official letter about Paul written by Claudius to Felix the governor is not known, but the document provides an important vindication of Paul's character and conduct in the face of his opponents' accusations.

CLEMENT
Coworker with Paul at Philippi who worked side by side with him in the furtherance of the gospel there (Phil 4:3). Paul includes him in the group of those whose names are written in the Book of Life. Even though some early church fathers identified this Clement with the third bishop of Rome, there is no evidence to substantiate their claims.

CLEOPAS
Follower of Jesus who conversed with him on the way to Emmaus (Lk 24:18). Some identify this Cleopas with the Clopas of John 19:25, but this is unlikely. *See* Clopas.

CLOPAS
Husband of Mary, one of the women who was present at Jesus' crucifixion (Jn 19:25). From the Greek it cannot be determined if Mary the wife of Clopas was also the sister of Jesus' mother or a different person. One tradition identifies Clopas as the brother of Joseph. Another links him with Cleopas of Luke 24:18, even though "Clopas" is of Hebrew origin and "Cleopas" is Greek. A third possibility is to equate him with Alphaeus. This is feasible only if James, son of Alphaeus (Mt 10:3; Lk 6:15; Acts 1:13) is the same as James, son of Mary (Mt 27:56; Mk 15:40), and Mary is the same person mentioned in John 19:25. These suggestions are theoretical; it is possible that Clopas, Cleopas, and Alphaeus are all separate individuals.

COL-HOZEH
The father of Shallum, who was ruler of the district of Mizpah (Neh 3:15). Col-hozeh, the son of Hazaiah in Nehemiah 11:5, may be another person.

CONANIAH
1. Levite and chief officer who supervised tithes, contributions, and the dedicated things given to the Temple during the reign of Hezekiah (2 Chr 31:12-13).

QUICKTAKE

CORNELIUS

STRENGTHS AND ACCOMPLISHMENTS
- A godly and generous Roman
- Although an officer in the occupying army, he seems to have been well-respected by the Jews
- He responded to God and encouraged his family to do the same
- His conversion helped the young church realize that the Good News was for all people, both Jews and Gentiles

LESSONS FROM HIS LIFE
- God reaches those who want to know him
- The gospel is for all people
- There are people everywhere eager to believe
- When we are willing to seek the truth and be obedient to the light God gives us, God will reward us richly

VITAL STATISTICS
Where: Caesarea
Occupation: Roman officer
Contemporaries: Peter, Philip, the apostles

KEY VERSE
"He was a devout, God-fearing man, as was everyone in his household. He gave generously to the poor and prayed regularly to God" (Acts 10:2).

Cornelius's story is told in Acts 10:1–11:18.

2. One of the chief Levites during the time of King Josiah (2 Chr 35:9); perhaps identifiable with Jeconiah in 1 Esdras 1:9.

CORNELIUS
Roman centurion and the first gentile Christian mentioned in the book of Acts.

The story of Cornelius's conversion through the preaching of the apostle Peter is recorded in Acts 10:1–11:18. Before his conversion, Cornelius was well known to the Jews as a person who feared God, prayed continually, and gave alms.

At first the church was composed only of Jews, who were reluctant to preach the gospel to Gentiles because law-abiding Jews never had fellowship with "pagans." Peter, a law-abiding

Jew, had scruples about entering a Gentile's house and eating "unclean" food. Through a vision, however, God led Peter to Cornelius's house to preach the gospel to him and his family and close friends. Before Peter had finished speaking, and before baptism or the laying on of hands could be administered, God dramatically demonstrated his acceptance of Gentiles into the fellowship of the church by giving them the gift of the Holy Spirit. Peter remained several days in Cornelius's house, no doubt rejoicing in the centurion's conversion and instructing him in his newfound faith.

Cornelius's conversion represented a significant step in the separation of the early church from Judaism. Cornelius did not have to submit to any of the Jewish practices, such as circumcision or eating only ritually "clean" animals. For the first time a gentile believer was accepted into the church on equal terms with Jewish Christians.

COSAM
Ancestor of Jesus, Addi's father and Elmadam's son, listed only in Luke's genealogy (3:28).

COZBI
Midianite woman with whom a Hebrew named Zimri entered into an illicit relationship. Phinehas, the grandson of Aaron, stopped a plague on Israel by executing Zimri and Cozbi (Nm 25:15-18).

CRESCENS
Coworker of the apostle Paul. Crescens went on to Galatia when Paul was imprisoned in Rome (2 Tm 4:10).

CRISPUS
Synagogue leader at Corinth who (along with all his household) was converted during the apostle Paul's 18-month missionary visit to the city (Acts 18:8, 11). Paul referred to Crispus as one of the few persons he personally baptized in Corinth (1 Cor 1:14).

CUSH
1. Eldest of Ham's four sons (Gn 10:6; 1 Chr 1:8). Because the other three (Egypt, Put, and Canaan) are place-names, it is likely that Cush also is a place. It is usually identified with Ethiopia.
2. Benjaminite and presumably David's enemy, mentioned in the title of Psalm 7.

CUSHAN-RISHATHAIM
King of Mesopotamia whom Israel served for eight years. The Lord raised up Othniel, Kenaz's son, to deliver Israel out of his hand; later, Cushan-rishathaim was defeated by Othniel in war (Jgs 3:8-10). His exact identity is uncertain.

CUSHI
1. Joab's messenger sent to David to announce Absalom's defeat (2 Sm 18:21-32). However, the Hebrew word transliterated "Cushi" should more likely be translated "Cushite."

2. Jehudi's great-grandfather. Jehudi was a prince in the court of King Jehoiakim of Judah in the time of Jeremiah the prophet (Jer 36:14).

3. Father of the prophet Zephaniah (Zep 1:1).

CYRUS (THE GREAT)

Persian king (559–530 BC) who founded the Achaemenid dynasty and the Persian Empire. Cyrus (II) was the son of Cambyses I (600–599 BC), who ruled the unified territories of Parshumash-anshan and Parsa. Cyrus's mother was Mandane, daughter of the Median king Astyages (585?–550 BC). The ancestor of the dynasty was Achaemenes. Cyrus succeeded his father and established himself in Pasargadae about 559 BC. Ambitious and daring, he aligned his kingdom with neighboring peoples and tribes into a solid block of Persian power, then revolted against Astyages of Media. When it became evident that Cyrus would win in the struggle to control Media, the troops of Astyages mutinied and deserted to Cyrus. When Cyrus conquered the Median kingdom, however, he came into conflict with Babylon, since the two kingdoms claimed much of the same territory.

Cyrus consolidated his power before fighting with Babylon. First, he conquered Asia Minor. Wealthy King Croesus of Lydia and the Lydians submitted to him. Then he overran the northern mountainous region between the Caspian Sea and the northwest corner of India.

By 539 BC, Cyrus was ready to move against Babylon. The Babylonian governor of Elam defected to Cyrus and joined his army. With a minimum of opposition, the armies of Cyrus entered the Babylonian capital in 539 BC. Nabonidus was taken prisoner but was treated with respect and mercy. Sixteen days later Cyrus himself entered the city, to the acclaim of many of its inhabitants.

Isaiah's prophecy spoke of Cyrus as the Lord's anointed (Is 45:1). Israel regarded him as called and empowered by their God to free them. Under Cyrus, the Jews were allowed to rebuild Jerusalem and its Temple (44:28). Documents preserved in the OT state that in his first year in Babylon, Cyrus issued a decree permitting the reconstruction of the house of God at Jerusalem (2 Chr 36:22-23; Ezr 1:1-3; 6:2-5). He also returned sacred vessels taken from the Temple by Nebuchadnezzar. Biblical descriptions of the decree say nothing about rebuilding the city, but that would be in harmony with the king's policy.

During excavations (1879–82) at Babylon, archaeologist Hormuzd Rassam discovered a clay barrel inscription on which Cyrus told of taking the city and of his resulting policies. Isaiah and Chronicles reflect the content of the inscription, which says that captured peoples were allowed to return home and build sanctuaries to their own gods.

Nothing is known about the death of Cyrus. Accounts that have been preserved make it clear that he was killed in battle, but the statements are conflicting. Probably the Greek historian Herodotus is right in indicating that Cyrus died in a terrible disaster that destroyed the Persian army fighting the Massagetae. The tomb of Cyrus can still be seen at Pasargadae in Iran.

D

DALPHON

Haman's son killed by the Jews in the aftermath of the plot against Mordecai (Est 9:7).

DAMARIS

Woman mentioned (Acts 17:34) as one of the first converts in the city of Athens, following Paul's preaching there. Since Luke singles her out by name, she may have been a person of importance (see Acts 13:50; 17:12).

DAN

Fifth son of the Jewish patriarch Jacob. Dan's mother was Bilhah, maid of Jacob's wife Rachel (Gn 30:1-6). Dan's descendants settled in Israel overlooking the Huleh Plain, in territory actually assigned to Naphtali, Dan's full brother (Gn 30:7-8; 35:25; Jos 19:32-48). The two brothers are mentioned together in a number of references (e.g., Ex 1:4).

Dan's name was given to him not by Bilhah but by Rachel, who considered the child her own. Rachel had long been childless—a shame to women in ancient cultures—and she was jealous of Jacob's other wife, Leah, who had already borne him four sons. Rachel viewed the birth of Bilhah's son as averting her shame and as God's vindication of her status as wife. The name Dan ("he judged") meant that God had judged her and had vindicated her through the child's birth (Gn 30:6).

Evidently Dan had only one son to continue his line, Hushim (Gn 46:23; "Shuham," Nm 26:42-43). In Jacob's patriarchal blessing, Dan was promised the role of "judge" among his people but was also spoken of as one who would be stealthy and dangerous, like a serpent (Gn 49:16-17). How that blessing worked out in the life of his descendants is unknown. The small amount of information given about Dan himself parallels the insignificance of his tribe in later times.

DANIEL

1. David's second son, the first by his wife Abigail (1 Chr 3:1); also called Kileab (2 Sm 3:3). *See also* Kileab.

2. Priest, descendant of Ithamar. He signed Ezra's covenant of faithfulness to God with Nehemiah and others after the Exile (Ezr 8:2; Neh 10:6).

3. Jewish statesman and seer in the Babylonian court whose career is recounted in the book of Daniel. Daniel's early life is cloaked in silence. Nothing is known of his parents or family, though he was probably descended from Jewish nobility (Dn 1:3). If born during the time of King Josiah's reforms (c. 621 BC), Daniel would have been about 16 when he and his three friends—Hananiah, Mishael, and Azariah—were deported from Jerusalem to Babylon by King Nebuchadnezzar. They may have been hostages to assure the cooperation of the royal family in Judah.

Daniel, renamed Belteshazzar (meaning "may Bel [god] protect his life"), was trained for court service. He quickly established a reputation for intelligence and for absolute fidelity to his God. After three years of instruction, he began a court career that lasted nearly 70 years (Dn 1:21). Daniel had hardly finished his training when he was called on to interpret one of Nebuchadnezzar's dreams, in which a great image collapsed and disintegrated when struck by a stone. God revealed its meaning to Daniel, who explained it to the king. In gratitude Nebuchadnezzar offered him the post of governor of Babylonia, but Daniel requested that the honor be conferred on his three companions in captivity.

Near the end of Nebuchadnezzar's life, Daniel was able to interpret a second dream (Dn 4). That dream intimated the king's impending insanity. Daniel urged the king to repent (4:27), but he did not, and subsequently for a period of time he became deranged.

After the death of Nebuchadnezzar in 562 BC, Daniel dropped from public view and evidently occupied an inferior position in the royal court. Although he received visions (Dn 7–8) in the first and third years of the Babylonian regent Belshazzar's reign (555 and 553 BC), it was not until 539 BC that Daniel made another public appearance. During a banquet hosted by Belshazzar, the king profaned the sacred vessels pillaged from the Jerusalem Temple. A disembodied hand suddenly appeared and wrote on the palace wall the mysterious words, "Mene, Mene, Tekel, Parsin." Summoned to explain the message, Daniel interpreted it as a forecast of the imminent end of the Babylonian kingdom. That same night Belshazzar was killed by the Persians, who attacked and successfully overtook the capital city (5:30).

Under Darius the Mede, Daniel became one of three "presidents" (administrators) of the realm (6:2). Daniel's rank, along with his capable and distinguished management, infuriated his political enemies. They persuaded Darius to pass a decree forbidding petition to any god or man but the king, under penalty of being cast into a lions' den. Daniel's religious integrity forced him to violate the law. Thrown to the lions, he remained miraculously unscathed. Vindicated, he was restored to office (vv 17-28).

The latter part of the book of Daniel describes several visions he received of future events. The visions dealt with four beasts (ch 7), future kingdoms (ch 8), the coming of the Messiah (ch 9), and Syria and Egypt (chs 11–12). The prophet Ezekiel alluded to Daniel's great wisdom (Ez 28:3) and ranked him in righteousness with Noah and Job (14:14, 20).

DARDA

Mahol's son (1 Kgs 4:31), a Judahite of the family of Zerah (1 Chr 2:6). With Ethan the Ezrahite and Heman and Calcol, also sons of Mahol, Darda is mentioned as the proverbial example of wisdom, though he is surpassed by Solomon (1 Kgs 4:31-32). First Chronicles 2:6 sometimes gives the name as Dara, probably the error of a copyist, and includes a fifth man, Zimri. That there are two different fathers (Mahol and Zerah) mentioned in the two passages may be explained by making Mahol the natural father and Zerah the Ezrahite an earlier ancestor.

DARIUS

Name of three emperors in the Persian dynasty of the legendary King Achaemenes. A Darius appears in the biblical books of Ezra, Nehemiah, Haggai, and Zechariah as a Persian king, and in the book of Daniel as a Mede who became king over the Chaldeans (Dn 9:1).

Darius I (521–486 BC)

Also known as Darius Hystaspes and Darius the Great, Darius I seized the throne of the Persian Empire after the death of Cambyses II. Although he was an Achaemenid, he was from a different branch of the royal family than Cyrus and Cambyses, and his authority was not accepted in all the provinces. After Darius quelled several revolts, however, his power was firmly established, and he turned his attention to expanding the empire. His military campaigns extended Persian borders to the Danube River in the west and to the Indus River in the east, making him ruler of the largest empire the world had known. Greco-Persian conflict, which continued until Alexander the Great conquered the empire in 330 BC, began when Darius launched two invasions of Greece after conquering Thrace and Macedonia. The first expedition was destroyed by a storm in the Aegean Sea; the second was defeated by the Athenians in the famous battle of Marathon in 490 BC.

An able administrator, Darius did much to promote trade and commerce. He instituted a uniform system of weights and measures. During his reign, a canal from the Nile River to the Red Sea was completed, and a sea route from the Indus River to Egypt was explored.

During Darius's reign, Persian architecture developed a style that continued until the end of the Achaemenid dynasty. Darius built at Babylon, Ecbatana, and Susa, his capital. A great royal road was constructed from Susa to the Lydian capital of Sardis. His greatest architectural accomplishment was the founding of Persepolis, a new royal city to replace the emperor's residence at Pasargadae. Darius also allowed temples to be built in Egypt and in Jerusalem, continuing Cyrus's policy of respecting the religious customs of his subjects.

Darius I is the Darius, king of Persia, mentioned in the books of Ezra, Haggai, and Zechariah. Ezra 5–6 record that Zerubbabel and Jeshua, with the help of Haggai and Zechariah, finished rebuilding the Temple during Darius's reign while Tattenai was governor of the province "Beyond the River" (Syria-Palestine). Zerubbabel and Jeshua had returned to Jerusalem under Cyrus II about 538 BC (Ezr 2:2). They completed the Temple in the sixth year of Darius (6:15). That must have been the sixth year of Darius I (516 BC), since the sixth year of Darius II would certainly be too late. That identification was confirmed by discovery of a Babylonian document, dated June 5, 502 BC, which refers to Tattenai as "the governor of Beyond the River."

In chapter 4 of Ezra three Persian rulers are mentioned: Darius (vv 5, 24); Ahasuerus (probably Xerxes I, v 6); and Artaxerxes (probably Artaxerxes I, vv 7-23). The chapter is a brief record of resistance to Jewish efforts to rebuild the city of Jerusalem and the Temple. Verse 24 states that work on the Temple stopped until "the second year of the reign of Darius," yet the Temple was completed in the sixth year of Darius I. Obviously, work on the Temple could not have stopped in the second year of Artaxerxes' son Darius II (421 BC) if it had already been finished in 515 BC. Therefore, Ezra 4:24 should be understood not as a chronological continuation of the first 23 verses but as an introduction to the next two chapters, which discuss the building of the Temple.

Darius II (423–404 BC)

Also known as Ochus (his real name) and Darius Nothus ("Darius the bastard"), Darius II was the son of Artaxerxes I by a Babylonian concubine. Before he became emperor, Ochus was a satrap (governor) of Hyrcania, a region on the southeast coast of the Caspian Sea. In 423 BC his half brother, Sogdianus (or Secydianus), killed Xerxes II. Ochus then seized the throne from Sogdianus, whom he executed, and adopted the name Darius II. His reign was plagued with revolution and corruption. His own full brother, Arsites, revolted soon after Darius seized the throne, and Darius had him executed.

After an alliance with Sparta was formed against Athens, Persia joined the Peloponnesian War. Several successful military campaigns succeeded in recovering the Greek coastal cities of Asia Minor and breaking Athenian power in the Aegean area. Darius II died in Babylon in 404 BC, the year the Peloponnesian War ended.

The Darius mentioned only once in the book of Nehemiah probably is Darius II. The passage states that Jewish priests were recorded "until the reign of Darius the Persian" (Neh 12:22b); descendants of Levi were recorded "until the days of Johanan son of Eliashib" (Neh 12:23). An Aramaic document found in Elephantine, Egypt, refers to Johanan the high priest in Jerusalem. The document was written in 407 BC, thus placing Johanan in the reign of Darius II.

Darius the Mede

Unknown in historical documents of the period of the Babylonian and Persian empires, this biblical Darius has been identified with several known figures. The most important efforts have identified Darius the Mede as another name for Cyrus II ("Cyrus the Persian," Dn 6:28); for Cambyses II, Cyrus's son; or for Gubaru, who was governor of Babylon and the province Beyond the River during the reigns of Cyrus II and Cambyses II.

According to the book of Daniel, "Darius the Mede received the kingdom" when Belshazzar, king of Babylon, was slain (Dn 5:30-31). Darius was about 62 years old (v 31) and was "the son of Ahasuerus, by birth a Mede" (9:1). Daniel never suggested that Darius was king of Media or of the whole Persian Empire, only of the Chaldean (Babylonian) kingdom. The Babylonian Empire included Mesopotamia (Babylonia and Assyria) and Syro-Palestine (Syria, Phoenicia, and Palestine). In the Persian Empire, that huge area became known as the province of Babylon (Mesopotamia) and Beyond the River (Syro-Palestine). Daniel also recorded that Darius appointed governors in the kingdom. By the third year of Cyrus the Persian (536 BC), the first year of Darius the Mede had already passed (Dn 10:1–11:1).

According to Nabonidus's Chronicle and the Persian Verse Account of Nabonidus (two cuneiform documents from Nabonidus's reign), Nabonidus was in Tema until

Cyrus's invasion of Babylonia. While he was away, he "entrusted the kingship" to his son Belshazzar. On October 12, 539 BC, Babylon fell to Ugbaru, general of Cyrus's army. Cyrus entered Babylon on October 29, 539 BC, and appointed a person named Gubaru governor of Babylon. Gubaru then appointed other governors under him. General Ugbaru died on November 6, 539 BC.

Clearly there is no place for Darius the Mede between the reigns of Nabonidus/Belshazzar and Cyrus II. Thus Darius the Mede must be Cyrus, a subordinate of Cyrus, or Cambyses, crown prince under Cyrus. But Cyrus II is mentioned as a separate person (Dn 6:28; 10:1–11:1), and it seems unlikely that the author would name the same figure both "Cyrus the Persian" and "Darius the Mede." Cambyses II could not have been 62 years old; also, since he was not made king of Babylon until he became king of the empire in 529 BC, Cambyses' first year could not precede Cyrus's third year (536 BC).

Darius the Mede was thus probably a subordinate of Cyrus who was made ruler of "the realm of the Chaldeans" after Belshazzar and who could have been considered a king by his subjects. Accordingly, the reign of Darius (Dn 6:28) should be understood as simultaneous with that of Cyrus, not as a preceding reign. Thus, Gubaru was made governor of Babylon immediately following the reign of Belshazzar, and he appointed governors, as did Darius the Mede. There is no record of Gubaru's age, nationality, or ancestry. He may well have been a 62-year-old Mede whose father was named Ahasuerus. The Ahasuerus of the book of Esther and of Ezra 4:6 should be identified with a later king, probably Xerxes I.

Many Babylonian texts record that Gubaru was governor of Babylon and the province Beyond the River for about 14 years (539–525 BC). The documents attribute much power to him. His name is a final warning to officials who might disobey the laws. In documents that mention Cyrus II or Cambyses II, crimes in Babylon are stated to be sins against Gubaru, not against Cyrus or Cambyses. The province of Babylon and Beyond the River was the richest and most populous in the Persian Empire, encompassing many nations and languages. For a powerful governor of such a region to be called "king" by his subjects seems only natural.

The case for Gubaru is admittedly circumstantial, but it remains the best solution to the problem. Until further evidence comes to light, it is safe to assume that Darius the Mede, "king over the realm of the Chaldeans," was actually Gubaru, the known governor of that realm.

DARKON
Ancestor of a group of people who returned to Judah with Zerubbabel after the Exile (Ezr 2:56; Neh 7:58).

DATHAN
Reubenite, son of Eliab and brother of Abiram; one of the leaders of Israel who, with Korah, rebelled against Moses during the wilderness wanderings (Nm 16:1-27; 26:9; Ps 106:17).

QUICKTAKE

DAVID

STRENGTHS AND ACCOMPLISHMENTS
- Greatest king of Israel
- Ancestor of Jesus Christ
- Listed in the Hall of Faith in Hebrews 11
- A man described by God himself as a man after his own heart

WEAKNESSES AND MISTAKES
- Committed adultery with Bathsheba
- Arranged the murder of Uriah, Bathsheba's husband
- Directly disobeyed God in taking a census of the people
- Did not deal decisively with the sins of his children

LESSONS FROM HIS LIFE
- Willingness to honestly admit our mistakes is the first step in dealing with them
- Forgiveness does not remove the consequences of sin
- God greatly desires our complete trust and worship

VITAL STATISTICS
Where: Bethlehem, Jerusalem
Occupations: Shepherd, musician, poet, soldier, king
Relatives: Father: Jesse. Wives: included Michal, Ahinoam, Bathsheba, Abigail.
    Sons: included Absalom, Amnon, Solomon, Adonijah. Daughters: included
    Tamar. Seven brothers
Contemporaries: Saul, Jonathan, Samuel, Nathan

KEY VERSES
"For you are God, O Sovereign LORD. Your words are truth, and you have promised these good things to your servant. And now, may it please you to bless the house of your servant, so that it may continue forever before you. For you have spoken, and when you grant a blessing to your servant, O Sovereign LORD, it is an eternal blessing!" (2 Samuel 7:28-29)

His story is told in 1 Samuel 16—1 Kings 2. He is also mentioned in Amos 6:5; Matthew 1:1, 6; 22:43-45; Luke 1:32; Acts 13:22; Romans 1:3; Hebrews 11:32.

DAVID

Israel's most important king. David's kingdom represented the epitome of Israel's power and influence during the nation's OT history.

The two books in the OT devoted to David's reign are 2 Samuel and 1 Chronicles. His earlier years are recorded in 1 Samuel, beginning at chapter 16. Almost half of the biblical psalms are ascribed to David. His importance extends into the NT, where he is identified as an ancestor of Jesus Christ and forerunner of the messianic king.

Preview

- Early Years
- Preparation for Kingship
- David as King
- David's Lasting Influence

Early Years

Family

David was the youngest son in Jesse's family, part of Judah's tribe. The family lived in Bethlehem, about six miles (10 kilometers) south of Jerusalem. His great-grandmother was Ruth, from the land of Moab (Ru 4:18-22). Genealogies in both the OT and the NT trace David's lineage back to Judah, son of the patriarch Jacob (1 Chr 2:3-15; Mt 1:3-6; Lk 3:31-33).

Training and Talents

Little is known about David's early life. As a boy, he took care of his father's sheep, risking his life to kill attacking bears and lions. Later, David publicly acknowledged God's help and strength in protecting the flocks under his care (1 Sm 17:34-37).

David was an accomplished musician. He had developed his ability as a harpist so well that, when a musician was needed at the royal court of King Saul, someone immediately recommended David.

In Jesse's family, David was regarded as unimportant. When the nationally known prophet Samuel visited Jesse's home, all the older sons were on hand to meet him; David was tending the sheep. Samuel had been instructed by God to anoint a king from Jesse's family, not knowing beforehand which son to anoint. Sensing divine restraint as seven brothers passed before him, he made further inquiry. When he learned that Jesse had one other son, David was immediately summoned. David was anointed by Samuel and endowed with the Spirit of the Lord (1 Sm 16:1-13). Whatever Jesse and his family understood by that anointing, it seems to have made no immediate change in David's pattern of living. He continued to tend the sheep.

Preparation for Kingship

During his youth, David was willing to serve others, even though he had been anointed king. It was his willingness to take supplies to three of his older brothers in the army that gave him his opportunity for national fame.

As a young man, David was also sensitive toward God. While greeting his brothers on the battlefield, he was disturbed by the Philistine Goliath's defiance of God's armies. Although rebuked by his brothers, David accepted the challenge to take on Goliath. He had a reasonable confidence that God, who had helped him encounter a lion and a bear, would aid him against a champion warrior. So, with faith in God and using his ability to sling stones, David killed Goliath (1 Sm 17:12-58).

National Fame
Killing Goliath made David a hero to the nation of Israel. It also brought him into close relationship with the royal family of Saul. But success and national acclaim brought on the jealousy of Saul and ultimately resulted in David's expulsion from the land of Israel.

In the Royal Court
Saul promised his oldest daughter, Merab, to David in marriage, but then Saul went back on the promise and offered David another daughter, Michal. The dowry of trophies from

DIGGING DEEPER

DAVID, A MAN OF GOD

David, one of the most gifted and versatile individuals in the OT, is second only to Moses in Israel's history. He was keenly conscious that God had enabled him to establish a kingdom (Ps 18; cf. 2 Sm 22); it was in that context that he was given the messianic promise of an eternal kingdom.

From David's own suffering, persecution, and nearness to death came prophetic psalms that portrayed the suffering and death of the Messiah (e.g., Pss 2; 22; 110; 118). Even the hope of the resurrection is expressed in Psalm 16, as the apostle Peter noted on the day of Pentecost (Acts 2:25-28).

Awareness of a vital personal relationship with God is expressed more consistently by David than by any of the faithful men and women who preceded him. He knew that it was not legalistic observance of rules or rituals that made him acceptable to God. Offering and sacrifice could not atone for sin if one had no accompanying contrition and humility. Many of David's prayers are as appropriate for Christians as they were for God-fearing people in the OT. David's writings show that "knowing God" was as real in OT times as it was for the apostle Paul, even though the full revelation of God in Jesus Christ was still in the future.

● ● ●

dead Philistines demanded by Saul was designed to bring about David's death at Philistine hands. But again David was victorious. Women sang praises of his exploits, intensifying Saul's jealousy and further endangering David's life (1 Sm 18:6-30).

In the meantime, David and Saul's son Jonathan developed a deep friendship. When they made a covenant, Jonathan gave David his choicest military equipment (sword, bow, and belt). Although Saul tried to turn Jonathan against David, the friendship deepened. Because Saul was trying to kill him, David had to flee from the court and live as a fugitive.

After Jonathan had warned David of Saul's continuing designs on his life, David went to Ramah to see the prophet Samuel. Together they went to Naioth, near Ramah. After sending several groups of men after David, Saul finally went with them himself. All his attempts to seize David were thwarted by the Spirit of God, who caused Saul and his men to prophesy all night in religious fervor (1 Sm 19).

Conferring again with Jonathan, David realized that Saul's jealousy had developed into hatred. Jonathan, aware that David would be the future king of Israel, requested assurance that his descendants would receive protection under David's rule (1 Sm 20).

Life as a Fugitive

Fleeing from Saul, David stopped at Nob. By deceiving Ahimelech, who was officiating as priest there, David obtained food supplies and Goliath's sword (kept as a trophy). An Edomite named Doeg, chief of Saul's herdsmen, saw what happened at Nob. David continued his flight, taking refuge temporarily in Gath with King Achish (1 Sm 21), then finding shelter in the cave of Adullam, located 10 miles (16.1 kilometers) southwest of Bethlehem. There his relatives and about 400 fighting men joined him. He went to Mizpeh in Moab, appealing to the Moabite king for protection, especially for his parents. When the prophet Gad warned him not to stay there, David moved back to Judah to the Hereth woods (1 Sm 22:1-5).

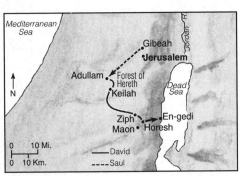

David Flees from Saul: David and his men attacked the Philistines at Keilah from the forest of Hereth. Saul came from Gibeah to attack David, but David escaped into the wilderness of Ziph. At Horesh he met Jonathan, who encouraged him. Then he fled into the wilderness of Maon and into the strongholds of En-gedi.

David's freedom of movement enraged Saul, who charged his own people with conspiracy. When Doeg reported what he had witnessed at Nob, Saul executed Ahimelech and 84 other priests, then massacred all of Nob's inhabitants. One priest named Abiathar escaped to report Saul's atrocities to David, who assured him of protection (1 Sm 22:6-23).

The Philistines were always ready to take advantage of any weakness in Israel. David's reprisal after a Philistine raid on Keilah, 12 miles (19.3 kilometers) southwest of Bethlehem, gave Saul an opportunity to attack David, who escaped to the wilderness of Ziph, a desert area near Hebron. David and Jonathan met for the last time in that wilderness. Pursued by Saul's army, David fled still farther south. He was almost encircled in uninhabited country near Maon when Saul had to march his army off to respond to a Philistine attack (1 Sm 23).

At his next place of refuge, En-gedi, on the western shore of the Dead Sea, David was attacked by Saul with 3,000 soldiers. David had an opportunity to kill Saul but refused to harm the "Lord's anointed" king of Israel. Learning of David's loyalty, Saul confessed his sin in seeking David's life (1 Sm 24).

During the years they roamed the wilderness in the Maon/Ziph/En-gedi area, David's band provided protection for Nabal, a rich man living in Maon with large flocks of sheep at Carmel. In exchange for that protection, David proposed that Nabal share some of his wealth. Nabal's scorn angered David, but Nabal's wife, Abigail, appealed to David not to take revenge. When Abigail told Nabal of his narrow escape, he was evidently so shocked that he had a heart failure. He died ten days later, and Abigail later became David's wife (1 Sm 25).

Once more Saul came with an army of 3,000 men into the Ziph Desert to find David, and David again passed up an opportunity to harm the king. Finally realizing the folly of seeking David's life, Saul abandoned pursuit (1 Sm 26).

DIGGING DEEPER

SOME PSALMS FROM DAVID'S EXPERIENCES

PSALM	HISTORICAL REFERENCE
59	1 Sm 19:11
56	1 Sm 21:10
34	1 Sm 21:13
142	1 Sm 22:1
52	1 Sm 22:9
54	1 Sm 23:19
57	1 Sm 24:1
7	1 Sm 24:11-12
18	2 Sm 7:1; 22
32	2 Sm 12:13-14
51	2 Sm 12:13-14
3	2 Sm 15:16
63	2 Sm 16:2

● ● ●

Refuge in Philistia

David continued to feel unsafe in Saul's kingdom. Returning to Gath in Philistine country, he was welcomed by King Achish. His followers were allotted the city of Ziklag, where they lived for about 16 months, attracting new recruits from Judah and the rest of Israel (1 Sm 27; 1 Chr 12:19-22).

The Philistine army, marching up to the Megiddo Valley to fight Saul's army, was uneasy with David's guerrillas in their rear column, so the commanders put pressure on Achish to dismiss David. When he returned to Ziklag, David found that the city had just been raided by the Amalekites. He pursued the enemy, rescued his people and goods, and divided the spoils with those who had remained behind to guard the supplies (1 Sm 29–30). Meanwhile, the Philistines routed the Israelites at Mt Gilboa, killing Jonathan and two of Saul's other sons in a fierce battle. Saul, badly wounded, killed himself with his own sword (ch 31).

David as King

David ruled over Israel for about 40 years, although the accounts of his reign do not contain enough information for an exact chronology. He began his rule at Hebron and reigned over Judah's territory for seven or eight years. With the death of Saul's successor, Ishbosheth, David was recognized as king by all the tribes and made Jerusalem his capital. During the next decade, he unified Israel through military and economic expansion. Then came approximately 10 years of disruption in the royal family. The last years of David's reign seem to have been devoted to plans for the Jerusalem Temple, which was built in the reign of his son Solomon.

The Years in Hebron

David was subjected to an unusually rugged period of training for his kingship. Serving under Saul, he gained experience in military exploits against the Philistines. Then, during his fugitive wanderings in the desert area of southern Judah, he ingratiated himself with the landholders and sheep raisers by giving them protection. Being recognized as an outlaw of Israel even enabled him to negotiate diplomatic relations with Moab and Philistia.

David was in Philistine country when news came to him that both Saul and Jonathan had been slain. In a beautiful elegy he paid tribute to his friend Jonathan as well as to King Saul (2 Sm 1).

Sure of God's guidance, David returned to his home, where the leaders of Judah anointed him king at Hebron. He sent a message of commendation to the men of Jabesh for providing a respectable burial for King Saul, probably also bidding for their support.

Confusion probably swept through Israel when Saul was killed, because the Philistines occupied much of the land. Various leaders gathered whatever fighting men they could find, as old tribal loyalties reasserted themselves. David had most of Judah's tribe firmly behind him.

A kind of civil war broke out between the followers of David and those of Saul, with David gaining the allegiance of more and more people. Saul's general, Abner, eventually negotiated peace with David, who requested the restoration of Michal as his wife, indicating that he held no animosity toward Saul's dynasty. With the consent of Saul's son Ishbosheth, whom Abner had enthroned as king, Abner went to Hebron and pledged Israel's support for David. But Abner was killed by Joab, one of David's captains, in a family vendetta, and soon afterward Ishbosheth was assassinated. David publicly mourned Abner's death and had Ishbosheth's two murderers executed. Thus, when Saul's dynasty ended, David was seen by the people not so much as a challenger but as a logical successor. Hence, he was recognized as king by all Israel (2 Sm 2–4).

Consolidation in Jerusalem

When the Israelites turned to David as king, the Philistines became alarmed and attacked (2 Sm 5; 1 Chr 14:8-17). David was strong enough to defeat them and thus unify the people of Israel.

In search of a more central location for his capital, David turned toward the city of Jerusalem, a Jebusite stronghold. Joab responded to his challenge to conquer the city and was rewarded by being made general of David's army. Jerusalem became known as the "city of David" (1 Chr 11:4-9).

In the same way that he had organized his earliest followers into an effective guerrilla band (1 Chr 11:1–12:22) at Hebron, David began organizing the whole nation (12:23-40). Once established in Jerusalem, he quickly gained recognition from the Phoenicians, contracting for their artisans to build him a magnificent palace in the new capital (14:1-2). He also made sure that Jerusalem would become Israel's religious center (2 Sm 6; 1 Chr 13–16). His abortive attempt to move the Ark of the Covenant by oxcart (cf. Nm 4) reminded the powerful king that he still had to do things God's way to be successful.

With Jerusalem well established as the nation's capital, David intended to build God a Temple. He shared his plan with the prophet Nathan, whose immediate response was positive. That night, however, God sent a message via Nathan that David should not build the Temple. David's throne would be established eternally, the prophet said, and unlike Saul, King David would have a son to succeed him and perpetuate the kingdom; that son would build the Temple (2 Sm 7; 1 Chr 17).

Prosperity and Supremacy

Little is recorded about the expansion of David's rule from the tribal area of Judah to a vast empire stretching from the Nile River of Egypt to regions of the Tigris-Euphrates valley. Nothing in secular history negates the biblical perspective that David had the most powerful kingdom in the heart of that "Fertile Crescent" about 1000 BC.

It is likely that skirmishes with the Philistines to the west were frequent until they finally became subservient to David and paid him tribute. In Saul's day the Philistines had enjoyed a monopoly on the use of iron (1 Sm 13:19-21). The fact that David freely used iron near the end of his reign (1 Chr 22:3) hints at profound economic changes in Israel.

David's kingdom expanded southward as he built military garrisons in Edomite territory. Beyond Edom, he controlled the Moabites and Amalekites, who paid him tribute in silver and gold. To the northeast, Israelite domination was extended over the Ammonites and the Arameans, whose capital was Damascus. David's treatment of both friends and enemies seemed to contribute to the strength of his kingdom (2 Sm 8–10). Although he was a brilliant military strategist who used all the means and resources available to bring Israel success, David was humble enough to glorify God (2 Sm 22; see Ps 18).

Sin in the Royal Family

A lengthy section of the book of 2 Samuel (chs 11–20) gives a remarkably frank account of sin, crime, and rebellion in David's family. The king's own imperfections are clearly portrayed; the king of Israel himself could not escape God's judgment when he did wrong.

Although polygamy was then a Near Eastern status symbol, it was forbidden for a king of Israel (Dt 17:17). David practiced polygamy, however; some of his marriages undoubtedly had political implications (such as his marriages to Saul's daughter Michal and to princess Maacah of Geshur). Flagrant sins of incest, murder, and rebellion in his family brought David much suffering and almost cost him the throne.

David's sin of adultery with Bathsheba, committed at the height of his military success and territorial expansion, led him further into evil: he planned a strategy to have Bathsheba's husband, Uriah, killed on the front line of battle. David seems to have excluded God from consideration in that segment of his personal life. Yet when the prophet Nathan confronted the king with his sins, David acknowledged his guilt. He confessed his sin and pleaded with God for forgiveness (as in Pss 32 and 51). God forgave him, but for nearly ten years David endured the consequences of his lack of self-restraint and his failure to exercise discipline in his family. Although unsurpassed in military and diplomatic strategy, David lacked strength of character in his domestic affairs. Evil fermented in his own house; the father's self-indulgence was soon reflected in Amnon's crime of incest, followed by Absalom's murder of his brother.

Having incurred his father's disfavor, Absalom took refuge in Geshur with his mother's people for three years. Joab, David's general, was eventually able to reconcile David with his alienated son. Absalom, however, having taken advantage of his position in the royal family to gain a following, went to Hebron, staged a surprise rebellion, and proclaimed himself king throughout Israel. His strong following posed such a threat that David fled from Jerusalem. David, still a master strategist, gained time through a ruse to organize his forces and put down his son's rebellion. Absalom was killed while trying to flee; his death plunged David into grief.

On his return to Jerusalem, David had to work at undoing the damage caused by Absalom's revolt. His own tribe of Judah, for example, had supported Absalom. Another rebellion, fomented by Sheba of Benjamin's tribe, had to be suppressed by Joab before the nation could settle down.

David's Last Years

Although David was not permitted to build the Temple in Jerusalem, he made extensive preparations for that project during the last years of his reign. He stockpiled materials and organized the kingdom for efficient use of domestic and foreign labor. He also outlined details for religious worship in the new structure (1 Chr 21–29).

The military and civic organization developed by David was probably patterned after Egyptian practice. The army, rigidly controlled by officers of proven loyalty to the king, included mercenaries. The king also appointed trusted supervisors over farms, livestock, and orchards in various parts of his empire (1 Chr 27:25-31).

David took, or at least began, a census of Israel (2 Sm 24; 1 Chr 21). The incompleteness of the accounts leaves unanswered such questions as the reason for God's punishment. The king overruled Joab's objection and insisted that the census be taken. Since David later seemed keenly aware that he had sinned in taking the census, it may be that he was motivated by pride to ascertain his exact military strength (approx. 1.5 million men). God may also have been judging the people for their support of the rebellions of Absalom and Sheba.

Through the prophet Gad, David was given a choice of punishments for his sin. He chose a three-day pestilence. As David and the elders repented, they saw an angel on the threshing floor of the Jebusite Ornan (Araunah). David offered sacrifice there and prayed for his people. Later he purchased the threshing floor, located just outside the city of Jerusalem, concluding that it should be the site for the Temple to be built by his son Solomon (1 Chr 21:28–22:1).

David's Lasting Influence
The Writer of Psalms

The OT book of Psalms became one of the most popular books in ancient Israel, and has remained so among countless millions of people throughout the centuries. These words of praise prepared by David were intended for use in the Temple worship (2 Chr 29:30). The 73 psalms ascribed to David generally grew out of his own relationship to God and to other persons.

David probably compiled Book I of the book of Psalms (1–41) and Book IV (90–106), since most of those psalms were written by David himself. Other psalms of his (Pss 51–71) are in Book II (42–72), which was probably

DAVID
The Times of David

1040 BC?
David is born in Bethlehem, the youngest of Jesse's eight sons (1 Samuel 16).

1025? BC
David is anointed by Samuel as Israel's next king, but he won't rule until Saul dies (1 Samuel 16:13).

1025? BC
David is brought into King Saul's court as a musician (1 Samuel 16:14-23).

1025? BC
David defeats Goliath (1 Samuel 17).

1025–1020? BC
David serves well in Saul's army, befriends Prince Jonathan, and marries Princess Michal (1 Samuel 18).

1020?–1010 BC
Jealous Saul tries to kill David, who flees. David has opportunities to kill Saul, but refuses (1 Samuel 18–30).

1010 BC
Saul dies, and David becomes king (1 Samuel 31:6; 2 Samuel 2, 5).

1010–970 BC
David's reign is marked by the defeat of the Philistines, but there is also family tension (2 Samuel).

1000 BC
David conquers Jerusalem and makes it his headquarters and center of worship (2 Samuel 5–6).

997? BC
David commits adultery with Bathsheba, murders her husband, and repents (2 Samuel 11–12).

985? BC
David's son Absalom rebels but is killed; David mourns (2 Samuel 13–19).

975? BC
David makes plans to build the Temple; God doesn't allow him to do so (2 Samuel 7).

970 BC
David dies and is succeeded by his son Solomon (1 Kings 1–2).

compiled by Solomon. As those psalms were used for worship in later generations, various people added others until the time of Ezra.

David's psalms provided much of the poetry that was set to music for Israel's worship. His organization of the priests and Levites and his provision of instruments for worship (2 Chr 7:6; 8:14) set the pattern for generations to come in the religious life of Israel.

David in the Writings of the Prophets

David, recognized as the greatest Israelite king, is often mentioned as a standard of comparison in the writings of the OT prophets. Isaiah (as in Is 7:2, 13; 22:22) and Jeremiah often referred to their contemporary kings as belonging to the "house" or "throne" of David. Contrasting David with some of his descendants who did not honor God, both Isaiah and Jeremiah predicted a messianic ruler who would establish justice and righteousness on the throne of David forever (Is 9:7; Jer 33:15). When Isaiah described the coming ruler, he identified him as being from the lineage of Jesse, David's father (Is 11:1-10). Predicting a period of universal peace, Isaiah saw the capital in "Zion," identified with the city of David (2:1-4).

Ezekiel promised the restoration of David as king in an eschatological and messianic sense (Ez 37:24-25), and of "my servant David" as Israel's shepherd (34:23). Hosea likewise identified the future ruler as King David (Hos 3:5). Amos assured the people that God would restore the "tabernacle" of David (Am 9:11, RSV) so that they could again dwell in safety. Zechariah referred five times to the "house of David" (in Zec 12–13, RSV), encouraging the hope of a restoration of David's glorious dynasty. The concept of the eternal throne promised to David during his reign was delineated in the message of the prophets even while they were announcing judgments to come on the rulers and people of their time.

David in the New Testament

David is frequently mentioned by the Gospel writers, who established Jesus' identity as the "son of David." The covenant God made with David was that an eternal king would come from David's family (Mt 1:1; 9:27; 12:23; Mk 10:48; 12:35; Lk 18:38-39; 20:41). According to Mark 11:10 and John 7:42, the Jews of Jesus' day expected the Messiah (Christ) to be a descendant of David. While stating that Jesus came from the lineage of David, the Gospels also clearly teach that Jesus was the Son of God (Mt 22:41-45; Mk 12:35-37; Lk 20:41-44).

In the book of Acts, David is recognized as the recipient of God's promises that were fulfilled in Jesus Christ. David is also seen as a prophet whom the Holy Spirit inspired to write the psalms (Acts 1:16; 2:22-36; 4:25; 13:26-39).

In the book of Revelation, Jesus is designated as having the "key of David" (Rv 3:7), and as being "the Lion of the tribe of Judah, the Root of David" (5:5). Jesus is quoted as asserting that "I am the root and the offspring of David, the bright morning star" (22:16).

See also Messiah.

DEBORAH the JUDGE

STRENGTHS AND ACCOMPLISHMENTS
• Fourth and only female judge of Israel
• Special abilities as a mediator, adviser, and counselor
• When called on to lead, was able to plan, direct, and delegate
• Known for her prophetic power
• A writer of songs

LESSONS FROM HER LIFE
• God chooses leaders by his standards, not ours
• Wise leaders choose good helpers

VITAL STATISTICS
Where: Canaan
Occupations: Prophet and judge
Relative: Husband: Lappidoth
Contemporaries: Barak, Jael, Jabin of Hazor, Sisera

KEY VERSE
"Deborah, the wife of Lappidoth, was a prophet who was judging Israel at that time" (Judges 4:4).

Her story is told in Judges 4–5.

DEBIR
One of the kings of Eglon who became an ally of Adoni-zedek, the king of Jerusalem. Debir was executed by Joshua (Jos 10:22-27).

DEBORAH
Name of two OT women. The word in Hebrew means "honeybee" (Ps 118:12; Is 7:18).
1. Rebekah's nurse (Gn 35:8). Deborah died as she was traveling to Bethel with her master Jacob's household. She was buried in a spot remembered as Allon-bacuth ("the oak of weeping"), indicating that she had been well loved. She was probably Rebekah's longtime companion (see 24:59-61).
2. Prophetess and judge (Jgs 4–5). Deborah's position as a prophetess, indicating that her message was from God, is not unique in the Bible, but it was unusual. Other

prophetesses included Miriam (Ex 15:20), Huldah (2 Kgs 22:14), and Anna (Lk 2:36). Deborah was unique in that only she is said to have "judged Israel" *before* the major event that marks her narrative (Jgs 4:4). Her husband, Lappidoth, is otherwise unknown.

Deborah, heralded as a "mother in Israel" (Jgs 5:7), remained in one location and the people came to her for guidance. Evidently over 200 years later, when the book of Judges was compiled, a giant palm tree still marked the spot. Though residing within the boundary of Benjamin (Jgs 4:5; cf. Jos 16:2; 18:13), Deborah was probably from the tribe of Ephraim, the most prominent tribe of northern Israel. Some scholars, however, place her in the tribe of Issachar (Jgs 5:14-15). At that early time, the tribes were loosely organized and did not always occupy the territory they had been allotted.

Under Deborah's inspired leadership, the poorly equipped Israelites defeated the Canaanites in the plain of Esdraelon (Jgs 4:15); flooding of the Kishon River evidently interfered with the enemy's impressive chariotry (5:21-22). The Canaanites retreated to the north, perhaps to Taanach near Megiddo (v 19), and never reappeared as an enemy within Israel. The Song of Deborah (ch 5) is a poetic version of the prose narrative in Judges 4.

See also Barak.

DEDAN

1. Grandson of Cush in the list of Noah's descendants. His father was Raamah, and his brother's name was Sheba (Gn 10:7; 1 Chr 1:9).

2. Grandson of Abraham through Keturah (Gn 25:3). His father was Jokshan, his brother was Sheba, and his descendants were the Asshurim, Letushim, and Leummim.

DELAIAH

1. Son of Elioenai who traced his line of descent through Zerubbabel to David (1 Chr 3:24, KJV "Dalaiah").

2. Priest in the time of David (1 Chr 24:18).

3. Head of a postexilic family that returned with Zerubbabel to Judea. The group was unable to prove true Israelite descent (Ezr 2:60; Neh 7:62).

4. Father of a fifth-century BC man named Shemaiah. Shemaiah opposed Nehemiah (Neh 6:10).

5. Counselor in the reign of Jehoiakim (609–598 BC) who urged the king not to destroy Jeremiah's scroll, which Baruch had just read (Jer 36:12, 25).

DELILAH

Samson's mistress, who betrayed him to his Philistine enemies (Jgs 16). Because Philistia held southern Israel in vassalage at the time (c. 1070 BC), Samson was chosen by God to begin the delivery of Israel. His success prompted the five Philistine rulers to offer Delilah a bribe if she would help capture him by discovering the secret of his enormous strength.

Delilah was from the valley of Sorek, in the southeast corner of Dan's territory, only a few miles from Samson's home in Zorah. It is clear from Judges 14:1 that she was a Philistine, although the large reward she accepted (5,500 pieces of silver) implies that her motivations were other than Philistine loyalty. Her unhindered contact with men probably indicates that she was a prostitute.

On her fourth attempt Delilah finally tricked Samson into revealing his secret. His strength was from God; his long hair, which signified that he was under a Nazirite vow (see Nm 6:1-8) and thus "set apart" by God for special service (Jgs 13:5), was never to be cut. Delilah lulled him to sleep, shaved his head, and delivered him (still unsuspecting) into the hands of his enemies.

See also Samson.

DEMAS

One of Paul's associates who was with him during one of his imprisonments. Little is known about Demas beyond the brief information given in the NT. Initially he supported Paul's ministry and was mentioned in the salutations of Paul's letters to the Colossians (Col 4:14) and to Philemon (Phlm 1:24). However, in 2 Timothy 4:10 Paul writes that Demas deserted him because of his love for the present world.

DEMETRIUS

Name ("Son of Demeter") of five persons in biblical times: three Syrian kings and two NT figures.

1. Successor to Antiochus V Eupator. Demetrius I was king (160–151 BC) when the Jewish uprising led by Judas Maccabeus was under way. He attempted several unsuccessful campaigns against the Jews (1 Macc 7:1-10; 2 Macc 14:1-15, 26-28). Toward the end of his reign Demetrius was challenged by Alexander Epiphanes and was killed in battle (1 Macc 10:46-50).

2. Son of Demetrius I. After his father's defeat and death, Demetrius II sought refuge in Crete, then challenged Alexander Epiphanes by invading Syria with an army of foreign mercenaries. Demetrius eventually concluded a treaty with the Jews and gained the Syrian throne in 145 BC (1 Macc 11:32-37). The Jews also helped Demetrius against another rival, Trypho, until he broke his word to them (vv 54-55). In the subsequent contest between Demetrius and Trypho, the Jews, under Jonathan's brother Simon Maccabeus, achieved independence (13:34-42). Demetrius was captured by Arsaces VI (Mithridates I), king of Parthia, around 138 BC (1 Macc 14:1-3). He returned to the Syrian throne 10 years later and reigned briefly until his assassination (125 BC).

3. Grandson of Demetrius II. Demetrius III ruled Syria (95–88 BC) in the turbulent years

of the Seleucid era. One ruling party in Israel, the Pharisees, unsuccessfully enlisted his aid in their contest with the priest-king Alexander Janneus.

4. Pagan silversmith in the city of Ephesus. He provoked a riot against Christian evangelists whose preaching had detrimental effects on his trade (Acts 19:23-41). The city of Ephesus was a center of the worship of Diana (Latin counterpart of the Greek goddess Artemis), the goddess of hunting. A huge temple, one of the seven wonders of the ancient world, had been erected there for her worship. Among the commercial enterprises connected with the cult of Diana was the making of religious images out of various materials, including silver.

Demetrius, speaking for the silversmiths, said that both his business and the worship of Diana were threatened by the preaching of the apostle Paul and his companions. Gathering the other silversmiths together, he denounced Paul. The meeting caused a general uproar, and a mob dragged three of Paul's companions to the amphitheater. Finally the town clerk, who was responsible to the Roman authorities for maintaining civic order, was able to quiet the mob, persuading them to take any grievances they might have to the courts.

5. Christian believer whom the apostle John commended in his third NT letter (3 Jn 1:12). Demetrius may have been the carrier of that letter.

See also John, The Apostle.

DEUEL
Eliasaph's father. Eliasaph led the tribe of Gad during the Israelites' wilderness wanderings (Nm 1:14; 7:42, 47; 10:20). In Numbers 2:14 the name is spelled Reuel in most manuscripts and Deuel in some others, due to a confusing similarity between the Hebrew letters for "d" and "r."

DIBLAIM
Father of Gomer, Hosea's wife (Hos 1:3). The name Diblaim is thought by some to be an allusion to Gomer's harlotry, since the name means "raisin cakes" and raisin cakes were used in ancient fertility-cult rites.

DIBRI
Father of Shelomith from Dan's tribe. Shelomith married an Egyptian man, and her son by this marriage was stoned in the wilderness for blaspheming the name of God (Lv 24:10-11).

DIKLAH
Son of Joktan in the list of nations descended from Noah's sons (Gn 10:27; 1 Chr 1:21); perhaps the name refers to an Arabian tribe or territory, living in or near a palm-bearing area, as the name suggests (Diklah is a variant of the Hebrew word *dikla*, which means date tree or palm tree).

DINAH

Daughter born to Jacob and Leah (Gn 30:21), whose name means "judgment." Living with her family at Shechem, a Canaanite city (33:18), Dinah went in to visit some neighboring pagan women (34:1). Shechem, the Hivite prince of the area, saw her and, while Dinah's brothers were away in the fields tending their herds, he raped her. Shechem then requested Dinah from Jacob as a wife.

Jacob's sons, enraged at the dishonor done to their sister, plotted revenge. They agreed to the marriage on the terms that all the Hivite males be circumcised. Hamor, Shechem's father, consented. While the Canaanite men were still incapacitated from their surgery, Dinah's brothers Levi and Simeon led a massacre in the city and killed every male. Dinah was retrieved and the city plundered. The brothers excused their action as a just retribution for one of the Canaanites having treated their sister as a harlot (Gn 34:27-31). For their use of weapons of violence (49:5), Simeon and Levi were later cursed by Jacob.

DIONYSIUS

Prominent citizen of Athens; a member of the Areopagus, the Athenian supreme court, and one of Paul's few converts during his brief ministry at Athens (Acts 17:34).

DIOTREPHES

A church member whom John reprimanded for his contentious behavior (3 Jn 1:9-10). He spoke against John; had resisted John's authority by refusing to receive an earlier letter; and refused to show Christian hospitality, urging others to do likewise. He may have been an official in the church who abused his position, since he liked to put himself first.

DISHAN

Chieftain in the land of Seir, a mountainous area southwest of the Dead Sea. Dishan's father was Seir the Horite (Gn 36:21; 1 Chr 1:38). The Horites were driven out of their territory by the Edomites (Dt 2:12). Later OT references often use Seir and Edom synonymously.

DISHON

1. Seir's fifth son and a Horite leader in Edom (Gn 36:21; 1 Chr 1:38), whose people were eventually displaced by the Edomites.

2. Grandson of Seir and son of Anah, a Horite leader. This Dishon was also the brother of Oholibamah, Esau's wife (Gn 36:25; 1 Chr 1:41).

DI-ZAHAB

Name, listed along with Paran, Tophel, Laban, and Hazeroth, meant to designate the locale of Moses' final address to Israel (Dt 1:1).

DODAI

Ahohi's descendant and a commander of one of Israel's 12 contingents of soldiers (24,000 men each) during David's reign (1 Chr 27:4). Dodai is perhaps alternately called Dodo, Eleazar's father, in 2 Samuel 23:9 and 1 Chronicles 11:12. *See* Dodo #2.

DODAVAHU

Inhabitant of Mareshah and father of Eliezer the prophet. Eliezer spoke against King Jehoshaphat of Judah because of his alliance with King Ahaziah of Israel (2 Chr 20:37, KJV "Dodavah").

DODO

1. Grandfather of Tola, a minor judge who judged Israel from his native city, Shamir (Jgs 10:1).

2. Father of Eleazar, one of David's mighty men known as "the thirty" (2 Sm 23:9; 1 Chr 11:12). Dodo is perhaps identifiable with Dodai the Ahohite in 1 Chronicles 27:4. *See* Dodai.

3. Father of Elhanan, one of David's mighty men known as "the thirty" (2 Sm 23:24; 1 Chr 11:26). Dodo lived at Bethlehem.

DOEG

Official of Saul who was commanded to kill the innocent priests at Nob (1 Sm 21–22). An Edomite, he was either a proselyte or a prominent Edomite chieftain captured by Saul (14:47). He was subsequently given supervision over Saul's flocks (21:7; cf. 1 Chr 27:30, where David had a foreign head over his herd). The reason for his presence at the sanctuary at Nob (1 Sm 21:7) is not clear, though he had some religious purpose in being there, maybe being detained while in a purification process (e.g., a Nazirite vow, Nm 6:13). Possibly he secretly hid there as a spy for Saul. Whatever the case, it is evident that he saw an opportunity to gain favor with Saul when he observed David hospitably treated by the priests, who even supplied him with a weapon—the sword of Goliath (1 Sm 21:9). Shortly thereafter, he had occasion to report this to Saul (22:9-10; Ps 52 title), hoping thereby to demonstrate his loyalty. His brutal killing of the priests and the inhabitants of the city of Nob (1 Sm 22:18-19) shows his ruthless character and intimates further that he was not an Israelite.

DORCAS

Christian woman in Joppa of Judea, noted for her acts of charity (Acts 9:36-41). Dorcas is called a disciple in Acts 9:36, which is the only instance where the feminine form of the word is used in the Greek NT. Her ethnic origins are not known, since Dorcas, her Greek name, was in common use among both Jews and Greeks. The Aramaic equivalent, Tabitha, meant "gazelle."

When Dorcas died, the apostle Peter was nearby at Lydda. In response to news of his healing ministry there, two men were sent to bring Peter to Joppa. When he arrived, the body had been prepared for burial and placed in an upper room. Peter sent the mourners from the room, knelt to pray, and raised Dorcas back to life. Her restoration was the first of such miracles performed by an apostle.

DRUSILLA

Third and youngest daughter of Herod Agrippa, king of Judea. A Jewess, Drusilla was born about AD 38 and had two sisters, Bernice and Mariamne. She became engaged to Epiphanes, prince of Commogene, but the engagement was broken as a result of his refusal to convert to Judaism.

Drusilla's brother Agrippa II, then arranged for her to marry Azizus, king of Emesa, who agreed to be circumcised. Soon after her marriage, Felix, a gentile governor of Judea, fell in love with the 16-year-old Drusilla. Around AD 54 he persuaded her to break the Jewish law and leave her husband to marry him.

Drusilla and Felix heard the apostle Paul's proclamation of the gospel, while Paul was held in custody at Caesarea (Acts 24:24). Their son, Agrippa, perished when the Italian volcano Vesuvius erupted in AD 79.

DUMAH

Ishmael's son, who founded an Arab tribe (Gn 25:14; 1 Chr 1:30).

E,F

EBAL

1. Shobal's son and descendant of Seir the Horite (Gn 36:23; 1 Chr 1:40).
2. Joktan's son and descendant of Shem (1 Chr 1:22). He is called Obal in Genesis 10:28.

EBED

1. Gaal's father (Jgs 9:26-35). Gaal led the men of Shechem in an unsuccessful revolt against Abimelech, judge of Israel.
2. Adin's descendant and son of Jonathan. Ebed was the head of a family that returned to Judah with Ezra after the Exile (Ezr 8:6).

EBED-MELECH

Ethiopian eunuch in King Zedekiah's court. He secured the king's permission to rescue the prophet Jeremiah out of a cistern where he had been thrown to die (Jer 38:6-13). For this righteous act, Ebed-melech was promised God's safety at the fall of Jerusalem (39:16).

EBENEZER

1. Site where the Israelite army encamped before a battle with the Philistines (1 Sm 4:1-11). It is thought to have been near Aphek, where the Philistines were encamped. The Israelite army was badly defeated in the battle, and 4,000 of its men were slain on the field. The elders of Israel tried to change their fortunes by bringing the Ark of the Covenant into their camp, but Israel was again defeated with a loss of 30,000 foot soldiers, and the Ark of God was captured (1 Sm 4:3-11; 5:1).
2. Site near Mizpah, where God gave Israel a great victory over the Philistines. To commemorate the victory Samuel set up a stone between Mizpah and Jeshanah and called its name Ebenezer, meaning "the stone of help," for the Lord had helped them get the victory (1 Sm 7:12).

EBER

1. Abraham's ancestor (Gn 10:21-25; 11:14-17; 1 Chr 1:18-25; Lk 3:35) from whom the word "Hebrew" may be derived. Eber lived 464 years and was the ancestor of the "sons of Eber," a phrase possibly equal to the "Hebrews," as "sons of Heth" equals the "Hittites" (Gn 23:10, NASB). However, the term "Hebrew" may be an indication of social class rather than of descent from Eber. Eber had a son in whose time the earth was divided, a division possibly into nomadic and sedentary groups.
2. Gadite leader registered during the reigns of Jothan, king of Judah (950–932 BC), and Jeroboam II, king of Israel (993–953 BC; 1 Chr 5:13, KJV "Heber").
3. Benjaminite and Elpaal's descendant (1 Chr 8:12).
4. Benjaminite and Shashak's descendant (1 Chr 8:22).
5. Head of Amok's priestly family during the days of the high priest Joiakim (Neh 12:20).

EDER

1. Member of Benjamin's tribe and the son of Beriah, a leader in the town of Aijalon (1 Chr 8:15).

2. Levite of Merari's clan and the son of Mushi (1 Chr 23:23; 24:30).

EGLAH

One of King David's wives and mother of Ithream (2 Sm 3:5; 1 Chr 3:3). Born while David was still in Hebron, Ithream was the sixth son.

EGLON

Moabite king who captured Jericho and held it for 18 years, exacting a tribute from Israel. Ehud, an Israelite judge pretending to bring tribute, killed Eglon (Jgs 3:12-30). *See* Moab.

EHI

Benjamin's son (Gn 46:21); perhaps a scribal error for Ahiram. *See* Ahiram.

EHUD

1. Judge of Israel from Benjamin's tribe who delivered Israel from Eglon, king of the Moabites (Jgs 3:12-30). He was notable because he was left-handed (Hebrew "hindered in the right hand"). Before taking Israelite tribute to Eglon, he made an iron dagger, with which he assassinated the unsuspecting Eglon during a private audience. He then rallied the Israelites west of the Jordan to encircle the Moabite troops before they could return south to Moab. When the 18-year rule of Eglon over the Israelites ended, an 80-year period of peace began.

2. Bilhan's son, a member of Benjamin's tribe (1 Chr 7:10; 8:6).

EKER

Jerahmeelite and the son of Ram from Judah's tribe (1 Chr 2:27).

ELA

Father of Shimei, one of the 12 officers appointed to requisition food for King Solomon's household (1 Kgs 4:18).

ELAH

1. Esau's descendant and a chief of Edom (Gn 36:41; 1 Chr 1:52).

2. KJV rendering of Ela, Shimei's father, in 1 Kings 4:18. *See* Ela.

3. Baasha's son and fourth king of Israel. Elah reigned for only two years (886–885 BC). While in a drunken stupor, he was murdered by one of his generals (1 Kgs 16:8-14).

4. Father of Hoshea, the last king of the northern kingdom of Israel (2 Kgs 15:30; 17:1; 18:1, 9).

5. Caleb's second son and father of Kenaz (1 Chr 4:15).

6. Uzzi's son, descendant of Benjamin (1 Chr 9:8). Elah was among the first to resettle in Jerusalem after the Babylonian exile. He is not mentioned in the parallel list of Nehemiah 11.

ELAM

1. Firstborn son of Shem and a grandson of Noah (Gn 10:22; 1 Chr 1:17).

2. Benjaminite and the son of Shashak (1 Chr 8:24).

3. Korahite Levite and the fifth son of Kore from the house of Asaph (1 Chr 26:3).

4. Forefather of 1,254 descendants who returned with Zerubbabel to Judah following the Exile (Ezr 2:7; Neh 7:12). Later, 71 members of Elam's house accompanied Ezra back to Palestine during the reign of King Artaxerxes I of Persia (464–424 BC; Ezr 8:7). In postexilic Judah, Shecaniah, Elam's descendant, urged Ezra to command the sons of Israel to divorce their foreign wives (10:2); a number from Elam's house eventually did so (v 26).

5. Another forefather of 1,254 descendants who returned with Zerubbabel to Judah (Ezr 2:31; Neh 7:34).

6. One of the chiefs of Israel who set his seal on Ezra's covenant (Neh 10:14).

7. One of the priestly musicians who performed at the dedication of the Jerusalem wall (Neh 12:42).

ELASAH

1. Priest of Pashhur's clan who obeyed Ezra's exhortation to divorce his pagan wife after the Exile (Ezr 10:22).

2. Shaphan's son and King Zedekiah's envoy to King Nebuchadnezzar of Babylon. On his trip to Babylon, Elasah also carried a letter of encouragement from the prophet Jeremiah to the Jewish exiles there (Jer 29:3).

ELDAAH

Midian's fifth son and a descendant of Abraham and his wife Keturah (Gn 25:4; 1 Chr 1:33).

ELDAD

One of the 70 elders of Israel who were commissioned to assist Moses in governing the people (Nm 11:26-27). Though Eldad and another elder, Medad, were not among the 68 elders who had gathered around the Tabernacle at Moses' command, they too received the Spirit and prophesied. When Joshua, out of concern for Moses' authority, asked Moses to stop them, Moses showed great humility and sensitivity to God's will by answering, "I wish that all the LORD's people were prophets" (Nm 11:29, NIV).

ELEAD
Ephraim's descendant who was killed in a raid against the Philistine city of Gath (1 Chr 7:21).

ELEADAH
Ephraim's descendant (1 Chr 7:20, KJV "Eladah").

ELEASAH
1. Helez's son and member of Judah's tribe (1 Chr 2:39-40).
2. Raphah's son and descendant of King Saul (1 Chr 8:37; 9:43).

ELEAZAR
1. Third of Aaron's four sons (Ex 6:23). Eleazar ("God has helped") was consecrated as a priest with his brothers and Aaron in the Sinai (Ex 28:1; Lv 8:2, 13). When his brothers Nadab and Abihu were killed by God as they offered "unholy fire" to the Lord (Lv 10:1-7), Eleazar and Ithamar took leading positions as Aaron's sons (Nm 3:1-4).

Eleazar is described as "chief of the leaders of the Levites" (Nm 3:32). Under his supervision were the sanctuary and its vessels (4:16; 16:37-39; 19:3-4). Eleazar was installed as high priest by Moses when Aaron died on Mt Hor (Nm 20:25-28; Dt 10:6). He was then considered Moses' assistant (Nm 26:1-3, 63; 27:2, 21). Joshua was commissioned by Moses in the presence of Eleazar (27:18-23). In the conquest of Canaan, Joshua and Eleazar served together as leaders. It was Eleazar's function as Joshua's counselor to inquire of the Lord (v 21). He also had his share in the census taking at Shittim. He took part in the partitioning of Canaan, the east bank (34:17), and the west bank (Jos 14:1; 17:4; 19:51; 21:1).

When Eleazar died, he was highly regarded and memorialized in the land of Ephraim (Jos 24:33); his son Phinehas followed him as high priest.

In the oversight of the priests, 16 divisions were assigned to Eleazar's descendants and eight to Ithamar's (1 Chr 24). The ancestry of the prominent priests Zadok and Ezra is traced to Eleazar (1 Chr 6:3-15, 50-53; 24:3; Ezr 7:1-5). In King Solomon's time the priests of Zadok replaced Abiathar, a descendant of Ithamar (1 Kgs 2:26-27, 35). The descendants of Eleazar would be the only ones permitted to minister in Ezekiel's ideal Temple (Ez 44:15). *See also* Aaron.

2. Abinadab's son, charged with caring for the Ark by the people of Kiriath-jearim, when it was brought from Beth-shemesh and placed in the "house of Abinadab on the hill" (1 Sm 7:1).

3. Dodo's son, one of the three mighty men whose exploits against the Philistines gained him great fame (2 Sm 23:9; 1 Chr 11:12).

4. Merarite Levite, son of Mahli. Eleazar died without sons, so his daughters were married to their first cousins (1 Chr 23:21-22; 24:28).

5. Priest descended from Phinehas. This Eleazar helped inventory the Temple treasure on returning from the Exile with Ezra (Ezr 8:33).

6. Parosh's son, listed with others who divorced their foreign wives in the reform under Ezra (Ezr 10:25).

7. Priest in attendance at the dedication of the rebuilt walls of Jerusalem following the Exile (Neh 12:42).

8. Person in the lineage of Joseph, husband of Mary (Mt 1:15).

ELHANAN

1. Hebrew soldier who distinguished himself by killing a Philistine giant. In one passage he is named as the son of Jaare-oregim of Bethlehem, and is said to have killed Goliath the Gittite (2 Sm 21:19). In another passage he is named as the son of Jair, and is said to have killed Lahmi, the brother of Goliath (1 Chr 20:5).

2. Dodo's son and warrior among King David's mighty men (2 Sm 23:24; 1 Chr 11:26).

ELI

Priest in the sanctuary of the Lord at Shiloh in the period of the judges (1 Sm 1:3, 9). Shiloh, about 10 miles (16 kilometers) north of Jerusalem, was the central shrine of the Israelite tribal confederation. Eli had two sons who were priests, Hophni and Phinehas (which are Egyptian names). No lineage is recorded for Eli, but there are two possible suggestions: he is a descendant of Ithamar, Aaron's younger son (1 Sm 22:20; 1 Kgs 2:27; 1 Chr 24:3); or he comes from the house of Eleazar (Ex 6:23-25; 2 Esd 1:2-3). In 1 Samuel 1, Eli blessed the childless Hannah, Elkanah's wife, after learning of her prayer for a son. Subsequently, Samuel was born, and when he was weaned, he was brought by his mother to Eli for service and training in the sanctuary, according to her promise to the Lord.

Hophni and Phinehas were corrupting the Israelites despite Eli's protests, and for this sin God promised judgment upon Eli's family (1 Sm 2:27, 36). The sons of Eli were to die on the same day (v 34), and the fulfillment came in a battle with the Philistines at Aphek (4:11, 17). Eli, too, died when he heard of the defeat and the loss of the Ark of the Covenant to the Philistines. At his death he was 98 years old, and besides being priest, he also had judged Israel for 40 years (vv 15-18). Eli's daughter-in-law, Phinehas's wife, died in childbirth, brokenhearted over the loss of her husband and the Ark. She named her son Ichabod because she felt that there was no more hope (vv 19-22).

Eli was not characterized by a firm personality. He was no doubt sincere and devout, but he was also weak and indulgent.

ELIAB

1. Helon's son and leader of Zebulun's tribe when the Israelites were roaming in the Sinai wilderness after their escape from Egypt (Nm 1:9; 2:7; 10:16).

As leader, he presented his tribe's offering at the consecration of the Tabernacle (7:24, 29).

2. Member of Reuben's tribe and son of Pallu. Eliab was the father of Nemuel, Dathan, and Abiram. Dathan and Abiram rebelled against Moses and Aaron in the wilderness (Nm 16:1, 12; 26:8-9; Dt 11:6).

3. Jesse's eldest son and brother of King David. An impressive person physically, he was rejected by God for the kingship in favor of David (1 Sm 16:6; 1 Chr 2:13). Eliab served King Saul when Goliath defied Saul's army (1 Sm 17:13, 28). He was appointed leader of Judah's tribe during David's reign (1 Chr 27:18). His granddaughter Mahalath married King Rehoboam of Judah (2 Chr 11:18).

4. Variant name for Elihu in 1 Chronicles 6:27. See Elihu #1.

5. Warrior from Gad's tribe who joined David at Ziklag in his struggle against King Saul (1 Chr 12:9). Eliab was an expert with the shield and spear (v 8).

6. Levite musician assigned to play the harp in the procession when King David brought the Ark to Jerusalem (1 Chr 15:18). He was assigned permanently to service in the Tabernacle (16:5).

ELIADA

1. One of King David's sons, born in Jerusalem (2 Sm 5:16; 1 Chr 3:8). He is also called Beeliada in 1 Chronicles 14:7.

2. Father of Rezon, the king of Damascus and an adversary of Solomon (1 Kgs 11:23).

3. General under King Jehoshaphat. Eliada and the 200,000 warriors he commanded were from Benjamin's tribe (2 Chr 17:17).

ELIAHBA

Warrior among David's mighty men who were known as "the thirty" (2 Sm 23:32; 1 Chr 11:33).

ELIAKIM

1. Hilkiah's son and a royal officer in the household and court of King Hezekiah (2 Kgs 18:18, 26, 37). His position had increased in importance since Solomon's reign (1 Kgs 4:2-6) until he was second only to the king. As such, Eliakim had absolute authority as the king's representative.

When Sennacherib of Assyria moved against Jerusalem in 701 BC, Eliakim was one of the diplomatic emissaries who conferred with the Assyrian officers on behalf of Hezekiah (2 Kgs 18:18, 26). He was also sent by Hezekiah in sackcloth to Isaiah to ask for prayer on Jerusalem's behalf (2 Kgs 19:1-5).

2. King Josiah's second son. When Eliakim was made king of Judah by Pharaoh Neco, his name was changed to Jehoiakim (2 Kgs 23:34; 2 Chr 36:4). See Jehoiakim.

3. One of the priests who assisted at the dedication of the Jerusalem wall after it was rebuilt by Zerubbabel (Neh 12:41).

4. Abiud's son in Matthew's genealogy of Jesus (Mt 1:13).

5. Melea's son in Luke's genealogy of Jesus (Lk 3:30).

ELIAM

1. Alternate name for Ammiel, Bathsheba's father, in 2 Samuel 11:3. *See* Ammiel #3.

2. Alternate name for Ahijah the Pelonite in 2 Samuel 23:34. *See* Ahijah #7.

ELIASAPH

1. Leader of Gad's tribe appointed by Moses. He was the son of Deuel (Reuel) (Nm 1:14; 2:14; 7:42, 47; 10:20).

2. Gershonite Levite and the son of Lael. His responsibility in the tribe was to take charge of the Tabernacle coverings, the curtains of the court and of the main altar (Nm 3:24-25).

ELIASHIB

1. Elioenai's son and a descendant of Zerubbabel in the royal lineage of David (1 Chr 3:24).

2. Aaron's descendant chosen by David to head the 11th of the 24 courses of priests taking turns in the sanctuary services (1 Chr 24:12).

3. High priest in the second succession from Jeshua (Neh 12:10). Eliashib assigned a chamber of the Temple to Tobiah the Ammonite, a relative by marriage. When Nehemiah returned from exile, he had Tobiah removed from his Temple lodging (Ezr 10:6; Neh 3:1, 20; 13:4, 7-8, 28).

4. Levite and Temple singer. He pledged to put away his foreign wife at Ezra's command (Ezr 10:24).

5, 6. Two men, a son of Zattu and a son of Bani, similarly persuaded by Ezra to put away their foreign wives (Ezr 10:27, 36).

ELIATHAH

Son of Heman appointed to assist in the Temple service during David's reign (1 Chr 25:4, 27).

ELIDAD

Benjaminite, of the sons of Kislon, appointed to work under Eleazar and Joshua in allotting Canaanite territory west of the Jordan to the 10 tribes (Nm 34:21).

ELIEHOENAI

1. Korahite Levite who, with his six brothers and his father, Meshelemiah, served as a Temple doorkeeper during David's reign (1 Chr 26:3).

2. Zerahiah's son, who came to Jerusalem with Ezra, bringing his family and others from Babylon (Ezr 8:4).

ELIEL

1. Warrior and head of a family of the half-tribe of Manasseh that lived east of the Jordan River (1 Chr 5:24).

2. Tola's son, a Kohathite who was one of the Levitical singers in the time of David (1 Chr 6:34); possibly the same as Eliab (1 Chr 6:27).

3. Shimei's son and a chief of Benjamin's tribe (1 Chr 8:20).

4. Shashak's son and a chief of Benjamin's tribe (1 Chr 8:22).

5. Warrior among David's mighty men (1 Chr 11:46), called a Mahavite.

6. Another warrior among David's mighty men (1 Chr 11:47).

7. Warrior from the Gadites who joined David at Ziklag in his struggle against King Saul. Eliel was one of those experts with a shield and spear. Whether the Eliel of 1 Chronicles 12:11 should be equated with either of the two Eliels of 1 Chronicles 11:46-47 is impossible to say.

8. Levite and chief of the family of Hebron, who was involved in bringing the Ark to Jerusalem in David's time (1 Chr 15:9).

9. Priest who assisted in bringing the Ark to Jerusalem (1 Chr 15:11); possibly the same as #8 above.

10. Levite who assisted Conaniah in the administration of the tithes, contributions, and dedicated things given to the Temple during Hezekiah's reign (2 Chr 31:13).

ELIENAI

Benjaminite and the son of Shimei (1 Chr 8:20). His name may be a contraction of Eliehoenai (see 1 Chr 26:3).

ELIEZER

1. Native of Damascus and Abraham's servant, who according to custom was the adopted heir before Ishmael and Isaac were born (Gn 15:2).

2. Moses and Zipporah's second son (Ex 18:4; 1 Chr 23:15-17).

3. Benjaminite and Becher's son (1 Chr 7:8).

4. One of the seven priests who blew a trumpet before the Ark of the Covenant when David moved it to Jerusalem (1 Chr 15:24).

5. Zichri's son and a chief officer in Reuben's tribe (1 Chr 27:16).

6. Son of Dodavahu of Mareshah, who prophesied against King Jehoshaphat of Judah because of his alliance with Ahaziah, king of Israel (2 Chr 20:37).

7. One of the leaders sent by Ezra to Iddo at Casiphia to request Levites for the house of God (Ezr 8:16).

8, 9, 10. Three men of Israel—a priest, Levite, and Israelite—who were encouraged by Ezra to divorce their foreign wives during the postexilic era (Ezr 10:18, 23, 31).

11. Ancestor of Christ (Lk 3:29).

ELIHOREPH

Prominent official in the time of Solomon (1 Kgs 4:3) who, with his brother Ahijah, was a royal secretary. Attempts to regard Elihoreph as the title of an official and not a personal name find no support in the Hebrew text.

ELIHU

1. Ephraimite, Tohu's son and an ancestor of Samuel the prophet (1 Sm 1:1); perhaps also called Eliab and Eliel in 1 Chronicles 6:27, 34, respectively.

2. One of the soldiers of Manasseh's tribe who joined up with David's army at Ziklag (1 Chr 12:20).

3. Korahite Levite and a gatekeeper of the Tabernacle during David's reign (1 Chr 26:7).

4. Alternate name for Eliab, David's eldest brother, in 1 Chronicles 27:18. See Eliab #3.

5. One of Job's friends, a Buzite, the son of Barachel (Jb 32:2). He spoke about suffering as a form of discipline after three of Job's friends failed to answer Job's arguments (chs 32–37).

ELIJAH

1. Ninth-century BC prophet of Israel. Elijah's name means "my God is the Lord"—appropriate for a stalwart opponent of Baal worship. The Scriptures give no information regarding his family background except that he was a Tishbite who probably came from the land of Gilead on the east bank of the Jordan River. He lived primarily during the reigns of kings Ahab (874–853 BC) and Ahaziah (853–852 BC) of Israel. The biblical account of Elijah runs from 1 Kings 17 to 2 Kings 2.

Elijah was called by God at a critical period in Israel's life. Economically and politically the northern kingdom was in its strongest position since its separation from the southern kingdom. Omri (885–874 BC) had initiated a policy of trade and friendly relations with the Phoenicians. To show his good faith, Omri gave his son Ahab in marriage to Jezebel, the daughter of Ethbaal, king of Tyre. She brought Baal worship with her to Israel, a false religion whose rapid spread soon threatened the kingdom's very existence. Elijah was sent to turn the nation and its leaders back to the Lord through his prophetic message and miracles.

Warning of Drought Elijah began his recorded ministry by telling Ahab that the nation would suffer a drought until the prophet himself announced its end

QUICKTAKE

ELIJAH

STRENGTHS AND ACCOMPLISHMENTS
• Was the most famous and dramatic of Israel's prophets
• Predicted the beginning and end of a three-year drought
• Was used by God to restore a dead child to his mother
• Represented God in a showdown with priests of Baal and Asherah
• Appeared with Moses and Jesus in the New Testament Transfiguration scene

WEAKNESSES AND MISTAKES
• Chose to work alone and paid for it with isolation and loneliness
• Fled in fear from Jezebel when she threatened his life

LESSONS FROM HIS LIFE
• We are never closer to defeat than in our moments of greatest victory
• We are never as alone as we may feel; God is always there
• God speaks more frequently in persistent whispers than in shouts

VITAL STATISTICS
Where: Gilead
Occupation: Prophet
Contemporaries: Ahab, Jezebel, Ahaziah, Obadiah, Jehu, Hazael

KEY VERSES
"At the usual time for offering the evening sacrifice, Elijah the prophet walked up to the altar and prayed, 'O LORD, God of Abraham, Isaac, and Jacob, prove today that you are God in Israel and that I am your servant. Prove that I have done all this at your command. O LORD, answer me! Answer me so these people will know that you, O LORD, are God and that you have brought them back to yourself.'"
"Immediately the fire of the LORD flashed down from heaven and burned up the young bull, the wood, the stones, and the dust. It even licked up all the water in the trench!" (1 Kings 18:36–38).

Elijah's story is told in 1 Kings 17:1—2 Kings 2:11. He is also mentioned in 2 Chronicles 21:12-15; Malachi 4:5, 6; Matthew 11:14; 16:14; 17:3-13; 27:47-49; Luke 1:17; 4:25, 26; John 1:19-25; Romans 11:2-4; James 5:17, 18.

(1 Kgs 17:1). He thus repeated Moses' warning (Lv 26:14-39; Dt 28:15-68) of the consequences of turning away from God.

Elijah then hid himself in a ravine on the east bank of the Jordan River by the brook Cherith (possibly the valley of the Yarmuk River in north Gilead). There he had sufficient water for his needs, and ravens brought him food twice daily. When the brook dried up, Elijah was directed to move to the Phoenician village of Zarephath near Sidon. A widow took care of him from her scanty supplies, and her obedience to Elijah was rewarded by a miraculous supply of meal and oil that was not depleted until the drought ended.

While Elijah was staying with the widow, her son became ill and died. By the power of prayer, the child was restored to life and good health.

In the drought's third year the Lord told Elijah to inform Ahab that God would soon provide rain for Israel. On his return, Elijah first encountered Ahab's officer, Obadiah, who was searching for water for the king's livestock. Elijah sent Obadiah to arrange a meeting with Ahab. At first Obadiah refused. For three years Ahab had searched Israel and the neighboring kingdoms in vain for the prophet, no doubt in order to force him to end the drought. Obadiah was certain that while he went to bring Ahab, Israel's most wanted "outlaw" would elude them again, thus enraging the king. When Elijah promised him that he would stay until he returned, the officer arranged for Ahab to meet the prophet.

In the subsequent meeting Elijah rejected the king's allegation that he was the "troubler of Israel" (1 Kgs 18:17-18). He was only obeying God, he insisted, in pointing out Ahab's idolatry. Ahab had even permitted Jezebel to subsidize a school of Baal and Asherah prophets. Elijah then requested a public gathering on Mt Carmel as a contest between the prophets of Baal and the prophets of the Lord to determine who was the true God.

Confrontation on Carmel One of the highlights of Elijah's ministry was the contest on Mt Carmel. Ahab assembled all Israel along with 850 prophets of Baal and Asherah. The famous challenge was issued: "How long are you going to waver between two opinions? If the LORD is God, follow him! But if Baal is God, then follow him!" (1 Kgs 18:21, NLT). Sacrificial animals were to be placed on two altars, one for Baal and one for the Lord, and the prophets representing each were to ask for fire from their God.

All day long the pagan prophets called in vain on Baal. They danced a whirling, frenzied dance, cutting themselves with knives until their blood gushed. But there was no answer. Finally, Elijah's turn came. He repaired the demolished altar of the Lord and prepared the sacrifice. For dramatic effect, he built a trench around the altar and poured water over the sacrifice until the trench overflowed. Then he said a brief prayer, and immediately fire fell from heaven and consumed the burnt offering, the wood, the stones, and the dust, and licked up the water that was in the trench (1 Kgs 18:38).

When the people saw it, they fell on their faces in repentance, chanting, "The LORD is God! The LORD is God!" (1 Kgs 18:39). At Elijah's command the people seized the prophets of Baal and killed them by the brook Kishon. Then Elijah, at the top of Carmel, began to pray fervently for rain. Dramatically, the sky became black with clouds and rain began to pour, ending the long drought. Ahab rode back in his chariot to Jezreel, 20 miles (32.2 kilometers) to the east. God's Spirit enabled Elijah to outrun Ahab, and he arrived in Jezreel first.

Jezebel, furious over the massacre of the Baal prophets, sent a message to Elijah: "May the gods strike me and even kill me if by this time tomorrow I have not killed you just as you killed them" (1 Kgs 19:2, NLT). When Elijah received her message, he panicked and fled to Beersheba.

Experience at Horeb Elijah left his servant in Beersheba, going another day's journey into the desert alone. There he lay down under a broom tree and, in despair and exhaustion, asked God to take his life.

Instead, an angel appeared, nourishing him twice with bread and water. After he had slept, Elijah continued on his way.

After 40 days, Elijah arrived at Mt Horeb, where he found shelter in a cave. There the Lord spoke to him, asking what he was doing there. The prophet explained that he was the only prophet of God left in Israel, and now even his life was threatened. In response, the mighty forces of nature—a great wind, an earthquake, and fire—were displayed before Elijah to show him that the omnipotent God could intercede on his behalf with a powerful hand. Finally God encouraged Elijah in a "still, small voice." The Lord had further tasks for him to accomplish. God also told Elijah that he was not the only faithful person in Israel; 7,000 others remained true to the Lord.

Elijah Flees from Jezebel: After killing Baal's prophets, Elijah fled from Jezebel to Beersheba, then to the wilderness, and then to Mt Horeb (Sinai).

Since Elijah had faithfully delivered God's message to Ahab, the Lord commissioned him to deliver another message, one of judgment on Israel's continuing failure to listen to God. The instruments of retribution were to be Hazael, who would become king in Syria (c. 893–796 BC), and Jehu, who would become king of Israel (841–814 BC). Elijah was instructed to anoint both of them. He was also told to anoint his successor, Elisha, to be his understudy until it was time for Elisha's full ministry to begin.

Confrontation concerning Naboth After his return to Israel, one of Elijah's boldest confrontations with King Ahab was over Naboth's vineyard. Although Ahab wanted Naboth's property, he was sensitive to the law regarding ownership of land. Further, Ahab never completely abandoned the faith of his fathers (1 Kgs 21:27-29). Jezebel, however, had no regard for the Mosaic law and conspired to have Naboth put to death on a false charge.

When Ahab then took possession of the vineyard, Elijah branded him as a murderer and a robber. He predicted divine judgment—the fall of Ahab's dynasty and Jezebel's horrible death (1 Kgs 21:17-24). Ahab repented, however, and the judgment was postponed.

Ahaziah's Folly The Lord's judgment on Ahab was finally executed when the king was killed in a battle with Syria in 853 BC. The dogs licked up Ahab's blood, as the prophet had predicted (1 Kgs 21:19). Shortly after Ahaziah had succeeded his father as king, he suffered a crippling fall. While lying ill, he sent messengers to ask Baal-zebub, the god of Ekron, whether he would recover. The Lord sent Elijah to intercept them and give them a message for the king: a rebuke for ignoring the God of Israel and a warning of the king's impending death.

Ahaziah angrily sent a captain with 50 soldiers to arrest Elijah. They were consumed by fire from heaven at Elijah's words. A second captain and another 50 soldiers were sent but met the same fate. The third captain who came begged the prophet to spare his and his soldiers' lives. Elijah went with this captain and delivered God's message to the king personally. The king would not recover but would die because he had inquired from pagan gods rather than from the true God.

Warning to Jehoram Elijah had been called primarily to minister to Israel, but he also delivered God's word of warning to Jehoram, king of Judah, rebuking him for following Israel in its idolatry and for not walking in the godly ways of his father and grandfather (2 Chr 21:12-15).

Elijah's Ascent into Heaven When the end of Elijah's ministry drew near, Elisha refused to leave him. After a journey that took them to schools of the prophets at Bethel and Jericho, the two crossed the Jordan River miraculously; Elijah struck the waters with his mantle and they parted. Elisha requested a double portion (the firstborn's share, cf. Dt 21:17) of his master's spirit, for he desired to be Elijah's full successor. Elisha knew his request was granted because he saw Elijah pass into the heavens in a whirlwind bearing a chariot and horses of fire. The young prophets who had accompanied Elisha searched in vain for Elijah in the mountains and valleys around the Jordan; God had taken his faithful prophet home. Elijah thus joined Enoch as the only other man in the Bible who did not experience death.

Elijah's Message and Miracles As the Baal worship of Tyre made inroads into Israel through Jezebel, Elijah was sent to check its spread by emphasizing again that Israel's God was the only God of the whole earth. He began a vital work that was continued by Jehu, who slaughtered many of the Baal worshipers among Israel's leaders (2 Kgs 10:18-28). Elijah's specific mission was to destroy heathen worship in order to spare Israel, thus preparing the way for the prophets who were to follow in his spirit.

Miracles were prominent in Elijah's ministry, given as a sign to confirm him as God's spokesman and to turn Israel's kings back to God. Some scholars have rejected these miracles or tried to explain them away. The OT, however, clearly testifies to their validity, and the NT affirms them.

Elijah and the New Testament Malachi named Elijah as the forerunner of the "great and terrible day of the LORD" who will "turn the hearts of fathers to their children and the hearts of children to their fathers" (Mal 4:5-6). Jewish writers have often taken up the same theme in their literature: Elijah will "restore the tribes of Jacob" (Ecclus 48:10); he is mentioned in the Qumran *Manual of Discipline* of the Dead Sea Scrolls; he is the central sign of the resurrection of the dead according to the Mishnah, the collection of Jewish oral law; and he is the subject of songs sung at the close of the Sabbath.

In the NT, Malachi's prophecy was interpreted in the angelic annunciation to Zechariah as pointing to John the Baptist, who was to do the work of another Elijah (Lk 1:17, KJV "Elias") and was confirmed by Jesus himself (Mt 11:14; 17:10-13).

Jesus also alluded to Elijah's sojourn in the land of Sidon (Lk 4:25-26), and the apostle Paul referred to the prophet's experience at Mt Horeb (Rom 11:2). The apostle James used Elijah to illustrate what it means to be a righteous man and a man of prayer (Jas 5:17).

Elijah appeared again on the Mt of Transfiguration with Moses as they discussed Jesus' approaching death (Mt 17:1-13; Lk 9:28-36). Some Bible scholars believe that Elijah will return as one of the two witnesses of the end times (Rv 11:3-12), in fulfillment of Malachi's prophecy that he is to come before the dreadful judgment day of God.

2. Chief of Benjamin's tribe (1 Chr 8:27, KJV "Eliah").

3. Priest who married a gentile wife (Ezr 10:21).

4. Layman who also married a foreign wife (Ezr 10:26).

ELIKA

Harodite, listed as one of David's mighty men (2 Sm 23:25). His name is not included in a similar list in 1 Chronicles 11:27.

ELIMELECH

Man from Bethlehem who took his wife, Naomi, and his sons, Mahlon and Chilion, to sojourn in Moab because of famine in Judah (Ru 1:2-3). While in Moab, he died; then his sons also died; and Naomi decided to return to Judah. One daughter-in-law, Orpah, preferred to remain in Moab; the other, Ruth, chose to accompany Naomi. Boaz, a kinsman of Elimelech, bought Elimelech's land and married Ruth (4:9-10). From this union came a great-grandson, David, and the royal line in which the Messiah would eventually be born. *See* Ruth.

ELIOENAI

1. Postexilic descendant of Solomon and the father of Hodaviah and Eliashib (1 Chr 3:23-24).
2. Simeonite chieftain (1 Chr 4:36).
3. Head of a Benjaminite family (1 Chr 7:8).
4. KJV spelling of the Levite Eliehoenai in 1 Chronicles 26:3. *See* Eliehoenai #1.
5. Man of the priestly family of Pashhur who divorced his foreign wife in Ezra's day (Ezr 10:22).
6. Zattu's son, who was encouraged by Ezra to divorce his foreign wife during the postexilic era (Ezr 10:27).
7. Postexilic priest who assisted in the dedication of the rebuilt Jerusalem wall (Neh 12:41).

ELIPHAL

Ur's son and one of David's mighty men (1 Chr 11:35); alternately called Eliphelet, son of Ahasbai, in 2 Samuel 23:34. *See* Eliphelet #2.

ELIPHAZ

1. Oldest son of Esau and his wife Adah (Gn 36:4-16; 1 Chr 1:35-36). He was the ancestor of a number of Edomite clans.
2. One of Job's friends, called the Temanite (see Jer 49:7). Teman was traditionally associated with wisdom; hence Eliphaz's speech depicts the orthodox view of sin and punishment. His three addresses (Jb 4, 15, 22) failed to grapple with the essence of Job's problem because he assumed previous major sin in Job's life. *See also* Job.

ELIPHELEHU

Levitical musician who played the lyre (harp) when the Ark was brought to Jerusalem in David's time (1 Chr 15:18, 21).

ELIPHELET

1. One of David's 13 sons born in Jerusalem (2 Sm 5:16; 1 Chr 3:8; 14:7).
2. Ahasbai's son and one of David's mighty men (2 Sm 23:34); perhaps the same as Eliphal, Ur's son, in 1 Chronicles 11:35. *See* Eliphal.
3. Another of David's sons born at Jerusalem but perhaps earlier than #1 above (1 Chr 3:6; 14:5).

4. Eshek's son and a descendant of Saul and Jonathan (1 Chr 8:39).

5. One of Adonikam's three sons who returned with Ezra from Babylon (Ezr 8:13).

6. Hashum's son whom Ezra persuaded to divorce his foreign wife during the postexilic era (Ezr 10:33).

ELISHA

Prophet in Israel during the ninth century BC.

Background and Call

Elisha is first mentioned in 1 Kings 19:16, where he is described as the son of Shaphat, who lived at Abel-meholah. That place has been tentatively identified with the modern Tel Abu Sifri, west of the river Jordan, though many scholars place it to the river's east. The prophet Elijah had been ordered by God to anoint Elisha as his successor, but the narrative does not make it clear whether Elisha was already one of Elijah's disciples. When the two met, Elisha was busy plowing a field, and he does not seem to have greeted Elijah with the respect that a disciple would normally show to his teacher.

Elisha's use of 12 yokes of oxen in his agricultural work has been taken as a sign that he was wealthy, for normally two yoked oxen would be handled by one person. When Elijah passed by and placed his cloak on Elisha's shoulder, the latter man knew it was a sign that he should inherit the great prophet's mission. The nation needed a prophet, for it was increasingly indulging in Canaanite idolatry with the encouragement of King Ahab and his Phoenician wife, Jezebel.

After Elijah commissioned him symbolically and strode away, Elisha hurried after the prophet to request a brief interval of time to announce his new vocation to his parents before leaving home. The prophet's reply, "Go back again; for what have I done to you?" (1 Kgs 19:20, RSV), helped Elisha to make up his mind immediately. Delay in implementing his vocation would almost certainly have been fatal for Elisha (cf. Mt 8:21-22; Lk 9:61-62).

To mark the change in his way of life, Elisha made a great feast for his neighbors, roasting two oxen. This is another hint that he came from a wealthy family. From that time, he was no longer a farmer; by associating with Elijah, he began to prepare for his own ministry. There is no record of Elisha being anointed to the prophetic office, but the transfer of prophetic authority by means of the cloak would leave no doubt in anyone's mind that Elisha was the next official prophet in Israel.

"Sons of the Prophets"

That there could have been some question of Elisha's authority is implied by the existence of groups of people known as "sons of the prophets." The phrase meant that those persons were heirs of the prophetic teachings and traditions, though apparently none of them was a major prophet. The prophet Amos even denied any connection with such groups, which seem to have died out in the eighth century BC (Am 7:14). In the time of Elisha, the "sons of the prophets" were located in Gilgal, Bethel, and Jericho, and seem to have exercised a primarily local ministry. They may have gone out under the instructions of Elijah and Elisha to teach people God's law and to pronounce divine revelations, as in the days of Saul (cf. 1 Sm 10:5, 10).

Just before Elijah was taken to heaven, he and Elisha visited such prophetic groups, and Elijah tried in vain to persuade Elisha to stay behind at Gilgal and at Bethel (2 Kgs 2:1-4). The prophetic group at Bethel may have been warned by God that Elijah would be taken from them, for they questioned Elisha about the matter and ascertained that he also was aware of the situation.

Successor to Elijah

After miraculously parting the waters of Jordan, Elijah asked his successor what he might do for him (2 Kgs 2:9). Elisha requested a "double share" of his spirit as they parted, the share of an inheritance normally given to a firstborn son (Dt 21:17). His request was granted when Elisha saw his master taken up to heaven in a fiery chariot, and it took immediate effect when Elisha parted the Jordan's waters and crossed over (2 Kgs 2:14).

His prophetic authority now recognized, Elisha began his ministry to Israel at approximately the end of King Ahab's reign (c. 853 BC). His work lasted for half a century, and in contrast with the harried, austere, and sometimes dramatic ministry of Elijah, the activities of Elisha were mostly quieter and took place among the ordinary people of Israel. But he also addressed the royal court, though not in conflicts with Canaanite priests, such as Elijah had experienced.

Miracles

The miraculous element was prominent in Elisha's ministry. When the people of Jericho reported that the local springwater was brackish, Elisha purified it (2 Kgs 2:19-22). To this day, it is the only significant freshwater spring in the area (Tell es-Sultan).

As the prophet left for Bethel, he encountered a group of youths who mocked his baldness (2 Kgs 2:23-24). He cursed them in the name of the Lord, and two bears came from the woods and mauled the offenders. What at first sight seems to be an immoral act on God's part was actually full of foreboding for the nation. The youths at Bethel were a generation of Israelites who had so absorbed the immoral, pagan culture of their city that they rejected both the person and the message of God's prophets. They were not merely irreligious but also unbelievably discourteous, according to ancient Near Eastern standards, in ridiculing a bald man instead of respecting his seniority.

The curses Elisha pronounced "in the name of the LORD" were not his own reactions to the treatment he had received, but instead were covenant curses (Dt 28:15-68) that would come upon all who rejected the Sinaitic laws and went back on their promises to God (see Ex 24:3-8). The two bears were also symbolic of Assyria and Babylonia, which would tear apart the nation at different times. One small incident was thus a somber forecast of what the future held for a wicked and disobedient people.

In one of his contacts with royalty Elisha gave a message (although unwillingly) from God to King Jehoram of Israel (853–841 BC). The king had allied with King Jehoshaphat of Judah (872–848 BC) and the Edomite ruler against Mesha, king of Moab. The allied forces were deep in Edomite territory when they ran out of water, and in despair they turned to Elisha, the local prophet. He refused to say anything at first, but finally predicted ample supplies of water and victory for the coalition. Both occurred on the following day (2 Kgs 3:1-27).

Miracles of Charity

The kind of work for which Elisha was justly renowned was usually performed for people who could not help themselves. Such a person was a poor widow who had almost pledged her two children to a creditor. Her only asset was a jar of oil. Elisha instructed her to borrow empty jars from her neighbors and fill them with the oil from her own jar. In a miraculous manner every jar was filled. Elisha then told her to sell the oil, pay her debts, and use the balance of the money for living expenses (2 Kgs 4:1-7).

A similar act of charity was performed for a Shunammite woman, who had persuaded her husband to provide a room where the prophet could stay when in the area. In return for her kindness Elisha predicted that the woman, previously childless, would have her own son. About a year later it happened (2 Kgs 4:8-17). The boy later contracted a severe ailment, perhaps meningitis, and died suddenly. His mother laid the body on Elisha's bed while she hurried to Mt Carmel to seek the prophet. Elisha was apparently unaware of the situation until the distraught mother informed him of the boy's death. As an emergency measure Elisha dispatched his servant Gehazi to put the prophet's staff on the child's face. That did not revive the child, but when Elisha arrived and lay down on the body, the boy was healed and returned to his parents (vv 18-37).

Another beneficial incident was the correction of a potentially disastrous situation. When some poisonous gourds were accidentally cooked and served, Elisha rendered the mixture harmless by adding meal to the contents of the cooking pot (2 Kgs 4:38-41). A miracle similar to Christ's multiplying of the bread loaves (see Mt 14:16-21; 15:32-38) occurred when someone brought the prophet several loaves of bread and fresh ears of corn. Elisha instructed his servant to set the food out for 100 people, and when that was done, the people ate and had food left (2 Kgs 4:42-44).

The healing of Naaman, a Syrian commander, came through the influence of a Hebrew maid in the man's household, who persuaded Naaman's wife that Elisha could heal her husband. The Assyrian king sent his general to the Israelite ruler with instructions for Naaman to be healed. The afflicted man was sent to Elisha, who ordered him to wash in the Jordan River. Reluctant at first, Naaman finally obeyed and was cured of his affliction. In gratitude the Syrian leader acknowledged the power of Israel's God (2 Kgs 5:1-19).

Encounters with Royalty

When Syria attacked Israel, Elisha revealed the movements of the Syrians to the Israelite king. Syrians tried to capture the prophet at Dothan, but God blinded them and Elisha led them to the Israelite capital of Samaria. Their sight returned, and Elisha advised the Israelite king to spare the captives, feed them well, and send them home. Because their evil was rewarded with good, the Syrians did not attack Israel for a while (2 Kgs 6:8-23).

When the Syrian king Ben-hadad besieged Samaria years later, famine conditions there became so severe that the king threatened to execute Elisha. In response, the prophet promised an abundance of food the following day. The Syrians fled from their camp for some unspecified reason, and the prophecy was fulfilled (2 Kgs 6:24–7:20). In an unusual encounter with the ailing king of Syria, Elisha was visited by Hazael, servant of Ben-hadad, who had been sent to ask about the prospects for his master's improvement. Elisha sent back a reassuring reply, but at the same time said that Hazael would shortly succeed Ben-hadad (8:7-13). On another occasion Elisha sent a prophet to Ramoth-gilead to anoint Jehu, son of Jehoshaphat, as king of Israel to replace Joram, whom Jehu proceeded to kill in battle (9:1-28).

Elisha's final contact with Israelite rulers came at the time of his own death, when Joash the king visited him to lament the prophet's illness. On that occasion, by the symbolic handling of arrows, the dying prophet promised Joash that he would defeat the Syrians in battle but would not exterminate them (2 Kgs 13:14-19).

The prophet also intervened a second time on behalf of the Shunammite woman whose son he had healed, instructing her to move her household into Philistine territory during a seven-year famine in Israel. When she came back, her house and property had apparently been occupied by others, so she appealed to the king for help in recovering it. Elisha's servant Gehazi told the ruler about her, and on interviewing her himself, the king ordered all her property to be returned (2 Kgs 8:1-6).

Continuing Influence

Elisha's final miracle occurred after his death, when a corpse that was tossed hurriedly into the prophet's tomb came abruptly to life (2 Kgs 13:21). Jesus mentioned Elisha once in connection with the healing of Naaman; Jesus declared that God's mercy was not restricted to the Israelites (Lk 4:27).

See also Elijah.

ELISHAH

Javan's son (Gn 10:4; 1 Chr 1:7). The Hebrew term for Greece is Javan; hence, Elishah could be the term for the western Aegean islands or coastlands (cf. Gn 10:5) that supplied dye stuffs to the inhabitants of Tyre (Ez 27:7). The Jewish historian Josephus identified Elishah with the Aeolians; other suggestions are Carthage in North Africa, Hellas, Italy, and Elis. A Mediterranean site seems probable from the context of Ezekiel 27:6-7, perhaps an area of Cyprus that exported copper.

ELISHAMA

1. Ammihud's son and leader of the Ephraimites at the beginning of the journey in the wilderness (Nm 1:10; 2:18; 7:48, 53). His was the ninth tribe in line during

the wilderness march (10:22). Elishama was the father of Nun and grandfather of Joshua (1 Chr 7:26).

2. One of David's 13 sons born in Jerusalem to a legitimate wife (2 Sm 5:16; 1 Chr 3:8; 14:7).

3. Ishmael's ancestor. Ishmael killed Gedaliah, the governor of Israel appointed by Nebuchadnezzar (2 Kgs 25:25; Jer 41:1).

4. Man of Judah descended through Jerahmeel and Sheshan (1 Chr 2:41).

5. Another of David's sons (1 Chr 3:6); alternately called Elishua in 2 Samuel 5:15 and 1 Chronicles 14:5. *See* Elishua.

6. Priest sent by Jehoshaphat to instruct the Judeans in the law of God (2 Chr 17:8).

7. Prince and scribe in Jeremiah's time (Jer 36:12). He heard Baruch read the words of God, and later the scroll of the Lord remained in Elishama's chamber until the king requested it to be read (vv 20-21).

ELISHAPHAT

Military commander in Judah who supported Jehoiada the priest in overthrowing Queen Athaliah and making the young Joash king (2 Chr 23:1).

ELISHEBA

Wife of Aaron (Ex 6:23), who bore him Nadab, Abihu, Eleazar, and Ithamar. Her father was Amminadab and her brother was Nahshon, the leader of Judah (Nm 1:7; 2:3), the tribe to which Elisheba also belonged. After Aaron died (Nm 20:28), Moses invested Eleazar, Elisheba's third son, with the office of chief priest.

ELISHUA

One of the 13 children fathered by David during his reign in Jerusalem (2 Sm 5:15; 1 Chr 14:5). In the parallel passage of 1 Chronicles 3:6, the name Elishama appears in Elishua's place in most Hebrew manuscripts.

ELIUD

Achim's son, Eleazar's father, and an ancestor of Jesus Christ according to Matthew's genealogy (Mt 1:14-15).

ELIZABETH

Woman of priestly descent (Lk 1:5) and mother of John the Baptist, she was a relative of Mary, mother of Jesus (v 36). The name Elizabeth, which derives from the same Hebrew word as Elisheba, wife of Aaron (Ex 6:23), means "my God is an oath." Only Luke's Gospel, which characteristically focuses greater attention upon the role of women, mentions Elizabeth and her husband, Zechariah.

Luke emphasized Elizabeth and Zechariah's godly character and blameless conduct (Lk 1:6) before stating that the elderly couple had not been favored with children. Although in Jewish culture childlessness was regarded as a reproach (Gn 30:22-23; Lk 1:25), the devout pair continued to steadfastly worship and serve God. Unexpectedly, an angel of the Lord appeared to Zechariah with the announcement that Elizabeth would conceive and bear a son, who would be the forerunner of the promised Messiah (Lk 1:13-17). When Elizabeth conceived, she withdrew from public life for five months, during which time her kinswoman Mary visited her.

See also John the Baptist.

ELIZAPHAN

1. Kohathite Levite and Uzziel's son (Nm 3:29-30), who assisted in removing the bodies of Nadab and Abihu from the camp (Lv 10:4). Elizaphan's descendants were responsible for caring for the Ark, the table, the lampstand, and vessels of the sanctuary (cf. 1 Chr 15:8; 2 Chr 29:13). His name is alternately spelled Elzaphan (Ex 6:22; Lv 10:4).

2. Parnach's son and a leader from Zebulun's tribe, who helped Eleazar and Joshua divide the Canaanite territory west of the Jordan among the 10 tribes (Nm 34:25).

ELIZUR

Shedeur's son and leader of Reuben's tribe at the start of Israel's wilderness journey (Nm 1:5; 2:10; 7:30-35; 10:18).

ELKANAH

1. Levite of Korah's family (Ex 6:24) from the house of Izhar (v 21). He was Assir's son, and fathered Ebiasaph (1 Chr 6:23).

2. Father of the prophet Samuel (1 Sm 1:19). He was the son of Jeroham of Ephraim, from Ramathaim-zophim (v 1). Elkanah had two wives, Hannah and Peninnah, the former being barren (v 2). Hannah begged God repeatedly for a son whom she would give to the Lord's service. Samuel was subsequently born, and after his weaning, he was brought to the aged priest Eli for training. Elkanah had other sons and daughters by Hannah (2:21), and became the forefather of Heman, a singer in David's time.

3, 4. Name of two Kohathite Levites descended from Korah's line and ancestors of Heman the singer (1 Chr 6:26, 35).

5. Levite who dwelt in the village of the Netophathites and later lived in Jerusalem in the postexilic era (1 Chr 9:16).

6. Benjaminite warrior who joined David's mighty men at Ziklag (1 Chr 12:6).

7. Gatekeeper (guard) for the Ark of the Covenant during David's reign (1 Chr 15:23). He is perhaps the same as #6 above.

8. One who held an authoritative post in King Ahaz's court. Elkanah was slain by Zichri, an Ephraimite, for having forsaken the Lord (2 Chr 28:7).

ELKOSH

Home or birthplace of the prophet Nahum (Na 1:1). Three sites have been suggested: (1) Hilkeesei, a village in Galilee, perhaps corresponding to modern el-Kauzeh; (2) Capernaum near the Sea of Galilee, where Jesus frequently taught; and (3) Bein Jebrin in southern Judea.

ELMADAM

Ancestor of Jesus Christ, according to Luke's genealogy (Lk 3:28, KJV "Elmodam").

ELNAAM

Father of two mighty warriors in David's army, Jeribai and Joshaviah (1 Chr 11:46).

ELNATHAN

1. Grandfather of King Jehoiachin. His daughter, Jehoiachin's mother, was Nehushta (2 Kgs 24:8).

2, 3, 4. Three Jewish leaders whom Ezra sent to Iddo at Casiphia to obtain Levites and Temple servants for the caravan of Jews returning to Palestine from Babylonia (Ezr 8:16).

5. Acbor's son, who was ordered by King Jehoiakim to bring back Uriah from Egypt to be executed for prophesying against the king (Jer 26:22-23). Elnathan was present with other princes when Baruch read the Lord's words of warning written at Jeremiah's dictation on a scroll (36:12); he tried unsuccessfully to prevent Jehoiakim from burning the scroll (v 25).

ELON

1. Hittite who was the father of Basemath (perhaps also called Adah, Gn 36:2), one of Esau's wives (26:34).

2. Second of Zebulun's three sons (Gn 46:14) and the founder of the Elonite family (Nm 26:26).

3. Judge from Zebulun who judged Israel for 10 years. He was buried in Aijalon (Jgs 12:11-12).

ELPAAL

Benjaminite and one of Shaharaim's sons (1 Chr 8:11-12, 18).

ELPELET

Alternative name of David's son Eliphelet in 1 Chronicles 14:5. See Eliphelet #3.

ELUZAI

One of the men of Benjamin who came to join David in Ziklag (1 Chr 12:5). Eluzai was an ambidextrous slinger and bowman.

ELYMAS

Another name for Bar-Jesus, a Jewish magician and false prophet, in Acts 13:8. *See* Bar-Jesus.

ELZABAD

1. Military leader from Gad's tribe who joined David at Ziklag (1 Chr 12:12).

2. Korahite Levite from Obed-edom's family, and a gatekeeper of the sanctuary (1 Chr 26:7).

ELZAPHAN

Alternate spelling of Elizaphan, a Levite chief, in Exodus 6:22 and Leviticus 10:4. *See* Elizaphan #1.

ENAN

Ahira's father. Ahira was appointed by Moses as the commander of the tribe of Naphtali during the first census of Israel in the desert of Sinai (Nm 1:15; 2:29; 7:78, 83; 10:27). The name is apparently preserved in the name Hazar-enan (-enon), a town somewhere between Damascus and Hauran (Nm 34:9; Ez 47:17; 48:1).

ENOCH

1. Cain's son and grandson of Adam (Gn 4:17, 19).

2. Jared's son among the descendants of Seth; Methuselah's father (Gn 5:18-24; 1 Chr 1:3). He lived in such close relationship to God that he was taken to heaven without having died.

ENOSH

Seth's son and the grandson of Adam (Gn 4:26; 1 Chr 1:1). He became the father of Kenan at 90 years of age, after which he fathered other sons and daughters, dying at the age of 905 (Gn 5:6-11). He is mentioned as Jesus' ancestor in Luke's genealogy (Lk 3:38; KJV, RSV "Enos").

EPAPHRAS

Coworker with the apostle Paul. Epaphras, a native of Colosse, was responsible for the city's evangelization, as well as that of Laodicea and Hierapolis. Through him Paul learned of the progress of the Colossian church and thus wrote his letter to the Colossians. Paul's high regard for Epaphras was evidenced by his use of such terms as "beloved fellow servant," "faithful minister of Christ" (Col 1:7), and "servant of Christ" (4:12), a title of esteem Paul bestowed only on one other person—Timothy (Phil 1:1). Epaphras was in prison with Paul at the time the letter to Philemon was written (Phlm 1:23).

EPAPHRODITUS

Leader in the Philippian church. Epaphroditus was sent to the apostle Paul during Paul's first Roman imprisonment; his mission was to deliver gifts (Phil 4:18) and to assist the apostle in his work (2:25). While in Rome, Epaphroditus became seriously ill and nearly died. After a period of convalescence, he returned to Philippi with Paul's letter instructing the church to receive him (v 29). Epaphroditus's devoted service endeared him to the Philippian believers and to Paul, who termed him "brother and fellow worker and fellow soldier" (v 25, RSV).

EPENETUS

Believer greeted by Paul in Romans 16:5 as "my dear friend" and "first person from the province of Asia to become a follower of Christ" (NLT). It is not known if Epenetus was a personal convert of Paul. Mention of his name has been used to promote the hypothesis that the letter was written for the Ephesians, but this is not sufficient grounds for making this identification.

EPHAH

1. Son of Midian, an offspring of Abraham through his concubine Keturah (Gn 25:4; 1 Chr 1:33). Isaiah mentions him as a gold trader (Is 60:6). Some manuscripts mention two sons of Midian with the same name, Ephah, but that is an error of misspelling.

2. Caleb's concubine, who bore him three sons (1 Chr 2:46).

3. Jahdai's son from Judah's tribe (1 Chr 2:47).

EPHAI

Netophathite (resident of the town Netophah, near Bethlehem) whose sons fought against the Babylonian army (Jer 40:8). They, with others, approached Gedaliah, the governor of Judah appointed by Babylon, and requested his protection. They died, along with Gedaliah, in an uprising led by Ishmael, the son of Nethaniah (41:3).

EPHER

1. Son of Midian and grandson of Abraham through his concubine Keturah, whose tribe was sent to the east. Some were supportive of Abraham's descendants and others became enemies (Gn 25:4; 1 Chr 1:33).

2. Son of Ezrah from Judah's tribe (1 Chr 4:17).

3. Head of a household and a great warrior in the half-tribe of Manasseh. He lived between Bashan and Mt Hermon (1 Chr 5:24).

EPHLAL

Jerahmeel's descendant, who could trace his ancestry through Perez to Judah (1 Chr 2:37).

EPHOD

Father of Hanniel, the prince of the children of Joseph (Nm 34:23). Hanniel was responsible for distributing Canaanite territory among the Israelite tribes.

EPHRAIM

Joseph's younger son, born of Joseph and Asenath before the seven years of famine in Egypt (Gn 41:52). He was the ancestor of an Israelite tribe, and his name came to designate the northern kingdom of Israel (Is 7:5, 8; Jer 31:18-20; Hos 5:3-5). Ephraim's boyhood overlapped the last 17 years of his grandfather, the patriarch Jacob, who migrated to Egypt during the years of famine. Thus Ephraim could learn of God's promises and blessings directly from Jacob. After Jacob exacted an oath from Joseph to bury him in Canaan he adopted his grandsons Ephraim and Manasseh. That adoption gave the two brothers the position and legal rights equal to Jacob's eldest sons, Reuben and Simeon (Gn 48:5).

EPHRATH

Mother of Hur and Caleb's second wife (1 Chr 2:19, 50).

EPHRON

Hittite from whom Abraham purchased the cave of Machpelah with its adjoining field for 400 shekels of silver (Gn 23:8-17). Sarah was buried there, as was Abraham (25:9) and Jacob (50:13).

ER

1. Eldest son of Judah and Bathshua, a Canaanite woman (Gn 38:3). The Lord killed him before he and his wife, Tamar, could have any children (Gn 38:7; 46:12; 1 Chr 2:3).

2. Grandson of Judah and father of Lecah (1 Chr 4:21); a nephew of #1 above.

3. Joshua's son and an ancestor of Joseph, the husband of Mary (Lk 3:28).

ERAN

Grandson of Ephraim and the oldest son of Shuthelah (Nm 26:36), from whom came the Eranite family. In 1 Chronicles 7:20, Eran was replaced by Eleadah, which may be a copyist's error.

ERASTUS

Name mentioned three times in the NT. Whether only one individual is being referred to cannot be ascertained, although in each case Erastus is an associate of Paul's. The three instances are (1) a helper of Paul sent with Timothy into Macedonia (Acts 19:22); (2) the city treasurer of Corinth (a steward of financial affairs, possibly a slave or freedman of some wealth and an important man in the Corinthian community), who sends greetings with Paul to the church in Rome (Rom 16:23); and (3) a friend of Paul's who stayed at Corinth (2 Tm 4:20).

ERI

Gad's fifth son (Gn 46:16) and founder of the Erite family (Nm 26:16).

ESARHADDON

King of Assyria (681–669 BC). Though probably not the eldest son of Sennacherib, he was the eldest surviving son following several interfamily murders. Sennacherib was assassinated by his sons Adram-melech and Sharezer, and civil war ensued between their supporters and those who accepted the youthful, newly proclaimed king, Esarhaddon. As the threat from the brothers was eliminated by death or exile, Esarhaddon solidified his position. He ruled from Nineveh and proclaimed his twin sons, Ashurbanipal and Samas-sumukin, crown princes of Assyria and Babylonia but his attempt thus to ensure a smooth changeover of rule at his own death was frustrated.

Esarhaddon's immediate task was to settle the rebellious border areas, which he did by launching military campaigns. He installed governors he could rely on, and he increased substantially the level of tribute required. Some kings were replaced and others subsequently restored. Of the latter, Manasseh (2 Chr 33:11), taken in chains to Babylon, later continued to reign in Jerusalem, although this incident may not have taken place until the reign of Ashurbanipal. Of the strong cities, Sidon was finally subdued, but Esarhaddon was forced to come to terms with Baslu, king of Tyre.

In 675 BC, Esarhaddon invaded Egypt and destroyed the royal city of Memphis, together with many other towns and cities. Prince Taharqa, who had fled to Nubia on the initial invasion, continued to rule over Egypt and subsequently led a rebellion against Esarhaddon. During his second Egyptian campaign, Esarhaddon succumbed to a fatal sickness.

Esarhaddon was a strong, cruel, and fearless ruler who was proud of his achievements. He maintained dominion over a vast area, claiming control not only of Babylonia and Syria but also of Egypt and Ethiopia, the lands bordering on Assyria, and some of the islands of the eastern Mediterranean. He built a palace at Kar-esarhaddon near Nineveh and restored the fabled temple of Ashur originally constructed by Shalmaneser I about 1250 BC. He commemorated the deeds of his reign on numerous stelae and prisms. Esarhaddon is mentioned in 2 Kings 19:37, Ezra 4:2, and Isaiah 37:38.

ESAU

Isaac's son, and the older twin brother of Jacob (Gn 25:24-26), who was given this name because of the hair on his body at birth. The reddish color of the baby, together with the color appearing in the episode of the lentil soup (v 30), led to the use of the term Edom, or "red." The Edomites claimed to be descended from Esau, and naming their land Seir may have been an attempt to retain an association with the word *sair,* meaning "hairy."

A proficient hunter, Esau brought tasty wild meat to his father, who enjoyed its stronger flavor much more than that of the mild meat provided from the family flocks by Jacob. On a certain day Esau returned home from an unsuccessful hunting expedition; he was very hungry. Esau was persuaded by Jacob to surrender his birthright in return for food (Gn 25:29-34).

Archaeological information from Nuzi shows that giving up the birthright to another member of the family was not unknown. Esau's marriage to two local women who were not descendants of Abraham made life extremely difficult for his parents (Gn 26:34-35). This may have been the reason why his mother, Rebekah, decided to coach Jacob to obtain the patriarchal blessing that normally belonged to his elder brother Esau (ch 27). Esau's anger on discovering the deception of his brother prompted Jacob to leave for Haran, though 20 years later, through the generous forgiveness of Esau, the brothers were reunited (33:4-16).

At birth Jacob had come into the world grasping the heel of Esau, an omen that was interpreted to show that the Edomite descendants of Esau would be subject to the offspring of Jacob. The subservient relationship between the Edomites and the Israelites in the time of David (2 Sm 8:11-15; 1 Chr 18:13) continued until the time of Jehoram (2 Kgs 8:20-22; 2 Chr 21:8-10). Following a rebellion in 845 BC, the Edomites gained their independence for a while but were reconquered by Amaziah (796–767 BC). Regaining their freedom in 735 BC, they subsequently remained independent of Judah.

ESHBAAL

King Saul's fourth son, who became Israel's king after his father's death. Eshbaal literally means "man of Baal," or "Baal exists" (1 Chr 8:33; 9:39). During the period of the judges and the early monarchy, many Hebrew names were compounded with "baal," a word that can mean "master" or "possessor." Later generations were reluctant to speak the name "baal," so "bosheth" (shame) was substituted (cf. Hos 2:16-17). Thus, Eshbaal was altered to Ishbosheth (2 Sm 2:8), which means "man of shame." Perhaps later copyists changed the name in the book of Samuel because it was read aloud in synagogue services, whereas Chronicles was not.

After the death of Saul and his older sons, Abner, commander of Saul's army, installed Ishbosheth as Israel's king (2 Sm 2:8-9). Judah's tribe, however, followed King David, who struggled with Ishbosheth for leadership of all the tribes. The conflict lasted a long time, but the house of David gradually overwhelmed the house of Saul (3:1). Abner deserted Ishbosheth and was murdered by Joab, one of David's men (v 27), thus removing an important leader of Israel and causing the people to despair (4:1). Soon afterward Ishbosheth was murdered by two of his captains (v 7). Although David disapproved of the deaths of Abner and Ishbosheth, the last obstacles to his kingship over all the tribes had been removed.

See also David; Saul #2.

ESHBAN

Dishon's second son and grandson of Seir the Horite (Gn 36:26; 1 Chr 1:41).

ESHCOL

Amorite who, with his brothers Mamre and Aner, helped the patriarch Abraham defeat the forces of Kedorlaomer and rescue Lot and his family (Gn 14:13, 24).

QUICKTAKE

ESTHER

STRENGTHS AND ACCOMPLISHMENTS
- Her beauty and character won the heart of Persia's king
- She combined courage with careful planning
- She was open to advice and willing to act
- She was more concerned for others than for her own security

LESSONS FROM HER LIFE
- Serving God often demands that we risk our own security
- God has a purpose for the situations in which he places us
- Courage, while often vital, does not replace careful planning

VITAL STATISTICS
Where: Persian Empire
Occupation: Xerxes' wife, queen of Persia
Relatives: Cousin: Mordecai. Husband: Xerxes. Father: Abihail

KEY VERSE
"Go and gather together all the Jews of Susa and fast for me. Do not eat or drink for three days, night or day. My maids and I will do the same. And then, though it is against the law, I will go in to see the king. If I must die, I must die" (Esther 4:16).

Esther's story is told in the book of Esther.

ESHEK
Descendant of Jonathan, Saul's son. Eshek's grandsons were mighty men of valor in the tribe of Benjamin (1 Chr 8:38-40).

ESHTEMOA
1. Ishbah's son from Judah's tribe (1 Chr 4:17).
2. Maacathite from Judah's tribe (1 Chr 4:19).

ESHTON
Mehir's son and the grandson of Chelub from Judah's tribe (1 Chr 4:11-12).

ESLI
Nahum's father and ancestor of Jesus, according to Luke's genealogy (3:25).

ESTHER

One of two names borne by the Jewish queen of Persia. Hadassah (Hebrew "Myrtle") apparently was her Jewish name (Est 2:7), and Esther (Persian "Star") her name as queen of Persia. Some scholars speculate about a connection with the Babylonian goddess Ishtar, since exiled Jews were occasionally given pagan names (see Dn 1:7).

Esther was an orphan from the tribe of Benjamin who lived with the Jewish exiles in Persia. She was reared by her cousin Mordecai, a minor government official and covert leader of the Jewish community (see Est 3:5-6) in Susa, capital of the Persian kingdom. Esther became queen after King Ahasuerus (Xerxes) became displeased with Queen Vashti when she refused to obey his command to attend a banquet (1:11-12).

After Esther's coronation, she discreetly won Xerxes' confidence by informing him of an assassination plot (Est 2:21-23). The favor she won in the king's eyes enabled her to deliver her family and her people from a massacre by Haman, a high official to the king.

The Feast of Purim was instituted to celebrate God's deliverance of his people through Esther and Mordecai. This festival is still observed annually by Jews.

ETHAN

1. Wise man comparable to Solomon (1 Kgs 4:31) and probably the author of Psalm 89. It is uncertain whether he was a contemporary of Solomon.

2. Descendant of Judah and son of Zerah (1 Chr 2:6), perhaps the same as #1 above. However, they are ascribed different fathers in the two passages.

3. Son of Zimmah, a descendant of Gershon, Levi's oldest son (1 Chr 6:42).

4. Descendant of Levi through his son Merari, and the son of Kishi (1 Chr 6:44) or Kushaiah (15:17). He was one of three outstanding musicians, along with Heman and Asaph, appointed by David (vv 16-19). It was probably this Ethan whose name is ascribed in the title to Psalm 39 (as "Jeduthun," which he is called in 1 Chr 16:41; 25:1) as "chief musician"; it is likely that he composed the music for the psalm.

ETHBAAL

King of Sidon whose daughter Jezebel entered into a political marriage with Ahab of Israel (1 Kgs 16:31). Ethbaal was credited with building Botrys in Phoenicia and founding the colony of Auza in Libya. He also established commercial relations with Damascus.

ETHNAN

Member of Helah's family from Judah's tribe (1 Chr 4:7).

ETHNI

Alternate name for Jeatherai, Zerah's son, in 1 Chronicles 6:41. *See* Jeatherai.

EUBULUS

Roman believer who sent greetings to Timothy during Paul's second Roman imprisonment (2 Tm 4:21). His Greek name indicates his probable gentile origin.

EUNICE

Timothy's mother, daughter of Lois (2 Tm 1:5), and the wife of a pagan Greek. She was a Jewish Christian (Acts 16:1). She apparently taught her son the OT Scriptures "from childhood" (2 Tm 3:15) and was converted to Christianity during Paul's first trip to her home in Lystra, previous to his visit mentioned in Acts 16:1.

EUODIA

Prominent woman in the Philippian church whom Paul asked to resolve her differences with Syntyche (Phil 4:2). The nature of their disagreement is not known, but it was of enough severity to reach Paul in Rome. Both women had labored with him in the work of the gospel (4:3).

EUTYCHUS

Common slave name, mentioned only in Acts 20:9. It was Eutychus's misfortune to become sleepy while sitting on a windowsill listening to the apostle Paul preach at Troas. He sank into a deep sleep and fell from the ledge, which was in the third loft. The apostle Paul revived him from the dead (vv 7-12).

EVE

First woman, "the mother of all living" (Gn 3:20). The book of Genesis recounts that after God had finished his creation of Adam, he saw that it was not good for Adam to be alone. He decided to create "a helper fit for him" (2:18). The woman is called *ezer* (in Hebrew lit. "help"), a word that appears elsewhere in the OT in reference to God as Israel's help. Causing Adam to fall into a deep sleep, God took one of his ribs and used it to fashion Eve (vv 21-25).

Eve was given two names by Adam. The first was "woman," a generic designation with theological connotations that denote her relationship to man (Gn 2:23). The second, Eve ("life"), was given after the fall and refers to her role in the procreation of the human race (3:20).

Adam and Eve are pictured as living in Eden, serving God and fulfilling each other's needs. Then evil entered when Eve was tempted by the serpent to disobey God's command, which forbade their eating the fruit of the tree of the knowledge of good and evil (Gn 2:17; 3:3). Tricked by the serpent's subtle persuasion, Eve transgressed God's will by eating the fruit. Adam did the same when she brought some to him, although he was not deceived as she had been. Both then recognized their nakedness and made garments of fig leaves.

When God came to commune with them, they hid from him. When he demanded an account, Adam blamed Eve, and Eve blamed the serpent. God told Eve that as a result of their sin, childbirth would be a painful experience and her husband would rule over her (Gn 3:16). Eve later became the mother of Cain, Abel, Seth, and other children (4:1-2, 25; 5:4).

Eve is mentioned twice in the NT. In his letter to Timothy, the apostle Paul referred to her when discussing whether or not women could teach (1 Tm 2:13). He said that a woman could not teach or have authority over a man because of man's priority in creation and Eve's responsibility for the original transgression (see 2 Cor 11:3).

See also Adam.

EVI

One of five Midianite kings killed in a battle against Israel under the leadership of Moses (Nm 31:8). Apparently, God directed Moses to go to battle against Midian because the Midianites had led the Israelites into pagan religious practices. In Joshua 13:21, Evi is called a prince of Sihon, the Midianite king.

EVIL-MERODACH

Son and successor of Nebuchadnezzar as king of Babylon, who reigned for two years (561–560 BC). During his reign, he released Jehoiachin, former king of Judah, from imprisonment (2 Kgs 25:27-30; Jer 52:31-34). Aside from this fact, little is known about his reign. He was killed by his brother-in-law Neriglissar, who succeeded him to the throne.

EZBAI

Father of Naarai, one of David's elite force known as "the thirty" (1 Chr 11:37). In 2 Samuel 23:35 he is called Paarai the Arbite. This has led some interpreters to suggest that "the son of Ezbai" in the 1 Chronicles passage is a corruption of "the Arbite" and that the correct reading of his name should be Naarai the Arbite.

EZBON

1. Gad's son (Gn 46:16), called Ozni in Numbers 26:16; perhaps an eponym of a Gadite family.

2. Benjamin's grandson (1 Chr 7:7). It has been proposed that 1 Chronicles 7:6-11 is a genealogy of Zebulun assigned to Benjamin by error, and that Ezbon suggests Ibzan (Jgs 12:8-10), a minor judge of Bethlehem.

EZEKIEL

Priest and prophet during Israel's Babylonian exile. Ezekiel was a descendant of the influential priestly family of Zadok (Ez 1:3). He was probably reared in Jerusalem and was familiar with the Temple ritual; it is unknown whether he served as a priest there. All that is known of his personal life is obtained from the OT book of Ezekiel.

Ezekiel was married (24:16-18) and lived at Tel-abib in Babylonia (3:15), in his own house (3:24; 8:1). Most of the Judean captives had settled by the Kebar Canal (1:3), which went from Babylon by Nippur to Erech. The elders of Israel there sought out Ezekiel for counsel (8:1; 14:1; 20:1). In the fifth year of the Exile, when Ezekiel was between 25 and 30 years old, he received God's call to the prophetic office (1:1–3:11). His wife died suddenly during the Exile, but he was forbidden to mourn for her in public (24:16-18). Her sudden

QUICKTAKE

EZEKIEL

STRENGTHS AND ACCOMPLISHMENTS
- Was a priest by training, a prophet by God's call
- Received vivid visions and delivered powerful messages
- Served as God's messenger during Israel's captivity in Babylon
- Became a tough and courageous man so he could reach a hard and stubborn people (Ezekiel 3:8)

LESSONS FROM HIS LIFE
- Even the repeated failures of his people will not prevent God's plan for the world from being fulfilled
- Each person's response to God determines his or her eternal destiny
- God has people through whom he can work even in seemingly hopeless situations

VITAL STATISTICS
Where: Babylon
Occupation: Prophet to the captives in Babylon
Relatives: Father: Buzi. Wife: Unknown
Contemporaries: Jehoiachin, Jeremiah, Jehoiakim, Nebuchadnezzar

KEY VERSES
"Then he added, 'Son of man, let all my words sink deep into your own heart first. Listen to them carefully for yourself. Then go to your people in exile and say to them, "This is what the Sovereign LORD says!" Do this whether they listen to you or not'" (Ezekiel 3:10, 11).

Ezekiel's story is told in the book of Ezekiel and 2 Kings 24:10-17.

death was meant to convey a striking and solemn warning of what would occur in the captives' homeland (vv 15-27).

The time of Ezekiel's ministry was unusual in many ways. It was a period of great prophetic activity. With the prophets Jeremiah and Daniel, Ezekiel spoke to the nation's needs at the time of the Babylonian captivity. It was an era of upheaval and uprooting for the southern kingdom of Judah, and a time of persistent apostasy, idolatry, and general disobedience to the Mosaic law. It was also a period of international conflict and shifting power balances throughout the Near East.

Ezekiel's ministry seems to have extended from 592 BC to at least the 27th year of the Exile (29:17). It falls into two main periods. During the first period (592–587 BC), his

QUICKTAKE

EZRA

STRENGTHS AND ACCOMPLISHMENTS
- Committed to study, follow, and teach God's Word
- Led the second group of exiles from Babylon to Jerusalem
- May have written 1 and 2 Chronicles
- Concerned about keeping the details of God's commands
- Sent by King Artaxerxes to Jerusalem to evaluate the situation, set up a religious education system, and returned with a firsthand report
- Worked alongside Nehemiah during the last spiritual awakening recorded in the Old Testament

LESSONS FROM HIS LIFE
- A person's willingness to know and practice God's Word will have a direct effect on how God uses his/her life
- The starting place for serving God is a personal commitment to serve him today, even before knowing what that service will be

VITAL STATISTICS
Where: Babylon, Jerusalem
Occupations: Scribe among the exiles in Babylon, king's envoy, teacher
Relative: Father: Seraiah
Contemporaries: Nehemiah, Artaxerxes

KEY VERSE
"This was because Ezra had determined to study and obey the Law of the LORD and to teach those decrees and regulations to the people of Israel." (Ezra 7:10).

Ezra's story is told in Ezra 7:1–10:16 and Nehemiah 8:1–12:36.

messages were repeated warnings—in prose discourse and symbolic acts—intended to lead the Exiles to repentance and faith in God. During the second period (586–570 BC), after Nebuchadnezzar's destruction of Jerusalem and the Temple, the prophet comforted the Exiles and encouraged them to look to the future in hope (chs 33–48). There were 13 years in which no prophetic utterances were delivered, namely 585 BC (32:1, 17; 33:21) to 572 BC (40:1). The prophet learned of the fall of Jerusalem while in Babylon (33:21-22).

The burden of Ezekiel's message was that Judah was ripe for judgment. His preparation for speaking God's message is given in the picture of his eating the written prophecies (2:8–3:3). At first the messages were not accepted, but later his prophecies were vindicated as they began to come true and as the nation was purged of its idolatry. Ezekiel has been called "the father of Judaism" because of his supposed influence on Israel's later worship. His greatest contribution to postexilic Jewish worship consisted in establishing the basis of the synagogue. He stressed the teaching of personal immortality, resurrection, and the ritual law.

Ezekiel carried out his messages with vivid and dramatic acts of symbolism (e.g., 4:1-8; 5:1-17). His style has been characterized as heavy and repetitious, but it was designed with the themes of apostasy and subsequent judgment in view.

The place and circumstances of his death are unknown, and Ezekiel is not mentioned elsewhere in the OT.

EZER

1. Chieftain of a Horite tribe (Gn 36:21; 1 Chr 1:38).

2. Descendant and probably the son of Ephraim. He was killed while making a raid on the cattle of the Philistines (1 Chr 7:21).

3. Man of Judah, descended from Hur (1 Chr 4:4).

4. Gadite who joined David at Ziklag (1 Chr 12:9).

5. Jeshua's son, who ruled Mizpah and repaired the Jerusalem wall (Neh 3:19).

6. Priest who took part in the ceremony at the dedication of the Jerusalem wall (Neh 12:42).

EZRA

1. Religious reformer following Israel's return from exile. Ezra's genealogy (Ezr 7:1-5; cf. 1 Chr 6:3-15) places him in the high priestly Aaron-Zadok family line, which accounts for the importance of his scribal and priestly activities. He is called "priest" (Ezr 10:10, 16; Neh 8:2), "scribe" (Ezr 7:6; Neh 12:36), and "priest and scribe" (Ezr 7:11-12; Neh 8:9; 12:26). The OT scribe was not a mere copyist, as in Christ's time, but a profound student of God's laws and commandments (Ezr 7:11-12; Jer 8:8). In the commission of the Persian king Artaxerxes to Ezra, the king described him as "priest" and "scribe" (Ezr 7:6-11). It was Ezra

EZRA
The Times of Ezra, Nehemiah, and Esther

539 BC
Cyrus leads Persian overthrow of Babylon's empire (Isaiah 45).

538–537 BC
Sheshbazzar and Zerubbabel lead the first group of Jews back to Jerusalem (Ezra 1–3).

537–536 BC
The Temple altar is rebuilt, and reconstruction of the Temple begins (Ezra 3).

530 BC
Work on the Temple stops, due to local opposition (Ezra 4).

520 BC
On order of King Darius, the Temple building resumes (Ezra 4–6).

516 BC
The Temple is completed (Ezra 6).

486 BC
Xerxes becomes king of Persia (Esther 1:1-3).

479 BC
Esther becomes Xerxes' queen (Esther 2).

474 BC
Esther and Mordecai foil Haman's plot to kill the Jews (Esther 3–8).

458 BC
Ezra leads a second group from Babylon to Judah and renews worship there (Ezra 7–10).

445 BC
Nehemiah leads a third group to Jerusalem to rebuild the city walls (Nehemiah 1–12).

445–432 BC
Nehemiah serves as governor of Judah (Nehemiah 13).

who began the traditional view of the scribe as a religious leader, a "bookman"; the view lasted until 200 BC. Scribes were qualified to teach and preach the Scriptures as well as interpret them, but by the first century AD, the scribe's function was more specialized.

As "Secretary of State for Jewish Affairs" in the Persian Empire, Ezra visited Jerusalem about 458 BC, and on his return reported his findings. Little was done, however, until Nehemiah went to Jerusalem in 445. Once the city walls had been rebuilt, Ezra instituted a religious reformation in which the ancient Torah (the Law) was made the norm for Jewish life. He also demanded that Jews who had married foreigners must divorce them to maintain the Jewish purity the Torah required. Ezra set an example of piety and dedication through prayer and fasting, and this placed his reforming zeal in proper spiritual perspective. He set the pattern for life in the postexilic Jewish commonwealth, making God's Word and worship central features. The date and place of his death are unknown.

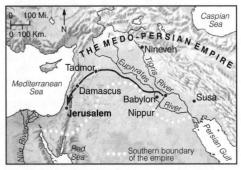

Ezra's Journey to Jerusalem: Ezra led a second group of exiles back to Judah and Jerusalem about 80 years after the first group. He traveled the dangerous route with a military escort (Ezr 8:22), but the people prayed and, under Ezra's godly leadership, arrived safely in Jerusalem after several months.

2. KJV rendering of Ezrah in 1 Chronicles 4:17. *See* Ezrah.

EZRAH
Father of four sons from Judah's tribe (1 Chr 4:17).

EZRI
Son of Kelub and one of the men who supervised the tilling of David's lands (1 Chr 27:26).

FELIX, ANTONIUS
Roman procurator (governor) of Judea (AD 52–60) succeeding Cumanus, appointed by Claudius and succeeded by Festus Porcius. Felix's brother, Pallas, a prominent, more influential Roman, interceded on his behalf after he was recalled from his procuratorship by Nero. During his oppressive rule, Felix utilized the aid of robbers to have Jonathan, the high priest,

murdered. His tyranny has been cited as the cause for the Jewish revolt that broke out six years after he was recalled. Felix had three wives: one unknown, another the granddaughter of Mark Antony and Cleopatra, and another the Jewish sister of Agrippa II, whose name was Drusilla. At the age of 16 Drusilla left her husband, King Azizus of Emesa, to marry Felix. She later bore him a son, Agrippa.

Felix was serving as governor when the apostle Paul was brought before him in Caesarea to answer charges against him after the riot in Jerusalem (Acts 23:24–24:27). After a five-day delay, Tertullus, spokesman for the Jews, and others arrived to state their charges. Felix put off a decision until he could hear from Lysias, the tribune. In the meantime Paul was placed in limited custody. Felix hoped to obtain bribe money for his release. As a result, Paul was detained for two years, during which time he and Felix often conversed. The apostle's message of "justice, self-control, and future judgment" alarmed Felix greatly (24:25). Record of his life after being recalled by Nero is not available.

FESTUS, PORCIUS

Roman procurator (governor) of Judea, who succeeded Felix Antonius and who was succeeded by Albinus. The precise date of Porcius Festus's accession to power is debatable but has been narrowed to sometime between AD 55 and 60. The only sources mentioning Festus are the book of Acts and the writings of Josephus, a Jewish historian who lived in Rome in the first century AD (*Antiquities* 20.8.9-11; 9.1).

Josephus wrote that Festus ruled wisely and justly, in contrast to Felix and Albinus. Sicarii bandits (named after the small swords they carried) who had terrorized the Palestinian countryside were eliminated under Festus's rule. In spite of this, he could not reverse the damage incurred by his predecessor, Felix, who had aggravated the conflict between pagans and Jews.

The NT recounts that the new procurator Festus traveled from Caesarea (where Paul was in custody) to Jerusalem (Acts 25:1). The Jewish leaders confronted him there and brought charges against Paul. Upon returning to Caesarea, Festus heard Paul's defense (v 6). He granted the apostle's appeal to be heard by Caesar (the right of any Roman accused of a capital offense) in an effort to avoid further religious disputes in his jurisdiction (vv 11-12). When King Agrippa arrived a few days later, Festus was in a quandary, unable to understand the Jews' charges against Paul (vv 25-27). After Paul's address before the king, Festus loudly declared him to be mad (26:24), though still agreeing that Paul had done nothing to deserve death or imprisonment (v 31).

FORTUNATUS

Member of the church at Corinth. Fortunatus is a Roman proper name written in Greek and found only once in the NT (1 Cor 16:17). Paul rejoiced that he, along with Stephanas and Achaicus, had come to be with him in Ephesus. The Textus Receptus has a subscript naming these three men as the carriers of Paul's letter to the Corinthians.

GAAL

Ebed's son, who persuaded the men of Shechem to revolt against Abimelech, the judge of Israel. The revolt, however, was quickly crushed and Shechem was destroyed (Jgs 9:26-41).

GABBAI

Head of a family that returned to Jerusalem with Zerubbabel after the Babylonian exile (Neh 11:8).

GAD

1. One of the 12 sons of Jacob (Gn 35:26; 1 Chr 2:2). He was the first of the two sons born to Jacob by Zilpah, Leah's maid. Delighted with giving Jacob another son, Leah named the boy Gad, meaning "good fortune" (Gn 30:11). Later, Gad moved his family with Jacob to Egypt (Ex 1:4). When Jacob blessed his sons, he predicted that Gad would constantly be troubled by foreign invaders but would successfully withstand them and put them to flight (see Gn 49:19). Gad became the father of seven sons (Gn 46:16) and the founder of the Gadites (Dt 3:12, 16), one of the 12 tribes of Israel (Nm 2:14).

2. Prophet and seer during the reign of David. He counseled David to leave Mizpeh of Moab and return to the land of Judah (1 Sm 22:5). Gad communicated David's punishment for numbering the fighting men of Israel (2 Sm 24:11-14, 18-19; 1 Chr 21:9-19), assisted David and Nathan in setting up the order of worship in the sanctuary (2 Chr 29:25) and later wrote an account of David's life (1 Chr 29:29).

GADDI

Man from Manasseh's tribe sent by Moses to search out the land of Canaan (Nm 13:11).

GADDIEL

Sodi's son from Zebulun's tribe, sent by Moses to search out the land of Canaan (Nm 13:10).

GADI

Father of Menahem. Menahem revolted and killed Shallum, king of Israel, placing himself on the throne as king (2 Kgs 15:14, 17).

GAHAM

Son of Nahor, Abraham's brother, and his concubine Reumah (Gn 22:24).

GAHAR

Ancestor of a group of Temple assistants that returned to Jerusalem with Zerubbabel after the Exile (Ezr 2:47; Neh 7:49).

GAIUS

1. Native of Macedonia and traveling companion of Paul during the apostle's third missionary journey. He and Aristarchus were both seized at Ephesus during the riot caused by Demetrius the silversmith (Acts 19:29).
2. Native of Derbe in Lycaonia, who traveled with Paul from Ephesus to Macedonia (Acts 20:4). Some have identified him with #1 above.
3. Prominent believer in Corinth and host to Paul and the whole church there (Rom 16:23). Since Romans was written in Corinth, the Gaius mentioned in 1 Corinthians 1:14 was probably the same person. If so, he was baptized by Paul.
4. Man to whom John addressed his third letter (3 Jn 1:1).

GALAL

1. Levite and Mica's son, who returned from exile in Babylon (1 Chr 9:15).
2. Levite and forefather of Obadiah (Abda). Obadiah returned from exile in Babylon (1 Chr 9:16; Neh 11:17).

GALLIO

Marcus Annaeus Seneca's son, and brother of the philosopher Seneca, who lived from 3 BC to AD 65. Born in Cordoba, Spain, Gallio came to Rome during Tiberius's reign. His given name was Marcus Annaeus Novatus, but he assumed the name Gallio after his adoption by the rhetorician Lucius Junius Gallio. The wealthy Lucius trained him for his career in administration and government.

Gallio served as Roman proconsul of Achaia sometime between AD 51 and 53. During the apostle Paul's first visit to Corinth, the Jews brought the apostle before the proconsul, accusing him of having persuaded people to practice religion in an unlawful manner (Acts 18:12-17). Gallio abruptly dismissed the charge since it dealt with Jewish and not Roman law. His action reflected the characteristic behavior of Roman governors toward religious disputes.

Forced to leave Achaia because of illness, Gallio returned to Rome as consul suffectus under Nero. His involvement in a conspiracy against Nero resulted in temporary pardon but eventual obligatory suicide.

GAMALIEL

1. Pedahzur's son and captain or prince of Manasseh's tribe (Nm 10:23). Gamaliel was chosen by Moses to help take the census in the wilderness near Mt Sinai (1:10) and to organize the tribe for the journey to the Promised Land (2:20). He participated in the special 12-day ceremonial offering by the princes at the dedication of the altar following completion of the Tabernacle (7:54, 59).
2. Jewish scholar. This man lived in the first century AD and died 18 years before the destruction of Jerusalem in AD 70 by Titus, the Roman general.

When Peter and the other apostles were brought before the enraged and threatening council in Jerusalem, Gamaliel, who was highly respected by the council, offered cautionary advice that probably saved the apostles' lives in that situation (Acts 5:27-40).

Gamaliel is also mentioned in Acts 22:3 as the rabbi with whom the apostle Paul studied as a youth in Jerusalem. During that period in Israel, a number of rabbinical schools evolved. Two of the most influential were the rival Pharisaic schools of Hillel and Shammai. Both of those teachers had vast influence on Jewish thinking. Hillel's school emphasized tradition even above the law. Shammai's school preserved the teaching of the law over the authority of tradition. Hillel's school was the more influential, and its decisions have been held by a great number of later rabbis.

Traditionally, Gamaliel is considered to be the grandson of Hillel, and he was thoroughly schooled in the philosophy and theology of his grandfather's teaching. Gamaliel was a member of the Sanhedrin, the high council of Jews in Jerusalem, and he served as president of the Sanhedrin during the reigns of the Roman emperors Tiberius, Caligula, and Claudius. Unlike other Jewish teachers, he had no antipathy toward Greek learning.

The learning of Gamaliel was so eminent and his influence so great that he is one of only seven Jewish scholars who have been honored by the title Rabban. He was called the "Beauty of the Law." The Talmud even says that "since Rabban Gamaliel died, the glory of the Law has ceased."

GAMUL
Priest assigned to Temple duty in David's time (1 Chr 24:17).

GAREB
Warrior among David's mighty soldiers (2 Sm 23:38; 1 Chr 11:40).

GATAM
Esau's grandson, the fourth son of Eliphaz and an Edomite chief (Gn 36:11, 16; 1 Chr 1:36).

GAZEZ
1. Caleb's son by his concubine Ephah, and the brother of Haran (1 Chr 2:46).
2. Son of Haran and the nephew of #1 above (1 Chr 2:46).

GAZZAM
Ancestor of a group of Temple assistants who returned to Jerusalem with Zerubbabel after the Exile (Ezr 2:48; Neh 7:51).

GEBER
1. Alternate name for Ben-geber, one of Solomon's commissariat officers, in 1 Kings 4:13. *See* Ben-geber.

G

2. Uri's son, who was responsible for providing food for Solomon's household. His territory was probably south of Ramoth-gilead (1 Kgs 4:19). Perhaps #1 and #2 were related.

GEDALIAH

1. Ahikam's son, and grandson of Shaphan (King Josiah's royal scribe). In 586 BC Nebuchadnezzar, the Babylonian king, appointed Gedaliah as governor over the Jews remaining in Israel to work the fields, vineyards, and orchards (2 Kgs 25:12, 22).

Gedaliah established his headquarters at Mizpah, where he was joined by the prophet Jeremiah and the Jewish commanders and their guerrilla forces who had escaped capture during the fall of Jerusalem (Jer 40:6-8). Gedaliah assured them that if they would settle down and live in peaceful subjection to Babylon, all would be well (2 Kgs 25:23-24; Jer 40:9-10). On the basis of that assurance, many of the Jews who were dispersed in the Transjordan and other countries returned to Israel to work the land into great productivity (Jer 40:11-12).

Though warned about a plot against him by Ishmael, Gedaliah entertained the schemer at a meal and was killed (2 Kgs 25:25; Jer 40:11-12; 41:1-3). Along with some pilgrims visiting the Temple, Ishmael fled with hostages to Ammon, escaping the vengeance of Johanan (Jer 41:10-15).

2. Temple musician in the time of King David (1 Chr 25:3, 9).

3. Jeshua's son and one called to divorce his foreign wife during Ezra's reforms (Ezr 10:18).

4. Pashhur's son and one of the Jerusalem officials who urged King Zedekiah to put the prophet Jeremiah to death for his pro-Babylonian prophetic pronouncements (Jer 38:1).

5. Amariah's son, grandson of King Hezekiah, and grandfather of the prophet Zephaniah (Zep 1:1).

GEDOR

Jeiel's son, who was an ancestor of King Saul. Gedor's family lived in Gibeon (1 Chr 8:31; 9:37).

GEHAZI

Servant of Elisha (2 Kgs 5:25) who instructed the prophet how best to recompense the generous Shunammite woman for her kindness to him (4:11-17). Gehazi took Elisha's staff to use in reviving the woman's dead son, but he was unsuccessful (v 31), and the prophet himself had to revive the child (vv 32-37). His greed in securing from Naaman presents declined by Elisha resulted in his contracting Naaman's leprosy (5:20-23, 27). In 2 Kings 8:1-6 Gehazi again encountered the Shunammite woman as she was petitioning the king of Israel.

GEMALLI

Father of Ammiel, one of the 12 spies sent by Moses to explore the land of Canaan (Nm 13:12).

GEMARIAH

1. Hilkiah's son and emissary to Nebuchadnezzar from King Zedekiah. He carried Jeremiah's letter to the Exiles in Babylon (Jer 29:3).

2. Son of Shaphan the scribe. In the Temple chamber of Gemariah, Baruch read Jeremiah's scroll (Jer 36:10-12, 25).

GENUBATH

Son of Hadad, the Edomite prince who, as a young lad, was taken to Egypt to escape Joab's slaughter. There Hadad married a sister of Queen Tahpenes. She bore Genubath, who was raised by the queen as a son of Pharaoh (1 Kgs 11:20).

GERA

1. One of Benjamin's sons (Gn 46:21). The name, however, does not appear in a similar list in Numbers 26:38-41.

2. Father of the judge Ehud (Jgs 3:15).

3. Shimei's father. Shimei cursed and threw stones at David during Absalom's rebellion; later, he sought David's pardon (2 Sm 16:5; 19:16-18; 1 Kgs 2:8).

4. Bela's son from Benjamin's tribe (1 Chr 8:3, 5); alternately called Heglam in verse 7.

GERSHOM

1. Moses' son by Zipporah, born in Midian during Moses' exile from Egypt (Ex 2:22; 18:3; 1 Chr 23:15-16).

2. Jonathan's father. He and his sons were priests to Dan's tribe. The Danites set up a graven image to worship and appointed Jonathan to be their priest (Jgs 18:30).

3. Alternate spelling of Gershon, Levi's oldest son (1 Chr 6:1, 16-17, 20, 43; 23:6-7). *See* Gershon.

4. Ancestor of Shebuel, the chief officer over the Temple treasury during David's reign (1 Chr 26:24).

5. Phinehas's son who returned with Ezra after the Exile (Ezr 8:2).

GERSHON

Levi's oldest son (also spelled Gershom) who went into Egypt with Israel (Gn 46:11; Nm 3:17; 1 Chr 6:1) and was ancestor of a division of Levites (Gershonites) who came out of Egypt with Moses (Ex 6:16-17; Nm 3:18, 21).

In the list of the allotment of Levitical cities, the Gershonites were listed as one of the largest Levitical groups in Israel (Jos 21:1-7). Some passages indicate that they were at times dominant among the functioning Levitical groups (Gn 46:11; Ex 6:16; Nm 3:17; 26:57; 1 Chr 6:1, 16; 23:6).

According to the book of Numbers, the Gershonites were encamped behind the Tabernacle to the west during the wilderness wanderings (Nm 3:23). Early in the second year after the Exodus from Egypt, the Gershonite males numbered about 7,500 (v 22). Only those between the ages of 30 and 50 could serve in the Tabernacle, which at the time of that early census totaled 2,630 men (4:39-40). They were responsible for the care and transportation of the external furnishings of the Tabernacle (3:25-26; 4:24, 27-28) and were given two wagons and four oxen for the purpose, being supervised by Aaron and his sons (4:27).

After the initial settlement of Canaan, the Gershonites were allotted 13 cities among the tribes of Issachar, Asher, Naphtali, and Manasseh in the northern part of Palestine (Jos 21:6).

During the time of King David, they were listed among the Levites appointed to service in the Temple (1 Chr 23:6-11). The Gershonite families of Ladan and Jehieli were in charge of the treasury of the house of God (26:20-22). At David's request, music in the Temple was directed in part by Asaph and his family, who were Gershonites (25:1-2). In the reign of King Hezekiah the Gershonites are mentioned among the Levites who cleansed the Temple (2 Chr 29:1-6, 12). In the postexilic period the descendants of Asaph celebrated the laying of the Temple foundation (Ezr 3:10) and the dedication of the city walls (Neh 12:31-36) with music.

GESHAN

Jahdai's son and a descendant of Judah through Caleb's line (1 Chr 2:47).

GESHEM

Arab opponent of Nehemiah who derided those seeking to rebuild the walls of Jerusalem (Neh 2:19; 6:1-6). He was likely an inhabitant of the north Arabian Desert and has been identified with Gashmu son of Shahr in a Dedanite Arabian inscription. Like Sanballat and Tobiah, his economic interests were threatened by the rebuilding of Jerusalem.

GETHER

Aram's son and the grandson of Shem (Gn 10:23). In 1 Chronicles 1:17 he is listed as one of the sons of Shem.

GEUEL

Maki's son from Gad's tribe, and one of the 12 spies appointed by Moses to search out the Promised Land of Canaan (Nm 13:15).

GIBBAR

Forefather of a family that returned to Jerusalem with Zerubbabel (Ezr 2:20). The parallel list in Nehemiah 7:25 reads "sons of Gibeon," suggesting that "Gibbar" may be a textual corruption. Some support for this view lies in the fact that Ezra 2:21 begins listing descendants by their home city rather than by family.

GIBEA
Caleb's grandson from Judah's tribe (1 Chr 2:49).

GIDDALTI
Heman's son and a Temple singer appointed by David to serve under the direction of his father (1 Chr 25:4). The 22nd of the 24 divisions of service was appointed to Giddalti (1 Chr 25:29, NLT mg).

GIDDEL
1. Ancestor of a group of Temple assistants who returned to Jerusalem with Zerubbabel after the Exile (Ezr 2:47; Neh 7:49).

2. Ancestor of a group of King Solomon's servants who returned with Zerubbabel after the Babylonian exile (Ezr 2:56; Neh 7:58).

GIDEON
Judge of Israel, son of Joash, of the clan of Abiezer and the tribe of Manasseh. Of the 12 judges of Israel, more verses are devoted to Gideon than any other—Samson running a close second. The narrative in which he is the central character antedates the Christian era by roughly 11 centuries.

Following seven years of cruel oppression by the Midianites, Israel cried out to the Lord for relief (Jgs 6:6). An unknown prophet informs the Israelites that their miserable conditions stem from their forgetting to give exclusive devotion to the one true God. God sends his angel to Gideon. A touch of humor earmarks the angel's greeting, for the "mighty warrior" (v 12) is threshing wheat secretly for fear of the Midianites. Yet God addresses Gideon in realization of what his mighty power is able to accomplish in him (vv 14-16, 34). Conscious of his own weakness and the formidable task before him, Gideon is an ideal vehicle for God's tremendous work of deliverance (cf. 1 Cor 1:27; 2 Cor 12:10).

Gideon's first task is to tear down his father's altar to Baal and the adjacent one to Asherah, Baal's female consort (cf. Is 42:8). Knowing that the people would resist such an act, Gideon and his servants destroy these images of debased Canaanite religion at night. The following day the men of Ophrah confront Gideon and seek his life in retaliation for the act. Joash pleads the cause of his son, inviting Baal,

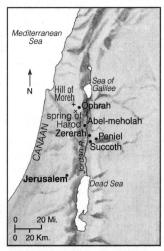

Gideon's Battle: Gideon routed thousands of Midianites, chasing them to Zererah and Abel-meholah.

QUICKTAKE

GIDEON

STRENGTHS AND ACCOMPLISHMENTS
- Israel's fifth judge. A military strategist who was expert at surprise
- A member of the Hall of Faith in Hebrews 11
- Defeated the Midianite army
- Was offered a hereditary kingship by the men of Israel
- Though slow to be convinced, acted on his convictions

WEAKNESSES AND MISTAKES
- Feared that his own limitations would prevent God from working
- Collected Midianite gold and made a symbol that became an evil object of worship
- Through a concubine, fathered a son who would bring great grief and tragedy to both Gideon's family and the nation of Israel
- Failed to establish the nation in God's ways; after he died they all went back to idol worship

LESSONS FROM HIS LIFE
- God calls in the middle of our present obedience. As we are faithful, he gives us more responsibility
- God expands and uses the abilities he has already built into us
- God uses us in spite of our limitations and failures
- Even those who make great spiritual progress can easily fall into sin if they don't consistently follow God

VITAL STATISTICS
Where: Ophrah, valley of Jezreel, spring of Harod
Occupations: Farmer, warrior, and judge
Relatives: Father: Joash. Son: Abimelech
Contemporaries: Zebah, Zalmunna

KEY VERSES
"'But Lord,' Gideon replied, 'how can I rescue Israel? My clan is the weakest in the whole tribe of Manasseh, and I am the least in my entire family!' The LORD said to him, 'I will be with you. And you will destroy the Midianites as if you were fighting against one man'" (Judges 6:15, 16).

His story is told in Judges 6–8. He is also mentioned in Hebrews 11:32.

if he indeed is deity, to contend for himself. Out of this confrontation the name Jerubbaal ("let Baal contend") is ascribed to Gideon (Jgs 6:32).

Yet Gideon is a man of inconstant faith, and his desire of further assurance is not rebuked as God graciously and patiently accedes to his requests concerning the dew and the fleece (Jgs 6:36-40). Subsequently Gideon is informed that mere numbers will not assure victory. Moreover, there must be no doubt whatever as to the true source of Israel's liberation (7:2). From 32,000, Gideon's troops are trimmed down to only 300 by an unusual method of reduction (vv 3-7). A secret reconnaissance mission to the outskirts of the oppositions' camp enables Gideon to receive further strengthening as he and his servant Purah overhear a Midianite soldier reveal his dream indicating Israel's imminent victory (vv 13-14). In response to this additional encouragement, he worships the Lord (Jgs 7:15; cf. 6:24).

Divided into three companies, Gideon's army stations itself at night outside the Midianite stronghold. At Gideon's signal each man blows a trumpet (made from an animal's horn) and smashes an empty jar containing a torch, shouting, "A sword for the LORD and for Gideon!" (Jgs 7:20). The effect of the clamor is overwhelming. Thinking themselves outnumbered, the confused and disheartened Midianites flee eastward across the Jordan. In hot pursuit, Gideon's men are joined by Israelites from Naphtali, Asher, and Manasseh, who follow the enemy into the Transjordan area. The men of Ephraim, whose efforts are now called upon for the first time, capture and kill two of the Midianite leaders. Angry with Gideon for failing to enlist their services earlier, the Ephraimites are nonetheless appeased by Gideon's tactful response to their queries (8:1-3).

Gideon's unselfishness shines in response to the people's desire to make him king, but he declines (Jgs 8:22-23). He does, however, receive an immense personal fortune from the spoils of war (vv 24-26). The unfortunate conclusion of Gideon's story relates to his making an ephod from the gold won in battle. Perhaps a garment patterned after the high priest's or a free-standing image, the object ensnares the people, and they worship it at Ophrah (v 27). In 2 Samuel 11:21 Gideon's alternate name, Jerubbaal, becomes Jerubbesheth, "Baal" being replaced with the Hebrew word for "shame" (*besheth*).

Gideon has been singled out in the Letter to the Hebrews as a hero of the faith whose trust in God brought glory to the Lord (Heb 11:32, KJV "Gedeon"). As far back as the time of Isaiah, "the day of Midian" had become proverbial for deliverance accomplished by the hand of God apart from human strength (Is 9:4).

GIDEONI
Abidan's father and leader of Benjamin's tribe when the Israelites were roaming in the Sinai wilderness after their escape from Egypt (Nm 1:11; 2:22; 10:24). As leader, Gideoni presented his tribe's offering at the consecration of the Tabernacle (7:60-65).

GILALAI
Musician present at the dedication of the Jerusalem wall, rebuilt during Ezra's time (Neh 12:36).

GILEAD

1. Makir's son from Manasseh's tribe (Nm 26:29-33) and head of the clan of his descendants (26:29; 27:1) during the time of Moses (36:1).

2. Father of Jephthah during the period of the judges (Jgs 11:1-2). Jephthah was the head of the Gileadites and judge over Israel.

3. Michael's son from Gad's tribe, who lived in Bashan during the initial settlement of Palestine (1 Chr 5:14).

GINATH

Tibni's father. Tibni unsuccessfully attempted to gain the throne of Israel; Omri became king instead (1 Kgs 16:21-22).

GINNETHON

1. Priest who set his seal on Ezra's covenant during the postexilic period (Neh 10:6).

2. Priest and head of Meshullam's household during the postexilic days of Joiakim the high priest (Neh 12:16).

GISHPA

Overseer of the Temple servants in Nehemiah's time (Neh 11:21, KJV "Gispa"); perhaps alternately called Hasupha in Ezra 2:43 and Nehemiah 7:46. *See* Hasupha.

GOD

God is the first person mentioned in the Bible (Ge 1:1). He is the eternal, self-existant being who made everything that exists. Through his revelation God is truly known by faith, yet no creature will ever fully comprehend God the Creator. Likewise, no one will ever fully understand any one of God's attributes. Acknowledgment of God's incomprehensibility should contribute to a spirit of humility in every consideration of God and his attributes (Pss 139:6; 145:3; Is 40:28; 55:8-9; Mt 11:25-27; Rom 11:33-36; 1 Cor 2:6-16; 13:8-13).

The Westminster Shorter Catechism (1647) describes God as "a Spirit, infinite, eternal, and unchangeable in his being, wisdom, power, holiness, justice, goodness and truth." God's *spirituality* indicates that God is not physical

GIDEON
The Times of the Judges

1367–1327 BC
Othniel defeats the Arameans and rules Israel (Judges 3:8-11).

1327–1309 BC
King Eglon of Moab subjects the Israelites (Judges 3:14).

1309–1229 BC
Ehud assassinates Eglon and begins an era of peace for Israel (Judges 3:14-30).

1229–1209 BC
King Jabin of Hazor oppresses Israel (Judges 4:2).

1209–1169 BC
Deborah leads an uprising against Jabin and rules Israel (Judges 4–5).

1169–1162 BC
Midianites take over Israel (Judges 6:1).

1162–1122 BC
Gideon defeats the Midianites with a band of 300 and rules Israel (Judges 6–8).

1122–1119? BC
Gideon's son Abimelech declares himself king and murders his own brothers (Judges 9).

1119–1095? BC
Tola, Jair, Jephthah, Ibzan, Elon, and Abdon rule Israel (Judges 10–12).

1105 BC
Samuel is born (1 Samuel 1:20).

1095–1055 BC
Philistines oppress Israel (Judges 13:1).

1075–1055 BC
Samson fights the Philistines (Judges 13–16).

and is invisible. Positively it means that God is personal, living, self-conscious, and self-determining. The invisible God cannot be seen by human eyes (Ex 33:20), so the second commandment forbids every visible representation of God (20:4). Because God is Spirit, he must be worshiped in spirit and in truth (Jn 4:24).

Also, because God is not visible, he must reveal himself to people if they are to know him. In the Bible, God describes himself and demonstrates his character. According to the Bible, the entire creation shows God's deity and eternal power (Ps 19:1-6; Rom 1:20). More of God's attributes are revealed implicitly in the biblical accounts of Creation, Fall, Flood, Babel, and the Exodus, and more fully in the various covenants God made with his people. To Israel, he identified himself as the God of Abraham, Isaac, and Jacob (Ex 3:15). To the pharaoh, he identified himself as the "God of Israel" or the "God of the Hebrews" (5:1-3).

At Mt Sinai, God himself proclaimed his name, *Yahweh*, (represented by LORD in most Bible translations) and described himself in some concrete terms: "Yahweh! The LORD! The God of compassion and mercy! I am slow to anger and filled with unfailing love and faithfulness. I lavish unfailing love to a thousand generations. I forgive iniquity, rebellion, and sin. But I do not excuse the guilty. I lay the sins of the parents upon their children and grandchildren; the entire family is affected—even children in the third and fourth generations." (Ex 34:6-7, NLT). This summary is repeated elsewhere with slight variations (Nm 14:18; Neh 9:17; Ps 103:8; Jer 32:18; Jon 4:2).

Finally, the fullest revelation of God's person is seen in the person of Jesus Christ (Jn 1:18; Heb 1:2-3). In his life and ministry as well as his death and resurrection, Jesus perfectly displayed the holiness, goodness, and mercy of God because he himself is God (Col 1:15-20).

With the revelation of Jesus as God and the teaching he passed on through his apostles, another aspect of God's person becomes clear: his triune nature. The word "Trinity" is used to describe God as he exists in three persons sharing one essence.

Throughout the Bible, God is presented as being Father, Son, and Holy Spirit—not three "gods" but three personas of the one and only God (see, e.g., Mt 28:19; 1 Cor 16:23-24; 2 Cor 13:13). The Scriptures present the Father as the source of creation, the giver of life, and God of all the universe (see Jn 5:26; 1 Cor 8:6; Eph 3:14-15); the Son as the Messiah-Redeemer (see Phil 2:5-6; Heb 1:1-3); and the Spirit as God in action, reaching people—influencing them, regenerating them, infilling them, and guiding them (see Jn 14:26; 15:26; Gal 4:6; Eph 2:18). All three are a tri-unity, inhabiting one another and working together to accomplish the divine design in the universe (see Jn 16:13-15).

We learn much about God by the different names and titles used for him in Scripture. In the Scriptures the name and person of God are inseparably related. This is in keeping with the biblical conception of what a name signifies.

In the Hebrew language, the term for "name" most probably meant "sign" or "distinctive mark." In the Greek language, "name" *(onoma)* is derived from a verb that means "to know." A name, therefore, indicates that by which a person or object is to be known. But the idea of name is not to be taken in the sense of a label or an arbitrary means of identifying or specifying a person, place, or object. "Name" in biblical usage correctly describes the person, place, or object and indicates the essential character of that to which the name is given. Adam named the animals according to their nature (Gn 2:19-20); Noah means "one who brings relief and comfort" (5:29); Jesus means "savior" (Mt 1:21). When a person was given a new position or a radical change took place in his life, a new name was given to indicate that new aspect—for example, Abraham ("father of many," Gn 17:5), and Israel ("one who strives with God" or "God strives," 32:28). The name of a person or people expressed what the person or people thought the proper description or statement of character was.

With regard to the names of God, there are considerable differences, and these are most clearly seen when biblical scholars and theologians confront the question of whether the names of God are ascriptions given by God concerning himself or they are ascriptions given to God by people who observed his acts and reflected on his character as discerned through a study of divine deeds. Here are some examples of various kinds of divine names:

1. Proper names: El, Yahweh, Adonai, Theos (God), Kurios (Lord).

2. Personal names: Father, Abba, Son, Jesus, Holy Spirit.

3. Titles: Creator, Messiah/Christ, Paraclete/Comforter.

4. Essential names: Light, Love, Spirit.

5. Descriptive names: Rock, Ba'al, Master, Rabboni, Shepherd.
   See also Jesus.

GOG

1. Reubenite, Shemaiah's son (1 Chr 5:4).

2. Individual described as the prince of Meshech who ruled over the land of Magog (Ez 38:2-21; 39:1-16). Magog was evidently a territory located far from Palestine whose inhabitants would attack Jerusalem in a final attempt to overthrow God's people. The Lord, through Ezekiel, promised Gog a catastrophic defeat.

   Attempts to identify Gog with some historical ruler have not been convincing. Gyges of Lydia, who drove out Cimmerian invaders, has been suggested, but equally probable are Gaga, mentioned in the Amarna tablets, and Gagi, king of the city-state of Sabi. Some have maintained a mythological interpretation, in which Gog is a symbol of evil actively opposing good. Certainly Gog—connected in Scripture with godless nations such as Gomer, Put, Persia, Sheba, and Tarshish—is depicted as leading an alliance of world powers in opposition to God. Gog also appears in Revelation (20:7-9), where Satan mobilizes Gog and Magog (i.e., the nations of the world) against God's saints in a final battle. A literal view contemplates an attack on Jerusalem by hostile forces (cf. Zec 14), while a symbolic interpretation envisions a climactic conflict between good and evil.

GOLIATH

Eleventh-century BC Philistine warrior from Gath, who challenged Israel to battle (1 Sm 17).

He was subsequently felled and decapitated by the youthful David. Goliath was over nine feet (2.7 meters) tall, wore armor weighing about 125 pounds (56.8 kilograms), and carried a spear of 15 pounds (6.8 kilograms). His sword, kept at Nob, was later given to David (1 Sm 21:9; 22:10). He may have descended from the Anakim (see Jos 11:22), but his height could have resulted from an anterior pituitary tumor. In 2 Samuel 21:19 his death is attributed to Elhanan, who in 1 Chronicles 20:5 is credited with killing Goliath's brother.

GOMER

1. Son of Japheth, who was a son of Noah (Gn 10:2; cf. 1 Chr 1:5). He had three sons: Ashkenaz, Riphath, and Togarmah (Gn 10:3; 1 Chr 1:6). He is the progenitor of the ancient Cimmerians, who according to Ezekiel's prophecy would join with Gog, the leader of the Magogites, in an effort to stamp out Israel (Ez 38:6).

2. Diblaim's daughter, a prostitute, who then became the wife of Hosea by divine command. Having borne Hosea children, she lapsed into immorality but was redeemed. Her behavior served as an illustration of Israel's infidelity to God (Hos 1–3). See also Hosea.

GUNI

1. Naphtali's son and the grandson of Jacob (Gn 46:24; 1 Chr 7:13).

2. Abdiel's father from Gad's tribe (1 Chr 5:15).

HAAHASHTARI
Naarah's son from Judah's tribe (1 Chr 4:6).

HABAKKUK
Author of the eighth book of the Minor Prophets. The meaning of Habakkuk's name is uncertain. It was probably derived from a Hebrew word meaning "to embrace."

Nothing is known about Habakkuk apart from what can be inferred from his book. Several legends purporting to give accounts of his life are generally regarded as untrustworthy. The apocryphal book Bel and the Dragon describes a miraculous transporting of Habakkuk to Daniel while Daniel was in the den of lions. A Jewish legend makes Habakkuk the son of the Shunammite woman mentioned in 2 Kings 4:8-37. That legend apparently is based on the tradition that she would "embrace" a son. Chronological difficulties make both accounts unlikely.

Habakkuk lived in the period during the rise of the Chaldeans (Hab 1:6), that is, during the reigns of the Judean kings Josiah and Jehoiakim. The dates 612–589 BC delineate the probable period of his prophetic activity.

The book of Habakkuk reveals a man of great sensitivity. His deep concern about injustice and his prayer (Hab 3) show that Habakkuk was characterized by profound religious conviction and social awareness.

HABAZZINIAH
Jaazaniah's grandfather. Jaazaniah was a leader of the Recabites, warriors tested by Jeremiah with regard to their forefather's command not to drink wine (Jer 35:3). They remained loyal to the command, and Jeremiah used their loyalty in an appeal to Judah to be faithful to God.

HACALIAH
Nehemiah's father (Neh 1:1; 10:1).

HADAD
1. Eighth of the 12 sons of Ishmael, and thus a grandson of Abraham (Gn 25:15; 1 Chr 1:30). The KJV reads "Hadar" in Genesis 25:15 and "Hadad" in 1 Chronicles 1:30, whereas RSV and NLT read "Hadad" in both passages.

2. Edomite ruler, son of Bedad, who reigned before the Hebrew captivity in Egypt and who won an important victory over the Midianites in the plain of Moab (Gn 36:35-36; 1 Chr 1:46-47).

3. Another king of Edom, one of the few whose wife, Mehetabel, was mentioned by name. His capital city was Pau (Gn 36:39; 1 Chr 1:50-51).

4. Prince of the royal house of Edom who fled to Egypt after David and Joab conquered Edom and occupied the land. He grew up in Egypt and gained favor with the pharaoh, who gave him his sister-in-law as a wife. Later, when David was dead, he desired to

return to Edom and lead a revolt against Solomon (1 Kgs 11:14-25). Some scholars have identified him with #3 above.

HADADEZER

King of Zobah in Syria during David's reign in Israel. He apparently ruled a region from Ammon in the south to the Euphrates in the east. According to 2 Samuel 8:3-12 (see also 1 Chr 18:3-10, KJV "Hadarezer"), Hadadezer attempted to restore his power. David engaged him in battle at the river Euphrates and defeated him. When the Syrians came to his aid, David defeated them and occupied Damascus. In 2 Samuel 10 David sent servants to comfort Hanun when his father—Nahash, king of Ammon—died. The servants were mistreated and humiliated (v 4). So David sent Joab against Ammon after Ammon allied with Syria as protection against Israel (v 6). Joab defeated the combined armies (vv 15-19; see also 1 Chr 19:16, 19). After Joab's victory, Hadadezer sent more troops from "beyond the river." The armies met at Helam, David was victorious, and Hadadezer begged for peace, thereby becoming a tributary to Israel.

HADAD-RIMMON

Combination of two storm deities, Hadad (mentioned in the Ugaritic texts) and Rimmon (Babylonian storm god). Hadad-rimmon was formerly thought to be a place. The Ras Shamra material equated Hadad with the vegetation god Baal, who was worshiped in an effort to ensure agricultural productivity. Canaanite fertility rituals included periodic mourning for the deceased Baal by the goddess Anat, his consort. It is to that rite that Zechariah 12:11 alludes. The messianic reference in the previous verse likens the grief in Jerusalem to the lamentation for Hadad-rimmon at the rites near Megiddo.

HADASSAH

Original name of Esther (2:7). *See* Esther.

HADLAI

Amasa's father from Ephraim's tribe (2 Chr 28:12). Amasa opposed the taking of prisoners from Judah's tribe after a battle.

HADORAM

1. Joktan's fifth son; Hadoram and his brothers were the sixth generation from Noah (Gn 10:27; 1 Chr 1:21).

2. Alternate spelling of Joram in 1 Chronicles 18:10 (KJV). *See* Joram #1.

3. Alternate spelling of Adoniram in 2 Chronicles 10:18 (KJV). *See* Adoniram.

HAGAB

Ancestor of a family of Temple servants returning with Zerubbabel to Palestine following the Exile (Ezr 2:46).

QUICKTAKE

HAGAR

STRENGTH AND ACCOMPLISHMENT
• Mother of Abraham's first child, Ishmael, who became founder of the Arab nations

WEAKNESSES AND MISTAKES
• When faced with problems, she tended to run away
• Her pregnancy brought out strong feelings of pride and arrogance

LESSONS FROM HER LIFE
• God is faithful to his plan and promises, even when humans complicate the process
• God shows himself as one who knows us and wants to be known by us
• The New Testament uses Hagar as a symbol of those who would pursue favor with God by their own efforts, rather than by trusting in his mercy and forgiveness

VITAL STATISTICS
Where: Canaan and Egypt
Occupation: Servant, mother
Relatives: Son: Ishmael

KEY VERSE
"The angel of the LORD said to her, 'Return to your mistress, and submit to her authority'" (Genesis 16:9).

Hagar's story is told in Genesis 16, 21. She is also mentioned in Galatians 4:24.

HAGABAH

Forefather of a family of Temple servants who returned to Jerusalem with Zerubbabel after the Babylonian exile (Neh 7:48; spelled "Hagabah" in Ezr 2:45).

HAGAR

Egyptian handmaid of Sarai, the wife of Abram. At Sarai's insistence, Abram took Hagar as his concubine, and she became the mother of his son Ishmael (Gn 16:1-16; 21:9-21).

When God commanded Abram to leave Mesopotamia, he promised to make a great nation of him and to give the new land to his seed (Gn 12:2, 7). After ten years in Canaan and still childless, Sarai suggested to Abram that he take Hagar as his concubine and have children by her. It was the custom in northeast Mesopotamia that, when a wife failed to produce an heir for her husband, she could give him a slave for that purpose. Any son born of the union of husband and concubine was considered the child of the wife (cf. 30:1-6).

During her pregnancy, Hagar became disrespectful to Sarai. Sarai dealt so harshly with Hagar that she fled to the desert. An angel of God appeared to her at a well in the desert and told her to return to Abram's house, promising that she would have a son, Ishmael ("God hears"), who would be a wild and quarrelsome man. Hagar then named the place Beerlahairoi, meaning "the well of one who sees and lives."

Ishmael was born when Abram was 86 years old, and 14 years later God gave Abraham and Sarah the promised son, Isaac. At the time of Isaac's weaning (at approximately three years of age), a feast was held. At the weaning feast Ishmael mocked Isaac (Gn 21:9), and Sarah in anger asked Abraham to send Hagar and Ishmael away. Abraham hesitated until God spoke to him and told him to do so (v 12).

Hagar and Ishmael left to wander in the wilderness of Beersheba. When their water was exhausted, God miraculously rescued Hagar and Ishmael from death and assured Hagar that Ishmael would be the father of a great nation (Gn 21:17-19). Ishmael lived in the wilderness of Paran, became a hunter, married an Egyptian, and became the father of the Ishmaelites.

In an allegory developed by Paul (Gal 4:22-31), Hagar represents the old covenant of Sinai. As Ishmael was Abraham's son by human arrangement, the Judaizing Christians who would bind all Christians to the law of Moses are like Hagar's children born in slavery. Sarah, the freewoman, represents the new covenant of Christ. As Isaac was Abraham's son by faith in the divine promise, Christians who are free of the fleshly ordinances of the law are spiritual children of Sarah. The contrast is between salvation by works, which is bondage to the law, and salvation by grace and faith, which is freedom.

See also Abraham; Sarah #1.

HAGGAI
Prophet whose book is the 10th in a series of 12 brief prophetic books concluding the OT. Haggai's name probably came from a word for "festival." We have no information concerning his family or social background. He is referred to merely as Haggai the prophet (Hg 1:1; Ezr 5:1; 6:14). His place in the postexilic community seems to have been a conspicuous one, and according to Jewish tradition, he was known as a prophet in Babylon during the Exile. The major concern of his prophetic ministry was to encourage the people to rebuild the Temple, which had been destroyed during the earlier years of the Exile.

HAGGEDOLIM
Father of Zabdiel, overseer of 128 "mighty men of valor" (RSV) who lived in Jerusalem in Nehemiah's day (Neh 11:14).

HAGGI
Gad's son and founder of the family of Haggites (Gn 46:16; Nm 26:15).

HAGGIAH
Merarite Levite, Shimea's son and the father of Asaiah (1 Chr 6:30).

HAGGITH

One of David's wives and the mother of Adonijah (2 Sm 3:4; 1 Kgs 1:5, 11; 2:13; 1 Chr 3:2). She gave birth to Adonijah in Hebron while David maintained his capital there. In 2 Samuel she and her son are fourth in the list of David's wives and sons.

HAGRI

Mibhar's father, according to 1 Chronicles 11:38. The parallel list in 2 Samuel 23:36, however, has "Bani, the Gadite" instead of "Mibhar, son of Hagri." Due to some textual difficulties in the 1 Chronicles passage, the 2 Samuel reading is preferred.

HAKKATAN

Member of Azgad's family, the father of Johanan, and one of the Exiles who returned to Jerusalem with Ezra (Ezr 8:12).

HAKKOZ

Name borne by a priestly family during the monarchy (1 Chr 24:10). In Ezra's time, the family pedigree could not be documented properly; consequently, the privilege of priestly service was withdrawn (Ezr 2:61; Neh 3:4, 21; 7:63; KJV "Koz").

HAKUPHA

Forefather of a family of Temple assistants who returned to Jerusalem with Zerubbabel after the Exile (Ezr 2:51; Neh 7:53).

HALLOHESH

Shallum's father (Neh 3:12) and one who set his seal on Ezra's covenant (10:24).

HAM

Second son of Noah (Gn 5:32; 6:10; 7:13; 9:18, 22; 10:1, 6, 20). Ham had four sons whose names were Cush, Mizraim (Hebrew for Egypt), Put, and Canaan (Gn 10:6; 1 Chr 1:8). Ham, then, is seen as the ancestor of the Egyptians (though a mixed race apparently occurs later), as well as of peoples in Africa, Arabia, and Canaan.

After the Flood, Noah began cultivating vineyards, and on one occasion exposed himself while drunk (Gn 9:20-24). Ham saw his father lying naked and related the incident to Shem and Japheth, who covered Noah up discreetly. When Noah awoke and learned what "his youngest son" (seen by some as Ham) had done, he cursed Ham's son Canaan, saying his brothers (Cush, Mizraim, and Put) and Shem and Japheth would rule over him. But if Ham is the one referred to in 9:24 as offending Noah, why should the curse fall on his son Canaan? The most likely answer is that Ham is not being referred to in verse 24. The expression is "his youngest son" (the "younger" of the KJV is hardly possible in Hebrew), whereas Ham is repeatedly seen as the second of the brothers, not the youngest (5:32; 6:10; 7:13; 9:18; 10:1), the explicit order of the sons indicating age. Instead, "his youngest son" refers to Canaan, and to some base deed not being recorded, on whom the curse falls. "Son" used for "grandson" is common Semitic material, and it seems to have been used here in this way since Canaan is the "youngest" of the (grand)sons. The curse, then, as the text clearly says, is on Canaan rather than Ham. Canaan (and his posterity) is to be subjugated by Japheth and Shem with the Canaanites, finally disappearing by NT times.

See also Noah #1.

HAMAN

Son of Hammedatha the Agagite, a high official under King Ahasuerus (Xerxes) in Persia during the time of Esther. Haman became angry with Mordecai, the uncle of Esther the queen, because Mordecai would not bow down to him as all others did. In anger he planned to exterminate all the Jews in Persia (Est 3:8). While he was plotting Mordecai's hanging, the king was reading about Mordecai's valuable services. Haman's plot to kill all Jews was revealed, and he went to the gallows made for Mordecai. Haman's ten sons were killed shortly after, and their bodies were strung up as well. In the Hebrew Bible the sons' names are written in a perpendicular manner, supposedly to show their relative positions on the gallows. The carnival atmosphere of the Feast of Purim sometimes resulted in Haman being hanged in effigy, or his name being written on the soles of shoes to express contempt.

See also Esther.

HAMMATH

Ancestor of the house of Rechab (1 Chr 2:55), about whom nothing else is known.

HAMMEDATHA

Father of Haman, a chief adviser to the Persian king Ahasuerus and a sworn enemy of the Jews, according to the book of Esther (3:1, 10; 8:5; 9:10, 24).

HAMMOLEKETH

Machir's daughter and Gilead's sister (1 Chr 7:18).

HAMMUEL

Member of Mishma's family from Simeon's tribe (1 Chr 4:26).

HAMOR

Hivite or Horite prince of the country about Shechem (Gn 34:2), from whom Jacob bought land when returning with his family from Paddan-aram. At this time Hamor's son Shechem committed fornication with Dinah, the daughter of Jacob. At his son's request Hamor asked Jacob for a marriage alliance between Shechem and Dinah, offering a dowry. Simeon and Levi, in pretended friendship, persuaded the males of the city to be circumcised, but then attacked and killed them before they were healed, taking revenge for their sister's humiliation.

"Hamor" is the Hebrew word that Jacob uses to denote Issachar in blessing his sons (Gn 49:14) and is the usual word for "ass" in the OT (e.g., Gn 42:26; Ex 20:17; Jgs 15:15; Is 1:3; Zec 9:9).

HAMUL

Perez's younger son (Gn 46:12; 1 Chr 2:5) and founder of the Hamulite family (Nm 26:21).

HAMUTAL

Daughter of Jeremiah of Libnah, one of King Josiah's wives, and the mother of two kings: Jehoahaz and Zedekiah (2 Kgs 23:31; 24:18; Jer 52:1).

HANAMEL

Shallum's son, from whom Jeremiah bought a field in Anathoth (Jer 32:7-12). This purchase signified that God would restore the nation and that possession of the land would again be possible.

HANAN

1. Shashak's son and one of the chief men of Benjamin (1 Chr 8:23).
2. Azel's son from Benjamin's tribe (1 Chr 8:38; 9:44).
3. Warrior among David's mighty men, who were known as "the thirty" (1 Chr 11:43).
4. Ancestor of a group of Temple assistants who returned to Jerusalem with Zerubbabel after the Exile (Ezr 2:46; Neh 7:49).
5. Levitical assistant who explained to the people passages from the law read by Ezra (Neh 8:7).
6. Levite who signed Ezra's covenant of faithfulness to God with Nehemiah and others after the Exile (Neh 10:10).
7, 8. Two political leaders who signed Ezra's covenant of faithfulness to God with Nehemiah and others after the Exile (Neh 10:22, 26).
9. One of the Levites whom Nehemiah appointed as treasurer over the storehouses (Neh 13:13).
10. Igdaliah's son and head of a prophetic guild occupying the room in the Temple where Jeremiah offered the Rechabites wine to drink (Jer 35:4).

HANANI

1. Seer who rebuked King Asa for giving treasure to Ben-hadad of Syria to persuade him to attack Israel. Hanani was imprisoned for his preaching (2 Chr 16:1-10). Hanani was the father of the prophet Jehu, who made protests against Baasha, king of Israel (1 Kgs 16:1-7), and Jehoshaphat, king of Judah (2 Chr 19:2).
2. Heman's son, David's seer, and a musician in the Temple (1 Chr 25:4, 25).

3. Priest who obeyed Ezra's exhortation to divorce his pagan wife after returning from exile (Ezr 10:20).

4. Brother of Nehemiah who induced him to act on behalf of the Jews when he reported the state of Jerusalem and Judah (Neh 1:2). Hanani was later given responsibility for the city of Jerusalem (7:2).

5. Priest and musician who participated in the dedication of the rebuilt walls of Jerusalem (Neh 12:36).

HANANIAH

1. Zerubbabel's son and a descendant of David (1 Chr 3:19, 21).

2. Benjaminite and the son of Shashak (1 Chr 8:24).

3. Heman's son and the leader of the 16th of 24 divisions of musicians trained for service in the house of the Lord (1 Chr 25:4, 23).

4. One of the commanders of King Uzziah's army (2 Chr 26:11).

5. Bebai's son, who returned with the Exiles from Babylon and was later encouraged by Ezra to divorce his foreign wife (Ezr 10:28).

6. Perfumer who helped Nehemiah rebuild the Jerusalem wall (Neh 3:8).

7. Shelemiah's son, who with Hanun repaired a section of the Jerusalem wall during the days of Nehemiah (Neh 3:30). He is perhaps identical with #6 above.

8. Commander of the citadel of Jerusalem who was assigned by Nehemiah to rule the city jointly with Hanani, Nehemiah's brother. Hananiah, described as a faithful and God-fearing man, was appointed the task of seeing that the city walls and gates were regularly guarded (Neh 7:2-3).

9. One of the leaders of the people who set his seal on the covenant of Ezra (Neh 10:23).

10. Head of the priestly family of Jeremiah during the days of Joiakim, the high priest, in postexilic Jerusalem (Neh 12:12).

11. One of the priests who blew a trumpet at the dedication of the Jerusalem wall during the days of Nehemiah (Neh 12:41).

12. Gibeonite and the son of Azzur. Hananiah prophesied during the fourth year of King Zedekiah of Judah's reign (597–586 BC). He openly declared in the Temple that in two years the Lord would break the yoke of Nebuchadnezzar, king of Babylon (605–562 BC), from the neck of Judah and return its exiles and sacred possessions to Palestine. Told by the Lord that Hananiah's prophecy was false, Jeremiah reproached Hananiah for lying and foretold his imminent death. Hananiah died two months later (Jer 28).

13. Father of Zedekiah, an official of King Jehoiakim of Judah (609–598 BC; Jer 36:12).

14. Grandfather of Irijah, the captain of the guards, who arrested Jeremiah at Jerusalem's Gate of Benjamin for apparently deserting to the Babylonians (Jer 37:13).

QUICKTAKE

HANNAH

STRENGTHS AND ACCOMPLISHMENTS
• Mother of Samuel, Israel's greatest judge
• Fervent in worship; effective in prayer
• Willing to follow through on even a costly commitment

WEAKNESS AND MISTAKE
• Struggled with her sense of self-worth because she was unable to have children

LESSONS FROM HER LIFE
• God hears and answers prayer
• Our children are gifts from God
• God is concerned for the oppressed and afflicted

VITAL STATISTICS
Where: Ephraim
Occupation: Homemaker
Relatives: Husband: Elkanah. Son: Samuel. Later, three other sons and two daughters
Contemporary: Eli the priest

KEY VERSES
"'Sir, do you remember me?' Hannah asked. 'I am the woman who stood here several years ago praying to the LORD. I asked the LORD to give me this boy, and he has granted my request. Now I am giving him to the LORD, and he will belong to the LORD his whole life.' And they worshiped the LORD there" (1 Samuel 1:26-28).

Her story is told in 1 Samuel 1–2.

---

15. One of the three Jewish friends of Daniel exiled in Babylon. He was assigned the Babylonian name Shadrach (Dn 1:6-19; 2:17). *See also* Shadrach, Meshach, and Abednego.

HANNAH

Wife of Elkanah from Ephraim's tribe and the mother of the prophet Samuel. The childless Hannah prayed annually at Shiloh for a son, whom she vowed to dedicate to the Lord.

The Lord answered her prayer, and she called her son Samuel. When he was weaned (probably about age three), she dedicated him at Shiloh to the service of the Lord in the sanctuary. Henceforth, Samuel lived with Eli the priest and was visited by his parents on their annual pilgrimages. Hannah had three more sons and two daughters (1 Sm 1:1–2:21). Her prophetic psalm (1 Sm 2:1-10) anticipates Mary's song of praise, the "Magnificat" (Lk 1:46-55).

HANNIEL

1. Ephod's son and leader of Manasseh's tribe who represented his tribe in apportioning land to Israel under Moses (Nm 34:23).

2. Ulla's son and warrior in the tribe of Asher (1 Chr 7:39).

HANOCH

1. Midian's third son, and grandson of Abraham by Keturah (Gn 25:4; 1 Chr 1:33).

2. Reuben's first son (Gn 46:9; Ex 6:14; 1 Chr 5:3) and ancestor of the Hanochites (Nm 26:5).

HANUN

1. Nahash's son and successor to the Ammonite throne. When King Nahash died, King David of Israel sent messengers to console Hanun and to express his continued friendship. But Hanun insulted David by humiliating his messengers and accusing them of spying. This action led to war and the defeat of Ammon (2 Sm 10:1-14; 11:1; 12:26-31; 1 Chr 19:1–20:3).

2. One who helped repair Jerusalem's Valley Gate during the time of Nehemiah (Neh 3:13).

3. Zalaph's son who repaired a section of the Jerusalem wall during the time of Nehemiah (Neh 3:30); perhaps the same as #2 above.

HAPPIZZEZ

Head of a division of priests whom David assigned to official duties in the Temple (1 Chr 24:15).

HARAN

1. Terah's son, brother of Abraham, and the father of Lot (Gn 11:26-31).

2. Caleb's son by his concubine Ephah, a member of Judah's tribe and the father of Gazez (1 Chr 2:46).

3. Shimei's son, a member of the Gershonite division of Levi's tribe (1 Chr 23:9).

HARBONA

One of King Ahasuerus's seven personal attendants. They were ordered by Ahasuerus to parade Queen Vashti before a drunken banquet to satisfy his vanity (Est 1:10). Harbona later suggested that Haman be hanged on the gallows he had built for Mordecai (7:9).

HAREPH

Caleb's descendant from Judah's tribe and founder (or perhaps father) of Beth-gader (1 Chr 2:51).

HARHAIAH

Father of Uzziel, a goldsmith who worked to rebuild the wall of Jerusalem in Nehemiah's time (Neh 3:8).

HARHAS

Shallum's grandfather. Shallum's wife was Huldah the prophetess (2 Kgs 22:14; spelled "Hasrah" in 2 Chr 34:22), who delivered an oracle for Josiah after the discovery of the Book of the Law by the high priest Hilkiah.

HARHUR

Ancestor of a group of Temple assistants who returned to Jerusalem with Zerubbabel after the Exile (Ezr 2:51; Neh 7:53).

HARIM

1. Priest whom King David appointed to official duties in the Temple (1 Chr 24:8).
2. Ancestor of a Jewish family who returned from the Babylonian exile with Zerubbabel (Ezr 2:32; Neh 10:5). Members of this family were guilty of marrying foreign women (Ezr 10:31), but they divorced their wives and a representative of the clan signed Ezra's covenant (Neh 10:27).
3. Ancestor of a family of priests who returned from the Exile with Zerubbabel (Ezr 2:39; Neh 7:42). Some identify him with #1 above. Members of this family were guilty of marrying foreign women.
4. Ancestor of Malkijah. Malkijah repaired a section of the Jerusalem wall during Nehemiah's time (Neh 3:11). This Harim could be the same as #2 above.
5. Priest who returned from the Exile with Zerubbabel (Neh 12:3; Hebrew "Rehum," see NLT mg). His son (or grandson) Adna is listed as a leading priest during the high priesthood of Joiakim (12:15). Later, under Ezra, a representative of the family (probably related to #3 above) signed the covenant of faithfulness to God (10:5).

HARIPH

Ancestor of a family who returned to Jerusalem with Zerubbabel after the Exile (Neh 7:24). The name Jorah appears in the parallel list of Ezra 2:18. A representative of this family signed Ezra's covenant of faithfulness to God with Nehemiah and others (Neh 10:19).

HARNEPHER

Zophah's son from Asher's tribe (1 Chr 7:36).

HAROEH

Alternate name of Reaiah, Shobal's son, in 1 Chronicles 2:52. *See* Reaiah #1.

HARSHA

Ancestor of a group of Temple assistants who returned to Jerusalem with Zerubbabel after the Exile (Ezr 2:52; Neh 7:54).

HARUM

Aharhel's father from Judah's tribe (1 Chr 4:8).

HARUMAPH

Jedaiah's father. Jedaiah helped repair the wall of Jerusalem during the time of Nehemiah (Neh 3:10).

HARUZ

Maternal grandfather of Amon, king of Judah (2 Kgs 21:19).

HASADIAH

One of Zerubbabel's sons (1 Chr 3:20).

HASHABIAH

1. Ancestor of Ethan, a Levite and descendant of Merari. Ethan was a musician in the Temple during the reign of David (1 Chr 6:45).

2. Ancestor of a group of Levites who helped rebuild the Temple after the Babylonian exile (1 Chr 9:14; Neh 11:15).

3. Jeduthun's son, a Levite and musician in the Temple during the time of David (1 Chr 25:3, 19).

4. Head of a group of Hebronites who was given the position of overseer of Israel west of the Jordan. He was in charge of both political and religious activities (1 Chr 26:30).

5. Kemuel's son, a Levite and head of a household during the reign of David (1 Chr 27:17).

6. Chief of the Levites who participated in the Passover kept by King Josiah in the kingdom of Judah (640–609 BC; 2 Chr 35:9).

7. Merarite Levite who returned to Jerusalem from Babylon with Ezra (Ezr 8:19).

8. Priest who returned to Jerusalem from Babylon with Ezra (Ezr 8:24); perhaps the same person as #7 above.

9. Parosh's son, who obeyed Ezra's exhortation to divorce his pagan wife after the Exile (Ezr 10:25); possibly the same as Asibias (1 Esd 9:26).

10. Ruler over half the district of Keilah (a city of Judah in the Shephelah district of Libnah-mareshah) who participated in rebuilding the Jerusalem wall for his district after the Exile (Neh 3:17).

11. Levite who signed Ezra's covenant of faithfulness to God (Neh 10:11).

12. Ancestor of Uzzi, an overseer of Levites in Jerusalem after the Exile (Neh 11:22).

13. Priest and head of a household in Palestine after the Exile during the time of the high priest Joiakim (Neh 12:21).

14. Chief of the Levites and a Temple musician after the Exile during the time of Joiakim the high priest (Neh 12:24); perhaps the same person as #11 above.

HASHABNAH

One of the leaders who signed Ezra's covenant of faithfulness to God with Nehemiah and others after the Exile (Neh 10:25).

HASHABNEIAH

1. Hattush's father. Hattush assisted in rebuilding the walls of Jerusalem during Nehemiah's day (Neh 3:10).

2. Levite who joined with others in an invocation at the covenant-signing ceremony (Neh 9:5).

HASHBADDANAH

Man, possibly of Levite origin, who stood on Ezra's left when Ezra read the law to the people (Neh 8:4).

HASHUBAH

One of Zerubbabel's sons (1 Chr 3:20).

HASHUM

1. Ancestor of a family who returned from Babylon with Zerubbabel after the Exile (Ezr 2:19; 10:33; Neh 7:22).

2. Israelite who stood to Ezra's left at the reading of the law (Neh 8:4).

3. Leader who signed Ezra's covenant of faithfulness to God with Nehemiah and others after the Exile (Neh 10:18).

HASSENAAH

Alternate name for Senaah in Nehemiah 3:3. *See* Senaah.

HASSENUAH

Ancestor of a Benjaminite family that returned to Judah with Zerubbabel after the Exile

(1 Chr 9:7; Neh 11:9, KJV "Senuah"); perhaps alternately called Senaah (Ezr 2:35; Neh 7:38), and Hassenaah (Neh 3:3). *See* Senaah.

HASSHUB

1. Merari clan leader of Levi's tribe. Hasshub was the father of Shemaiah, a settler in Jerusalem after the return from captivity (1 Chr 9:14; Neh 11:15).
2. Pahath-moab's son, who repaired a section of the Jerusalem wall and the Tower of the Ovens during the time of Nehemiah (Neh 3:11).
3. Another Hasshub who repaired the Jerusalem wall opposite his house (Neh 3:23).
4. Leader who signed Ezra's covenant of faithfulness to God with Nehemiah and others after the Exile (Neh 10:23).

HASSOPHERETH

Ancestor of a family of Temple assistants who returned to Jerusalem with Zerubbabel after the Exile (Ezr 2:55). He is perhaps identifiable with Sophereth in Nehemiah 7:57 (see NLT mg).

HASUPHA

Ancestor of a group of Temple assistants who returned to Jerusalem with Zerubbabel after the Exile (Ezr 2:43; Neh 7:46). He is perhaps the same person as Gishpa in Nehemiah 11:21. *See* Gishpa.

HATHACH

Eunuch appointed by the Persian king Ahasuerus to wait on Esther. Hathach brought Esther messages from Mordecai. In this way Esther learned of Haman's plot against the Jews (Est 4:5-10).

HATHATH

Othniel's son and the grandson of Kenaz (1 Chr 4:13).

HATIPHA

Ancestor of a family of Temple servants who returned to Jerusalem with Zerubbabel after the captivity (Ezr 2:54; Neh 7:56).

HATITA

Ancestor of a family of gatekeepers who returned to Jerusalem with Zerubbabel after the Exile (Ezr 2:42; Neh 7:45).

HATTIL

Forefather of a family of King Soloman's servants who returned to Jerusalem with Zerubbabel after the Exile (Ezr 2:57; Neh 7:59).

HATTUSH

1. Shemaiah's son and a descendant of David (1 Chr 3:22). Hattush returned from the Babylonian exile with Ezra (Ezr 8:3).

2. Son of Hashabneiah, who helped Nehemiah rebuild the walls of Jerusalem (Neh 3:10).

3. Priest who returned from Babylon with Zerubbabel (Neh 12:2). One of his descendants signed Ezra's covenant of faithfulness to God (Neh 10:4). His name is omitted from Nehemiah 12:14 through scribal error.

HAVILAH

1. Descendant of Cush (Gn 10:7; 1 Chr 1:9).

2. Descendant of Shem through Joktan (Gn 10:29; 1 Chr 1:23).

HAZAEL

King of Syria (843?–796? BC) who came to power by assassinating his ruler, Ben-hadad (2 Kgs 8:7-15), and establishing a new dynasty. An inscription of Shalmaneser speaks of Hazael as a "son of a nobody," and mentions that he had "seized the throne." The Hebrew prophet Elijah was told to anoint Hazael as the next king of Syria (1 Kgs 19:15).

Upon becoming king, Hazael continued the policy of Ben-hadad in resisting the Assyrian military influence in Palestine. Although most of Palestine came under Assyrian control in 841 BC, Hazael was able to retain independence by withstanding the siege of Damascus. Failing in a final attempt to subdue Damascus in 837 BC, the Assyrians withdrew. This allowed Hazael the freedom to begin a series of attacks against Israel that resulted in Syrian domination of most of Palestine.

Toward the end of Jehu's reign in Israel, Hazael occupied Israelite territory in the hills of Galilee and east of the Jordan (2 Kgs 10:32). After Jehu's death, the Syrian king continually harassed Israel, captured much of Philistia, and spared Jerusalem only because Joash, king of Judah, asked for peace and was willing to pay heavy tribute (12:17-18). The Syrian oppression continued during the reign of Hazael's son until Adad-nirari III, king of Assyria, marched into Syria, causing Damascus to submit and pay heavy tribute. This took the pressure off Israel and provided opportunity for her to regain territory taken by Hazael (13:24-25).

Archaeologists found the remains of a bed at Arslan Tash (Hadathah) that may have been included in the tribute taken from Damascus. Part of the inscription on a piece of ivory inlay from the bed reads "to our Lord Hazael." Evidently there was a high level of culture in Damascus under Hazael. According to Josephus, Hazael was long remembered for his part in building temples in Damascus.

HAZAIAH

Maaseiah's descendant from Judah's tribe, who was one of the leaders in Jerusalem after the Exile (Neh 11:5).

HAZARMAVETH

Descendant of Shem through Joktan (Gn 10:26; 1 Chr 1:20) whose progeny lived in southern Arabia (Gn 10:30) in the Wadi Hadhramaut. Excavations there revealed a flourishing economy in the fifth century BC, based on frankincense trade. This trade, revived in the second century BC, made the area prosperous and influential.

HAZIEL

Levite and son of Shimei during David's time (1 Chr 23:9).

HAZO

Nahor's fifth son (Gn 22:22); probably used as the name for a Nahorite clan. It has been identified with the name Hazu, which designated a mountainous region in northern Arabia mentioned in an inscription telling of Esarhaddon's Arabian campaign.

HAZZELELPONI

Etam's daughter from Judah's tribe (1 Chr 4:3).

HEBER

1. Descendant of Jacob through Asher and Beriah (Gn 46:17) and father of the family of Heberites (Nm 26:45; 1 Chr 7:31-32).

2. Husband of Jael, the woman who deceptively killed Sisera, known as Heber the Kenite (Jgs 4:11-21; 5:24).

3. Judahite, Mered's son and the father of Soco (1 Chr 4:18).

4. Elpaal's son from Judah's tribe (1 Chr 8:17).

5. KJV spelling for Eber in 1 Chronicles 5:13; 8:22; and Luke 3:35. *See* Eber #1, #2, #4.

HEBRON

1. Third of Kohath's four sons, Hebron was a descendant of Levi (Ex 6:18; Nm 3:19; 1 Chr 6:2, 18; 23:12). Hebron's sons were Jeriah, Amariah, Jahaziel, and Jekameam (1 Chr 23:19). Hebron's descendants were called the Hebronites. They are mentioned in a census taken in the plains of Moab (Nm 26:58). The Hebronites are mentioned in connection with the transfer of the Ark to Jerusalem in David's time (1 Chr 15:9; 26:23, 30-31).

2. Mareshah's son and Korah's father (1 Chr 2:42-43).

HELAH

One of Ashhur's wives who bore him Zereth, Izhar, and Ethnan from Judah's tribe (1 Chr 4:5-7).

HELDAI

1. Baanah's son, described as a Netophathite in the line of Othniel. He appears first as one of David's mighty men (2 Sm 23:29; 1 Chr 11:30, "Heled"). In 1 Chronicles 27:15, he is

called a commander of an army division of 24,000 that served during the 12th month of the year.

2. One of the Exiles returning from Babylon from whom the prophet Zechariah took gold and silver to make a crown for Joshua, the high priest (Zec 6:10).

HELECH

Term mentioned in Ezekiel's prophecy against the city of Tyre (Ez 27:11), perhaps referring to Cilicia or to mercenaries from Cilicia, which was southeast of Asia Minor. Assyrian texts indicate that Cilicia was once called Hilakku, but little is known about the people. They are first mentioned by Shalmaneser III, king of Assyria (854–824 BC), in his conquest of Asia Minor. Their history under the Assyrians was quite violent. Sargon, Sennacherib, and Esarhaddon had to put down revolts from the Hilakku. Later, they gave tribute to Ashurbanipal.

HELED

Alternate name for Heldai, Baanah's son, in 1 Chronicles 11:30. *See* Heldai #1.

HELEK

Gilead's son from Manasseh's tribe (Jos 17:2) and founder of the Helekite family (Nm 26:30).

HELEM

1. Member of Asher's tribe (1 Chr 7:35), called Hotham in verse 32.
2. KJV rendering for Heldai in Zechariah 6:14. *See* Heldai #2.

HELEZ

1. One of David's valiant warriors, called a Paltite in 2 Samuel 23:26 and a Pelonite in 1 Chronicles 11:27. The former is probably correct and refers to a person from Bethpelet. Most scholars think he is the same man as the officer in charge of the seventh course during David's reign (1 Chr 27:10).
2. Jerahmeel's descendant from Judah's tribe (1 Chr 2:39).

HELI

Ancestor of Joseph in Luke's genealogy of Christ (Lk 3:23).

HELKAI

Head of Meraioth's priestly house in the time of Joiakim the high priest (Neh 12:15).

HELON

Father of Eliab, prince of Zebulun's tribe at the taking of the first census (Nm 1:9; 2:7; 7:24, 29; 10:16).

HEMAN

1. Lotan's son, the brother of Hori and a descendant of Seir the Horite (Gn 36:22); alternately spelled Homam in 1 Chronicles 1:39, reflecting a later scribal error.

2. Mahol's son, descendant of Zerah from Judah's tribe and one of the sages whose wisdom was surpassed by King Solomon's (1 Kgs 4:31; 1 Chr 2:6). He is perhaps the Ezrahite and author of Psalm 88.

3. Kohathite Levite, Joel's son and one appointed, along with Asaph and Ethan (also called Jeduthun), by David to lead the musicians in the sanctuary (1 Chr 6:33; 15:17; 16:41). During the transport of the Ark from Obed-edom's house to Jerusalem, he was responsible for sounding the bronze cymbals (1 Chr 15:19; 2 Chr 5:12). Heman fathered 14 sons and 3 daughters, all of whom served as musicians in the Lord's house (1 Chr 25:1-6). Later, his descendants participated in the cleansing of the Temple during King Hezekiah's reign (715–686 BC; 2 Chr 29:14) and assisted with the Passover celebration initiated by King Josiah (640–609 BC; 2 Chr 35:15).

HEMDAN

Dishon's son and a descendant of Seir the Horite (Gn 36:26). He is also called Hamran in 1 Chronicles 1:41 (KJV "Amram").

HENADAD

Head of a Levite family that participated in the rebuilding of the Temple (Ezr 3:9). Members of this family also helped to build the Jerusalem wall (Neh 3:18, 24), and signed Ezra's covenant of faithfulness to God together with Nehemiah (10:9).

HEPHER

1. Manassite and founder of the Hepherite family (Nm 26:32).

2. Ashhur's son from Judah's tribe (1 Chr 4:6).

3. One of David's valiant warriors (1 Chr 11:36).

HEPHZIBAH

1. Mother of Manasseh, king of Judah (2 Kgs 21:1).

2. Symbolic name (KJV) for the restored city of Jerusalem, meaning "my delight is in her" (Is 62:4).

HERESH

Levite who returned to Jerusalem following the Exile (1 Chr 9:15).

HERMAS

Christian to whom Paul sent greetings in his letter to the Romans (Rom 16:14).

HERMES

Christian to whom Paul sent greetings in his letter to Rome (Rom 16:14).

HERMOGENES

Prominent Asian believer who "turned away" from Paul (2 Tm 1:15). His actions may have been the result of doctrinal disagreement but more likely involved his unwillingness to come to Paul's defense during the apostle's second Roman imprisonment for fear of suffering the same fate himself.

HEROD

Name of various political rulers during the lifetime of Christ. Christ was born when Herod the Great was ruling. Herod's son Herod Antipas was the ruler of Galilee and Perea, the territories in which Jesus and John the Baptist carried out most of their ministries. It was this ruler who beheaded John the Baptist and tried Christ just before his death. Herod Agrippa I is the persecutor of the church in Acts 12, and Herod Agrippa II heard Paul's testimony (Acts 26) just before he went to Rome to be tried by Caesar. Without a knowledge of the Herodian family, one can hardly have a proper understanding of the times of Christ.

Preview

- The Herodian Dynasty
- Herod the Great
- Archelaus
- Antipas
- Philip the Tetrarch
- Agrippa I
- Agrippa II

The Herodian Dynasty (67–47 BC)

The Herodian dynasty became prominent during the confusion that resulted in the decay of the Hasmonean dynasty, the transference of Syria and Palestine to Roman rule, and the civil wars that marked the decay of the nation. Much of what we know about the Herods comes from the historian Josephus's writings: *Antiquities of the Jews* and *The Jewish War*.

Herod the Great (47–4 BC)

As Governor of Galilee (47–37 BC)

Herod the Great became governor of Galilee at 25 years of age. Although he gained the respect of both the Romans and the Galilean Jews for quickly capturing and executing the bandit leader Ezekias, some in Hyrcanus's court thought that he was becoming too powerful and arranged to have him brought to trial. He was acquitted and released and

QUICKTAKE

HEROD the GREAT

STRENGTHS AND ACCOMPLISHMENTS
- Was given the title king of the Jews by the Romans
- Held on to his power for more than 30 years
- Was an effective, though ruthless, ruler
- Sponsored a great variety of large building projects

WEAKNESSES AND MISTAKES
- Tended to treat those around him with fear, suspicion, and jealousy
- Had several of his own children and at least one wife killed
- Ordered the killing of the baby boys in Bethlehem
- Although claiming to be a God-worshiper, he was still involved in many forms of pagan religion

LESSONS FROM HIS LIFE
- Great power brings neither peace nor security
- No one can prevent God's plans from being carried out
- Superficial loyalty does not impress people or God

VITAL STATISTICS
Occupation: King of Judea from 37 to 4 BC
Relatives: Father: Antipater. Sons: Archelaus, Antipater, Antipas, Philip, and others. Wives: Doris, Mariamne, and others
Contemporaries: Zechariah, Elizabeth, Mary, Joseph, Mark Antony, Augustus

KEY VERSE
"Herod was furious when he realized that the wise men had outwitted him. He sent soldiers to kill all the boys in and around Bethlehem who were two years old and under, based on the wise men's report of the star's first appearance" (Matthew 2:16).

Herod the Great is mentioned in Matthew 2:1-22 and Luke 1:5.

thereafter fled to Sextus Caesar at Damascus. Sextus Caesar, governor of Syria, appointed Herod governor of Coele-Syria, and thus he became involved with Roman affairs in Syria. He remained in this position under a series of rulers and was successful in collecting taxes and suppressing various revolts. Thus, in 41 BC when Antony came to power under Octavius Caesar, after asking the advice of Hyrcanus II, Sextus appointed Herod and Phasael as tetrarchs of Judea.

As King (37–4 BC)

The reign of Herod is divided by most scholars into three periods: (1) consolidation from 37 to 25 BC; (2) prosperity from 25 to 13 BC; and (3) domestic troubles from 13 to 4 BC.

The period of consolidation extended from his accession as king in 37 BC to the death of the sons of Babas, the last male representatives of the Hasmonean family. During this period, he had to contend with many powerful adversaries.

The first adversaries, the people and the Pharisees, objected to his being an Idumean, a half Jew, and a friend of the Romans. Those who opposed him were punished, and those who took his side were rewarded with favors and honors.

The second adversaries were those of the aristocracy who sided with Antigonus. Herod had executed 45 of the wealthiest and had confiscated their properties to replenish his own coffers.

The third group of adversaries was the Hasmonean family. Herod's chief problem was his mother-in-law, Alexandra. She was upset that he had not appointed another Hasmonean to the high priesthood to replace Hyrcanus, specifically her son Aristobulus. She wrote to Cleopatra, asking her to influence Antony to force Herod to remove the appointed high priest, Ananel, and replace him with Aristobulus. Finally, Herod gave way to the pressure. In the end, after a celebration of the Feast of Tabernacles, Herod had Aristobulus drowned, making it look like an accident. Herod put Alexandra in chains and placed her under guard to keep her from causing him more trouble.

Herod's fourth adversary was Cleopatra. When civil war broke out between Antony and Octavius, Herod wanted to help Antony. But Cleopatra persuaded Antony to set Herod in battle against the Arabian king Malchus, who had failed to pay tribute to her. When she saw Herod winning, she ordered her troops to help Malchus, hoping to weaken both parties to the breaking point so that she could absorb them both. After a catastrophic earthquake in his domain in 31 BC, Herod defeated the Arabs and returned home. Soon after, on September 2, 31 BC, Octavius defeated Antony in the Battle of Actium, resulting in the suicides of Antony and Cleopatra.

The second period of Herod's reign was one of prosperity (25–14 BC). It was a period of splendor and enjoyment interrupted by occasional disturbances. According to Josephus, the most noble of all Herod's achievements was the rebuilding of the Temple in Jerusalem, begun in 20/19 BC (*Antiquities* 15.8.1). Rabbinic literature claims, "He who has not seen the Temple of Herod has never seen a beautiful building" (Babylonian Talmud: *Baba Batra* 4a). Prior to this, he had built theaters, amphitheaters, and racecourses for both men and horses. In 24 BC Herod built himself a royal palace and built or rebuilt many fortresses and gentile temples, including Strato's Tower, later renamed Caesarea.

During this time, he became very interested in culture and gathered around him men accomplished in Greek literature and art. Greek rhetoricians were appointed to the highest offices of the state. One of these was Nicolas of Damascus, Herod's instructor and adviser in philosophy, rhetoric, and history. In late 24 BC he married Mariamne, daughter of Simon, a well-known priest in Jerusalem (she will be referred to as Mariamne II).

During this period, Herod's rule was favorably accepted by the people. They were annoyed, however, by two things. First, he violated Jewish law by his introduction of the quinquennial games in honor of Caesar; and second, he built theaters and racecourses. He demanded a loyalty oath from his subjects, except for a privileged few. Also, he would not allow them to congregate freely for fear of a revolt. Despite these things, he had good control of the people and twice favored them by lowering taxes (in 14 BC he reduced taxes by one-fourth).

The third period of Herod's rule was clearly marked by domestic troubles (13–4 BC). By now he had married ten wives. His first wife, Doris, had only one son, Antipater. He repudiated Doris and Antipater when he married Mariamne I, allowing them to visit Jerusalem only during the festivals. He married Mariamne I in 37 BC. She was the granddaughter of Hyrcanus and had five children, two daughters and three sons. The youngest son died while in Rome, and the remaining two sons were to play an important role in this part of Herod's reign. In late 24 BC he married his third wife, Mariamne II, to whom one child was born, Herod (Philip). Malthace, his fourth wife, was a Samaritan and mother of two sons, Archelaus and Antipas. His fifth wife, Cleopatra of Jerusalem, was the mother of Philip the tetrarch. Of the remaining five wives, only Pallas, Phaedra, and Elpsis are known by name, and none played a significant part in the events of this period.

Alexander and Aristobulus, the sons of Mariamne I, were his favorites. Immediately following their own marriages, troubles began within the Herodian household. Salome, Herod's sister and mother of Berenice (wife of Aristobulus), hated these two sons, mainly because she wanted the position and favor they enjoyed for her own son. Herod decided to recall his exiled son Antipater to show Alexander and Aristobulus there was another heir to the throne. Antipater took full advantage of the situation and used every conceivable means to acquire the coveted throne. Finally, a man of bad character, Eurycles from Lacedaemon, took it upon himself to inflame the father against his two sons and vice versa. Soon other mischief makers joined Eurycles, and Herod's patience became exhausted. He put Alexander and Aristobulus in prison and named Antipater heir.

In his impatience to gain the throne, Antipater attempted to poison Herod. This plot failed when Pheroras, Herod's brother, drank the poison by mistake. Herod put Antipater in prison and reported the matter to the emperor (c. 5 BC). At this time Herod became very ill with an incurable disease. He drew up a new will that bypassed his older sons, Archelaus and Philip, because Antipater had poisoned his mind against them also. He chose his youngest son, Antipas, as his sole successor.

It was during this time that the wise men arrived in Judea, searching for the newborn king of the Jews. Herod instructed them to report to him the whereabouts of this child as soon as they found him. Being warned in a dream, they did not do so, but rather returned to their homes by another route. God warned Joseph (husband of the mother of Jesus) to flee to Egypt because of Herod's intention to kill Jesus. Joseph took his family and left Bethlehem. Shortly after, Herod killed all the male children in Bethlehem who were two years old and under.

Herod's disease grew increasingly worse. Permission came from Rome to execute Antipater, which he promptly did. He again altered his will, making Archelaus king of Judea, Idumea, and Samaria; Antipas tetrarch of Galilee and Perea, and Philip tetrarch of territories east of Galilee. On the fifth day after Antipater's execution, Herod died at Jericho in the spring of 4 BC. The people acclaimed Archelaus as their king.

Archelaus (4 BC–AD 6)

Archelaus was the son of Herod the Great and Malthace (a Samaritan) and was born around 22 BC. Archelaus was faced with a multitude of problems. He had killed 3,000 people in putting down a revolution led by people avenging the blood of those killed by his father, Herod. Thus his rule got off to a bad start. At Pentecost in 4 BC, another revolt broke out, which lasted about two and a half months and during which the Temple porticoes were burned and the treasury was pillaged by the Romans. This unrest spread to the countryside of Judea and to Galilee and Perea.

Archelaus treated both the Jews and the Samaritans brutally (*War* 2.7.3), a fact borne out by the Gospels. When Joseph returned from his flight to Egypt and learned that Archelaus was ruling Judea, he was afraid to go there and was warned against it by God; he took the infant Jesus to Galilee instead (Mt 2:22).

Archelaus's tyranny finally caused the Jews and Samaritans to send a delegation to Rome and complain formally to Augustus. The fact that such bitter enemies as the Jews and Samaritans could cooperate in this matter indicates the serious nature of the complaint. Antipas and Philip also went to Rome to complain about him. Presumably they resented his neglect as their Roman representative for Palestine. Thus in AD 6 Archelaus was deposed and exiled to Vienna in Gaul (modern Vienne on the Rhône, south of Lyons). Antipas and Philip were allowed to continue their respective rules, and Archelaus's territories were reduced to a province ruled by prefects or procurators.

Antipas (4 BC–AD 39)

Antipas was the younger brother of Archelaus, born around 20 BC. Of all the Herodians, he is mentioned most in the NT because he ruled over Galilee and Perea, where both Jesus and John the Baptist concentrated their ministries.

Antipas's domain was in turmoil caused by the rebellion begun at Pentecost in 4 BC. He immediately set out to restore order and rebuild what had been destroyed. Following the example of his father, Herod the Great, Antipas founded cities. Sepphoris was his first project; it was the largest city in Galilee and his capital city until he built Tiberias. Since Nazareth was only four miles (6.4 kilometers) south-southeast of Sepphoris, it is quite possible that Joseph, Mary's husband, was employed as a carpenter (Mt 13:55; Mk 6:3) to help rebuild that city.

Of the 12 cities built by the Herodian family, Tiberias is the most important. It was the first city in Jewish history to be founded with the municipal framework of a Greek *polis*. It was built in honor of the reigning emperor, Tiberius. Due to the fact that a cemetery was destroyed in the process of building, Tiberias was considered unclean by the Jews. Antipas offered free houses, land and tax exemptions for the first few years to anyone who would move into the city. He completed the city in AD 23 and made it his capital.

In the Christian world the incident for which Antipas is most remembered is his beheading of John the Baptist (Mt 14:3-12; Mk 6:17-29; Lk 3:19-20; *Antiquities* 18.5.2.116-119). There was a tangle of family events leading up to the death of John the Baptist. Antipas had married the daughter of Aretas IV (the daughter's name is unknown). Aretas IV was the Nabatean king, and Augustus may have encouraged this marriage since he favored intermarriages between various rulers to promote peace in his empire.

Around AD 29 Antipas took a trip to Rome, and on the way he paid a visit to his half brother Herod Philip, who must have lived in a coastal city in Palestine. Antipas fell in love with Herodias, Philip's wife, who was also Antipas's niece. The idea of becoming the wife of a tetrarch appealed to her, and she agreed to marry him when he returned from Rome if he would oust Aretas's daughter. Antipas agreed to the plan, and when Aretas's daughter heard of it, she fled to her father. This was a breach of political alliance as well as a personal insult, which led to retaliation by Aretas.

The marriage of Antipas and Herodias was in violation of the Mosaic law that forbade marriage to a brother's wife (Lv 18:16; 20:21) except in order to raise children for a deceased childless brother by a levirate marriage (Dt 25:5; Mk 12:19). In this case, Philip not only had a child, Salome, but he was still alive. This is the situation that John the Baptist spoke so boldly against, and Antipas threw him in prison. Herodias's hatred of John the Baptist was too great merely to settle for his incarceration. At an appropriate time, possibly Antipas's birthday, she planned a banquet at Machaerus in Perea. Her daughter, Salome, danced for the king, and in an impulsive moment Antipas promised her under oath that he would give her anything, up to half of his kingdom. Following her mother's advice, she asked for John the Baptist's head on a platter. Immediately Antipas was sorry for his rash promise, but in order to save face in the presence of his underlords, he granted the request. Thus, John's ministry ended around AD 31 or 32.

There are three specific times when Antipas and Jesus are mentioned together in the Gospels.

Early in Jesus' ministry Antipas heard of him and commented, perhaps with irony, that Jesus was John the Baptist resurrected (Mt 14:1-2; Mk 6:14-16; Lk 9:7-9). It was obvious to Antipas that Jesus' ministry was even more remarkable than John's, but he was reluctant to use force to bring about the meeting for fear of once more arousing the people against him. Eventually, Jesus withdrew from Antipas's territories without the two meeting.

Later, as Jesus became more popular, Antipas saw a potential threat to his own power and threatened to kill Jesus. Thus it was that on Jesus' final trip to Jerusalem he was warned by some of the Pharisees that he should leave Antipas's territories for his own safety (Lk 13:31-33). Jesus sent as answer to "that fox" that he would continue his ministry of healing and casting out demons for a little longer, and when he had finished, he would then go to Jerusalem to die. The lion and fox were often contrasted in ancient literature. The Lion of Judah, Jesus Christ, was not going to be coerced by the crafty coward, Antipas.

The final encounter between the two occurred when Jesus was tried by Antipas in AD 33 (Lk 23:6-12). Since this event is mentioned only by Luke, some scholars consider it legendary. It must be remembered, however, that Luke's addressee was Theophilus, probably a Roman officer, who would be especially interested in the reconciliation between Pilate and Antipas mentioned in this passage.

According to Luke's account, when Pilate could find no fault in Jesus, he sent him to Antipas (who was celebrating the Passover in Jerusalem). Pilate thus freed himself from an awkward situation. A more subtle reason may have been to reconcile himself to Antipas. Their relationship had been rather strained since the Galilean massacre (Lk 13:1), and because Pilate brought votive shields into Jerusalem, arousing the anger of the Jews (Philo's *Legatio ad Gaium* 299–304). When Jesus was brought before Antipas, the ruler only mocked him and sent him back to Pilate. The main political accomplishment of the incident was Antipas and Pilate's reconciliation.

Philip the Tetrarch (4 BC–AD 34)

Philip the tetrarch was the son of Herod the Great and Cleopatra of Jerusalem and was born around 22 BC. When Herod's will was resolved, Philip was made tetrarch over Gaulanitis, Auranitis, Batanea, Trachonitis, and Iturea, all in the northern part of Herod the Great's domain (Lk 3:1). His subjects were mainly Syrian and Greek. Thus he was the first and only Herodian to have his image on his coins.

He built two cities. First, he rebuilt and enlarged Paneas and renamed it Caesarea Philippi. Here Peter made his confession of faith to Jesus and was given the revelation of the church (Mt 16:13-20; Mk 8:27-30). Next, he rebuilt and enlarged Bethsaida and renamed it Julias. Here Jesus healed the blind man (Mk 8:22-26), and in a nearby desert place he fed the 5,000 (Lk 9:10-17).

Philip was not as politically ambitious as his brothers. His rule was marked by tranquility and the loyalty of his subjects. When Philip died in AD 34, Tiberius annexed his territories to Syria. After Caligula became emperor in AD 37, he gave the territories to Agrippa I, brother of Herodias.

Agrippa I (AD 37–44)

Agrippa I was the son of Aristobulus (son of Herod the Great and Mariamne I) and Berenice. He was born in 10 BC and was the brother of Herodias.

Agrippa I might be considered the black sheep of the Herodian family. While at school in Rome, he lived a wanton life, incurring many debts. In Rome he became a friend of Gaius Caligula and at one point stated that he wished Caligula were king rather than Tiberius. This was overheard and reported to Tiberius, who imprisoned him. He remained in prison until Tiberius's death six months later.

Upon Caligula's accession to the throne, he released Agrippa and gave him Philip the

Tetrarch's territories and the northern part of Lysanias's territory as well as the title of king. The title of king aroused the jealousy of his sister Herodias, and that eventually led to her husband, Antipas's, downfall. At that time (AD 39) Agrippa acquired all of Antipas's territories and property.

When Caligula died in AD 41, Agrippa curried the favor of the new emperor Claudius, whereupon Claudius added Judea and Samaria to Agrippa's territory. This territory was once ruled by Agrippa's grandfather, Herod the Great.

Agrippa I is mentioned in the NT for his persecution of the early church in order to gain favor with the Jews (Acts 12:1-19). He killed James, the son of Zebedee, and imprisoned Peter. When Peter was released by an angel, Agrippa put the sentries to death.

Agrippa died in AD 44 in Caesarea. Accounts of this incident are recorded both by Josephus (*Antiquities* 19.9.1.274–275; *War* 2.11.5.214–215) and the Scriptures. The incident occurred at Caesarea; he was wearing a sparkling silver robe, and when the people flattered him by calling him a god, he was suddenly struck with a mortal illness and died a horrible death. He was survived by his daughters, Bernice, Mariamne, and Drusilla, and by a son, Agrippa, who was 17 at the time. Because of Agrippa II's youth, his father's territories were temporarily made a province.

Agrippa II (AD 50–100)

Agrippa II was the son of Agrippa I and Cypros. In AD 50, six years after his father's death, Claudius made him king of Chalcis.

Agrippa II was in control of the Temple treasury and the vestments of the high priest and thus could appoint the high priest. The Romans consulted him on religious matters, which is probably why Festus asked him to hear the apostle Paul at Caesarea (AD 59), where he was accompanied by his sister Bernice (Acts 25–26).

In May AD 66 the Palestinian revolution began (*War* 2.14.4.284). When Agrippa's attempt to quell the revolt failed, he became a staunch ally of the Romans throughout the entire war (AD 66–70). During this time, Nero committed suicide, the new emperor Galba was murdered, and Vespasian became the emperor. After pledging his allegiance to the new emperor, Agrippa remained with Titus, Vespasian's son, who was in charge of the war (Tacitus's *History* 5.81). After the fall of Jerusalem (August 6, AD 70), Agrippa was probably present to celebrate the destruction of his own people.

Following this, Vespasian added new territories to Agrippa's kingdom, though just which ones is not known. In AD 79 Vespasian died and Titus became emperor. Little is known of Agrippa's rule after this, except that he wrote to the historian Josephus praising him for *The Jewish War*, and he purchased a copy of it (Josephus's *Life* 65.361–367; *Apion* 1.9.47–52).

Although the Talmud implies that Agrippa II had two wives (Babylonian Talmud: *Sukkah* 27a), Josephus gives no indication that he had any wives or children. Rather, he was known for his incestuous relationship with his sister Bernice. He died around AD 100. His death marked the end of the Herodian dynasty.

HERODIAS

Daughter of Aristobulus, the son of Herod the Great, and Berenice. Born between 9 and 7 BC, her older brother was Herod Agrippa I. In 6 BC, while still in her infancy, she was betrothed by her grandfather, Herod the Great, to his son by Mariamne II named Herod Philip. Herodias was the mother of Salome, born between AD 15 and 19.

Herodias and Herod Philip lived on the seacoast of Judea, possibly at Azotus or Caesarea. In AD 29 Herod Antipas visited Herodias's (his niece) residence on his way to Rome. They were attracted to each other and Herodias agreed to marry him provided he would divorce his present wife, the daughter of Aretas IV, the Nebatean king of Petra. Herodias, being a Hasmonean, did not want to share the house with an Arab—longtime foes of the Hasmonean dynasty. When Aretas's daughter got word of this plot, she secretly escaped to her father, and Herodias and Antipas were married. This incident was the beginning of hostilities between Antipas and Aretas, which eventually led to Aretas's war against and defeat of Antipas in AD 36.

John the Baptist openly denounced this marriage (Mt 14:3-12; Mk 6:17-29; Lk 3:19-20) because Jewish law forbade marriage with one's brother's wife (Lv 18:16; 20:21), except in order to raise children for a deceased childless brother by a levirate marriage (Dt 25:5; Mk 12:19). In this case the brother, Herod Philip, was still alive and had a child, Salome. The bold denunciation by John the Baptist led to Antipas's imprisoning him around AD 30 or 31. Herodias wanted more than this. She arranged, possibly at Herod Antipas's birthday, to have her daughter dance before him and his magistrates. In appreciation, Herod Antipas promised Salome up to half of his kingdom. At her mother's bidding, she asked for John the Baptist's head on a platter.

Herodias last appears in history involved in an intrigue between her brother, Agrippa I, who had been designated king by the emperor Caligula, and her husband Antipas, who had long wanted such a title. Antipas, at his wife's insistence, went to Rome to plead his case, but he lost and was banished. Herodias, however, did remain faithful and followed him into exile, even though Caligula would not have punished her because she was Agrippa's sister.

See also Herod.

HERODION

Christian of Jewish ancestry to whom Paul sent greetings at the conclusion of his Epistle to the Romans (Rom 16:11).

HEZEKIAH

1. King of Judah from 715–686 BC. The account of Hezekiah's reign is in 2 Kings 18:1–20:21, 2 Chronicles 29:1–32:33, and Isaiah 36:1–39:8.

   Chronology Hezekiah succeeded to Judah's throne at 25 and ruled for 29 years (2 Kgs 18:2; 2 Chr 29:1). His mother was Abi (2 Kgs 18:2; 2 Chr 29:1; "Abijah," a longer

QUICKTAKE

HEZEKIAH

STRENGTHS AND ACCOMPLISHMENTS
- Was the king of Judah who instigated civil and religious reforms
- Had a personal, growing relationship with God
- Developed a powerful prayer life
- Noted as the patron of several chapters in the book of Proverbs (Proverbs 25:1)

WEAKNESSES AND MISTAKES
- Showed little interest or wisdom in planning for the future and protecting for others the spiritual heritage he enjoyed
- Rashly showed all his wealth to messengers from Babylon

LESSONS FROM HIS LIFE
- Sweeping reforms are short-lived when little action is taken to preserve them for the future
- Past obedience to God does not remove the possibility of present disobedience
- Complete dependence on God yields amazing results

VITAL STATISTICS
Where: Jerusalem
Occupation: 13th king of Judah, the southern kingdom
Relatives: Father: Ahaz. Mother: Abijah. Son: Manasseh
Contemporaries: Isaiah, Hoshea, Micah, Sennacherib

KEY VERSES
"Hezekiah trusted in the LORD, the God of Israel. There was no one like him among all the kings of Judah, either before or after his time. He remained faithful to the LORD in everything, and he carefully obeyed all the commands the LORD had given Moses" (2 Kings 18:5, 6).

Hezekiah's story is told in 2 Kings 16:20–20:21; 2 Chronicles 28:27–32:33; Isaiah 36:1–39:8. He is also mentioned in Proverbs 25:1; Isaiah 1:1; Jeremiah 15:4; 26:18, 19; Hosea 1:1; Micah 1:1.

form), a daughter of Zechariah. The chronology of Hezekiah's reign is difficult to establish with certainty. The Bible says the Assyrian siege of Samaria, capital of the northern kingdom of Israel, began in the fourth year of his reign and that Samaria fell in the sixth year (2 Kgs 18:9-10), which would make his reign begin about 728 BC and end about 699 BC. Assyrian king Sennacherib besieged the fortified Judean cities during Hezekiah's 14th year (2 Kgs 18:13), which would have been 714 BC. Assyrian records, however, indicate that Sennacherib came to the Assyrian throne in 705 BC and that his Judean campaign took place in 701 BC. The most generally accepted solution to the discrepancy is that Hezekiah came to the throne in 715 BC, probably after a co-regency with his father, Ahaz, that began in 728 BC. That solution harmonizes with the statement that Sennacherib's siege took place in the 14th year of Hezekiah's reign, or 701 BC.

Hezekiah's Religious Reforms Hezekiah came to the throne at a critical juncture in Judah's history. Sargon II had taken Samaria in 722 BC, and Judah was militarily weakened from wars and raids by surrounding nations during the reign of Ahaz. Perhaps motivated by warnings to the northern kingdom delivered by the prophets Amos and Hosea that punishment would come if Israel did not turn back to God, Hezekiah began his religious reforms soon after becoming king.

In the first month of his reign, Hezekiah opened the Temple doors and repaired them. He brought the Levites together and ordered them to sanctify themselves and the Temple and to reinstate the religious ceremonies that had long been neglected. Hezekiah brought sacrifices, and the priestly Temple service was restored (2 Chr 29).

Hezekiah then sent invitations throughout Judah and Israel for the Passover celebration in Jerusalem (held a month later than the prescribed time because the priests and people could not be ready earlier). It was hoped that religious unification would be a prelude to political reunification of the northern kingdom of Israel and the southern kingdom of Judah. However, most of the northern tribes mocked the Judean messengers who brought the invitations, and only a few persons from the tribes of Asher, Manasseh, and Zebulun went to Jerusalem for the celebration (2 Chr 30).

After the Passover observance, the worshipers set about destroying the high places and altars. They broke the pillars and cut down the Asherim throughout Judah and Benjamin, and also went into Ephraim and Manasseh (2 Chr 31:1). Hezekiah even smashed the bronze serpent that Moses had made (Nm 21:6-9), for it had become an object of worship and was identified with a serpent deity, Nehushtan (2 Kgs 18:4). Because of his sweeping reforms, later generations said of Hezekiah, "There was never another king like him in the land of Judah, either before or after his time" (2 Kgs 18:5, NLT).

The Assyrian Threat Hezekiah knew that Assyria's growing international dominance was a serious threat to his kingdom, but following his father's policy of submission, Hezekiah did not attempt any resistance at first.

The inscriptions of the Assyrian king Sargon II record his victorious campaign in 711 BC against a revolt by Aziru, king of Ashdod, who requested help from Egypt and Judah. Perhaps a prophecy received by Isaiah warned Hezekiah not to interfere with the Ashdod siege (Is 20), and so no punitive action was taken against Judah by Assyria. Sargon died in 705, and his son Sennacherib came to the throne. This triggered widespread rebellion throughout the Assyrian provinces. Hezekiah withheld tribute from the new Assyrian ruler and, taking advantage of the confused situation, made raids against the Philistines (2 Kgs 18:8). After subduing rebellious elements in the East, Sennacherib began his campaign against the "land of Hatti" (the Assyrian name for the western countries) in 701 BC. In preparation Hezekiah repaired Jerusalem's city wall, raised towers on it, built another wall outside it, and strengthened the Millo in the City of David. He also stockpiled abundant quantities of weapons and shields (2 Chr 32:5). Knowing the necessity of an adequate water supply for a city under siege, Hezekiah had a 1,777-foot (542-meter) tunnel cut through solid rock from the spring of Gihon to the Siloam Pool to bring water into the city and to prevent the Assyrians from gaining access to the spring water outside the city (2 Kgs 20:20; 2 Chr 32:3-4). The Siloam inscription, carved inside the tunnel itself, records the completion of that remarkable conduit and is one of the oldest preserved examples of the Hebrew language.

Sennacherib invaded Palestine and, after an extensive campaign, put down the rebellion there. That campaign is well documented in Assyrian records, including a description of his siege on Jerusalem in 701, and this documentation is supplemented by the biblical account (2 Kgs 18:13–19:37; 2 Chr 32:1-22; Is 36–37). Sidon, the cities of Phoenicia, and the immediate neighbors of Judah (including Byblos, Arnon, Moab, Edom, and Ashdod) submitted to the Assyrians. Resistant Philistine cities were also taken. Sennacherib laid siege against Ekron, whose king, Padi (a loyal subject of Sennacherib), had been taken prisoner by his own subjects and turned over in chains to Hezekiah. A large Egyptian and Ethiopian army failed to relieve the Ekronites, who were defeated by the Assyrians in the vicinity of Eltekah. Ekron was captured, and Padi was recalled to his throne by Sennacherib.

Sennacherib then turned his attention to the fortified cities of Judah and took them one by one (2 Kgs 18:13). Assyrian records claim that he captured 46 walled cities and countless villages, including Lachish and Debir (southwest of Jerusalem), 200,150 people, homes, cattle, and flocks without number. While Lachish was still under siege, Hezekiah saw that it was hopeless to resist and sent word to Sennacherib offering to surrender and pay whatever tribute he would impose. The Assyrian ruler demanded an enormous tribute of 300 talents of silver (800 talents according to Assyrian records, either an exaggerated figure or computed by a different standard) and 30 talents of gold. In order to pay that tribute, Hezekiah took all the silver in the Temple and the royal treasuries, and stripped the gold from the Temple doors and doorposts (2 Kgs 18:14-16). This treasure was sent to Sennacherib along with other gifts that, according to the Assyrian account, included some of Hezekiah's own daughters as concubines.

The account in 2 Kings 18:17–19:37 raises the question of whether there was another invasion of Judah at a later date, or whether this passage gives additional details about the invasion of 701. Although Hezekiah had already submitted and paid tribute, these verses describe further Assyrian demands. Those who believe it was a single invasion suggest that this is an account of the Assyrian deputation sent by Sennacherib to demand Jerusalem's surrender while Lachish was still under siege. The deputation included the Tartan, Rabsaris, and Rabshakeh (titles of court officials rather than personal names). They warned the citizens that their God was no more able to save them than the gods of other cities defeated by the Assyrians. In distress Hezekiah sent word to the prophet Isaiah, who assured the king that Sennacherib would hear a rumor and return to his own land and there die by the sword (2 Kgs 19:1-7). Shortly afterward Sennacherib received word of Babylon's revolt in his eastern provinces, so he departed at once without taking Jerusalem. Assyrian records do not claim that Jerusalem was taken but only say that Hezekiah was "shut up in Jerusalem like a bird in a cage." Judah's surrounding neighbors celebrated their deliverance and brought gifts of gratitude to Hezekiah (2 Chr 32:23).

Later, the Assyrian king heard that Tirhakah, king of Ethiopia, was advancing against him, so he sent another threatening message to Hezekiah, probably to warn him against making an alliance with Tirhakah. Hezekiah took the matter before the Lord and received word from Isaiah that the Assyrian king would return the same way he came and that Jerusalem would be untouched. Soon afterward, in a miraculous intervention by God, 185,000 Assyrian troops were killed, and the Assyrian monarch abandoned his plans to conquer Hezekiah. That embarrassing calamity understandably is not mentioned by the Assyrian records. In 681 Sennacherib was killed by two of his sons as Isaiah had predicted (2 Kgs 19:7, 37).

Sometime prior to 701, Hezekiah became seriously ill, and Isaiah told him to prepare for death. The king earnestly prayed for an extension of life, and God promised him 15 more years as well as deliverance from the Assyrians. Hezekiah asked Isaiah for a sign that he would be healed, and a shadow cast by the sun moved backward 10 steps contrary to its normal direction (2 Kgs 20:1-11).

Sometime after his recovery Hezekiah received a delegation with presents from Merodach-baladan of Babylon, ostensibly to congratulate Hezekiah on his return to health. The real object of the visit was probably to enlist Hezekiah as an ally in a conspiracy being formed against Assyria. The king showed the Babylonian envoys all the gold, silver, and other valuables he possessed. This act brought a warning from Isaiah that the day would come when all those treasures would be carried away to Babylon (2 Kgs 20:12-19).

Hezekiah lived the remainder of his life in peace and prosperity. It may have been during this time that he encouraged literary efforts in Judah, which included copying some of Solomon's proverbs (Prv 25–29). Upon his death in 686, he was succeeded by his son Manasseh, who probably had become co-regent 10 years earlier.

2. KJV form of Hizkiah, Neariah's son, in 1 Chronicles 3:23. *See* Hizkiah #1.

3. Head of a family of exiles (the sons of Ater), 98 of whose descendants returned from the Babylonian exile with Zerubbabel (Ezr 2:16; Neh 7:21; 10:17).

4. Ancestor of the prophet Zephaniah, possibly King Hezekiah himself (Zep 1:1).

HEZION
Tabrimmon's father and the grandfather of Ben-hadad, king of Syria. Ben-hadad formed an alliance with King Asa of Judah (910–869 BC) and opposed Israel's King Baasha (908–886 BC; 1 Kgs 15:18).

HEZIR
1. Levite and head of the 17th of 24 divisions of priests for sanctuary service formed during David's reign (1 Chr 24:15).

2. Israelite leader who set his seal on Ezra's covenant during the postexilic era (Neh 10:20).

HEZRO
One of David's mighty warriors (2 Sm 23:35; 1 Chr 11:37), a Carmelite by birth.

HEZRON
1. Reuben's son (Gn 46:9; Ex 6:14; 1 Chr 5:3) and founder of the Hezronite family in Reuben's tribe (Nm 26:6).

2. Perez's son (Gn 46:12; Ru 4:18-19; 1 Chr 2:5-25; 4:1), founder of the Hezronite family in Judah's tribe (Nm 26:21), and an ancestor of Jesus Christ (Mt 1:3; Lk 3:33).

HIEL
Bethelite in the days of King Ahab who fulfilled Joshua's curse upon the city of Jericho (Jos 6:26; 1 Kgs 16:34). Joshua had said centuries before that anyone attempting to rebuild the city would suffer the loss of his oldest and youngest sons. It is unclear whether Hiel's sons died a natural death or were killed in a punitive ritual.

HILKIAH
1. Father of Eliakim, an overseer in King Hezekiah's household (2 Kgs 18:18, 26; Is 22:20; 36:3, 22).

2. High priest and Shallum's son in the reign of King Josiah who, during the repair of the Temple, found the Book of the Law (2 Kgs 22:3-14; 1 Chr 6:13; 9:11; 2 Chr 34:14-22). According to Ezra 7:1 (cf. 1 Esd 8:1), he was also an ancestor of Ezra. He is an important figure in the events surrounding Josiah's religious reform, not only because he found the Book of the Law, but also because he led the king's messengers to consult Huldah the prophetess regarding God's Word (2 Kgs 22:14) and later presided over the purification of the Temple (23:4).

3. Merarite Levite, the son of Amzi and Amaziah's father (1 Chr 6:45).

4. Merarite Levite and Hosah's son, who was appointed as a gatekeeper in the Temple by David (1 Chr 26:11).

5. Companion of Ezra at the public reading of the law (Neh 8:4). Scholars disagree as to whether he was a layman or a priest.

6. Priest among the returned exiles (Neh 12:7).

7. Anathoth priest who was the father of Jeremiah (Jer 1:1).

8. Father of Gemariah whom King Zedekiah sent to Babylon with a letter of assurance from Jeremiah (Jer 29:3).

HILLEL
Father of Abdon, one of the judges (Jgs 12:13-15).

HIRAH
Adullamite and friend of Judah to whose house Judah went after he and his brothers sold Joseph (Gn 38:1). He accompanied Judah to the sheepshearing after Judah's wife died (v 12), and he served as the messenger to carry a kid from Judah to Tamar (v 20).

HIRAM
1. King of Tyre during the time of David and Solomon. After David had conquered Jerusalem and moved his capital there, Hiram sent cedarwood, masons, and carpenters to build David's palace (2 Sm 5:11; 1 Chr 14:1). Hiram remained David's friend throughout his life (1 Kgs 5:1), and after David's death, he sought to continue that friendship with Solomon. When Solomon was ready to build the Temple, Hiram provided wood from the forests of Lebanon, gold, and skilled craftsmen to help build and furnish the Temple; Solomon, in return, gave Hiram wheat and oil for his household. Moreover, Solomon gave Hiram 20 cities in Galilee, although Scripture indicates that Hiram was not pleased with them (1 Kgs 5:1-11; 9:10-14).

    Although the Israelites were not a maritime people, Solomon did maintain a fleet of ships at Ezion-geber (1 Kgs 9:26-28). Hiram gave his assistance to Solomon by supplying sailors and perhaps ships to make Solomon's fleet operable. The Phoenicians were noted sailors, who sailed the Mediterranean Sea as far west as Tarshish in Spain.

    Hiram was probably the son of Abibal. Hiram reigned in Tyre for 34 years and died at the age of 53. Phoenician historians record that Solomon married the daughter of Hiram.

2. Craftsman from Tyre who worked on Solomon's Temple. He was said to be the son of a man of Tyre and a woman from the tribe of Naphtali (1 Kgs 7:13-14), although 2 Chronicles 2:14 says that his mother was from "the daughters of Dan." (Possibly

her ancestors were from Dan's tribe; cf. Ex 38:23.) He was responsible for the creation of various furnishings in the Temple: 2 bronze pillars, the capitals that adorned the pillars, the molten sea and the 12 oxen on which it stood, the 10 lavers with their bases, as well as shovels, pots, and basins.

His name is also spelled Huram in 2 Chronicles 4:11. He is called Huram-abi (abi meaning "master") in 2 Chronicles 2:13 and 4:16.

HIZKI
Elpaal's son from Benjamin's tribe (1 Chr 8:17).

HIZKIAH
1. Neariah's son and a descendant of David through Rehoboam's line (1 Chr 3:23). *See* Hezekiah #2.

2. KJV spelling of Hezekiah, Zephaniah's forefather, in Zephaniah 1:1. *See* Hezekiah #4.

HOBAB
Name associated with Moses' father-in-law (Nm 10:29; Jgs 4:11, NLT mg), who was a priest of Midian (Ex 18:1) and ancestor of the Kenites (Jgs 4:11). He is usually called Jethro (Ex 3:1; 4:18; 18:1-12), but also Reuel (Ex 2:18).

The confusion surrounding the name Hobab has never been satisfactorily resolved. Judges 4:11 seems to identify Hobab with Jethro; there is some manuscript evidence for adding "Hobab" to "the Kenite, Moses' father-in-law" in Judges 1:16, and to the mention of Reuel in Exodus 2:18. But Hobab could be Jethro's son, on one reading of Numbers 10:29a: "Hobab the son of Reuel the Midianite, Moses' father-in-law." In this passage Moses requests that Hobab accompany Israel as guide and adviser in the wilderness.

See also Jethro.

HOBAIAH
Head of a priestly family who returned to Palestine with Zerubbabel after the Exile. He was unable to prove his priestly genealogy and so was not allowed to do priestly service (Ezr 2:61; Neh 7:63).

HOD
Zophah's son from Asher's tribe (1 Chr 7:37).

HODAVIAH
1. Postexilic descendant of David (1 Chr 3:24).

2. Chieftain of Manasseh's half-tribe east of the Jordan (1 Chr 5:24).

3. Hassenuah's son and the father of Meshullam from Benjamin's tribe (1 Chr 9:7).

4. Progenitor of a family of Levites who returned with the Exiles from Babylon (Ezr 2:40); alternately called Judah in Ezra 3:9 and Hodevah in Nehemiah 7:43.

HODESH

Name given to Shaharaim's wife from Benjamin's tribe in 1 Chronicles 8:9 (a textually corrupt passage).

HODIAH

1. A man of Judah mentioned in 1 Chronicles 4:19.

2, 3, 4. Three of the men who signed the covenant of Ezra (Neh 10:10, 13, 18) bear this name; two of them are perhaps among those who interpreted the covenant to the people at Ezra's public reading of the law (8:7) and stood upon the stairs of the Levites during the service of covenant renewal (9:5).

HOGLAH

One of Zelophehad's five daughters (Nm 26:33; 27:1; Jos 17:3). Zelophehad, who was of Manasseh's tribe, had no sons, so that his inheritance passed to his daughters. They married within their own tribe according to God's command, so that their land remained in the tribe of the family of their father (Nm 36:11-12).

HOHAM

Amorite king of Hebron, confederate with four other kings in reprisals against Gibeon for making peace with Joshua (Jos 10:3). They were defeated and put to death at the cave of Makkedah (vv 16-27).

HOPHNI

Brother of Phinehas, with whom he served as a priest at Shiloh (1 Sm 1:3). He was an evil man who flouted the sacrificial rituals (2:12-17) and behaved immorally (v 22). Condemned by God, Hophni died during a Philistine attack on Shiloh and its sanctuary (4:11).

HOPHRA

Son of Psammis, ruler over Egypt from 589–570 BC during the 26th dynasty. Called Pharaoh Hophra in Jeremiah 44:30, although he is alluded to several other times during the divided kingdom period (Jer 37:5; 43:8-13; Ez 29:1-3; 31:1-18).

He came to power after the death of his father, and in 589 BC marched into Judah against Nebuchadnezzar and the Babylonians in order to assist Zedekiah. Apparently he retreated before superior forces, Jerusalem was overthrown in 586 (Jer 37:5-8), and Hophra was killed as prophesied (Jer 44:30). This occurred in 566 BC, at the hands of Amasis (Ahmose II), who had usurped the throne of Egypt in 569 BC. Both Jeremiah (Jer 43:9-13; 46:13-26) and Ezekiel (Ez 29–30) foretold this defeat.

HORAM

King of Gezer who, while coming to the aid of Lachish, was defeated and killed by Joshua (Jos 10:33).

HORI

1. Lotan's first son. Lotan was the founder of a Horite subclan in Edom (Gn 36:22; 1 Chr 1:39).

2. Shaphat's father and a member of Simeon's tribe. Shaphat was one of the 12 spies (Nm 13:5).

HOSAH

Merarite Levite who guarded the gate of the tent where the sacred Ark was kept (1 Chr 16:38) when David brought it to Jerusalem. His gatekeeping responsibilities were shared by his sons (26:10-16).

HOSEA

Prophet of ancient Israel whose sphere of activity was the northern kingdom. Little is known of him outside of the prophetic book that bears his name. His prophetic ministry is best placed in the third quarter of the eighth century BC. His name means "help" or "helper," and is based on the Hebrew word for salvation.

The evidence for placing Hosea in the northern kingdom is basically internal. The book is concerned mainly with the northern tribes, whom he frequently identifies as "Ephraim," a common appellation for the northern kingdom. And the dialect of Hebrew in which the book was written seems to be of a northern cast.

The circumstances surrounding the marriage of Hosea form the catalyst for his prophetic message. He was commanded by God to marry Gomer, who apparently was a harlot; his marriage provided an analogy with Israel, who was guilty of spiritual adultery.

Scholars differ as to the interpretation of this controversial account but there is little reason for doubting that it was a literal event. The act of sacrifice involved in Hosea's obedience to God forms a marvelous picture of God's sacrificial love for man.

HOSHAIAH

1. Prince of Judah who led a contingent of princes in procession at the dedication of the walls of Jerusalem after they were rebuilt (Neh 12:32).

2. Father of Azariah (Jer 42:1; 43:2). Azariah was a leader of the people of Judah after the fall of Jerusalem.

HOSHAMA

Jeconiah's descendant (1 Chr 3:18).

HOSHEA

1. Original name of Joshua, the son of Nun and Moses' successor, before his name was changed by Moses (Nm 13:8, 16). See Joshua #1.

2. Son of Elah and the last of the 20 kings of the northern kingdom of Israel (2 Kgs 17:1-6).

He reigned for nine years (732–723 BC) before being taken captive by the Assyrians. In the later years of the northern kingdom, Assyria (under the rule of Tiglath-pileser III) had gained control of most of the Middle East and had reduced the scope of the northern kingdom to Ephraim, Issachar, and the half of Manasseh west of the Jordan.

Earlier, the northern kingdom, under Pekah (740–732 BC), entered into an alliance with Rezin of Damascus (Syria) and attempted to coerce King Ahaz of Judah (735–715 BC) to join them in action against Tiglath-pileser (2 Kgs 16:5; Is 7:1-6). Assyria came to Judah's aid, and at this point Hoshea was one of a group of conspirators who assassinated Pekah (2 Kgs 15:30). Tiglath-pileser rewarded Hoshea by making him king over the remnant of the northern kingdom. Hoshea ruled only as a vassal of Assyria and paid heavy tribute, remaining loyal to Assyria until the death of Tiglath-pileser in 727 BC. When Shalmaneser V succeeded to the throne of Assyria, he did not trust Hoshea's loyalty and marched against him, thereby continuing the forced annual tribute (2 Kgs 17:3). In a short time Hoshea attempted to assert independence. He withheld tribute and entered into negotiations with So, king of Egypt (v 4), finding a favorable response, because Egypt would be in a precarious position if Assyria were to control Palestine. Therefore, Egypt was quite willing to support Hoshea in his resistance to Assyria in the hope that Samaria would remain a buffer between Egypt and Assyria. Soon, Shalmaneser directed his army against Samaria (724 BC), and Hoshea discovered that the alliance with Egypt was of little value. Hoshea was taken prisoner, and Assyria apparently besieged Samaria for three years. The city fell in 722 BC, and Sargon II, who had succeeded Shalmaneser about 726 BC, deported many Israelites to various places in Assyria, thus ending the northern kingdom.

3. Son of Azaziah and one of King David's officers set over the Ephraimites (1 Chr 27:20).

4. One who set his seal on Ezra's covenant (Neh 10:23).

5. Eighth-century prophet of Israel better known as Hosea. *See* Hosea.

HOTHAM

1. Variant form of Helem in 1 Chronicles 7:32. *See* Helem #1.

2. Shama and Jeiel's father. Shama and Jeiel were two of David's mighty men (1 Chr 11:44).

HOTHIR

Levite and the head of the 21st of 24 divisions of priests for sanctuary service, formed during David's reign (1 Chr 25:4, 28).

HUBBAH

Shemer's son from Asher's tribe (1 Chr 7:34).

HUL

Son of Aram and grandson of Shem (Gn 10:23; 1 Chr 1:17).

HULDAH

Prophetess living in Jerusalem; a contemporary of the prophets Jeremiah and Zephaniah. Huldah is introduced as the wife of Shallum, the wardrobe keeper in King Josiah's court (2 Kgs 22:14; 2 Chr 34:22). Josiah sent his officers to ask Huldah's counsel concerning the book of the Mosaic law that had been found during the Temple repair. She prophesied that disaster would strike the nation (2 Kgs 22:16), but that Josiah would be spared because he was penitent and had humbled himself before the Lord (vv 18-19). She declared the destruction would come after his death and that he would be buried in peace (v 20). Although Josiah later died in battle, he was properly entombed (23:30), avoiding the indignity of becoming prey for carrion feeders. It was after receiving Huldah's advice that Josiah carried out his religious reform (2 Chr 35:1-25).

HUPHAM

Benjaminite and the founder of the Huphamite family (Nm 26:39); he is perhaps identifiable with Huppim (Gn 46:21; 1 Chr 7:12, 15) and Huram (1 Chr 8:5).

See also Huppim; Huram #1.

HUPPAH

One of the chief men appointed in charge of the 13th division of priests in the time of David and Solomon (1 Chr 24:13).

HUPPIM

Perhaps the son of Ir (Iri) and a descendant of Benjamin through Bela's line (Gn 46:21; 1 Chr 7:12, 15). Huppim is probably an alternate spelling of Hupham, the father of the Huphamite family from Benjamin's tribe (Nm 26:39). His precise lineage is difficult to determine.

HUR

1. Aaron's assistant in supporting Moses' hands until the Amalekites were defeated at Rephidim (Ex 17:8-13). He is mentioned again as assisting Aaron in overseeing Israel while Moses was on Mt Sinai (24:14). According to Josephus, Hur was the husband of Miriam, the sister of Moses (*Antiquities* 3.2.4).

2. Fourth of the five kings of Midian who was killed with Balaam by the Israelites under Moses (Nm 31:8). He is also referred to as one of the "princes of Midian" and "Sihon" (Jos 13:21).

3. Father of one of the 12 officers whom Solomon appointed to provide food for the king's household (1 Kgs 4:8, KJV; NLT "Ben-hur").

4. Son of Caleb and Ephrath and the grandfather of Bezalel (1 Chr 2:19-20; cf. Ex 31:2; 38:22). Although some interpreters regard the Hur discussed in #1 as the grandfather of Bezalel, others think that the Hur who assisted Moses and the Hur who was Bezalel's grandfather were different men.

5. Father (or perhaps family name) of Rephaiah, a postexilic leader who assisted Nehemiah in rebuilding the Jerusalem wall (Neh 3:9).

HURAI
Name of one of King David's mighty men (2 Sm 23:30, NLT mg; see also 1 Chr 11:32).

HURAM
1. Bela's son from Benjamin's tribe (1 Chr 8:5); perhaps the same person as Hupham (Nm 26:39).

2. Alternate spelling of Hiram, the Phoenician king of Tyre who was an ally of David and Solomon and who supplied materials for the building of the Temple (2 Chr 2:3, 11-12; 8:2, 18; 9:10, 21). *See* Hiram #1.

3. Alternate spelling of Hiram, a craftsman from Tyre who worked on Solomon's Temple (2 Chr 4:11, NLT "Huram-abi"). *See* Hiram #2.

HURAM-ABI
Alternate name for Hiram, Solomon's Temple craftsman, in 2 Chronicles 2:13 and 4:16. *See* Hiram #2.

HURI
Abihail's father from Gad's tribe who inhabited Gilead in Bashan (1 Chr 5:14).

HUSHAH
Ezer's son (1 Chr 4:4) or perhaps a town that Ezer founded. The warriors Sibbecai (2 Sm 21:18; 1 Chr 11:29; 20:4; 27:11) and Mebunnai (2 Sm 23:27) were described as Hushathites. Whether this designates genealogical ancestry or geographical locality (or perhaps both) is uncertain.

HUSHAI
Friend and adviser who remained faithful to David when his other adviser, Ahithophel, defected to join the rebelling Absalom. According to David's instructions, Hushai pretended loyalty to Absalom and slipped information to David regarding Absalom's plans. Ahithophel urged Absalom to attack the fleeing David before he had a chance to strengthen his forces, but Absalom followed Hushai's advice, which gave David time to escape over the Jordan and ultimately to defeat Absalom's party. When his counsel was not followed, Ahithophel hanged himself, probably anticipating the disastrous outcome

(2 Sm 15:32-37; 16:15–17:23). Hushai belonged to the Archite family from Ataroth, a town on Ephraim and Benjamin's border (Jos 16:2, 7).

HUSHAM
Temanite who succeeded Jobab as king of Edom (Gn 36:34-35; 1 Chr 1:45-46).

HUSHIM
1. Dan's son (Gn 46:23), alternately called Shuham in Numbers 26:42, where he is mentioned as the founder of the Shuhamite family.
2. Benjaminite descendant of Aher (1 Chr 7:12).
3. One of the Benjaminite Shaharaim's three wives (1 Chr 8:8-11).

HYMENAEUS
Believer, probably of Ephesus, cited by Paul as one who "rejected conscience" (1 Tm 1:19-20) and "swerved from the truth" (2 Tm 2:18). In the first instance, Hymenaeus (mentioned with Alexander) is viewed as having rejected correct beliefs and made a shipwreck of his faith. The seriousness of his offense is evident, as Paul sternly relates that he has delivered him over to Satan. The meaning of this phrase is uncertain, although it might have involved physical affliction, as well as severance from the body of other Christians. The harsh action was meant to bring about, not ultimate destruction, but eventual and lasting benefit to Hymenaeus so he might learn not to blaspheme (cf. 1 Cor 5:5). Apparently, this censure was not successful. In 2 Timothy 2:17-18, Hymenaeus appears as one who is "upsetting the faith." He (along with Philetus) was teaching that the resurrection had already taken place. Most probably, he was teaching that the resurrection takes place at the time of spiritual rebirth and baptism, based on a faulty interpretation of Romans 6:1-11 and Colossians 3:1. Hymenaeus thus sought to teach a spiritualized resurrection taking place as the soul awakens from sin.

IBHAR

Son born to David during his reign in Jerusalem (2 Sm 5:15; 1 Chr 3:6; 14:5).

IBNEIAH

Jeroham's son from Benjamin's tribe (1 Chr 9:8).

IBNIJAH

Forefather of Meshullam from Benjamin's tribe (1 Chr 9:8).

IBRI

Merarite Levite and Jaaziah's son, who lived during David's time (1 Chr 24:27).

IBSAM

Tola's son from Issachar's tribe (1 Chr 7:2).

IBZAN

Judge who ruled over Israel, or part of it, for seven years (Jgs 12:8-10). Ibzan was a native of Bethlehem, probably of Zebulun, and was buried in his place of birth. Jewish tradition identified Ibzan with Boaz and consequently understood his native city to be Bethlehem in Judah. Ibzan had 30 sons and 30 daughters and was a man of wealth and high social standing.

ICHABOD

Name given to Phinehas's son (Eli's grandson) to commemorate the glory that had departed from Israel, after the Ark of God was taken by the Philistines (1 Sm 4:19-22; 14:3).

Phinehas was killed in the battle of Aphek, at the same time the Philistines had captured the Ark. When Phinehas's wife heard of the tragedy, she went immediately into labor, and when the child was born, she named him Ichabod (meaning "no glory") to express her despair.

IDBASH

One of the descendants of Etam from Judah's tribe (1 Chr 4:3).

IDDO

1. Father of Ahinadab, Solomon's official at Mahanaim, who provisioned the royal household (1 Kgs 4:14).

2. Gershonite Levite, descendant of Joah and forefather of Zerah (1 Chr 6:21); perhaps alternately called Adaiah in verse 41. See Adaiah #2.

3. Zechariah's son and the chief officer of Manasseh's half-tribe in Gilead during David's reign (1 Chr 27:21).

4. Prophet and seer who recorded the events of Solomon's reign concerning Jeroboam son of Nebat in a book of visions (2 Chr 9:29), Rehoboam's acts in his genealogical records (12:15), and Abijah's life as part of a commentary (13:22).

5. Grandfather of Zechariah the prophet (Zec 1:1, 7). Iddo was a well-known priest who returned to Jerusalem from exile in 538 BC, and whose household was headed by Zechariah during Joiakim's reign as high priest during the postexilic era (Neh 12:16). According to Ezra 5:1 and 6:14, Zechariah, and not Berechiah his father, was considered Iddo's successor. *See* Zechariah #20.

6. Leading Levite at Casiphia in Babylonia to whom Ezra sent a delegation of men requesting priests and Temple servants to join Ezra's caravan returning to Palestine for service in the Jerusalem Temple (Ezr 8:17).

IEZER

Contraction of Abiezer. *See* Abiezer #1.

IGAL

1. Joseph's son from Issachar's tribe and one of the 12 spies sent by Moses to search out Canaan (Nm 13:7).

2. Nathan's son and one of David's mighty men (2 Sm 23:36). In 1 Chronicles 11:38 he is called Joel, Nathan's brother (in Hebrew, only one letter different from Igal).

3. Shemaiah's son and a descendant of King David through King Jehoiachin (1 Chr 3:22).

IGDALIAH

Hanan's father. Hanan's sons had a room adjacent to the Temple during Jehoiakim's reign (Jer 35:4).

IKKESH

Man from Tekoa whose son Ira was one of David's mighty men (2 Sm 23:26; 1 Chr 11:28), and head of a division of 24,000 men during the sixth month of the year (1 Chr 27:9).

IMLAH

Father of Michaiah, a prophet during King Ahab's reign, whom the king despised for speaking the truth (1 Kgs 22:8-9; 2 Chr 18:7-8).

IMMANUEL

Hebrew masculine name that means "God with us." It appears only twice in the OT (Is 7:14; 8:8) and once in the NT (Mt 1:23), where it is sometimes transliterated "Emmanuel." In the OT the name was given to a child born in the time of Ahaz as a sign to the king that Judah would receive relief from attacks by Israel and Syria. The name symbolized the fact that God would demonstrate his presence with his people in this deliverance. The greater application is that this is a prophecy of the birth of the incarnate God, Jesus the Messiah, as shown in Matthew.

The Prophecy in Isaiah's Day

In focusing on the birth of Jesus as Immanuel, there has been some neglect of the historical fulfillment that occurred in the time of Ahaz. Ahaz was the son of a good king, Jotham and the grandson of another godly ruler, Uzziah, but his reign was marked by apostasy and idolatry. He made "molten images" for the Baals, offered incense in the Hinnom Valley, and even burned his sons as an offering (2 Chr 28:2-4). Because of this, the Lord gave him into the hand of Rezin, king of Syria, and of Pekah, king of Israel. The Edomites also invaded Judah, and the Philistines attacked the Shephelah and the Negev and took several cities (vv 17-18).

Ahaz appealed to Tiglath-pileser III of Assyria (745–727 BC) for help against Israel and Syria. Tiglath-pileser accepted tribute from Ahaz, but attacked him instead of helping him (2 Chr 28:20-21). When he went to Damascus to meet the Assyrian king, Ahaz saw an altar, upon which he made offerings to the gods of Syria (v 23). He had a replica of this made and placed in the Temple of Jerusalem (2 Kgs 16:10-12). The prophet Isaiah was directed to accost Ahaz at the end of the conduit of the upper pool. God's message to the king was to "take heart," for the attacking kings would fall (Is 7:7-9). Isaiah directed Ahaz to ask the Lord for a sign of this, but the king demurred, having a sudden attack of piety (v 12).

Upon this refusal, the Lord gave to Ahaz a sign: a young woman would conceive and bear a son and call his name Immanuel (Is 7:14). That son would be able to distinguish good from evil by the time he was old enough to eat curds and wild honey, but even before that, the two kings would be removed and the king of Assyria would devastate their lands. The people would be taken away captive, so that the land would lie desolate and uncultivated. A man would have a cow to provide milk for curds, and wild honey would be gathered from the tangle of brush in the untended land.

The identity of this woman and child in Isaiah's time is uncertain. It has been proposed that the woman was Abijah, the wife of Ahaz, and that their son, Hezekiah, was this Immanuel. This is not demonstrable, and it seems inappropriate that a man like Ahaz should be the father of Immanuel.

It has also been suggested that the wife of Isaiah was the mother of Immanuel. Isaiah 7:14 tells of the prospective birth of Immanuel; 8:3 tells of the conception and birth of Isaiah's son, whose name, Maher-shalal-hash-baz ("swift to plunder and quick to spoil") is related to the prediction of the fall of Judah's enemies, for before the child would learn to talk, the lands of Syria and Israel would be taken by the king of Assyria (Is 8:4). Isaiah's statement that he and his children were "signs and portents in Israel from the LORD" (v 18, RSV) enhances the view that it was his son who was also named Immanuel.

The Lord then directed a message to Immanuel (Is 8:5-10). Because the people had refused the gracious invitation of the Lord, the Assyrians would scourge and fill the land of Immanuel. The plotting and plans of the people would come to nothing, for "God is with us" (*'immanu'el*). This is a play on words, using the name Immanuel to express the truth of the Lord's presence.

The Prophecy Fulfilled in Jesus

In the fullness of time God sent forth his son; more than 700 years after Ahaz, Jesus was born and here all ambiguities fade away. His mother was a virgin from Nazareth named Mary (Miriam), betrothed to a solid citizen named Joseph. Matthew 1:23 cites Isaiah 7:14 as being fulfilled in the birth of Jesus. The Scripture is very explicit in stating that Mary had no sexual contact with her husband prior to the birth of Jesus (Mt 1:25). The same precision is seen in the Gospel of Luke. When the announcement of this child's conception was made to Mary, she asked, "How can this be, since I have no husband?" (Lk 1:34, RSV). The angelic messenger explained that this conception would be brought about by the coming of the Holy Spirit upon her and by the overshadowing power of the Most High (v 35). For this reason the child would be not only Jesus and Immanuel but he would be called holy, the Son of God, God manifest in the flesh (Jn 1:18); the child would be unique, being both God and man.

There were great distinctions between the Immanuel of Isaiah's day and Immanuel the son of Mary. The first was a type; the other, the antitype. The first was the shadow; the other, the reality. The one symbolized deliverance from foreign oppression; the second was the Deliverer from the oppressor. The first represented God's presence for but a few years; the second Immanuel is the son who lives forever.

The concept of "God with us" was often reiterated by Jesus. He told his disciples that where two or three gathered in his name he would be present (Mt 18:20). Before his ascension, he assured them that he would be with them until the end of the age (28:20).

He spoke also of the promise of the Holy Spirit, who "lives with you now and later will be in you" (Jn 14:17, NLT), who will abide with them forever (v 16). The "God with us" indwelling is spoken of in Colossians 1:27: "Christ lives in you." In the consummation of all things, as shown to the apostle John, the Lord said: "Look, the home of God is now among his people! He will live with them, and they will be his people. God himself will be with them" (Rv 21:3, NLT).

See also God; Jesus.

IMMER

Priest in the time of David. He became the ancestral head of a house of priests: Pashhur, the priest who had Jeremiah arrested and placed in stocks, was a descendant of Immer (Jer 20:1). There were 1,052 priests of the subclan of Immer who returned from the Exile (1 Chr 9:12; Ezr 2:37; Neh 7:40). A descendant of Immer helped rebuild the Jerusalem wall (Neh 3:29) and 128 priests under Amashsai (also a descendant) helped resettle the city and tend the Temple (Neh 11:13-14).

IMNA

Helem's son from Asher's tribe (1 Chr 7:35).

IMNAH

1. Asher's son (Gn 46:17; 1 Chr 7:30) and founder of the Imnite family (Nm 26:44).
2. Levite and Kore's father. Kore was a Temple assistant during King Hezekiah's reign (2 Chr 31:14).

IMRAH

Zophah's son, a chief of Asher's tribe (1 Chr 7:36, 40).

IMRI

1. Ancestor of Uthai, one of the postexilic Jews of Judah's tribe (1 Chr 9:4). In the genealogy of Nehemiah 11:4, Imri and Amariah are probably the same person.
2. Father of Zaccur, a rebuilder of the Jerusalem wall (Neh 3:2).

IPHDEIAH

Shashak's son from Benjamin's tribe (1 Chr 8:25).

IR

Benjaminite father of Shuppim and Huppim (1 Chr 7:12), perhaps identical with Iri (v 7). In Numbers 24:19, the name is translated "the city" (KJV, NIV; cf. NLT).

IRA

1. David's priest or chief official in service at the time of Sheba's revolt (2 Sm 20:26).
2. Warrior among David's mighty men, known as "the thirty" (2 Sm 23:26). He was the son of Ikkesh of Tekoa (1 Chr 11:28; 27:9) and became commander of the sixth division of David's militia.
3. Warrior among David's mighty men, "the thirty," identified as an Ithrite (2 Sm 23:38; 1 Chr 11:40; NLT "from Jattir").

IRAD

Enoch's son, a member of Cain's line (Gn 4:18).

IRAM

Chieftain in Edom (Gn 36:43; 1 Chr 1:54).

IRI

Bela's son from Benjamin's tribe (1 Chr 7:7).

IRIJAH

Benjaminite guard who apprehended Jeremiah as he left Jerusalem to see property that was his by redemption (Jer 32:6-7) and charged him before the princes with deserting to the Chaldeans; as a consequence, Jeremiah was beaten and imprisoned (37:13-14).

IR-NAHASH

Son of Tehinnah, Eshton's son from Judah's tribe (1 Chr 4:12). Some translations note the alternate rendering, "city of Nahash" (mg NIV, KJV).

IRU

Caleb's son from Judah's tribe (1 Chr 4:15).

ISAAC

Son of Abraham and Sarah, father of Jacob and Esau, one of the patriarchs of Israel.

The name Isaac has an interesting etymology. It is the Anglicized form of the Hebrew *Yitshaq,* in Greek *Isaak.* If taken as an imperfect form, it means "he laughs"; as a perfect form, it means "he laughed." Scholars have debated this problem and also the absence of an antecedent subject. If God is implied, the name could indicate divine amusement at an aged couple ridiculing the prospect of having a child (Gn 17:17; 18:12) and then suddenly becoming parents, as God had promised.

Isaac's pedigree is also interesting, for Sarah was not only the wife of Abraham but also his half sister (Gn 20:12), and this fact alone may have interfered with conception in their earlier years. Because of this relationship, Isaac belonged to both sides of Terah's family. According to prevailing custom, the son of the legal wife took precedence over the male offspring of concubines, so that Isaac had priority of inheritance over Ishmael. The gifts that Abraham subsequently gave to the sons of his concubines (25:6) were without prejudice to the inheritance of Isaac.

Following God's instructions (Gn 17:10-14), Isaac was circumcised on the eighth day as a member of the covenant community. The next ceremony came when he was old enough for weaning, probably around three years old. In eastern countries where this procedure is still observed, the child's transition from milk to solid protein and carbohydrates is normally celebrated in the context of a feast. During the celebration the mother chews a mouthful of solid food and then pushes it into the baby's mouth with her tongue. The infant is often so shocked by this treatment that it promptly expels the food, whereupon the mother repeats the process. For an observer the procedure can be hilarious, and Ishmael may have been laughing at such a spectacle when he incurred Sarah's wrath (21:8-10).

During the years of Isaac's adolescence, Abraham was living in Philistine territory (Gn 21:34). The supreme test of the father's faith and obedience came in this period. Having watched this son of God's promise grow up into a healthy young man, Abraham is asked by God to offer him as a sacrifice. Isaac was familiar with sacrificial rituals and helped

QUICKTAKE

ISAAC

STRENGTHS AND ACCOMPLISHMENTS
- He was the miracle child born to Sarah and Abraham when she was 90 years old and he was 100
- He was the first descendant in fulfillment of God's promise to Abraham
- He seems to have been a caring and consistent husband, at least until his sons were born
- He demonstrated great patience

WEAKNESSES AND MISTAKES
- Under pressure he tended to lie
- In conflict he sought to avoid confrontation
- He played favorites between his sons and alienated his wife

LESSONS FROM HIS LIFE
- Patience often brings rewards
- Both God's plans and his promises are larger than people
- God keeps his promises! He remains faithful though we are often faithless
- Playing favorites is sure to bring family conflict

VITAL STATISTICS
Where: Various places in the southern part of Palestine, including Beersheba (Genesis 26:23)
Occupation: Wealthy livestock owner
Relatives: Parents: Abraham and Sarah. Half brother: Ishmael. Wife: Rebekah. Sons: Jacob and Esau

KEY VERSE
"But God replied, "No—Sarah, your wife, will give birth to a son for you. You will name him Isaac, and I will confirm my covenant with him and his descendants as an everlasting covenant" (Genesis 17:19).

Isaac's story is told in Genesis 17:15–35:29. He is also mentioned in Romans 9:7-10; Hebrews 11:17-20; James 2:21.

with the preparations, though probably not without some misgivings, for he was also familiar with the patriarchal traditions that gave the head of the family power of life or death over everyone and everything in the family. If he voiced any protest as he lay bound on the sacrificial altar, it is not recorded. When Abraham's faith did not waver, God intervened at the crucial moment and provided another offering in the form of a ram. Because of his obedience, God promised Abraham great blessing, blessing in which Isaac also participated (Gn 22; 25:11). It was this act of faith and obedience that Paul honored centuries later by calling Abraham the forefather of the Christian church (Rom 4).

After Sarah's death (Gn 23), Abraham set about securing a bride for Isaac, as it was the custom for parents to arrange marriages for their children. Rather than have Isaac marry a local pagan woman, Abraham sent his household steward to Nahor in Mesopotamia to seek a bride for his son from among his relatives. In an account that emphasizes faith, perseverance, and divine blessing, Genesis 24 describes how the servant met Rebekah and betrothed her to Isaac even before he had met the rest of her family. Bethuel, her father, and Laban, her brother, assented to this arrangement, and she left with the family's blessing to take up her new responsibilities in Palestine as Isaac's wife.

When Abraham died at a ripe old age, Isaac and Ishmael buried him in the cave of Machpelah (Gn 25:8-9). Isaac was now patriarch of the family. He pleaded with God that his wife, Rebekah, might bear children, and as a result, she bore twin sons, Esau ("the hairy one") and Jacob ("supplanter"). Esau became a hunter, and Isaac favored him, while Jacob was more of a settler and agriculturalist and was favored by his mother. Jacob was also crafty and took advantage of Esau's extreme hunger one day, bargaining with his older brother to exchange his birthright for some lentil stew. Possession of the birthright secured for Jacob a double portion of the inheritance (Dt 21:17).

When famine gripped the land, God instructed Isaac not to visit Egypt (Gn 26:2), but to stay in Palestine, where he would enjoy great prosperity. When the men of the area asked about Rebekah, Isaac became fearful and said she was his sister. When the deception was uncovered, Abimelech the king rebuked Isaac and forbade anyone to interfere with him. Isaac prospered so greatly that Abimelech finally asked him to relocate, so he moved to Beersheba, where there was sufficient water for his flocks, and his fortune increased.

Although Esau was Isaac's favorite son, he displeased his father by marrying two Hittite women. When Isaac felt that the end of his life was approaching, he wanted to bless his firstborn in the traditional patriarchal manner (Gn 27). Rebekah overheard his instructions to Esau, and she encouraged Jacob to deceive the blind old man by disguising himself as Esau and taking his brother's blessing. The deception succeeded, and Isaac gave Jacob the blessing of the firstborn. When Esau appeared to receive his blessing he was too late, and he was very bitter against Jacob because of what had happened. Rebekah sent Jacob away to her brother Laban in Mesopotamia, to escape Esau's anger and also to obtain a wife. Esau did receive a blessing from Isaac, but a lesser one. Two decades later a rich and prosperous Jacob returned with his family. He made peace with Esau before Isaac died, and the brothers buried Isaac in Hebron (Gn 35:27-29).

Isaac is given less prominence in the patriarchal narratives than Abraham or Jacob, but his importance for covenantal faith was recognized in such NT passages as Acts 7:8, Romans 9:7, Galatians 4:21-31, and Hebrews 11:9-20.

ISAIAH

Eighth-century BC prophet during the reigns of the Judean kings Uzziah, Jotham, Ahaz, and Hezekiah; author of the biblical book of Isaiah. Isaiah was the son of Amoz (Is 1:1) and may have been a relative of King Amaziah. Growing up in Jerusalem, Isaiah received the best education the capital could supply. He was also deeply knowledgeable about people, and he became the political and religious counselor of the nation. He had easy access to the monarchs and seems to have been the historiographer at the Judean court for several reigns (2 Chr 26:22; 32:32).

Isaiah's wife is referred to as a prophetess (Is 8:3) and they had at least two sons, Shear-jashub (7:3) and Maher-shalal-hash-baz (8:3). Isaiah's customary attire was a prophet's clothing, that is, sandals and a garment of goat's hair or sackcloth. At one point during his ministry, the Lord commanded Isaiah to go naked and bare-foot for a period of three years, (wearing only a loincloth) (20:2-6). This must have been humiliating in a society that measured status by meticulous dress codes.

Isaiah worked to reform social and political wrongs. Even the highest members of society did not escape his censure. He berated soothsayers and denounced wealthy, influential people who ignored the responsibilities of their position. He exhorted the masses to be obedient rather than indifferent to God's covenant. He rebuked kings for their willfulness and lack of concern.

Isaiah's writings express a deep awareness of God's majesty and holiness. The prophet denounced not only Canaanite idolatry but also the religious observances of his own people that were external ceremonies only and lacking sincerity (1:10-17; 29:13). He preached impending judgment on the idolatrous Judeans, declaring that only a righteous remnant would survive (6:13).

Isaiah foretold the coming of the Messiah, the "peaceful prince," and the ruler of God's kingdom (11:1-11; cf. 9:6-7). He also depicted this Messiah as a suffering, obedient servant (53:3-12). Isaiah was preeminent among the prophets for the variety and grandeur of his imagery. His imagination produced forceful, brilliant figures of speech.

Isaiah prophesied during the last three decades of the northern kingdom of Israel but because he lived in Jerusalem, in Judah, he made little direct reference to Israel. However, when that kingdom fell, Judah lay open to conquest by Assyria. Isaiah advised King Ahaz to avoid foreign entanglements and depend on God to protect his people. Ignoring that advice, Ahaz made an alliance with Assyria.

It was Hezekiah, Ahaz's pious son, who sought to remove Judah from this dangerous situation. When the Assyrians under Sennacherib approached Jerusalem, Isaiah inspired Hezekiah and the Judeans to rely on the Lord for the city's defense, and "the angel of the Lord" destroyed Sennacherib's army (37:36-38), securing a short period of peace for Hezekiah and the Judeans.

Hebrew prophecy reached its pinnacle with Isaiah, who was greatly esteemed in both OT and NT times. One indication of that esteem is the collection of apocryphal literature associated with his name.

QUICKTAKE

ISAIAH

STRENGTHS AND ACCOMPLISHMENTS
- Considered the greatest Old Testament prophet
- Quoted at least 50 times in the New Testament
- Had powerful messages of both judgment and hope
- Carried out a consistent ministry even though there was little positive response from his listeners
- His ministry spanned the reigns of five kings of Judah

LESSONS FROM HIS LIFE
- God's help is needed in order to comfort people while effectively confronting sin
- One result of experiencing forgiveness is the desire to share that forgiveness with others
- God is purely and perfectly holy, just, and loving

VITAL STATISTICS
Where: Jerusalem
Occupations: Scribe, prophet
Relatives: Father: Amoz. Sons: Shear-jashub, Maher-shalal-hash-baz
Contemporaries: Uzziah, Jotham, Ahaz, Hezekiah, Manasseh, Micah

KEY VERSE
"Then I heard the Lord asking, 'Whom should I send as a messenger to this people? Who will go for us?

"I said, 'Here I am. Send me'" (Isaiah 6:8).

Isaiah's story is told in 2 Kings 19:2–20:19. He is also mentioned in 2 Chronicles 26:22; 32:20, 32; Matthew 3:3; 8:17; 12:17-21; John 12:38-41; Romans 10:16, 20, 21.

ISCAH
Haran's daughter and Milcah's sister (Gn 11:29).

ISCARIOT
See Judas #1.

ISHBAH
Mered's son by Bithiah, the daughter of the pharaoh (1 Chr 4:17).

ISHBAK
One of the sons of Abraham by Keturah (Gn 25:2; 1 Chr 1:32).

ISHBI-BENOB
Giant who nearly killed David. During one of his many battles with the Philistines, David grew faint and was nearly killed by Ishbi-benob. Abishai killed the giant, saving David's life (2 Sm 21:16).

ISHBOSHETH
Alternate name for Eshbaal, Saul's son and successor to Israel's throne (2 Sm 2–4). *See* Eshbaal.

ISHHOD
Hammoleketh's son from Manasseh's tribe (1 Chr 7:18).

ISHI
1. Appaim's son, the father of Sheshan and a descendant of Judah through Jerahmeel's line (1 Chr 2:31).
2. Man from Judah's tribe whose descendants were Zoheth and Ben-zoheth (1 Chr 4:20).
3. Simeonite whose four sons led 500 men to Mt Seir, where they destroyed the remnant Amalekites and settled their own people (1 Chr 4:42).
4. One of the leaders of the half-tribe of Manasseh east of the Jordan (1 Chr 5:24).
5. Name of God, meaning "my husband," by which Israel will one day address him (Hos 2:16). *See also* God.

ISHIJAH
Harim's son, who obeyed Ezra's exhortation to divorce his pagan wife (Ezr 10:31).

ISHMA
Etam's son from Judah's tribe (1 Chr 4:3).

ISHMAEL
1. Abraham's first son, born of Hagar, Sarah's Egyptian handmaid, at the instigation of Sarah herself. God promised to make a great nation of the childless Abraham (Gn 12:2), assuring him that his son would be his heir (15:4). But when Sarah was past 75 years old and still barren, she invoked the custom whereby a childless wife gave her maid to her husband as concubine and laid claim to the offspring of their union (16:1-2). When Hagar conceived, the reproach attendant on barrenness prompted the maid to behave contemptuously toward her mistress, and with Abraham's consent Sarah dealt harshly with her and she fled. An angel sent Hagar

QUICKTAKE

ISHMAEL

STRENGTHS AND ACCOMPLISHMENTS
• One of the first to experience the physical sign of God's covenant, circumcision
• Known for his ability as an archer and hunter
• Fathered 12 sons who became leaders of warrior tribes

WEAKNESS AND MISTAKE
• Failed to recognize the place of his half brother, Isaac, and mocked him

LESSON FROM HIS LIFE
• God's plans incorporate people's mistakes

VITAL STATISTICS
Where: Canaan and Egypt
Occupation: Hunter, archer, warrior
Relatives: Parents: Hagar and Abraham. Half brother: Isaac

KEY VERSES
"But God heard the boy crying, and the angel of God called to Hagar from heaven, 'Hagar, what's wrong? Do not be afraid! God has heard the boy crying as he lies there. Go to him and comfort him, for I will make a great nation from his descendants'" (Genesis 21:17, 18).

Ishmael's story is told in Genesis 16–17; 21:8-20; 25:12-18; 28:8, 9; 36:1-3. He is also mentioned in 1 Chronicles 1:28-31; Romans 9:7-9; Galatians 4:21-31.

back to submit to her mistress and promised her a son to be named Ishmael meaning "God hears" (16:9-11). The boy was born near Hebron when Abraham was 86 years old (13:18; 16:16).

Abraham and Sarah received him as the son of God's promise, as attested by their disbelief when the forthcoming birth of Isaac was announced (17:17; 18:12), and by Abraham's subsequent wish that Ishmael should be accepted of God (17:18). At age 13 he participated in the institution of circumcision as a witness of God's covenant with Abraham (17:9-14, 22-27), and the Lord promised to make Ishmael the father of 12 princes, from which would come a great nation, though the covenant was to be established with Isaac (17:20-21).

There is no evidence that Ishmael was out of favor until Isaac's weaning at about three years of age. When Sarah saw Ishmael "making fun" of her son Isaac, she determined that the son of a slave woman should not be heir with her son Isaac, and she demanded that Ishmael and Hagar be banished. Although vexed, Abraham received reassurance from the Lord and sent them away with some provisions. It was then clear to Abraham that Isaac, not Ishmael, was the son of God's promise.

Hagar survived in the wilderness with the guidance of an angel, and Ishmael became a hunter of wild animals. He settled in the wilderness of Paran and married an Egyptian woman (21:20-21). Little else is recorded of him, except that he lived to assist in the burial of Abraham (25:9-10), gave his daughter Mahalath in marriage (28:9), and died at the age of 137 (25:17). The names of his 12 sons and their settlements are recorded in Genesis 25:13-16. In subsequent history, a caravan of Ishmaelite traders (also called Midianites, cf. Jgs 8:22-24) bought Joseph from his brothers and sold him in Egypt (Gn 37:25-28; 39:1).

Though Isaac, rather than Ishmael, inherited the covenantal blessings, it is clear that the covenant was not the only means whereby divine favor could be bestowed. Abraham and Sarah overestimated the importance of Ishmael in God's plan by mistaking him for the heir of covenant promises, but they also underrated God's intentions for him by excluding him altogether from inheritance with Isaac.

In the NT, Paul alludes to Ishmael while urging the Galatians not to see the law as a yoke (Gal 4:22). He states that those who trust the law instead of putting their faith in God's promises do not inherit the kingdom, just as the son of the slave woman did not receive inheritance with the son of the free woman (v 30).

2. Son of Nethaniah, son of Elishama, of the royal family of Zedekiah (2 Kgs 25:25). He was prompted by Baalis, king of the Ammonites, to assassinate Gedaliah, Judean governor of the puppet regime, which Nebuchadnezzar left behind at Mizpah at the time of the Babylonian exile. Gedaliah ignored advance warning of the plot and refused to allow Johanan to assassinate Ishmael first (Jer 40:14-16). While sharing a meal with Gedaliah, Ishmael and ten companions killed him, along with the Babylonian troops accompanying him. The next day he persuaded a group of 80 pilgrims passing from the north to the Temple at Jerusalem to enter Mizpah, where he killed all but 10 who ransomed their lives with stores of food. Hiding all the bodies in a cistern, Ishmael took captive the rest of the population of Mizpah, including Jeremiah and women of the royal family, and set out to join the Ammonites. But Johanan, with an armed force, overtook Ishmael at Gibeon and rescued the captives, whereupon Ishmael fled to Ammonite territory (Jer 41).

3. Son of Azel, a Benjaminite of the family of Saul (1 Chr 8:38; 9:44).

4. Father of Zebadiah, the governor of the house of Judah under Jehoshaphat (2 Chr 19:11).

5. Son of Jehohanan, and one of the commanders who allied with Jehoiada the priest to enthrone the child Joash and thus end the reign of Athaliah (2 Chr 23:1).

6. Son of Pashhur, and one of the priests who put away foreign wives during Ezra's reforms (Ezr 10:22).

ISHMAIAH

1. Warrior from Benjamin's tribe who joined David at Ziklag in his struggle against King Saul. Ishmaiah was one of David's ambidextrous archers and slingers (1 Chr 12:4).

2. Obadiah's son, a chief officer in Zebulun's tribe in David's time (1 Chr 27:19).

ISHMERAI

Elpaal's son and a chief in Benjamin's tribe (1 Chr 8:18).

ISHPAH

Beriah's son from Benjamin's tribe (1 Chr 8:16).

ISHPAN

Shashak's son and a leader in Benjamin's tribe (1 Chr 8:22).

ISHVAH

Asher's son (Gn 46:17; 1 Chr 7:30).

ISHVI

1. Asher's third son (Gn 46:17; 1 Chr 7:30) and founder of the Ishvite family (Nm 26:44).

2. A variant form of Ishbosheth, one of King Saul's sons (1 Sm 14:49).

ISMAKIAH

Levite overseer of things dedicated at the Temple during Hezekiah's reform (2 Chr 31:13).

ISRAEL

Name meaning "one who struggles with God" or "God struggles" (Gn 32:28, NLT mg). It was given to Isaac's son Jacob, whose descendants were then called "Israelites" (35:9-12; cf. Dt 6:1-4). See Jacob #1.

ISSACHAR

1. Jacob's ninth son, the fifth by his wife Leah (Gn 30:17-18); his name perhaps means "reward." Jacob, in his final message to his 12 sons says, "Issachar is a strong donkey, lying down between the sheepfolds" (49:14, NASB); the picture suggested is a loaded donkey who refuses to move his burden, a lazy man who is unwilling to do his share of the work. Little is known about Issachar except what he did along with the other sons

of Israel. He had four sons (46:13), who headed clans in the tribe (1 Chr 7:1-5). His family went with Jacob to Egypt, where they died (although Issachar's remains were subsequently moved to Shechem with the other 12 patriarchs—Acts 7:16).

The descendants of Issachar numbered 54,400 at the first census (Nm 1:29), increased to 64,300 at the second (26:25), and to 87,000 during David's reign (1 Chr 7:5). Issachar was the main tribe involved in the fighting led by Deborah, herself a member of the tribe (Jgs 5:15). During the time of David, there were men of the tribe of Issachar who had understanding of what Israel ought to do in warfare (1 Chr 12:32). These men supported David as king to replace Saul.

Issachar was assigned the fourth lot of land after the Ark was taken to Shiloh (Jos 19:17). This included the cities of Jezreel, Shunem, and En-gannim, and it lay between the mountains of Gilboa and Tabor. Their allotment was bordered on the south and west by the tribe of Manasseh, on the north by Zebulun and Naphtali, and on the east by the river Jordan. This territory was largely a fertile plain and was often threatened by the Canaanites nearby as well as by foreign invaders.

2. Obed-edom's son, who was a Levite gatekeeper during David's reign (1 Chr 26:5).

ISSHIAH

1. Izrahiah's son from Issachar's tribe (1 Chr 7:3).

2. Warrior from Benjamin's tribe who joined David in his struggle against King Saul. Isshiah was one of David's ambidextrous archers and slingers (1 Chr 12:6).

3. Uzziel's son from Levi's tribe (1 Chr 23:20; 24:25).

4. Rehabiah's son from Levi's tribe and a descendant of Moses (1 Chr 24:21).

ITHAI

Alternate spelling of Ittai, a Benjaminite warrior, in 1 Chronicles 11:31. *See* Ittai #2.

ITHAMAR

Aaron's fourth and youngest son, who served as a priest to the tribes of Israel during the wilderness period (Ex 6:23; Nm 3:2-4; 26:60; 1 Chr 6:3; 24:2). After the death of two of his brothers, he was given the special duty of overseeing the moving of the Tabernacle (Nm 4:28, 33; 7:8). During David's reign, the descendants of Ithamar and Eleazar were organized as the formal Temple priesthood (1 Chr 24:3-6). Later, some of his descendants returned with Ezra from Babylon (Ezr 8:2).

ITHIEL

1. Ancestor of Sallu, a Benjaminite who lived in Jerusalem after the Babylonian exile (Neh 11:7).

2. One of the two persons to whom Agur spoke his proverbs (Prv 30:1, NLT mg).

ITHMAH

Warrior of Moabite origin and one of David's mighty men (1 Chr 11:46).

ITHRAN

1. Dishon's son, who was a Horite chief (Gn 36:26; 1 Chr 1:41).

2. One of Zophah's sons (1 Chr 7:37). He is probably the same as Jether mentioned in 1 Chronicles 7:38.

ITHREAM

David's sixth son, borne by his wife Eglah at Hebron (2 Sm 3:5; 1 Chr 3:3).

ITTAI

1. Philistine from Gath who, with 600 other Gittites, remained loyal to David and accompanied him on his flight from Absalom (2 Sm 15:18-22). Ittai commanded a third of David's army in the battle against Absalom's forces (18:2, 5).

2. Benjaminite warrior among David's mighty men (2 Sm 23:29; 1 Chr 11:31, "Ithai").

IZHAR

1. One of Kohath's sons from Levi's tribe (Ex 6:18, 21; Nm 3:19; 16:1; 1 Chr 6:2, 18, 38; 23:12, 18), and father of the Izharite family (Nm 3:27; 1 Chr 24:22; 26:23, 29); alternately called Amminadab in 1 Chronicles 6:22. One of Izhar's sons was Korah, who led the rebellion against Moses and Aaron (Nm 16:1-11).

2. Helah's son from Judah's tribe (1 Chr 4:7).

IZLIAH

Elpaal's son from Benjamin's tribe (1 Chr 8:18).

IZRAHIAH

Uzzi's son and a leading member of Issachar's tribe (1 Chr 7:3).

IZZIAH

Parosh's son, who was encouraged by Ezra to divorce the foreign woman he married during the postexilic period (Ezr 10:25).

JAAKAN

Esau's descendant and a son of Ezer the Horite (1 Chr 1:42, NLT mg); alternately called Akan in Genesis 36:27.

JAAKOBAH

Leader in Simeon's tribe (1 Chr 4:36).

JAALAH

Servant of King Solomon and head of a family who returned to Jerusalem with Zerubbabel after the Babylonian exile (Ezr 2:56; Neh 7:58).

JAARESHIAH

Jeroham's son, a Benjaminite leader who lived in Jerusalem (1 Chr 8:27).

JAASIEL

1. Warrior among David's mighty men. He is called "the Mezobaite" (1 Chr 11:47).

2. Abner's son and the leader of Benjamin's tribe during David's reign (1 Chr 27:21).

JAASU

Bani's son, who obeyed Ezra's exhortation to divorce his pagan wife after the Exile (Ezr 10:37).

JAAZANIAH

1. Son of Hoshaiah, who was a Maacathite and a leader in the armies of Judah at the beginning of the Exile. These troops received assurance of safety in return for loyalty to the Babylonians (2 Kgs 25:23). Jaazaniah is alternately called Jezaniah in Jeremiah 40:8 and Azariah in Jeremiah 42:1 (NLT mg) and 43:2.

2. Son of Jeremiah (not the prophet), who was taken by Jeremiah the prophet into the Lord's house, where he refused to drink wine because of the command of his ancestor Jonadab the Recabite (Jer 35:3-11).

3. Shaphan's son, who led a group of elders in worshiping idols in the Temple (Ez 8:11).

4. Azzur's son and one of a group of 25 men seen by Ezekiel in a vision who gave bad counsel and plotted evil in Jerusalem near the time of the Exile (Ez 11:1).

JAAZIAH

Descendant of Merari in a list of family leaders among Levites assigned to Temple duty in David's reign (1 Chr 24:26-27).

JAAZIEL

One of the eight men appointed to play harps or lyres when the Ark was brought up to Jerusalem by David (1 Chr 15:18-20; and probably 16:5a, "Jeiel," which is most likely a copyist's error). He is called Aziel in verse 20.

JABAL
Descendant of Cain and the first son of Lamech and Adah. He was the father of a nomadic people who dwelt in tents (Gn 4:20).

JABESH
Shallum's father. Shallum assassinated Zechariah, king of Israel (2 Kgs 15:10-14).

JABEZ
Member of Judah's tribe who was noted for his godliness. He prayed for God's protection, and his prayer was answered (1 Chr 4:9-10).

JABIN
1. King of Hazor who led a coalition against Joshua at Merom. Jabin and his allies were destroyed in the battle, and Hazor was burned to the ground (Jos 11:1-14).
2. King of Hazor during the period of the judges (Jgs 4). God allowed him to oppress Israel for 20 years because of their wickedness. His army included 900 chariots of iron. Eventually, God delivered Israel through the prophetess Deborah and her captain, Barak, who defeated Sisera, the captain of Jabin's army. While resting after his flight from battle, Sisera himself was killed by a woman. Jabin was no longer a threat after Sisera's death and was soon killed (Jgs 4:24; Ps 83:9).

JACAN
Member of Gad's tribe who lived in Bashan during the reign of Jotham, king of Judah (1 Chr 5:13).

JACOB
1. Younger of twin sons born to Isaac and Rebekah (Gn 25:24-26). Isaac had prayed for his barren wife, Rebekah, and she conceived the twins, who jostled each other in the womb. When she asked the Lord about this, he told her that she was carrying two nations and that the older son would serve the younger (v 23). Esau was hairy and red (later he was called Edom, "red," 25:30; 36:1), but Jacob was born holding the heel of his brother, so that he was named Jacob, "he takes by the heel" (cf. Hos 12:3), with the derived meaning "to supplant, deceive, attack from the rear."

Personal History Esau and Jacob were very different from each other. Esau was an outdoorsman, the favorite of his father, while Jacob stayed around the tents and was loved by his mother.

One day when Jacob was preparing red pottage, Esau came in famished and asked Jacob for some food. Jacob offered to sell Esau some stew in exchange for his birthright as firstborn, and Esau agreed, thus repudiating his birthright (cf. Heb 12:16). The significance of this episode of the red pottage is demonstrated by its association with Esau's second name, Edom ("red") (Gn 25:30).

QUICKTAKE

JACOB

STRENGTHS AND ACCOMPLISHMENTS
• Father of the 12 tribes of Israel
• Third in the Abrahamic line of God's plan
• Determined, willing to work long and hard for what he wanted
• Good businessman

WEAKNESSES AND MISTAKES
• When faced with conflict, relied on his own resources rather than going to God for help
• Tended to accumulate wealth for its own sake

LESSONS FROM HIS LIFE
• Security does not lie in the accumulation of goods
• All human intentions and actions—for good or evil—are woven by God into his ongoing plan

VITAL STATISTICS
Where: Canaan
Occupation: Shepherd, livestock owner
Relatives: Parents: Isaac and Rebekah. Brother: Esau. Father-in-law: Laban. Wives: Rachel and Leah. Twelve sons and one daughter are mentioned in the Bible

KEY VERSE
"What's more, I am with you, and I will protect you wherever you go. One day I will bring you back to this land. I will not leave you until I have finished giving you everything I have promised you" (Genesis 28:15).

Jacob's story is told in Genesis 25–50. He is also mentioned in Hosea 12:2-5; Matthew 1:2; 22:32; Acts 7:8-16; Romans 9:11-13; Hebrews 11:9, 20, 21.

Isaac became old and blind. One day he asked Esau to take his weapons and get some wild game, of which Isaac was very fond (Gn 27:6-7; cf 25:28), so that he could eat and then confer his blessing upon Esau. Rebekah overheard this, so she called Jacob and told him to go to the flock and select two good kids. She would prepare a dish that would pass for the game while Esau was out hunting. Jacob feared that Isaac would detect the deception, for Esau was very hairy, but Rebekah had everything planned. She placed the skins of the kids on Jacob's hands and neck to give the impression of hairiness (27:16) and clothed him in Esau's best garments, which had the smell of the outdoors on them. Although Isaac recognized the voice of Jacob, his other senses failed him, and he was deceived by the feel of the skins and the smell of the garments. He proceeded to give the blessing to Jacob (vv 27-29).

No sooner had Jacob left than Esau arrived with the game he had cooked. Jacob's ruse was discovered, but the deed could not be undone (Gn 27:33), for, as the Nuzi tablets show, an oral blessing had legal validity and could not be revoked. Esau was heartbroken (cf. Heb 12:17). Isaac gave him a blessing inferior to the one given to Jacob (Gn 27:39-40).

The animosity between the brothers deepened, and Esau plotted to kill Jacob after the death of their father. Rebekah learned of this, so she instructed Jacob to flee to her brother Laban in Haran (Gn 27:42-45). Esau's Hittite wives, meanwhile, had been making life miserable for Rebekah; she complained to Isaac, who called Jacob and sent him to Laban to marry one of his uncle's daughters (27:46–28:4).

Jacob set out for Haran. Using a stone for a pillow, he dreamed one night of a ladder reaching up to heaven, with the angels of God ascending and descending on it. God spoke to Jacob and gave to him the promise he had given to Abraham and Isaac concerning the land and descendants. The next morning Jacob took his stone pillow and set it up as a pillar, anointing it with oil. He named the place Bethel ("house of God") and made a vow that if the Lord would be with him and provide for him, he would give a tithe to the Lord (Gn 28:10-22).

When Jacob reached the area of Haran, he met shepherds who knew Laban. Rachel, Laban's younger daughter, arrived with her father's flock, and Jacob rolled the large stone from the mouth of the well and watered the sheep for her (Gn 29:1-10). When Rachel learned that Jacob was from their own family, she ran to tell her father, who greeted Jacob warmly. After staying with them for a month, Jacob was hired to tend Laban's flocks. When wages were discussed, Jacob proposed to work seven years to earn Rachel as his wife (vv 15-20).

At the end of seven years Jacob was set to claim his wages, but on the night of the wedding feast, Laban gave his older daughter, Leah, to Jacob; Jacob did not discover the substitution until morning. He felt cheated and protested to Laban, but Laban insisted that according to custom the older daughter must marry first and proposed that Jacob work another seven years for Rachel. Jacob agreed to this and put in his time (Gn 29:21-30).

Genesis 29 and 30 relate the births of most of Jacob's children. Leah bore Jacob four sons: Reuben, Simeon, Levi, and Judah (Gn 29:31-35). She named her first son Reuben ("see, a son") since she felt that her husband would love her because she bore a son. Simeon is derived from the root "hear," since Leah thought that God had given her this son because he had heard that she was hated. Levi is related to the verb "join," for Leah thought that her husband would be joined to her because of this third son. Judah means "praise," for she praised the Lord at the birth of her fourth son.

Rachel had not conceived any children, so she gave her maid Bilhah to Jacob. She bore him Dan and Naphtali (Gn 30:1-8). Rachel named the first son Dan ("he judged") because God had judged, that is, vindicated her. Naphtali means "my struggle, my wrestling," for Rachel said she had wrestled with and overcome her sister.

Thereupon Leah gave her maid Zilpah to Jacob as a wife; she brought forth Gad and Asher (Gn 30:11). Gad means "fortune"; Leah said, "Good fortune," when he was born. Asher ("happy") was so named because Leah said, "Now the women will call me happy."

Reuben found some mandrakes in the field, and Leah traded them to Rachel for Jacob's services. Leah then bore sons five and six, Issachar and Zebulun, followed by a daughter, whom she named Dinah (Gn 30:14-21). Issachar perhaps means "reward," for Leah said that God had rewarded her for giving her maidservant to her husband. Zebulun probably means "honor"; Leah thought that now her husband would honor her.

At last Rachel herself conceived and bore her first child, a son whom she named Joseph. "Joseph" means "he will add" or "may he add," for Rachel wanted God to add another son to her.

Jacob wanted to leave and go back to Canaan, but Laban wanted him to stay, for through divination he had learned that the Lord had blessed him because of Jacob (Gn 30:27). They discussed the matter of wages, and Jacob proposed that every speckled and spotted sheep and goat and every black lamb become his (vv 32-33). Laban agreed to this, but he quickly removed all the animals marked in that fashion and put them under the care of his sons, some three days' distance from the rest of the flocks (vv 35-36).

Jacob also contrived to gain an advantage; he tried to influence the genetics of the animals by putting speckled and streaked wooden rods by the water troughs when the best animals were breeding. The Lord blessed Jacob and he became rich in flocks and herds (Gn 30:37-43).

The sons of Laban became very bitter toward Jacob, and Laban's attitude toward him changed also. Jacob noticed this, and now the Lord spoke to Jacob and told him to return to Canaan (Gn 31:3-16). Jacob held a family council with his two wives and told them how God had blessed him, even though their father had cheated him and had changed his wages ten times. Jacob organized his caravan while Laban was away shearing sheep. Rachel stole her father's household gods, for their possession would make the holder heir to Laban's estate (see Nuzi Tablets). The party took off, crossed the Euphrates, and headed for Gilead. Laban and his relatives pursued them, but God spoke to Laban in a dream, warning him not to say anything to Jacob.

When Laban caught up with Jacob, he upbraided him for sneaking away and inquired about his household gods. Jacob did not know what Rachel had done, so he said that the one found with the gods should be put to death (Gn 31:32). Rachel had hidden them in a camel saddle and was sitting on the saddle when her father searched the tent. Laban did not find the idols. After this, Jacob became angry and complained that he had served Laban for 20 years and that Laban had reduced his wages ten times.

Laban suggested a covenant of peace, so the two men gathered stones to make a monument and called it "heap of witness." Early the next morning Laban said his farewells and returned home.

As Jacob and his household journeyed on, he was met by the angels of God ("God's camp," Gn 32:2), so he named that place Mahanaim, "the two camps." Jacob sent messengers ahead to inform Esau of his return. They came back with the news that Esau was approaching with 400 men. Jacob was afraid and sought the Lord's protection. To win Esau's favor, Jacob sent ahead gifts of animals, and that night he sent his family and possessions across the ford of the Jabbok River. Jacob was left alone, and "a man" wrestled with him throughout the night. Toward dawn the man touched Jacob's thigh, and his hip was dislocated, but Jacob would not give up until the "man" blessed him. Here the Lord changed Jacob's name to Israel ("he strives with God"), and Jacob named the place Peniel ("face of God") because he had seen God face to face and lived (Gn 32:30).

Esau was getting near, so Jacob arranged his family and went forward, bowing low before his brother. But Esau was gracious and forgiving and the meeting was a happy one (Gn 33:4). Esau was surprised at Jacob's large family and property and made every gesture of friendship. Esau returned to Seir, and Jacob moved on to Shechem, where he bought a piece of land from Hamor, the father of Shechem. Jacob built an altar there and named it El-Elohe-Israel, "God, the God of Israel" (v 20).

Acting on the Lord's instructions, Jacob moved to Bethel and expelled the foreign gods from his household. At Luz (Bethel) the Lord again met him and reaffirmed his new name, renewing his promise of land and descendants (Gn 35:9-15). As they journeyed south, Rachel died while giving birth to her second son (vv 16-20). She named him Ben-oni ("son of my sorrow"), but Jacob changed his name to Benjamin ("son of the right hand"). Jacob went on to Hebron and found that Isaac was still living. Isaac died at age 180 and was buried by Esau and Jacob.

Although the story of Jacob continues in the book of Genesis, the central figure of chapters 37–50 is Joseph, Jacob's favorite son, the firstborn of Rachel. Jacob showed this favoritism so openly that the other sons became jealous of Joseph. They plotted to kill Joseph but instead sold him to a caravan of traders on their way to Egypt (Gn 37:9-28). They took Joseph's coat, dipped it into the blood of a goat, and took it to their father, telling him that they had found the robe. Jacob recognized the coat he had given his son and concluded that he was dead. Jacob was heartbroken and would not be comforted.

When a famine hit Canaan, Jacob sent his sons to Egypt to buy grain (Gn 42:1-5), keeping Benjamin at home. When the brothers returned to Canaan, they reported to Jacob that the governor (who was really Joseph) had kept Simeon as a hostage and demanded that they bring Benjamin with them when they came again for grain. The famine continued, and Jacob again sent his sons to Egypt for grain. Very reluctantly, he permitted Benjamin to go with them, also sending a gift for the Egyptian governor (43:11-14).

The next news Jacob received was that Joseph was alive in Egypt and wanted his father and all his family to join him (Gn 45:21-28). Jacob went first to Beersheba and made offerings to the Lord. The Lord spoke to Jacob, telling him to go down to Egypt and confirming once more the promises he had previously made. Jacob and his descendants who were in Egypt numbered 70, including the two sons of Joseph.

When Jacob reached Goshen, Joseph came to meet him, and there was a joyous reunion (Gn 46:28-30). Joseph reported the arrival of his father and brothers to the pharaoh (47:1) and took five of the brothers and his father to meet the ruler. Israel settled in the area of Goshen and prospered there. Jacob spent 17 years in Egypt and reached the age of 147.

When Jacob sensed his death was near, he called Joseph and made him swear that he would bury him with his forebears in Canaan. Joseph took his two sons, Manasseh and Ephraim, to his father for the patriarchal blessing. He presented the boys so that Manasseh, the firstborn, would be on Jacob's right and Ephraim on his left. Jacob, however, crossed his hands and gave the younger son the greater blessing (48:13-20). Jacob prophesied that his people would return to Canaan, and he gave Joseph a double portion of the land. Then Jacob called for all his sons and gave to each of them a blessing (49:1-28). Judah received the place of preeminence, and it is he who appears in the genealogies of Jesus (vv 8-12). The blessing of Joseph shows the mark of special favor (vv 22-26). Jacob also charged his sons to bury him in the cave of Machpelah near Hebron, then he drew his feet up on the bed and died.

Joseph summoned the physicians to embalm his father according to Egyptian practice; there were 40 days for embalming and 70 days for the period of mourning (Gn 50:1-3). Arrangements were made to go to Canaan to bury Jacob as Joseph had promised, and a large funeral procession, including many Egyptian officials as well as the family of Jacob, went up from Egypt. The company mourned for seven days at the threshing floor of Atad; then the sons of Jacob buried him in the cave of Machpelah as he had requested. The entire group returned to Egypt, and Joseph assured his brothers that he had no intention of avenging the wrong they had done him. God had meant the whole episode for good (vv 15-21).

Jacob as the Nation Israel God made the same promises concerning the land and the nation to Abraham, Isaac, and Jacob, but it is by Jacob's God-given name, Israel, that the nation is known.

The name Jacob is used for the nation about 100 times (e.g., Nm 24:5, 19; Dt 32:9; Ps 59:13). It is often found as a parallel to Israel (e.g., Nm 23:7; Dt 33:10; Is 14:1).

"Jacob" is also used specifically of the northern kingdom of Israel (Am 7:2, 5). In Isaiah 41:21 "the King of Jacob" refers to God himself.

2. Father of Joseph, the husband of Mary and earthly father of Jesus according to Matthew's genealogy (Mt 1:16). Luke, however, names Heli as Joseph's father (Lk 3:24).

JADA

Onam's son from Judah's tribe (1 Chr 2:28, 32).

JADAH

Ahaz's son and a descendant of King Saul through Jonathan's line (1 Chr 8:36). Variant of Jehoaddah (1 Chr 8:36) and Jarah (1 Chr 9:42).

JADDAI

Nebo's descendant, who was encouraged by Ezra to divorce his foreign wife during the postexilic era (Ezr 10:43).

JADDUA

1. Leader who set his seal on Ezra's covenant during the postexilic era (Neh 10:21).

2. Eliashib's descendant and a contemporary of Nehemiah (Neh 12:11, 22). Jaddua's father, Jonathan (v 11), is mentioned in the Elephantine papyri as Johanan (see also v 22).

JADON

Workman on the Jerusalem wall after the return from exile. Jadon worked on the section near the Old Gate of the city with men from Gibeon and Mizpah. He was a Meronothite (Neh 3:7).

JAEL

Wife of Heber. Though her husband was from the Kenite tribe, a longtime ally of Israel, he had chosen to side with Jabin, the Canaanite king. Jael demonstrated her loyalty to Israel, Jabin's enemy, however, by inviting Sisera, Jabin's general, into her tent, giving him milk instead of water, providing him a place to sleep, and then driving a tent peg into

JACOB
The Times of Jacob

C. 2006 BC
Jacob and Esau are born to Isaac and Rebekah (Genesis 25:21-26).

C. 1981 BC?
Esau sells Jacob his rights as firstborn for a bowl of stew (Genesis 25:29-34).

C. 1961 BC?
Jacob deceives Isaac to get his blessing and escapes Esau's wrath by fleeing to Haran (Genesis 27).

C. 1960–1953 BC?
Jacob works seven years to win Rachel as his wife but gets Leah instead (Genesis 29:18-25).

C. 1953–1946 BC?
Jacob works another seven years to wed Rachel (Genesis 29:26-30).

C. 1940 BC?
Jacob leaves Haran with his substantial family to return to Canaan. Along the way, he wrestles with God and reconciles with Esau (Genesis 31–32).

C. 1915 BC
Jacob's eleventh (and favorite) son, Joseph, is born (Genesis 30:22-24).

C. 1876 BC
Jacob moves to Egypt, where Joseph rules, and settles there with his family (Genesis 46).

C. 1859 BC
Jacob dies in Egypt (Genesis 49:33).

his temple (Jgs 4:17-18, 21-22). Deborah, the inspired poetess, reflecting on the God-given victory over the Canaanites, praises Jael for this deed (5:6, 24-31).

JAHATH

1. Reaiah's son and the father of Ahumai and Lahad, Zorathites from Judah's tribe (1 Chr 4:2).
2. Gershonite Levite (1 Chr 6:20), whose descendant Asaph was appointed by King David to serve as a musician in the Temple (v 43).
3. A descendant of Shimei, who was a descendant of Gershon from Levi's tribe (1 Chr 23:10-11).
4. Shelomith's son from Levi's tribe (1 Chr 24:22).
5. Merarite Levite, who was one of the supervisors of the Temple repairs under Josiah (2 Chr 34:12).

JAHAZIEL

1. Warrior from Benjamin's tribe who joined David at Ziklag in his struggle against King Saul. Jahaziel was one of David's ambidextrous archers and slingers (1 Chr 12:4).
2. One of the two priests David appointed to blow trumpets before the Ark as it was brought into the tent in Jerusalem, where it remained until the completion of the Temple by Solomon (1 Chr 16:6).
3. Levite belonging to the Kohathite division appointed by David to Temple duties (1 Chr 23:19; 24:23).
4. Levite of the sons of Asaph who encouraged Jehoshaphat and the army of Judah not to be dismayed by the size of Moabite and Ammonite armies coming against them but to stand still and see the victory of the Lord (2 Chr 20:14). Jehoshaphat's response exemplified a godly king encouraging his people to have faith in the Lord their God (vv 18-21).
5. Shecaniah's father. Shecaniah returned to Jerusalem with Ezra after the Exile (Ezr 8:5).

JAHDAI

Caleb's descendant from Judah's tribe (1 Chr 2:47).

JAHDIEL

One of the family heads of Manasseh's tribe dwelling east of the Jordan following the allotment of the land (1 Chr 5:24). He was noted as one of the mighty warriors in his tribe.

JAHDO

Gadite, son of Buz and a forefather of a number of valiant men who were registered during the reigns of King Jeroboam of Israel (793–753 BC) and King Jotham of Judah (750–735 BC; 1 Chr 5:14).

JAHLEEL

Zebulun's son (Gn 46:14) and the founder of the Jahleelite family (Nm 26:26).

JAHMAI

Tola's son from Issachar's tribe (1 Chr 7:2).

JAHZEEL

Naphtali's son (Gn 46:24; 1 Chr 7:13) and founder of the Jahzeelite family (Nm 26:48).

JAHZEIAH

Tikvah's son and one of the persons named in connection with the divorce proceedings between the Israelites and their foreign wives (Ezr 10:15). Opinions differ as to whether he was for or against the proceedings. While the Hebrew text can be justifiably read either way, the grammar favors the interpretation that Jahzeiah opposed the proceedings (see NLT).

JAHZERAH

Ancestor of a priest who returned to Judah after the Babylonian exile (1 Chr 9:12). He is called Ahzai in Nehemiah 11:13. Little else is known about him except that he was a great-grandson of a priest named Immer who lived in Jerusalem before the Exile.

See also Ahzai.

JAIR

1. Descendant of Manasseh (Nm 32:41), who at the time of the Conquest took several villages in the Argob region of Bashan and Gilead and called them after his own name, Havvoth-jair, meaning "Towns of Jair" (Dt 3:14; cf. Jos 13:30; 1 Kgs 4:13; 1 Chr 2:23).

2. One of the judges of Israel. He judged Israel 22 years. His being a Gileadite makes it probable that he was a descendant of #1 above (Jgs 10:3-5).

3. Father of Elhanan, who killed Lahmi, Goliath's brother (1 Chr 20:5). In 2 Samuel 21:19 he is called Jaare-oregim.

4. Father of Mordecai (Est 2:5). Because of the time lapse from the capture of Jeconiah, king of Judah (597 BC), to the beginning of the reign of Xerxes, king of Persia (486 BC), Jair was either the one taken captive with Jeconiah or his father, Shimei, was, in which case Jair would have been born during the Captivity.

JAIRUS

Leader of the synagogue, perhaps at Capernaum. Jairus sought Jesus among the crowds and petitioned him to come and heal his critically ill daughter. While delayed by another healing, Jesus learned that Jairus's daughter had died. Encouraging Jairus not to fear but to believe,

Jesus went on to the leader's house, dismissed the mourners, and brought the child back to life (Mk 5:22, 35-42; Lk 8:41, 49-55).

JAKEH
Agur's father. Agur authored a series of proverbs addressed to Ithiel and Ucal (Prv 30:1).

JAKIM
1. Shimei's descendant from Benjamin's tribe (1 Chr 8:19).
2. Family leader of the 12th group of Aaron's descendants assigned to Temple duty in David's time (1 Chr 24:12).

JAKIN
1. Son of Simeon and leader of the Jachinites, who immigrated to Egypt with his grandfather Jacob (Gn 46:10; Ex 6:15; Nm 26:12). He is called Jarib in 1 Chronicles 4:24.
2. Priest who lived in Jerusalem after the Exile (1 Chr 9:10; Neh 11:10). The name Jachin may possibly designate a family of priests of which Jachin was the head.
3. Descendant of Aaron and head of the 21st course of priests assigned to Temple duty in David's reign (1 Chr 24:17).

JALAM
Esau's son and chief of an Edomite clan (Gn 36:5, 14, 18; 1 Chr 1:35).

JALON
Ezrah's son from Judah's tribe (1 Chr 4:17).

JAMBRES
Enemy of Moses, who, along with Jannes, is used by Paul as an example of the type of person to avoid (2 Tm 3:8-9). *See* Jannes and Jambres.

JAMES
1. James, son of Zebedee. One of the 12 apostles; the first of them to be martyred (AD 44).
   James was a Galilean fisherman whose circumstances we can suppose to have been comfortable (Mk 1:19-20) and who was called to be one of the disciples at the same time as his brother John (Mt 4:21; Mk 1:19-20). It is reasonable to assume that he was older than John, both because he is nearly always mentioned first and because John is sometimes identified as "the brother of James" (Mt 10:2; 17:1; Mk 3:17; 5:37).
   James, John, and Simon Peter, who were part of a fishing partnership that included Andrew, Simon's brother (Lk 5:10), were a trio who attained in some sense a place of primacy among the disciples. They are found at the center of things—for example,

QUICKTAKE

JAMES

STRENGTHS AND ACCOMPLISHMENTS
• One of the 12 disciples
• One of a special inner circle of three with Peter and John
• First of the 12 disciples to be killed for his faith

WEAKNESSES AND MISTAKES:
• Two outbursts from James indicate struggles with temper (Luke 9:54) and selfishness (Mark 10:37). Both times, he and his brother, John, spoke as one

LESSON FROM HIS LIFE:
• Loss of life is not too heavy a price to pay for following Jesus

VITAL STATISTICS:
Where: Galilee
Occupations: Fisherman, disciple
Relatives: Father: Zebedee. Mother: Salome. Brother: John
Contemporaries: Jesus, Pilate, Herod Agrippa

KEY VERSES:
"Then James and John, the sons of Zebedee, came over and spoke to him.'Teacher,' they said,'we want you to do us a favor.'

"'What is your request?' he asked.

"They replied,'When you sit on your glorious throne, we want to sit in places of honor next to you, one on your right and the other on your left'" (Mark 10:35-37).

James's story is told in the Gospels. He is also mentioned in Acts 1:13 and 12:2.

when Jairus's daughter was raised (Mk 5:37; Lk 8:51), at the Transfiguration (Mt 17:1; Mk 9:2; Lk 9:28), on the Mount of Olives (Mk 13:3), and in the Garden of Gethsemane (Mt 26:37; Mk 14:33). It was James and John, moreover, who had earlier accompanied Jesus to the home of Simon and Andrew (Mk 1:29).

James and John were given by Jesus the nickname Boanerges, or "sons of thunder" (Mk 3:17), when they were rebuked by the Lord for impetuous speech and for having totally misconceived the purpose of his coming. This may have been the consequence of the suggestion made by them that they should pray for the destruction of the Samaritan village, the inhabitants of which had rejected the Lord's messengers (Lk 9:54; cf. Mk 9:38; Lk 9:49).

The presumptuous and ill-considered thinking of the two brothers was obvious also when, after asking with his brother for a place of honor in the kingdom, James was corecipient of the prophecy that they would drink the cup their Master was to drink (Mk 10:35-40; cf. Mt 20:20-23). The two sons of Zebedee are also assumed to have been present with the other disciples when the risen Christ appeared by the Sea of Galilee (Jn 21:1), though curiously James's name is nowhere mentioned in the fourth Gospel.

We know nothing about James's career subsequently until about the year 44, when Jesus' prophecy was fulfilled: James was killed "by the sword" by Herod Agrippa I, and thus became the first of the Twelve whose martyrdom was referred to in the NT (Acts 12:1-2).

The wife of Zebedee was Salome (Mt 27:56; Mk 15:40), who may have been a sister of the Lord's mother (Jn 19:25). If this were so, it would mean that James and John were first cousins of Jesus and that they may have considered themselves to have been in a privileged position.

2. James, brother of Jesus; leading elder in the church at Jerusalem; author of the epistle bearing his name.

The only two references to James in the Gospels mention him with his brothers Joseph (Greek Joses), Simon, and Judas (Mt 13:55; Mk 6:3). This James may have been, after Jesus, the oldest of the brothers. The question has been raised about whether these were indeed full brothers of Jesus by Mary, for such a situation has created difficulty for those who cannot square it with their views on the perpetual virginity of Mary. But there seems to be no good reason to challenge the fact from Scripture. As with the other brothers, James apparently did not accept Jesus' authority during his earthly life (Jn 7:5).

There is no specific mention of James's conversion; it may have dated from Jesus' appearance to him and the others after Jesus' resurrection (1 Cor 15:7). He became head of the church at Jerusalem (Acts 12:17; 21:18; Gal 2:9). Although Jesus had always taught the relative subordination of family ties (Mt 12:48-50; Mk 3:33-35; Lk 8:21), it is hard to believe that James's authority was not somehow enhanced because of his relationship to the Master.

James was regarded as an apostle (Gal 1:19), although he was not one of the Twelve. Some suggest he was a replacement for the martyred son of Zebedee; others infer his apostleship by widening the scope of that term to embrace both "the Twelve" and "all the apostles" (see the two separate categories cited in 1 Cor 15:5, 7).

Tradition stated that James was appointed the first bishop of Jerusalem by the Lord himself as well as the apostles. What is certain is that he presided over the first Council of Jerusalem, called to consider the terms for admission of Gentiles into the

Christian church, and he may have formulated the decree that met with the approval of all his colleagues and was sent to the churches of Antioch, Syria, and Cilicia (Acts 15:19-20). James evidently regarded his own special ministry as being to the Jews, and his was a mediating role in the controversy that arose in the young church around the place of the law for those who had become Christians, from both Gentile and Jewish origins.

That he continued to have strong Jewish-Christian sympathies is apparent from the request made to Paul when the latter visited Jerusalem for the last time (Acts 21:18-25). This was also the last mention in Acts of James's career. His name also occurs in the NT as the traditional author of the Epistle of James, where he describes himself as "a slave of God and of the Lord Jesus Christ" (Jas 1:1).

According to Hegesippus (c. 180), James's faithful adherence to the Jewish law and his austere lifestyle led to the designation "the Just." It seems clear that James suffered martyrdom. Josephus places it in the year 61, when there was a Jewish uprising after the death of Festus the procurator and before his successor had been appointed.

3. James, son of Alphaeus; one of the 12 apostles.

James, son of Alphaeus, is always listed as one of the 12 apostles (Mt 10:3; Mk 3:18; Lk 6:15; Acts 1:13), but nothing is known for certain about him. Levi (also known as Matthew) is also described as the son of Alphaeus (Mk 2:14), but it is improbable that he and James were brothers. Many scholars have identified him with the one called "James the less" or "James the smaller." The description "the less" seems to have been given to distinguish him from the son of Zebedee, and it may signify that he was either smaller or younger than Zebedee's son (the Greek word can cover both interpretations).

JAMIN

1. Simeon's son (Gn 46:10; Ex 6:15; 1 Chr 4:24) and founder of the Jaminite family (Nm 26:12).

2. Ram's son from Judah's tribe (1 Chr 2:27).

3. One of the men (perhaps a Levite) who taught and explained the law to the people following Ezra's public reading (Neh 8:7).

JAMLECH

Leader in Simeon's tribe (1 Chr 4:34).

JANAI

Gadite chief who settled, along with his kinsmen, in the land of Bashan (1 Chr 5:12).

JANIM

City in the hill country of the territory assigned to Judah's tribe for an inheritance (Jos 15:53). Its location is presumably southwest of Hebron.

JANNAI

Ancestor of Jesus recorded in Luke's genealogy (Lk 3:24).

JANNES AND JAMBRES

Two of Pharaoh's magicians, who opposed Moses and tried to show that they were as effective as he at working miracles (Ex 7–9). Jewish legend regarded Jannes and Jambres (somewhat improbably) as sons of Balaam, the Midianite prophet of Numbers 22–24. Curiously, the Exodus chapters do not identify them by name. The only biblical reference to them appears in the NT. The apostle Paul saw similarity between Jannes and Jambres and the false teachers of debased intellect who were enemies of the truth in his day (2 Tm 3:6-8).

Much speculation has arisen about the two names. They are apparently Semitic, but their precise derivation is unclear. They are referred to in the Qumran documents and in late Jewish, pagan, and early Christian literature. Variations include "Yohanneh and his brother" (Qumran), "Yohane and Mamre" (Babylonian Talmud), and "Mambres" (the translation in most Latin and some Greek manuscripts of 2 Tm 3:8). The names appear also in the writings of Pliny (first century AD) and of Apuleius and Numenius (both second century), though both names are not always cited.

Origen, an Alexandrian church father, twice referred to an apocryphal work entitled The Book of Jannes and Jambres, suggesting that it was the source of Paul's words in 2 Timothy. A Latin church document called the Gelasian Decree (fifth or sixth century?) mentions Penitence of Jannes and Jambres, possibly the work mentioned by Origen.

JANOAH

1. City defining the eastern border of Ephraim's territory, located southeast of Shechem and northeast of Shiloh (Jos 16:6-7). It has been identified with modern Khirbet Yanun.

2. Town (modern Yanuh) of Naphtali's tribe captured by Tiglath-pileser, king of Assyria, during the reign of King Pekah of Israel in 732 BC (2 Kgs 15:29).

JAPHETH

One of Noah's three sons (Gn 5:32; 7:13; 9:18, 23, 27; 10:1-5; 1 Chr 1:4-5) who, along with his wife, was among the eight human survivors of the great Flood. Because Japheth and his brother Shem acted with respect and modesty in covering their father's nakedness while he was in a drunken condition (Gn 9:20-23), they were both blessed in Noah's prophetic pronouncement of Genesis 9:26-27. Of Japheth, Noah said, "God enlarge Japheth, and let him dwell in the tents of Shem; and let Canaan be his slave" (RSV). There are two interpretations of the meaning of this prophecy. Some understand the enlargement of Japheth to be a reference to a great increase in numbers of descendants. "To dwell in the tents of Shem" is understood as Japheth's sharing in the blessing of Shem. According to this view, there is to be a time when God will work primarily with Shem (the people of Israel), but then, at a later time, Japheth will be brought into connection with the faith of Israel and share in its promises. In this view fulfillment is found in the opening of the gospel to the Gentiles at the inception of the NT church. Others understand the "enlargement of Japheth" to refer to territorial enlargement, and the "dwelling in the tents of Shem" as the conquest of Shemite territory by Japhethites. In this view, fulfillment is found in the Greek and Roman conquests of Palestine.

In the "table of nations" in Genesis 10:2, Japheth is listed as the father of Gomer, Magog, Madai, Javan, Tubal, Meshech, and Tiras. These are the ancestors of peoples who lived to the north and west of Israel and who spoke what today are classified as Indo-European languages.

See also Noah #1.

JAPHIA

1. King of Lachish who joined an alliance of four other Amorite kings to punish Gibeon for its treaty with the Jews. Joshua dealt a total defeat to the Amorites at the battle of Beth-horon (aided by hailstones and the sun standing still). Japhia and the four kings hid in a cave at Makkedah but were discovered and hung by Joshua (Jos 10:3-27).

2. Son born to David while he was king in Jerusalem (2 Sm 5:15; 1 Chr 3:7; 14:6).

JAPHLET

Heber's son and chief in Asher's tribe (1 Chr 7:32-33).

JARED

Mahalalel's son and a descendant of Seth. He was the father of Enoch (Gn 5:15-20; 1 Chr 1:2; Lk 3:37).

JARHA

Egyptian servant of Sheshan, Jerahmeel's descendant, who was given his master's daughter in marriage. Sheshan did this because he had no sons (1 Chr 2:34-35).

JARIB

1. Alternate name for Jachin, Simeon's son, in 1 Chronicles 4:24.

2. Man who assisted Ezra in securing Temple servants before the return to Palestine from exile (Ezr 8:16).

3. From Jeshua's family, a priest who obeyed Ezra's exhortation to divorce his pagan wife after the Exile (Ezr 10:18).

JARMUTH

1. Fortified city in the northern part of the Shephelah given to Judah's tribe for an inheritance (Jos 15:35). It was one of five Amorite cities that banded together to attack Gibeon after they had made peace with Joshua and Israel (10:3-5). Jarmuth was reinhabited after the Exile by people of Judah (Neh 11:29), and possibly maintained a population

throughout the Dispersion. It is identified with Khirbet Yarmuk, 18 miles (29 kilometers) southwest of Jerusalem. Archaeological evidence suggests that the area of the Bronze Age city was six to eight acres (2.4 to 3.2 hectares) and had a population of about 1,500 to 2,000 people. It is mentioned in the Amarna letters as receiving aid from Lachish.

2. One of four cities of Issachar given to the Levites for their inheritance (Jos 21:28-29). It is apparently identifiable with Ramoth in 1 Chronicles 6:73 and Remeth in Joshua 19:21. A stele of Pharaoh Seti I was found at Beth-shan, referring to the whole area as Mt Jarmuth.

JAROAH
Gilead's son from Gad's tribe (1 Chr 5:14).

JASHEN
One of David's mighty men known as "the thirty" (2 Sm 23:32). The Hebrew text reads "the sons of Jashen," and 1 Chronicles 11:34 reads "the sons of Hashem the Gizonite." Scholars are generally agreed that the phrase "the sons of" is dittographic and repeats the last three letters of the preceding word. The reading in the original text probably was either "Jashen the Gizonite" or "Hashem the Gizonite," making him, and not his son, the mighty man of David's army.

JASHOBEAM
1. Zabdiel's son who was put in charge of David's three mightiest men (1 Chr 11:11) and also appointed chief of a division (24,000 soldiers) on duty in the first month of the year (1 Chr 27:2). He is the same person as Josheb-basshebeth, the Tahkemonite (2 Sm 23:8, NLT mg). Jashobeam gained renown by killing 300 men, according to 1 Chronicles 11:11, or 800, according to 2 Samuel 23:8.
2. One of the ambidextrous warriors who joined David at Ziklag (1 Chr 12:6).

JASHUB
1. Issachar's third son (1 Chr 7:1; alternately called Iob in Gn 46:13), and founder of the Jashubite family (Nm 26:24).
2. Bani's descendant, who obeyed Ezra's exhortation to divorce his pagan wife after the Exile (Ezr 10:29).

JASHUBI-LEHEM
Mentioned along with Moab in 1 Chronicles 4:22.

JASON
1. Jewish high priest (174–171 BC) who brought about the decline of the priesthood by Hellenizing Jerusalem, making her inhabitants "citizens of Antioch" (2 Macc 4:9ff.). He was deposed by his cousin Onias Menelaus, but when a false report told of the

death of Antiochus Epiphanes, Jason attacked Jerusalem without mercy for his own people. Antiochus, returning from an aborted attack on Egypt, retook Jerusalem and Jason was forced to flee to Transjordan and thence from city to city. Second Maccabees reports that at his death, "[Jason] who had cast out many to lie unburied had no one to mourn for him; he had no funeral of any sort and no place in the tomb of his fathers" (5:10, RSV).

2. Jewish Christian at Thessalonica who hosted Paul and Silas (Acts 17:1, 5-9). He and others were called before the city officials on charges of harboring seditionists. He was released when he put up bail.

3. Christian at Corinth who, along with Paul, sent greetings to the church at Rome (Rom 16:21).

JATHNIEL
Fourth son of Meshelemiah the Korahite and doorkeeper of the Temple in David's time (1 Chr 26:2).

JAVAN
Japheth's son whose seafaring descendants migrated to the north and west of Canaan (Gn 10:2-4; 1 Chr 1:5-7).

JAZIZ
One of David's royal stewards in charge of the flocks (1 Chr 27:30-31).

JEATHERAI
Zerah's son, a Gershonite Levite (1 Chr 6:21), called Ethni in 1 Chronicles 6:41.

JEBEREKIAH
Father of Zechariah the scribe. Zechariah, with Uriah the priest, witnessed Isaiah's prophecy of the Assyrian conquest of Israel (Is 8:2).

JECOLIAH
Mother of King Azariah, or Uzziah (2 Kgs 15:2; 2 Chr 26:3).

JEDAIAH
1. Shimri's son and the father of Allon. He is listed in the genealogical tables of the Simeonites who settled in the valley of Gedor in Hezekiah's time (1 Chr 4:37).

2. Harumaph's son, who helped repair the Jerusalem wall after the Exile (Neh 3:10).

3. Aaron's descendant and head of the second of the 24 priestly divisions for Temple service in David's time (1 Chr 24:7). His descendants are listed among the returned exiles (1 Chr 9:10; Ezr 2:36; Neh 7:39). The individuals and families listed below

are probably a part of this priestly line, but their exact relationships are difficult to determine.

4. Provincial priest who agreed to resettle in postexilic Jerusalem (Neh 11:10; cf. v 2).

5. Priest who returned with Zerubbabel after the Exile (Neh 12:6-7). In the next generation this was the name of a family (v 21).

6. One of the Exiles taken by Zechariah as witness to the symbolic crowning of Joshua (NLT "Jeshua"). He may be the same as #4 or #5 above. He came back from captivity bringing gifts for the Temple in the days of the high priest Joshua (Zec 6:10-14).

JEDIAEL

1. Benjamin's son (1 Chr 7:6, 10-11), whose descendants were warriors, numbering 17,200 by David's time. Some suggest that he is identifiable with Ashbel, also Benjamin's son (Gn 46:21).

    See also Ashbel.

2. Shimri's son, listed among David's mighty men (1 Chr 11:45).

3. One who deserted Saul to join David at Ziklag (1 Chr 12:20). He may be the same as #2 above.

4. Member of the Levitical family of Korah, appointed a doorkeeper of the Temple during David's reign (1 Chr 26:2).

JEDIDAH

Adaiah's daughter, the wife of King Amon of Judah and the mother of King Josiah (2 Kgs 22:1).

JEDIDIAH

Name meaning "beloved of the LORD [Yahweh]." God told Nathan the prophet to give Solomon, David's second son by Bathsheba, this name soon after his birth (2 Sm 12:24-25).

JEDUTHUN

Member of the Levitical family of Merar who, along with Asaph and Heman, presided over the music in the sanctuary in David's reign (1 Chr 25:1; 2 Chr 5:12; called "Ethan" in 1 Chr 6:44; 15:17). Jeduthun is mentioned in the titles of Psalms 39, 62, and 77. Some of his sons were set apart to prophesy with lyres, harps, and cymbals (1 Chr 25:1-3), apparently following the example of their father, who was called "the king's seer" (2 Chr 35:15). In 1 Chronicles 16:38 and 42, he is listed as Obed-edom's father.

JEHALLELEL

1. Descendant of Judah who had four sons (1 Chr 4:16).

2. Levite of the family of Merari whose son Azariah participated in the cleansing of the Temple in Hezekiah's time (2 Chr 29:12).

JEHDEIAH

1. Shubael's son, a Levite in David's time (1 Chr 24:20).

2. Royal steward from Meronoth who was in charge of David's donkeys (1 Chr 27:30).

JEHEZKEL

Levite assigned to Temple duty in David's time; leader of the 20th division (1 Chr 24:16).

JEHIAH

Levite who, along with Obed-edom, was appointed as doorkeeper for the Ark when David brought it to Jerusalem (1 Chr 15:24).

JEHIEL

1. A Levite musician who, along with other Levites appointed by David, played a psaltery at the removal of the Ark to Jerusalem (1 Chr 15:18-20). Afterward, he was appointed to a permanent ministry of music in the sanctuary (1 Chr 16:5).

2. Levite of the family of Gershon; a chief of the house of Ladan (1 Chr 23:8, NLT mg). He was in charge of the Temple treasury during David's reign—an office that seems to have continued in the family (29:8)—and founder of a priestly family called Jehieli or Jehielites (26:21-22).

3. Hacmoni's son who, with David's uncle Jonathan (a counselor and a scribe), was appointed to take care of the king's sons as a tutor and adviser (1 Chr 27:32).

4. Son of King Jehoshaphat of Judah, placed by his father over one of the fortified cities of Judah (2 Chr 21:2). He and five brothers were slain by Jehoram when Jehoram became king.

5. One of the Kohathite Levites from the family of Heman who assisted in King Hezekiah's reforms (2 Chr 29:14, RSV "Jehuel"). He may be the same Levite who was assigned to oversee the reception and distribution of the sacred offerings (2 Chr 31:13).

6. One of the chief officers of the Temple at the time of Josiah's religious reformation (2 Chr 35:8); he contributed many sacrifices for the great Passover service.

7. Father of Obadiah from Joab's house; he returned with Ezra from Babylon (Ezr 8:9).

8. One of the sons of Elam and father of Shecaniah. He was associated with Ezra's marriage reforms (Ezr 10:2) and was perhaps the same Jehiel who was among those who divorced their foreign wives (v 26).

9. Priest who was among those Ezra persuaded to divorce their foreign wives (Ezr 10:21).

10. KJV spelling of Jeiel, King Saul's ancestor, in 1 Chronicles 9:35. See Jeiel #2.

11. KJV spelling of Jeiel, Hotham's son, in 1 Chronicles 11:44. See Jeiel #3.

JEHIZKIAH

Shallum's son and a chief of Ephraim during the reign of Ahaz in Judah. He opposed the enslavement of the men of Judah by victorious Israel (2 Chr 28:12).

JEHOADDIN

Mother of Amaziah, king of Judah (2 Kgs 14:2; 2 Chr 25:1).

JEHOAHAZ

1. Twelfth king of Israel, succeeding his father, Jehu, and ruling from 814 BC to 798 BC. Because he was an evil king, God punished Israel by subjecting them to the Aramean kings Hazael and his son Ben-hadad. The military force in Israel was reduced to 50 cavalrymen, 10 chariots, and 10,000 infantrymen. The oppression became so severe that Jehoahaz prayed to God, who listened to him and delivered Israel from the Arameans, but not until the reign of Joash (Jehoash) (2 Kgs 13:2-7, 25). During Jehoahaz's reign, relations between Judah and Israel seem to have been fairly good, since Jehoahaz (14:1, "Joahaz") named his son Joash after his contemporary, Joash king of Judah (2 Kgs 13:1, 9; 14:1).

2. Seventeenth king of Judah, ruling three months in 609 BC. The people chose him to succeed his father, Josiah, who was killed in the battle of Megiddo. His mother's name was Hamutal. Jehoahaz was 23 years old at his coronation. He is also called Shallum (1 Chr 3:15), and Jehoahaz may well be a throne name. He is characterized as an evil king before God. His rule ended when Pharaoh Neco imprisoned him at Riblah in Hamath. Later he was taken to Egypt, where he died (2 Kgs 23:30-34). Jeremiah prophesied that Jehoahaz would never return to Israel but would die in the land of his captivity (Jer 22:11-12).

3. Another form of the name of Ahaziah, the sixth king of Judah, who ruled in 841 BC (2 Chr 21:17; cf. 22:1). Both forms of the name have the same meaning. The difference is the placement of the divine name. In Jehoahaz it comes first, "Jeho-" and in Ahaziah it comes last, "-iah" (-yah). *See* Ahaziah #2.

4. Full name of Ahaz, the 12th king of Judah, according to an inscription of Assyrian king Tiglath-pileser III. *See* Ahaz #1.

JEHOASH

Name of two OT kings, occurring only in the book of 2 Kings. The name means "the LORD is strong" or "the LORD hath bestowed." Joash, the shorter form of the name, frequently appears in the Kings and Chronicles narratives.

1. Son of Ahaziah and seventh king of Judah (835–796 BC). Jehoash ascended the throne after the wicked Athaliah had been killed at the command of Jehoiada the priest. As an infant, he was hidden by his aunt Jehosheba in the Temple and thus survived the slaughter of the king's household by Athaliah (2 Kgs 11:1-3; 2 Chr 23:10-12). After

remaining six years within the Temple precinct, Jehoash was declared king at the age of seven and ruled for 40 years (11:21–12:1; 2 Chr 24:1-3).

His major activity during his reign was the renovation of the Temple (2 Kgs 12:4-5; 2 Chr 24:4-5). When, by his 23rd year, little progress had been made (2 Kgs 12:6), he revised the taxation schedule, commanded the people of Judah to bring their contributions directly to the Jerusalem Temple, and soon restored the Lord's house to its proper condition (2 Chr 24:13).

After the death of the priest Jehoiada, Jehoash and Judah forsook the Lord and served the Asherim and the idols (2 Chr 24:15-18). Not heeding the prophetic warning of divine judgment (v 20), Jehoash and his people were conquered by the Arameans. Though Jehoash had once been able to avert a siege of Judah by paying tribute to Hazael (2 Kgs 12:17-18), the same strategy did not work a second time. The Arameans plundered Judah and Jerusalem, sending the spoil to Hazael in Damascus (2 Chr 24:23-24). Jehoash was assassinated by his servants Jozacar (Jozabad/Zabad) and Jehozabad while recuperating from wounds incurred in battle with the Arameans (2 Kgs 12:20-21; 2 Chr 24:25-26).

2. Son of Jehoahaz and 13th king of Israel (798–782 BC). Jehoash enjoyed a measure of military success that had eluded his father. No longer subject to punitive military exploits from Hazael of Aram, he was able to establish political stability in the northern kingdom. In fact, he subjugated the southern kingdom of Judah while Amaziah was king in Jerusalem (796–767 BC). The conflict between Amaziah and Jehoash was precipitated mainly by Amaziah. Overconfident with his victories in Edom, Amaziah initiated a military conflict with Israel (2 Chr 25:17-19). The battle was fought near Beth-shemesh in the Judean Shephelah. King Jehoash routed the army of Judah, captured Amaziah, and moved on to Jerusalem. Destroying the outer wall from the Ephraim Gate to the Corner Gate, he entered the capital city and plundered the treasures of both the palace and the Temple (vv 21-24). He was apparently used as an instrument of the Lord to subdue Judah (v 20).

A contemporary of Jehoash was Elisha the prophet. In spite of the pervasive wickedness in Israel and the apostasy of the king himself (2 Kgs 13:10-11), Jehoash still sought the counsel of this prophet of the Lord. While Elisha was on his deathbed, Jehoash sought the prophet's blessing (v 14). Elisha assured the king that the Arameans would be defeated by Israel at Aphek and that Israel would enjoy three decisive victories over this same enemy (vv 15-19). During his 16-year reign, Jehoash achieved political stability in the northern kingdom. Though considered an evil king, he was used as an instrument of judgment against Amaziah of Judah and enjoyed the blessing of Yahweh against Aram.

JEHOHANAN

1. Korahite Levite who was a gatekeeper of the sanctuary during David's reign (1 Chr 26:3).

2. Commander of thousands in King Jehoshaphat's army (2 Chr 17:15).

3. Father of Ishmael, commander of a unit of soldiers who helped the priest Jehoiada overthrow the wicked queen Athaliah of Judah (2 Chr 23:1).

4. Eliashib's descendant who owned a chamber into which Ezra retired to pray, fast, and mourn for his people (Ezr 10:6). He is possibly the same as Johanan, a grandson of Eliashib the high priest (Neh 12:22-23, NLT), and Jonathan (a textual variant), Joiada's son, in Nehemiah 12:11.

5. One of Bebai's four sons, who was exhorted by Ezra to divorce his foreign wife (Ezr 10:28).

6. Son of the Ammonite official Tobiah and a contemporary of Nehemiah. He married a Jewish woman whose father, Meshullam, had helped repair the Jerusalem wall (Neh 6:18; KJV "Johanan").

7. Priest and family leader in postexilic Jerusalem during the time Joiakim was high priest (Neh 12:13).

8. One of the priests who participated as a singer in the dedication of the rebuilt Jerusalem wall (Neh 12:42).

JEHOIACHIN

King of Judah for a very brief time (598–597 BC). He was the son of Jehoiakim and Nehushta, the daughter of Elnathan of Jerusalem (possibly the Elnathan mentioned by Jeremiah, cf. Jer 26:22; 36:12, 25). The name Jehoiachin means "Yahweh will uphold," and variations include Coniah (Jer 22:24, 28; 37:1), Jeconiah (1 Chr 3:16-17; Est 2:6; Jer 24:1; 27:20; 28:4; 29:2), and Jechoniah (Mt 1:11-12; KJV "Jechonias"). Jehoiachin was 18 years old when he was installed as king upon his father's death, and he ruled for only three months and ten days in Jerusalem (2 Kgs 24:8; cf. 2 Chr 36:9, NLT mg). He inherited a vassal kingdom in revolt. Besieged by the armies of the Babylonian overlord Nebuchadnezzar, Jehoiachin had little choice but to capitulate in the face of insurmountable odds. According to the Babylonian Chronicle, records based on the official annals of the Babylonian kings, Nebuchadnezzar entered Syro-Palestine in December of 598 BC and took Jerusalem on March 16, 597. The Babylonians plundered the palace and Temple treasuries. Along with Jehoiachin, his family, prominent military leaders, royal officials, and artisans were taken prisoner and led away to exile in Babylon. Before returning to Babylon, the victorious king placed Jehoiachin's uncle Mattaniah, now named Zedekiah, on the throne in Jerusalem (2 Kgs 24:12-17; cf. 2 Chr 36:10).

According to Jeremiah, the trauma caused by the Babylonian invasion of Judah, and the consequent political upheaval prompted by a succession of three kings in four months, had little impact on the people spiritually (Jer 37–38). This same prophet of God forecast Jehoiachin's exile and predicted he would have no descendants succeeding him on the throne (22:24-30). In contrast, the false prophet Hananiah prophesied Jehoiachin would be restored to the throne of Judah within two years (28:3-4, 11; cf. vv 12-17).

Jehoiachin's continuing royal status as the legitimate claimant to the Judahite kingship was reflected in the fact that Ezekiel's oracles are dated to the year of Jehoiachin's exile, not Zedekiah's reign (Ez 1:2; 8:1; 20:1; etc.). Babylonian records confirm this recognition of Jehoiachin's former position; he retained his title of king and received favorable treatment from the Babylonians. He is certainly the "Yaukin, king of the land of Yahuda" listed in one of the cuneiform tablets; this tablet contains inventories of rations of oil and barley for the king and his five sons and implies they were not imprisoned but living a fairly normal life in Babylonia. At some point Jehoiachin must have been imprisoned, however, because later, during the reign of Evil-merodach, he was released from prison and granted dining privileges with the Babylonian king (c. 562 BC; cf. 2 Kgs 25:27-30; Jer 52:31-34). Whether he was imprisoned for attempting to escape or because of Judah's rebellion against Babylon under Zedekiah is unclear.

Jehoiachin's name appears in Matthew's genealogy of Jesus Christ (Mt 1:11-12), and some contend that this contradicts Jeremiah's oracle of judgment against the king's descendants (Jer 22:30). Yet it is possible to understand Haggai's blessing of Zerubbabel (Hg 2:20-23) as a reversal of Jeremiah's curse and the reinstatement of Jehoiachin's line on the Davidic—and ultimately messianic—throne (cf. Is 56:3-5).

JEHOIADA

1. Father of Benaiah, a high military officer during the reigns of David and Solomon. Jehoiada was a priest (1 Chr 27:5) who joined forces with David at Hebron and was identified with the house of Aaron (12:27). See Benaiah #1.

2. High priest in Jerusalem who organized and led the coup that overthrew Queen Athaliah of Judah, together with the Baal cult she supported, and established his nephew Joash (Jehoash) on the throne (2 Kgs 11:4-21; 2 Chr 23:1-15). As long as he lived, Jehoiada kept the king true to the Lord (2 Kgs 12:1-16; 2 Chr 23:16–24:14). He died at the age of 130 and was buried in the city of David among the kings.

3. Benaiah's son, who succeeded Ahithophel as King David's counselor (1 Chr 27:33-34); he was probably a grandson of #1 above, although some believe these to be the same.

4. KJV spelling of Joiada, Paseah's son, in Nehemiah 3:6. See Joiada #1.

5. Alternate name for Joiada, son of Eliashib the high priest, in Nehemiah 13:28. See Joiada #2.

6. Priest during the time of Jeremiah who was succeeded by Zephaniah as overseer of the Temple (Jer 29:26).

JEHOIAKIM

Second son of Josiah by Zebidah (2 Kgs 23:36; 1 Chr 3:15; 2 Chr 36:4) who became king of Judah in 609 BC. He replaced his younger brother Jehoahaz as king when he was deposed and exiled by Pharaoh Neco after a three-month reign (2 Kgs 23:31-35). Jehoiakim was installed as king at age 25, and he ruled for 11 years in Jerusalem. His given name, Eliakim, means "God will establish." Upon enthroning him, Neco changed his name to Jehoiakim, meaning "Yahweh will establish" (2 Kgs 23:34), perhaps seeking to claim Yahweh's support for his action.

Neco laid a heavy tribute on Judah, which Jehoiakim raised by levying a tax on the whole land (2 Kgs 23:35; cf. Jer 22:13-17, where the woe oracle against Jehoiakim implies that he appropriated some of these funds for personal use). Jehoiakim remained subservient to the Egyptians until the battle of Carchemish in 605 BC, when Nebuchadnezzar and the Neo-Babylonians routed Neco. Judah then became a vassal state of Babylon for three years (2 Kgs 24:1-2). After Nebuchadnezzar's failure to completely subdue Neco in a second fierce battle in 601 BC, Jehoiakim seized the opportunity to throw off the Babylonian yoke when the Babylonian king returned home to reorganize his army. This ill-advised decision proved costly, as Nebuchadnezzar invaded Judah in 598 BC to punish the rebellious vassal king (2 Kgs 24:3-7). The expected help from Egypt never came, and the Babylonians destroyed the important Judahite cities of Debir and Lachish, seized control of the Negev, and deported several thousand of Judah's ablest citizens. This no doubt crippled the economy and left Judah virtually leaderless. Jehoiakim died during the Babylonian siege (probably late in 598 BC). His son Jehoiachin was placed on the throne.

Although the details of Jehoiakim's death are not reported, the biblical historian does pass judgment on this reign as one that perpetuated the evils of his fathers (see 2 Kgs 23:37; 2 Chr 36:5, 8; cf. Jer 22:18-19 and 36:27-32, which predicted that Jehoiakim's dead body would be cast on the ground outside of Jerusalem without proper burial and he would have no descendants upon the throne). Presumably the reference to "fathers" is to his predecessors Manasseh, Amon, and Jehoahaz. Jeremiah specifies the evils that characterized Jehoiakim's rule, including idolatry, social injustice, robbery of the wage earner, greed, murder, oppression, extortion, and forsaking of the covenant of the Lord (Jer 22:1-17). Despite Jeremiah's extensive activity during his reign (chs 25–26, 36), Jehoiakim remained disobedient, unrepentant, smug, and self-sufficient in his ill-gotten prosperity (22:18-23).

JEHOIARIB

1. Alternate form of Joiarib, a priestly family in Jerusalem, in 1 Chronicles 9:10. See Joiarib #1.

2. Priest in the time of King David, assigned to head the first of 24 divisions of priests for annual Temple duty (1 Chr 24:7).

JEHONADAB

Alternate name for Jonadab, Recab's son. See Jonadab #2.

JEHONATHAN

1. KJV spelling of Jonathan, Uzziah's son, in 1 Chronicles 27:25. See Jonathan #7.

2. One of the Levites appointed by Jehoshaphat to travel about Judah teaching the law to the people as part of his national religious reform (2 Chr 17:8).

3. Head of Shemaiah's priestly house in postexilic Jerusalem during the days of Joiakim the high priest (Neh 12:18).

JEHORAM

1. Jehoshaphat's son and Judah's fifth king (853–841 BC; also called Joram). Prior to the rule of the Omride dynasty in the northern kingdom of Israel (885–841 BC), the relationship between Judah and Israel had been strained. The political influence and economic stability of the united monarchy had long since vanished. Power and wealth had been diminished by Egyptian overlordship under Shishak (2 Chr 12) and by civil war: the unsuccessful Shechem conference (ch 10); Rehoboam of Judah versus Jeroboam of Israel (12:15); Abijah of Judah versus Jeroboam of Israel (13:1-22); and Asa of Judah versus Baasha of Israel (16:1-4). The Omride dynasty in the mid-ninth century BC, however, cast aside familial rivalry and sought to forge a new alliance between the two nations.

The two kingdoms of Judah and Israel were increasingly threatened by the surrounding peoples—the Ammonites, Moabites, Edomites, Syrians, Philistines, Arabs, and Assyrians. In response to this threat Ahab, the second king of the Omride dynasty, secured diplomatic relations with Phoenicia (1 Kgs 16:31) and Judah (22:4). During this time, joint military expeditions by Israel and Judah were not infrequent (1 Kgs 22; 2 Kgs 3; 8:28), though these political alliances were not without their liabilities. The intrusion of the worship of Baal and Asherah led to religious apostasy in Judah and Israel (1 Kgs 16:31-33; 2 Kgs 3:2; 2 Chr 21:11). It was within this political-religious context that Jehoram reigned over Judah.

Though he may have served as co-regent as early as 853 BC, Jehoram was the sole ruler for eight years (848–841 BC). His reign was marked by unnecessary internecine fighting and religious apostasy. His father had generously provided for his six brothers, a decision that Jehoram quickly reversed once he had secured the throne (2 Chr 21:2-3). He executed not only his brothers but also several Israelite princes, thereby removing any political threat to himself (v 4). In addition, he reverted to the idolatrous practices that his father had tried to eliminate by restoring forbidden worship sites, "the high places" (v 11). Jehoram had apparently fallen under the influence of his wife, Athaliah, the daughter of Jezebel (2 Kgs 8:18). As her mother had done in Israel, Athaliah imported Baal worship into Judah. As a result, Elijah the prophet pronounced judgment on Jehoram and the people of Judah—a curse that brought a great plague upon Jehoram's people, children, wives, and possessions, and a gross intestinal disorder upon the king himself. In spite of this pervasive wickedness in Judah, the Lord did not destroy the southern kingdom, because of his promise to David (2 Kgs 8:19; cf. 2 Sm 7:12-16).

Politically, Judah was vulnerable, having lost its control of Edom (2 Chr 21:9) and having sustained attacks by the Philistines and the Arabs. Jehoram was left bereft of possessions, wives, and sons except for Jehoahaz (Ahaziah), his youngest (vv 16-17). At his death Jehoram was not honored and was deprived of burial in the tomb of the kings within the city of David (vv 19-20).

2. Ahab and Jezebel's son, and Israel's tenth king (852–841 BC; also called Joram). He succeeded his brother Ahaziah, whose premature death led to Jehoram's ascension to the throne in Samaria (2 Kgs 1:2, 17); he was a contemporary of the Judean kings Jehoshaphat, Jehoram, and Ahaziah.

Jehoram was preoccupied with the political resurgence of the two neighboring kingdoms of Moab and Syria. When Moab withheld its annual tribute to Israel, he sought assistance from both Jehoshaphat and Judah's vassal kingdom, Edom. Jehoram and Jehoshaphat joined forces with the king of Edom but were halted in their attack on Moab when they encountered a serious lack of water. Hesitant to advance with their troops, they summoned Elisha the prophet and asked him to inquire of the Lord's will regarding the expedition. Because of the high regard that Elisha held for Jehoshaphat, the prophet sought the Lord on their behalf, gaining both the Lord's blessing and an abundance of water. The account of the battle records the slaughter of the Moabites as well as the horrible incident of a human sacrifice by the Moabite king. Having won the battle, Israel withdrew (2 Kgs 3:4-27).

Jehoram's conflict with Syria was less successful because the Israelite king sustained a battle wound. Retreating from Ramoth-gilead in Transjordan to his palace in Jezreel (2 Kgs 8:29), he found his problems compounded when one of his generals, Jehu, led an insurrection against him. Commissioned by the Lord and declared to be king of Israel, Jehu confronted Jehoram and his nephew, Ahaziah, king of Judah. The incident culminated in the death of the two reigning monarchs of Israel and Judah (2 Kgs 9:14-24, 27). While Ahaziah was buried in the tomb of the kings in Jerusalem (v 28), Jehoram's corpse was cast into Naboth's field outside the city of Jezreel. His end was the appropriate judgment against the last king of the wicked Omride dynasty (vv 25-26).

3. Levite member of a traveling group of scholars who taught the people from the Book of the Law during the reign of Jehoshaphat (2 Chr 17:7-9).

JEHOSHAPHAT

1. The fourth king of Judah (872–848 BC), son and successor of Asa (910–869 BC).

Jehoshaphat was 35 years of age when he began his reign; he ruled 25 years, during which time he maintained the stability of the Davidic dynasty (1 Kgs 22:41-42). He was contemporary with King Ahab of Israel (874–853 BC), since his first year on the throne corresponds with the fourth year of the reign of Ahab (v 41). He was also contemporary with Ahaziah (853–852 BC), son of Ahab, and his brother Jehoram (852–841 BC), who succeeded Ahaziah when he died childless (2 Kgs 1:17).

Jehoshaphat is held in high esteem by the Chronicler, along with Hezekiah and Josiah. His successful rule was due to his religious policy. He continued the religious reformation initiated by his father; therefore, the Lord firmly established the kingdom under his control. Everyone in Judah brought tribute to Jehoshaphat, so that he had great riches and honor (2 Chr 17:1-5). The Chronicler praised Jehoshaphat's courageous heart, evidenced in his removing the high places and the Asherim from Judah (v 6). Jehoshaphat is also reported to have closed all the Temples of prostitution (1 Kgs 22:46).

The biblical record informs us that Jehoshaphat reversed his father's foreign policy. During his reign, Asa warred against Baasha of Israel (908–886 BC), who exterminated the house of Jeroboam I (930–909 BC) and usurped the throne for himself, keeping it for nearly a quarter of a century. The two kingdoms engaged in warfare over the boundaries between the kingdoms. Jehoshaphat, however, discontinued this war and made peace with the king of Israel (1 Kgs 22:2). To confirm this state of peace, he made an alliance with Ahab and married his son and successor, Jehoram, to Ahab's daughter Athaliah (2 Kgs 8:18; 2 Chr 18:1-2). In accordance with this alliance Jehoshaphat fought on the side of Ahab in his battle against Aram, which took place a Ramoth-gilead (1 Kgs 22; 2 Chr 18). He also was an ally of Jehoram, the younger son of Ahab, against Mesha the king of Moab (2 Kgs 3:4-27).

In his domestic reforms Jehoshaphat sent Ben-hail, Obadiah, Zechariah, Nethanel, and Micaiah to teach the law in the cities of Judah (2 Chr 17:7-9). He is also reported to have organized the use of tribute paid to Judah. The surrounding nations, observing the strength of Jehoshaphat and recognizing the presence of the Lord with him, not only refrained from attacking Judah but even brought tribute to him. He used this tribute to fortify the cities of Judah (vv 10-13). Jehoshaphat also reorganized the army and made arrangements for the defense of the kingdom. He had a standing army in the capital as well as garrisons in the fortified cities. It is evident that the organization centered about the tribal association of Judah and Benjamin (vv 14-19).

A prophet by the name of Jehu rebuked Jehoshaphat for his alliances with Ahab (2 Chr 19:1-3). Evidently, Jehoshaphat took this rebuke to heart and ruled Judah wisely. He swept most of the Asherim from the land and determined in his mind to seek God. He is reported to have gone regularly among the people from Beersheba to Mt Ephraim to convert them to the Lord. He appointed judges in each of the fortified cities of Judah and admonished them to judge as the Lord's representatives. He also appointed Levites, priests, and family heads to handle cases pertaining to the worship of the Lord and to make decisions in disputes arising among citizens (vv 4-11).

In addition to the fortified cities in Judah, Jehoshaphat placed military forces in the cities of Ephraim that his father, Asa, had taken (2 Chr 17:1-2). Though his alliances with Phoenicia and Israel were not approved by the prophets and proved dangerous in the long run, they still brought relative peace and temporary prosperity to his realm. He was held in high esteem by the neighboring Philistines and the Arabs (vv 10-13), and it is also evident that Edom submitted to him. He won victory over the Moabites, Ammonites, and Meunites at En-gedi (20:1-30). Wishing to emulate Solomon, he constructed ships at Ezion-geber to go to Tarshish, but this did not prove a successful venture (vv 35-37).

Jehoshaphat died when he was about 60 years of age and was buried with his fathers in the city of David. His son Jehoram became king in his place (2 Chr 21:1). His name is listed in Matthew's genealogy of Jesus Christ (Mt 1:8).

2. Son of Ahilud who held the position of "recorder" (the Hebrew word may imply an official historian or a spokesman for the king) in the days of David and Solomon (2 Sm 8:16; 20:24; 1 Kgs 4:3; 1 Chr 18:15).

3. Son of Paruah and one of Solomon's 12 administrative officials who requisitioned food from the people for the king's household. Each of them arranged provisions for one month of the year. Jehoshaphat was the officer assigned for the tribe of Issachar (1 Kgs 4:7, 17).

4. Son of Nimshi and the father of Jehu, who exterminated the dynasty of Omri and became king of Samaria around 842–815 BC (2 Kgs 9:2, 14).

5. KJV spelling of Joshaphat in 1 Chronicles 15:24, a priest during David's reign.

JEHOSHEBA

Daughter of King Jehoram of Judah (853–841 BC) and Queen Athaliah, sister of King Ahaziah (841 BC), and wife of Jehoiada the high priest. Upon Ahaziah's death, Athaliah attempted to kill all the remaining royal heirs to the throne; Jehosheba, however, hid young Joash, Ahaziah's son, in a Temple bedroom for the duration of Athaliah's reign (841–835 BC; 2 Kgs 11:2). Jehosheba is alternately spelled Jehoshabeath in 2 Chronicles 22:11.

JEHOZABAD

1. Shomer's son, who was a servant of King Joash and later, with another assailant, murdered the king at Millo (2 Kgs 12:21). In a parallel passage, Jehozabad is called the son of Shimrith the Moabitess (2 Chr 24:26). King Amaziah, Joash's son, eventually executed Jehozabad for the murder (25:3).

2. Obed-edom's second son and a member of a Levitical Korahite family appointed by King David to be gatekeepers in the Temple (1 Chr 26:4).

3. Benjaminite military commander who served under King Jehoshaphat of Judah and commanded 180,000 men in his army (2 Chr 17:18).

JEHOZADAK

Seraiah's son and one of the Exiles transported by Nebuchadnezzar to Babylonia (1 Chr 6:14-15). He was the father of Jeshua (also called Joshua), the high priest in postexilic Jerusalem during the days of Zerubbabel (Ezr 3:2, 8; 5:2; 10:18; Neh 12:26; Hg 1:1-14; 2:2-4; Zec 6:11).

JEHU

1. Prophet and son of the "seer" Hanani (2 Chr 16:7), who denounced Baasha for following in the ways of Jeroboam (1 Kgs 16:1-7). In addition to continuing the heretical worship of the golden calves at Bethel and Dan, Baasha also assassinated Nadab, the son of Jeroboam (15:25-32).

   Jehu later rebuked Jehoshaphat, king of Judah, for helping Ahab the king of Israel in his wars against the Arameans (2 Chr 19:1-2). The writings of this prophet were included in one of the records of the reign of Jehoshaphat, *The Book of the Kings of Israel* (2 Chr 20:34).

2. Important army officer during the reigns of Ahab and Jehoram (2 Kgs 9:25), who in reaction to the economic and religious abuses of the house of Omri was anointed as king of the northern kingdom of Israel (1 Kgs 19:16-17). In the following revolution he exterminated the royal house of Israel, the king of Judah, and a royal party from the south (2 Kgs 9–10). He executed the worshipers of Baal in order to revive true worship in Israel. As king, he ruled in Samaria 28 years (841–814 BC) and began a dynasty that lasted some 100 years.

   In the time of Jehu the prophets were engaged in a religious equivalent of war with the adherents of the Tyrian Baal. Elijah met and defeated the Canaanite priests on Mt Carmel (1 Kgs 18:17-40). Later he and then Elisha were commissioned to anoint Jehu as king. The prophets waited until the time was right (2 Kgs 9:1-10), at which time Elisha sent a "son of the prophets" to Ramoth-gilead to designate Jehu as the monarch.

   Jehu left his siege of Ramoth-gilead in northern Transjordan to meet the king of Israel in Jezreel. There he killed King Jehoram and Ahaziah, the king of Judah (2 Kgs 9:17-28). His bloody ways continued as he extinguished the royal house of Ahab (10:1-17) and 42 ambassadors of goodwill from Judah (apparently without provocation, vv 12-14). Israel's bloodbath finally ended in Samaria. There Jehu cunningly vowed to serve Baal with a zeal greater than that of Ahab. Unsuspecting devotees of Baal gathered in great numbers to join in a festival sacrifice. Instead, the devotees themselves became the sacrifice, and the house of Baal in Samaria was destroyed and desecrated by turning its ruins into a latrine (vv 18-27).

   Political and economic problems also contributed to the unrest. Under the reign of Ahab and Jezebel, justice was corrupted. The poor lost their land in the drought and their property rights were ignored (1 Kgs 18:5-6). Jehu threw the body of Jehoram into the field of Naboth the Jezreelite (2 Kgs 9:25-26) as justice for the crime of Ahab and Jezebel (1 Kgs 21:19; cf. v 13). But religious passions dominated the cause. Jehu called his slaughter of the house of Omri his "zeal for the Lord." Jehonadab, a Recabite, joined Jehu as he traveled toward Samaria (2 Kgs 10:15-17). Recabites opposed social and economic developments that took place in the northern kingdom under Ahab. They followed a strict moral code and lived a simple life (Jer 35). Since Recabites represented the most conservative elements of Yahwism, they became natural allies for the reform of Jehu.

Jehu's revolution seriously weakened the worship of Baal. Although not all of the adherents were eliminated, Baalism no longer remained the official religion of the state (2 Kgs 10:28). Rather, Baalism united with Yahwism to form the sinister syncretistic religion that was denounced by Hosea.

Politically, the revolt of Jehu was disastrous. The triple alliance between Tyre, Israel, and Judah was shattered by the atrocities. Israel, now isolated, became easy prey for Assyria and Syria. Jehu attempted to buy some help from Assyria by paying tribute to Shalmaneser III. That event is pictured on the Black Obelisk in a relief from the campaign of 841 BC. An inscription names "Jehu, son of Omri," as the one kneeling before Shalmaneser.

After the Assyrian threat dissipated in 838 BC, Hazael, king of Aram-Damascus, conquered all of Israelite Transjordan as far as the Arnon (2 Kgs 10:32-33). In a second campaign in 815 BC, Hazael moved across the Jordan River, through the Jezreel plain, and down the coast, conquering the land as far as Gath in the northern Shephelah. There the son of Jehu, Jehoahaz, paid tribute to Hazael (12:18). The revolution weakened Israel both politically and economically.

Later generations spoke of the massacre of the house of Omri with horror (Hos 1:4). Jehu did not destroy the golden calves of Jeroboam, and so continued the syncretistic worship at Bethel and Dan. In the final analysis the revolution, which was meant to purge Israel of oppression and false religion, succeeded in doing neither.

3. Member of Judah's tribe, the son of Obed and Azariah's father (1 Chr 2:38).

4. Prince of Simeon's tribe, and the son of Joshibiah, who, along with others, migrated from the approaches to the valley of Gedor eastward in search of good pasture (1 Chr 4:35).

5. One of the skilled warriors who joined David at Ziklag. Interestingly, he was of Saul's tribe, Benjamin, and from Anathoth, to which Abiathar of the priests of Eli was later banished (1 Chr 12:3).

JEHUCAL

Son of Shelemiah who was sent by King Zedekiah to request Jeremiah's prayers for Judah (Jer 37:3; 38:1). Later he tried to kill Jeremiah, who continued to prophesy the invasion of Jerusalem by the Babylonians, thereby undermining the confidence of the people and the army (38:1-6).

JEHUDI

Son of Nethaniah and a messenger of King Jehoiakim of Judah. He was sent by a number of princes to summon Baruch to read Jeremiah's scroll privately to them. Later, Jehoiakim ordered Jehudi to read the same scroll publicly before him and all the court, after which the writing was burned (Jer 36:14-23).

JEIEL

1. Chief in Reuben's tribe (1 Chr 5:7).

2. Benjaminite who lived at Gibeon and an ancestor of Israel's first king, Saul (1 Chr 8:29; 9:35).

3. One of David's mighty men (1 Chr 11:44). He is perhaps identical with #1 above.

4. Levite gatekeeper in the sanctuary. He seems to have served as a musician also (1 Chr 15:18, 21; 16:5b). The Jeiel of 1 Chronicles 16:5a is probably a different musician.

5. Levite descended from Asaph and an ancestor of a prophet named Jahaziel (2 Chr 20:14).

6. Secretary for King Uzziah's army, who kept or made military "rolls" or "musters" of the king's troops (2 Chr 26:11).

7. KJV and NLT spelling of Jeuel, Elizaphan's descendant, in 2 Chronicles 29:13. See Jeuel #2.

8. Levite leader who contributed Passover offerings during King Josiah's reign (2 Chr 35:9).

9. KJV spelling of Jeuel, Adonikam's descendant, in Ezra 8:13. See Jeuel #3.

10. Nebo's descendant who was encouraged to divorce his foreign wife during the postexilic era (Ezr 10:43).

JEKAMEAM

Hebron's son from the Kohathite division of Levi's tribe (1 Chr 23:19; 24:23).

JEKAMIAH

1. Shallum's son from Judah's tribe (1 Chr 2:41).

2. One of King Jehoiachin's sons (1 Chr 3:18).

JEKUTHIEL

Zanoah's father from Judah's tribe (1 Chr 4:18).

JEMIMAH

First of the three daughters born to Job when he was restored after his affliction (Jb 42:14).

JEMUEL

Simeon's first son (Gn 46:10; Ex 6:15). He is called Nemuel in 1 Chronicles 4:24 and is the founder of the Nemuelite family (Nm 26:12).

JEPHTHAH

Illegitimate son of Gilead (Jgs 11:1) and a leader in the period of the judges. The son of a harlot, Jephthah was dispossessed by his father's other sons and refused a share in their father's home. He moved to the land of Tob, a small Aramean state east of the Jordan River (Jgs 11:3-5), and became leader of a band of malcontents and adventurers who went raiding with him.

When war broke out between the Israelites and the Ammonites, the leaders of Gilead begged Jephthah to return and lead their army. At first he refused because of their previous mistreatment of him. When they promised to make him Gilead's ruler, he accepted and became commander in chief and ruler (Jgs 11:4-10). The agreement was ratified before the Lord at a general assembly of the people at Mizpah (v 11) in Gilead, probably just south of the Jabbok River.

After diplomatic negotiations with the king of Ammon failed, Jephthah waged war against the Ammonites. Before the fighting started, he vowed to the Lord that if he was victorious, on his return home he would sacrifice to God whoever met him at the door of his house. Then he successfully led his army against the Ammonites, destroying them with a terrible slaughter (Jgs 11:29-33).

When Jephthah returned home, he was shocked to find that the first person to meet him was his only child, his daughter, playing a tambourine and dancing for joy. When he saw her, he tore his clothes and said, "Alas, my daughter! you have brought me very low, and you have become the cause of great trouble to me; for I have opened my mouth to the LORD, and I cannot take back my vow" (Jgs 11:35, RSV). She submitted to her destiny but begged that it might be postponed for two months so that she and her companions could retreat to the mountains and lament that she must die a virgin (vv 34-38). A woman in ancient Israel could suffer no greater disgrace than to die unmarried and childless. When she returned, her father fulfilled his vow (vv 38-39).

Jephthah also led Gilead against the Ephraimites, who were resentful that they had not been included in the fight against Ammon. They had been given a previous chance to ally with Gilead but had refused. Jephthah captured the fords of the Jordan behind the Ephraimites and prevented their escape by an ingenious strategy. Gileadite guards put fugitives to a test, demanding that they say "Shibboleth." If they could not pronounce the "sh," they were revealed as Ephraimites and killed. The account says that 42,000 Ephraimites died at that time (Jgs 12:1-6).

Jephthah was judge over Gilead for six years (Jgs 12:7), and when he died, he was buried in one of the cities of Gilead. In the Letter to the Hebrews, Jephthah is named with Gideon, Barak, and others as a hero of faith (Heb 11:32).

JEPHUNNEH

1. Father of Caleb, one of the 12 spies sent by Moses to search out the land of Canaan (Nm 13:6; 14:6; 26:65; 1 Chr 4:15; 6:56). He is identified variously as a Judahite and a Kenizzite (Jos 14:6).

2. Jether's son from Asher's tribe (1 Chr 7:38).

JERAH

Son of Joktan and nephew of Peleg, during whose lifetime the earth was divided, probably a reference to the dispersion following Babel. Jerah is likely also the name of an Arabian tribe or district (Gn 10:25-26; 1 Chr 1:20).

JERAHMEEL

1. Firstborn of Hezron's three sons, the father of six sons and a descendant of Judah through Perez's line (1 Chr 2:9-42). He was the founder of the family of Jerahmeelites, who in David's time lived in the Negev region and occupied a number of cities (1 Sm 27:10; 30:29).

2. Kish's son and a Levite family leader who served in the sanctuary during David's reign (1 Chr 24:29).

3. Son of King Jehoiakim of Judah and one who, with Shelemiah and Seraiah, was ordered by the king to seize Baruch and Jeremiah (Jer 36:26).

JERED

1. KJV spelling of Jared in 1 Chronicles 1:2. *See* Jared.

2. Ezrah's son from Judah's tribe (1 Chr 4:18).

JEREMAI

Hashum's son who obeyed Ezra's exhortation to divorce his foreign wife after the Exile (Ezr 10:33).

JEREMIAH

1. Prophet to Judah before its fall in 586 BC; his name is also spelled "Jeremias" (Mt 16:14) and "Jeremy" (Mt 2:17; 27:9) in the KJV.

   Jeremiah was born in the village of Anathoth, about three miles (4.8 kilometers) northeast of Jerusalem. His father's name was Hilkiah, and he belonged to the tribe of Benjamin. His call came in the 13th year of King Josiah (640–609 BC). He refers to himself as "a child" when called (Jer 1:6), but the Hebrew word is not the same as used in Jeremiah 30:6 and 31:8 and cannot be limited to preadolescence. He was probably referring to his inexperience rather than to his age. Jeremiah was born about 657 BC during the reign of the wicked king Manasseh, while the great Ashurbanipal, who had shaken the world by sacking the ancient Egyptian city of Thebes in 663 BC, ruled a world empire from Assyria.

   God informed Jeremiah that he had consecrated and appointed him before birth (Jer 1:4-5). Jeremiah first shrank with a sense of inadequacy and fear: "O Sovereign LORD, . . . I can't speak for you! I'm too young!" (v 6, NLT). God would not allow Jeremiah to excuse himself. He was assured that words would be given him to speak, and guidance given for the way (v 7). He was promised protection (v 18) and deliverance (v 8) despite opposition (v 19). God touched his mouth, signifying divine inspiration of his words, and gave the sign of a branch from an almond tree, explaining that the Lord is watching (see NLT mg). The third sign was the boiling pot (v 13) facing from the north, picturing the source and fury of impending disaster.

Thus the tone of Jeremiah's life ministry was set: judgment, disaster, danger, defeat, and impending death for the nation.

Early Ministry The messages given by Jeremiah during his first five years of ministry may have been instrumental in the great revival of 622 BC. Those cooperating with King Josiah in the reformation and friendly with Jeremiah included Ahikam and his father, Shaphan (Jer 26:24); Gedaliah, Ahikam's son (39:14), who later became governor; Acbor, son of Micaiah, also called Abdon, whose son Elnathan joined the opposition (26:22) but later repented (36:25); and Asaiah (2 Chr 34:20). The prophets Nahum and Zephaniah also influenced the reform movement, which must have climaxed under the preaching of Habakkuk and Jeremiah, the priestly ministry of Hilkiah, and the prophecies of Huldah the prophetess. During the reign of King Josiah, Jeremiah spoke without the fear of persecution that plagued his later ministry. Though the content of the book of Jeremiah sometimes appears to be fragmentary, most of chapters 1–19 date to the time of Josiah.

The finding of the lost Book of the Covenant in the Temple debris may be the reason for the words in Jeremiah 15:16: "Your words are what sustain me. They bring me great joy and are my heart's delight" (NLT). The words "So be it, LORD" (Jer 11:5) in a context recalling the words of Moses in the Torah may be Jeremiah's response after hearing King Josiah read the newly found book.

Small towns and rural areas, including his hometown, heard Jeremiah's denunciation of high places and idolatry. They sought to kill the young prophet, or at least to intimidate him (11:21). Instead of being silent, Jeremiah asserted that his motivation was for their good and condemned their resistance to the truth as their greatest danger.

Shortly after Jeremiah began his ministry, a number of world-changing events took place. Ashurbanipal died and the Assyrian Empire rapidly declined. Nabopolassar began a 21-year reign in Babylon, leading an expansion that culminated in his son Nebuchadnezzar's subjugation of the known world. As the world news filtered in, Jeremiah turned more toward Jerusalem. His first Temple speeches (chs 7–10) may have been uttered at this time.

Nabopolassar felt his strength sufficient to launch an attack against Assyrian territory in 616 BC, but he advanced cautiously because Psamtik I (Psammeti-chus) of Egypt appeared ready to aid Assyria. Cyaxares of Media pounced on Assyria when Babylon hesitated and took its most sacred city, Asshur, in 614 BC. Babylon joined Media, along with Scythia, and waged an assault against Nineveh, which fell late in the summer of 612 BC. The Assyrian Empire had shriveled to two small holdings, Haran and Carchemish.

Nabopolassar took Haran in 610, and Ashuruballit, having escaped, appealed to Egypt for help at Carchemish. Neco, who had become pharaoh within the year, responded immediately. He marched through Judah without giving Josiah prior notice and asked that the Jews not bother him in view of his haste to go northward (2 Chr 35:21). Ignoring the request, Josiah pursued them to Megiddo and was wounded in the ensuing battle; he died in Jerusalem.

Ministry during the Reign of Jehoiakim In place of Jehoahaz, Josiah's fourth son, who reigned only three months, Pharaoh Neco enthroned Jehoiakim (Eliakim). Neco demanded heavy indemnity payments from Judah and took Jehoahaz prisoner as collateral to assure payment (2 Kgs 23:31-33).

Early in the reign of Jehoiakim, Jeremiah, moved by God's Spirit, delivered his third Temple speech (Jer 26) on the occasion of one of the annual Jewish feasts. He called for the people to repent and to act on the basis of the revelation they had heard repeatedly from the Book of the Law. The barb of the sermon came in the warning: "This is what the LORD says: If you will not listen to me and obey the law I have given you, and if you will not listen to my servants, the prophets—for I sent them again and again to warn you, but you would not listen to them—then I will destroy this Temple as I destroyed Shiloh, the place where the Tabernacle was located. And I will make Jerusalem an object of cursing in every nation on earth" (26:4-6, NLT). Shiloh had been the heart of Jewish worship from Joshua to Samuel, but after being destroyed by the Philistines, it never revived. It served as an example of complete desolation following God's judgment in the days of Eli.

Crowds gathered rapidly and reacted angrily against Jeremiah. Priests and princes hurried to the New Gate, where a court was established to bring order and to control violence. Jehoiakim would be no help to Jeremiah, for he had refused to listen to God's messages (Jer 22:21). The priests and false prophets spoke against Jeremiah, calling him a traitor. Then some of the elders spoke to the people about Uriah, who had prophesied the same message. Rather than risk disaster, Ahikam persuaded the court to spare Jeremiah.

Egypt controlled Palestine and Syria after the decay of the Assyrian Empire. In 606 BC Egypt succeeded in annihilating a garrison city of Babylonian soldiers south of Carchemish and then reoccupied Carchemish to await the return blow from Babylon. This Egyptian victory meant persecution for Jeremiah, who was often accused of false prophecy (cf. Jer 20).

Jeremiah never had confidence in Egypt. Each time a Jewish leader would call for a new alliance with Egypt, Jeremiah repeated God's message against it. Whenever a Jewish group fled to Egypt for security, Jeremiah warned of worse things in that land of false refuge (see Jer 44:26-27). Jeremiah's ode and prophecy in chapter 46 poetically describe Egypt's defeat at Carchemish, when Nabopolassar sent his son Nebuchadnezzar to destroy them (605 BC). After smashing the Egyptian army at

Carchemish, Nebuchadnezzar pursued the enemy through Judah. "Not a single man escaped to his own country," reads the exaggerated Babylonian record. His father's death, however, prevented him from invading Egypt, and he returned to Babylon to assume the throne. The following year Nebuchadnezzar, now king of Babylonia, returned to accept the homage of the rulers of Judah, Syria, and Phoenicia. On this occasion God gave Jeremiah his great 70-year prophecy (Jer 25:11-12), which became the basis of Daniel 9:2, 24-27.

A year after the decisive battle at Carchemish, Baruch, Jeremiah's scribe, finished recording all the dictated words of Jeremiah and was reading from this scroll at the Temple. A report reached the king, who sent Jehudi, a servant, to fetch the scroll and read it to him. When this was done, Jehoiakim burned the scroll in spite of his counselors, who pleaded that the king not do it (Jer 36:23-25). God's message, soon rewritten, added a promise of fearful judgment on Jehoiakim (vv 27-31).

Ambitious young Nebuchadnezzar determined to add Egypt to his dominion. In 601 BC he led his forces through Judah again, but Neco had advance warning and was prepared for the onslaught. In the desert of Shur, Nebuchadnezzar suffered defeat. Encouraged by this display of Egyptian defensive strength, the pro-Egyptian parties in Judah asserted themselves, persuading Jehoiakim to lead them to freedom from Babylon by making an alliance with Egypt (2 Kgs 24:1). But help from Egypt did not come (v 7).

In 599 BC, Nebuchadnezzar armed those surrounding the rebel Jewish kingdom to harass the Jews, which they willingly did (2 Kgs 24:2). Evidently Jehoiakim lost his life in one of these raids. Since the people despised him, his body was thrown out without honorable burial, as Jeremiah had predicted (Jer 22:19).

Ministry during the Reign of Zedekiah Nebuchadnezzar's siege of Jerusalem in 598 BC lasted only a short time because the new king, Jehoiachin, crowned at age 18, knew resistance was useless. He gave himself up, with all his family and court, in March of 597 BC, after serving as king about three months. The Babylonian Chronicle reads: "He [Nebuchadnezzar] seized the city and captured the king."

Jehoiachin was carried to Babylon along with 8,000 (2 Kgs 24:16; cf. v 14) officers, artisans, and executives (Ezekiel among them) and much booty. In his place Nebuchadnezzar appointed Zedekiah, Jehoiachin's uncle, to rule. Zedekiah proceeded to organize his government with the less capable and inexperienced help left after the deportation.

Jeremiah took up his thankless ministry, calling on the Jews to believe God, obey the laws of Babylon, and reject false hopes in Egypt. Zedekiah turned a deaf ear to these appeals, listening rather to the unwise advice of his counselors (Jer 37:1-2). During the first year of Zedekiah's rule, Jeremiah received the vision of the two baskets of figs. The Jews carried to Babylon were like good figs, while Zedekiah and those who trusted in Egypt were like rotten figs (24:1-8). The reason for this reproachful description was that the Jews began plotting rebellion against Babylon along with Edom, Moab, Ammon, Tyre, and Sidon from the beginning of the reign of Zedekiah (27:1-3), thus breaking their oath of loyalty to Nebuchadnezzar and repudiating God's message through Jeremiah.

In Egypt the pharaoh began to renew plans to organize dissidents within the Babylonian Empire to revolt. He hired Jewish soldiers to aid him in protecting his southern border. The Jewish soldiers settled on a Nile island called Elephantine, or Yeb (593–410 BC). Jeremiah addressed an oracle to these Jews (ch 44). The treaty for Jews to help in Egypt evidently also assumed that Egyptians would aid Israel. When the Babylonians besieged Jerusalem in 589, Pharaoh Hophra came to the aid of Zedekiah. Nebuchadnezzar, ruling from Riblah, commanded that the siege against Jerusalem be lifted in order to make a surprise attack on Hophra (37:5). The release gave Jeremiah an opportunity to journey to Anathoth to secure some family property (v 12). However, Irijah, captain of the guard, arrested Jeremiah in the Gate of Benjamin for defecting to the enemy, and he was beaten and flung into a dungeon. King Zedekiah brought him out after many days to obtain a prognostication. With characteristic boldness, Jeremiah told the king he would shortly become a captive. At the same time, Jeremiah requested relief from injustice for himself. He gained part of his request but continued as prisoner in the court of the guard.

The Babylonian army chased Pharaoh Hophra back to Egypt and returned to crush Jerusalem without further mercy. The siege, which began in 589 BC, was restored with rigor in January of 588, Zedekiah's ninth year (39:1). During this time, the Lord gave Jeremiah foreknowledge of a visit from a cousin who wished to sell a field near Anathoth (32:7-9; cf. 37:12). Jeremiah bought the field as an object lesson to verify the message of restoration after a captivity of 70 years (29:10).

The armies of Babylon cut off all supplies from Jerusalem and were able to destroy the last two outlying Jewish fortresses of Lachish and Azekah (34:7). Food became scarce. Disease spread. Undisposed-of sewage and impure cistern water caused pestilence. With increased distress came Jeremiah's increased appeal for the city to surrender.

Jeremiah remained in the prison court until the Babylonians breached the city wall in July of 586 BC. The king escaped by night and succeeded in reaching the plains of Jericho but was captured there and taken to Riblah. Zedekiah's family and counselors were killed; he himself was blinded and taken in chains to Babylon, where he died soon after (39:6-7).

Back in Jerusalem, Nebuzaradan, the Babylonian general, sent most of the Jews into captivity. Jeremiah, however, was granted special consideration; after being released from prison, he was placed under the care of Gedaliah, son of Ahikam.

After the Fall of Jerusalem A month after the fall of Jerusalem, the city was burned and the walls broken down. Gedaliah was appointed governor of the remaining agricultural community, with headquarters at Mizpah. Jeremiah returned to Jerusalem, where, according to tradition, he took up his abode in a grotto near what is now known as Gordon's Calvary. There he wrote the book of Lamentations. The Ammonite king Baalis, plotting rebellion against Babylon, instigated the murder of Gedaliah (40:13). In the reaction that followed, the remaining people followed the leader Johanan ben Kareah to a camp near Bethlehem, intending to go to Egypt. They asked Jeremiah, at Jerusalem, to give guidance from the Lord, promising obedience. Jeremiah's message required that they remain in Israel and not go to Egypt. Disobedience was complete and immediate. Fearing Babylon, they departed from Judah, taking Jeremiah with them, and entered Egypt (41:16–43:7).

Jeremiah did not stop his ministry in Egypt. His message at Tahpanhes (43:8-12) assured a victorious conquest of the land by Nebuchadnezzar, which took place in 568–567 BC.

Jews from all parts of Egypt gathered to discuss their future as exiles. Jeremiah took the opportunity to denounce their idolatry. Jewish women as well as men argued that they had enjoyed prosperity while serving idols but had suffered since stopping. Jeremiah condemned their obdurate blindness to reality and gave God's indictment. For a verifying sign, Jeremiah predicted that Pharaoh Hophra of Egypt would be assassinated (44:30), which happened in 466 BC. No later record of Jeremiah's acts exists in the Bible. Tradition says Jeremiah was stoned to death by the people of the Jewish exile settlement in Tahpanhes.

Though Jeremiah suffered continued rejection during his life, he has been honored by numerous apocryphal and traditional embellishments to his history. Jesus could well have had Jeremiah in mind when he said, "You build tombs for the prophets your ancestors killed and decorate the graves of the godly people your ancestors destroyed.... [You are] the descendants of those who murdered the prophets" (Mt 23:29-31, NLT).

2. Family head in the Transjordan portion of Manasseh whom Tiglath-pileser took captive (1 Chr 5:23-26; cf. 2 Kgs 15:29).

3. Father of Hamutal, a wife of King Josiah (2 Kgs 23:31; 24:18).

4. Ambidextrous Benjaminite bowman and slinger who joined David at Ziklag (1 Chr 12:4).

5, 6. Two Gadite soldiers who joined David's army (1 Chr 12:10, 13).

7. Postexilic priest who, with Nehemiah, set his seal to the covenant, renewing the people's promise to obey God's laws (Neh 10:2). He is mentioned again (12:34) as part of the procession for the dedication of the new wall of Jerusalem.

8. Priest who returned from exile with Zerubbabel (Neh 12:1) and became head of a family of priests (v 12).

9. Father of Jaazaniah, a Recabite who refused to drink wine (Jer 35:3).

JEREMOTH

1. One of Beker's nine sons and a leader in Benjamin's tribe (1 Chr 7:8). His name is rendered Jerimoth in some versions.

2. Benjaminite, the son of Beriah and head of his family living in Jerusalem (1 Chr 8:14).

3. Levite of the family at Merari and one of Mushi's three sons registered during David's reign (1 Chr 23:23). His name is alternately spelled Jerimoth here and in 1 Chronicles 24:30.

4. Heman's son and the leader of the 15th of 24 divisions of musicians trained for service in the house of the Lord (1 Chr 25:22, NLT mg). Here and also in 1 Chronicles 25:4 his name is spelled Jerimoth.

5. Azriel's son and the chief official of Naphtali's tribe during David's reign (1 Chr 27:19). His name is spelled Jerimoth in some texts.

6. One of Elam's descendants who was encouraged by Ezra to divorce his foreign wife during the postexilic period (Ezr 10:26).

7. One of Zattu's descendants who was encouraged by Ezra to divorce his foreign wife (Ezr 10:27).

8. One of Bani's descendants who was encouraged by Ezra to divorce his foreign wife (Ezr 10:29). He is named "Ramoth" in the KJV.

JERIAH

Levite of the family of Kohath and head of Hebron's house (1 Chr 23:19; 24:23). David organized Jeriah and other Levites to manage the religious and civil affairs of the kingdom (26:31).

JERIBAI

Elnaam's son and one of David's mighty men (1 Chr 11:46).

JERIEL

Tola's son from Issachar's tribe (1 Chr 7:2).

JERIMOTH

1. One of Bela's five sons and a leader in the tribe of Benjamin (1 Chr 7:7).

2. Alternate spelling of Jeremoth, Beker's son, in 1 Chronicles 7:8. *See* Jeremoth #1.

3. Benjaminite and one of the ambidextrous warriors who came to David's support at Ziklag (1 Chr 12:5).

4. Alternate spelling of Jeremoth, Mushi's son, in 1 Chronicles 23:23 and 24:30. *See* Jeremoth #3.

5. Alternate spelling of Jeremoth, Heman's son, in 1 Chronicles 25:4 and 25:22. *See* Jeremoth #4.

6. Alternate spelling of Jeremoth, Azriel's son, in 1 Chronicles 27:19. *See* Jeremoth #5.

7. David's son and Mahalath's father. Mahalath was married to King Rehoboam of Judah (2 Chr 11:18).

8. One of the Levites who assisted with the administration of the Temple contributions during King Hezekiah's reign (2 Chr 31:13).

JERIOTH
One of Caleb's wives, according to 1 Chronicles 2:18.

JEROBOAM
Name of two kings who reigned in the northern kingdom of Israel: Jeroboam I (930–909 BC), the originator and first monarch of the 10 tribes of Israel, and Jeroboam II (793–753 BC), the 14th king of the northern kingdom.

1. Jeroboam I was the son of Nebat from Ephraim's tribe. He also served King Solomon (1 Kgs 11:26) and his efforts had been rewarded by his placement as the supervisor of an Ephraimite work force. Jeroboam, therefore, helped rebuild an important section of the defenses of Jerusalem (vv 27-28). This efficient and energetic young man did not remain in the employ of Solomon for long, however. Jeroboam's background, his tribe's pride, and the oppression of Solomon had produced a young rebel. Ahijah, the prophet of Shiloh, met Jeroboam outside Jerusalem one day and did a startling thing—he tore a new garment he was wearing into 12 pieces and gave 10 of them to Jeroboam (1 Kgs 11:29-30). Ahijah had symbolically shown Jeroboam that God would give him 10 tribes and would leave the Davidic line intact (vv 31-39). Solomon's idolatry had brought this judgment upon the Davidic line (v 33). Although precise details of a revolt are not given (v 7), Jeroboam fled to Egypt in order to save his life (v 40).

After Solomon's death, Jeroboam returned to Palestine and approached Rehoboam, Solomon's son, with a request that his program of oppression cease (1 Kgs 12:1-4). Rehoboam asked for three days to consult with his advisers before answering (vv 5-11). The counsel of the older advisers was toward clemency, but younger hotheads prevailed with their counsel of increased taxation and forced labor (vv 12-14).

The Israelites responded by rejecting Rehoboam. Jeroboam was quickly elected king of the northern tribes (1 Kgs 12:20), and an uneasy cease-fire temporarily stabilized relationships between the two kingdoms at their division (930 BC).

Being ambitious and skillful, Jeroboam built two capital cities, one at Shechem (cf. Gn 12:6-8; Jos 8:30-35), in the territory west of the Jordan, and one at Penuel (cf. Gn 32:30; Jgs 8:17), east of the Jordan (1 Kgs 12:25). He reinstituted the cult of the golden calves, substituting an ancient religion for the worship of Jehovah. He changed the centers of worship, the object of worship, the priesthood, and the time of worship. The new centers became Bethel and Dan (v 29); Bethel was a place of patriarchal

QUICKTAKE

JEROBOAM

STRENGTHS AND ACCOMPLISHMENTS
• An effective leader and organizer
• First king of the 10 tribes of Israel in the divided kingdom
• A charismatic leader with much popular support

WEAKNESSES AND MISTAKES
• Erected idols in Israel to keep people away from the Temple in Jerusalem
• Appointed priests from outside the tribe of Levi
• Depended more on his own cunning than on God's promises

LESSONS FROM HIS LIFE
• Great opportunities are often destroyed by small decisions
• Careless efforts to correct another's errors often lead to the same errors
• Mistakes always occur when we attempt to take over God's role in a situation

VITAL STATISTICS
Where: The northern kingdom of Israel
Occupations: Project foreman, king of Israel
Relatives: Father: Nebat. Mother: Zeruah. Sons: Abijah, Nadab
Contemporaries: Solomon, Nathan, Ahijah, Rehoboam

KEY VERSES
"But even after this, Jeroboam did not turn from his evil ways. He continued to choose priests from the common people. He appointed anyone who wanted to become a priest for the pagan shrines. This became a great sin and resulted in the utter destruction of Jeroboam's dynasty from the face of the earth" (1 Kings 13:33, 34).

Jeroboam's story is told in 1 Kings 11:26–14:20. He is also mentioned in 2 Chronicles 10–13.

worship (Gn 28:10-22; 31:13; 35:1-7), and Dan was the site of a renegade Levitical worship established for the tribe of Dan in the days of the judges (Jgs 18).

The object of worship became the idol calf (1 Kgs 12:28). The worship was based upon Aaron's participation in the first instance of this idolatry in Israel. Aaron had presented the golden calf at Sinai as a visible representation of the invisible Yahweh who had brought Israel out of Egypt (Ex 32:4-5). This compromise religion would yet have an appeal to Yahweh worshipers. Aaron's prior establishment of this worship added to the appeal for those who were reluctant to separate from Levitical methodology. The Levites in Dan would also add to the authentication of the calf worship. Doubtless, the Egyptian sojourn of Jeroboam contributed to this turn of events. The Egyptians' worship of Amon-Re, the sun god, included his representation as a bull. The bull in Egyptian worship was intended to visibly represent an invisible deity. This concept could have easily been transferred by the Israelites to their worship of the invisible Yahweh.

Jeroboam's idolatry would result in the ultimate destruction of his line (1 Kgs 13:33-34). An immediate result was the death of his son Abijah (14:1-18). Jeroboam's plan to deceive the prophet Ahijah failed and became the means of pronouncing judgment upon the house of Jeroboam and the northern kingdom (vv 7-16). One manifestation of the gradual decline of Israel was the defeat Jeroboam suffered at the hand of Abijah of Judah (2 Chr 13:1-20).

Jeroboam I died after reigning 22 years over Israel (1 Kgs 14:19-20). His remaining son, Nadab, ruled for only two years before he was assassinated by Baasha of the tribe of Issachar (1 Kgs 14:20; 15:25-31). The whole household of Jeroboam was then killed by Baasha, fulfilling the prophecy of Ahijah concerning the end of the dynasty of Jeroboam. Yet even Baasha walked in the footsteps of Jeroboam's apostasy (1 Kgs 15:34).

2. Jeroboam II, the son of Joash (or Jehoash, 798–782 BC), reigned over Israel longer than any other northern king even though he followed the evil example of his ancestral namesake, Jeroboam I (2 Kgs 14:23-24). His reign of 41 years included an 11-year co-regency with his father. Evidently, Joash had taken steps to ensure the stability of his kingdom before meeting Amaziah of Judah in battle (2 Kgs 14:8-14; 2 Chr 25:5-24).

Jeroboam II ruled in the city of Samaria (2 Kgs 14:23). The archaeological evidence at Samaria indicates a reconstruction program in the royal palace during the prosperous reigns of Joash and Jeroboam II. In 1910 excavators found over 60 inscribed potsherds that were invoices or labels for oil and wine sent to the royal stores for use in the king's service. The limited number of place-names (27) on the potsherds indicates that the shipments of these commodities were not a nationwide levy of taxes but were probably all from properties belonging to the royal house. These illustrate the extensive holdings and opulence of the royal house in Israel during the reign of Jeroboam II.

Large numbers of carved decorative plaques and panels of ivory were also found in the ruins of Samaria, a reminder of the wealth of the northern kingdom in its latter days. The influence of the pagan societies of Syria, Assyria, and Egypt can be seen by the various figures of deities on the ivories.

The prophet Jonah, son of Amittai, had prophesied the acquisition of power by Jeroboam II (2 Kgs 14:25). Although Jeroboam's reign was late in the history of the northern kingdom, God still desired to exhibit his long-suffering and faithful covenant-keeping love, offering Israel repentance (vv 26-28).

The northern kingdom reached its greatest extension since the time of Solomon as the result of God's care for Israel during Jeroboam's reign. The boundaries stretched from Hamath on the Orontes River in the north to the Gulf of Aqaba, with its cities of Elath and Ezion-geber, in the south. Prosperity did not suffice to deliver Israel from internal and external problems, however. The extensive corruption in government and the degenerate spiritual state of the people propelled Israel into the tumultuous days that would end in the utter destruction of the northern kingdom. Jeroboam's own life must have been in danger from conspirators. Amaziah, a priest at Bethel, even accused the prophet Amos of conspiring to assassinate Jeroboam (Am 7:8-17). Amos had actually prophesied the captivity of Israel and the fall of Jeroboam's dynasty. The word of God had become a threat to Jeroboam because of the hardness of the hearts of all in Israel, including the king.

Economic depression, moral deterioration, political weakness, and governmental corruption served to hasten the fall of Israel. The rich landowners, including Jeroboam II, had oppressed the less wealthy citizens and had forced small landowners to migrate from their farms to the cities.

Within six months of the death of Jeroboam II, the prophecy concerning the end of the dynasty of Jehu (Jeroboam was the fourth king of that line) was fulfilled (2 Kgs 14:29; 15:8-12; cf. 10:12-31). As the son of Jeroboam I, Nadab, was assassinated, so the son of Jeroboam II, Zechariah, was assassinated. Thirty-one years after the death of Jeroboam II, the prophecies concerning the captivity of Israel were fulfilled (722 BC; 2 Kgs 17:5-41).

JEROBOAM
The Kings of Israel (Northern Kingdom)

930–909 BC
Jeroboam I (1 Kings 12:25–14:20)

909–908 BC
Nadab (1 Kings 15:25-31)

908–886 BC
Baasha (1 Kings 15:32–16:7)

886–885 BC
Elah (1 Kings 16:8-14)

885 BC
Zimri (1 Kings 16:15-20)

885–882 BC
Tibni (1 Kings 16:21-22)

885–874 BC
Omri (1 Kings 16:23-28)

874–853 BC
Ahab (1 Kings 16:29-22:40)

853–852 BC
Ahaziah (1 Kings 22:5
1-2 Kings 1:18)

852–841 BC
Joram (2 Kings 1:17; 3:1-8:15)

841–814 BC
Jehu (2 Kings 9:30–10:36)

814–798 BC
Jehoahaz (2 Kings 13:1-9)

798–783 BC
Jehoash (2 Kings 13:10-25)

793–753 BC
Jeroboam II (2 Kings 14:23-29)

753 BC
Zechariah (2 Kings 15:8-12)

752 BC
Shallum (2 Kings 15:13-15)

752–742 BC
Menahem (2 Kings 15:16-22)

742–740 BC
Pekahiah (2 Kings 15:23-26)

740–732 BC
Pekah (2 Kings 15:27-31)

732–722 BC
Hoshea (2 Kings 17)

JEROHAM

1. Levite of the family of Kohath, father of Elkanah and a forefather of the prophet Samuel and Heman

the singer. Heman was a musician in the sanctuary during David's reign (1 Sm 1:1; 1 Chr 6:27, 34).

2. Benjaminite whose sons lived in Jerusalem and were leaders among their people (1 Chr 8:27). He is perhaps identical with #3 below.

3. Benjaminite and Ibneiah's father. Ibneiah, head of his family, returned to Jerusalem from exile in Babylon (1 Chr 9:8).

4. Descendant of Pashhur and the father of Adaiah the priest. Adaiah returned to Jerusalem after the Exile (1 Chr 9:12; Neh 11:12).

5. Benjaminite from Gedor whose two sons, Joelah and Zebadiah, came to David's support at Ziklag (1 Chr 12:7).

6. Father of Azarel, the chief official of the Danites during David's reign (1 Chr 27:22).

7. Father of Azariah, one of the commanders who was instrumental in removing Queen Athaliah from Judah's throne to make way for Joash (Jehoash), the rightful claimant (2 Chr 23:1).

JERUBBAAL
Name given to Gideon after he destroyed an altar to Baal (Jgs 6:32). The name means "let Baal contend against him." *See* Gideon.

JERUSHA
Zadok's daughter, wife of King Uzziah of Judah and mother of King Jotham (2 Kgs 15:33; 2 Chr 27:1, alternately spelled "Jerushah").

JESHAIAH
1. Hananiah's son; the father of Rephaiah and a descendant of David through Zerubbabel's line, who lived in postexilic Palestine (1 Chr 3:21).

2. Jeduthun's son and the leader of the eighth of 24 divisions of musicians trained for service in the sanctuary during David's reign (1 Chr 25:3, 15).

3. Rehabiah's son and one of the Levites in charge of the Temple treasury during David's reign (1 Chr 26:25).

4. Son of Athaliah from the house of Elam, who returned with Ezra to Judah following the Babylonian captivity (Ezr 8:7).

5. Levite of the family of Merari, who returned with Ezra to Jerusalem after the Exile (Ezr 8:19).

6. Benjaminite, Ithiel's father, and an ancestor of Sallu. Sallu resettled in Jerusalem during the postexilic era (Neh 11:7).

JESHEBEAB
Levite family leader assigned to Temple duty during David's reign (1 Chr 24:13).

JESHER
Caleb's son from Judah's tribe (1 Chr 2:18).

JESHISHAI
Descendant of Gad in the days of Jotham, king of Judah (1 Chr 5:14).

JESHOHAIAH
One of the 13 Simeonite princes in the days of Hezekiah who participated in the invasion of the valley of Gedor; they killed the inhabitants of the territory and took the land for the pasture of their sheep (1 Chr 4:36).

JESHUA

1. Levite and head of the ninth of 24 divisions of priests formed during David's reign (1 Chr 24:11). He was perhaps the forefather of 973 descendants who returned with Zerubbabel to Judah following the Exile (Ezr 2:36; Neh 7:39).

2. One of the Levites assisting Kore in the distribution of the offerings among his fellow priests living in the priestly cities of Judah during the days of King Hezekiah (2 Chr 31:15).

3. Son of Jozadak (alternately "Jehozadak") the high priest. Jozadak was deported by Nebuchadnezzar to Babylon (1 Chr 6:14-15). Jeshua, Jozadak's successor as high priest, returned with Zerubbabel to Jerusalem after the Exile (Ezr 2:2; Neh 7:7; 12:1). Upon arrival, he led his fellow priests in making the altar of God (Ezr 3:2; 5:2) and eventually headed up a construction program to rebuild the Temple (3:8). Confirmed as God's leader by Haggai and Zechariah (Hg 1:1-14; 2:2, 4; Zec 3:1-9; 6:11), Jeshua (alternately "Joshua" in these passages) resolutely resisted attempts by adversaries to infiltrate his people and hinder the work on the Temple (Ezr 4:3). Joiakim was Jeshua's son and successor as high priest, serving in the days of Nehemiah and Ezra (Neh 12:12, 26).

4. Descendant of Pahath-moab and the forefather of a family of Jews who returned with Zerubbabel to Judah following the Babylonian captivity (Ezr 2:6; Neh 7:11).

5. Father of a family of Levites who returned to Jerusalem with Zerubbabel (Ezr 2:40; Neh 7:43; 12:8). He and his sons were responsible for overseeing the workmen building the Temple (Ezr 3:9; this Jeshua may be identical with #3 above).

6. Levite and Jozabad's father. Jozabad assisted Meremoth, Eleazar, and Noadiah with taking inventory of the Temple's precious metals and vessels during the days of Ezra (Ezr 8:33).

7. Ezer's father. Ezer was ruler of Mizpah, who repaired a section of the Jerusalem wall during the days of Nehemiah (Neh 3:19).

8. Azaniah's son and a leader of the Levites in the days of Ezra and Nehemiah. Jeshua assisted Ezra with teaching the people the law (Neh 8:7) and later set his seal on Ezra's covenant (10:9).

9. Alternate spelling of Joshua, the son of Nun, in Nehemiah 8:17. *See* Joshua #1.

JESIMIEL

One of the 13 Simeonite princes who participated in the invasion of the valley of Gedor in King Hezekiah's day, killing the inhabitants and taking the land for the pasture of their sheep (1 Chr 4:36).

JESSE

Son of Obed and grandson of Ruth and Boaz (Ru 4:17, 22). Jesse was a shepherd from Bethlehem. He had eight sons, of whom David was the youngest. He had at least two daughters, Zeruiah and Abigail, who became mothers of famous warriors.

When Samuel went to Jesse's home to search for and anoint a king, Jesse did not at first feel it worthwhile to call David for examination (1 Sm 16:11). Later he sent David to play the lyre for Saul (vv 19-21). After David became a fugitive from Saul, Jesse and others of the family came to David in the cave of Adullam. David then brought his father and mother to Mizpah in Moab (22:3). Nothing further is heard of Jesse.

After Saul broke with David, he commonly spoke of David derisively as a "son of Jesse" to underscore his humble origins (1 Sm 20:31; 22:7). This same emphasis on Jesse's modest station in life is found in such messianic references as Isaiah 11:1 and 10, which speak of the "shoot from the stump of Jesse" and "the root of Jesse" (RSV).

See also David.

JESUS

1. Name meaning "savior" or "Jehovah [Yahweh] is salvation" given to the Messiah. *See* Jesus Christ.

2. KJV translation of Joshua, son of Nun, in Acts 7:45 and Hebrews 4:8. *See* Joshua #1.

3. Jewish Christian, surnamed Justus, who sent his greetings to the believers at Colosse in the salutation of Paul's Letter to the Colossians (Col 4:11).

JESUS CHRIST

Messiah, Savior, and founder of the Christian church.

The following sections present the main events in what may be regarded as the chief stages of the life of Jesus. These stages show a definite progression from Christ's incarnation to his cross. The amount of space devoted to each stage in each of the Gospels is dictated by theological rather than biographical interest. The whole presentation of Christ's life centers on the cross and the subsequent triumphant resurrection and is more an account of God's message to humanity than a plain historic account of the life of Jesus.

Preview
- The Incarnation
- Preparation for Ministry
- Public Ministry
- The Final Journey to Jerusalem
- The Trial and Crucifixion
- The Burial, Resurrection, and Ascension

The Incarnation

The major event of this initial stage was the Incarnation. Only Matthew and Luke give accounts of Jesus' birth. John goes back and reflects on what preceded the birth.

It may seem strange that John began his Gospel with a reference to the Word (Jn 1:1), but it is in this way that he delivers to the reader an exalted view of Jesus. John saw Jesus as existing even before the creation of the world (v 2). In fact, he saw him as having a part in the act of creation (v 3). Therefore, when Jesus was born, it was both an act of humiliation and an act of illumination. The light shone, but the world preferred to remain in darkness (vv 4-5, 10). Therefore, anyone coming to John's records of the life of Jesus would know at once, before even being introduced to the man named Jesus, that here was the record of no ordinary man. The account of his life and teachings that followed could not be properly understood except against this background of his preexistence.

John says that the Word became flesh and dwelt among us. Matthew and Luke fill in some of the details of how this happened. There is little in common between the two accounts. Each approaches the subject from a different point of view, but the supernatural is evident in both. The coming of Jesus is announced beforehand, through dreams to Joseph in Matthew's account (Mt 1:20-21) and through an angel to Mary in Luke's account (Lk 1:26-33). Matthew leaves his readers in no doubt that the one to be born had a mission to accomplish—to save people from their sins (Mt 1:21). Luke sets his story of Jesus' coming in an atmosphere of great rejoicing. This is seen in the inclusion of some exquisite songs, which have formed part of the church's worship ever since (Lk 1:46-55, 68-79). The homage of the wise men in Matthew 2:1-12 is significant because it sets the scene for a universalistic emphasis that links the beginning of the Gospel to its ending (cf. Mt 28:19-20). A similar emphasis is introduced in the angel's announcement to the shepherds in Luke 2:14 and in Simeon's song (Lk 2:32), where he predicts that Jesus would be a light for Gentiles as well as a glory for Israel. The flight into Egypt for safety (Mt 2:13-15) shows the contribution of a gentile nation in providing protection for a Jewish child.

Preparation for Ministry

All four Gospels refer to a brief preparatory period that immediately preceded the commencement of Christ's public ministry. This period focused on three important events: the preaching of John the Baptist, the baptism of Jesus, and the temptation of Jesus.

John the Baptist appeared in the wilderness and caused an immediate stir in Judea, particularly as a result of his call to repentance and to baptism (Mt 3:1-6). John was like one of the OT prophets, but he disclaimed any importance in his own office except as the herald of a greater person to come. He announced the imminent coming of the kingdom (Mt 3:2) as did Jesus (4:17). He set the stage in stern terms for the initial public act of Jesus—his willingness to be baptized (Mt 3:13-15; Lk 3:21).

John's baptism was a baptism of repentance. Since Jesus submitted to this, are we to suppose that Jesus himself needed to repent? If this were the case, it would involve the assumption that Jesus had sinned. This is contrary to other evidence in the NT (John was, in fact, hesitant to baptize Jesus; Mt 3:14-15). If Jesus did not need to repent, what was the point of his requesting baptism at the hands of John? Jesus had come on a mission to others, and it is possible that he deliberately submitted to John's baptism in order to show that he was prepared to take the place of others. This explanation is in line with Paul's later understanding of the work of Jesus Christ (2 Cor 5:21). The most important part of the baptism of Jesus was the heavenly voice, which declared pleasure in the beloved Son (Mt 3:17). This announcement by God was the real starting point of the public ministry of Jesus. It revealed that the ministry was no accident or sudden inspiration on the part of Jesus. He went into his work with the full approval of the Father. A further important feature is the part played by the Holy Spirit in this scene. The dovelike description is full of symbolic meaning (v 16). It was not just an inner experience that Jesus had. The activity of the Spirit in the ministry of Jesus, although not much emphasized in the Gospels, is nevertheless sufficiently evident to be indispensable to a true understanding of Jesus Christ.

Jesus' baptism showed the nature of his mission. The temptation showed the nature of the environment in which he was to minister (Mt 4:1;

Important Places in Jesus' Ministry in Galilee: After returning to his hometown, Nazareth, from Capernaum, Jesus preached in the villages of Galilee and sent his disciples out to preach as well. After meeting back in Capernaum, they left by boat to rest, only to be met by the crowds who followed the boat along the shore.

Lk 4:1-2). Confrontation with adverse spiritual forces characterized Jesus' whole ministry. The Temptation presented shortcuts that, if pursued, would have deflected Jesus from his vocation. The record leaves us in no doubt that Jesus gained the victory. Both Gospels show that he accomplished this by appealing to Scripture. Jesus is also seen in this event as a genuine human who, like all other humans, was subject to temptation. The writer of the Letter to the Hebrews notes that this fact qualified Jesus to act as High Priest and to intercede on behalf of his people (Heb 2:18; 4:15).

Public Ministry

Jesus' public ministry occured mainly in Galilee and included the choosing of his Twelve apostles, preaching and miracles, a time spent north of Galilee, a final departure for Jerusalem, and his death and resurrection. While the synoptic Gospels concentrate exclusively on the events in Galilee, John's account indicates that there were some visits by Jesus to Jerusalem before the Crucifixion.

Calling the Twelve

In the synoptic Gospels there is an account of the initial call to four of the disciples to leave their fishing boats and to become fishers of men (Mt 4:18-22; Mk 1:16-20; Lk 5:1-11). They had already met Jesus and must have had some idea what was involved in following him. Jesus did not at this time appoint them to be apostles, but this call was an indispensable step toward the establishment of the Twelve as a group. Setting apart a particular number of disciples formed an important part of the ministry of Jesus. The miraculous catch of fish, which preceded the call of the disciples in Luke's account, served to highlight the superiority of the spiritual task of catching people rather than fish.

Jesus accepted his chosen disciples as they were and molded them into men who later came to learn how to be totally dependent on God and the power of his Spirit. The synoptic Gospels supply full lists of the 12 apostles (Mt 10:2-4; Mk 3:16-19; Lk 6:14-16). Both Matthew and Mark name them in the context of their exercising authority over evil spirits, thereby showing that these men were being called to enter the same spiritual conflict as Jesus. The synoptic Gospels also give details of the instructions Jesus gave to these disciples before sending them to minister in Israel (Mt 10:5-42; Mk 6:7-13; Lk 9:1-6). They were to proclaim the kingdom as he had done, but they were not to suppose that all would respond to it. They were warned about coming hostility and even persecution. It is important to note that Jesus warned his disciples against encumbering themselves with material possessions. Although the instructions given related immediately to a ministry tour, he was laying the foundation for the future work of the church.

Public Teaching

The Gospel of Matthew presents a substantial sample of Jesus' teachings commonly called the Sermon on the Mount (Mt 5:1–7:29). This may be taken as a fair sample of the kind of discourses that must have abounded in the ministry of Jesus. Additionally, Jesus often taught in parables or stories. Matthew grouped together some of the parables that concern the theme of the kingdom (ch 13). Luke tends to preserve parables of a different kind that are not specially linked to the kingdom. Reading the Gospels, one senses that the parable was a form of teaching particularly characteristic of Jesus. In addition, Jesus interspersed even his discourses with metaphors akin to the parabolic form. The parable was valuable because it could stimulate thought and challenge the hearer. This is because the form of the parable is easy to retain in the mind. Jesus did not speak in parables in order to obscure his meaning. This would be contrary to all that he aimed to do through his work and teaching.

Jesus as Healer

Throughout the Gospels there are records of miracles involving Jesus healing people. There are more of these miracles than any other type. In a section in Matthew devoted to a sequence of healings (Mt 8:1–9:34), a leper, a centurion's servant, Peter's mother-in-law, a demoniac, a paralytic, a woman with a hemorrhage, blind men, and a man who was mute—all were healed. In addition, Jairus's daughter was raised from the dead. This concentration of healings focuses on Jesus as a miracle worker, but throughout the Gospels there is no suggestion that Jesus healed by magical means. In some cases an individual's faith was acknowledged (8:10; 9:22). In at least one incident, the healing was accompanied by an announcement of the forgiveness of the sins of the one healed (Mt 9:2; Mk 2:5). This shows that Jesus considered spiritual needs to be of greater consequence than the physical problems.

In view of the widespread belief in the powerful influence of evil spirits over human lives, it is of great significance that Jesus is seen exercising his power of exorcism over demons. Jesus' ministry was set in an atmosphere of spiritual conflict, so the confrontations between the forces of darkness and the Light of the World were to be expected. Those who explain away these cases of demon-possession in psychiatric terms miss this key feature of Jesus' ministry. Each time he exorcised a demon, he was demonstrating victory, which reached its most dramatic expression in his victory over death at his resurrection.

In addition to the healing miracles in this early section, one nature miracle is recorded, that of the stilling of the storm (Mt 8:23-27; Mk 4:35-41; Lk 8:22-25). This miracle focused both on the lack of faith in the disciples and the mysterious power of the presence of Jesus.

The Reaction to Jesus by His Contemporaries

In the early stages of his ministry, Jesus was very popular with the ordinary people. There are several notices to this effect (Mt 4:23-25; Mk 3:7-8). This popularity showed no appreciation of the spiritual purpose of Jesus' mission (Lk 13:17). Nevertheless, it stands in stark contrast to the nit-picking opposition of the religious leaders, who even plotted to kill Jesus in the early period of his ministry (Mk 3:6).

Jesus and the religious leaders often clashed over the observance of the Sabbath (Mt 12:1-14; Lk 13:10-17; Jn 5:9-18). Jesus adopted a more liberal view than the rigid and often illogical interpretation of some of his religious contemporaries—as in the instances when he was criticized for healing on the Sabbath even though the Jewish law allowed the rescuing of trapped animals on the Sabbath (Mt 12:11; Lk 13:15). To the Pharisaic mind, Jesus was a lawbreaker. The Pharisees feared that it would undermine their authority if his teaching were permitted to permeate popular opinion.

Leaving Northern Galilee

Jesus spent a brief time in the region of Tyre and Sidon, where he performed further healings and made it clear that his main mission was to the house of Israel (Mt 15:21-28). He then moved on to Caesarea Philippi; this was the turning point of his ministry (Mt 16:13-20; Mk 8:27-38; Lk 9:18-27). It was there that Jesus asked his disciples: "Who do people say the Son of Man is?" This caused Peter to confess: "You are the Christ, the Son of the living God." This impressive confession led Jesus to promise that he would build his church on "this rock." There has been much discussion about the meaning of this saying. It is open to some doubt whether Jesus intended to build his church on Peter, on his confession, or on Peter making the confession. Historically, Peter was the instrument God used for the entrance into the church of both Jews and Gentiles (Acts 2; 10). There is no doubt about Jesus' intention to found a church, since the word occurs again in Matthew 18:17. Despite the glorious revelation of Jesus on this occasion, he took it as an opportunity to begin to inform his disciples of his death and resurrection (Mt 16:21-23).

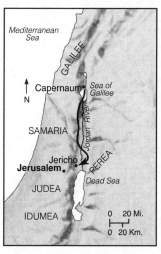

This revelation of Jesus was considerably reinforced by the event known as the Transfiguration, when Jesus was transformed in the presence of three of his disciples (Mt 17:1-8). It was natural for them to want to keep this glorious vision of Jesus for themselves, but the vision vanished as rapidly as it came. Its purpose was evidently to show the three leading disciples something of the nature of Jesus, which was obscured by his normal human form. A further feature of the vision was the appearance with Jesus of Moses and Elijah, representatives of the Law and the Prophets.

Jesus Travels toward Jerusalem: Jesus left Galilee for the last time, heading toward Jerusalem and death. He again crossed the Jordan, spending some time in Perea before going on to Jericho.

After the Transfiguration, Jesus made two predictions concerning his approaching death. These announcements were a total perplexity to the disciples. In Matthew 16, when Jesus mentioned his death, Peter attempted to rebuke Jesus and was rebuked by Jesus in kind. When Jesus mentioned his death again in chapter 17, Matthew noted that the disciples were greatly distressed (Mt 17:23), while Mark and Luke mentioned the disciples' lack of understanding (Mk 9:32; Lk 9:45). Jesus was approaching the cross with no support from those closest to him. It is not surprising that when the hour arrived they all forsook him.

After the Transfiguration revealed that Jesus was greater than Moses and Elijah and in fact was the beloved Son of God, he was asked to pay the Temple tax (Mt 17:24-27). This incident illustrates the attitude of Jesus toward the authorities and practical responsibilities. He paid the tax, although he did not acknowledge any obligation to do so. The method of payment was extraordinary, for it involved the miracle of the coin in the fish. But the greater importance of the incident is the light it throws on Jesus' independence from the Jewish law.

JESUS
The Last Week of Jesus' Earthly Life

SUNDAY
Triumphal entry (Matthew 21:1-11)

MONDAY
Moneychangers thrown out of Temple (Matthew 21:12-19)
Jesus meets with Greek pilgrims (John 12:20-36)

TUESDAY
Fig tree withers at Jesus' curse (Matthew 21:18-19)
Leaders challenge; Jesus responds with parables, wit (Matthew 21:23–22:46)
Jesus preaches about the misdeeds of the Pharisees (Matthew 23)
At the Mount of Olives, Jesus preaches about future events (Matthew 24)
Dining with a Pharisee, Jesus is anointed by a woman (Matthew 26:6-13)
Judas makes plans to betray Jesus (Matthew 26:14-16)

THURSDAY
Preparations are made for the Passover (Matthew 26:17-19)
Jesus washes his disciples' feet (John 13:1-20)
Passover eaten, Jesus institutes Lord's Supper (Matthew 26:20, 26-29)
Judas leaves (Luke 22:21-23)
Jesus gives final instructions and prays with disciples (John 14-17)

THURSDAY NIGHT/FRIDAY EARLY MORNING
Jesus prays in the Garden of Gethsemane (Luke 22:39-46)
Jesus is betrayed and arrested (Luke 22:47-53)

FRIDAY
Jesus interrogated by high priest Annas (John 18:12-14, 19-23)
Jesus is tried by Caiaphas and the Sanhedrin (Luke 22:54, 63-71)
Peter denies Jesus (Luke 22:54-62)
Jesus appears before the Roman governor, Pilate (Luke 23:1-5)
Pilate sends Jesus to Herod (Luke 23:6-12)
Herod sends Jesus back to Pilate, and he is interrogated again (Luke 23:13-25)
Pilate defers to the crowd, which clamors for crucifixion
Jesus is led to Golgotha and crucified (Luke 19:16-30)
Jesus is buried in the tomb of Joseph of Arimathea (Luke 19:31-42)

SUNDAY
Women visit the tomb to anoint the body, find it empty (Luke 24:1-11)
Peter and John rush to the empty tomb (John 20:1-10)
Jesus appears to Mary Magdalene (John 20:11-18)
Jesus appears to two disciples on the road to Emmaus (Luke 24:13-35)
Jesus appears to his disciples, with Thomas absent (John 20:19-25)

The Final Journey to Jerusalem

On the approach to Jerusalem, Jesus visited both Jericho and Bethany. At Jericho he healed Bartimaeus (Lk 18:35-43) and had a fruitful encounter with Zacchaeus, who reformed his ways as a tax collector (19:1-10). Bethany was the home of Mary, Martha, and their brother, Lazarus, whom Jesus had raised from the dead (Jn 11). Jesus spent his remaining days in Jerusalem but returned each night to stay at Simon the Leper's house in Bethany in the presence of those who loved him (Mt 26:6). It was there that a woman anointed his body with costly ointment. This was a controversial and prophetic act preparing Jesus for his burial and enhancing the gospel with loving consecration (vv 6-13).

All four Gospels relate the entry of Jesus into Jerusalem (Mt 21:1-11; Mk 11:1-10; Lk 19:29-38; Jn 12:12-15). At this time multitudes greeted Jesus with praises acclaiming him as their king. This welcome stands in stark contrast with the crowd's later cry for his crucifixion. In fact, it was the second crowd that was doing God's bidding, since Jesus had not come to Jerusalem to reign but to die.

The synoptic Gospels place the cleansing of the Temple as the first main event following Jesus' entry into the city (Mt 21:12-13; Mk 11:15-17; Lk 19:45-46). The clouds of opposition had been thickening, but the audacity of Jesus in clearing out the money changers from the Temple area was too much for the authorities (Mk 11:18; Lk 19:47). The die was cast and the Crucifixion loomed closer.

It was during this period that further controversies developed between Jesus and the Pharisees and Sadducees (Mt 21:23–22:45). In several cases trick questions were posed in order to trap Jesus, but with consummate skill he turned their questions against them. His opposers eventually reached the point where they dared not ask him any more questions (22:46).

Nearing his final hour, Jesus took the opportunity to instruct his disciples about future events, especially the end of the world. He reiterated the certainty of his return and mentioned various signs that would precede that coming (Mt 24–25; Mk 13; Lk 21). The purpose of this teaching was to provide a challenge to the disciples to be watchful (Mt 25:13) and diligent (vv 14-30). This section prepares the way for the events of the arrest, the trial, the scourging, and the cross carrying and crucifixion that followed soon after. But first we must note the importance of the Last Supper.

When Jesus sat at the table with his disciples on the night before he died, he wished to give them a simple means by which the significance of his death could be grasped (Mt 26:26-30; Mk 14:22-25; Lk 22:19-20; 1 Cor 11:23-26). The use of the bread and wine for this purpose was a happy choice because they were basic elements in everyday life. Through this symbolic significance Jesus gave an interpretation of his approaching death—his body broken and his blood poured out for others. It was necessary for Jesus to provide this reminder that his sacrificial death would seal a completely new covenant. It was to be an authentic memorial to prevent the church from losing sight of the centrality of the cross.

John's Gospel does not relate the institution of the Last Supper. Nevertheless, it does record a significant act in which Jesus washed the feet of the disciples as an example of humility (Jn 13:1-20). He impressed on the disciples the principle of service to others. John follows this display of humility with a series of teachings Jesus gave on the eve of the Passion (chs 14–16). The most important feature of this teaching was the promise of the coming of the Holy Spirit to the disciples after Jesus had gone. Even with his mind occupied by thoughts of approaching death, Jesus showed himself more concerned about his disciples than about himself. This is evident in the prayer of Jesus in John 17. All the Evangelists refer in advance to the betrayal by Judas (Mt 26:21-25; Mk 14:18-21; Lk 22:21-23; Jn 13:21-30), which prepares readers for the final stages of the way of Jesus to the cross.

The Trial and Crucifixion

After being betrayed by Judas, Jesus was first taken to the house of Annas, one of the high priests, for a preliminary examination (Jn 18:13). During his trial, he was scorned by his enemies, and one of his disciples, Peter, denied him three times (Mt 26:69-75, Mk 14:66-72; Lk 22:54-62; Jn 18:15-27), as Jesus predicted he would (Mt 26:34; Mk 14:30; Jn 13:38). The official trial before the Sanhedrin was presided over by Caiaphas, who was nonplussed when Jesus at first refused to speak. At length Jesus predicted that the Son of Man would come on the clouds of heaven; this was enough to make the high priest charge him with blasphemy (Mk 14:62-64). Although he was spat upon and his face was struck, Jesus remained calm and dignified. He showed how much greater he was than those who were treating him with contempt.

The further examinations before Pilate (Mt 27:1-2; Mk 15:1; Lk 23:1; Jn 18:28) and Herod (Lk 23:7-12) were no better examples of impartial justice. Again Jesus did not answer when asked about the charges before either Pilate (Mt 27:14) or Herod (Lk 23:9). He remained majestically silent, except to make a comment to Pilate about the true nature of his kingship (Jn 18:33-38). The pathetic governor declared Jesus innocent, offered the crowds the release of either Jesus or Barabbas, and then publicly disclaimed responsibility

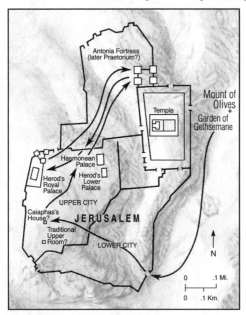

The Last Evening: After Judas singled Jesus out for arrest, the mob took Jesus first to Annas and then to Caiaphas, the high priest. This trial, a mockery of justice, convened at daybreak and ended with their decision to kill him, but the Jews needed Rome's permission for the death sentence. Jesus was taken to Pilate (who was probably in the Praetorium), then to Herod (Lk 23:5-12), and back to Pilate, who sentenced him to die.

by washing his hands. Pilate then cruelly scourged Jesus and handed him over to be crucified. This judge has ever since been judged by the prisoner.

The reader of this scene cannot help but see man's inhumanity to man—even the man of all men, Jesus Christ. The soldiers' ribald mockery of Jesus (Mt 27:27-30), mixing a royal robe with a hurtful crown of thorns (Mk 15:17), compelling a passerby to carry the cross (Lk 23:26), the cruel procedure of nailing Jesus to the cross, the callous casting of lots for his garment (Jn 19:23-24), and the scornful challenge to him to use his power to escape (Mt 27:40-44)—all expose the cruelty of Jesus opponents. But against this is Jesus' concern about the repentant criminal who was crucified with him (Lk 23:39-43), his concern for his mother (Jn 19:25-27), his prayer for forgiveness for those responsible for the Crucifixion (Lk 23:34), and his final triumphant cry (Mk 15:37)—all of which show a nobility of mind that contrasted strongly with the meanness of those about him. A few observers showed a better appreciation, like the centurion who was convinced of Jesus' innocence (Mk 15:39) and the women who followed him and stood at a distance (Mt 27:55-56). There was one dark moment, as far as Jesus was concerned—his forsaken cry, which quickly passed (Mk 15:34). There was an accompanying darkness and an earthquake, as if nature itself were acknowledging the significance of the event. Even the Temple veil was torn in two, as if it had no longer any right to bar the way into the Holy of Holies (Mt 27:51).

The Burial, Resurrection, and Ascension

Jesus' body was placed in a tomb that belonged to Joseph of Arimathea, who was assisted by Nicodemus in laying the body to rest (Mt 27:57-60; Jn 19:39). But the tomb played only an incidental part in the resurrection. The Evangelists concentrate on the appearances of Jesus not only on the day of resurrection but also subsequently. The disciples were convinced that Jesus was alive. Some, like Thomas, had doubts to overcome (Jn 20:24-29). Others, like John, were more ready to believe when they saw the empty tomb (vv 2-10). It is not without significance that the first to see the risen Lord was a woman, Mary Magdalene (Mt 27:61; 28:1, 5-9), whose presence at the cross put to shame those disciples who had run away (Mt 26:56; Jn 19:25).

We may note that in his glorified, risen state Jesus was in a human form, although he was not at once recognized (Jn 20:15-16). There was a definite continuity with the Jesus the disciples had known. The appearances were occasions of both joy and instruction (cf. Lk 24:44 and Acts 1:3). The resurrection, in fact, had transformed the Crucifixion from a tragedy into a triumph. Forty days after his resurrection, Jesus ascended into heaven to join his Father in glory (Lk 24:51; Jn 20:17; Acts 1:9-11).

JESUS JUSTUS

Jewish Christian. *See* Jesus #3.

JETHER

1. Firstborn son of Gideon who, because of his youth, was afraid to execute the Midianite kings Zebah and Zalmunna at his father's request (Jgs 8:20).

2. Ishmaelite and the father of Amasa (1 Kgs 2:5, 32; 1 Chr 2:17). He is alternately called Ithra in 2 Samuel 17:25.

3. Firstborn son of Jada, the brother of Jonathan, and a descendant of Judah through Hezron's line. He fathered no children (1 Chr 2:32).

4. Judahite and the firstborn of Ezrah's four sons (1 Chr 4:17).

5. Asherite, the father of three sons (1 Chr 7:38) and probably identical with Ithran, Zophah's son, in 1 Chronicles 7:37.

JETHETH
Chief of Edom (Gn 36:40; 1 Chr 1:51).

JETHRO
Father-in-law of Moses. Zipporah, Jethro's daughter, became Moses' wife while he was a fugitive in the wilderness (Ex 2:21). When Moses departed for Egypt, he took Zipporah and his sons with him (4:20), but he must have sent them back. Jethro brought them to Moses after the Israelites arrived in Sinai (18:1-7). Through this familial relationship with Moses, Jethro became involved with Israel.

Jethro's relationship with Israel has been variously interpreted. Jethro was a priest of Midian (Ex 2:16; 3:1). It is not definitely known what the religion of the Midianites was, but some scholars have suggested that the Kenites, who were a tribe included in the nation of Midian (Jgs 1:16), had a tribal god named Yahweh whom Jethro served as priest. Scholars who have suggested that Jethro's tribal god, Yahweh, was introduced to Israel by Moses have not been able to establish their case. Biblical evidence does not support this interpretation. That Jethro was a god-fearing and god-serving man is quite clear. The biblical record could be understood to teach that Jethro knew of Israel's God because he was a descendant of Abraham (Gn 25:2). Having heard of Yahweh's deliverance of his people from Egypt, Jethro acknowledged him as God, greatest of all gods. He also brought a burnt offering and sacrifices, thereby worshiping Yahweh and identifying with Israel (Ex 18:11). This action has been interpreted as Jethro's acceptance of a covenant with Israel, but the interpretation rests upon a faulty reading of what Jethro actually did and the meaning of sacrifice and a fellowship meal. Upon receiving Jethro's good counsel concerning procedures for judging disputes among the people, Moses appointed able men as heads and judges over the people (vv 13-27). Jethro departed to his own land and seems to have had no further interaction with Israel, but his son (Nm 10:29-33) and other descendants later became a part of Israel (Jgs 1:16; 4:11).

Jethro is referred to by other names, both in the Scriptures and later. The Talmud records that his name was Jether originally, but after his conversion it became Jethro; there is no definite evidence to support this. He is called Reuel, the father of seven daughters whom Moses met at a well (Ex 2:16-18; Nm 10:29). He is also referred to by the name Hobab (Jgs 4:11); and he is said to be the son of Reuel (Nm 10:29). The Scriptures do not explain the use of the different names. Suggestions include the following: (1) each Midianite tribe he served as a priest knew him by a different name; (2) Reuel was a tribal name, not personal; (3) Hobab, the son's name, was used to refer to the father; (4) a gloss appears in the text at Exodus 2:18 and Judges 4:11. It can be quite clearly established, however, that Jethro had a son named Hobab.

See also Moses.

JETUR

Son of Ishmael (Gn 25:15; 1 Chr 1:31) whose descendants fought the Israelite tribes who settled east of the Jordan (1 Chr 5:19). Also called Itureans, they survived into NT times, giving their name to Iturea, an area northeast of Galilee (Lk 3:1).

JEUEL

1. Descendant of Judah residing in postexilic Jerusalem (1 Chr 9:6).

2. Levite who took part in Hezekiah's reforms (2 Chr 29:13).

3. Head of a family who returned to Jerusalem with Ezra after the Exile (Ezr 8:13).

JEUSH

1. Eldest of three sons born to Esau by Oholibamah, daughter of the Canaanite Anah, and a chief among Esau's descendants in Edom (Gn 36:5-18; 1 Chr 1:35).

2. Bilhan's son from Jediael's house and a leader in Benjamin's tribe (1 Chr 7:10).

3. Benjaminite, Eshek's son and a descendant of Saul (1 Chr 8:39).

4. Levite from the family of Gershon and the third of Shimei's four sons. Since he and his youngest brother, Beriah, had few sons, they were together considered one house during David's reign (1 Chr 23:10-11).

5. Eldest of three sons born to King Rehoboam by Mahalath, Eliab's granddaughter (2 Chr 11:19).

JEUZ

From Benjamin's tribe, Shaharaim's son by his wife Hodesh (1 Chr 8:10).

JEZANIAH

Alternate form of Jaazaniah, one of the Judean captains in Jerusalem during the Exile (Jer 40:8 NLT mg; 42:1) *See* Jaazaniah #1.

JEZEBEL

Daughter of Ethbaal, king of Sidon (1 Kgs 16:31). She became the wife of Ahab, king of the northern kingdom of Israel. The marriage was probably a continuation of the friendly relations between Israel and Phoenicia begun by Omri; it confirmed a political alliance

QUICKTAKE

JEZEBEL

WEAKNESSES AND MISTAKES
- Systematically eliminated the representatives of God in Israel
- Promoted and funded Baal worship
- Threatened to have Elijah killed
- Believed kings and queens could rightfully do or have anything they wanted
- Used her strong convictions to get her own way

LESSONS FROM HER LIFE
- It is not enough to be committed or sincere. Where our commitment lies makes a great difference
- Rejecting God always leads to disaster

VITAL STATISTICS
Where: Sidon, Samaria
Occupation: Queen of Israel
Relatives: Husband: Ahab. Father: Ethbaal. Sons: Joram, Ahaziah
Contemporaries: Elijah, Jehu

KEY VERSE
"No one else so completely sold himself to what was evil in the LORD's sight as Ahab did under the influence of his wife Jezebel" (1 Kings 21:25).

Jezebel's story is told in 1 Kings 16:31—2 Kings 9:37. Her name is used as a synonym for great evil in Revelation 2:20.

between the two nations. Jezebel exerted a strong influence over the life of Israel, as she insisted on establishing the worship of Baal and demanded the absolute rights of the monarchy. So strong was her pagan influence that Scripture attributes the apostasy of Ahab directly to Jezebel (vv 30-33).

Jezebel's efforts to establish Baal worship in Israel began with Ahab's acceptance of Baal following the marriage (1 Kgs 16:31). Ahab followed Jezebel's practices by building a house of worship and altar for Baal in Samaria, and by setting up a pole for worship of the Asherah. A campaign was then conducted to exterminate the prophets of God (18:4), while Jezebel organized and supported large groups of Baal prophets, housing and feeding large numbers of them in the royal palace (v 19). To meet this challenge, God sent Elijah to prophesy a drought that lasted three years (17:1; 18:1).

Elijah's confrontation with Jezebel and Ahab culminated on Mt Carmel, where Elijah demanded that the prophets of Baal meet him (1 Kgs 18:19-40). As they and the people of Israel gathered, Elijah issued the challenge to Israel to follow the true God. To demonstrate who was the true God, Baal's prophets and Elijah each took a bull for sacrifice. The prophets of Baal then prepared the sacrifice and called on their god to send fire to consume it. But no answer came. Elijah prepared his sacrifice and had it drenched in water. After his prayer, God sent fire that consumed the sacrifice, the wood, the stones of the altar, the dust, and the water in the trench. Following this, the Israelites fell down in tribute to God. Then Elijah directed the people to take the prophets of Baal to the brook Kishon, and he slaughtered all of them. When Jezebel heard of this, she flew into a rage and threatened Elijah with the same fate. In fear, Elijah fled for his life to the wilderness.

Jezebel's unscrupulous nature is revealed in the account of Ahab's desire for Naboth's vineyard (1 Kgs 21:1-16). Although Ahab desired the vineyard, he recognized Naboth's right to retain the family property. Jezebel recognized no such right in view of a monarch's wishes. She arranged to have Naboth falsely accused of blaspheming God and consequently executed, leaving the vineyard for Ahab to seize. For this heinous crime, Elijah pronounced a violent death for Ahab and Jezebel (21:20-24), a prophecy which was ultimately fulfilled (1 Kgs 22:29-40; 2 Kgs 9:1-37).

The corrupt influence of Jezebel spread to the southern kingdom of Judah through her daughter Athaliah, who married Jehoram, king of Judah. Thus the idolatry of Phoenicia infected both kingdoms of the Hebrews through this evil Sidonian princess.

In Revelation 2:20 the name of Jezebel is used (probably symbolically) to refer to a prophetess who seduced the Christians of Thyatira to fornication and to eating things sacrificed to idols.

See also Ahab #1; Elijah #1.

JEZER

Naphtali's third son and the founder of the family of Jezerites (Gn 46:24; Nm 26:49; 1 Chr 7:13).

JEZIEL

Warrior from Benjamin's tribe who joined David at Ziklag in his struggle against King Saul. Jeziel was one of David's ambidextrous archers and slingers (1 Chr 12:3).

JEZRAHIAH

Leader of the Temple singers who participated in the dedication of the rebuilt Jerusalem wall (Neh 12:42).

JEZREEL

1. Descendant of Etam from the tribe of Judah (1 Chr 4:3). Another possible reading suggests that Jezreel was one of the founding fathers of the town of Etam. Due to

numerous scribal alterations within the Hebrew text, it is difficult to discern the original intent of the author.

2. Firstborn son of the prophet Hosea and his wife, Gomer. Jezreel's name, meaning "God sows," prefigured the outpouring of God's wrath on the disobedient kingdom of Israel under Jehu (Hos 1:4-5) and ultimate restoration (2:21-22).

JIDLAPH
Seventh son of Nahor and Milcah (Gn 22:22).

JOAB
1. Son of Zeruiah, the half sister of David (1 Chr 2:16), who, along with his brothers Abishai and Asahel, was well known for his military valor in Judah (2 Sm 2:18; cf. 1 Sm 26:6). According to 2 Samuel, Joab rose to prominence and distinguished himself at the battle of Gibeon when Saul's troops under Abner were vanquished (2 Sm 2:8-32). Because Abner had slain Joab's brother Asahel (v 23), Joab later killed Abner in revenge (3:26-30), despite Abner's new loyalty to David (vv 12-19). Possibly Joab sensed that Abner would be his rival. Nevertheless, David praised the slain commander as a prince and a great man (vv 31-39) and set a curse on the house of Joab for his insubordination (vv 26-29, 39). This incident illumines Joab's sometimes unscrupulous and ruthless behavior.

Joab spearheaded David's siege of the Jebusite city of Jerusalem, and when David consolidated his reign there, Joab became the commander of the king's army (2 Sm 8:16; 11:1; cf. 1 Chr 11:6-8; 18:15). He suppressed a rebellion among the Syrians and Ammonites (2 Sm 10:7-14; 1 Chr 19:8-15). At Rabbah he not only conquered the city (2 Sm 11–12) but arranged for the death of Uriah the Hittite so that David could take Uriah's wife, Bathsheba.

Joab's loyalties to David and shrewd control of the army are seen during Absalom's rebellion (2 Sm 15). Joab suppressed the conspiracy (ch 18), but ignoring a direct order from David not to kill his son (18:5), brutally killed him anyway (vv 10-17). When David mourned, Joab rebuked the king, urging that a crisis with the army was imminent (19:5-7). This insubordination led David to replace Joab with Amasa as commander (v 13), but later, at Gibeon, Joab also killed him dishonorably (20:8-10). Joab's influence in the army must have been great, since he regained his former role as military commander (2 Sm 20:23, 24:2; 1 Kgs 1:19).

At the end of David's reign, Joab supported the conspiracy of Adonijah and Abiathar against the throne (1 Kgs 1:7). David's distrust of him led the king to warn Solomon specifically about Joab's repeated treacheries (2:5-9). Solomon had to resolve the problem of an untrustworthy army. Therefore, upon his father's death, Solomon pursued the conspirators Adonijah (v 23), Abiathar (v 26), and Joab (v 28). Solomon's officer Benaiah found Joab at the altar seeking refuge and killed him there (vv 28-35), thus cleansing Solomon's reign from the wrongdoing of Joab.

2. KJV translation ("Ataroth, the house of Joab") of Atroth-beth-joab in 1 Chronicles 2:54.

3. Judahite, Seraiah's son from the house of Kenaz and forefather of the residents of the valley of craftsmen (1 Chr 4:14).

4. Forefather of a clan of Jews who returned to Palestine with Zerubbabel following the Exile (Ezr 2:6; Neh 7:11).

5. Forefather of a family of which 219 members returned with Ezra to Palestine following the Exile (Ezr 8:9). He is perhaps identifiable with #4 above.

JOAH

1. Asaph's son and a court official under King Hezekiah (2 Kgs 18:18, 26; Is 36:3, 11, 22). He was one of the officers sent by Hezekiah to deal with the Assyrians during the siege of Jerusalem.

2. Zimmah's son from Levi's tribe (1 Chr 6:21).

3. Levite, Obed-edom's son and a gatekeeper of the sanctuary in David's time (1 Chr 26:4).

4. Joahaz's son and a recorder under King Josiah; he was one of the deputies overseeing the Temple repairs (2 Chr 34:8).

JOAHAZ

1. Variant spelling or contraction of Jehoahaz, Jehu's son, in 2 Kings 14:1. See Jehoahaz #1.

2. Joah's father. Joah was King Josiah's recorder (2 Chr 34:8).

JOANAN

Ancestor of Jesus mentioned in Luke's genealogy (Lk 3:27).

JOANNA

1. KJV form of Joanan in Luke 3:27. See Joanan.

2. Wife of Chuza, a steward of Herod the tetrarch. She was among those healed of evil spirits and sickness by Jesus, and contributed to his support (Lk 8:2-3). She probably witnessed the Crucifixion and prepared spices for the body; later she found Jesus' tomb empty (23:55–24:10).

JOASH

1. Abiezrite who lived at Ophrah and the father of Gideon. Joash built an altar to Baal and an image of Asherah, which Gideon later destroyed (Jgs 6:11-31; 7:14; 8:13, 29-32).

2. Son of King Ahab of Israel (1 Kgs 22:26; 2 Chr 18:25).

3. Alternate name for Jehoash, Ahaziah's son and king of Judah (835–796 BC), in 2 Kings 11:2-3 and 1 Chronicles 3:11. See Jehoash #1.

QUICKTAKE

JOB

STRENGTHS AND ACCOMPLISHMENTS
- Was a man of faith, patience, and endurance
- Was known as a generous and caring person
- Was very wealthy

WEAKNESS AND MISTAKE
- Allowed his desire to understand why he was suffering overwhelm him and make him question God

LESSONS FROM HIS LIFE
- Knowing God is better than knowing answers
- God is not arbitrary or uncaring
- Pain is not always punishment

VITAL STATISTICS
Where: Uz
Occupation: Wealthy landowner and livestock owner
Relatives: Wife and first 10 children not named. Daughters from the second set of children: Jemimah, Keziah, Keren-happuch
Contemporaries: Eliphaz, Bildad, Zophar, Elihu

KEY VERSES
"For examples of patience in suffering, dear brothers and sisters, look at the prophets who spoke in the name of the Lord. We give great honor to those who endure under suffering. For instance, you know about Job, a man of great endurance. You can see how the Lord was kind to him at the end, for the Lord is full of tenderness and mercy" (James 5:10, 11).

Job's story is told in the book of Job. He is also referred to in Ezekiel 14:14, 20 and James 5:11

4. Alternate name for Jehoash, Jehoahaz's son and king of Israel (798–782 BC), in 2 Kings 13:10-13. *See* Jehoash #2.

5. Judahite from the house of Shelah (1 Chr 4:22).

6. Second of Beker's nine sons and a leader in Benjamin's tribe (1 Chr 7:8).

7. Benjaminite warrior who supported David at Ziklag (1 Chr 12:3).

8. One of David's officials (1 Chr 27:28).

JOB

1. Central character of the book of Job. The intense suffering endured by Job provides the framework for the main theme of the book, which deals with the role of suffering in the life of a child of God.

The etymology of the name is difficult. Some have seen it as a derivative of a Hebrew word meaning "to be hostile" and have suggested that it reflects Job's adamancy in refusing to bow to God's will. The name occurs in several West Semitic texts as a proper name, however, and it seems best to understand it simply as a common name. The meaning of the name in West Semitic is either "no father" or "where is my father?"

The lack of certainty surrounding the authorship and geographical provenance of the book makes it difficult to place Job in history. The occurrence of Job's name in Ezekiel 14:14, 20 seems to support the possibility that he was a personage of great antiquity.

2. KJV rendering of Iob, an alternate form of Jashub, Issachar's third son, in Genesis 46:13. *See* Jashub #1.

JOBAB

1. Joktan's son in Eber's line (Gn 10:29; 1 Chr 1:23).

2. Early Edomite king. He was the son of Zerah of Bozrah (Gn 36:33-34; 1 Chr 1:44-45).

3. King of Madon who, along with other Canaanite kings, joined Jabin of Hazor in a northern confederacy to stop the Israelites from taking over the northern section of Canaan. He was killed in battle at the waters of Merom (Jos 11:1; 12:19).

4. Shaharaim's son by his wife Hodesh, a member of Benjamin's tribe (1 Chr 8:9).

5. Elpaal's son from Benjamin's tribe (1 Chr 8:18).

JOCHEBED

Amram's wife and the mother of Moses, Aaron, and Miriam (Ex 6:20; Nm 26:59).

JODA

Joanan's son, the father of Josech, and a forefather of Jesus Christ living in Palestine during the postexilic era (Lk 3:26).

JOED

Descendant of Benjamin living in Jerusalem during the days of Nehemiah (Neh 11:7). His name, meaning "Yahweh is witness," does not appear in a parallel list in 1 Chronicles 9:7.

JOEL

1. Levite from the family of Kohath. He was Azariah's son and an ancestor of Elkanah, the father of Samuel the prophet (1 Sm 1:1; 1 Chr 6:36).

2. Oldest son of Samuel the prophet. He and his brother Abijah so corrupted the office of judge that the elders increased their demands for a king (1 Sm 8:2-5). He was the father of Heman the singer (1 Chr 6:33; 15:17). His name has been mistakenly translated "Vashni" in the KJV in 1 Chronicles 6:28.

3. Prince from one of the Simeonite families that emigrated to the valley of Gedor (1 Chr 4:35).

4. Member of Reuben's tribe (1 Chr 5:4, 8).

5. Chief of Gad's tribe residing in Bashan (1 Chr 5:12).

6. Third of Izrahiah's four named sons and a chief of Issachar's tribe in David's time (1 Chr 7:3).

7. Nathan's brother and one of David's mighty men (1 Chr 11:38). He is alternately called Igal the son of Nathan in 2 Samuel 23:36. *See* Igal #2.

8. Levite from the family of Gershon who participated in the royal procession that brought the Ark of God to Jerusalem during David's reign (1 Chr 15:7-11). He may have administered the treasuries of the Temple in Jerusalem (1 Chr 26:22).

9. Pedaiah's son, who acted as tribal chieftain over the west half of Manasseh's tribe during David's reign (1 Chr 27:20)

10. Levite from the family of Kohath who assisted in King Hezekiah's reform of the Temple in Jerusalem (2 Chr 29:12).

11. Nebo's son, who was encouraged by Ezra to divorce his foreign wife during the postexilic period (Ezr 10:43).

12. Zicri's son and the supervisor of 128 Benjaminites who moved to postexilic Jerusalem (Neh 11:9).

13. Prophet who wrote the second book of the Minor Prophets. Little is known about him except that he was Pethuel's son (Jl 1:1; Acts 2:16).

JOELAH
Warrior who joined David at Ziklag in his struggle against King Saul. Joelah was one of David's ambidextrous archers and slingers (1 Chr 12:7).

JOEZER
Warrior who joined David at Ziklag in his struggle against King Saul. He was one of David's ambidextrous archers and slingers (1 Chr 12:6). He was called a Korahite, which probably refers to his place of origin.

JOGLI
Father of Bukki, a Danite leader who helped oversee the distribution of the Promised Land west of the Jordan River (Nm 34:22).

JOHA

1. Benjaminite and one of Beriah's nine sons (1 Chr 8:16).
2. Tizite, the brother of Jediael and one of David's mighty men (1 Chr 11:45).

JOHANAN

Name meaning "Yahweh has been gracious." It occurs also in the alternate form of Jehohanan. The name John is derived from these names. Several men of this name appear in the OT.

1. Son of Kareah (2 Kgs 25:23). Johanan was a Jewish leader, a contemporary of Jeremiah, and supportive of Gedaliah, the governor of Judah after the fall of Jerusalem (Jer 40:8, 13). He forewarned Gedaliah of Ishmael's plan to assassinate him (vv 13-16). When the warning was ignored and Johanan was refused permission to execute the would-be assassin, Gedaliah was murdered. Johanan took vengeance against Ishmael and rescued those who had been captured (41:14-18), but he was unable to pursue Ishmael. In fear of a Babylonian reprisal, he made plans to seek asylum in Egypt. Jeremiah, whom he consulted, gave God's word against this move (42:1-22), but Johanan was unwilling to take counsel (43:2-3). He led the Judeans, including Jeremiah and Baruch, to Egypt (vv 5-7).
2. Eldest son of Josiah, king of Judah (1 Chr 3:15). Possibly he died young, for he did not succeed his father on the throne, even though he was the firstborn.
3. Son of Elioenai (1 Chr 3:24), a descendant of Jehoiachin, one of the last kings of Judah.
4. Grandson of Ahimaaz. He was the father of Azariah, who served as high priest in the Temple of Solomon (1 Chr 6:9-10).
5. Warrior from Benjamin's tribe. He joined David's special forces of 30 men at Ziklag (1 Chr 12:4). The special forces could shoot arrows and sling stones with either hand (v 2).
6. Gadite who joined David in the wilderness (1 Chr 12:8-12). He was also specially trained for war, in that he could handle both shield and spear, could endure hardship, and was quick on his feet.
7. Ephraimite whose son was a leader in the northern Kingdom during the regime of Pekah and protested against the enslavement of 200,000 Judeans (2 Chr 28:12; NLT "Jehohanan"), who were subsequently freed.
8. Son of Hakkatan ("the younger" or "the smaller"). The designation may be read as "Johanan the younger." He was head of a family who claimed their descent from Azgad (Ezr 8:12). He joined Ezra with 110 men in traveling from Babylonia to Judah.
9. Priest under Joiakim. He was one of the priests during whose ministry the Levites and priests formally registered (Neh 12:22). He is alternately called Jehohanan in Ezra 10:6 and Jonathan in Neh 12:11. *See* Jehohanan #4.
10. KJV spelling of Jehohanan, Tobiah's son, in Nehemiah 6:18. *See* Jehohanan #6.

JOHN

1. Father of Simon Peter and Andrew (Jn 1:40-42; 21:15-17). According to Matthew 16:17, Peter's father was named Jona (Jonas, Jonah). Either Jona was an alternate form of the name John or, more probably, two independent traditions existed regarding his name.

2. Member of the high priestly family who, along with Annas, Caiaphas, and Alexander, questioned Peter and John after the two apostles had healed a lame man (Acts 4:6).

3. According to the early church bishop Papias, a member of the larger group of Jesus' disciples outside the Twelve (cf. Lk 10:1). Known as "John the elder" (the presbyter), he is often credited with the authorship of 2 and 3 John (2 Jn 1:1; 3 Jn 1:1), although the term "elder" there more likely refers to John the apostle.

4. The apostle. *See* John, The Apostle.

5. The Baptist. *See* John the Baptist.

6. An early disciple known as John Mark, author of the second Gospel. *See* Mark, John.

JOHN, THE APOSTLE

The apostle known as "the disciple whom Jesus loved"; author of the fourth Gospel, three epistles, and probably Revelation.

The apostle John has a high reputation among Christian people, and his influence has been felt throughout the centuries. Despite this, he is a surprisingly shadowy figure. When he appears in the pages of the NT, it is almost always in company with Peter or James, and if there is speaking to be done, it is usually his companion Peter who does it; thus, there is not a great deal on which to base a biography.

John's father's name was Zebedee, and John had a brother called James (Mt 4:21). Among the women at the cross, Matthew names Mary Magdalene, Mary the mother of James and Joseph, and "the mother of Zebedee's children" (27:56). Mark names the two Marys and adds Salome (Mk 15:40). This indicates that Salome may be the name of John's mother. If Matthew and Mark are naming the same women as does John, then Salome was Jesus' "mother's sister" (Jn 19:25). This would make John a cousin of Jesus. We cannot be certain of this, for there were many women there (Mt 27:55) and there is no way of being sure that Matthew, Mark, and John all name the same three. Many accept the identification, but we can scarcely say more.

John was among those whom Jesus called by the Sea of Galilee (Mt 4:21-22; Mk 1:19-20). This makes him one of the first disciples. It is also possible that he was the unnamed companion of Andrew when that apostle first followed Jesus (Jn 1:35-37). John was important in the little group around Jesus since he was one of three who were especially close to the Master. These disciples were selected to be with Jesus on many great occasions. John, along with his brother James and Peter, was present at the Transfiguration (Mt 17:1-2; Mk 9:2; Lk 9:28-29). Jesus also took just these three into the house of Jairus when he brought that

QUICKTAKE

JOHN the APOSTLE

STRENGTHS AND ACCOMPLISHMENTS
- Before following Jesus, was one of John the Baptist's disciples
- One of the 12 disciples and, with Peter and James, one of the inner three, closest to Jesus
- Wrote five New Testament books: the Gospel of John; 1, 2, and 3 John; and Revelation

WEAKNESSES AND MISTAKES
- Along with James, shared a tendency to outbursts of selfishness and anger
- Asked for a special position in Jesus' Kingdom

LESSONS FROM HIS LIFE
- Those who realize how much they are loved are able to love much
- When God changes a life, he does not take away personality characteristics, but puts them to effective use in his service

VITAL STATISTICS
Occupations: Fisherman, disciple
Relatives: Father: Zebedee. Mother: Salome. Brother: James
Contemporaries: Jesus, Pilate, Herod

KEY VERSES
"Dear friends, I am not writing a new commandment for you; rather it is an old one you have had from the very beginning. This old commandment—to love one another—is the same message you heard before. Yet it is also new. Jesus lived the truth of this commandment, and you also are living it. For the darkness is disappearing, and the true light is already shining" (1 John 2:7, 8).

John's story is told throughout the Gospels, Acts, and Revelation.

man's daughter back to life (Mk 5:37; Lk 8:51). Before Jesus' arrest, it was this trio that he took to pray with him in the Garden of Gethsemane (Mt 26:37; Mk 14:33). Though the three were admonished for sleeping instead of watching in prayer, we must not overlook the fact that in that time of great difficulty, when Jesus faced the prospect of death on a cross, it was to these three that he looked for support.

There are other occasions when John is mentioned in the Gospels. Luke tells us of John's surprise when the miraculous catch of fish took place (Lk 5:9-10). This is especially noteworthy since John was a fisherman. Toward the close of Jesus' ministry, we find John coming to Jesus with Peter, James, and Andrew to ask when the end would come and what would be the sign when all things come to their climax (Mk 13:3-4). And on the last evening, Jesus sent Peter and John to prepare the Passover meal (Lk 22:8).

Passages like these show that John was highly esteemed among the apostles and that he stood especially close to Jesus. But there are indications that at first John was far from appreciating what Jesus stood for. When Mark gives his list of the Twelve, he tells us that Jesus gave to James and John the name "Boanerges," which means "sons of thunder" (Mk 3:17). Some in the early church understood this name as a compliment, thinking it meant that James's and John's witness to Jesus would be as strong as thunder. But most see it as pointing to their tempestuousness of character. We see this, for example, when John encounters a man who was casting out demons in Jesus' name. John instructs him not to, "for he isn't one of our group" (Mk 9:38; Lk 9:49).

Mark also tells us of an occasion when the sons of Zebedee asked Jesus for the two chief places in his kingdom, one to be on his right and the other on his left (Mk 10:35-40). Matthew adds the point that the words were spoken by the men's mother, but he leaves us no doubt that James and John were in on it (Mt 20:20-22). Jesus proceeded to ask them whether they could drink the cup he would drink and be baptized with the baptism he would receive. (Clearly, these are metaphors for the suffering Jesus would in due course undergo.) James and John affirmed that they could, and Jesus assured them that they would indeed do this. However, he gave them no assurance about their places in the Father's kingdom. (But it is plain that James and John would suffer for Christ.) At that time they also failed to understand the loving spirit that moved their Master and was required of them as well.

Another incident that shows the same tempestuous spirit is one involving Samaritan villagers who refused to receive the little band as they traveled. When James and John heard of it, they asked Jesus whether he wanted them to call down fire from heaven to consume the villagers (Lk 9:54). They were clearly at variance with Jesus, and indeed he rebuked them. But we should not miss the zeal they displayed for their Lord, nor their conviction that if they did call down fire it would come. They were sure that God would not fail to answer the prayer of those who asked for vengeance on the opponents of Jesus. There is zeal here and faith, though also a spirit of lovelessness.

The synoptic Gospels thus show us John as a zealous and loyal follower of Jesus. He is not depicted as gentle and considerate. At this time, he knew little of the love that should characterize a follower of Jesus, but he did have faith and a passionate conviction that God would prosper Jesus and those who served him.

John is not mentioned by name in the fourth Gospel, but there are passages that speak about "the disciple whom Jesus loved" (Jn 13:23; 19:26; 20:2; 21:7, 20). We are not told who this was, but the evidence seems to indicate that it was the apostle John. For example, there is an account of a fishing trip in chapter 21, with a listing of those who went fishing. It includes Peter, who must be ruled out as "the disciple whom Jesus loved" because he is often mentioned along with the beloved disciple. Thomas and Nathanael were there, but there seems to be no reason for seeing either as a likely candidate. Two unnamed men and the sons of Zebedee make up the remainder of the party. James is excluded as being the author because of his early death—around AD 44 (Acts 12:2). This leaves us with John or one of the unnamed men. John is favored by the fact that the beloved disciple is linked with Peter on a number of occasions (Jn 13:23-24; 20:2; 21:7). We know from the other Gospels that Peter and John (together with James) were especially close (see also Acts 3; 8:14; Gal 2:9). Of course, one of the unnamed disciples may have been the beloved disciple, but we have no reason to assume this. Further, such a supposition faces the problem of the omission of the name of John the apostle throughout the entire fourth Gospel. If John wrote this book, we can understand his not mentioning himself. But if it was written by someone else, why would that person omit all mention of a man as prominent in the apostolic band as the other Gospels show John to have been? In addition, if John is the author, it would explain why John the Baptist is called simply "John."

It is argued that "the disciple whom Jesus loved" is not the kind of title a man would naturally use of himself, but it must be said also that it is not the kind of title a man would naturally use of someone else, either. And it may be that John uses it in a modest fashion— partly because he did not want to draw attention to himself by using his name, and partly because he wanted to emphasize the truth that it was the fact that Jesus loved him that made him what he was.

If this identification may be accepted, we learn more about the apostle. We should not, of course, read the words "the disciple whom Jesus loved" as though they meant that Jesus did not love the other disciples. He loved them all. But as applied to John, they mean that he was indeed beloved, probably also that he recognized that he owed all he had and all he was to that love. That he was specially close to Jesus is indicated by the fact that he leaned on Jesus' breast at the Last Supper (Jn 13:23). It also tells us something of his relationship to the Master that he was at the cross when Christ was crucified and that it was to him that Jesus gave the charge to look after his mother (19:26-27). One would have expected that Jesus would have selected one of his family for this responsibility. But his brothers did not believe in him, whereas both John and Mary did. This event certainly shows that a close relationship existed between Jesus and the disciple he loved.

On the first Easter morning, John raced with Peter to the tomb when Mary Magdalene told them it was empty. He won the race but stood outside the tomb until Peter came. Peter, the leader of men, went right in, and John followed. We read that he "saw and believed" (Jn 20:8). Then in chapter 21 we read of the beloved disciple fishing with the others. Significantly, it was he who recognized that it was Jesus who stood on the shore and told them where to cast the net (21:7).

There is not much to add to this picture when we turn to Acts. At the beginning, John's name occurs in a list of the Twelve (Acts 1:13); and later, when we are told of James's death, it is noted that he was John's brother (12:2). In every other reference to John, he is in the company of Peter. These two were the instruments God used in bringing healing to a lame man (ch 3). At that time, they were going to the Temple at the hour of prayer. This says something about their habits of devotion. Prayer at the ninth hour apparently refers to the Jewish service of prayer that was held at the same time as the evening offering (i.e., at about three o'clock in the afternoon). Evidently, Peter and John were continuing the devotional habits of pious Jews with an interest in the Temple and all its doings. On another occasion, these two were arrested and jailed on account of their preaching about Jesus' resurrection (4:1-3). They were brought before the council, where Peter spoke for them. The council saw that these two men were "uneducated, common men" (v 13). This means that they had never had the normal rabbinic education. By the standards of the council, they were uneducated. The council forbade them to speak about Jesus, but the apostles' reply displays John's typical boldness: "Whether it is right in the sight of God to listen to you rather than to God, you must judge; for we cannot but speak of what we have seen and heard" (vv 19-20, RSV).

John was associated with Peter again when the gospel was first preached in Samaria. Philip was the evangelist to the Samaritans, but the apostles in Jerusalem decided to send Peter and John to Samaria when they heard how the people had accepted the gospel message. "As soon as they arrived, they began praying for these new Christians to receive the Holy Spirit" (Acts 8:15, TLB), a revealing illustration of apostolic priorities. In due course, they laid their hands on the new believers and they received the Holy Spirit (8:17). John is not specifically mentioned, but he no doubt was included in "the apostles" who were arrested and jailed because of the jealousy of prominent Jews (5:17-18). But that imprisonment did not last long, for an angel released them at night, so that they resumed their preaching in the early morning (v 21). John is mentioned by name in Galatians 2:9, where he is joined with Peter and James and the three are called "the pillars of the church."

This appears to be the extent of the NT's record of the apostle John. Clearly he was an important figure in the little band of early Christians. On almost every occasion when he comes before us in the record, he is in the company of someone else and normally the speaking is done by his companion, not by John. But we may justly conclude that he stood very close to Jesus. Perhaps he had entered into the mind of Jesus more than any of the others. The best evidence of this is the Gospel of John. Clearly the man who wrote this had great spiritual insight. John may have been more the thinker than a man of action and leader of men.

We have seen that there is good reason to think that the fourth Gospel was written by the apostle John. The epistles of John probably came from him also (though, as they stand, they are anonymous). All the Johannine writings probably emanated from the province of Asia. The heretics alluded to in 1 John resemble the Cerinthians (followers of the heretic Cerinthus), who were in Asia Minor at the end of the first century, and tradition connects the author of 1 John with Ephesus. It is certain that the same person wrote all three letters, and reasonably certain that this author also wrote the Gospel of John; the Gospel and the letters certainly represent the same mind at work in different situations.

An author named John wrote the book of Revelation (Rv 1:1), though it is not clear whether this is the apostle or another John. Tradition has identified the John of Revelation (see Rv 1:1, 9; 22:8) with John the apostle, the author of the Gospel of John and the three letters of John. This view was held by Justin Martyr as early as 140. The main objection to this view is that the original Greek is unlike that of the other Johannine writings, showing scant respect for the rules of the language. Some have suggested that a different John wrote Revelation, others that John's disciples wrote the Gospel and letters and that John himself wrote Revelation. But it is still plausible that the apostle John (or one of his close disciples) wrote the Gospel and the letters.

Assuming John the apostle wrote Revelation, he was exiled to Patmos (Rv 1:9). But the date of this is uncertain. Some probably unreliable evidence from the late fifth century suggests that John was martyred at about the same time as his brother James (c. 44; see also Acts 12:2). Jesus' prophecy in Mk 10:39 need not imply that both met with a simultaneous and violent end. Much stronger is the tradition reflected by Polycrates, bishop of Ephesus (c. 190), that John died a natural death in Ephesus, and by Irenaeus (c. 175–195) that John lingered on in Ephesus until the time of the emperor Trajan (ruled c. 97–117).

JOHN THE BAPTIST

Forerunner of the Messiah who prepared the people for Jesus' coming, proclaimed the need for forgiveness of sins, and offered a baptism symbolizing repentance. His ministry included the baptism of Jesus in the Jordan River, where he testified to Jesus being the Expected One from God. John was arrested and beheaded by Herod Antipas in approximately AD 29, while Jesus was still ministering.

Preview
- Birth, Infancy, and Boyhood
- Appearance and Identity
- John's Proclamation
- John's Baptism
- John's View of Jesus
- Jesus' View of John
- Arrest, Imprisonment, and Martyrdom
- The Disciples of John

Birth, Infancy, and Boyhood

Luke's Gospel is our only source of information concerning the birth and boyhood of John. The Gospel writer states that John was born in the hill country of Judah (Lk 1:39) of priestly descent, being the son of Zechariah, a priest of the order of Abijah, and Elizabeth, a descendant of Aaron (v 5). Both parents were righteous in the sight of God, following all the commandments closely (v 6). Like the birth of Jesus, only to a much lesser degree, the birth of John the Baptist is described in Luke as extraordinary. The angel Gabriel announced the coming birth to Zechariah in the Temple; to the older, barren Elizabeth it came as an answer to prayer (vv 8-13). John's name is announced to Zechariah by the angel, even as his purpose as forerunner is revealed before birth (vv 13-17). Such a consecration from birth is reminiscent of the call of the OT prophet Jeremiah (cf. Jer 1:5).

There existed some familial relationship between the families of John and Jesus. Elizabeth is described as a relative of Mary (Lk 1:36), which may connote cousin or aunt, or may only mean being from the same tribe.

John's childhood, as that of Jesus, is left quite vague in the Gospel account. All that is said is that "John grew up and became strong in spirit. Then he lived out in the wilderness until he began his public ministry to Israel" (Lk 1:80, NLT). Some scholars have suggested that John might have been adopted as a boy by the Essenes (as was their practice) at Qumran and reared in their wilderness community, adjacent to the Dead Sea and near the Jordan River. There are some similarities between the activities of the Qumran sect, known through the Dead Sea Scrolls, and the later ministry of John the Baptist. Both

QUICKTAKE

JOHN the BAPTIST

STRENGTHS AND ACCOMPLISHMENTS
- The God-appointed messenger to announce the arrival of Jesus
- A preacher whose theme was repentance
- A fearless confronter
- Known for his remarkable lifestyle
- Uncompromising

LESSONS FROM HIS LIFE
- God does not guarantee an easy or safe life to those who serve him
- Doing what God desires is the greatest possible life investment
- Standing for the truth is more important than life itself

VITAL STATISTICS
Where: Judea
Occupation: Prophet
Relatives: Father: Zechariah. Mother: Elizabeth. Distant relative: Jesus
Contemporaries: Herod, Herodias

KEY VERSE
"I tell you the truth, of all who have ever lived, none is greater than John the Baptist. Yet even the least person in the Kingdom of Heaven is greater than he is!" (Matthew 11:11).

John's story is told in all four Gospels. His coming was predicted in Isaiah 40:3 and Malachi 4:5; and he is mentioned in Acts 1:5, 22; 10:37; 11:16; 13:24, 25; 18:25; 19:3, 4.

practiced a type of asceticism and removed themselves from the life of Jerusalem. Both practiced baptism and associated this rite with initiation and repentance. Finally, John and the Qumran group were both eschatologically minded, awaiting God's final end-time activity in history. Nevertheless, many significant differences exist between John and the Qumran sect.

Appearance and Identity

Mark's Gospel begins with an account of John the Baptist's appearance: "John the Baptist ... lived in the wilderness and was preaching that people should be baptized to show that they had turned from their sins and turned to God to be forgiven" (Mk 1:4, NLT). A rich OT background lies behind John's association with the wilderness, in this case the wilderness of Judea. It was in the wilderness that God revealed himself to Moses (Ex 3), gave the law, and entered into the covenant with Israel (ch 19). It was also the site of refuge for David (1 Sm 23–26; Ps 63) and Elijah (1 Kgs 19), and in this light became the anticipated site of God's future deliverance (Is 40:3-5; Ez 47:1-12; Hos 2:14-15).

The unusual dress of John the Baptist—"clothing made of camel's hair, with a leather belt around his waist" (Mk 1:6, NIV)—may have suggested to his audience an association with Elijah in particular (2 Kgs 1:8) or with the prophets in general (Zec 13:4). His diet, "locusts and wild honey" (Mk 1:6), was Levitically clean, reflecting one who lived off the desert (such food was also eaten at Qumran) and formed part of the broader asceticism practiced by John and his disciples (Mt 9:14; 11:18).

Who did John understand himself to be? In answer to questions by the multitude whether he was the Messiah, Elijah, or the expected prophet (Jn 1:20-23), John only identified himself as "a voice crying in the wilderness, 'Prepare the way of the Lord'" (Is 40:3). The background for the question lies at the end of the OT period. Prophecy, on the one hand, was considered to have ceased (Zec 13:2-6); yet, on the other hand, it was expected to appear again before the coming of the messianic kingdom (see Jl 2:28-29; Mal 3:1-4). Some anticipated this final prophet to be one who was like Moses (Dt 18:15), others a returning Elijah as foretold in Malachi 4:5-6. While John personally refrained from identifying himself with these specific expectations (Jn 1:20-23), it is clear that his dress, lifestyle, and message caused the people to identify him with this end-time prophet (Mt 14:5; Mk 11:32). Jesus also saw John as this final "Elijah-like" prophet (Mt 11:7-15), who from Malachi's prophecy was to be a forerunner to the coming of the Lord (Mal 3:1-4; 4:5-6).

John's Proclamation

John's proclamation involved three elements: a warning of imminent judgment at the hands of the Coming One, a call for repentance in light of the coming kingdom of heaven, and a demand to express this repentance in concrete ethical terms. Many Jews looked forward confidently to the messianic judgment as a time of blessing for themselves and destruction for the gentile oppressors. John, however, warned that Jewish ancestry was false security in the coming judgment (Lk 3:8); true repentance was the only means of escaping destruction

(Mt 3:2). John anticipated this judgment at the hands of the Coming One, who would baptize the nation with "the Holy Spirit and with fire" (Lk 3:16). Fire represented the OT means of destruction in the end time (Mal 4:1) as well as purification (Mal 3:1-4), while the outpouring of the Holy Spirit in the end time connoted blessing (Is 32:15; Ez 39:29; Jl 2:28) and purification (Is 4:2-4). The judgment anticipated by John was therefore twofold: destruction for the unrepentant, and blessing for the penitent and righteous (Mt 3:12).

In light of this imminent event John called for repentance on the part of his listeners (Mt 3:2), a true "turning back" or "turning toward" God in obedience that would bring forgiveness of sin. Such a turnabout in an individual's relation with God should be lived out in one's everyday dealings: fairness on the part of tax collectors (Lk 3:12-13) and soldiers (v 14), and the general requirement of compassion for the poor (vv 10-11).

John's Baptism

The Gospels record that John baptized those repentant of their sins at several locations: the Jordan River (Mk 1:5), Bethany beyond the Jordan (Jn 1:28), and Aenon near Salim (Jn 3:23). This practice was an integral part of John's call for repentance, given in light of the approaching judgment and the appearance of the Coming One. The baptism of the penitent symbolized desire for forgiveness of sin, a renunciation of past life, and a desire to be included in the coming messianic kingdom.

What was the background for John's practice of baptism? From the OT we know of ceremonial lustrations or washings that guaranteed ritual purity (Lv 14–15; Nm 19). Unlike John's baptism, these washings were repetitive in nature and referred predominantly to ritual rather than moral cleansing. The prophets, however, urged a moral purification associated with the washing of water (Is 1:16-18; Jer 4:14). More significantly, the prophets anticipated a cleansing by God in the end times preceding the Day of Judgment (Ez 36:25; Zec 13:1; cf. Is 44:3), an eschatological element that John may have assumed was being fulfilled in his water baptism.

Another precedent for John's practice may have been proselyte baptism, a rite (along with circumcision and the offering of sacrifices) that constituted the conversion of a Gentile to Judaism. Common to both proselyte baptism and John's baptism were the emphasis on an ethical break with the past, a once-for-all character, and the similarity of immersion. Notable differences were that John's baptism was for Jews, not Gentile converts, and that it had a marked eschatological character as a preparation for the new age. Unless John, in light of the imminence of the messianic age, consciously treated all Jews as "pagan" in need of a baptism of repentance (cf. Mt 3:7-10), it is doubtful that proselyte baptism formed the primary background for John's baptismal ministry.

If John's baptism had a clear association with the forgiveness of sin, the question naturally arises as to why Jesus, the Son of God, sought baptism from John. John himself asks this very question of Jesus (Mt 3:14), to which Jesus responds, "It must be done, because we must do everything that is right" (v 15, NLT). First, it is clear that Jesus' baptism represented an act of obedience on his part to God's will as he saw it. Second, by submitting to the baptism of John, Jesus was clearly validating the ministry and message of John. The imminent coming of the kingdom and its Messiah, and the need for repentance in anticipation of this event that John proclaimed, were affirmed by Jesus through baptism. Third, by being baptized, Jesus condemned the self-righteous for their lack of repentance and took a stand with the penitent publicans and sinners awaiting the kingdom of God (Lk 7:29-30). Fourth, Jesus stepped forward for baptism not as an individual in need of forgiveness but as one who represented the people of God. His baptism, therefore, demonstrated solidarity with the people in their need of deliverance, even as he is judged in their place on the cross. Finally, the voice from heaven (Mk 1:11) and the descent of the Spirit (Lk 3:21-22) signify the inauguration of Jesus' own ministry through his baptism by John.

John's View of Jesus

Throughout his ministry John pointed beyond himself to one "who is far greater than I am—so much greater that I am not even worthy to be his slave" (Mk 1:7, NLT). His self-understanding apparently sprang from the application of Isaiah 40:3 to himself, that he was the preparer or forerunner for God's coming activity through the Messiah (Lk 3:4-6). When asked by curious spectators, John firmly denied that he was the Messiah, and according to the Gospel accounts, subordinated himself to the Coming One (Mk 1:7-8; Jn 1:26-28; 3:28-31). The coming of Jesus to baptism seems to represent the first time John identified these expectations with Jesus himself (Jn 1:35-36). His recognition of Jesus as the Messiah prior to baptism (Mt 3:14) was confirmed by the descent of the Holy Spirit as a dove and the voice from heaven quoting a phrase from an OT messianic psalm (Mk 1:11a, from Ps 2:7), together with a phrase from a Suffering Servant song of Isaiah (Mk 1:11b, from Is 42:1). In the fourth Gospel, John the Baptist goes even further in acknowledging Jesus to be the "Lamb of God" (Jn 1:29), in anticipation of Jesus' sacrificial role on the cross. And John recognized him as "God's Chosen One" (v 34, NEB—another term for the Messiah; Ps 2:7, see Mk 1:11).

In light of John's strong affirmation, it is at first difficult to understand his questioning of Jesus while imprisoned: "Are you he who is to come, or shall we look for another?" (Mt 11:3, RSV). Some have suggested that John was merely asking for the sake of his disciples, or that the question reflected John's despondency with being imprisoned. It is more likely, however, that the question represents John's own confusion with the activity expected of the Messiah. John had proclaimed a Coming One who would bring a baptism of fire and judgment upon the wicked (Lk 3:16). It may have been difficult for him to understand Jesus' different emphases on forgiveness and acceptance of sinners (Mt 9:9-13) and his healing of the sick (Mt 8–9). When John's disciples brought their master's question to Jesus, asking whether or not he was the Messiah, Jesus responded by quoting Isaiah 35:5-6 (see also Is 61:1). This text proclaims the activities of healing and proclaiming salvation to the poor to be fulfillments of the Messiah's role, even though they may not have been what John or countless other Jews expected.

Jesus' View of John

That Jesus highly regarded John the Baptist is indicated by his baptism by John. It is also explicitly stated on several occasions. Jesus called him the greatest man to have ever lived (Lk 7:28). (Of course, he was not as great as Jesus, the God-man.) Jesus also said that John was a burning and shining lamp (Jn 5:33-35) and that he practiced a baptism divinely ordained (Lk 20:1-8).

John's uniqueness, however, lies in the fact that he stood at the turning of the ages. He was the last of the old era, the period of the law and the prophets (Lk 16:16), which was to precede the coming of the messianic age (the kingdom of God). John was the last of the prophets, the greatest of them, the Elijah figure who would prepare the way for the judgment of God (Mt 11:13-15; Lk 1:17). Because John belonged to the era of the law and the prophets, however, he was not as great as the "least" already in the kingdom of God (Mt 11:11)—that is, those who belonged to the era of the kingdom's appearance in Jesus.

Arrest, Imprisonment, and Martyrdom

To understand why John was arrested and beheaded by Herod Antipas, one has to grasp the messianic excitement caused by John's appearance and message (Lk 3:15-18). Herod and other secular rulers were obviously suspicious of anyone who might stir up the crowds with predictions of a coming messianic ruler. Other messianic movements had arisen before John, which resulted in outbreaks of violence against the Roman-Herodian rulership. Moreover, Herod Antipas was under heavy criticism for his marriage with Herodias, the ex-wife of his brother Philip. His first marriage, with the daughter of Aretus II, constituted a political alliance between the Herodian family and the Nabatean kingdom of Perea. His new relationship with Herodias was perceived as a breach of the political alliance and led to friction between the two families. John's denunciation of Herod's new marriage (Mt 14:3-12) could thus have been interpreted by Herod as a subversive rousing of sentiment against his authority. The Jewish historian Josephus states that Herod did, in fact, arrest John because he feared John's influence over the crowds. According to Josephus, John was imprisoned at the fortress Machaerus on the eastern side of the Dead Sea. That he was not killed immediately was due to Herod's personal fear of the righteous John (Mk 6:2) and of the people's reaction (Mt 14:5). On a point about which Josephus is silent, the Gospels record that it was Herodias's feelings against John (Mk 6:17) and her plot, through the dancing of her daughter, which brought about the beheading of John (vv 21-29). John was beheaded at Herodias's request in approximately AD 29 or 30.

The Disciples of John

While it is clear that a band of disciples formed around John in his lifetime (Jn 1:35), to suggest that he intended to begin a continuing movement is contradicted by his message on the imminent Day of Judgment. Apparently, John's disciples consisted of a small group of those who had been baptized by him and were awaiting the coming Messiah. Some transferred their loyalty to Jesus after John had identified Jesus as the Coming One (Jn 1:37). Others, however, apparently stayed on with their teacher, communicating with the imprisoned John concerning the activities of Jesus (Lk 7:18-23) and, after his death, taking the body for burial (Mk 6:29).

We know little about the activities and practices of the band of disciples clustered around John. We do know, however, that fasting was one practice specifically associated with the group, and one that marked them as similar to the Pharisees (Mt 9:14). In this practice they no doubt followed the example of John himself (Lk 7:33). Prayer and fasting were often linked in late Judaism. The disciples of John were also known for the prayers taught by their master (11:1). Seeing this practice, the disciples of Jesus asked the Lord to teach them to pray, to which Jesus responded with the Lord's Prayer (vv 2-4).

After his death it is likely that other disciples of John joined the followers of Jesus (see Lk 7:29-30). Not all did so, however, as disciples of John were encountered by Paul and other Christians approximately 25 years later in Ephesus (Acts 18:24–29:7). Upon hearing witness to Jesus, these followers of John proclaimed Jesus as Messiah. When Paul baptized them in the name of Jesus they received the Holy Spirit (19:4-7). Even so, it is apparent from later documents that various groups continued to honor John, even considering him the Messiah, centuries after the NT period.

JOHN MARK
See Mark, John.

JOIADA
1. Paseah's son who, with Meshullam, repaired the Old Gate in the Jerusalem wall during the days of Nehemiah (Neh 3:6).
2. Levite and high priest in Jerusalem during the postexilic era, the great-grandson of Jeshua, son of Eliashib, and father of Jonathan ("Johanan" or "Jehohanan," Neh 12:10-11, 22). He is alternately called Jehoiada in Nehemiah 13:28, where we read that one of his sons was expelled from the priesthood for marrying a daughter of Sanballat, governor of Samaria.

JOIAKIM
Levite high priest in a family of high priests. Jeshua's son and the father of Eliashib the high priest, a contemporary of Nehemiah (Neh 12:10-12, 26).

JOIARIB
1. One of the Jewish leaders whom Ezra sent to Iddo at Casiphia to gather Levites and Temple servants for the caravan of Jews returning to Palestine from Babylon (Ezr 8:16). He is alternately called Jehoiarib in 1 Chronicles 9:10.
2. Zechariah's son, the father of Adaiah, and an ancestor of a Judahite family that resettled in Jerusalem during the postexilic era under Nehemiah (Neh 11:5).

3. Father of Jedaiah, a priest who served in the Temple during the days of Nehemiah (Neh 11:10). Perhaps Joiarib's forefather was Jehoiarib, who was the head of the first course of priests ministering in the sanctuary during David's reign (1 Chr 24:7; cf. 9:10).

4. One of the leaders of the priests who returned with Zerubbabel and Jeshua to Judah after the Exile (Neh 12:6). His family in the next generation was headed by Mattenai (v 19).

JOKIM
Descendant of Judah through Shelah's line (1 Chr 4:22).

JOKSHAN
Son of Abraham and Keturah, and the father of Sheba and Dedan (Gn 25:2-3; 1 Chr 1:32).

JOKTAN
Eber's son and younger brother of Peleg. A number of Arabian groups descended from him (Gn 10:25-29; 1 Chr 1:19-23).

JONADAB
1. King David's nephew, the son of David's brother Shimeah. As a friend to David's son Amnon, he devised a scheme by which Amnon seduced his half sister Tamar (2 Sm 13:3-5). Absalom, Tamar's brother, sought revenge, eventually killing Amnon.

2. Recab's son; descendant of the Kenites (1 Chr 2:55; NLT "Jehonadab"). He founded the religious order of Recabites, who maintained a nomadic tradition. He encouraged Jehu in his bloody reform of the house of Ahab (2 Kgs 10:15, 23).

JONAH
Prophet of Israel; Amittai's son (Jon 1:1) of the Zebulunite city of Gath-hepher (2 Kgs 14:25). The historian who wrote 2 Kings recorded that Jonah had a major prophetic role in the reign of King Jeroboam II (793–753 BC). Jonah had conveyed a message encouraging expansion to the king of Israel, whose reign was marked by prosperity, expansion, and unfortunately, moral decline.

In the midst of all the political corruption of Israel, Jonah remained a zealous patriot. His reluctance to go to Nineveh probably stemmed partially from his knowledge that the Assyrians would be used as God's instrument for punishing Israel. The prophet, who had been sent to Jeroboam to assure him that his kingdom would prosper, was the same prophet God chose to send to Nineveh to forestall that city's (and thus that nation's) destruction until Assyria could be used to punish Israel in 722 BC. It is no wonder that the prophet reacted emotionally to his commission.

No other prophet was so strongly Jewish (cf. his classic confession, Jon 1:9), yet no other prophet's ministry was so strongly directed to a non-Jewish nation. Jonah's writing

QUICKTAKE

JONATHAN

STRENGTHS AND ACCOMPLISHMENTS
- Brave, loyal, and a natural leader
- The closest friend David ever had
- Did not put his personal well-being ahead of those he loved
- Depended on God

LESSONS FROM HIS LIFE
- Loyalty is one of the strongest parts of courage
- An allegiance to God puts all other relationships in perspective
- Great friendships are costly

VITAL STATISTICS
Occupation: Military leader
Relatives: Father: Saul. Mother: Ahinoam. Brothers: Abinadab and Malkishua. Sisters: Merab and Michal. Son: Mephibosheth

KEY VERSE
"How I weep for you, my brother Jonathan!
    Oh, how much I loved you!
And your love for me was deep,
    deeper than the love of women!" (2 Samuel 1:26).

His story is told in 1 Samuel 13–31. He is also mentioned in 2 Samuel 9.

is also unusual among the prophets. The book is primarily historical narrative. His actual preaching is recorded in only five words in the Hebrew—eight words in most English translations (Jon 3:4b).

See also Jeroboam #2.

JONAM
Ancestor of Jesus mentioned in Luke's genealogy (Lk 3:30).

JONATHAN
1. Benjaminite, the firstborn son of Saul and the father of Meribbaal (1 Sm 14:49; 1 Chr 8:33-34). Jonathan was a valiant warrior (1 Sm 13:2-4; 14:1-15; 2 Sm 1:22) and a devoted friend to David (1 Sm 18:1-5).

2. Levite from Bethlehem in Judah, a descendant of Gershom, son of Moses (cf. 1 Chr 23:14-15); he was a priest first to Micah in Ephraim and later to Dan's tribe during the period of the judges (Jgs 17:7-10; 18:30; 19:1-7). He was eventually killed, along with his brothers, by the Philistines at Mt Gilboa (1 Sm 31:2; 1 Chr 10:2).

3. Son of the high priest Abiathar and one of David's loyal servants (2 Sm 15:27, 36; 17:17, 20; 1 Kgs 1:42-43).

4. Shimei's son and the nephew of David (2 Sm 21:21; 1 Chr 20:7).

5. Son of Shagee the Hararite and one of David's mighty warriors (2 Sm 23:33; 1 Chr 11:34).

6. Judahite, Jada's son, the brother of Jether, and the father of Peleth and Zaza (1 Chr 2:32-33).

7. Son of Uzziah and one of David's treasurers (1 Chr 27:25).

8. David's relative who served as counselor and scribe in the royal household (1 Chr 27:32).

9. Ebed's father. Ebed returned with Ezra to Judah following the Babylonian captivity (Ezr 8:6).

10. Asahel's son, who, with Jahzeiah, opposed Ezra's suggestion that the sons of Israel should divorce the foreign woman they had married since returning to Palestine from Exile (Ezr 10:15).

11. Levite, the son of Joiada, the father of Jaddua, and a descendant of Jeshua, the high priest (Neh 12:11). He is perhaps the same man as Jehohanan (or Johanan), Eliashib's grandson, in Ezra 10:6 (cf. Neh 12:23, NLT). See Jehohanan #4.

12. Priest and the head of Malluch's house during the days of Joiakim the high priest (Neh 12:14).

13. Priest, father of Zechariah, and a descendant of Asaph (Neh 12:35).

14. Secretary in whose house Jeremiah was at one point imprisoned during the reign of King Zedekiah of Judah (Jer 37:15, 20; 38:26).

15. Kareah's son who sought protection under Gedaliah (Jer 40:8).

JORAH
Alternate name for Hariph in Ezra 2:18 and Nehemiah 7:24. See Hariph.

JORAI
Member of Gad's tribe (1 Chr 5:13).

JORAM
1. Toi's son and king of Hamath. He was sent by Toi to offer congratulations to David when David won a victory over Hadadezer of Zobah (2 Sm 8:9-12). He is also called Hadoram in 1 Chronicles 18:10.

2. Alternate name for Jehoram, king of Judah (853–841 BC). *See* Jehoram #1.

3. Alternate name for Jehoram, king of Israel (852–841 BC). *See* Jehoram #2.

4. Jeshaiah's son from Levi's tribe (1 Chr 26:25).

JORIM

Ancestor of Jesus listed in Luke's genealogy (Lk 3:29).

JORKEAM

Identified with Raham, a descendant of Judah through Caleb's line (1 Chr 2:44; KJV "Jorkoam"), the name should perhaps be understood as a place-name and be identified with Jokdeam (Jos 15:56).

JOSECH

Ancestor of Jesus mentioned only in Luke's genealogy (Lk 3:26).

JOSEPH

1. Jacob's 11th son and the firstborn son of Rachel. Rachel named the boy Joseph, meaning "may he add," expressing her desire that God would give her another son (Gn 30:24).

   Nothing more is said about Joseph until, at the age of 17, he is seen tending his father's flocks with his brothers (Gn 37:2). Joseph was the favorite of his father, since he was the son of his old age (v 3) and the firstborn son of his favorite wife. Because of this, his brothers hated Joseph. This envy was magnified when Jacob gave Joseph a ground-length, long-sleeved, multicolored robe (vv 3-4). (This type of garment is illustrated by the paintings in the Asiatic tombs of Khnumhotep II at Beni Hasan and of the nobles at Gurneh, near Luxor.) The animosity of his brothers increased still more when Joseph revealed to them his dreams of dominion over them (vv 5-11). Subsequently, when Joseph was sent to check on his brothers and the flocks near Shechem, his brothers sold him to a caravan of traders going down to Egypt

JOSEPH
The Times of Joseph

C. 1915 BC
Joseph is born to Rachel, the eleventh of twelve sons of Jacob (Genesis 30:22-24).

C. 1898 BC
Joseph is sold into slavery in Egypt; becomes head of Potiphar's household (Genesis 37; 39).

C. 1893 BC?
Joseph is falsely accused of attacking Potiphar's wife, and he is imprisoned (Genesis 39).

C. 1887 BC
In prison, Joseph interprets dreams of the Pharaoh's butler and baker (Genesis 40).

C. 1885 BC
Joseph is appointed Egypt's second-in-command (Genesis 41).

C. 1885–1878 BC
Joseph helps Egypt store food through seven bountiful years, and then famine hits (Genesis 41:47-57).

C. 1877 BC
Joseph's family suffers from famine in Canaan and visits Egypt seeking food (Genesis 42).

C. 1876 BC
Joseph is reunited with his family; they move to Egypt (Genesis 43–46).

C. 1805 BC
Joseph dies (Genesis 50:26).

(vv 25-28). His brothers then took his robe, dipped it in goat's blood, and brought it to Jacob, who concluded that Joseph had been killed by wild animals (vv 31-33); Jacob was overwhelmed with grief (vv 34-35).

In Egypt, Joseph was sold to Potiphar, an Egyptian officer of the guard (Gn 37:36; 39:1), who eventually put Joseph in charge of his entire household. However, trouble arose from Potiphar's wife, who was attracted to the young Hebrew and tried to seduce him (39:6-10). He steadfastly resisted her advances, protesting that to comply with her wishes would be a disservice to his master and a sin against God (v 9). One day she seized his garment, but he left the garment behind and fled. Potiphar's wife accused Joseph of attempted rape; her report was believed, and Joseph was incarcerated in the king's prison (v 20), where Pharaoh's butler and baker were also confined. While in prison, Joseph, with the Lord's help, interpreted these men's troublesome dreams. As Joseph had foretold, the baker was executed and the butler was restored to royal favor (ch 40).

Two years later Pharaoh had two dreams that his magicians and wise men could not interpret. The butler, remembering Joseph, had him summoned from prison. God revealed to Joseph that the dreams foretold seven years of abundance, followed by seven years of famine (Gn 41:25-36). Pharaoh, impressed with Joseph's interpretation, made him ruler of Egypt, second only to himself (vv 39-44). Joseph was given a new name, Zaphenath-paneah, and a wife, Asenath, the daughter of Potiphera (v 45).

Joseph was 30 years old when he became ruler of Egypt. During the seven years of prosperity, he gathered the good supplies for the seven years of famine to come (Gn 41:53-56). When the famine eventually became severe in Palestine, Jacob sent all his sons, except Benjamin, his youngest son, to Egypt to purchase grain. Appearing before Joseph in Egypt, they did not recognize him. But he knew them and remembered his dreams of years before (42:8-9). After listening to the report of their family, he accused them of being spies (vv 9-14) and insisted that they leave one of their brothers as hostage and return with Benjamin to verify the truthfulness of their report (vv 19-20). Thus Simeon was bound and left in Egypt (v 24).

After the famine worsened in Palestine, Jacob asked his sons to go back to Egypt to buy more grain (Gn 43:1-2); reluctantly agreeing to the conditions that the Egyptian administrator had placed on them, Jacob allowed Benjamin to go with them (vv 11-13). When they arrived in Egypt, they were taken to Joseph's house, where Simeon was restored to them (v 23) and a meal was prepared for them (v 33). Joseph at last disclosed his identity and declared that God had sent him before them to preserve their lives (45:4-8). Arrangements were then made to send for Jacob; wagons were provided, along with provisions for the journey (v 21). When Jacob came to Goshen in the Nile Delta, Joseph went out to meet him, and another great reunion took place (46:28-29). He also presented his father and brothers to Pharaoh, who let them live in the land of Goshen (47:6).

Upon learning that his father was ill, Joseph took his two sons, Manasseh and

QUICKTAKE

JOSEPH

STRENGTHS AND ACCOMPLISHMENTS
• Rose in power from slave to ruler of Egypt
• Was known for his personal integrity
• Was a man of spiritual sensitivity
• Prepared a nation to survive a famine

WEAKNESS AND MISTAKE
• His youthful pride caused friction with his brothers

LESSONS FROM HIS LIFE
• What matters is not so much the events or circumstances of life, but your response to them
• With God's help, any situation can be used for good, even when others intend it for evil

VITAL STATISTICS
Where: Canaan, Egypt
Occupation: Shepherd, slave, convict, ruler
Relatives: Parents: Jacob and Rachel. Eleven brothers and one sister. Wife: Asenath. Sons: Manasseh and Ephraim

KEY VERSE
"So Pharaoh asked his officials 'Can we find anyone else like this man so obviously filled with the spirit of God?'" (Genesis 41:38).

Joseph's story is told in Genesis 30–50. He is also mentioned in Hebrews 11:22.

Ephraim, to him for his blessing. He presented the sons so that the older would be at Jacob's right hand and the younger at his left in order that Manasseh would receive the blessing of the firstborn. Jacob, however, crossed his hands and with his right hand on Ephraim gave him the greater blessing (Gn 48:14-20). He also gave to Joseph the land that he had taken from the Amorites (v 22). At Jacob's death, Joseph made the funeral arrangements; and after the customary funerary practices were carried out, a great funeral procession went to Canaan, where Jacob was buried by his sons in the cave of Machpelah near Hebron (50:1-12).

When Joseph was 110 years old, he called his brothers and told them that he was about to die. He made them take an oath that when they returned to Canaan they would take his bones with them. So he died, was embalmed, and was placed in a coffin in Egypt (Gn 50:26). Many years later, during the Exodus, Moses took the bones of Joseph with him from Egypt (Ex 13:19). Joseph's remains were eventually interred at Shechem in the parcel of land that Jacob had bought from Hamor, the father of Shechem (Gn 33:18-20; Jos 24:32).

2. Igal's father from Issachar's tribe. Igal was one of the 12 spies sent by Moses to search out the land of Canaan (Nm 13:7).

3. Asaph's second son and the leader of the first course of priests serving in the sanctuary during David's reign (1 Chr 25:2, 9).

4. One of Binnui's descendants who was encouraged by Ezra to divorce his foreign wife during the postexilic era (Ezr 10:42).

5. Priest and family leader from Shebaniah's line during the days of Joiakim, the high priest (Neh 12:14).

6. Descendant of David (Mt 1:16; Lk 3:23) and the husband of Mary, the mother of Jesus. Joseph was betrothed to Mary, a young woman of the city of Nazareth. Mary had learned from the angel Gabriel that she was to bear the Son of God, whom she was to name Jesus (Lk 1:31) and that this conception was to be a work of the Holy Spirit (v 35). Joseph was not aware of this, so when he learned that Mary was pregnant, he decided to divorce her quietly, for he was a just man and did not want to humiliate her publicly (Mt 1:19). An angel subsequently appeared to him in a dream to tell him what was happening (Mt 1:21; cf. Is 7:14). The text of Matthew makes it clear that there was no sexual union between Joseph and Mary until after Jesus was born (Mt 1:18, 25; see also Lk 1:34-37).

When Caesar Augustus issued a decree that everyone had to register in his native city for purposes of taxation, Joseph and Mary returned to Bethlehem, where Jesus was subsequently born (Lk 2:1-6). Later, Joseph and Mary took the infant Jesus to the Temple to present him to the Lord (vv 22, 33). After the visit of the wise men, an angel appeared to Joseph in a dream and instructed him to take Jesus and Mary to Egypt to protect the child from King Herod (Mt 2:13). Upon the death of Herod, an angel similarly advised him to return to Israel, so the family went to live in Nazareth. The last recorded event that involves Joseph is the incident of Jesus at the Temple at age 12 (Lk 2:41-51). Joseph is not mentioned by name, but Mary told Jesus that she and his father had been looking for him anxiously.

Jesus was identified by people around Nazareth as "Joseph's son" (Lk 4:22; Jn 1:45; 6:42). It is only through references identifying Jesus that we learn of Joseph's trade. Twice Jesus is referred to as "the carpenter's son" (Mt 13:55; Mk 6:3). Joseph was not a carpenter in our sense of the word, for houses were built mostly of stone and earth. He was a woodworker or artificer in wood, and probably most of his work was with furniture and agricultural implements.

During the ministry of Jesus, it was his mother and his brothers who came to look for him (Mt 12:46-50; Mk 3:31-35), so it is assumed that by this time Joseph was dead. Joseph was most likely the father of James, Joseph, Simon, Judas, and unnamed sisters (Mt 13:55; Mk 6:3).

7. Joseph and Mary's son and the brother of Jesus (Mt 13:55); alternately called Joses in Mark 6:3.

8. Native of Arimathea and the follower of Jesus who provided for his burial. He was a rich man from the town of Arimathea and a respected member of the Sanhedrin, or council (Mk 15:43). He was a good and righteous man and did not go along with the decision to crucify Jesus (Lk 23:50-51). Joseph had been a secret follower of Jesus because he was afraid of the Jews (Jn 19:38), but after the Crucifixion he took courage and went to Pilate to ask for Jesus' body. He and Nicodemus took the body, treated it with spices, and wrapped it in linen cloths, according to the Jewish burial customs. In a nearby garden was Joseph's own new rock-cut tomb in which no one had ever been buried. Here they placed Jesus and sealed the tomb with a large stone.

9. Mattathias's son and an ancestor of Jesus (Lk 3:25).

10. KJV rendering of Josech, an ancestor of Jesus, in Luke 3:26. *See* Josech.

11. Jonam's son and an ancestor of Jesus (Lk 3:30).

12. Disciple of Jesus who was "called Barsabbas" and "surnamed Justus" (Acts 1:23). Joseph was one of the candidates put forward by the 11 apostles to replace Judas Iscariot. It was Matthias, however, who was chosen.

13. Cypriot Levite who sold a field and gave the proceeds to the apostles. He was surnamed "Barnabas," meaning "son of encouragement," by the apostles (Acts 4:36). *See* Barnabas.

JOSEPH BARSABBAS
See Joseph #12.

JOSEPH OF ARIMATHEA
See Joseph #8.

JOSHAH
Prince in Simeon's tribe (1 Chr 4:34).

JOSHAPHAT
1. Mithnite (NLT "from Mithna") and one of David's mighty men (1 Chr 11:43).

2. One of the seven priests assigned to blow a trumpet before the Ark of God in the procession led by David when the Ark was brought to Jerusalem (1 Chr 15:24).

QUICKTAKE

JOSHUA

STRENGTHS AND ACCOMPLISHMENTS
• Moses' assistant and successor
• One of only two adults who experienced Egyptian slavery and lived to enter the Promised Land
• Led the Israelites into their God-given homeland
• Brilliant military strategist
• Faithful to ask God's direction in the challenges he faced

LESSONS FROM HIS LIFE
• Effective leadership is often the product of good preparation and encouragement
• The persons after whom we pattern ourselves will have a definite effect on us
• A person committed to God provides the best model for us

VITAL STATISTICS
Where: Egypt, the wilderness of Sinai, and Canaan (the Promised Land)
Occupations: Special assistant to Moses, warrior, leader
Relative: Father: Nun
Contemporaries: Moses, Caleb, Miriam, Aaron

KEY VERSES
"So Moses did as the LORD commanded. He presented Joshua to Eleazar the priest and the whole community. Moses laid his hands on him and commissioned him to lead the people, just as the LORD had commanded through Moses" (Numbers 27:22, 23).

Joshua is also mentioned in Exodus 17:9-14; 24:13; 32:17; 33:11; Numbers 11:28; 13–14; 26:65; 27:18-23; 32:11, 12, 28; 34:17; Deuteronomy 1:38; 3:21, 28; 31:3, 7, 14, 23; 34:9; the book of Joshua; Judges 2:6-9; and 1 Kings 16:34.

JOSHAVIAH
Elnaam's son, the brother of Jeribai and one of David's 30 valiant warriors (1 Chr 11:46).

JOSHBEKASHAH
Heman's son and head of the 17th of 24 divisions of priestly musicians for ministry in the sanctuary during David's reign (1 Chr 25:4, 24).

JOSHIBIAH
Simeonite prince, Seraiah's son, and the father of Jehu (1 Chr 4:35).

JOSHUA

1. Son of Nun, Moses' assistant and successor, and the military leader whom God chose to lead the Israelites in the conquest of Canaan (Nm 13:16, KJV "Jehoshua"; also spelled "Jehoshuah" in 1 Chr 7:27 and "Jeshua" in Neh 8:17).

Early in the Exodus, Joshua was sent by Moses to fight against the Amalekites (Ex 17:8-15). Joshua defeated Amalek, and Moses wrote of the event and built an altar that he called "The LORD Is My Banner" (v 15).

When Moses sent 12 men from Kadesh-barnea to spy out the land of Canaan, Joshua represented the tribe of Ephraim (Nm 13:8). At that time Joshua was called Hoshea, but Moses changed his name to Joshua (vv 8, 16). Joshua and Caleb were the only two spies to bring back an affirmative report concerning an Israelite invasion of the land (14:6-9). Consequently, of all the adult Israelite males to leave Egypt in the Exodus, only these two crossed the Jordan River and entered the Promised Land (v 30).

When the Lord announced to Moses his impending death, Moses asked about his successor, and the Lord appointed Joshua to that position (Nm 27:12-23). After the death of Moses on Mt Nebo, Joshua's leadership was confirmed (34:17), and the Lord told Joshua to go over the Jordan and take the land (Jos 1:1-2).

From the Transjordan, Joshua sent two men across the river to reconnoiter Jericho (ch 2). In Jericho they were concealed by Rahab and later safely made their way back to Joshua to report that the people of the land were fainthearted because of the Israelites (vv 23-24).

When Israel had crossed the river, the Lord instructed Joshua to set up a circle of 12 stones at Gilgal to commemorate this passage (Jos 4:1-7). The Lord then commanded all of the males who had been born during the Exodus to be circumcised (5:2-9).

While camped at Gilgal, near Jericho, Joshua was confronted by a man with a drawn sword. When Joshua challenged the man, he learned that it was the Lord, who told him to remove his shoes, for the

JOSHUA
The Times of Joshua

C. 1485 BC?
Joshua is born, while Israelites are slaves in Egypt.

C. 1446 BC
On the way to Mount Sinai, the Israelites fight the Amalekites; Joshua leads the army (Exodus 17).

C. 1444 BC
Joshua is one of 12 scouts exploring Canaan, and one of two scouts to file a positive report (Numbers 14).

C. 1407 BC
Joshua is appointed as the new leader of Israel, succeeding Moses (Deuteronomy 34:9).

C. 1406 BC
Under Joshua's command, the Israelites cross the Jordan River (Joshua 3).

C. 1406 BC
Joshua fights the battle of Jericho, and "the walls come tumblin' down" (Joshua 6).

C. 1406 BC
Due to Achan's sin, the Israelites lose a battle against the village of Ai, but then they win (Joshua 7–8).

C. 1406–1405 BC?
The Gibeonites trick Joshua into an unwise treaty (Joshua 9).

C. 1405 BC?
Joshua leads a covenant service at Mount Ebal and Mount Gerizim (Joshua 8:30-35).

C. 1405–1399 BC
Joshua leads the Israelites against southern Canaan; then they attack northern Canaan (Joshua 10–12).

C. 1399 BC
Joshua divides the land among the tribes of Israel (Joshua 13–21).

C. 1376 BC?
Joshua leads a recommitment service at Mount Ebal and Mount Gerizim (Joshua 24).

C. 1375 BC?
Joshua dies (Joshua 24:29).

ground was holy (Jos 5:13-15). The Lord gave Joshua directions for the destruction of Jericho; these were followed explicitly and the city fell (ch 6). The attack on Ai ended in temporary defeat, until the matter of Achan's sin was discovered and judged (7:10-26). Then Ai was taken and destroyed.

Joshua built an altar on Mt Ebal (Jos 8:30-32), and the blessings and curses were read, as commanded by God through Moses (Jos 8:33-35; cf. Dt 27–28).

Because the Israelites failed to ask direction from the Lord (Jos 9:14), Joshua was tricked into making a covenant of peace with the Hivites of Gibeon. Joshua then reduced them to doing menial tasks in Israel (vv 21-27).

Joshua's Final Days: Joshua gave his final speech at Shechem, then went to his hometown, Timnath-serah, where he died.

The kings of the various Canaanite cities allied themselves against the Israelite threat (Jos 9:1-2) and a league of five Amorite cities (Jerusalem, Hebron, Jarmuth, Lachish, and Eglon) attacked Gibeon (10:1-5). The Gibeonites appealed to Joshua for help; he responded quickly against this Amorite confederation and routed the Amorite forces. It was on this occasion that Joshua commanded the sun and the moon to stand still so that Israel could have more time to defeat these adversaries (vv 12-14). This victory was followed by a series of successful attacks on enemy towns (vv 28-43).

A northern alliance headed by Jabin, king of Hazor, was the next opposition (Jos 11:1-5). The Lord assured Joshua of success, and the city of Hazor was taken and destroyed by fire (vv 6-15). Joshua 11:23 summarizes the conquest of the land, and chapter 12 enumerates the kings who were conquered.

Joshua was now old, and the Lord told him that much land remained to be possessed. These territories are listed, but the Lord directed Joshua to proceed with the division of the land among the nine and a half tribes (Jos 13:7; cf. 13:8–18:28). Joshua himself was given the city he asked for, Timnath-serah, in the hill country of Ephraim, which he rebuilt and settled (19:49-50).

The Lord told Joshua to appoint cities of refuge to which a person guilty of manslaughter could flee to escape the avenger of blood (Jos 20). Then the Levites came to Eleazar the priest and Joshua to request that they be given their cities, as the Lord had commanded through Moses (21:1-42).

In his advanced years Joshua summoned all Israel and solemnly charged them to continue in faithfulness to the Lord (Jos 23). Finally, he called all Israel to Shechem, where he gave them his farewell message. He summed up the Lord's dealings with them from the time of Abraham and again challenged them to serve the Lord, putting before them the well-known choice and decision: "Choose today whom you will serve. ...As for me and my family, we will serve the LORD" (24:15, NLT).

Joshua died at the age of 110 years and was buried in the land of his inheritance at Timnath-serah (Jos 24:29-30; the parallel account in Jgs 2:8-9 reads "Timnath-heres," NLT mg). Israel served the Lord during all the days of Joshua and the elders who outlived him (Jos 24:31; Jgs 2:7).

2. Inhabitant of Beth-shemesh. It was his grainfield into which the cart carrying the Ark sent by the Philistines came. It stopped by a large stone which was then used to commemorate this event (1 Sm 6:14, 18).

3. Governor of Jerusalem during King Josiah's reign (2 Kgs 23:8).

4. Jozadak's son and high priest during the days of Zerubbabel in postexilic Jerusalem (Hg 1:1-14; 2:2-4; Zec 3:1-9; 6:11; NLT "Jeshua"). Joshua is alternately called Jeshua in Ezra and Nehemiah. *See* Jeshua #3.

5. Eliezer's son and an ancestor of Jesus Christ (Lk 3:29).

JOSIAH

1. Sixteenth king of the southern kingdom of Judah (640–609 BC). A godly man, he stood in marked contrast to his grandfather Manasseh and his father, Amon. In fact, Scripture declares there was no king either before or after him who was as obedient to the law of Moses (2 Kgs 23:25). The Greek form of his name, Josias, appears in Matthew 1:10-11 (KJV).

The Times of Josiah When Josiah became king in 640 BC, the international scene was about to change drastically. After the great Assyrian king Ashurbanipal died in 633 BC, mediocre rulers followed him on the throne, and there was considerable unrest in the empire. Nabopolassar, father of Nebuchadnezzar, seized the kingship in Babylon and established the Neo-Babylonian Empire late in 626 BC. Soon Babylonians and Medes combined forces to topple the Assyrian Empire, and in 612 BC completely destroyed the city of Nineveh. As Babylonian power rose in the east, Assyrian control over the province that had once been the kingdom of Israel relaxed and Assyrian pressure on Judah virtually ceased. After the fall of Nineveh, the Assyrians established their capital at Haran. There they were defeated by Babylonians and Scythians in 610 BC. At that point Pharaoh Neco II of Egypt decided to support Assyria. In the late spring of 609 BC he advanced through Judah, defeated and killed Josiah, and spent the summer campaigning in Syria.

Before Josiah's reign, Judah had capitulated to gross idolatry during the reign of Manasseh (697–642 BC). Baalism, Molech worship, and other pagan religions had invaded the land, as had occultism and astrology. A false altar even stood in the Temple in Jerusalem, and human sacrifice to pagan deities was practiced near Jerusalem. The nation was thoroughly corrupt. Although some reform occurred in Manasseh's latter days, conditions reverted to their former baseness during the reign of his son Amon (642–640 BC). In 640 BC officials of Amon's household assassinated him, and the "people of the land" put Josiah on the throne (2 Kgs 21:26; 22:1; 2 Chr 33:25–34:1).

Josiah's Reform Activities Josiah was only eight years old when he became king. Evidently he had spiritually motivated advisers or regents; by the time he was 16, he began of his own accord "to seek the God of his ancestor David" (2 Chr 34:3). When he was 20, he became greatly exercised over the idolatry of the land and launched a major effort to eradicate the pagan high places, groves, and images from Judah

QUICKTAKE

JOSIAH

STRENGTHS AND ACCOMPLISHMENTS
- Was king of Judah
- Sought after God and was open to him
- Was a reformer like his great-grandfather Hezekiah
- Cleaned out the Temple and revived obedience to God's law

WEAKNESS AND MISTAKE
- Became involved in a military conflict that he had been warned against

LESSONS FROM HIS LIFE
- God consistently responds to those with repentant and humble hearts
- Even sweeping outward reforms are of little lasting value if there are no changes in people's lives

VITAL STATISTICS
Where: Jerusalem
Occupation: 16th king of Judah, the southern kingdom
Relatives: Father: Amon. Mother: Jedidah. Son: Jehoahaz
Contemporaries: Jeremiah, Huldah, Hilkiah, Zephaniah

KEY VERSE
"Never before had there been a king like Josiah, who turned to the LORD with all his heart and soul and strength, obeying all the laws of Moses. And there has never been a king like him since" (2 Kings 23:25).

Josiah's story is told in 2 Kings 21:24–23:30; 2 Chronicles 33:25–35:27. He is also mentioned in Jeremiah 1:1-3; 22:11, 18.

and Jerusalem. So intense was Josiah's hatred of idolatry that he even opened the tombs of pagan priests and burned their bones on pagan altars before the altars were destroyed.

Josiah carried his reform movement beyond the borders of Judah, venting his fury especially on the cult center at Bethel, where Jeroboam had set up his false worship. In fulfillment of prophecy (1 Kgs 13:1-3), he destroyed the altar and high place and burned the bones of officiating priests to desecrate the site (2 Kgs 23:15-18). What he did at Bethel he did everywhere else in the kingdom of Samaria (vv 19-20).

When Josiah was 26, he launched a project to cleanse and repair the Temple in Jerusalem (2 Kgs 22:3). Shaphan, the king's administrative assistant, commissioned the work; Hilkiah the priest supervised the renovation and construction. In the process of restoring the Temple, Hilkiah found the Book of the Law, the nature and contents of which are otherwise unknown. Possibly in the dark days of Manasseh a deliberate attempt had been made to destroy the Word of God. At any rate, there was little knowledge of Scripture in Judah.

When Shaphan read the Book of the Law to Josiah, the king was devastated by the pronouncements of judgment against apostasy contained in it. He sent a delegation to Huldah the prophetess to find out what judgments awaited the land. The prophetess replied that the condemnation of God would indeed fall on Judah for its sin, but she sent word to Josiah that because his heart was right toward God, the punishment would not come during his lifetime.

The king called together a large representative group for a public reading of the law—evidently sections especially concerned with obligations to God. The king and the people made a covenant before God to keep his commandments.

Faced with the importance of maintaining a pure monotheistic faith, the king was spurred on to even more rigorous efforts to cleanse the Temple and Jerusalem. He destroyed the vessels used in Baal worship, the monument of horses given by the kings of Judah for sun worship, the chariots dedicated to the sun, the homosexual community near the Temple, and shrines built by Solomon and in use since his day. Moreover, he made stringent efforts to eliminate the pagan shrines and high places in all the towns of Judah (2 Kgs 23:4-14).

The Death of Josiah Precisely why Josiah opposed Pharaoh Neco's advance through Judean territory is unknown. He may have wanted to prevent aid from reaching the hated Assyrians or to maintain his own independence. Josiah was mortally wounded in the conflict and was greatly lamented by Jeremiah and all the people (2 Chr 35:25). Well they might weep, for their godly king was gone, and within a few years the judgment withheld during his lifetime would descend on the nation.

2. Son of Zephaniah, who returned to Jerusalem with other Jews after the captivity (Zec 6:10, 14; Hebrew "Hen").

JOSIPHIAH
Father of Shelomith, leader of a family of which 160 members accompanied Ezra back to Palestine (Ezr 8:10).

JOTHAM
1. Youngest of Gideon's 70 sons and the only survivor of Abimelech's slaughter of Jotham's brothers at Ophrah (Jgs 9:5). Upon learning of Abimelech's intrigue with the Shechemites, which led to the death of his brothers, Jotham traveled to Shechem and addressed its people from atop nearby Mt Gerizim. Using a parable, he portrayed Abimelech's rise as king and concluded his denunciation by issuing a curse on both his half brother (see 8:31) and the people of Shechem for their treachery (9:7). Jotham then fled to Beer for fear of a reprisal from Abimelech (v 21). Later, God fulfilled Jotham's curse; the people of Shechem were killed in a revolt and Abimelech was struck down at the hands of a woman (v 57).

2. Eleventh king of Judah (750–735 BC). He was the son of King Azariah (Uzziah) of Judah and Jerusa, daughter of Zadok (2 Kgs 15:7; 2 Chr 26:21; 27:1), and the father of Ahaz. Jotham, at 25 years of age, ascended to Judah's throne in the second year of King Pekah of Israel (752–732 BC) and ruled for 16 years in Jerusalem. Initially he reigned as co-regent with Azariah, who was stricken with leprosy for tolerating pagan worship, until his father's death (2 Kgs 15:5).

   Jotham was considered a righteous king in the eyes of the Lord. However, he also failed to cleanse the Temple of its pagan influences, and subsequently the people of Judah continued in their evil ways (2 Chr 27:2-6). His building projects included the Upper Gate of the Temple, work on the wall of Ophel, and the fortification of numerous towns in Judah's hill country (vv 3-4). Jotham also defeated the troublesome Ammonites in battle (v 5) and registered by genealogy the families of Gad living east of the Jordan (1 Chr 5:17). He was buried in Jerusalem after his death (2 Chr 27:9). The prophets Isaiah and Micah ministered to Judah, and Hosea to Israel, during his tenure as king. Jotham is listed as an ancestor of Jesus Christ in Matthew's genealogy (Mt 1:9).

3. Second of Jahdai's five sons (1 Chr 2:47).

JOZABAD
1. Benjaminite from Gederah and one of the military men who came to David's support at Ziklag (1 Chr 12:4).

2, 3. Leaders and mighty warriors from Manasseh's tribe who joined David at Ziklag to fight against Saul (1 Chr 12:20).

4. One of the Levites who assisted with the administration of the Temple contributions in Jerusalem during King Hezekiah's reign (2 Chr 31:13).

5. One of the Levitical chiefs who generously gave animals to the Levites for the celebration of the Passover feast during King Josiah's reign (2 Chr 35:9).

6. Levite, the son of Jeshua, and one who helped Meremoth, Eleazar, and Noadiah take inventory of the Temple's gifts and precious metals during the days of Ezra (Ezr 8:33).
7. Priest and one of the six sons of Pashhur who was encouraged by Ezra to divorce his foreign wife during the postexilic era (Ezr 10:22).
8. One of the Levites who was encouraged by Ezra to divorce his foreign wife (Ezr 10:23).
9. One of the Levites who assisted Ezra with teaching the people the law during the postexilic period (Neh 8:7).
10. One of the Levites who relocated to Jerusalem and was put in charge of the work of the Temple during the days of Nehemiah (Neh 11:16).
11. Alternate rendering for Shimeath's son in 2 Kings 12:21. *See* Jozacar.

JOZACAR
Son of Shimeath the Ammonitess and one of the royal servants who conspired against the murdered King Joash of Judah (2 Kgs 12:21). He is alternately called Zabad in 2 Chronicles 24:26. *See* Zabad.

JUBAL
Son of Adah, wife of Lamech, a descendant of Cain. He is credited with being the first musician, the inventor of the harp and flute (Gn 4:19-21).

JUDAH
1. Fourth of Jacob's 12 sons (Gn 35:23; 1 Chr 2:1) and the fourth son born to Jacob by Leah, who, overjoyed with the thought of bearing Jacob another son, named him Judah, meaning "praise" (Gn 29:35). Judah fathered five sons: Er, Onan, and Shelah by Bathshua the Canaanitess (Gn 38:3-5; 1 Chr 2:3); and the twins Perez and Zerah by Tamar, his daughter-in-law (Gn 38:29-30; 1 Chr 2:4). He eventually settled his family in Egypt with his father and brothers (Ex 1:2), although his first two sons, Er and Onan, were divinely killed in Canaan for their disobedience (Gn 46:12). Judah became the founder of one of Israel's 12 tribes (Nm 1:26-27).

   Though reckless in his behavior with Tamar (Gn 38:6-30), Judah showed firm resolve in taking personal responsibility for Benjamin's safety in Egypt and acting as intercessor for his brothers before Joseph (44:14-18). At the time of Jacob's blessing, Judah was granted the birthright privileges of the firstborn; the leadership of Jacob's family would come through Judah's seed, as would the promised Messiah of Abraham's covenant (49:8-12). Later, Judah's family was praised at the time of Ruth's engagement to Boaz (Ru 4:12), and both the Davidic lines of kings (1 Chr 2:1-15; 3:1-24) and Jesus Christ's ancestors traced their descent from Judah (Mt 1:2-3; Lk 3:33).
2. Forefather of a family of Levites who assisted Jeshua, the high priest, with rebuilding

QUICKTAKE

JUDAH

STRENGTHS AND ACCOMPLISHMENTS
• Was a natural leader—outspoken and decisive
• Thought clearly and took action in high-pressure situations
• Was willing to stand by his word and put himself on the line when necessary
• Was the fourth son of 12, through whom God would eventually bring David and Jesus, the Messiah

WEAKNESSES AND MISTAKES
• Suggested to his brothers they sell Joseph into slavery
• Failed to keep his promise to his daughter-in-law, Tamar

LESSONS FROM HIS LIFE
• God is in control, far beyond the immediate situation
• Procrastination often makes matters worse
• Judah's offer to substitute his life for Benjamin's is a picture of what his descendant Jesus would do for all people

VITAL STATISTICS
Where: Canaan and Egypt
Occupation: Shepherd
Relatives: Parents: Jacob and Leah. Wife: The daughter of Shua (1 Chronicles 2:3).
    Daughter-in-law: Tamar. Eleven brothers, at least one sister, and at least
    five sons

KEY VERSES
"Judah, your brothers will praise you.
    You will grasp your enemies by the neck.
    All your relatives will bow before you.
Judah, my son, is a young lion
    that has finished eating its prey.
Like a lion he crouches and lies down;
    like a lioness—who dares to rouse him?
The scepter will not depart from Judah,
    nor the ruler's staff from his descendants,
until the coming of the one to whom it belongs,
    the one whom all nations will honor" (Genesis 49:8-10).

Judah's story is told in Genesis 29:35–50:26. He is also mentioned in 1 Chronicles 2–4.

the Temple during the postexilic era (Ezr 3:9, NLT mg). He is alternately called Hodaviah in Ezra 2:40 and Hodevah in Nehemiah 7:43. *See* Hodaviah #4.

3. One of the Levites who was encouraged by Ezra to divorce his foreign wife (Ezr 10:23).

4. Benjaminite, son of Hassenuah, who was second in command over the city of Jerusalem during the days of Nehemiah (Neh 11:9).

5. One of the leaders of the Levites who returned with Zerubbabel and Jeshua to Judah after the Exile (Neh 12:8).

6. One of the princes of Judah who participated in the dedication of the Jerusalem wall during the postexilic period (Neh 12:34).

7. One of the priests who played a musical instrument at the dedication of the Jerusalem wall during the days of Nehemiah (Neh 12:36). He is perhaps identical with #5 above.

8. Joseph's son, father of Simeon and an ancestor of Jesus Christ (Lk 3:30).

JUDAS

1. Simon's son, surnamed Iscariot; one of the 12 disciples of Jesus. The derivation of Iscariot is uncertain. In all probability it designated the place of his birth, the town of Kerioth. His childhood home was perhaps Kerioth of Moab, east of the Jordan (Jer 48:24; Am 2:2), or Kerioth-hezron of southern Judah, also known as Hazor (Jos 15:25). A less feasible suggestion identifies Iscariot with an Aramaic word meaning "assassin," a word eventually attached to Judas's name because of his betrayal of Jesus.

Judas Iscariot's name appears last in the list of disciples (Mt 10:4; Mk 3:19; Lk 6:16), perhaps indicating his ignominy in the minds of later believers rather than his original importance among the Twelve. During Jesus' public ministry, he managed the treasury of the group (Jn 13:29), from which he was known to pilfer money (12:4). As a betrayer, Judas contracted to turn Jesus over to the chief priests for 30 pieces of silver. He accomplished this act of treachery by singling out Jesus with a kiss in the Garden of Gethsemane (Mt 26:14-47; Mk 14:10-46; Lk 22:3-48; Jn 18:2-5).

Various suggestions have been offered to explain Judas's traitorous deed. (1) In keeping with his patriotic zeal, Judas turned Jesus over to the authorities after realizing that his Master did not intend to overthrow the Roman order and establish a Jewish state. (2) Judas believed Jesus to be the Messiah and planned his arrest in hope of urging Jesus to usher in his kingdom. (3) He was a scoundrel who had plotted wickedness since the start of Jesus' public ministry. (4) Prompted by a satanic impulse, Judas betrayed Jesus; however, after recognizing that he was deceived, out of remorse he took his own life. (5) With damaged pride and humiliated ego from Jesus' caustic rebukes, Judas, originally a loyal disciple, turned against him. (6) Judas, moved by his own greed, yielded to his selfish instincts, not realizing that Jesus would consequently be tried and killed; upon learning the outcome of his betrayal, he repented in despair and committed suicide.

Judas, despondent over his act of betrayal, went out and hung himself in a field bought with his 30 pieces of silver (Mt 27:3-10). Acts 1:18 gruesomely adds that his body burst open, spilling out his intestines; for this reason the field was called the "Field of Blood" (Acts 1:19). Matthias later took Judas Iscariot's place among the Twelve (v 26).

2. Son of Joseph and Mary, and the brother of Jesus, James, Joseph, and Simon (Mt 13:55; Mk 6:3). Evidently Judas and his brothers rejected Jesus as Messiah (Jn 7:5) until after his resurrection (Acts 1:14). Later, it is thought, Judas (English "Jude") authored the epistle named Jude.

3. Son of James and one of the 12 disciples (Lk 6:16; Jn 14:22; Acts 1:13). He is identifiable with Thaddeus in Matthew 10:3 and Mark 3:18. See Thaddaeus, The Apostle.

4. Galilean who led a Jewish revolt against the Romans because of the census taken by Quirinius in AD 6. In Acts 5:37 the Pharisee Gamaliel mentioned Judas as an example of one who unsuccessfully tried to gain the support of the Jewish people. Josephus credited him with founding the Jewish Zealot party, an extreme revolutionary movement that attempted to throw off Roman rule and to reestablish Jewish autonomy (*War* 2.8.1).

5. Owner of a house along the street called Straight in Damascus. Here, following his conversion, Saul (Paul) found lodging and had his vision restored by Ananias (Acts 9:11).

6. Prophet and leader in the early Jerusalem church. Judas, surnamed Barsabbas, was selected with Silas to accompany Paul and Barnabas to Antioch, where they confirmed the Jerusalem Council's decision regarding the gentile church and subsequently encouraged its believers (Acts 15:22-32). See Joseph #12.

7. KJV spelling of Judah, Jacob's son (Mt 1:2-3). See Judah #1.

JUDAS BARSABBAS
See Judas #6.

JUDAS ISCARIOT
See Judas #1.

JUDAS OF GALILEE
See Judas #4.

JUDE
Brother of James and author of the general epistle named Jude. Jude is the English form of the Greek name Judas (Hebrew Judah). Most scholars think Jude was the brother of Jesus called Judas. See Judas #2.

JUDITH
Daughter of Beeri the Hittite and one of Esau's wives (Gn 26:34). In Genesis 36:2 she is alternately called Oholibamah. *See* Oholibamah.

JULIA
1. Woman greeted by the apostle Paul (Rom 16:15). Her name follows that of Philologus, who may have been her brother or husband.
2. According to a variant reading, a woman noted by Paul as being one of his coworkers, as well as a distinguished apostle (Rom 16:7, NLT mg). She was probably Andronicus's wife. The couple, like Aquila and Priscilla, formed an apostolic team. In other manuscripts, the reading is Junia—which, in the Greek, can be understood as a masculine name or feminine, depending on the accent. However, the most ancient manuscripts do not have an accent mark on this name; therefore, the interpreter must decide if this apostle was male or female.

JULIUS
Roman centurion of the Augustan cohort who escorted the apostle Paul and other prisoners from Palestine to Rome (Acts 27:1). Jewish leaders in Jerusalem accused Paul of teaching false doctrine and defiling the Temple. Because indecision by two successive Roman governors kept Paul in prison for more than two years, he finally appealed to Caesar. Julius was a kind man. He allowed Paul to leave the ship in Sidon to be comforted by his friends (v 3). However, in his eagerness to get his prisoners to Rome, Julius ignored Paul's advice to spend the winter in Fair Havens. Instead, he ordered the ship to sail to Phoenix, another harbor in Crete, which was more suitable for harboring in winter (vv 9-12). During the trip, a storm wrecked the ship. The soldiers on board wanted to kill the prisoners for fear of their escaping, but Julius prevented that massacre, ordering all to jump ship and swim to shore. This decision spared Paul's life (vv 42-44). Some scholars have conjectured that Julius was the soldier who stayed with Paul in Rome (28:16).

JUNIA
A Jew who, along with Andronicus, was greeted by Paul in his letter to the church in Rome—according to the reading of some manuscripts (Rom 16:7). Paul recognized Junia as an apostle who had been a prisoner with Paul for the sake of the gospel. This person could have been a male or female. *See* Julia #2.

JUSHAB-HESED
One of Zerubbabel's seven sons (1 Chr 3:20). Jushab-hesed means "loving-kindness is returned."

JUSTUS
1. Surname for Joseph Barsabbas (Acts 1:23). *See* Joseph #12.

2. Godly Corinthian man (presumably a convert of Paul), who opened his home to Paul and the Christians after the Jewish synagogue was closed to Paul's preaching (Acts 18:7). There is disagreement among the manuscripts as to the exact form of his name. Various readings are Justus or Titius Justus. He has also been identified as the Gaius of Romans 16:23.

3. Surname of a believer named Jesus, a Jewish Christian (Col 4:11). *See* Jesus #3.

K

KADMIEL

Head of a Levite family who returned from the Exile with Zerubbabel (Ezr 2:40; Neh 7:43; 12:8). His name appears in the list of those who supervised the Temple rebuilding project (Ezr 3:9), participated in sealing the covenant (Neh 10:9), and were prominent in the praise service (9:4-5; 12:24).

KALLAI

Priest and the head of Sallu's (Sallai's) priestly family during the days of Joiakim the high priest (Neh 12:20).

KANDAKE

Title given to ancient Ethiopian queens. Often rendered "Candace" and mistaken for a name, this term occurs in Acts 8:27 when Philip, a leader in the early church, met and baptized an Ethiopian eunuch, who was a minister under Candace, queen of the Ethiopians (Acts 8:27). That Kandake, whose name was probably Amanitere, ruled over Nubia (the northern region of modern Sudan) from AD 25 to 41.

KAREAH

Father of Jonathan and Johanan (2 Kgs 25:23). After Jerusalem fell to Nebuchadnezzar's army, his sons joined Gedaliah at Mizpah (Jer 40:8–43:5).

KEDAR

1. Second son of Ishmael, Abraham's son (Gn 25:13; 1 Chr 1:29).

2. Tribe or area appearing mainly in the prophetic writings from Solomon to the Exile. In Isaiah's prophecy against Arabia, Kedar is mentioned twice (Is 21:13-17). Along with Arabia, Dedan, and Tema, the Kedarites are threatened with destruction. The pomp attributed to them in verse 16 indicates some degree of affluence (see also Ez 27:21), and the militaristic tone of verse 17 points to the fact that they were a warring people. In Jeremiah 49:28 Kedar is linked with Hazor as victims of Nebuchadnezzar's conquests. Although there is no extrabiblical record of Nebuchadnezzar's march on Kedar, Ashurbanipal, the king of Assyria, does mention the conquest of Kedar. That would have been about 650 BC, or a half a century earlier than the Babylonian conquest. Apart from Ashurbanipal's account, the only other ancient extrabiblical reference to Kedar is found on a silver bowl offered to the Arabian goddess Han'ilat in the Egyptian Delta. The inscription on the bowl reads, "Cain, son of Geshem, king of Kedar," and the date is firmly fixed in the fifth century BC. This Geshem was very likely the enemy of Nehemiah (Neh 2:19; 6:1-6).

   The picture the Bible gives of Kedar is that of a desert nomadic people descended from Ishmael. They were not initially believers in Yahweh but are included in Isaiah's prophecy of the future kingdom of God (cf. Is 42:11; 60:7). Their desert environment limited their work to sheep herding and trading. Because of unpredictable water supplies in the desert, they were constantly moving—a way of life best handled by living in tents rather than permanent houses (cf. Ps 120:5; Song 1:5). For this reason archaeologists have found no site named Kedar. All we can surmise is that the area of Kedar lay to the east and slightly to the south of Israel in what is today the southern part of Jordan. The people of Kedar presumably died out or were assimilated into the surrounding nations.

KEDEMAH
Son of Ishmael (Gn 25:15) who gave his name to the tribe he fathered (1 Chr 1:31).

KEDORLAOMER
King of Elam who participated with three other kings in a campaign against five cities near the southern end of the Dead Sea plain (Gn 14). Although Kedorlaomer is initially third in the list (v 1), he was evidently the leader of the four kings. Elsewhere in the chapter his name comes first or stands alone.

For 12 years the five cities of the plain were vassals of Kedorlaomer. In the 13th year the cities rebelled, and the next year Kedorlaomer enlisted allies to enforce his lordship. The victorious kings looted the cities and took prisoners. Because the patriarch Abram's nephew Lot was among the captives, Abram mustered his servants and allies and pursued Kedorlaomer as far as Damascus. Kedorlaomer was defeated, and the captured loot and prisoners were rescued.

The first half of the name Kedorlaomer is a common Elamite word meaning "servant." The second half is probably the name of an Elamite deity. Although both elements of the name are known outside the Bible, the combination is not. It fits, however, with an early second-millennium BC date for the encounter, coinciding with the biblical account.

KEILAH
Caleb's descendant from Judah's tribe, called the Garmite in 1 Chronicles 4:19. Some identify this reference with the city in Judah instead of a person.

KELAIAH
A Levite who was guilty of marrying a pagan wife (Ezr 10:18). According to verse 23 Kelaiah is also called Kelita. A Levite named Kelita is also found in Nehemiah 8:7, 10:10, and 1 Esdras 9:48, where he is one who helped Ezra in expounding the law and who set his seal on Ezra's covenant. It cannot be determined with certainty whether Kelaiah and Kelita are the same individual.

KELAL
Pahath-moab's son, who obeyed Ezra's exhortation to divorce his pagan wife after the Exile (Ezr 10:30).

KELITA
A Levite sometimes thought to be the same as Kelaiah. See Kelaiah.

KELUB

1. Shuhah's brother and the father of Mehir from Judah's tribe (1 Chr 4:11).
2. Father of Ezri. Ezri oversaw the tilling of soil in King David's fields (1 Chr 27:26).

KELUHI

One of Bani's sons, who was encouraged by Ezra to divorce his foreign wife after the Exile (Ezr 10:35).

KEMUEL

1. Third son of Nahor (Abraham's brother) and the father of Aram (Gn 22:21).
2. Shiphtan's son from Ephraim's tribe; one of 12 men appointed to divide the land among the Israelite tribes (Nm 34:24).
3. Hashabiah's father, a ruler of the Levites during David's reign (1 Chr 27:17).

KENAANAH

1. Father of Zedekiah, the false prophet who incorrectly prophesied victory for kings Ahab and Jehoshaphat over the Syrians (1 Kgs 22:11, 24; 2 Chr 18:10, 23).
2. Bilhan's son, who was chief of the subclan of Jediael in Benjamin's tribe in the time of King David (1 Chr 7:10-11).

KENAN

Fourth-generation descendant of Adam (Gn 5:9-14; 1 Chr 1:2); alternately called Cainan in Luke's genealogy of Christ (Lk 3:37, RSV).

KENANI

Levite who participated in Ezra's public reading of the law after the Exile (Neh 9:4).

KENANIAH

1. Levite chief who led processional singing when King David brought the Ark of the Covenant to the new Tabernacle in Jerusalem (1 Chr 15:1-3, 22, 27).
2. Public administrator during David's reign. His sons also served as public officials (1 Chr 26:29).

KENAZ

Singular form of the name of the Kenizzite tribe, whose land was promised to Abraham's descendants (Gn 15:19). The appearance of three men by this name in the OT may be explained by the spread of the Kenizzite tribe over Edom and southern Judah before the Israelite conquest.

1. Grandson of Esau and chieftain of Edom (Gn 36:11, 15, 42; 1 Chr 1:36, 53).

2. Father of Othniel (Jos 15:17; Jgs 1:13; 3:9-11) and Seraiah (1 Chr 4:13).

3. Caleb's descendant (1 Chr 4:15).

KERAN
Dishon's son, a member of the Horite tribe during Esau's time (Gn 36:26; 1 Chr 1:41).

KEREN-HAPPUCH
Job's third daughter and the sister of Jemimah and Keziah. She was listed as a member of Job's family at the time of his restoration (Jb 42:14).

KEROS
One of the Temple servants whose descendants returned to Jerusalem with Zerubbabel (Ezr 2:44; Neh 7:47).

KERUB
One of five Babylonian cities from which Israelites who could not trace their ancestry returned after the Exile (Ezr 2:59; Neh 7:61).

KESED
Son of Milcah and Nahor, Abraham's brother (Gn 22:22).

KETURAH
Second wife of Abraham. It is unclear whether he married her before or after Sarah's death (Gn 25:1). He had six sons with her: Zimran, Jokshan, Medan, Midian, Ishbak, and Shuah (v 2). Keturah's status was not identical to that of Sarah. She is called a concubine (Gn 25:6, cf. 1 Chr 1:32), and her sons were presented with gifts instead of receiving a share in the inheritance. Keturah's sons were the ancestors of tribes with which Israel came into contact after the Conquest, especially Midian and Jokshan's sons Sheba and Dedan (Gn 25:3). As far as can be determined, the tribes settled in the north and central regions of the northern Euphrates, as far as the central sections of the Arabian Desert. They were merchants (ch 37) and shepherds (Ex 2:16). They were involved in international trade (Is 60:6). For example, the queen of Sheba, a descendant of Jokshan (Gn 25:3), came to Solomon to initiate trade relations (1 Kgs 10:2).

See also Abraham.

KEZIAH
Job's second daughter, born after his restoration (Jb 42:14).

KILEAB
David's second son, and the first born to him by Abigail (2 Sm 3:3); alternately called Daniel in 1 Chronicles 3:1.

KILION

One of the two sons of Elimelech and Naomi (Ru 1:2). He married a Moabite girl named Orpah (v 4) and eventually died in Moab (v 5).

KIMHAM

Son of Barzillai (according to Josephus), a very wealthy man who supplied David and his men with food while they were in Mahanaim during their flight from Absalom (2 Sm 19:32). David offered to take Barzillai back to Jerusalem with him, but Barzillai declined and suggested that David show kindness to Kimham instead (vv 37-40). David accepted the proposal and ordered his son and successor, Solomon, to grant Kimham a pension at the palace (1 Kgs 2:7). His name is reflected centuries later in Geruth-kimham, a place near Bethlehem where the people Johanan had rescued from Ishmael stayed, intending to go to Egypt later (Jer 41:17).

KISH

1. Benjaminite of Gibeah, father of King Saul and a man of some position in the community (1 Sm 9:1). His genealogy is traced for four generations, as is that of Elkanah, the father of Samuel, who would anoint Saul king (1:1).

   There is some obscurity in the genealogical information about Kish. His father's name is listed as Abiel in 1 Samuel 9:1. If the Kish mentioned in 1 Chronicles 8:30 is the same person, then we must conclude that Abiel was also known as Jeiel. But it may be that this second Kish was an uncle of Saul's father. A further obscurity results from 1 Chronicles 8:33 and 9:39, where Ner, not Abiel, is said to be the father of Kish. Yet in 1 Samuel 14:51 Abiel is said to be the father of two sons whose names were Ner and Kish. The solution probably lies in the assumption that Ner in the Chronicles references was an earlier ancestor, probably Abiel's father or grandfather. If that should be the case, then the father-son relationship between Ner and Kish should be taken in an extended sense, as elsewhere in the OT. No other details of Kish's life are available. His grave was in Zela of Benjamin (2 Sm 21:14). The KJV of Acts 13:21 spells his name Cis.

2. Levite, grandson of Merari, Mahli's son and the father of Jerahmeel (1 Chr 23:21-22; 24:29).

3. Abdi's son, another Levite of the family of Merari. He was one of the Levites who assisted Hezekiah in the cleansing of the Temple (2 Chr 29:12).

4. Benjaminite and the great-grandfather of Mordecai. Mordecai was carried into exile by Nebuchadnezzar in 597 BC (Est 2:5), together with King Jehoiachin and the prophet Ezekiel.

KISHI

Levite of Merari's family whose son Ethan was a singer and musician in the sanctuary during David's reign (1 Chr 6:44). He is also known as Kushaiah in 15:17.

KISLON

Father of Elidad, leader of Benjamin's tribe during the Israelites' wilderness wanderings and one of those appointed by Moses to divide the land of Canaan among the tribes (Nm 34:21).

KOA

People probably living northeast of Babylonia. They are named along with Babylon, Pekod, and Shoa as people who would come against Jerusalem as instruments of God's judgment on Israel (Ez 23:23). They are perhaps identifiable with the Kutu, mentioned frequently in Assyrian inscriptions.

KOHATH

Son of Levi (Gn 46:11; Ex 6:16), father of Amram, Izhar, Hebron, and Uzziel (Ex 6:18; Nm 3:19, 27; 1 Chr 6:2), and progenitor of the Kohathite branch of Levitical families who were responsible for the Tabernacle service (Nm 3:31-32). Moses, Aaron, and Miriam were descendants of Kohath (Ex 6:18-20; Nm 26:59; 1 Chr 6:3; 23:13-17).

The three main divisions of the tribe of Levi bore the names of Gershon, Kohath, and Merari, who were traditionally the original sons of Levi (Gn 46:11; Ex 6:16; Nm 3:17; 1 Chr 6:1, 16; 23:6). The Kohathites, therefore, were a prominent Levitical family. The order of their names in Numbers 4, Joshua 21, 1 Chronicles 6:16, and 2 Chronicles 29:12 indicates that they were assigned a more honorable office than either Gershon or Merari. Their position and responsibilities—whether referred to as "the Kohathites," or "the sons of Kohath"—are noted throughout the early writings of the Hebrews (Ex 6:18; Nm 3:19, 27-30; 4:2-4, 15, 18, 34, 37; 7:9; 10:21; 26:57; Jos 21:4-5, 10, 20, 26; 1 Chr 6:2, 18, 22, 33, 54, 61, 66, 70; 15:5; 23:12; 2 Chr 20:19; 29:12; 34:12).

During the wandering of the Israelites in the desert following their Exodus from Egypt, the Kohathites were assigned a position on the southern side of the Tabernacle (Nm 3:29). When the Tabernacle was moved, they were to carry the Ark and other sacred things on their shoulders (7:9). At the time of the building of the Tabernacle, a census was taken to determine the number of male Kohathites who would be involved in the service of the Lord (3:27-28; 4:1-4, 34-37).

After the settlement of the tribes in the land of Canaan, the service of the Kohathites appeared to have ended. God, however, specifically stated that they should be cared for in the same manner as the other Levitical families. The Kohathites were given numerous cities (Jos 21:4-5, 20-26; 1 Chr 6:66-70).

When David became king, he organized the Levites into three divisions (1 Chr 23:6). Heman, who represented the Kohathites, was charged with the musical service in the house of the Lord (6:31), and another group of Kohathites was made responsible for the "bread of the presence" each Sabbath (9:32). When David brought the Ark of the Covenant to Jerusalem, Uriel, a Kohathite, was commissioned to supervise its transportation (15:3-5).

During the period of the divided kingdom, the combined forces of the Moabites and

Ammonites attacked Judah. King Jehoshaphat admitted his inability to repulse the aggressors and sought the aid of the Lord. The Kohathites led the people in a song of praise and probably led the army when, the next morning, the king and the fighting men of Judah went out against the invaders (2 Chr 20:19-22).

Two important reform movements characterized the declining years of the kingdom of Judah. The first took place during the reign of Hezekiah (715–686 BC; 2 Kgs 18; 2 Chr 29–30); the second in the reign of Josiah (640–609 BC; 2 Kgs 22–23; 2 Chr 34). The climax of Josiah's reform came in 621 BC with the discovery of the Book of the Law. In both these movements the Kohathites played an important role. In the reign of Hezekiah they were numbered among those who cleansed the house of the Lord (2 Chr 29:12-16), and in Josiah's time two notable Kohathites were among those appointed to supervise the work of the Temple (34:12).

Following the Exile, mention is again made of the Kohathites. The paucity of evidence precludes any judgment of the significance of their ministry. In all probability they were numbered among those who attempted to serve the Lord faithfully in the midst of general spiritual decline. The few whose names are forever enshrined in Scripture were appointed to humble offices. In the absence of evidence to the contrary, it may be assumed that they discharged their duties faithfully (1 Chr 9:19, 31-32; Ezr 2:42; Neh 12:25).

See also Priests and Levites.

KOLAIAH

1. Benjaminite; forefather of a family who lived in Jerusalem after the Exile (Neh 11:7).

2. Father of Ahab, the false prophet who, along with Zedekiah, prophesied falsely in the name of God during Jeremiah's day (Jer 29:21).

KORAH

1. Third son of Esau by Oholibamah, daughter of Anah (Gn 36:5, 14, 18; 1 Chr 1:35).

2. Esau's grandson; fifth son of Eliphaz (Gn 36:16).

3. Eldest son of Izhar, Kohath's son from Levi's tribe (Ex 6:21, 24), who led a rebellion against Moses and Aaron in the wilderness, accusing them of exalting themselves above the assembly of the Lord (Nm 16:1-3). Numbers 16:1 also records a revolt led by two brothers, Dathan and Abiram, and a man named On, all of the tribe of Reuben, who also challenged the authority of Moses. Dathan and Abiram accused Moses of making himself a prince over the people and then failing to lead them into the Promised Land (vv 12-14). The stories of the two rebellions are interwoven in such a way that it is difficult to separate them. It may be that the two revolts occurred simultaneously.

Moses challenged Korah and his followers to a trial by ordeal. Together with Aaron, they were to take censers filled with fire and incense to the tent of meeting the next day; the Lord would then select from among them whoever should be the

QUICKTAKE

KORAH the LEVITE

STRENGTHS AND ACCOMPLISHMENTS
• Popular leader; influential figure during the Exodus
• Mentioned among the chief men of Israel (Exodus 6)
• One of the first Levites appointed for special service in the Tabernacle

WEAKNESSES AND MISTAKES
• Failed to recognize the significant position God had placed him in
• Forgot that his fight was against someone greater than Moses
• Allowed greed to blind his common sense

LESSONS FROM HIS LIFE
• There is sometimes a fine line between goals and greed
• If we are discontented with what we have, we may lose it without gaining anything better

VITAL STATISTICS
Where: Egypt, Sinai peninsula
Occupation: Levite (Tabernacle assistant)

KEY VERSES
"Then Moses spoke again to Korah: 'Now listen, you Levites! Does it seem insignificant to you that the God of Israel has chosen you from among all the community of Israel to be near him so you can serve in the LORD's Tabernacle and stand before the people to minister to them? Korah, he has already given this special ministry to you and your fellow Levites. Are you now demanding the priesthood as well?'" (Numbers 16:8-10).

Korah's story is told in Numbers 16:1-40. He is also mentioned in Numbers 26:9; Jude 1:11.

holy priest before the Lord (Nm 16:4-10, 15-17). Moses accused Korah and his company of rebelling against God rather than against Aaron (v 11). When the men gathered as Moses had instructed, the glory of the Lord appeared to all the people. The Lord ordered Moses to tell the congregation to separate themselves from the tents of Korah, Dathan, and Abiram (vv 19-24). Moses proposed a test to show the source of his authority, but while he was still speaking, the earth opened and swallowed all the rebels, their families, and their possessions. Fire consumed the 250 men who were offering the incense. The rest of the Israelites were terrified and fled from the scene (vv 31-35). Numbers 26:11 adds, however, that "the sons of Korah did not die that day" with the others.

Then, through Moses, the Lord instructed Eleazar, the son of Aaron, to take the censers of the men who had died and have them made into hammered plates to be used as a covering for the altar; thus, they would serve as a reminder to the Israelites that no one who was not a priest and a descendant of Aaron should ever draw near to burn incense before the Lord, lest that person meet the same fate as Korah and his company (Nm 16:36-40).

Instead of being convinced that God had vindicated Moses and Aaron, the next day the congregation began complaining that they had killed the Lord's people. For this act of rebellion God threatened to destroy the congregation and sent a plague among them. Moses interceded and averted complete catastrophe, but not before 14,700 Israelites had died (Nm 16:41-50). The rebellious incident of the Korahites is last mentioned in Jude 1:11.

4. Eldest son of Hebron, included in the genealogy of Caleb (1 Chr 2:43); the reference has been understood as a geographical name, possibly a town in Judah.

5. Aminadab's son and grandson of Kohath, second son of Levi (1 Chr 6:22).

KORE

1. Kohathite Levite who, with his brothers, was responsible for the service at the entrance to the tent of meeting in David's time (1 Chr 9:19; 26:1).

2. KJV alternate name for Korahite in 1 Chronicles 26:19.

3. Imnah's son, a Levite who was a keeper of the East Gate in Hezekiah's reign. He had charge of the freewill offerings of the people (2 Chr 31:14).

KOZ

1. Descendant of Judah and possibly an ancestor of the priestly house of Hakkoz (1 Chr 4:8).

2. KJV rendering of the priestly family of Hakkoz (Ezr 2:61; Neh 3:4, 21; 7:63); perhaps identifiable with #1 above. *See* Hakkoz.

KUSHAIAH

Alternate name for Kishi, a Merarite Levite, in 1 Chronicles 15:17. *See* Kishi.

LAADAH

Shelah's son and the father of Mareshah from Judah's tribe (1 Chr 4:21).

LABAN

Bethuel's son (Gn 24:24, 29), brother of Rebekah (vv 15, 29), father of Leah and Rachel (29:16), and the uncle and father-in-law of Jacob. Laban's forebears lived in Ur, but his father, Bethuel, was called the Aramean of Paddan-aram, and Laban also is referred to as the Aramean (KJV "Syrian," 25:20; cf. 28:5). Their hometown was Haran, which was in Syria and which, like Ur, was a center of the worship of the moon god, Sin or Nannar.

When Isaac came of age, Abraham sent his servant Eliezer back to Haran to find a wife for Isaac. Laban greeted Eliezer hospitably and made provision for him and his camels (Gn 24:29-33, 54). Laban acted as the head of the house; he made the decision concerning Rebekah's marriage to Isaac (vv 50-51), and it was to him and his mother that Eliezer made gifts of costly ornaments (v 53).

Laban figures largely in the narrative of his nephew Jacob in his quest for a wife. After the deception of Isaac by Rebekah and Jacob, Rebekah feared that Esau would kill Jacob, so she suggested that he flee to her brother, Laban (Gn 27:43); meanwhile, she persuaded Isaac that Jacob should go to Haran to find a wife from among their own people. When Jacob arrived in the area of Haran, he met Rachel, the younger daughter of Laban, and was warmly welcomed (29:13). Laban hired Jacob to tend his flocks, and it was agreed that after seven years of work Jacob would receive Rachel as his wages. At the end of that period Laban substituted Leah, his older daughter. Jacob protested, but the two men finally decided that Jacob should serve another seven years for Rachel.

Both Jacob and Laban were schemers and had serious disputes about wages. Jacob proposed that his wages should be a certain portion of the flocks. When this was accepted, the Lord blessed Jacob and his flocks, and Laban became angry. Jacob claimed that Laban had changed his wages ten times (Gn 31:7, 41).

Jacob fled from Haran. Laban pursued him because he was missing his household gods, whose possession made the holder heir to Laban's estate. Rachel had taken them but adroitly concealed them from her father's search.

Laban and Jacob parted after making a covenant of peace and erecting a pillar of stones to serve as a witness between them (Gn 31:46-50).

See also Jacob #1.

LADAN

1. Member of Ephraim's tribe who was Joshua's ancestor (1 Chr 7:26).
2. Gershonite Levite, named as the head of several families (1 Chr 23:7; 26:21). He is also called Libni. See Libni #1.

LAEL

Levite of the family of Gershon and father of Eliasaph (Nm 3:24).

LAHAD
Jahath's son from Judah's tribe (1 Chr 4:2).

LAHMI
Brother of Goliath the Gittite. According to 1 Chronicles 20:5, he was killed by Elhanan. However, 2 Samuel 21:19 says that Elhanan killed Goliath rather than his brother Lahmi. Most interpreters accept the 1 Chronicles passage as the correct reading, the 2 Samuel text being a textual corruption.

LAISH
Father of Paltiel (Palti), to whom Saul gave his daughter Michal, who was formerly David's wife (1 Sm 25:44; 2 Sm 3:15-16).

LAMECH
1. Methushael's son, a descendant of Cain, and the husband of Adah and Zillah. Lamech's sons by Adah were Jabal, "the father of those who dwell in tents and have livestock," and Jubal, "the father of all those who play the lyre and pipe." A son, Tubal-cain, "the forger of all instruments of bronze and iron," and a daughter, Naamah, were Lamech's children by Zillah (Gn 4:18-22). In the account of beginnings given in the early chapters of Genesis, the sons of Lamech are the first herdsmen, musicians, and metalworkers. His song of vengeance (vv 23-24) is an example of early Hebrew poetry. In the song Lamech declares that he has killed a man for wounding him and compares the act to his forebear Cain's slaying of Abel (cf. vv 8-12). He asserts that "if anyone who kills Cain is to be punished seven times, anyone who takes revenge against me will be punished seventy-seven times!" Lamech's song indicates that, as civilization became more complex, pride and the propensity for violence increased. Jesus' word about forgiving "seventy times seven" (Mt 18:22) stands in sharp contrast to Lamech's example.

2. Methuselah's son, and the father of Noah (Gn 5:25-31; 1 Chr 1:3). When Noah was born, Lamech expressed his hope that the child would bring relief to humanity from the curse placed upon Adam (Gn 5:29; cf. 3:17). His life span—777 years—is one of the longest in the listing of those who lived before the Flood. Fanciful conversations in old age between Lamech and his father, Methuselah, are recorded in the Dead Sea Scrolls. Lamech is listed as an ancestor of Jesus in the genealogy recorded in Luke 3:36.

LAPPIDOTH
Husband of Deborah the prophetess (Jgs 4:4).

LAZARUS
1. Lazarus the beggar. In one of Jesus' most familiar parables (Lk 16:19-31), he contrasted the earthly circumstances of a beggar named Lazarus with that of a nameless rich man. From the adjective for "rich" in the Latin Vulgate, the rich man came to be called in English "Dives." The rich man relished the luxury of his wealth, while he

ignored an ulcerated blind beggar lying at his gate. Jesus said that Lazarus died and went to Abraham's bosom, while Dives suffered everlasting torment.

The parable of Lazarus has been misinterpreted sometimes as a condemnation of wealth instead of a warning against enjoyment of wealth without regard for the poor. It teaches that decisions in the present life determine eternal destiny.

In no other parable did Jesus identify a character by name. Some Bible students have therefore concluded that he was telling a true story. The name's symbolism, however, seems to account for its use, since Lazarus was cast in the role of one "whom God helped." In the Middle Ages the beggar Lazarus was venerated as the patron saint of lepers. Leper hospitals were called lazar-houses.

2. Lazarus of Bethany. Jesus performed the most spectacular of all his miracles (excluding his own resurrection) when he restored Lazarus of Bethany to life four days after death. Lazarus lived with his two sisters, Mary and Martha. They were among Jesus' most intimate friends (Jn 11:3-5, 36). On several occasions he visited in their home, which also served as his headquarters during his final week on earth (Mt 21:17; Lk 10:38-42; Jn 11:1–12:11). Lazarus was at the banquet in Jesus' honor when Mary anointed Jesus' feet with costly ointment (Jn 12:1-3).

The raising of Lazarus, the climax of the signs in John's Gospel, receives the fullest treatment of Jesus' miracles. It produced three notable results: (1) many Jews in the vicinity of Jerusalem believed in Jesus (Jn 11:45) and some weeks later escorted him into the city (12:17-18); (2) the Jewish leaders, hardened in their rejection of Jesus, resolved that he must die (11:53); (3) those leaders also plotted Lazarus's death (12:10-11). The miracle not only showed Jesus' power over death but set the stage for his own resurrection.

LEAH

Laban's daughter, the wife of Jacob, and the older sister of Rachel.

After deceiving his father, Isaac, into giving him the blessing intended for Esau (Gn 27:5-40), Jacob left home and went to his uncle Laban (27:43; 28:2) in distant Mesopotamia, in order to find a wife (27:46–28:2) and escape the revenge of Esau, who had determined to kill him (27:41-42). Here he fell in love with his cousin Rachel and arranged with her father to marry her in exchange for seven years of work (29:17-18). When the time for the wedding feast came, Laban deceived Jacob in an apparent scheme to keep his services for seven more years; he gave Leah instead of Rachel to Jacob on the wedding night (vv 21-25). His lame excuse that custom required the giving of the older daughter in marriage before the younger (v 26) was hardly appropriate at that point and certainly should have been explained from the beginning. Leah is described as "weak-eyed," perhaps to be understood as "dull-eyed," in contrast with Rachel, who is described as "beautiful and lovely" (v 17).

Jacob's love for Rachel (Gn 29:20) induced him to agree to work for another seven years in order to receive her also as his wife. Because of the intense rivalry between the two sisters and Jacob's favoring of Rachel, the Lord blessed Leah with six sons and a daughter (Reuben, Simeon,

Levi, Judah, Issachar, Zebulun, Dinah) before Rachel was given any children (29:31–30:22). This barrenness became a great burden for Rachel over the years. At one point she bargained with Leah for mandrakes, a plant believed to ensure conception, in exchange for conjugal rights. The result was to increase her sister's advantage, however, because Leah conceived and bore her fifth son, Issachar (30:14-17).

Leah was given the honor of being the mother of the two tribes that played the most significant roles in the history of the nation of Israel. The tribe of Levi became the tribe of the priesthood. The tribe of Judah became the tribe of royalty through which the promised seed (Gn 3:15; 12:2-3; 2 Sm 7:16; Mt 1:1) ultimately came in the person of Jesus Christ.

See also Jacob #1.

LEBANAH

Head of a family who returned to Jerusalem with Zerubbabel following the Exile (Ezr 2:45; Neh 7:48).

LECAH

Either a person, descendant of the Judahite Er, or an otherwise unknown place in Judah settled by Er, depending on one's understanding of "father" (1 Chr 4:21).

LEMUEL

King credited with writing Proverbs 31:1-9. In these verses he sets forth teachings given him by his mother on good government, sexual relations, and wine. Although he has been identified with Solomon, most modern interpreters reject this identification.

LEVI

1. Jacob's third son by Leah (Gn 29:34). The etymology of the name is uncertain. Levi's name is associated with the tragedy at Shechem, where the male inhabitants of the city were ruthlessly murdered when Levi and Simeon sought to avenge the violation of their sister Dinah by Shechem the Hivite. Jacob condemned the act and before his death pronounced a judgment on Levi's behavior (49:5-7). According to these words, Levi's descendants were to be dispersed among the tribes.

   The tribe of Levi was composed of the descendants of Levi's three sons: Gershon (Gershom), Kohath, and Merari. Moses, Aaron, and Miriam traced their genealogy to Kohath (Ex 6:16). The Levites remained faithful to Yahweh at the occasion of the golden calf by Mt Horeb. They were rewarded with the right to special service in and around the Tabernacle (ch 32) and later in the Temple.

2. Tax collector in Capernaum (Mk 2:14); one of the 12 disciples who was also named Matthew (Mk 2:14; Lk 5:27; cf. Mt 9:9). *See* Matthew.

3. Son of Melki and ancestor of Jesus (Lk 3:24).

4. Son of Simeon and ancestor of Jesus (Lk 3:29).

LIBNI

1. Gershon's son, the grandson of Levi, and Shimei's brother (Ex 6:17; Nm 3:18; 1 Chr 6:17, 20). He was the father of three sons and the founder of the Libnite family (Nm 3:21). Libni is alternately called Ladan in 1 Chronicles 23:7-9 and 26:21.

2. Mahli's son, the father of Shimei, and a descendant of Levi through Merari's line (1 Chr 6:29).

LIKHI

Shemida's son from Manasseh's tribe (1 Chr 7:19).

LINUS

Christian at Rome who joined Paul in sending salutations to Timothy (2 Tm 4:21). According to Irenaeus and Eusebius, the apostles Peter and Paul made a man named Linus bishop of Rome. Eusebius identified him with the Linus referred to by Paul at the end of 2 Timothy and said that he served for 12 years. The *Apostolic Constitutions,* along with other early church documents, also makes this identification.

LO-AMMI

Symbolic name, meaning "Not My People" (Hos 1:9), given by the prophet Hosea to his son.

LOIS

Maternal grandmother of Timothy (2 Tm 1:5), whose family, including Timothy's mother, Eunice, lived at Lystra (Acts 16:1). Lois was a deeply committed Jew who probably converted to Christianity during Paul's first missionary trip (ch 14). Paul comments that Timothy shared the faith of his grandmother and mother.

LO-RUHAMAH

Symbolic name, meaning "Not pitied" (Hos 1:6-8), given by the prophet Hosea to his daughter, indicating God's rejection of Israel. *See* Ruhamah.

LOT

Abraham's nephew; progenitor of both the Moabites and the Ammonites. Like Abraham, he was born in Ur. When his father died, he was put in the care of his grandfather Terah, and accompanied him and his uncle Abram to Haran (Gn 11:27-32). After the death of Terah, he joined Abram in the journey to Canaan and subsequently to Egypt and back to Canaan.

By the time the pair returned to Canaan, their flocks and herds were too numerous for them to live together in a single area. Generously, Abram gave Lot his choice of where he would like to settle; Lot chose the fertile plain of the Jordan, which was like a "garden of the Lord" (Gn 13:10) before the divine judgment and catastrophe fell on the region. Thus, Lot became increasingly involved with and contaminated by the corruption of the cities of the plain and took up his residence in Sodom.

QUICKTAKE

LOT

STRENGTHS AND ACCOMPLISHMENTS
• He was a successful businessman
• Peter calls him a righteous man (2 Peter 2:7, 8)

WEAKNESSES AND MISTAKES
• When faced with decisions, he tended to put off deciding, then chose the easiest course of action
• When given a choice, his first reaction was to think of himself

LESSON FROM HIS LIFE
• God wants us to do more than drift through life; he wants us to be an influence for him

VITAL STATISTICS
Where: Lived first in Ur of the Chaldeans, then moved to Canaan with Abram. Eventually he moved to the wicked city of Sodom
Occupation: Wealthy sheep and cattle rancher; also a city official
Relatives: Father: Haran. Adopted by Abram when his father died. The name of his wife, who turned into a pillar of salt, is not mentioned

KEY VERSE
"When Lot still hesitated, the angels seized his hand and the hands of his wife and two daughters and rushed them to safety outside the city, for the LORD was merciful" (Genesis 19:16).

Lot's story is told in Genesis 11–14; 19. He is also mentioned in Deuteronomy 2:9; Luke 17:28-32; 2 Peter 2:7, 8.

While Lot was living in Sodom, four Mesopotamian kings (probably of small city-states) defeated the kings of the five towns in the area in battle, and in the subsequent plundering they carried off Lot and his family and possessions. When word of the loss reached Abram, he launched a rearguard action against the invaders and recovered all the prisoners and the loot at Hobah, north of Damascus (Gn 14).

Subsequently, two angelic visitors called on Lot in Sodom to hasten his departure from the doomed city. The homosexual attack on them illustrated the depravity of the city, and Lot's willingness to sacrifice his daughters shows how the corruption of his environment was rubbing off on him. As further evidence of the evil influence, Lot was unwilling to leave

Sodom; his future sons-in-law refused to accompany him; and his wife looked back and was turned to a pillar of salt (Gn 19).

The sequel to the story was as sordid as the scene at Lot's door. His daughters, despairing of husbands of their own, got him drunk enough to engage in sexual relations with them. The result was the birth of two sons, Moab and Ben-ammi, ancestors of the Moabites and Ammonites, inveterate enemies of Israel (Gn 19:30-38).

In spite of his waywardness the NT declares that Lot was a "righteous man" (2 Pt 2:7-9), apparently meaning that his faith in God was sufficient to guarantee his salvation. To critics who question the historicity of Lot and the destruction of Sodom, it must be noted that Jesus vouched for both in Luke 17:28-29.

LOTAN

Seir's eldest son (Gn 36:20) and a chief of the native Horite inhabitants of Edom (vv 22, 29). Lotan had two sons, Hori and Homam (1 Chr 1:38-39).

LUCIUS

1. Man from Cyrene, listed among the prophets and teachers in Antioch (Acts 13:1). He may have been among the Jewish Christians from Cyprus and Cyrene who preached to the Gentiles in Antioch in the face of persecution (11:19-21). Various attempts have been made to identify him with Luke, the author of Acts, or with the Lucius of Romans 16:21, but these have been unsuccessful.

2. Jewish believer (cf. Rom 9:3) and one of the companions of Paul who sent greetings to those in Rome (16:21). This casts doubt on Origen's identification of this Lucius with the Luke of the Gospel and Acts, who was most likely a Gentile (Col 4:12-14).

LUD

The fourth son of Shem (Gn 10:22). There is little question that Lud is to be associated with Lydia. Josephus makes this identification (*Antiquities* 1.6.4.). In Isaiah 66:19, it is listed among other nations of Asia Minor. Lud is often mentioned in contexts that suggest the men were well known as good soldiers. According to Jeremiah 46:9, they fought with the Egyptians against the Babylonians at the battle of Carchemish in 605 BC. In the lament over Tyre in Ezekiel 27:10, they are listed among others who were mercenaries in the army of Tyre. Perhaps Ezekiel 30:5 is another case of Lydians serving as mercenaries—this time in the Egyptian army. Such military aid to Egypt goes back to the Assyrian period when Gyges sent military aid to Psammetichus of Egypt against the Assyrians.

LUKE

Companion of the apostle Paul; author of the third Gospel and Acts.

Accepting the author of Luke-Acts as Luke the companion of Paul, much can be learned about him from this two-volume work. The preface to the Gospel indicates that Luke was not an eyewitness or immediate disciple of the Lord. Luke states that he had carried out extensive research and had written an orderly account about Jesus.

Luke's writings have some features not found in the other Gospels. The extraordinary feature of Luke's work is the inclusion of the book of Acts as a sequel to the Gospel. The two books together—Luke and Acts—show the actual fulfilling of the prophecies of Isaiah in the proclamation of the gospel to the ends of the earth. This inclusion of the Gentiles is often referred to as Luke's universalism or concern for all humanity (Luke 2:14; 24:47). The Gospel of Luke displays a keen interest in individuals, social outcasts, women, children, and social relationships, especially situations involving poverty or wealth. This Gospel has a special stress on prayer and the Holy Spirit, which results in a striking note of joyfulness and praise. These features tell us something about Luke as a person and his understanding of Christianity.

If Luke is accepted as the companion of Paul, then the "we" passages of Acts disclose that

QUICKTAKE

LUKE

STRENGTHS AND ACCOMPLISHMENTS
- A humble, faithful, and useful companion of Paul
- A well-educated and trained physician
- A careful and exact historian
- Writer of both the Gospel of Luke and the book of Acts

LESSONS FROM HIS LIFE
- The words we leave behind will be a lasting picture of who we are
- Even the most successful person needs the personal care of others
- Excellence is shown by how we work when no one is noticing

VITAL STATISTICS
Where: Probably met Paul in Troas
Occupations: Doctor, historian, traveling companion
Contemporaries: Paul, Timothy, Silas, Peter

KEY VERSES
"Many people have set out to write accounts about the events that have been fulfilled among us. They used the eyewitness reports circulating among us from the early disciples. Having carefully investigated everything from the beginning, I also have decided to write a careful account for you, most honorable Theophilus, so you can be certain of the truth of everything you were taught" (Luke 1:1-4).

Luke includes himself in the we sections of Acts 16–28. He is also mentioned in Luke 1:3; Acts 1:1; Colossians 4:14; 2 Timothy 4:11; Philemon 1:24.

Luke was in Philippi (possibly his hometown) when he first joined Paul (Acts 16:10-17). Then he later rejoined Paul when the latter returned to Philippi (20:5-15). Luke then journeyed with Paul on his way to Jerusalem and stayed with Philip at Caesarea (21:1-18). Then, after Paul's two-year imprisonment in Caesarea, Luke sailed with him to Rome (27:1–28:16).

Further references to Luke in the epistles of Paul (Col 4:14; 2 Tm 4:11; Phlm 1:24) give some valuable information about Luke. Colossians 4:11 and 14 seem to indicate that Luke was a Gentile and a physician. The latter is supported, but not proved, by the interest shown by Luke in medical matters, as in Luke 4:38, 5:12, and 8:43. It is also interesting that early tradition adds that Luke was a physician of Antioch who wrote his Gospel in Achaia and died at the age of 84.

LYDIA

Gentile woman who was converted under the preaching of Paul in Philippi (Acts 16:14, 40). Lydia was a dealer in purple cloth and came from the city of Thyatira in the region of Lydia in the western part of the Roman province of Asia (commonly known as Asia Minor). The description of her as "a worshiper of God" (or "God-fearer") indicates that she was a Gentile who had been attracted to Judaism. After her conversion to Christianity and her baptism, she hosted Paul and Silas during their stay in Philippi.

LYSANIAS

Tetrarch of Abilene (the area west of Damascus) in AD 27–28. The Gospel of Luke mentions Lysanias as among those who ruled at the beginning of John the Baptist's ministry (Lk 3:1). This is the only reference to him in the NT.

Josephus mentions a Lysanias who succeeded his father, Ptolemaeus, as the king of Chalcis. However, he was killed by Mark Antony in 36 BC. Since there is no other known reference to a Lysanias in the writings of antiquity, and since this second Lysanias could not have lived during John the Baptist's lifetime, some biblical scholars assume Luke was inaccurate in his chronology. In defense of Luke, other scholars indicate that Josephus mentions "Abila of Lysanius," an area given to Agrippa II by Claudius in AD 53; however, that reference may be to the Lysanias who ruled Chalcis 90 years earlier.

The most conclusive evidence in support of Luke is found in an inscription that records the dedication of a temple at Abila, "for the salvation of the Lord Imperial and their whole household by Nymphaeus, a freedman of Lysanias the tetrarch." The title "Lord Imperial" was bestowed jointly only on Emperor Tiberius and his mother, Livia, Augustus's widow. That would fix Lysanias's date between AD 14 (when Tiberius became emperor) and AD 29 (when Livia died). On that basis Luke's chronology may be assumed accurate.

LYSIAS

Roman commander who wrote a letter to Felix concerning the apostle Paul (Acts 23:26). See Claudius Lysias.

M

MAACAH
Common Hebrew name, often spelled Maachah in the KJV.

1. Last of the four children of Nahor, Abraham's brother, by Reumah his concubine (Gn 22:24).

2. Daughter of Talmai, king of Geshur, a wife of David, and Absalom's mother (2 Sm 3:3; 1 Chr 3:2).

3. Achish's father. Achish, king of Gath, housed two of Shimei's slaves during Solomon's reign (1 Kgs 2:39). He is identified with Maoch in 1 Samuel 27:2. *See* Maoch.

4. Daughter of Absalom (Abishalom) (1 Kgs 15:2, 10), the wife of Rehoboam, king of Judah (930–913 BC), and the mother of King Abijah (913–910 BC) and grandmother of King Asa (910–869 BC) of Judah (1 Kgs 15:10; 2 Chr 11:20-22). Later, Asa removed her as queen mother because she had an idol made for Asherah (1 Kgs 15:10-13; 2 Chr 15:16). Maacah is spelled Micaiah (Michaiah) in 2 Chronicles 13:2.

5. Caleb's concubine and the mother of four sons (1 Chr 2:48).

6. Sister of Huppim and Shuppim, the wife of Makir the Manassite and mother of Peresh and Sheresh (1 Chr 7:15-16).

7. Benjaminite, the wife of Jeiel, and an ancestress of King Saul (1 Chr 8:29; 9:35).

8. Father of Haman, one of David's mighty warriors (1 Chr 11:43).

9. Father of Shephatiah, chief officer of Simeon's tribe during David's reign (1 Chr 27:16).

MAADAI
Bani's son, who obeyed Ezra's exhortation to divorce his pagan wife after the Exile (Ezr 10:34).

MAAI
Priestly musician who participated in the dedication of the rebuilt Jerusalem wall (Neh 12:36).

MAASAI
Priest who returned to Jerusalem with Zerubbabel after the Exile (1 Chr 9:12).

MAASEIAH
1. One of the singers appointed by the Levites to accompany David when he brought the Ark from Obed-edom's house to Jerusalem (1 Chr 15:18-20).

2. Commander who agreed to assist Jehoiada the priest in crowning Joash king (2 Chr 23:1).

3. Officer who served King Uzziah by assisting in the organization of the king's army (2 Chr 26:11).

4. Son of Judah's royal house who was slain when Pekah the king of Israel invaded Judah (2 Chr 28:7).

5. Ruler in Jerusalem whom Josiah appointed to assist in repairing the Temple (2 Chr 34:8).

6–8. Three priests who obeyed Ezra's exhortation to divorce their foreign wives during the postexilic era (Ezr 10:18-22).

9. Pahath-moab's son (Ezr 10:30).

10. Father of Azariah, a repairman of the Jerusalem wall (Neh 3:23).

11. Ezra's attendant when he read the law to the people (Neh 8:4).

12. Levite who, with others, helped the people to understand the law Ezra read (Neh 8:7).

13. Leader who set his seal on Ezra's covenant under Nehemiah's leadership (Neh 10:25).

14. Judahite leader and the son of Baruch, who lived in Jerusalem with those chosen by lot to inherit the rebuilt city (Neh 11:5). He is sometimes identified with the Asaiah mentioned in 1 Chronicles 9:5.

15. Ithiel's son from Benjamin's tribe who was chosen to live in Jerusalem (Neh 11:7).

16. Priestly trumpeter at the dedication of the Jerusalem wall (Neh 12:41).

17. Priestly singer at the dedication of the Jerusalem wall (Neh 12:42).

18. Father of Zephaniah the priest. Zephaniah, with Pashhur, was sent to Jeremiah by King Zedekiah to inquire of the Lord concerning the future of Nebuchadnezzar's war against Jerusalem (Jer 21:1-2; 29:25) and to request that Jeremiah pray for Jerusalem (37:3).

19. Father of Zedekiah the false prophet, an opponent of Jeremiah's prophecy about Jerusalem's fall under Nebuchadnezzar's siege (Jer 29:21).

20. KJV form of Mahseiah, Baruch's forefather, in Jeremiah 32:12 and 51:59. *See* Mahseiah.

21. Keeper of the threshold during Jehoiakim's reign (Jer 35:4).

MAATH
Ancestor of Jesus in Luke's genealogy (Lk 3:26).

MAAZ
Ram's son from Judah's tribe (1 Chr 2:27).

MAAZIAH
1. Levite who served in the Temple during David's reign (1 Chr 24:18).

2. Levite who set his seal on Ezra's covenant (Neh 10:8); sometimes identified with Maadiah, a postexilic priest (Neh 12:5).

MACBANNAI
Warrior from Gad's tribe who joined David at Ziklag in his struggle against King Saul (1 Chr 12:13).

MACNADEBAI
A son of Bani (Binnui), who obeyed Ezra's exhortation to divorce his foreign wife during the postexilic era (Ezr 10:40).

MADAI
Third of Japheth's seven sons (Gn 10:2; 1 Chr 1:5).

MADMANNAH
Shaaph's son and a grandson of Caleb (1 Chr 2:49).

MAGDALENE, MARY
Name of one of several Marys who followed Jesus. This Mary was the first to see the risen Christ (Jn 20:11-18). *See* Mary #3.

MAGDIEL
One of the chiefs of Edom (Gn 36:43; 1 Chr 1:54).

MAGOG
Term found only five times in the Bible but significant because of its use in the well-known prophetic passages of Ezekiel 38–39 and Revelation 20. In the register of nations in Genesis 10:2 (see also 1 Chr 1:5), Magog was listed among the sons of Japheth, identifying both an individual and the nation that came forth from him. In Ezekiel and Revelation, Magog came to refer either to a land, a people, or both (see Ezekiel 38–39; Revelation 20).

MAGPIASH
Political leader who signed Ezra's covenant during the postexilic period (Neh 10:20).

MAHALALEL
1. Kenan's son and the father of Jared in Seth's line (Gn 5:12-17; 1 Chr 1:2), also mentioned in Luke's genealogy (Lk 3:37).
2. Perez's son and a postexilic Judahite (Neh 11:4).

MAHALATH
1. Daughter of Ishmael, Nebaioth's sister, Esau's third wife, and Reuel's mother (Gn 28:9); alternately called Basemath (KJV "Bashemath") in Genesis 36:3-17.
2. Jerimoth's daughter and King Rehoboam's first wife (2 Chr 11:18).

MAHARAI

One of David's mighty men and a Zerahite from Netophah in the hill country of Judah. He was appointed commander of a division (24,000 soldiers) during the 10th month of the year (2 Sm 23:28; 1 Chr 11:30; 27:13).

MAHATH

1. Levite, son of Amasai, and ancestor of Heman the Temple singer in David's time (1 Chr 6:35).

2. Levite who assisted in the cleansing of the Temple during Hezekiah's time (2 Chr 29:12). He was appointed an overseer of the contributions, the tithes, and the things dedicated to God (31:13).

MAHAZIOTH

One of the 14 sons of Heman the Kohathite, and head of the 23rd course of Tabernacle musicians who ministered with cymbals, harps, and lyres (1 Chr 25:4, 30).

MAHER-SHALAL-HASH-BAZ

Name of Isaiah's son, meaning "swift to plunder and quick to spoil" (NLT mg), which prophetically described the imminent destruction to befall Damascus and Samaria by the hand of the Assyrians (Is 8:1, 3).

MAHLAH

1. Manassite; one of Zelophehad's five daughters. She, with her sisters, appealed to Moses to work out an arrangement that would allow them to retain their inheritance in spite of having no brothers (Nm 26:33; 27:1; 36:11; Jos 17:3).

2. Hammoleketh's son from Manasseh's tribe (1 Chr 7:18).

MAHLI

1. Merari's son and Levi's grandson (Ex 6:19; Nm 3:20; 1 Chr 6:19, 29; 23:21; 24:26-28; Ezr 8:18), and the founder of the Mahlite family (Nm 3:33; 26:58). The Mahlites, along with the other families of Merari, were appointed to carry the frames of the Tabernacle and the pillars of the court (Nm 4:29-33).

2. Mushi's son and the nephew of #1 above (1 Chr 6:47; 23:23; 24:30).

MAHLON

Son of Elimelech and Naomi, and Chilion's brother. While with his family in Moab, he married Ruth, the Moabitess. He died in Moab, however, and Ruth later married Boaz (Ru 1:2, 5; 4:9-10).

MAHOL

Father of three famous wise men (Heman, Calcol, and Darda) during the Solomonic era (970–930 BC; 1 Kgs 4:31).

MAHSEIAH

Forefather of Baruch (Jer 32:12) and Seraiah (51:59), spelled Maaseiah in the KJV.

MAKI

Father of Geuel from Gad's tribe. Geuel was one of the 12 spies sent to search out the land of Canaan (Nm 13:15).

MAKIR

1. Joseph's grandson and the firstborn son of Manasseh through his Aramean concubine (Gn 50:23; 1 Chr 7:14). Machir was the father of Gilead and the founder of the Machirite family (Nm 26:29). His descendants dispossessed the Amorites living in the land of Gilead east of the Jordan during the days of Moses (Nm 32:39); later, they were assigned this land along with Bashan for an inheritance (Dt 3:15; Jos 17:1-3). In Judges 5:14, the whole tribe of Manasseh is called by this name.

2. Ammiel's son living at Lo-debar, a town east of the Jordan. Machir provided shelter for Mephibosheth (2 Sm 9:4-5) and later, with Shobi and Barzillai, took care of David's domestic needs during his flight from Absalom (2 Sm 17:27).

MALACHI

Author of the last book of the OT (Mal 1:1). The prophet Malachi lived about 500–460 BC. His name means "my angel" or "my messenger" and is so translated in Malachi 3:1 and elsewhere. Apart from the book that bears his name, nothing else is known about him from the Bible. In the apocryphal book of 2 Esdras 1:40 he is identified as "Malachi, who is also called a messenger of the Lord." Rabbinic tradition suggests that Malachi may be another name for Ezra the scribe, although there is no supporting evidence for this identification.

MALCAM

Shaharaim's son from Benjamin's tribe (1 Chr 8:9).

MALCHUS

Name of a slave of the high priest in John 18:10. At the time of Jesus' arrest, Peter struck Malchus with a sword, cutting off his right ear. In Matthew 26:51, Mark 14:47, and Luke 22:50-51, no name is given for this person. According to Luke, Jesus immediately healed the wound.

MALKIEL

Beriah's son, a grandson of Asher (Gn 46:17; 1 Chr 7:31), and the founder of the Malkielite family (Nm 26:45).

MALKIJAH

1. Gershon's descendant, appointed by David, along with the rest of his family, to serve as a Temple musician (1 Chr 6:40, KJV "Malchiah").

2. Priest who served in the time of David (1 Chr 9:12). His descendants were among those who returned to Jerusalem with Zerubbabel (Neh 11:12).

3. Priest in David's reign (1 Chr 24:9); perhaps the same as #2 above.

4. Parosh's son, who obeyed Ezra's exhortation to divorce his pagan wife after the Exile (Ezr 10:25, KJV "Malchiah").

5. KJV rendering of Hashabiah, another of Parosh's sons, in Ezra 10:25. *See* Hashabiah #9.

6. Harim's son, who obeyed Ezra's exhortation to divorce his pagan wife after the Exile (Ezr 10:31, KJV "Malchiah"). He repaired part of the Jerusalem wall under Nehemiah (Neh 3:11).

7. Recab's son and the ruler of Beth-hakkerem. Under Nehemiah's direction, he repaired the Dung Gate of the Jerusalem wall (Neh 3:14).

8. Goldsmith who worked under Nehemiah's direction to help repair the Jerusalem wall (Neh 3:31).

9. One who stood to Ezra's left during the public reading of the law (Neh 8:4).

10. Priest who signed Ezra's covenant of faithfulness to God with Nehemiah and others after the Exile (Neh 10:3).

11. Participant in the dedication of the rebuilt Jerusalem wall (Neh 12:42).

12. Royal prince who owned a cistern in which the prophet Jeremiah was imprisoned (Jer 38:6). Malchijah's son Pashhur (21:1; 38:1) was one of those who, after hearing the harsh prophecies of Jeremiah, appealed to King Zedekiah to put Jeremiah to death. The princes attempted to do so by throwing him into Malchijah's cistern.

MALKIRAM

Son of Jeconiah (Jehoiachin), and a descendant of David (1 Chr 3:18).

MALKISHUA

King Saul's third son (1 Sm 14:49; 1 Chr 8:33; 9:39). He was killed by the Philistines at the battle of Gilboa (1 Sm 31:2; 1 Chr 10:2).

MALLOTHI

One of Heman's 17 children (1 Chr 25:4-5), who became leader of the 19th of 24 divisions of singers for service in the sanctuary during David's reign (v 26).

MALLUCH

1. Merarite Levite and ancestor of Ethan the singer in Solomon's Temple (1 Chr 6:44).

2. Bani's son, whom Ezra required to divorce his foreign wife (Ezr 10:29).

3. Harim's son, whom Ezra required to divorce his foreign wife (Ezr 10:32).

4. Priest who set his seal on Ezra's covenant (Neh 10:4).

5. Another priest who set his seal on Ezra's covenant (Neh 10:27).

6. Priest who returned from the Exile with Zerubbabel (Neh 12:2).

MAMRE

Owner of a parcel of land called "the plain of Mamre." He was an Amorite and is recorded as having two brothers: Aner and Eshcol (Gn 14:13). These became confederates of Abraham when he fought to save his nephew Lot.

MANAEN

One of the prophets and teachers in the church at Antioch (Acts 13:1), identified as a close companion of Herod the tetrarch. The name is a Greek form of the Hebrew name Menahem.

MANAHATH

One of Shobal's five sons (Gn 36:23; 1 Chr 1:40).

MANASSEH

1. Firstborn son of Joseph and his Egyptian wife, Asenath (Gn 41:50-51). Manasseh, along with Ephraim his brother, visited their grandfather Jacob on his deathbed. Jacob announced that Manasseh and Ephraim were to be considered his own, not Joseph's sons (Gn 48:5-6), and that Manasseh, the firstborn, would have descendants not quite as great as those of Ephraim (vv 13-20). This explains why Ephraim and Manasseh (in that order) provided their names for two of the 12 tribes of Israel but Joseph did not, at least in most listings (cf. Rv 7:6). Manasseh also founded the Manassite family (Dt 4:43; 2 Kgs 10:33).

2. KJV translation for Moses in Judges 18:30. In Hebrew the two names differ by only one letter. Apparently an early scribe was offended that this verse connected Moses' grandson with idolatry, so he changed the name to Manasseh to preserve Moses' reputation. *See* Moses.

3. Thirteenth king of Judah (697–642 BC) and Jesus' ancestor (Mt 1:10); notorious for his long and wicked reign, described in 2 Kings 21:1-26 and 2 Chronicles 33:1-20. His father was the godly king Hezekiah, and his mother was Hephzibah (2 Kgs 21:1).

   At the age of 12 he became co-ruler with his father. In 686 BC his father died and he became sole monarch at only 23. His 55-year reign (2 Kgs 21:1) is dated from the beginning of his co-regency, so he ruled 11 years as co-regent and 44 years as sole king—longer than any other king in Judah or in Israel. Regrettably, he was the most wicked of all the Judean kings, even resorting to a series of murders, presumably to stay in power (21:16; 24:4). In addition to murder, among his sins listed in 2 Kings 21:2-9 are rebuilding the high places for pagan worship; encouraging Baal, sun, moon, and star worship; and burning his son as a child sacrifice (21:6; cf. 23:10; Jer 7:31).

Second Chronicles 33:11-16 indicates that he was taken as a prisoner of war to Babylon, that he genuinely repented there, that God restored him as king, and that he tried to abolish his former pagan practices and to restore proper worship of God alone. Skepticism about this account is not warranted, even though unparalleled in 2 Kings. Surviving Assyrian records twice mention Manasseh, saying that he faithfully provided men to transport timber from Lebanon to Nineveh for the Assyrian king Esar-haddon (681–669 BC) and that he paid tribute to King Ashurbanipal (669–627 BC) after an Assyrian military campaign in Egypt in 667 BC. Though Pharaoh Neco's similar captivity and release is mentioned, Manasseh's is not.

When Manasseh died in 642 BC, at the age of 67, he was buried in his own garden (2 Kgs 21:18), rather than with highly regarded kings like Jehoiada and Hezekiah (2 Chr 24:16; 32:33). His son Amon reverted to his father's wicked practices, but reigned only two years (642–640 BC) before being assassinated. It was his godly grandson Josiah (640–609 BC) who led the people back to the true worship of Yahweh (2 Kgs 23:4-14). But even his reforms could not avert the judgment promised on account of Manasseh's sins (vv 26-27).

4. Pahath-moab's son, who obeyed Ezra's exhortation to divorce his pagan wife after the Exile (Ezr 10:30).

5. Hashum's son, who obeyed Ezra's exhortation to divorce his pagan wife after the Exile (Ezr 10:33).

MANOAH

Danite from Zorah whose wife was barren. Through encounters with the Angel of the Lord, the couple learned that God was about to give them a son who would judge the Philistines and deliver Israel from its oppression. Manoah later fathered Samson, who fulfilled these promises (Jgs 13; 16:31).

MAOCH

Father of Achish, the Philistine king of Gath. David sought refuge with this king in order to escape Saul's plots to kill him (1 Sm 27:2). See Maacah #3.

MAON

Son of Shammai, and Bethzur's father (1 Chr 2:45). He was either the founding father of the people of Bethzur and/or the founder of the city. His descendants are perhaps the Maonites of Judges 10:12.

MARA

A name, meaning "bitter," which Naomi gave to herself when she returned as a widow to Judah from Moab (Ru 1:20). See Naomi.

MARESHAH

1. Caleb's firstborn son and the father of Hebron (1 Chr 2:42; RSV, based on the Greek text). He is alternately called Mesha in the Hebrew text (RSV mg). *See* Mesha #2.
2. Perhaps a Judahite son of Laadah (1 Chr 4:21).

QUICKTAKE

MARK, JOHN

STRENGTHS AND ACCOMPLISHMENTS
- Wrote the Gospel of Mark
- Provided the family home as one of the main meeting places for the Christians in Jerusalem
- Persisted beyond his youthful mistakes
- Was an assistant and traveling companion to three of the greatest early missionaries

WEAKNESSES AND MISTAKES
- Probably the nameless young man described in the Gospel of Mark who fled in panic when Jesus was arrested
- Left Paul and Barnabas for unknown reasons during the first missionary journey

LESSONS FROM HIS LIFE
- Personal maturity usually comes from a combination of time and mistakes
- Mistakes are not usually as important as what can be learned from them
- Effective living is not measured as much by what we accomplish as by what we overcome in order to accomplish it
- Encouragement can change a person's life

VITAL STATISTICS
Where: Jerusalem
Occupations: Missionary-in-training, Gospel writer, traveling companion
Relatives: Mother: Mary. Cousin: Barnabas
Contemporaries: Paul, Peter, Timothy, Luke, Silas

KEY VERSE
"Only Luke is with me. Bring Mark with you when you come, for he will be helpful to me in my ministry" (Paul writing in 2 Timothy 4:11).

John Mark's story is told in Acts 12:25–13:13 and 15:36-39. He is also mentioned in Colossians 4:10; 2 Timothy 4:11; Philemon 1:24; 1 Peter 5:13.

MARK, JOHN

Cousin of Barnabas; companion to both Paul and Peter; author of the second Gospel.

A member of a Jewish family in Jerusalem who were early believers in Jesus Christ, John Mark had both a Jewish and a Roman name. The Roman name Mark was perhaps a badge of Roman citizenship, as in Paul's case, or was adopted when he left Jerusalem to serve the gentile church in Antioch (Acts 12:25). When an angel of the Lord freed Peter from prison, the apostle went directly to "the house of Mary, the mother of John whose other name was Mark" (v 12, NRSV). This house, described as having an outer gate, being of adequate size to accommodate a gathering of many believers and served by a slave named Rhoda (vv 12-13), was obviously the dwelling of a wealthy family. By the time of this event (c. AD 44), Mark may have already been converted through the personal influence of Peter (1 Pt 5:13). The fact that he was chosen to accompany Barnabas and Saul (Paul) to Antioch indicates that Mark was held in high esteem by the church in Jerusalem (Acts 12:25).

John Mark accompanied Barnabas and Saul to assist them on their evangelistic expedition (Acts 13:5). He soon left the apostles, however, and returned to Jerusalem (v 13). Scripture does not reveal the cause of this desertion. Perhaps the rigors and hardships of the journey overwhelmed the young man. Another possible explanation was that at Paphos, shortly into the journey, Paul stepped to the front as leader and spokesman (v 13). Thereafter, Acts (with the natural exception of 15:12, 25) speaks of Paul and Barnabas rather than Barnabas and Paul. Perhaps it offended Mark to see his kinsman Barnabas, who had preceded Paul in the faith (4:36-37) and had ushered him into the apostles' fellowship (9:27), take second place in the work of the gospel. But there may have been a deeper and more significant cause for Mark's withdrawal. Like Paul, Mark was "a Hebrew born of Hebrews" (Phil 3:5, NRSV). Because of this, Mark may have objected to Paul's offer of salvation to the Gentiles based only on faith without the prerequisite of keeping the Jewish law. It is noteworthy that the Bible uses only the Hebrew name John when recording Mark's presence on the gospel journey (Acts 13:5) and his departure at Perga in Pamphylia (v 13). Also important is the fact that John Mark returned, not to the gentile church in Antioch, the site of his former service, but to the Jewish church in Jerusalem (v 13). Luke's history records that "the disagreement [between Paul and Barnabas over Mark] became so sharp that they parted company" (Acts 15:39, NRSV). Nothing stirred Paul's feelings more than the question of justification by faith, and Barnabas had demonstrated his weakness on this point (Gal 2:13). Therefore, it may have been the cause of their separation: Barnabas and Mark to Cyprus, and Paul and Silas into Asia Minor to strengthen the new churches (Acts 15:39-41).

About 11 years pass before Mark again appears in the biblical record. In Colossians 4:10 and Philemon 1:24, he is in Rome with "Paul the aged," who is there as "a prisoner of Jesus Christ" (Phlm 1:19). The fracture had been healed, such that Paul says that Mark and others are "the only ones of the circumcision [the Jews] among my co-workers for the kingdom of God" (Col 4:11, NRSV). Paul, in his last epistle, pays Mark his final tribute. He tells Timothy, "Do your best to come to me soon.... Only Luke is with me. Get Mark and bring him with you, for he is useful in my ministry" (2 Tm 4:9, 11, NRSV). Although all had deserted Paul in his trial before Caesar Nero (v 16), Mark, who in his youth had also deserted the apostle, traveled from Ephesus to Rome, endeavoring to come to the beloved Paul with Timothy.

According to 1 Peter 5:13, the apostle Peter sent Mark's greeting along with that of the church in Babylon (signifying Rome), indicating Mark's close relationship with the apostle to the circumcision (Gal 2:9). The most important and reliable extrascriptural tradition concerning Mark is that he was the close attendant of Peter. The early church fathers said this association produced the Gospel of Mark, inasmuch as Mark took account of Peter's teachings about Jesus and then used them to shape his Gospel, perhaps written in Rome between AD 60 and 68.

MARSENA

One of the seven princes of Persia and Media who served Ahasuerus, ranking next to him in authority in the kingdom (Est 1:14).

MARTHA

Sister of Mary and Lazarus, and friend of Jesus. Martha's family lived in Bethany, a small town on the eastern slope of the Mt of Olives.

Luke gives an account of an incident concerning Martha when she was busy preparing and serving food while her sister, Mary, was listening to Jesus. Martha complained to Jesus that Mary was not helping her; Jesus corrected Martha gently: "My dear Martha, you are so upset over all these details! There is really only one thing worth being concerned about. Mary has discovered it—and I won't take it away from her" (Lk 10:41-42, NLT). In saying this, Jesus challenged Martha's anxiousness by pointing out that fellowship with him was life's highest and most rewarding priority.

In John's account of the death and resurrection of Lazarus, it is Martha who, upon Jesus' arrival, goes out to meet him while Mary remains in the house (Jn 11:20). Once again, Martha complains to Jesus, this time saying that if he had come earlier Lazarus would not have died (v 21). When Jesus replied that her brother would rise again, Martha naturally assumed that Jesus was speaking of the future resurrection. Jesus reassured Martha that he was the resurrection and the life and that she must trust in him (vv 23-26). Martha then confessed her belief that Jesus was the Christ (v 27). When Jesus asked that the tomb be opened, Martha protested that the smell would be unpleasant. Jesus replied firmly to her doubts, "Did I not tell you that if you would believe you would see the glory of God?" (v 40, RSV). Jesus then proceeded to raise Lazarus from the dead.

In John 12:1-11 Martha is again serving a meal for Jesus and Lazarus; this time she does not protest Mary's elaborate show of affection for Jesus.

MARY

Popular feminine name among first-century Jews, borne by six (or seven) women in the NT.

1. Mary, the mother of Jesus. According to the infancy narratives of Matthew and Luke, Mary was a young Jewish virgin, probably from the tribe of Judah, who during her

QUICKTAKE

MARY

STRENGTHS AND ACCOMPLISHMENTS
• The mother of Jesus, the Messiah
• The one human who was with Jesus from birth to death
• Willing to be available to God
• Knew and applied Old Testament Scriptures

LESSONS FROM HER LIFE
• God's best servants are often ordinary people who make themselves available to him
• God's plans involve extraordinary events in ordinary people's lives
• A person's character is revealed by his or her response to the unexpected

VITAL STATISTICS
Where: Nazareth, Bethlehem
Occupation: Homemaker
Relatives: Husband: Joseph. Relatives: Zechariah and Elizabeth. Children: Jesus, James,
    Joseph, Judas, Simon, and daughters

KEY VERSE
"Mary responded, 'I am the Lord's servant. May everything you have said about me come
true.' And then the angel left her" (Luke 1:38).

Mary's story is told throughout the Gospels. She is also mentioned in Acts 1:14.

engagement to Joseph (of Davidic descent from the tribe of Judah) was discovered to be pregnant. This was due to her submission to the Holy Spirit (Mt 1:18-25; Lk 1:26-38). The couple married and lived first in Nazareth of Galilee, then traveled to Bethlehem (Joseph's hometown) for a census, where Jesus was born (Mt 2:1; Lk 1:5; 2:4-5). Matthew informs us that shortly after the birth the family had to flee to Egypt to escape Herod (Mt 2:13-14). Later, the family resided again in Nazareth (Mt 2:23; Lk 2:39).

We have little other information about Mary. She was certainly a concerned mother (as her scolding of Jesus in Lk 2:48 shows), and she later had a high estimate of Jesus' ability (as at the wedding in Cana, Jn 2:1-4). She had several other sons and daughters to care for. She appeared at the foot of the cross, where Jesus asked "the beloved disciple" to care for her in her grief (Jn 19:25-27). After the resurrection she and Jesus' brothers were among the disciples who experienced the outpouring of the Spirit on Pentecost (Acts 1:14). No further mention is made of her.

Mary's song of praise, "The Magnificat" (Lk 1:46-55) displays her sterling humility and trust in God's will. She is truly "blessed among women" (v 42).

2. Mary, the mother of James and Joseph. This woman goes by several names, but in each account she appears among Jesus' faithful female disciples, standing by the cross and witnessing the empty tomb. Matthew calls her "Mary the mother of James and Joseph" or just "the other Mary" (27:56, 61; 28:1); Mark names her "Mary the mother of James the younger and of Joses," "Mary the mother of Joses," or "Mary the mother of James" (15:40, 47; 16:1); in John's Gospel, she is "Mary wife of Clopas" (19:25), though she may possibly be a separate Mary. Tradition has it that this Mary was Jesus' aunt, as Clopas was Joseph's brother (Eusebius's *Ecclesiastical History* 3.11).

3. Mary Magdalene. We know little about this woman other than that her name indicates that she was from Magdala in Galilee. Somewhere in Galilee she met Jesus, who cast seven demons out of her. She then joined the band of disciples and followed Jesus wherever he went (Lk 8:2), ending up in Jerusalem at the foot of the cross when all the male disciples had fled (Mk 15:40; Jn 19:25). She observed Jesus' burial (Mk 15:47) and witnessed the events surrounding the resurrection. Matthew 28:1, Mark 16:1, and Luke 24:10 group her with the other women who went to the tomb. John says that she was the first among these women to discover the empty tomb, the first to report to the disciples, and the first to see the risen Christ as she lingered by the tomb after all the others had left (Jn 20:1-2, 11-18). This faithful disciple, however, was not allowed to touch her Lord (v 17).

4. Mary of Bethany. This Judean Mary was the sister of Martha and Lazarus. We know three facts about her. First, she was such a devoted follower of Jesus that she neglected her household duties to listen to him (Lk 10:38-42; Jesus approved this). Second, she was apparently upset with Jesus when he did not come to heal her brother before he died (Jn 11:20, 28-33). Finally, before Jesus died, she anointed him with an expensive ointment while he feasted at her home in Bethany (Mt 26:6-13; Mk 14:3-9; Jn 12:1-8).

5. Mary, mother of John Mark. This woman appears only once in Scripture (Acts 12:12). Her house was the meeting place of the persecuted church. Since it was apparently large and she had servants, she was a wealthy woman, probably a widow (since no husband is mentioned). In her house the church prayed for Peter, and Peter came there after being released from prison. Her son John Mark accompanied Paul and probably Peter as well.

6. Mary of Rome. In Romans 16:6 Paul greets a woman in Rome named simply "Mary, who has worked hard among you." At some time she had been in Greece or Asia Minor, perhaps being expelled from Rome with Aquila and Priscilla (Acts 18:2; c. AD 49). While there she had met Paul, perhaps being converted by him, and had worked hard with him in his work of evangelism or caring for the church. By AD 56 (a probable

date for the book of Romans), she had returned to Rome. She was distinguished by the praise Paul heaped upon her and his other coworkers living in Rome.

MARY MAGDALENE
See Mary #3.

MASH
Aram's fourth son (Gn 10:23), a descendant of Shem. He is called Meshech in 1 Chronicles 1:17. *See* Meshech #2.

MASHAL
Alternate spelling of Mishal, a Levitical town in Asher, in 1 Chronicles 6:74.

MASSA
Ishmael's seventh son and Abraham's grandson (Gn 25:14; 1 Chr 1:30). His descendants inhabited northwestern Arabia. Tiglath-pileser III mentions these people, along with the inhabitants of Tema (cf. Gn 25:15) and others who were ruled by him and paid tribute to him. The people of Tema probably were descendants of Massa's brother Tema.

Massa forms part of the titles of Proverbs 30:1 and 31:1. The definite article precedes it in 30:1 and can be translated "the burden" or "the oracle." It is frequently used in prophetic passages in the ominous sense of God's impending judgment (Is 13:1; Na 1:1; Hab 1:1).

MATRED
Mother of Mehetabel, the wife of King Hadad (Hadar) of Edom (Gn 36:39; 1 Chr 1:50).

MATTAN
1. Priest of Baal killed at the time when Jehoiada the priest had Queen Athaliah killed and Joash placed on the throne of Judah (2 Kgs 11:18; 2 Chr 23:17).

2. Father of Shephatiah, a prince under King Zedekiah and among those who persecuted Jeremiah (Jer 38:1-6).

MATTANIAH
1. Last king of Judah, whom King Nebuchadnezzar of Babylon enthroned in place of his nephew Jehoiachin; his name subsequently was changed to Zedekiah (2 Kgs 24:17), and as such he was known in the other references to him in 2 Kings, 2 Chronicles, and Jeremiah. *See* Zedekiah.

2. Asaph's descendant, named among the Levites living in postexilic Jerusalem (1 Chr 9:15; Neh 11:17, 22; 12:8, 35).

3. Heman's son, who helped lead music in the sanctuary during David's reign (1 Chr 25:4, 16).

4. Levite of the sons of Asaph, who was an ancestor of Jahaziel, a messenger of God in the days of King Jehoshaphat (2 Chr 20:14).

5. Another Levite of the sons of Asaph who helped cleanse the Temple during King Hezekiah's reign (2 Chr 29:13).

6–9. Four men of Israel who were exhorted by Ezra to divorce their foreign wives during the postexilic era (Ezr 10:26-27, 30, 37).

10. One of the gatekeepers at the time of the dedication of the reconstructed wall of Jerusalem in Nehemiah's day (Neh 12:25).

11. Grandfather of Hanan, a treasurer of the Temple storehouse in Nehemiah's day (Neh 13:13).

MATTATHA
Ancestor of Jesus, according to Luke's genealogy (Lk 3:31).

MATTATHIAS
1. Member of the priestly family of Joarib (his genealogy can be traced in 1 Macc 2:1 and in Josephus's *Antiquities* 12.6.3). He was a native of Jerusalem who settled in Modein and became the father of the nationalistic leaders, the Maccabeans, who led the Jewish revolt against the Syrians (167 BC). In his attempt to wipe out Judaism and establish Hellenism, Antiochus Epiphanes, king of Syria, outlawed Jewish sacrifices, built pagan altars (including one to Zeus in the Temple), and executed anyone who possessed the law (1 Macc 2:1-49). Mattathias ignited the revolt against this oppression when Greek officers set up a pagan altar at Modein and ordered that sacrifices be offered to heathen gods. Mattathias refused, killed the Jew who volunteered, killed the Greek officer, destroyed the altar, and fled to the hills with a band of followers. He led guerrilla warfare against the Syrians, continued to circumcise children, and made strenuous efforts to preserve the law. His motto was "Let everyone who is zealous for the law come after me."

He led the revolt for about a year and died, probably in 167 BC. His last bequest to his sons was "Obey the ordinance of the law." He was succeeded in military leadership by his son Judas, and the Hasmonean dynasty of priests were his descendants. He is remembered in special Hanukkah prayers because of his zeal in fighting for religious freedom.

2. Amos's son and an ancestor of Jesus, according to Luke's genealogy (Lk 3:25).

3. Semein's son and an ancestor of Jesus, according to Luke's genealogy (Lk 3:26).

MATTATTAH
Hashum's son, who obeyed Ezra's exhortation to divorce his pagan wife after the Exile (Ezr 10:33).

MATTENAI

1. Hashum's son, who obeyed Ezra's exhortation to divorce his pagan wife after the Exile (Ezr 10:33).

2. Bani's son, who obeyed Ezra's exhortation to divorce his pagan wife after the Exile (Ezr 10:37).

3. Head of Joiarib's priestly house during the days of Joiakim the high priest in postexilic Jerusalem (Neh 12:19).

MATTHAN

Ancestor of Jesus (Mt 1:15); perhaps identifiable with Matthat in Luke 3:24.

MATTHAT

1. Ancestor of Jesus (Lk 3:24), perhaps the same as Matthan (Mt 1:15).

2. Ancestor of Jesus (Lk 3:29).

MATTHEW

Son of Alphaeus; a tax collector by occupation; chosen by Jesus to be one of the 12 apostles; credited with the authorship of the Gospel of Matthew.

Matthew is listed in each of the four rosters of the 12 (Mt 10:3; Mk 3:18; Lk 6:15; Acts 1:13). Aside from these lists, Matthew is mentioned only in the account of his calling (Mt 9:9; Mk 2:13-14; Lk 5:27). Before his apostolic call, the Gospels refer to Matthew as Levi (Mk 2:14; Lk 5:27; compare Mt 9:9). The identity of Levi as Matthew is beyond all doubt. It is improbable that Matthew was the brother of James the Less whose father was also named Alphaeus (Mt 10:3), since this fact would have been mentioned in the record of Scripture, as it is in the cases of Peter and Andrew and the sons of Zebedee.

Matthew served King Herod Antipas in Capernaum of Galilee, collecting tariffs on goods passing on the road from Damascus to the Mediterranean Sea. To function in this capacity Matthew would have been an educated man, acquainted with the Greek language as well as the native Aramaic, thus qualifying him to write the Gospel of Matthew. As a tax collector, Matthew may have been a man of wealth, but this occupation also caused him to be despised by the Jews and to be considered among the lowest of people. The Pharisees consistently spoke of tax collectors in the same breath with sinners (Mt 11:19; Mk 2:16; Lk 7:34; 15:1).

Matthew was called while he was working at his tax booth. Jesus passed by on the road and said to him, "Follow me" (Mk 2:14). Matthew left everything and did so (Lk 5:28). Immediately he gave Jesus a great banquet at his house, and a large crowd of his fellow tax collectors and others were there to enjoy it. It was at this feast that the Pharisees and their scribes made the well-known complaint "Why do you eat and drink with tax collectors and sinners?" (Lk 5:30, NLT mg).

QUICKTAKE

MATTHEW

STRENGTHS AND ACCOMPLISHMENTS
- Was one of Jesus' 12 disciples
- Responded immediately to Jesus' call
- Invited many friends to his home to meet Jesus
- Compiled the Gospel of Matthew
- Clarified for his Jewish audience Jesus' fulfillment of Old Testament prophecies

LESSONS FROM HIS LIFE
- Jesus consistently accepted people from every level of society
- Matthew was given a new life, and his God-given skills of record keeping and attention to detail were given new purpose
- Having been accepted by Jesus, Matthew immediately tried to bring others into contact with Jesus

VITAL STATISTICS
Where: Capernaum
Occupations: Tax collector, disciple of Jesus
Relative: Father: Alphaeus
Contemporaries: Jesus, Pilate, Herod, other disciples

KEY VERSE
"As Jesus was walking along, he saw a man named Matthew sitting at his tax collector's booth. 'Follow me and be my disciple,' Jesus said to him. So Matthew got up and followed him" (Matthew 9:9).

Matthew's story is told in the Gospels. He is also mentioned in Acts 1:13.

It is not certain when Matthew was called, but it is probable that the first six disciples were present on that day, since the Pharisees complained to Christ's disciples during Matthew's feast. Unlike the first men Jesus called, Matthew was not originally a follower of John the Baptist.

MATTHIAS

Disciple of Jesus, mentioned by name only in Acts 1:23-26, chosen to take the place of Judas Iscariot.

Shortly after Jesus' ascension, Peter voiced the need for another apostle, the stipulations being that the candidate must have been a follower of Jesus from his baptism to his ascension and have been a witness to his resurrection. The assembly put forward two men who met these criteria: Joseph called Barsabbas, surnamed Justus, and Matthias. They then cast lots (some scholars believe they cast ballots). Whatever the method, Matthias was chosen. Later, the apostolate was widened to include others such as Paul, Andronicus, and Junias. Scripture never mentions Matthias again, though tradition says that he preached in Judea and was finally stoned to death by the Jews.

MATTITHIAH

1. Levite and Shallum's firstborn son, who was in charge of making the baked cakes that accompanied the offerings in the Temple (1 Chr 9:31).
2. Musician appointed by the Levites to play the lyre, along with five others, when the Ark was brought to Jerusalem in David's time (1 Chr 15:18, 21; 16:5).
3. One of Jeduthun's six sons, who was a musician in David's time (1 Chr 25:3, 21); perhaps identifiable with #2 above.
4. Nebo's son, who divorced his foreign wife as commanded by Ezra (Ezr 10:43).
5. One who stood to Ezra's right when Ezra read the law to the people after the Exile (Neh 8:4).

MEDAD

Elder of Israel who, with Eldad, prophesied in the wilderness to Joshua's consternation. Moses, however, defended Medad's right to speak in God's name (Nm 11:26-27).

MEDAN

Third son of Abraham by his second wife, Keturah (Gn 25:2; 1 Chr 1:32).

MEHETABEL

1. Matred's daughter and the wife of Hadar (Gn 36:39; 1 Chr 1:50), king of Edom in pre-Israelite times.
2. Shemaiah's grandfather. Shemaiah was hired by Tobiah and Sanballat to discredit Nehemiah by frightening him into fleeing into the Temple (Neh 6:10).

MEHIDA

Head of a family of Temple servants in Ezra's time (Ezr 2:52; Neh 7:54).

MEHIR

Kelub's son from Judah's tribe (1 Chr 4:11).

MEHUJAEL

Irad's son and the father of Methushael in Cain's line (Gn 4:18).

QUICKTAKE

MELCHIZEDEK

STRENGTHS AND ACCOMPLISHMENTS
• The first priest/king of Scripture—a leader with a heart tuned to God
• Good at encouraging others to serve God wholeheartedly
• A man whose character reflected his love for God
• A person in the Old Testament who reminds us of Jesus and who some believe really was Jesus

LESSON FROM HIS LIFE
• Live for God and you're likely to be at the right place at the right time. Examine your heart: To whom or what is your greatest loyalty? If you can honestly answer God, you are living for him

VITAL STATISTICS
Where: Ruled in Salem, site of the future Jerusalem
Occupation: King of Salem and priest of God Most High

KEY VERSES
"This Melchizedek was king of the city of Salem and also a priest of God Most High. When Abraham was returning home after winning a great battle against the kings, Melchizedek met him and blessed him.... Consider then how great this Melchizedek was. Even Abraham, the great patriarch of Israel, recognized this by giving him a tenth of what he had taken in battle" (Hebrews 7:1, 4).

Melchizedek's story is told in Genesis 14:17-20. He is also mentioned in Psalm 110:4; Hebrews 5–7.

MEHUMAN
One of the seven chamberlains King Ahasuerus sent to bring Queen Vashti to the royal banquet (Est 1:10).

MELATIAH
Descendant of Gideon who helped repair the Jerusalem wall next to the Old Gate during Nehemiah's time (Neh 3:7).

MELCHIZEDEK
Mysterious biblical personality whose name means "king of righteousness." The historical record about this priest-king is contained in Genesis 14:18-20, and he is spoken of in Psalm 110:4 and Hebrews 5:10; 6:20; 7:1-17.

In Genesis 14:18-20

Kedorlaomer, king of Elam, with three other Mesopotamian kings, raided a vassal confederacy of five kings near the shores of the Dead Sea. In the ensuing massacre and rout by the Mesopotamian confederacy, Abraham's nephew Lot and his family and possessions were captured (Gn 14:1-12). Abraham led an attacking force in pursuit of Lot's captors, achieved victory, retrieved the plunder, and secured the release of Lot and his family (vv 13-16).

Upon his return, Abraham was greeted not only by the grateful kings of the Dead Sea confederacy but also by Melchizedek, king of Salem, who gave Abraham bread and wine along with his blessing as "priest of the most high God" *(El Elyon)* (Gn 14:18). Salem is Jerusalem (cf. Ps 76:2). El Elyon is not the pagan deity of Canaanite worship by the same name but rather the title of the true God who created heaven and earth—an idea foreign to Canaanite religion (cf. Gn 14:22; Pss 7:17; 47:2; 57:2; 78:56). Melchizedek correctly viewed Abraham as worshiping this same God (Gn 14:22) and praised God for giving victory to Abraham. Abraham identified himself with the worship of the one true God represented by Melchizedek in that he received his gifts and blessing and gave him a tenth of everything, thus recognizing Melchizedek's higher spiritual rank as a patriarchal priest. In contrast, Abraham disassociated himself from Canaanite polytheism by declining gifts from the king of Sodom.

It is interesting to speculate whether Melchizedek's knowledge of the true God was received by tradition from the past ages closer to the Flood, or whether he, like Abraham, had been uprooted from paganism to monotheism by direct divine revelation. It is at least clear from Hebrews 7:3 that his priesthood was isolated and not received through a priestly pedigree.

In Psalm 110:4

In this messianic psalm, David envisioned one greater than himself whom he called "Lord" (v 1; cf. Mk 12:35-37). Thus the perfect messianic king was not an idealization of the present ruler but someone to come. Also, he was to be not merely a man but more than this. The Messiah would be the Son of God as well as the son of David. The divine oracle of Psalm 110:4 is addressed to the Messiah: "You are a priest forever in the line of Melchizedek." The significance of this statement is left for the inspired author of the letter to the Hebrews to develop.

In Hebrews 5:6-11; 6:20–7:28

The argument of the writer of Hebrews is that the priesthood of Aaron has been superseded by the superior priesthood of Christ and that the superiority of Christ's priesthood is demonstrated by its Melchizedekian character. First, both Christ and Melchizedek are kings of righteousness and kings of peace (Heb 7:1-2). Second, both have a unique priesthood that does not depend on family pedigree (v 3). Third, both exist as priests continually (v 3).

Melchizedek was superior to Abraham, the father of Levi, because Melchizedek gave gifts to and blessed Abraham, and received tithes from him (7:4-10); David predicted the succession of the Melchizedekian priesthood over the Levitical priesthood, showing the imperfection of the latter (vv 11-19); the Melchizedekian priesthood of the Messiah was confirmed by a divine oath, which was not true of the Levitical priesthood (vv 20-22); and the Melchizedekian priesthood possessed an unchangeable and permanent character (vv 23-25).

Certain scholars have thought that Melchizedek was an appearance of the preincarnate Christ in the OT (technically called a Christophany). They argue this on the basis of Hebrews 7:3, which says that there is no record of his father or mother or any of his ancestors—no beginning or end to his life. However, this statement is simply to be understood in the sense that his priesthood was not connected to any priestly family line. Melchizedek had a priestly office by special divine appointment, and was thus a type of Jesus Christ in his priesthood. The writer of Hebrews says that Melchizedek was one "resembling the Son of God" (7:3); this clearly indicates that he was not himself the Son of God.

See also Priests and Levites.

MELEA
Ancestor of Jesus, according to Luke's genealogy (Lk 3:31).

MELECH
Micah's son from Benjamin's tribe (1 Chr 8:35; 9:41).

MELKI
1. Jannai's son, according to Luke's genealogy (Lk 3:24).
2. Addi's son, according to Luke's genealogy (Lk 3:28).

MEMUCAN
One of the seven princes of Persia and Media under King Ahasuerus (Est 1:14-21). He brought charges against Vashti, the Persian queen, who had refused to make a royal appearance that the king had commanded (v 16). Memucan proposed that she be divested of her position and the queenship given to another; the king took his counsel and issued a decree to that effect (v 21). Hence Esther was chosen as queen over Media and Persia.

MENAHEM
King of Israel who ruled from 752–742 BC. He was the son of Gadi, a name not attested in the OT except in 2 Kings 15:14-22.

Virtually everything that the OT records about the career of Menahem is contained in a few brief verses in 2 Kings 15. Three important points may be noted from these verses.

First, 2 Kings 15:14 records the assassination of Shallum, which enabled Menahem to seize the throne. Verse 16 then recounts the actions of Menahem against the town of Tappuah (Tiphsah). The entire verse is troublesome but may be translated as follows (NLT): "At that time Menahem destroyed the town of Tappuah and all the surrounding countryside as far as Tirzah, because its citizens refused to surrender the town. He killed the entire population and ripped open the pregnant women." Two things are unusual. First, the actions of Menahem are quite without precedent in Israelite history. Second, the location and identity of the town that Menahem attacked are uncertain. The Hebrew text reads "Tiphsah" (see NLT mg), using the spelling of a town normally identified as Thapsacus on the Euphrates. Menahem's reasons for attacking a town this far away from his own territory and interests would be difficult to determine. Accordingly, some scholars have followed the Lucianic version of the Greek Bible that reads the Hebrew letters as if they were "Tappuah," a town 14 miles (22.5 kilometers) southwest of Menahem's hometown of Tirzah. If this reading is correct, and the textual evidence for it is limited to the one version, the meaning of 2 Kings 15:16 is that Menahem began just outside the boundaries of his hometown (Tirzah) and put to the sword the entire population of a neighboring town (including its citizens who lived outside the city proper) that failed to support his bid to become king.

Second, 2 Kings 15:19-20 provides the biblical view of the way in which Menahem dealt with the Assyrian crisis posed by the campaign of Tiglath-pileser III into the Syro-Palestinian region (c. 744). Evidently hoping to persuade the Assyrians to support his claims to the throne in Israel, Menahem levied a stiff tax upon the wealthy citizens of his nation to be used to pay tribute to Tiglath-pileser (called by his Babylonian name "Pul" in v 19). Evidently Menahem hoped this payment would convince the Assyrian king "to gain his support in tightening his grip on royal power" (v 19). Politically at least, Menahem appears to have guessed correctly, because the Assyrians withdrew (v 20) and Menahem was left in power.

Finally, the reign of Menahem is introduced (2 Kgs 15:17) and concluded by the standard literary forms employed throughout the books of Kings. Despite the fact that Menahem was judged to be just as sinful as the original apostate (Jeroboam I) had been, 2 Kings 15:22 appears to attest an unusual fact about his death. Of the last six kings of Israel, only he died a peaceful death.

MENNA
Ancestor of Jesus, according to Luke's genealogy (Lk 3:31).

MEONOTHAI
Othniel's son from Judah's tribe (1 Chr 4:13-14).

MEPHIBOSHETH
1. Son of Jonathan, David's friend. The original form of the name was undoubtedly Merib-baal (1 Chr 8:34; 9:40), but when the word *baal* became predominantly associated with the chief male deity of the Canaanite fertility cult, it was replaced, in some instances, by the Hebrew word *bosheth* (meaning "shame"). As the grandson of Saul, Mephibosheth was born into a situation of privilege, which changed dramatically when the Philistines attacked. Saul, Jonathan, and two of his brothers were killed in

the battle on Mt Gilboa (1 Sm 31:1-6). When news of the catastrophe reached the Israelite palace at Jezreel, the five-year-old Mephibosheth was snatched up by his nurse. In a panicked scramble for safety, she fell, dropping Mephibosheth, whose legs or ankles were broken. The lack of adequate medical attention meant that he became completely crippled (2 Sm 4:4). Eventually, he found refuge at Lo-debar in Transjordan, with Makir, who later on befriended David himself (9:4; 17:27).

Mephibosheth's uncle, Ishbosheth (Saul's only surviving son), who had been made Israel's puppet king (2:8-10) was murdered (ch 4). Mephibosheth, although apparently next in succession, appears not to have been considered. When David was established on the throne of a now united kingdom and wished to show kindness to any surviving members of Jonathan's family, he was informed of Mephibosheth's existence by Ziba, once an influential steward in Saul's palace (9:1-13). Summoned to Jerusalem, Mephibosheth was naturally apprehensive, probably fearing that David might want to eliminate all possible rivals (see 19:28). But David's generous nature showed itself in restoring to Mephibosheth all of Saul's original land, with Ziba and his family continuing to manage the estate, and in granting the cripple a permanent place at the royal table.

When Absalom's rebellion broke out, Ziba met the fleeing David and supplied him with welcome provisions, taking the opportunity to curry favor at the expense of his master. Mephibosheth, he suggested, even entertained hopes of gaining the kingdom for himself. David, in the stress of the crisis, was taken in by this unlikely story and promised Ziba all Mephibosheth's property (2 Sm 16:1-4). The civil war over, Mephibosheth himself came to David with clear evidence of his grief at the latter's exile and therefore of Ziba's duplicity. But David, not willing to alienate Ziba and probably grateful for his earlier gift, compromised, dividing the land between the two. Mephibosheth's genuine joy at the king's restoration was such that the loss of his land was of no account in comparison (19:24-30). Later, when seven descendants of Saul were slain to appease the Gibeonites, David's continuing remembrance of Jonathan resulted in Mephibosheth's being spared (21:7). Mephibosheth's son, Mica (9:12), became the head of a considerably large family (1 Chr 8:35; 9:41).

2. Son of Rizpah, Saul's concubine. Unlike his better-known namesake, he was one of Saul's seven descendants who had to be hung in order to appease the Gibeonites, whose ancient treaty with Israel had been violated by Saul, causing a three-year famine (2 Sm 21:8; see Jos 9:3-27). In the sequel (2 Sm 21:10-14), Rizpah's untiring vigil over the corpses prompted David to give them a decent burial, together with the remains of Saul and Jonathan, in the family sepulcher.

MERAB
Eldest of Saul's two daughters (1 Sm 14:49), who was promised as a wife to David (18:17-18). Saul unexplainedly did not keep the agreement, instead giving him Michal.

MERAIAH

Head of Seraiah's priestly family during the priesthood of Joiakim in postexilic Jerusalem (Neh 12:12).

MERAIOTH

1. Levite, six to seven generations removed from Aaron (1 Chr 6:6-7; Ezr 7:3).
2. Ahitub's son and the father of Zadok (1 Chr 9:11; Neh 11:11); perhaps identifiable with #1 above, despite differences in genealogy.
3. Priestly house whose head was Helkai during the days of Joiakim in postexilic Jerusalem (Neh 12:15). Its forebear is given as Meremoth (v 3). Some regard Nehemiah 12:15 as a scribal error and identify the names in verses 3 and 15 as the same person.

MERARI

Transliteration of a Hebrew word meaning "bitter," "bitter drink," or "to be bitter." It means the same in Arabic and Akkadian, but in Ugaritic it means "to strengthen, to bless." Traditionally, the word has been understood to be derived from the Hebrew and thus to mean "gall" or "bitterness." But the Ugaritic root meaning "to strengthen, to bless" is not foreign to the Hebrew way of thinking. When used as a person's name, it probably should be understood to mean "strength" or "blessing." Such an understanding may be preferred in many biblical references. In the case of Merari, the third son of Levi, this understanding is preferable in noting his importance and that of his family. It is inconsistent for the youngest son to have a name meaning "gall" or "bitterness" and then to have the greatest responsibility and the greatest reward for his service.

The Bible makes numerous references to Merari the son of Levi. He was the youngest of Levi's three sons (Gn 46:11; Ex 6:16-19; Nm 3:17-20, 33; 1 Chr 6:1). He was the father of two sons, Mahli and Mushi (Ex 6:19; Nm 3:20), who had the responsibility of carrying the frames (KJV "boards"), bars, pillars, bases (KJV "sockets"), vessels, and accessories of the Tabernacle (Nm 3:36-37; 4:31-33; 7:8; 10:17; Jos 21:7, 34, 40). His descendants are known as Merarites. Chronicles makes numerous references to Merari's family as an indication of its importance (1 Chr 6; 9; 15; 23; 26; 2 Chr 29; 34).

MERED

Ezrah's son from Judah's tribe, who had two wives. One wife, Bithiah, was the daughter of Pharaoh, and one was a Jewess (1 Chr 4:17-18).

MEREMOTH

1. Priest, son of Uriah, grandson of Hakkoz (Ezr 8:33; Neh 3:4, 21). The family of Hakkoz was unable to prove its descent; therefore, they were excluded from the priesthood. Meremoth appears to be an exception. He weighed silver and gold (a priestly function

[Ezr 8:24-30]), repaired part of the Jerusalem wall (Neh 3:4, 21), and sealed the covenant (10:5).

2. Priest and Bani's son, who severed ties with his foreign wife and children at Ezra's request (Ezr 10:36).

3. Priest who returned from Babylon with Zerubbabel (Neh 12:3) and established the house of priests called Meraioth in Nehemiah 12:15 (though some identify the two references as the same person).

MERES
One of the seven princes of Persia and Media who acted as personal adviser to King Ahasuerus (Est 1:14).

MERIBAH
1. Noun meaning "strife," named for a place at Horeb, near Rephidim (Wadi Feiran), where Israel contended with Moses for water near the beginning of the wilderness wanderings (Ex 17:7). This is the place probably alluded to in Deuteronomy 33:8 and Psalm 95:8, and is alternately called Massah.

2. Another place, near Kadesh-barnea in the wilderness of Zin, where Israel also quarreled with Moses for water, and God again provided it from a rock (Nm 20:13, 24; 27:14); alternately called Meribath-kadesh in Deuteronomy 32:51. This episode took place toward the close of the desert wanderings. The waters of Meribah were waters of contention. Here God's anger was provoked against Moses and Aaron because they did not listen to him and sanctify him before Israel. Instead of speaking to the rock as God commanded, Moses—angered at Israel's hardness of heart—struck the rock twice with his rod. The psalmist records that here God tested Israel (Ps 81:7), and Israel's subsequent rebellion prodded Moses to sin (106:32). Meribah-kadesh is mentioned as a place on Israel's southern border (Ez 47:19; 48:28).

MERIBBAAL
Original name for Mephibosheth, the handicapped son of Jonathan (1 Chr 8:34; 9:40). The name means "Baal contends" and is displaced by the later name (Mephibosheth, meaning "idol breaker") in 2 Samuel 4:4 and 9:6. The substitution of *bosheth* ("shame") for *baal* ("lord") was not uncommon when the term acquired its idolatrous connotation (cf. 2 Sm 11:21). See Mephibosheth #1.

MERODACH-BALADAN
Name meaning "Marduk has given a son!" Second Kings 20:12-19 and Isaiah 39 present a parallel account of Merodach-baladan, son of Baladan, king of Babylon, sending envoys to King Hezekiah of Judah.

Shalmaneser V, king of Assyria, captured Samaria in 722 BC and threatened King Hezekiah in Jerusalem but then died within a year's time. Sargon II succeeded him in 722 BC. At that time Merodach-baladan, living south of Babylon in the land called Bit-Yakin, formed an alliance with the Elamites and seized the throne of Babylon, referred to as the second jewel of the Assyrian crown. Sargon II immediately made efforts to regain Babylon as a province in the Assyrian Empire. He must not have been successful initially, for Merodach-baladan reigned over Babylon for 10 years. In 710 BC Sargon succeeded in defeating him and captured the Babylonian fortresses. Merodach-baladan escaped. After Sargon died in 705 BC, Merodach-baladan, in 703 BC, was able to recapture and hold the throne of Babylon for a short period. It is considered most plausible that during this short reign Merodach-baladan sent envoys to Hezekiah in Jerusalem, as he also is thought to have sent them to Edom, Moab, Ammon, and others, seeking to form an alliance against Assyria. The Arabian desert between Babylon and Palestine made such an alliance ineffective, and the new king of Assyria, Sennacherib, thoroughly destroyed Merodach-baladan and then turned to the nations on Palestinian soil.

Isaiah rebuked Hezekiah for receiving the envoys from Babylon, the province that had broken away from the Assyrian Empire and that in a very short time was again forced into the Assyrian Empire. In Isaiah's rebuke lies the prediction that Babylon would become the invading and despoiling nation in the future. Hezekiah, knowing Assyria's power and Babylon's inability to cope with it at that time, felt quite safe as far as Babylon was concerned (2 Kgs 20:19).

MESHA

1. King of Moab in the ninth century BC whose name is derived from a root meaning "to save or deliver." According to 2 Kings 3:4-5, Mesha was a sheep breeder who paid heavy tribute to Israel during the time of Ahab but rebelled after Ahab's death (2 Kgs 1:1). Later, Jehoram the son of Ahab joined with Jehoshaphat of Judah and the king of Edom in an attempt to reestablish hegemony over Moab. When the battle went against the Moabites, Mesha took his eldest son and offered him as a human sacrifice upon the wall of the city to the Moabite god Chemosh (3:27).

2. Caleb's son and the father of Ziph (1 Chr 2:42). In the Greek text the latter part of this verse appears to say that Mesha was the father of Hebron, though the Hebrew text here substitutes the name Mareshah for Mesha. The RSV (following the Septuagint) reads Mareshah in both places. *See* Mareshah #1.

3. Benjaminite and one of the sons of Shaharaim born by Hodesh in the land of Moab (1 Chr 8:9).

MESHACH

One of the three companions of the prophet Daniel who was thrown into the fiery furnace (Dn 1:7; 2:49; 3:12-30). *See* Shadrach, Meshach, and Abednego.

MESHECH

1. Son of Japheth and Noah's grandson (Gn 10:2). His descendants are usually mentioned in connection with Tubal, Gog, or Magog (Ps 120:5; Ez 27:13; 32:26; 38:2-3; 39:1). They are called Muski in Assyrian records and inhabited the mountains north of Assyria during the reigns of Tiglath-pileser I (1115–1102 BC), Shalmaneser III (859–824 BC), and Sargon (722–705 BC). The people of Meshech are characterized as aggressive and pagan, traders in bronze and slaves with Tyre.

2. Shem's son according to 1 Chronicles 1:17, but rendered Mash in the parallel passage in Genesis 10:23. The latter is generally accepted.

MESHELEMIAH

Korahite Levite, Kore's son from the house of Asaph, and a gatekeeper of the sanctuary with his sons in the time of David (1 Chr 9:21; 26:1-2, 9); alternately called Shelemiah in 1 Chronicles 26:14.

MESHEZABEL

1. Ancestor of Meshullam who helped repair the Jerusalem wall (Neh 3:4).

2. Political leader who signed Ezra's covenant of faithfulness to God during the postexilic period (Neh 10:21).

3. Father of Pethahiah, an adviser to King Artaxerxes regarding the people in Judah (Neh 11:24).

MESHILLEMITH

Alternate spelling of Meshillemoth in 1 Chronicles 9:12. *See* Meshillemoth #2.

MESHILLEMOTH

1. Father of Berekiah, a chief of Ephraim (2 Chr 28:12).

2. Ancestor of the postexilic priest Amashsai (Neh 11:13); alternately spelled Meshillemith in 1 Chronicles 9:12.

MESHOBAB

Prince of Simeon's tribe in the days of Hezekiah, who, with 12 other princes, moved to Gedor, dispossessed its pagan people (the Meunim), and settled his family there (1 Chr 4:34).

MESHULLAM

1. Forefather of Shaphan, the royal secretary to King Josiah of Judah (2 Kgs 22:3).

2. Zerubbabel's son and a descendant of David (1 Chr 3:19).

3. Gadite leader registered during the reigns of Jotham, king of Judah (950–932 BC), and Jeroboam II, king of Israel (993–953 BC; 1 Chr 5:13).

4. Benjaminite and a descendant of Elpaal (1 Chr 8:17).

5. Benjaminite and the father of Sallu, a resident in Jerusalem during the postexilic period (1 Chr 9:7; Neh 11:7).

6. Benjaminite and the son of Shephatiah, who resided in Jerusalem during the postexilic period (1 Chr 9:8).

7. Priest, the son of Zadok and the father of Hilkiah, whose descendants served in Jerusalem's sanctuary during the postexilic era (1 Chr 9:11; Neh 11:11). He is probably identical with Shallum in 1 Chronicles 6:12-13.

8. Priest, the son of Meshillemith and a forefather of Adaiah. Adaiah served in Jerusalem's sanctuary during the postexilic era (1 Chr 9:12).

9. Kohathite Levite who was appointed to oversee the repair of the Temple during King Josiah's reign (2 Chr 34:12).

10. One of the Jewish leaders whom Ezra sent to Iddo at Casiphia to gather Levites and Temple servants for the caravan of Jews returning to Palestine from Babylonia (Ezr 8:16).

11. One who opposed Ezra's suggestion that the sons of Israel should divorce the foreign women they had married since returning to Palestine from exile (Ezr 10:15).

12. Bani's son, who was encouraged by Ezra to divorce his foreign wife during the postexilic era (Ezr 10:29).

13. Berekiah's son, who rebuilt a section of the Jerusalem wall during the days of Nehemiah (Neh 3:4, 30). His daughter married Jehohanan, the son of Tobiah the Ammonite (6:18).

14. Besodeiah's son, who with Joiada repaired the Old Gate in the Jerusalem wall (Neh 3:6).

15. One of the men who stood to Ezra's left when Ezra read the law to the people (Neh 8:4).

16. One of the priests who set his seal on the covenant of Ezra (Neh 10:7).

17. One of the leaders of Israel who set his seal on the covenant of Ezra (Neh 10:20).

18. Head of Ezra's priestly family during the days of Joiakim, the high priest, in postexilic Jerusalem (Neh 12:13).

19. Head of Ginnethon's priestly family during the days of Joiakim (Neh 12:16).

20. One of the gatekeepers during the days of the high priest Joiakim (Neh 12:25); perhaps identifiable with Shallum in 1 Chronicles 9:17.

21. One of the princes of Judah who participated in the dedication of the Jerusalem wall during the postexilic era (Neh 12:33).

MESHULLEMETH

Mother of Amon, king of Judah (642–640 BC) and the daughter of Haruz of Jotbah (2 Kgs 21:19).

MESSIAH

Title derived from the Hebrew, *mashiach,* a verbal adjective meaning "anointed one." Along with its NT equivalent, *christos* (Christ), it refers to an act of consecration whereby an individual is set apart to serve God and then anointed with oil. The verbal root *(mashach)* conveys this idea as well.

Israel's practice of ceremonially anointing with oil is present in several contexts. Priests were regularly anointed prior to their divinely given service at the altar of sacrifice (Lv 4:3). While there is evidence for a literal anointing of prophets (1 Kgs 19:16), this does not appear to have been a standard practice. The anointing of Saul and David by Samuel established the act as a significant prerequisite for Hebrew kings before they assumed their positions of royal leadership. The king was especially considered to be the Lord's anointed and as such was viewed to hold a secure position before men (1 Sm 12:14; 2 Sm 19:21) and God (Pss 2:2; 20:6). Along with numerous messianic prophecies, these proceedings helped inform the Jews of the Anointed One, par excellence, who would eventually come to bring salvation to Israel.

Concluding the 13 articles of Hebraic faith attributed to Moses Maimonides (13th century AD) is the statement still found in many Hebrew prayer books: "I believe with a perfect heart that the Messiah will come; and although his coming be delayed, I will still wait patiently for his speedy appearance."

Messiah in the Old Testament

Jewish hope for the advent of the Messiah developed dynamically from the period of David's reign, when it was prophesied that his kingdom would endure to the end of time (2 Sm 7:16). Israel was told that, through David's descendants, his throne would exert a never-ending dominion over all the earth (2 Sm 22:48-51; Jer 33). It is with this aspect of messianic salvation that Jewish minds have traditionally been preoccupied (cf. Acts 1:6).

Among Orthodox rabbis there has never been a lack of conjecture respecting the details of the Messiah's ministry. At one time the rabbis applied no less than 456 passages of Scripture to his person and salvation. Preoccupation with the Messiah is evident in the tractate *Sanhedrin* (Babylonian Talmud), where passages state that the world was created for him and that all the prophets prophesied of his days (*Sanhedrin* 98b, 99a). By and large, Orthodoxy still retains its time-worn belief in the Messiah's reign in Jerusalem, the rebuilding of the Temple, and the reestablishment of both priesthood and sacrifice.

While later Judaism looked for the Messiah as an eschatological figure who will reign at the end of time, modern Jewish thought has largely jettisoned the traditional notion of a personal Messiah in favor of belief in a messianic age. Prevalent liberal Judaism envisions the world ultimately perfected through the influence of the twin Judaic ideals of justice and compassion. Such conviction, ignoring the plight of fallen humans and the teaching of Scripture, substitutes humanistic thinking for miraculous heavenly intervention.

While the Messiah's origin is linked firmly to the house of David (2 Sm 7:14; Hos 3:5), the promise for a Messiah was given long before David lived. In fact, the hope for the Messiah is implicit in the first promise of the establishment of the kingdom of God. Addressed to Satan, Genesis 3:15 declares that God will place hostility between the serpent and the woman until, in the fullness of time, the "seed" of the woman inflicts a fatal blow to the head of the serpent.

The nature of messianic prophecy is progressive; each prophecy casts more light on the subject. This occurs, for example, respecting the concept of the "seed": Messiah is to be born of a woman (Gn 3:15), through the line of Shem (9:26) and specifically through Abraham (22:18). Yet even as late as Genesis 22:18, the "seed" is not clearly presented as a person, since *zerah* (seed) may indicate a singular or plural object. Still less apparent in these early stages of messianic prophecy is the nature of the "bruising" that is to occur. Yet the idea of the Messiah being crushed for sin is implicit in the Genesis pronouncement, as is the violence associated with that act. Chief among the messianic prophets, Isaiah gives full range to the axiom that the Anointed One must endure extensive suffering (Is 53:1). Under the figure "the Servant of the Lord," four "servant songs" delineate the mission of the future deliverer (Is 42:1-7; 49:1-9; 50:4-11; 52:13–53:12). While it is true that Isaiah does not explicitly link the title Messiah with the Servant of the Lord, identifying both figures as one and the same person is justifiable. Both figures are uniquely anointed (61:1); each brings light to the Gentiles (55:4; cf. 49:6); neither is pretentious in his first appearance (7:14-15; 11:1; cf. 42:3; 53:1); and the title of Davidic "branch" rests upon them both (11:1-4). Equally significant are the dual facts of their humiliation and exaltation (49:7; 52:13-15). Jewish scholars of the early Christian era in the Aramaic Targum on the prophets paraphrase Isaiah 42:1, "Behold my Servant Messiah" and begin Isaiah 53, "Behold my Servant Messiah will prosper." While Cyrus may be spoken of as "anointed," no final salvific work is attributed to him (45:1-5). Israel, although elect and loved by God (41:8), is ill-equipped as God's servant to bring his redeeming work to mankind (42:18). The collapse of David's dynasty points eloquently to Israel's need for an anointed monarch who will heal the apostasy and disobedience (Ex 33:5; Hos 4:1). More and more, OT history presents Israel's comprehensive moral failure. Her problem, which she shares with mankind, can only be solved by the making of a covenant whose surety and focal point is both a personal Savior and sovereign Lord (Jer 31:31-34). The advent of such a champion lives in the recorded promise of a shoot from the stump of Jesse's fallen tree, who will bring the light of life to God's benighted people (Is 9:2; 11:1).

It is difficult to get away from the idea that the concept of servanthood and lowliness belongs within the sphere of royalty (Zec 9:9). The concept of the Messiah filling the complementary offices of priest and king is incontrovertible (Ps 110:1-4); a suffering priest-king is far less obvious. Some among the Talmudic writers apparently recognized the likelihood that the Messiah would have to suffer. In the Babylonian Talmud, tractate *Sanhedrin* 98b, the Messiah is said to bear sicknesses and pain. Among the prayers for the Day of Atonement may be found the words of Eleazar ben Qalir (perhaps as late as AD 1000): "Our righteous Messiah has departed from us; we are horror-stricken, and there is none to justify us. Our iniquities and the yoke of our transgressions he carries, and is wounded for our transgressions. He bears on his shoulders our sins to find pardon for our iniquities. May we be healed by his stripes." In a similar vein Rabbi Eliyya de Vidas writes, "The meaning of 'He was wounded for our transgressions, bruised for our iniquities,' is that since the Messiah bears our iniquities, which produce the effect of His being bruised, it follows that whosoever will not admit that the Messiah thus suffers for our iniquities must endure and suffer for them himself." For all this, it is highly doubtful that anyone imagined the Messiah would accomplish his salvational work by means of his own death (cf. Is 53:12). When rabbinic speculation failed to satisfactorily harmonize the paradoxical facts of humiliation and exaltation, some hypothesized that God would send a Messiah to suffer as well as a Messiah to reign. Biblically, it is evident that the Anointed One's terrible ordeal of suffering is but the necessary prelude to infinite glory. He is pictured not only as a great king (52:13; 53:12) but also as humble (53:2), humiliated (52:14), rejected (53:3), and bearing the consequences of mankind's rebellion (vv 5-6). Yet he is raised up to intercede for, and richly bless, his people (v 12). The Messiah, having accomplished that full obedience that Adam and Israel failed to achieve, will bring Israel and the nations back to God (42:18-19; 49:3, 6).

The writings of Daniel contain important messianic data. Daniel is unique in that he boldly speaks of "Messiah the Prince" (Dn 9:25), identifies him as the "Son of Man" (7:13), and says he suffers ("cut off," 9:26). This statement of the cutting off (i.e., death) of the Messiah makes possible his work of atonement (9:24). The doctrine of a vicarious substitutionary atonement is the only doctrine of atonement found in the Bible (cf. Lv 17:11). Israel understood that to bear sin meant enduring the consequences, or penalty, for sin (cf. Nm 14:33). The same penal substitution is evident in the working principle of the Messiah's atoning sacrifice. He is the victim's substitute to whom is transferred the suffering due the sinner. The penalty having been thus borne vicariously, the suppliant is fully pardoned.

Psalm 22:1 records the plaintive cry of the Messiah bearing man's penalty for sin (cf. Mt 27:46) as he becomes sin on behalf of his people (2 Cor 5:21). Yet his cry, "My God," indicates an intimate relationship that cannot be radically severed. Once again the motif of messianic humiliation prior to great exaltation is in view (Ps 22:27). In the so-called "royal psalms" (e.g., 2; 72; 110) it is the priestly intercessor who is also ordained to function as monarch and judge.

Jeremiah brings the portrait a step further. The one who will enable humans to enter into a salvational covenant with God conveys God's imputed righteousness: the Messiah, God's righteous branch, becomes "the Lord our Righteousness." Paradoxically, under the law no one could be crucified who was not guilty of sin (Dt 21:22). But it is Christ the righteous one who was crucified, thereby forever undermining any supposed legalistic confidence (Dt 21:23; Gal 3:13). More than forgiven, believers are deemed righteous in him (Jer 23:5-6).

While the birthplace of the Messiah was well established (Mi 5:2), his deity was a hotly contested matter. Although few in ancient Israel disputed the belief in a superhuman Messiah, it is doubtful that anyone imagined him to be "God with us" in the fullest sense of the expression (cf. Heb 1:3).

Messiah in the New Testament

The NT writers present the picture that he who was the child of supernatural origins (Is 7:14; Mi 5:2) carried the full weight of divinity (Is 9:6; Phil 2:6; Col 1:19). He is the Son of God, worthy to receive the worship of all people (Ps 45:6-7; cf. Heb 1:8-9).

The Jews of first-century Palestine knew that the messianic promise would be fulfilled in the coming of one like Moses (Dt 18:18). Parallels between Jesus and Moses are abundant. As mediators, innovators, and propagators of new phases of spiritual life for the people, they are unexcelled. Specifically, both are miraculously spared in infancy (Ex 2; Mt 2:13-23); both renounce a royal court for the sake of serving the people of God (Phil 2:5-8; Heb 11:24-28); both exhibit intense compassion for others (Nm 27:17; Mt 9:36); both commune "face to face" with God (Ex 34:29-30; 2 Cor 3:7); and each mediates a covenant of redemption (Dt 29:1; Heb 8:6-7). But, as Luther observes, "Christ is no Moses." In the final analysis Moses is but a household servant; the Messiah is the maker and master of all things (Heb 3:3-6; cf. Jn 1:1-2, 18).

Family genealogies are important in Scripture. Rabbis agreed upon the absolute necessity of the Messiah's Davidic lineage based on Hosea 3:5 and Jeremiah 30:9. The angelic announcement immediately establishes the correct lineage for Jesus (Lk 1:32-33; cf. 2:4), as does Matthew's (Mt 1:1-17). The Lukan list, like that of Matthew, sets forth the exclusive kingly descent verifying Jesus as Messiah (Lk 3:23-38). Although variations occur between the two genealogies, there is a firm solidarity emphasizing an ancestry within the unique messianic stock. Fully aware of the messianic focus of Scripture (Jn 5:46; 8:56), Jesus acknowledged himself to be the Christ on numerous occasions. He accepted the title from blind Bartimaeus (Mk 10:46-48); from the crowds when he entered Jerusalem (Mt 21:9); from the children at the Temple (v 15); and in other contexts as well (Mt 16:16-18; Mk 14:61-62; Lk 4:21; Jn 4:25-26). Nonetheless, he warned his disciples not to broadcast his mighty acts as Messiah prior to his resurrection (Mt 17:9; cf. Lk 9:20-21). Owing to the commonly held (but false) notion that the Messiah's role was primarily that of a political liberator, Jesus actually avoided use of that term and preferred to identify himself as "the Son of Man." It was by no means assumed that both designations referred to the same person (cf. Mk 14:61-62). Borrowing essentially from Daniel's vision of a heavenly conqueror (Dn 7:13-14), Jesus consistently employed this less-known title and filled it with the true character and scope of messianic salvation. Jesus' teaching in this regard enabled his disciples to correct their erroneous views concerning his mission (Mt 16:21-23). In the fullness of time they would come to see him not only as Messiah but also as the theme of the entire OT (Mt 5:17; Lk 24:27, 44; Jn 5:39; cf. Heb 10:7). When Jesus expounded the Scriptures beginning with the Torah (Lk 24:27), he did so as the living exegesis of God, the Word made flesh (Jn 1:14, 18). Legitimate messianic exposition is found in a host of texts, such as Psalms 2; 16; 22; 40; 110; Isaiah 7:14; 9:6; 11:1; 40:10-11; 50:6; 52:13–53:12; 61:1; 63:1-6; Jeremiah 23:5-6; 33:14-16; Ezekiel 34:23; 37:25; Daniel 9:24-27; Hosea 11:1; Micah 5:2; Zechariah 9:9; 11:13; 12:10; 13:7; Malachi 3:1; 4:2.

The messiahship of Jesus is firmly proclaimed by all four evangelists (Mt 1:1; Mk 1:1; Lk 24:26; Jn 20:31). Peter on Pentecost, Philip before the Ethiopian eunuch, and Apollos in open debate all argue convincingly that Jesus is the Messiah (Acts 2:36; 8:35; 28:28). Peter says he was "made" both Lord and Christ (2:36), signifying that the resurrection rightfully confirms him as such. Similarly, the apostle Paul speaks of Jesus' resurrection as a patent declaration of his inalienable right to the title (Rom 1:4). For the ex-Pharisee and former persecutor of the church, "Jesus the Christ" is the very heart and soul of Paul's preaching. Nothing is worthy to be compared to the glory of the Messiah; everything pales by comparison (Phil 3:5-10). The apostle's all-consuming passion is for others to know the fullness of God in the person of his only Son (Eph 3:14-19).

The Holy Spirit in Scripture speaks of Jesus with wide-ranging appellatives—Holy One, Judge, Righteous One, King, Son of God, and Lord—but these are not exhaustive. In him all the lines of messianic prediction converge; he is the touchstone whereby their validity is firmly established. The Lord Jesus Christ is himself the heart and substance of that covenant through which sinful people may be reconciled to a holy God (Is 42:6; Jn 14:6). That Jesus is the Messiah of Israel, God incarnate, exhaustively fulfills prophecy, type, and symbol—all shadows of his coming. Therefore, all should trust in him, the source of all grace, the only abiding treasure (Mt 12:21; Jn 1:16-17; Col 2:3). Anointed as prophet, he leads us into all truth (Jn 6:14; 7:16); as priest he intercedes for us (Heb 7:21); and as king he reigns over us (Phil 2:9-10).

METHUSELAH
Son of Enoch, Lamech's father, and the grandfather of Noah through Seth's line (Gn 5:21-27; 1 Chr 1:3). Living 969 years, Methuselah is the oldest recorded person in the Bible. His lineage is included in Luke's genealogy of Christ (Lk 3:37).

METHUSHAEL
Mehujael's son and the father of Lamech in Cain's line (Gn 4:18).

MEZAHAB
Matred's father and the grandfather of Mehetabel, the wife of the Edomite king Hadar (or Hadad) (Gn 36:39; 1 Chr 1:50).

MIBHAR
Warrior among David's mighty men, who were known as "the thirty" (1 Chr 11:38).

MIBSAM

1. One of Ishmael's sons and the founder of a tribe named after him (Gn 25:13; 1 Chr 1:29).

2. Shallum's son and the father of Mishma (1 Chr 4:25).

MIBZAR

Chief of Edom (Gn 36:42; 1 Chr 1:53). The name means "fortress." Eusebius connects Mibzar with Mibsara, a large town in Edom.

MICA

Common name interchangeable with Micah and probably a contracted form of Micaiah.

1. Mephibosheth's son. He shared in the fortunes of David's generosity to his father, and in Ziba's treachery (2 Sm 9:12).

2. Levite and Zicri's son from Asaph's clan (1 Chr 9:15), who performed musical service in the Temple. He appears to have been one of the Exiled priests whose son Mattaniah was among the first group of returning exiles (also called "the son of Zabdi," Neh 11:17, 22, and Micaiah, the son of Zaccur, 12:35).

3. One who set his seal on Ezra's covenant during the postexilic era (Neh 10:11).

MICAH

1. Ephraimite judge who had idols made and then hired a Levite to become his priest (Jgs 17–18).

2. Shimei's descendant from Reuben's tribe (1 Chr 5:5).

3. Alternate spelling of Mica, Mephibosheth's son and the great-grandson of King Saul, in 1 Chronicles 8:34-35; 9:40-41. See Mica #1.

4. KJV spelling of Mica, Zicri's son, in 1 Chronicles 9:15. See Mica #2.

5. Levite and Uzziel's son from Kohath's clan, whose Temple responsibilities included care of the furniture and equipment (1 Chr 23:20; 24:24-25).

6. Alternate spelling of Micaiah, Acbor's father, in 2 Chronicles 34:20. See Micaiah #2.

7. Prophet and author of the OT book that bears his name (Mi 1:1). A native of Moresheth, a town about 21 miles (33.8 kilometers) southwest of Jerusalem, Micah prophesied to both northern and southern kingdoms during the reigns of Jotham, Ahaz, and Hezekiah (750–686 BC). According to Micah 1:9, he was still prophesying in 701 BC when the Assyrian armies under Sennacherib (cf. Is 36–37) besieged Jerusalem. About 100 years later, Micah is used as an example of an early prophet who predicted the destruction of Jerusalem (cf. Jer 26:16-19).

MICAIAH

1. Prophet and Imlah's son, called by Ahab to forecast the result of projected battles

against the Syrians. At first Micaiah mocks him with glad news, then tells the cruel truth. Ahab casts the prophet into prison as a kind of ransom, but the wicked ruler dies in battle, just as Micaiah predicted (1 Kgs 22:8; 2 Chr 18:7-25).

2. Father of Acbor, one of the court officials whom King Josiah sent to the prophetess Huldah to get an opinion on the Book of the Law that Hilkiah the high priest had found in the Temple (2 Kgs 22:12; 2 Chr 34:20, "Abdon, son of Micah").

3. Alternate rendering of Maacah, mother of Judah's King Abijah, in 2 Chronicles 13:2. *See* Maacah #4.

4. Teacher commissioned by King Jehoshaphat to teach the law of the Lord throughout Judah (2 Chr 17:7).

5. Alternate spelling of Mica, Zicri's son, in Nehemiah 12:35. *See* Mica #2.

6. Priest who blew a trumpet at the dedication of the Jerusalem wall (Neh 12:41).

7. Gemariah's son, who reported the words of the Lord to Jewish princes during the reign of King Jehoiakim (Jer 36:11-13).

MICHAEL

Name meaning "Who is like God?" used of 10 men in Scripture and also of a supernatural being who is described as an archangel.

1. Father of one of the spies sent by Moses into Canaan (Nm 13:13).

2–3. Gadites named in the lists of those who settled in the land of Bashan (1 Chr 5:13-14).

4. Forefather of Asaph, a Temple singer in the days of David (1 Chr 6:40).

5. Chief man of Issachar in the Temple lists (1 Chr 7:3).

6. Benjaminite named in the Temple lists (1 Chr 8:16).

7. Man of Manasseh who joined David in Ziklag when he was fleeing from Saul (1 Chr 12:20).

8. Father of Omri, a top political officer in the days of David (1 Chr 27:18).

9. Son of King Jehoshaphat of Judah (2 Chr 21:2).

10. Father of Zebadiah, a returnee with Ezra to Jerusalem (Ezr 8:8).

11. Angel in the OT, intertestamental literature, and the NT. In Daniel 10:13 it is said that "the spirit prince of the kingdom of Persia" sought to oppose the purpose of God, but Michael, "one of the archangels," contended against this evil spirit at the Lord's side (Dn 10:21). His conflict on behalf of Israel is referred to further in Daniel 12:1.

In the book of Enoch, Michael is one of four (Enoch 9:1; 40:9) or of seven (20:1-7) special angels or "archangels." In Enoch, in the War Scroll (of the Dead Sea Scrolls), and in other intertestamental literature, Michael regularly is presented either as the champion of the cause of the righteous or as the patron angel of Israel.

The book of Jude, apparently alluding to the Assumption of Moses, speaks of the archangel Michael as having contended with the devil in a dispute about the body of Moses (Jude 1:9; cf. 2 Pt 2:10-11; see also the reference to "the archangel" in 1 Thes 4:16). The only other reference to Michael in the NT is Revelation 12:7-8, where it is said, "Then there was war in heaven. Michael and the angels under his command fought the dragon and his angels. And the dragon lost the battle and was forced out of heaven" (NLT).

MICHAL

Younger daughter of Saul (1 Sm 14:49). She fell in love with David after his defeat of Goliath (18:20). Saul, jealous of David, offered his first daughter, Merab, to David, but the recent victor graciously declined. When Michal's love became known to Saul, he renewed his offer of a wife, providing David produce evidence of having killed 100 Philistines—a condition Saul felt would surely lead to David's death.

David met Saul's condition in double measure and married Michal. Saul's jealousy was only fanned, and he plotted to have David murdered. Michal heard of the plot and assisted in her husband's escape (1 Sm 19:8-17). During David's exile, Saul gave Michal to Palti (25:44).

Following Saul's death, Abner negotiated with David, part of the agreement being the return of Michal to David's household. This was done despite Palti's remorse (2 Sm 3:12-16). But youthful ardor had apparently suffered strain. When David returned with the Ark to Jerusalem, dancing before it, Michal voiced her harsh criticism. David's reply was equally severe. Michal would remain childless as punishment for her candidness. (The KJV, using inferior manuscripts, reports Michal as the mother of five sons in 2 Samuel 21:8. Adriel, however, was the husband of Merab—a correction reflected in modern versions.)

David's overwhelming popularity should not overshadow the courage and passion displayed by Michal. She let her love be known when women hardly took the initiative in courtship, saved David's life at the risk of her own, was emotionally victimized by her forced marriage to and separation from Palti, and voiced her critical convictions against the tide of public opinion.

MICRI

Ancestor of a family who returned to Jerusalem with Zerubbabel after the Babylonian captivity (1 Chr 9:8).

MIDIAN

Person whose descendants figure prominently only in the early history of Israel, in connection with Abraham (Gn 25:1-6), Joseph (37:25-36), Moses (Ex 2:15–3:1), Balaam (Nm 22:1-6; 25; 31:1-20), and Gideon (Jgs 6:1–8:28).

Midian was Isaac's younger half brother, the fourth of six sons born to Keturah, whom Abraham married as an old man (Gn 25:1-2; cf. 23:1-2; 24:67; 1 Chr 1:32). By calling Midian and his full brothers "the sons of Keturah" (Gn 25:4; 1 Chr 1:32-33), the Bible carefully distinguishes them from Isaac, the son of Sarah, who was the one through whom God's promise to Abraham would be fulfilled (Gn 12:1-3; 17:15-21). In fact, Abraham and the Israelites regarded these other sons as having no more inheritance rights than a concubine's sons (Gn 25:5-6; 1 Chr 1:31).

MIJAMIN

1. Priest who ministered during the time of David (1 Chr 24:9).
2. Parosh's son, who was encouraged by Ezra to divorce his foreign wife during the postexilic period (Ezr 10:25).
3. One of the priests who signed Ezra's covenant during the postexilic period (Neh 10:7).
4. Priest who returned to Jerusalem with Zerubbabel after the Exile (Neh 12:5, NLT "Miniamin").

MIKLOTH

1. Resident of Gibeon, son of the Benjaminite Jeiel, and father of Shimeah (1 Chr 8:32; 9:37-38).
2. Officer in David's army who served under Dodai (1 Chr 27:4), according to some manuscripts.

MIKNEIAH

Levite of the second order who was a gatekeeper and musician during David's reign (1 Chr 15:18, 21).

MILALAI

Participant in the dedication of the rebuilt Jerusalem wall (Neh 12:36).

MILCAH

1. Daughter of Haran and half sister of Nahor who became Nahor's wife (Gn 11:29). She bore Nahor eight sons (22:20-23). Through her son Bethuel she was the grandmother of Rebekah (24:15-47).
2. One of the five daughters of Zelophehad. Because Zelophehad had no sons, his daughters petitioned Moses to allow them to receive their father's inheritance in west Manasseh after their father's death (Nm 26:33; 27:1-11; 36:5-13; Jos 17:3-4).

MINIAMIN

1. Levite who assisted Kore, the son of Imnah, with the distribution of the "contribution reserved for the Lord" among the priests in the cities of Judah (2 Chr 31:14-15).
2. Head of a priestly house during the postexilic era (Neh 12:17). He was also called "Mijamin" (12:5).
3. Participant in the dedication of the Jerusalem wall (Neh 12:41).

MINNI

People mentioned in Jeremiah 51:27, along with Ararat and Ashkenaz, as aggressors against Babylon. The Minni first appear in Assyrian inscriptions during the reign of Shalmaneser III (858–824 BC), who pillaged and subdued the people. They lived between Lake Urmia and Lake Van, north of Babylon, and are identified with the Mannean people, regularly associated with Urarteans (Ararat) in Assyrian manuscripts. The Minni were restless subjects. They revolted against Assyria in 716 and 715 BC. Further agitation occurred in the reign of Ashurbanipal (669–627 BC). After Nineveh's fall to the Babylonians in 612 BC, the Minni disappear from the extrabiblical record.

MIRIAM

1. Daughter of Amram and Jochebed and the sister of Aaron and Moses (Ex 15:20; Nm 26:59; 1 Chr 6:3). Miriam first appears in Scripture as a young girl commissioned with the task of watching her infant brother's cradle hidden in the reeds of the Nile River (Ex 2:4)—the result of a scheme conceived by her parents (Heb 11:23)—to escape the pharaoh's edict that all Hebrew males be drowned at birth (Ex 1:22). Miriam evidences not only courage and concern, but also displays a certain wisdom when her brother is discovered by the Egyptian princess (2:5-6). Taking the initiative, she offers to secure a nurse for the child, and when this plan is accepted, she gets her mother (vv 7-8).

   Miriam first appears by name after the Israelites have crossed the Red Sea (Ex 15:20). She is given the title of "prophetess" and is, with her brothers, appointed a leader in the nation (Mi 6:4). Following the death of the Egyptian charioteers she leads the women of Israel in an anthem of praise accompanied with dancing and instrumental music (Ex 15:21).

   Miriam appears in disgrace after her jealousy of and rebellion against Moses. With Aaron she murmurs against Moses because of his superior influence in the nation and because of his marriage to a Cushite woman (Nm 12:1-2). For this attack against God's chosen spokesman, she is struck with leprosy (v 10). Moses, however, intercedes on her behalf (Nm 12:9-13), and she was restored, but only after seven shameful days spent outside the camp while Israel waits to resume its march (Nm 12:14-15). This sad incident is the last recorded event in Miriam's public life. She died near the close of the wilderness wanderings at Kadesh and was buried there (20:1).

2. Child of Mered, descended from Ezra of Judah's tribe (1 Chr 4:17).

MIRMAH

Son of Shaharaim and Hodesh from Benjamin's tribe (1 Chr 8:10).

MISHAEL

1. Uzziel's son (Ex 6:22), who, with his brother Elzaphan, was summoned by Moses

to remove the bodies of Nadab and Abihu after they were killed for defiling the altar of the Lord (Lv 10:1-5).

2. One who stood beside Ezra when the law was read (Neh 8:4).

3. Hebrew name for one of Daniel's companions in Babylon (Dn 1:6), who, with Daniel and two others, remained faithful to God (vv 11, 19) and was delivered from the fiery furnace into which he had been cast for refusing to obey the king's edict (ch 3). His Babylonian name was Meshach (1:7).
   See also Shadrach, Meshach, and Abednego.

MISHAM

Elpaal's son from the tribe of Benjamin, who helped to build Ono and Lod with its towns (1 Chr 8:12).

MISHMA

1. Son of Ishmael, Abraham's grandson, and the father of an Arabian tribe (Gn 25:14; 1 Chr 1:30).

2. Mibsam's son from Simeon's tribe (1 Chr 4:25-26). His omission in Genesis 25 and inclusion in the 1 Chronicles genealogy may indicate either that he was born after Jacob moved his family to Egypt or that he represented an Arabian tribe that affiliated with Simeon when Simeon's tribe expanded to the south (1 Chr 4:38-43).

MISHMANNAH

Warrior from Gad's tribe who joined David at Ziklag in his struggle against King Saul (1 Chr 12:10).

MISHRAITE

Descendant of Caleb and a member of Kiriath-jearim's family from Judah's tribe (1 Chr 2:53).

MISPAR

One of the men who returned with Zerubbabel to Palestine following the Babylonian captivity (Ezr 2:2); alternately called Mispereth in Nehemiah 7:7.

MITHREDATH

1. Name of the treasurer of King Cyrus of Persia, who was given charge of the sacred vessels to give to the Judean prince Sheshbazzar as the Exiles prepared to return to Jerusalem (Ezr 1:8).

2. Persian officer stationed in Samaria who, along with others, wrote a letter to King Artaxerxes of Persia, protesting the restoration of the city and walls of Jerusalem (Ezr 4:7).

MIZZAH

Reuel's son and a chief of an Edomite clan (Gn 36:13, 17; 1 Chr 1:37).

MNASON

Name of a Christian in Jerusalem (Acts 21:16). He is identified as a native of the island of Cyprus and a disciple of long standing. On their arrival at Jerusalem, Paul and his traveling party were entertained as guests by Mnason.

MOAB

A son of Lot (Gen 19:37) and his descendants who later dwelt in a small kingdom in central Transjordan. Ruth (for whom the book of Ruth is named) is perhaps the Bible's best known Moabite.

The land of Moab was situated on the high plateau immediately east of the Dead Sea; the escarpment of the Jordan Rift formed an effective boundary between Moab and Judah. Even at its peak, ancient Moab encompassed a relatively small territory, measuring only about 60 miles (96.5 kilometers) north-south by about 20 miles (32.2 kilometers) east-west. Most of Moab was gently rolling tableland that is divided by numerous ravines. Running through the heart of Moab is the King's Highway, a route that probably had military and commercial importance throughout this region's history (Nm 21:21-22; Jgs 11:17). The plateau has always been famous for its abundant pasturage (2 Kgs 3:4), and Moab's soil and climate are quite suitable for growing wheat and barley.

Origin and History

According to Genesis 19:37, the Moabites descended from Moab, the son of Lot and his oldest daughter. Deuteronomy 2:10-11, a passage whose context relates to the Moabites at the time of the Hebrew invasion, says that the pre-Moabite inhabitants of this region were the Emim, but the connection between Lot's descendants, the Emim, and the occupants of Moab at the time of the Hebrew invasion is not identified. There is thus far no specific information concerning the establishing of the Moabite kingdom proper, which existed from around 1300 BC to 600 BC. Knowledge of this period of Moabite history and culture is derived from archaeological and textual sources, including Egyptian, Assyrian, and OT texts.

Prior to the Israelites' passage through Transjordan, the Moabites had lost control of the land north of the Arnon and were dominated by Sihon, the Amorite king who ruled at Heshbon (Nm 21:13, 26). After the Israelites defeated Sihon, King Balak of Moab feared they might take his land and waged war against the Hebrews (Nm 22:6; Jos 24:9). He hired the Mesopotamian diviner, Balaam, to pronounce a curse upon his enemies (Nm 22–24).

Later, the Moabite king Eglon oppressed the Hebrew tribes on both sides of the Jordan (Jgs 3:12-30). By Jephthah's day, northern Moab was once again under Israelite control (11:26). Obviously, as the book of Ruth indicates, there were also periods in which Moab and Israel lived in peace.

During the reigns of Saul and David, from the late-11th until the mid-10th centuries BC,

Moab and Israel were at war, with Israel usually holding the upper hand (1 Sm 14:47; 2 Sm 8:2). Solomon's harem included Moabite women, and he also built a high place for Chemosh, the chief god of the Moabites (1 Kgs 11:1,7). Following the division of the Israelite monarchy in 930 BC, Moab experienced a brief period of independence, but this ended when Omri and Ahab dominated the Moabites and their king, Mesha, during the ninth century BC. (The famous Moabite Stone, which describes Mesha's conflict with the Omride dynasty, and several shorter texts demonstrate that the language of Moab was closely related to OT Hebrew.) Conflict between Moab and her neighbors (e.g., Israel, Judah, Edom, and most importantly, Assyria) continued until the Babylonian king Nebuchadnezzar destroyed the Moabite kingdom early in the sixth century BC (Ez 25:8-11). This conflict is documented in the Assyrian literature, which indicates that Moab became an Assyrian vassal in the late eighth century BC, and in the OT (2 Kgs 3; 10:32-33; 13:20; 24:2). Indeed, the enmity between Moab, Israel, and Judah is especially evident in a series of prophetic oracles leveled against the Moabites (Is 15–16; Jer 9:25-26; 48; Am 2:1-3; Zep 2:8-11). These passages call attention to some of the major towns in ancient Moab (Nebo, Medeba, Heshbon, Dibon, Ar, Kir, and Horonaim).

Following the Babylonian conquest, the region of Moab fell under Persian control and was occupied by various Arab peoples, most notably the Nabateans. Although a Moabite state was never reestablished, people of Moabite ancestry were recognized in late OT times (Ezr 9:1; Neh 13:1,23), since the postexilic Jewish community was concerned about observing the law recorded in Deuteronomy 23:3-6.

Religion

During the third and second millennia BC, Moabite religion was probably similar to that practiced by the Canaanites, though the religion of Moab eventually developed into a relatively distinct system. Although other deities were worshiped by the Moabites, Chemosh was their national god. The OT refers to the Moabites as "people of Chemosh" (Nm 21:29; Jer 48:46), and the frequent appearance of "Chemosh" in Moabite personal names points to this god's elevated status. In general, the Moabite Stone's dozen references to Chemosh portray him as a god of war who leads his people against their enemies.

Divine guidance and favor were sought, and diviners and oracles were respected (Nm 22–24). A priesthood (Jer 48:7) and sacrificial system (Nm 22:40–23:30; 25:1-5; 2 Kgs 3:27; Jer 48:35) were important aspects of Moabite religion. No Moabite sanctuary has been discovered, but their existence is mentioned in the Moabite Stone and the OT (1 Kgs 11:7; 2 Kgs 23:13). Elaborately furnished tombs, like those found at Dibon, point to the Moabites' belief in the afterlife.

MOADIAH

Head of a family of postexilic priests, whose house was headed by Piltai during the days of Joiakim the high priest (Neh 12:17); alternately called Maadiah in verse 5. He is perhaps identifiable with the priest Maaziah, who set his seal on Ezra's covenant (10:8).

QUICKTAKE

MORDECAI

STRENGTHS AND ACCOMPLISHMENTS
- Exposed an assassination plot against the king
- Cared enough to adopt his cousin
- Refused to bow to anyone except God
- Took Haman's place as second-in-command under Xerxes

LESSONS FROM HIS LIFE
- The opportunities we have are more important than the ones we wish we had
- We can trust God to weave together the events of life for our best, even though we may not be able to see the overall pattern
- The rewards for doing right are sometimes delayed, but they are guaranteed by God himself

VITAL STATISTICS
Where: Susa, one of several capital cities in Persia
Occupation: Jewish official who became second in rank to Xerxes
Relatives: Adopted daughter: Esther. Father: Jair
Contemporaries: Xerxes, Haman

KEY VERSE
"Mordecai the Jew became the prime minister, with authority next to that of King Xerxes himself. He was very great among the Jews, who held him in high esteem, because he continued to work for the good of his people and to speak up for the welfare of all their descendants" (Esther 10:3).

Mordecai's story is told in the book of Esther.

MOLID

Son of Abishur and Abihail from Judah's tribe (1 Chr 2:29).

MORDECAI

1. Jewish leader during the Exile. Our knowledge of Mordecai comes exclusively from the book of Esther, which, according to some rabbinic sources, Mordecai himself wrote. Mordecai's activities are set against the period in which Xerxes (Ahasuerus) reigned over ancient Persia, a vast empire stretching over 127 provinces. Mordecai

was a Benjaminite descendant of Kish, the father of King Saul. His relatives were among those Jews who left Palestine during the captivity of Nebuchadnezzar. While his name reveals a Babylonian etymology, his heart burned with love for his countrymen who, notwithstanding the decree of Cyrus permitting their return to the Holy Land (538 BC), determined to colonize in dispersion rather than face the hardships of resettling in Palestine.

His remarkable life's drama is intertwined with Hadassah (Esther), his cousin, who became his ward following the death of her parents. Esther's sudden, unexpected exaltation to the position of queen following Vashti's deposition was an essential link to the deliverance of her people; Mordecai's forceful influence upon this beautiful Jewess was another. Behind them both, however, moved their sovereign God, whose love for Israel provided protection against the malevolent designs of Xerxes' prime minister, Haman.

Haman, the very incarnation of evil, had determined to exterminate the Jews of Persia because of Mordecai's unwillingness to pay him homage. Mordecai, learning of the plot, communicated the matter to Esther by way of Hathach, one of the king's officers. Her initial hesitancy to intervene on behalf of her people was met with her cousin's concise and stern answer: "Do not think that because you are in the king's house you alone of all the Jews will escape. For if you remain silent at this time, relief and deliverance for the Jews will arise from another place, but you and your father's family will perish. And who knows but that you have come to royal position for such a time as this?" (Est 4:13-14, NIV).

Several days elapsed during which Haman erected an enormous "gallows" upon which to hang (or possibly impale) Mordecai. On the evening of its completion, Xerxes, being unable to sleep, ordered the book containing the record of his reign to be read to him. Upon hearing of the actions of Mordecai in frustrating an earlier assassination attempt against him, he inquired as to what honors Mordecai had received in recognition of his service. Finding he had not been rewarded, Xerxes summoned Haman and asked him what fitting thing should be done for the man the king had purposed to honor. Haman, thinking that he was the object of the king's query, responded with three grand ideas (Est 6:7-9). Ironically, Haman was chosen to carry out his recommendations on behalf of Mordecai. A final touch of irony is seen in the execution of Haman on the very instrument he had prepared for Mordecai.

Following Haman's death, Mordecai and Esther had to act quickly to counteract the irrevocable edict directed against the Jews at Haman's instigation. Xerxes, now solicitous of the Jews' well-being, issued another edict allowing the Jews the freedom both to defend themselves and to retaliate against any aggressors. Apparently, the Persian officials to whom Mordecai forwarded this follow-up directive cooperated fully in protecting the Jews from their adversaries, thousands of whom were slain.

Consequently, Mordecai instructed all Jews to celebrate the time of their deliverance annually on the 14th and 15th days of Adar (roughly, March). The name of

QUICKTAKE

MOSES

STRENGTHS AND ACCOMPLISHMENTS
- Egyptian education; wilderness training
- Greatest Jewish leader; set the Exodus in motion
- Prophet and lawgiver; recorder of the Ten Commandments
- Author of the Pentateuch

WEAKNESSES AND MISTAKES
- Failed to enter the Promised Land because of disobedience to God
- Did not always recognize and use the talents of others

LESSONS FROM HIS LIFE
- God prepares, then uses. His timetable is life-sized
- God does his greatest work through frail people

VITAL STATISTICS
Where: Egypt, Midian, wilderness of Sinai
Occupations: Prince, shepherd, leader of the Israelites
Relatives: Sister: Miriam. Brother: Aaron. Wife: Zipporah. Sons: Gershom and Eliezer

KEY VERSES
"It was by faith that Moses, when he grew up, refused to be called the son of Pharaoh's daughter. He chose to share the oppression of God's people instead of enjoying the fleeting pleasures of sin" (Hebrews 11:24, 25).

Moses' story is told in the books of Exodus through Deuteronomy. He is also mentioned in Acts 7:20-44; Hebrews 11:23-29.

the festival, Purim, is derived from the word *pur* ("lot"), which was cast by Haman to determine the day for the Jews' annihilation.

2. One of the 10 leaders who returned with Zerubbabel after the Exile (Ezr 2:2; Neh 7:7).

MOSES
Great leader of the Hebrew people who brought them out of bondage in Egypt to the Promised Land in Canaan; also the one who gave them the law at Mt Sinai that became the basis for their religious faith through the centuries. Focused in this one person are the figures of prophet, priest, lawgiver, judge, intercessor, shepherd, miracle worker, and founder of a nation.

The meaning of his name is uncertain. It has been explained as a Hebrew word meaning "to draw out" (Ex 2:10; cf. 2 Sm 22:17; Ps 18:16). If, however, it is an Egyptian name given him by the daughter of Pharaoh who found him, it is more likely from an Egyptian word for "son" (also found as part of many well-known Egyptian names such as Ahmose, Thutmose, and Ramses). No one else in the OT bears this name.

Without question, the greatest figure in the OT (mentioned by name 767 times), his influence also extends to the pages of the NT (where he is mentioned 79 times). The first 40 years of his life were spent in the household of Pharaoh (Acts 7:23), where he was instructed in all the wisdom of the Egyptians. The next 40 years he spent in Midian as a fugitive from the wrath of Pharaoh, after killing an Egyptian who was mistreating a Hebrew. His last 40 years were devoted to leading the Israelites out of bondage in Egypt to the land God had promised to Abraham and his descendants (Gn 12:1-3). He died at the age of 120 after leading the Israelites successfully through 40 years of wandering in the wilderness to the very edge of the Promised Land on the east side of the Jordan River (Dt 34:7). He is one of the great figures in all of history, a man who took a group of slaves and, under inconceivably difficult circumstances, molded them into a nation that has influenced and altered the entire course of history.

Preview

- Background
- The First 40 Years—In Egypt
- The Second 40 Years—In Midian
- The Third 40 Years—From Egypt to Canaan
- Moses in the New Testament

Background

The only source of information for the life of Moses is the Bible. Archaeology confirms the credibility of the events associated with Moses, but it has never provided any specific confirmation of his existence or work. His story begins with the arrival in Egypt of Jacob, his sons, and their families during a time of famine in Canaan. Invited by Joseph and welcomed by Pharaoh, the family settled down in northeast Egypt in an area known as Goshen, where they remained for 430 years (Ex 12:40). With the passing of time, their numbers grew rapidly, so that the land was filled with them (1:7). A new king arose over Egypt who did not know Joseph. The biblical account does not give the name of this pharaoh, and there has never been agreement as to his identity. He has most frequently been identified as Thutmose III (1504–1451 BC), Seti I (1304–1290 BC), or Ramses II (1290–1224 BC). Out of fear that their growing numbers might become a threat to the security of his nation, Pharaoh determined to take measures to reduce their number. He put them to work building the store cities of Pithom and Rameses, but the severity of the work did not diminish them. He next tried to enlist the cooperation of the midwives to destroy the male babies, but they would not carry out his orders. He then ordered his own people to drown the male infants in the Nile River. Against the background of this first-known Jewish persecution, the baby Moses was born.

The First 40 Years—In Egypt
Birth and Early Life
A man of the family of Levi named Amram married his father's sister Jochebed (Ex 6:20; cf. 2:1). Their first son, Aaron, three years older than Moses, was born before the command to drown the Hebrew babies was given, as there is no indication that his life was in danger. However, the cruel order was in force when Moses was born, and after three months, when his mother could no longer hide him, she took a basket made of bulrushes and daubed it with bitumen and pitch. She put the baby into the basket and placed it among the reeds along the banks of the river. An older sister, Miriam, stayed near the river to see what would happen. Soon the daughter of Pharaoh (identified by Josephus as Thermuthis and by others as Hatshepsut, but whose actual identity cannot be determined) came to the river to bathe, as was her custom. She discovered the baby, recognized it as one of the Hebrew children, and determined that she would raise the child as her own. Miriam emerged from her hiding place and offered to secure a Hebrew woman to nurse the child, an arrangement that was agreeable to the princess. Miriam took the baby to his own mother, who kept him for perhaps two or three years (cf. 1 Sm 1:19-24). Nothing is recorded of those formative years. Whether his mother continued seeing him during his later childhood and young manhood or revealed his true identity to him or taught him the Hebrew faith are matters of speculation. Moses was instructed in all the wisdom of the Egyptians, as would befit a member of the royal household, and he became mighty in his words and deeds (Acts 7:22).

Identification with His Own People
Just when Moses became aware that he was a Hebrew rather than an Egyptian cannot be known, but it is clear that he knew it by the time he was 40 years old. One day he went out to visit his people and to observe their treatment, for the cruel measures taken against them by Pharaoh at the time of Moses' birth had not been lifted. Seeing an Egyptian beating a Hebrew, Moses in great anger killed the Egyptian and buried him. He thought the deed had gone unnoticed until the next day when he encountered two Hebrews fighting with each other. When he tried to act as peacemaker, they both turned on him and accused him of murder: "Who made you a prince and a judge over us? Do you mean to kill me, as you killed the Egyptian?" (Ex 2:14, RSV). Acts 7:25 adds: "He supposed that his brethren understood that God was giving them deliverance by his hand" (RSV). Aware that being a member of Pharaoh's household would not exempt him from punishment now that the deed was known, Moses fled for his life to the land of Midian.

The Second 40 Years—In Midian
Marriage into the Family of Jethro
Soon after arriving in Midian, Moses sat down by a well, where he observed the seven daughters of the priest of Midian who had come to the well to draw water for their father's

flock. Shepherds came and drove them away, but Moses intervened and helped them water their animals. When Jethro (Ex 3:1; also called Reuel, 2:18; Hobab, Nm 10:29) learned what had happened, he invited Moses to stay with his family and gave him Zipporah as his wife. (There is some disagreement among scholars regarding the identity of Hobab in Numbers 10:29; some think he was Moses' father-in-law, while others maintain that Hobab was Moses' brother-in-law. *See also* Hobab). Two children, Gershom (Ex 2:22) and Eliezer (18:4), were born to Moses and Zipporah during the years in Midian. Forty years passed, and Moses' thoughts about his former life in Egypt must have faded into the past. He could not have foreseen that God would soon thrust him back into the midst of the court in Egypt, where he would confront the son of the now-dead pharaoh with the demand to release the Hebrew people from the bondage they had endured for so many years. God had not forgotten his people and was now ready to deliver them.

Encounter with God at the Burning Bush

One day, while Moses was taking care of the flocks of his father-in-law, he led them to Mt Horeb (known also as Sinai), where God appeared to him in a flame of fire out of the midst of a bush that burned but was not consumed. Moses approached to observe the strange sight more closely and heard God speak to him out of the bush, "Moses, Moses!" Moses replied, "Here am I." Before he could come any nearer to the bush, God said, "Do not come near; put off your shoes from your feet, for the place on which you are standing is holy ground" (Ex 3:4-5, RSV). He further identified himself as the God of Abraham, Isaac, and Jacob. He assured Moses that he was aware of the cruel afflictions of his people and had heard their cries. Then he told of his plan to send Moses to Egypt to deliver his people from their bondage.

Faced with a challenge that seemed beyond his capabilities, the aged Moses began making excuses for not accepting the task. God assured Moses that he would be with him (Ex 3:11-12). To his excuse that he would not be able to give an answer if the people asked him the name of the God he represented, God revealed his name in the cryptic statement, "'I AM WHO I AM' . . . Just tell them, 'I AM has sent me to you'" (vv 13-14, NLT). Many interpretations have been proposed for the name. Whatever else it means, it undoubtedly suggests the self-existence and all-sufficiency of God. Moses then argued that the people would not believe him when he told them that God had sent him to deliver them from Egypt. In response God gave him three signs: When he cast his shepherd's rod to the ground, it became a serpent. When he put his hand to his bosom, it became leprous. He was also told that when he would pour water from the Nile on the ground, it would become blood (Ex 4:1-9). Even armed with these powerful evidences of the presence of God with him, Moses raised still another objection, "O Lord, I'm not very good with words. I never have been, and I'm not now, even though you have spoken to me. I get tongue-tied, and my words get tangled" (v 10, NLT). God told him that he would teach him what to say, but despite such assurance, Moses asked God to send someone else. In anger mingled with compassion, God made Moses' brother, Aaron, the spokesman, but said his instructions would still be given directly to Moses.

Return to Egypt

Moses took his wife and sons and set out for Egypt, telling his father-in-law only that he wanted to go back to Egypt to visit his kinsmen there (Ex 4:18). The biblical account says he put his wife and sons on the same donkey to journey back to Egypt (v 20). The fact that all three rode the same animal indicates that both children were quite young and had not been born in the early years of Moses' marriage. At a lodging place along the way a strange thing happened. The Lord met him and sought to kill him (v 24), apparently because Moses had failed to circumcise the baby before leaving Midian. When Zipporah realized that Moses' life was in danger, she performed the rite herself and said to her husband, "Now you are a bridegroom of blood to me!" (v 25, NLT). Whatever else may have been involved in this unusual encounter with God, it was a solemn reminder that the one who was to be the leader of the covenant people must not himself neglect any part of the covenant (Gn 17:10-14).

God told Aaron (who was still in Egypt) to go to the mountain where Moses had encountered God at the burning bush and meet his brother there. Moses told Aaron everything that had happened, and together they went to Egypt, gathered the elders together, and informed them of these matters. When Moses and Aaron performed the signs in the presence of the people, they believed these leaders had been sent by God to deliver them from their affliction (Ex 4:30-31).

The Third 40 Years—From Egypt to Canaan
The Encounter with Pharaoh

Soon after his return to Egypt, Moses, accompanied by Aaron, went to Pharaoh and repeated the demands of the Lord, "Let my people go so they may hold a festival in my honor in the wilderness" (Ex 5:1, NLT). Pharaoh rejected the demand with the observation that he had never heard of this God of Moses. When one realizes that Egyptian kings considered themselves to be gods, the affront to Pharaoh becomes even more acute. Not only did he reject Moses' demands, but he intensified the burdens of the Hebrews. Their work had up until then required them to make brick

MOSES
The Times of Moses

C. 1526 BC
Moses is born to Israelite slaves in a time when Israelite babies are being killed (Exodus 1–2).

C. 1526–1486 BC
Moses is "adopted" by Pharaoh's daughter and raised in Egyptian royal court (Exodus 2:5-10).

C. 1486 BC
Moses kills an Egyptian taskmaster and must flee to desert (Exodus 2:11-15).

C. 1486–1446 BC
Moses lives in the Sinai Desert as a nomadic shepherd (Exodus 2:16–3:1).

C. 1447 BC
Moses meets God at the burning bush and is called to free Israel from Egypt (Exodus 3–4).

C. 1446 BC
Moses meets with Pharaoh and demands, "Let my people go." (Exodus 5–11).

C. 1446 BC
After ten plagues, Pharaoh releases the Israelites; the first Passover (Exodus 12).

C. 1446 BC
Moses parts the Red Sea for the Israelites to cross (Exodus 14).

C. 1446–1445 BC
Moses receives the law from God at Mount Sinai (Exodus 19–32).

C. 1444–1406 BC
Moses leads the Israelites as they wander the wilderness (Numbers 1–36).

C. 1406 BC
Moses dies on Mount Nebo, overlooking the Promised Land (Deuteronomy 34).

using straw provided for them, but now Pharaoh said they would have to gather their own straw and still produce the same number of bricks. The Hebrews turned in anguish and anger to Moses and blamed him for making them offensive in the sight of Pharaoh. Even Moses could not understand the turn of events and complained bitterly to God. God reassured Moses that he would deliver the Hebrews from their bondage, and moreover, he would bring them into the land he had promised Abraham, Isaac, and Jacob. He then instructed Moses to return to Pharaoh and repeat the demand to release the Hebrews upon threat of severe reprisal if the demand were ignored.

Ushered again into Pharaoh's presence, Moses repeated his request for release of the Israelites. He attempted to impress Pharaoh by turning his rod into a serpent, but the Egyptian wise men, through their secret arts, were able to duplicate the miracle, so Pharaoh's heart remained hardened and he would not listen to Moses. In rapid succession Moses brought nine plagues upon the land of Egypt to show the omnipotence of God to force the compliance of Pharaoh. These included a plague in which the water of the Nile turned to blood, a plague of frogs, one of gnats, then of flies, a plague on the livestock, boils on the people, plagues of hail, locusts, and complete darkness. During the plagues of the frogs, flies, hail, locusts, and darkness, Pharaoh was distraught and would temporarily relent and agree to Moses' demands, but as soon as the plague was lifted, his heart hardened and he would retract his promise. The outcome of the first nine plagues was terrible devastation of the land of Egypt, but the Israelites were not released. There was yet one more plague in store, the most terrible of all.

The First Passover

God told Moses that there remained one more plague in store for the Egyptians: "All the firstborn sons will die in every family in Egypt, from the oldest son of Pharaoh, who sits on his throne, to the oldest son of his lowliest servant girl who grinds the flour. Even the firstborn of all the livestock will die" (Ex 11:5, NLT). Furthermore, he assured Moses that the plague would not touch a single household of the Hebrews, "Then you will know that the LORD makes a distinction between the Egyptians and the Israelites" (v 7, NLT).

God instructed the people through Moses and Aaron to make their preparations for leaving the land in haste. They were to go to the Egyptians and ask them for their jewels of silver and gold (Ex 11:2-3), a request to which the Egyptians agreed, perhaps out of fear of the Hebrews and in the belief that the gifts would bring about an end of the terrors that had struck the land. The Hebrews were also instructed to prepare a lamb for each family— small families could share—for the last meal to be eaten in the land of Egypt (a rite that became the pattern for the Jewish observance of the Passover for many centuries). Blood of the lamb was to be put on the doorposts and lintels of the houses in which the Passover meal was being eaten that night. The Hebrews were promised that wherever the blood was on the door, no harm would come to that household. They were also instructed to prepare unleavened bread. At midnight the death angel of the Lord killed all the firstborn in the land of Egypt, from the firstborn of Pharaoh himself to the lowest captive in a dungeon; not a single house of the Egyptians escaped tragedy. When Pharaoh saw what had happened, he ordered Moses and the people to leave the land at once (12:31-32). The biblical record says that about 600,000 Hebrew men left Egypt. Together with women and children, the total would have been in excess of 2 million people.

The Exodus from Egypt

The Exodus is the central event of the OT and marks the birth of Israel as a nation. The Jewish people still look back to that event as the great redemptive act of God in history on behalf of his people, much as Christians look upon the cross as the great redemptive act of their faith.

The exact route taken by the Hebrews out of Egypt cannot be determined today, though many possibilities have been proposed. They did not take the shortest, most direct route to Canaan (which would have been about a 10 days' journey along the Mediterranean coastline), but set out in the direction of Mt Sinai, where Moses had earlier met God at the burning bush. As a sign that Moses had been sent to deliver the people, God told Moses he would bring them to that same spot, where they would worship God (Ex 3:12). The Hebrews did not forget the request of Joseph to carry his bones with them when they returned to their own land (Gn 50:25; Ex 13:19).

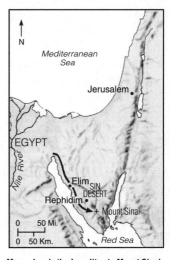

Moses Leads the Israelites to Mount Sinai

As the people journeyed, they were preceded by a pillar of cloud during the day and a pillar of fire at night. The cloud represented the presence of God with his people and guided them along the route they should travel.

Back in Egypt, Pharaoh was having second thoughts about letting the Hebrews leave the land and decided to pursue them with his army and bring them back. When the Hebrews saw the approaching cloud of dust and realized that the Egyptian army was pursuing them, they were terrified. The sea lay ahead of them and the Egyptians were behind; there seemed to be no way of escape. The people turned on Moses, blaming him for bringing them out of Egypt. God again assured them that they did not need to be afraid or do anything to defend themselves. He promised to fight the battle for them and give them victory (Ex 14:14).

The Lord parted the water of the Sea of Reeds (traditionally but erroneously referred to as the Red Sea) by a strong east wind and allowed the Israelites to pass through the sea on dry ground to the other side. The Egyptians rushed after the Israelites, following them into the dry bed of the sea. But before they reached the other side, the waters rushed back together, destroying the Egyptian army in the midst of the sea and leaving the Israelites safe on the other side. The people celebrated their great deliverance in song (Ex 15) and then continued their journey. The narrative that follows describes the struggle of the Israelites to survive in the desert—problems of food and water, internal dissension, murmurings against Moses, and battles with enemies. Through all their experiences, Moses towers as the unifying force and great spiritual leader.

In spite of having seen God's great act of deliverance so recently, the faith of the Israelites was not strong. Three days later they came to a place where the water was not fit to drink, and they began complaining against Moses. The Lord showed Moses how to purify the water, and the people's needs were satisfied (Ex 15:22-25). When they reached the wilderness of Sin, they complained again, this time because of lack of food. God met their need by supplying manna, a breadlike substance that would serve as their food until they came to Canaan (16:1-21). Later, camped at Rephidim, the people complained again, this time for lack of water. Once again God met their needs by supplying water from the rock at Horeb (17:1-7). The Amalekites attacked them while they were still camped at Rephidim, but God gave a great victory to the Israelites (vv 8-13).

Moses and the people reached Sinai and camped there. Jethro came to visit, bringing Moses' wife and sons. Zipporah had apparently decided to return with her children to stay with her father rather than to go on to Egypt with Moses. It was a joyful reunion, and Jethro made a burnt offering and sacrifices to God (an act that has evoked the suggestion that Jethro was a true worshiper of God, though nothing is known of his links to the Hebrew faith). When Jethro observed Moses trying to settle all the disputes and problems of the Hebrews unaided, he proposed that Moses delegate responsibility for some of the lesser matters to able men chosen from among the people. Moses accepted the suggestion, and shortly afterward Jethro returned to his own land. He did not remain at Sinai to participate in the ratification of the covenant (Ex 18:13-27).

Giving of the Law at Sinai

God had kept his promises to Moses. He had delivered the Hebrews from their Egyptian bondage and brought them to the very place where he had commissioned Moses to be their leader. He was now ready to enter into a covenant relationship with Israel. Amid a spectacular and terrifying scene of lightning, thunder, thick clouds, fire, smoke, and earthquake, God descended to the top of Sinai and called Moses to come up the mountain, where he remained 40 days to receive the law that would become the basis of the covenant.

At Sinai, God was revealed as the God who demands exclusive allegiance in all areas of life and, at the same time, as the God who desires personal fellowship with his people.

Apostasy of the People

While Moses tarried on Mt Sinai, the people below became impatient and skeptical about his return, so they went to Aaron and asked him to make idols for them to worship. They contributed the gold earrings they were wearing. "Then Aaron took the gold, melted it down, and molded it into the shape of a calf. When the people saw it, they exclaimed, 'O Israel, these are the gods who brought you out of the land of Egypt!'" (Ex 32:4, NLT). The next day they joined in the worship of the idol with sacrifices and revelry. God told Moses what was taking place below and angrily declared that he was going to destroy the people but would make a great nation of Moses and his descendants. Moses immediately interceded on behalf of the people, and God's wrath abated. Moses descended the mountain, carrying the two tablets of stone on which the law had been written, but when he entered the camp and saw what was taking place, he could not restrain his anger. He threw the stone tablets to the ground, ground the golden calf to powder, mixed it with water, and forced the people to drink it. He turned angrily to Aaron and demanded an explanation for the great sin that had been committed. Aaron lamely tried to shift the blame by minimizing his own role: "I simply threw it [the gold] into the fire—and out came this calf!" (v 24, NLT). Moses called for volunteers to carry out God's judgment on the people for the great sin they had committed. Men of the tribe of Levi responded and executed about 3,000 men. Later they were commended and rewarded (Dt 33:9-10). Moses again interceded for the people, requesting that he be destroyed with the rest if God could not forgive them. God relented and promised Moses that the angel of the Lord would go with them still (Ex 32:34).

Then Moses made a special request that he might be allowed to see the glory of the Lord. God instructed Moses to hew out two more tablets of stone like the ones he had destroyed and to return to the top of the mountain the next day. There the Lord passed before him and proclaimed his name: "Yahweh! The LORD! The God of compassion and mercy! I am slow to anger and filled with unfailing love and faithfulness" (Ex 34:6, NLT). Moses remained on the mountain another 40 days, where he received renewed warnings against idolatry and further instructions from the Lord, together with another copy of the Ten Commandments on tablets of stone. When Moses came down from the mountain, he was not aware that the skin of his face shone as a result of talking with God. At first the people were afraid to come near him, but he called them together and repeated all the Lord had said to him on the mountain. Afterward, he covered his face with a veil, which he removed only when he went into the presence of the Lord. Paul said the purpose of the veil was to prevent the people from seeing the heavenly light gradually fade from Moses' face (2 Cor 3:13).

The Tabernacle and Establishment of the Priesthood

When Moses went up to the mountain the first time to receive the law from God, he was instructed to collect materials to be used in the construction of the Tabernacle or tent. Gold, silver, bronze, blue and purple and scarlet yarn, fine twined linen, goats' hair, tanned rams' skins, goatskins, and acacia wood would be needed, along with oil for the lamps, spices for the anointing oil and for the fragrant incense, onyx stones, and stones for setting (Ex 25:3-7). The pattern for construction was also given to him, together with the ritual to be used for the consecration of the priests. A man named Bezalel was put in charge of the construction of the Tabernacle, assisted by Oholiab (31:1-6). The Tabernacle was portable like a tent so that it could be taken down and moved from place to place as the Hebrews continued their journey toward Canaan.

In addition to giving Moses directions for the Tabernacle, God also instructed him concerning the sacrifices that were to be brought: the burnt offering, grain offering, peace offering, sin offering, and guilt offering (Lv 1–7). The solemn ceremony for ordaining Aaron and his sons as priests and for inaugurating the worship practices were to be performed by Moses (chs 8–9).

Sometime after this solemn inauguration of the religious ritual actually took place, Nadab and Abihu, two of Aaron's four sons, offered unauthorized fire before the Lord. A fire came out from the Lord and destroyed them. Moses forbade Aaron and his sons Eleazar and Ithamar to express grief because of the sinfulness of the act (Lv 10:1-7). The nature of their sin is difficult to determine, but it surely involved a violation of God's holiness. Therefore, it is appropriate that a large part of the remainder of the book of Leviticus gives regulations that stress the holy living that God expected from his people.

From Sinai to Kadesh

A year had elapsed from the time the Israelites left Egypt until the census was taken (Nm 9:1). God reminded the people that it was time to observe the Passover, which they did, and a month later they set out from Sinai and came to the wilderness of Paran. Along the way they complained about the unvarying diet of manna and they longed for the fish, cucumbers, melons, leeks, onions, and garlic they had eaten in Egypt (11:4-6). In anger God sent quail in abundance, but even while the people were devouring the meat, God sent a great plague that killed many Israelites. The complaining attitude of the people was shared even by Miriam and Aaron. They began to speak against the Cushite woman Moses had married (12:1-2). It is not certain whether the Cushite was an Ethiopian or whether this was another way of referring to Zipporah. If Moses did marry a second time, no mention is made of it elsewhere in the OT. Moses made no reply to the accusations of his brother and sister. It was not necessary, for God intervened in defense of his servant. He smote Miriam with leprosy for her part in speaking against Moses, and when Aaron saw what had happened to Miriam, he acknowledged that they both had sinned. Miriam's leprosy was removed in response to Moses' fervent intercession.

While the people were encamped at Kadesh (also called Kadesh-barnea—Nm 32:8) in the wilderness of Paran, Moses sent 12 men into Canaan, one from each tribe, to spy out the land in preparation for the Israelite entry. After 40 days the spies returned and, though they acknowledged that the land was fertile and inviting, 10 of them were afraid of the Canaanite inhabitants and advised against going into the land. Only Joshua and Caleb were willing to go ahead and occupy the territory. The entire congregation joined the protest against going in and determined to choose a new leader and return to Egypt rather than risk death by the sword in Canaan. They threatened to stone Moses and Aaron. At that moment God intervened and would have destroyed all the people on the spot except for the intervention of Moses (13:1–14:19). He declared that, if God did not bring the people into Canaan, the nations round about would conclude that the God of the Israelites was unable to bring them into the land. Once again God acquiesced to Moses' request to pardon the people but said that none of them 20 years and older who had complained against him would be allowed to enter the land. All the people would wander in the wilderness for 40 years until that generation died, and then their children would be allowed to enter Canaan (14:29-33). When they heard the Lord's sentence upon them, the people quickly decided to lift the sentence of judgment by entering the land at once, but God was not with them, and they suffered a disastrous defeat at the hands of the Amalekites and Canaanites.

Forty Years in the Wilderness

Very little is known about events during the 40 years of wilderness wanderings. In spite of the judgment that had already come upon them, the people did not seem to change their ways. A man named Korah led another rebellion against the authority of Moses and Aaron. God would not listen to the pleas of Moses and Aaron on behalf of these dissidents (Nm 16:22-24), but told the congregation to separate itself from the tents of Korah and his conspirators. While the people watched, the ground split open and swallowed up the rebellious factions together with their households and all their possessions. Though the rest of the Israelites witnessed the fate of the rebels, it did not deter them from again turning on Moses and Aaron. At this, God told Moses to remove himself from the murmuring congregation in order that he could take vengeance. Though Moses offered atonement for the people's sins, 14,700 died by plague before the punishment was ended. To demonstrate further to the people that Moses was his chosen leader, the Lord instructed Moses to take rods, one for each tribe, and to deposit them in the tent of meeting. God would cause the rod of the man chosen by him to sprout, and so silence the murmurings of the people. The rod belonging to Aaron sprouted and budded and bloomed, but the people only complained more.

As the people neared the end of their years of wilderness wanderings, Miriam died in Kadesh and was buried there (Nm 20:1). Soon after, the people began to complain once more for lack of water. God instructed Moses to speak to a rock that would bring forth water to satisfy the needs of the people. Instead of speaking to the rock, Moses struck it twice with his rod. The water came forth, but God rebuked Moses and Aaron: "Because you did not trust me enough to demonstrate my holiness to the people of Israel, you will not lead them into the land I am giving them!" (v 12, NLT). The nature of the sin is not clear, but Moses and Aaron were apparently taking to themselves honor that belonged to God alone. Because of the sin, they were denied the privilege of leading the Israelites into the Promised Land. The punishment may seem too severe for the sin, but it shows that the privileged role of leadership given to Moses and Aaron carried with it an unusual measure of responsibility.

The people then journeyed from Kadesh to Mt Hor on the border of the land of Edom, where Aaron died. Moses took his priestly garments from him and gave them to Eleazar, his son, thereby transferring the priestly office (Nm 20:28).

As the people came closer to their destination, resistance on the part of the native population increased. There was a skirmish with the king of Arad and his forces at Hormah, resulting in a victory for Israel (Nm 21:1-3). As they journeyed around Edom, some of the Israelites began speaking against God and Moses because there was no food or water and they were tired of eating manna. This time the Lord sent poisonous snakes among the people, and many of them died of the venomous bites. Those who had not yet been bitten came to Moses, acknowledged their sin, and asked that the serpents be removed from their midst. God instructed Moses to make a serpent of bronze and set it on a pole. If a person bitten by a serpent looked up at the bronze serpent, he or she would live.

As the Israelites approached the territory of Sihon, king of the Amorites, they sent messengers asking permission to pass peaceably through his land. Instead of granting the request, Sihon gathered his army together and fought against Israel. He was killed in the battle, and his land and cities were taken and occupied by the Hebrews (Nm 21:21-25).

Arrival at the Jordan River

After their victory over Sihon, the Israelites set out again and encamped in the plains of Moab on the east side of the Jordan River facing Jericho, in full view of the Promised Land. The Moabites were terrified by the presence of these people because they had heard what happened to the Amorites. Their king, Balak, hired a magician named Balaam to curse the Israelites. Three times Balaam attempted to curse them, but each time God turned his words into a blessing (Nm 22–24). Though unable to curse the Israelites, Balaam was responsible for an even greater calamity. He advised the Moabites to entice the Israelites to sacrifice to their gods and bow down to them (Nm 25:1-3; 31:16; 2 Pt 2:15; Rv 2:14). While the people were worshiping the Moabite deity, Baal of Peor, God's anger was kindled against them, and he sent a plague that killed 24,000 of them (Nm 25:9). It was Israel's first encounter with the seductive allurement of licentious idolatry and an ominous foreview of what would happen after they settled down in Canaan. Their continued attraction to idolatry would be their final undoing.

After the plague, God instructed Moses and Eleazar to take another census of the people like the one almost 40 years earlier. A whole generation of Israelites had died in the wilderness, but they had been replaced by an almost equal number, so that now there were 601,730 men 20 years and older who were able to go to war (Nm 26:51). Not a man remained of those who had been counted in the first census, except Caleb and Joshua.

The Lord instructed Moses to lay hands on Joshua and commission him as the new leader in the sight of Eleazar the priest and all the congregation (Nm 27:12-23). In addition, the Lord gave Moses instructions concerning feasts and offerings and vows (chs 28–30). God ordered Moses, as his last act as leader, to avenge the Israelites on the Midianites. In that battle the armies of Israel gained a great victory over the Midianites, killing their kings, their men, and also Balaam.

The Lord gave instructions to Moses concerning the boundaries that would mark the Promised Land and named the men who would divide the land among the tribes (Nm 34). He also ordered that 48 cities be given to the Levites, the priestly tribe, as their portion. Six of these were designated as cities of refuge where murderers could flee so that they would not be killed by those seeking vengeance without having an opportunity to stand before the congregation for judgment (ch 35).

Moses' Death

The book of Deuteronomy has often been called Moses' valedictory speech to the people, for in it Moses is not merely the chief speaker but the only speaker. With the congregation of his people gathered before him, he rehearsed all that God had done for them since leaving Sinai, and he reminded them of their failure to enter the Promised Land 38 years earlier (Dt 2:14). He recalled his plea that God would let him cross the Jordan and see the land that was to be the home of the people, but God responded that Moses would only be allowed to view the land from the top of Pisgah. Moses then exhorted the people to obey the statutes and ordinances that had been given to them in order to experience God's blessings in the land.

As the day of Moses' death approached, the Lord ordered Moses and Joshua to present themselves at the tent of meeting in order for Joshua to be commissioned as the new leader (Dt 31:14-23). Before his death, Moses pronounced a blessing upon all the Israelites (ch 33). Having completed these tasks, Moses went up from the plains of Moab to Mt Nebo, and to the top of Pisgah. From there God showed him the land promised long ago to Abraham, Isaac, and Jacob—the land that was soon to be the home of the wandering Israelite tribes. Again God told him that he would not be allowed to cross over the Jordan. Moses died there and God buried him somewhere in the valley in the land of Moab opposite Beth-peor (34:6). Moses was 120 years old when he died, and the Israelites mourned his death for 30 days. The finest tribute to Moses is found in the closing words of the book of Deuteronomy, "There has never been another prophet in Israel like Moses, whom the LORD knew face to face" (v 10).

Moses in the New Testament

All Jews and Christians in apostolic times considered Moses the author of the Pentateuch. Such expressions as "the law of Moses" (Lk 2:22), "Moses commanded" (Mt 19:7), "Moses said" (Mk 7:10) "and Moses wrote" (12:19) shows that his name was synonymous with the OT books attributed to him. He is mentioned in the NT more than any other OT figure, a total of 79 times. His role as lawgiver is emphasized more than any other aspect of his life (Mt 8:4; Mk 7:10; Jn 1:17; Acts 15:1). He appears at the transfiguration of Jesus as the representative of OT law, along with Elijah as the representative of OT prophets (Mt 17:1-3).

Moses' role as prophet is also mentioned in the NT. As a prophet, he spoke of the coming Messiah and his sufferings (Lk 24:25-27; Acts 3:22). The NT also draws from the life and experiences of Moses to show patterns of life under the new covenant. The nativity story of Jesus parallels the Mosaic story of the infant deliverer being rescued from the evil designs of an earthly despot (Mt 2:13-18). Jesus' proclamation of a new law in his Sermon on the Mount parallels the giving of the law at Sinai (Mt 5–7) and presents Jesus as the authoritative interpreter of the will of God. Contrast between the old law and the new relationship with God is especially marked in the book of Galatians. The comparison of Moses with Christ is an important emphasis of the book of Hebrews (Heb 3:5-6; 9:11-22). John contrasted the law that was given through Moses with the grace and truth that came through

Jesus Christ (Jn 1:17). He also contrasted the manna in the wilderness to Jesus as "the bread of life" (6:30-35).

Other references to Moses or to events associated with him include his birth (Acts 7:20; Heb 11:23), the burning bush (Lk 20:37), the magicians of Egypt (2 Tm 3:8), the Passover (Heb 11:28), the Exodus (3:16), crossing of the sea (1 Cor 10:2), the covenant sacrifice at Sinai (Mt 26:28), the manna (1 Cor 10:3), the glory on Moses' face (2 Cor 3:7-18), water from the rock (1 Cor 10:4), the bronze serpent (Jn 3:14), and the song of Moses (Rv 15:3).

MOZA

1. Caleb's son by his concubine Ephah (1 Chr 2:46).

2. Zimri's son, the father of Binea and a descendant of Saul and Jonathan (1 Chr 8:36-37; 9:42-43).

MUPPIM

One of Benjamin's 10 sons (Gn 46:21). He is elsewhere called Shephupham (Nm 26:39) and Shuppim (1 Chr 7:12) and is perhaps identifiable with Shephuphan (1 Chr 8:5). *See* Shephuphan.

MUSHI

Son of Merari, the grandson of Levi, and Mahli's brother (Ex 6:19; Nm 3:20; 1 Chr 6:19, 47). He was the father of Mahli, Eder, and Jeremoth (1 Chr 23:21-23; 24:26, 30) and the founder of the family of Mushites (Nm 3:33; 26:58).

NAAM
Caleb's descendant from Judah's tribe (1 Chr 4:15).

NAAMAH
1. Daughter of Zillah and Lamech in the list of Cain's descendants (Gn 4:22).
2. One of Solomon's many wives, an Ammonitess (1 Kgs 14:21, 31; 2 Chr 12:13). She was surely responsible in part for Solomon's idolatry. Her son Rehoboam ruled Judah after Solomon's death (1 Kgs 14:21-24).

NAAMAN
1. Grandson of Benjamin and son of Bela, who gave his name to the Naamite clan (Gn 46:21; Nm 26:38-40; 1 Chr 8:4, 7).
2. Commanding general of the Aramean army during the reign of Ben-hadad, king of Syria (2 Kgs 5). He was held in honor by the king, evidently for his character as well as for military achievements, "but he had leprosy." This did not exclude him from society, as it would have done in Israel (cf. Lv 13–14), but the possibility of a cure suggested by a captive Israelite girl sent Naaman, with Ben-hadad's approval and gifts, to the court of his highly suspicious neighboring monarch (unnamed, but probably Jehoram). Elisha the prophet intervened and prescribed an unlikely mode of healing. The reluctant Naaman followed through because of the good sense of his servants, who said, "If the prophet had told you to do some great thing, would you not have done it?" Naaman confessed that the one true God is in Israel, and he returned home with two mule-loads of earth, perhaps on the assumption that this was a God who could be worshiped only on his own ground (cf. Ex 20:24). In Luke 4:27 Jesus reminds his synagogue listeners of how Naaman, a non-Israelite, was the only one of his time to be cleansed of leprosy.

NAARAH
One of Ashhur's two wives, who bore him four sons (1 Chr 4:5-6).

NABAL
Wealthy, successful farmer of Maon in the southern wilderness of Judah. Unlike his godly forefather, Caleb, Nabal was hard of heart and wicked in all his ways (1 Sm 25:3).

When he enters the story of David (1 Sm 25), it is sheep-shearing time, which seems to have been a time of festivity and hospitality. Fleeing from Saul, who wanted to kill him, David decided to ask Nabal for a gift, not only to mark the occasion, but also because David's presence in the area had served to protect Nabal's flocks. Nabal refused in a most insulting way, suggesting that David was no better than a runaway slave.

David decided on revenge. But Abigail, Nabal's quick-witted wife, saved Nabal by bringing David the presents he had asked for and by begging him not to stain his record by acting in anger. David agreed. But when Nabal heard what had happened, he was struck down by what appears to have been a stroke and died 10 days later.

Nabal, whose name means "fool," stands as a reminder of the deep folly of opposing God. God himself, not David, took revenge.

NABOTH

Owner of a vineyard that Ahab, king of Israel, coveted (see the story in 1 Kgs 21). Ahab's request was perhaps not unreasonable, and Naboth's refusal may have been a little curt. While Ahab sulked, however, Jezebel had two scoundrels accuse Naboth of blasphemy, the greatest crime an Israelite could commit, which was punishable by death (Lv 24:10-23). Two witnesses secured a conviction, according to the law of Moses (Dt 17:6-7). The murder that was carried out had the appearance of being a legal and just execution. A fast was proclaimed and held according to royal instructions. The accusation and trial of Naboth was supervised by the elders of the city, and he was stoned to death in accordance with the law.

The prophet Elijah, however, knew the real wickedness that lay behind the deed. He faced Ahab with it and prophesied that he and Jezebel and all their family would be wiped out because of it.

The words came true. Ahab got a temporary reprieve when he repented but was later killed in battle (1 Kgs 22:34-40). The blood of Jezebel was indeed licked up by dogs (2 Kgs 9:36), and the body of Joram, their son, was flung into Naboth's vineyard (v 25).

NADAB

1. Eldest son of Aaron and Elisheba, the daughter of Amminadab (Ex 6:23; Nm 3:2; 1 Chr 24:1), who became one of Israel's first priests together with his brothers and father. He participated in the ratification of the covenant with God on Mt Sinai (Ex 24:1, 9) and was ordained to the priesthood (28:1).

   Nadab and his brother Abihu, Aaron's second son, died because they offered "strange fire" to the Lord (Lv 10:1-2; Nm 3:4; 1 Chr 24:2). Incense offered in the morning usually preceded the cutting up of the sacrifice. In this case "fire from the Lord devoured them." The offering of "strange fire" does not appear anywhere else in the Bible.

   Rabbis have offered various explanations of the offense committed by Nadab and Abihu. Since an admonition against drinking wine in the tent of meeting follows this tragedy (Lv 10:9), an early tradition held that the brothers were drunk. Death was the penalty for any priest drinking in this sacred tent.

   An interesting point arises in the instructions that Moses gave to the grieving father of Nadab and Abihu. Moses exhorted Aaron not to mourn or to interrupt his priestly functions. Since Aaron had been sanctified by the sacred anointing oil, he had to continue serving God. He was not allowed to go out of the door of the tent "lest he die." Instead, the rest of Israel mourned for Nadab and Abihu (Lv 10:3-7).

2. Son of Jeroboam, whom he succeeded to the throne of Israel (909–908 BC). Nadab ruled two years (1 Kgs 14:20; 15:25), coming to power in the second year of Asa's reign in Judah; he was succeeded in the third year of Asa's reign (15:28). His rule may have been arranged before the death of Jeroboam, for he surely recognized the dangers of the charismatic ideal that continued among the northern tribes. However, Nadab was not successful in stabilizing the kingdom. To gain the acclamation of the army, he went into battle against the Philistines at Gibbethon, about two and a half miles (4 kilometers) southwest of Gezer. Baasha from the tribe of Issachar, presumably a military officer, assassinated Nadab and all his sons and usurped the throne. So he fulfilled the prophecy predicted by Ahijah the Shilonite against the house of Jeroboam (v 29).

3. Jerahmeelite, the son of Shammai and grandson of Onam, and the great-grandson of Jerahmeel. Nadab in turn had two sons, Seled and Appaim (1 Chr 2:26-30).

4. Son of Jeiel and Maacah, a Gibeonite (1 Chr 8:30; 9:36).

NAGGAI
Ancestor of Jesus, according to Luke's genealogy (Lk 3:25, KJV "Nagge").

NAHAM
Judahite chief and the brother of Hodiah's wife (1 Chr 4:19).

NAHAMANI
One of the leading officials who returned with Zerubbabel to Palestine following the Exile (Neh 7:7). His name is omitted in the parallel list of returning officials in Ezra 2:2.

NAHARAI
One of David's mighty warriors, who was also Joab's armor bearer. Naharai was from the city of Beeroth (2 Sm 23:37; 1 Chr 11:39).

NAHASH
1. King of the Ammonites who laid siege to Jabesh-gilead during the days of Saul. The men of the city, offering themselves in servitude, petitioned Nahash to make a treaty with them; he agreed to do so on the condition that he gouge out each one's right eye to shame all of Israel. Given a week's reprieve from his threat, the men of Jabesh organized a secret war plan with Saul and Israel, resulting in the destruction of Nahash's Ammonite army (1 Sm 11:1-2; 12:12). He later honored a reconciliation with David, which his son Hanun, on bad counsel, disregarded (2 Sm 10:2; 1 Chr 19:1-2).

2. Father of Abigail and Zeruiah (2 Sm 17:25). In 1 Chronicles 2:16, Abigail and Zeruiah are listed as the daughters of Jesse and the sisters of David and his brothers. Various

theories have been offered to resolve this difference. The most feasible suggests that Nahash's wife bore him Abigail and Zeruiah; after his death, his widow married Jesse and subsequently bore David.

3. Father of Shobi from Rabbah, the chief Ammonite city east of the Jordan. Shobi, along with Makir and Barzillai, took care of David's domestic needs during his flight from Absalom (2 Sm 17:27). He is perhaps identifiable with #1 above.

NAHATH

1. Chief of a clan in Edom and Reuel's firstborn son (Gn 36:13, 17; 1 Chr 1:37).

2. Levite of the family of Kohath and Elkanah's grandson (1 Chr 6:26).

3. Levite who oversaw the Temple during King Hezekiah's reign (2 Chr 31:13).

NAHBI

Son of Vophsi; the head of Naphtali's tribe and one of the 12 spies sent to search out the land of Canaan (Nm 13:14).

NAHOR

1. Abraham's grandfather (Gn 11:22-25; 1 Chr 1:26); also an ancestor of Jesus according to Luke's genealogy (Lk 3:34, where some English translations follow the Greek spelling, Nachor). The Genesis and 1 Chronicles passages show that Nahor is from Shem's line. Hence, Abraham and his descendants are part of the Semitic family of nations.

2. Son of Terah and Abraham's brother (Gn 11:26-29; Jos 24:2). He married Milcah, Haran's daughter, and his family is named in Genesis 22:20-23. Abraham sent his servant to seek a wife for Isaac at Nahor's residence in Mesopotamia (see Gn 24:10, which possibly suggests that the city itself was called Nahor). There he found Rebekah, Nahor's granddaughter (Gn 24:1-51). Nahor is also named as the father (perhaps grandfather) of Laban, to whom Jacob went when he fled from his brother Esau (Gn 29:5). Both of these texts link Abraham's family with related Semitic people. In Genesis 31:53 God is spoken of as "the God of Abraham and Nahor."

NAHSHON

Amminadab's son; brother of Elisheba and Salmon's father (Ex 6:23; 1 Chr 2:10-11). Nahshon, the prince of Judah's tribe at the start of Israel's wilderness wanderings (Nm 1:7; 2:3; 10:14), represented his kinsmen at the altar's dedication (7:12). In Ruth 4:20 he is listed as David's forefather and a descendant of Judah through the line of Perez, and in Matthew and Luke's genealogies as an ancestor of Jesus Christ (Mt 1:4; Lk 3:32).

NAHUM

1. A prophet of Judah whose name means "consolation" or "consoler." This name fits his message, as he wrote to encourage the people of Judah while they were being

oppressed by the Assyrians (Na 1:1). Other than being the prophet who wrote the book of Nahum, nothing is known of him except that he came from the village of Elkosh. Its exact location is unknown, but four suggestions have been made. First, it was the town of Alqush, near Mosul on the Tigris River just north of Nineveh. A tradition declares this to be the site of Nahum's tomb, but it is first mentioned by Masius in the 16th century. The tomb and its location have no archaeological confirmation, and its authenticity is highly suspect. Second, Jerome recounts a Jewish tradition identifying it with "a village in Galilee called 'Helcesaei'" (Helcesei or Elcesi), and writes, "A very small one, indeed, and containing in its ruins hardly any traces of ancient buildings, but one which is well known to the Jews and was also pointed out to me by my guide." This village is located about 15 miles (24.1 kilometers) northwest of the Sea of Galilee. Third, on the northern edge of the Sea of Galilee rest the ruins of Capernaum, meaning "village of Nahum." But there is no proof that this name goes back to the prophet. Finally, some believe it should be identified with Elcesi, near Bet-gabre, about halfway between Gaza and Jerusalem in the territory of Judah. Internal evidence seems to support this position (Na 1:15).

It is entirely possible that Nahum may have been a member of the northern tribes but migrated to Judah after the conquest of 722 BC and ministered there.

2. Ancestor of Jesus, according to Luke's genealogy (Lk 3:25).

NAOMI

Wife of Elimelech and the mother of Mahlon and Chilion. A member of Judah's tribe, she lived in Bethlehem during the period of the judges. Her story is told in the book of Ruth. Because of a severe famine in Canaan, Naomi temporarily resettled with her family in the land of Moab, east of the Dead Sea (Ru 1:1-2). Following the death of her husband and two sons in Moab (vv 3-5), Naomi returned to Bethlehem with Ruth, her Moabitess daughter-in-law (vv 8-22). Upon meeting her friends, she told them not to call her Naomi, meaning "pleasant," but Mara, meaning "bitter," for she said, "I went away full, but the LORD has brought me home empty" (vv 20-21, NLT). Naomi's domestic problems were eventually resolved when Ruth married Boaz, Elimelech's near kin (chs 2–4).

NAPHISH

Eleventh of Ishmael's 12 sons (Gn 25:15; 1 Chr 1:31) and the founder of a tribe that later went to war against the tribes of Israel living east of the Jordan (1 Chr 5:19).

NAPHTALI

One of Jacob's 12 sons (Gn 35:25; 1 Chr 2:2). He was the second of two sons borne to Jacob by Bilhah, Rachel's maid. Overjoyed with giving Jacob another son, Rachel named the boy Naphtali, meaning "my wrestling," for her conflict with Leah—"with mighty wrestlings

QUICKTAKE

NAOMI

STRENGTHS AND ACCOMPLISHMENTS
- A relationship where the greatest bond was faith in God
- A relationship of strong mutual commitment
- A relationship in which each person tried to do what was best for the other

LESSON FROM THEIR LIVES
- God is compassionate and can work through life's most unlikely and difficult circumstances.

VITAL STATISTICS
Where: Moab, Bethlehem
Occupation: Wife, mother, widow
Relatives: Elimelech, Mahlon, Kilion, Orpah, Boaz

KEY VERSES
"Don't call me Naomi," she responded. "Instead, call me Mara, for the Almighty has made life very bitter for me." (Ruth 1:20).
"Then the women of the town said to Naomi, "Praise the LORD, who has now provided a redeemer for your family! May this child be famous in Israel" (Ruth 4:14).

Her story is told in the book of Ruth.

I have wrestled with my sister, and have prevailed" (Gn 30:8, RSV). Naphtali eventually moved his family with Jacob to Egypt (Gn 46:24; Ex 1:4). He fathered four sons (Nm 26:50; 1 Chr 7:13) and founded one of the 12 tribes of Israel (Nm 1:43).

NARCISSUS
Christian whose household knew the Lord and received greetings from Paul in his letter to Rome (Rom 16:11).

NATHAN
1. Son of David by Bathsheba, the third son to be born in Jerusalem (2 Sm 5:14; 1 Chr 3:5; 14:4). Nathan, Solomon's older brother, is featured in the apocalyptic oracle of Zechariah 12:12 and Christ's line of descent via Joseph (Lk 3:31).

2. One of the early prophets and adviser of David. When David's military campaigns were almost completed, he shared with Nathan his desire to erect a suitable dwelling place for God. Nathan's immediate reaction was favorable, but on receiving direct instructions from the Lord, he countermanded his initial approval. He foretold that one of David's sons would build God a house, and that God would establish a house (dynasty) for David through his son Solomon. The prophecy includes not only the Davidic line but also the messianic king. Nathan's oracle, therefore, was of vital importance, since it dealt with two great institutions, the Temple and the Davidic monarchy (2 Sm 7:1-7; 1 Chr 17:1-15).

During the Ammonite war, David, having fathered an illegitimate child, tried to cover his sin by involving the woman's husband, Uriah (2 Sm 11:1-13; 23:39). When this attempt failed, he had Joab, the general of the army, engineer Uriah's death, whereupon David took Bathsheba openly as his wife (11:14-27). Nathan confronted the king, courageously exposing the enormity of David's crime by a parable that provoked the king's righteous anger and turned the finger of condemnation upon David himself (12:1-9). Nathan foretold the fearful consequences for David's family resulting from his sin and evil example (vv 10-12). This prophecy was fulfilled in rape, the deaths of three of David's sons, and civil war (2 Sm 13–18; 1 Kgs 1). Bathsheba's child also would not live (2 Sm 12:14).

When David was near death, one of his sons, Adonijah, seized power (1 Kgs 1:1, 10). Nathan prompted Bathsheba to remind David of an earlier promise concerning Solomon's succession, supporting her by his own timely intervention (vv 10-27). David immediately authorized Solomon's coronation (vv 28-53).

Nathan was an important chronicler (1 Chr 29:29; 2 Chr 9:29). With David he played a vital part in developing the musical aspects of Temple worship (2 Chr 29:25).

3. Man of Zobah and the father of Igal, one of David's 30 heroes (2 Sm 23:36). He was possibly the Nathan noted as the brother of Joel (1 Chr 11:38).

4. Father of two important court officials (1 Kgs 4:5); probably either the prophet or David's son.

5. Descendant of Judah, in the clan of Jerahmeel, the son of Attai and the father of Zabad (1 Chr 2:36).

6. One of a deputation sent by Ezra to secure Levitical reinforcements for the Israelites returning to Jerusalem (Ezr 8:16). Possibly Nathan was among those who covenanted to divorce their foreign wives (10:39), but the name, meaning "gift," was a very common one.

NATHANAEL

Jew from Cana of Galilee whom Jesus called to be a disciple (Jn 1:45-50; 21:2). Initially skeptical when Philip described Jesus as the fulfillment of the whole OT (1:45-46), Nathanael proclaimed Jesus to be the Son of God and the King of Israel (v 49) after an astonishing personal encounter.

The fact that the only NT references to Nathanael occur in the Gospel of John has led some scholars to identify him with several personalities appearing in the synoptic Gospels. Because his call appears with those of Andrew, Peter, and Philip, some have speculated that he was one of the 12, possibly Bartholomew. Three pieces of evidence are cited in support of this position: (1) the name Bartholomew is patronymic (literally "son of Tolmai") and would be accompanied by another name; (2) each of the Synoptic lists of the 12 apostles place Bartholomew after Philip (Mt 10:2-4; Mk 3:16-19; Lk 6:14-16), paralleling the call of Nathanael after Philip in John's account; and (3) Bartholomew's name does not appear in the fourth Gospel.

A second position identifies Nathanael as James, the son of Alphaeus. According to this view, Jesus' comment in John 1:47 should read "Behold, Israel [not "an Israelite"] indeed, in whom is no guile!" Israel is the name God gave to Jacob, and the NT form of Jacob is James. John addressed James, the son of Alphaeus, as Nathanael in order to distinguish him from others who had become prominent in the early church.

Two less plausible identifications equate Nathanael with either Matthew or Simon the Cananaean. The first is precariously founded on the similar etymologies of the names Matthew ("gift of Yahweh") and Nathanael ("Yahweh has given"). The second identifies the two on the basis of the common hometown of Cana.

In the final analysis, Nathanael was most likely a disciple who was not a member of the 12 and was known only to John. This suggestion conforms to early patristic evidence. In the fourth Gospel, Nathanael serves as a symbol for the true Jew who overcomes initial skepticism to believe in Christ. This is confirmed by three observations: (1) his initial reaction to Jesus parallels that of others who believed in the Law and the Prophets (Jn 7:15, 27, 41; 9:41); (2) Jesus' perception of Nathanael under a fig tree (1:48) identifies the latter's devotion to the Torah (in rabbinic literature the proper place to study the Torah is under a fig tree); and (3) Jesus identifies Nathanael with Jacob, the father of the Israelite nation. In Genesis 25–32, Jacob is certainly sly and cunning in his dealings with Esau and Laban. John 1:51 strengthens the ties between Nathanael and Jacob by presenting the imagery of angels ascending and descending, reminiscent of Jacob's dream, and by locating the event in Galilee close to Bethel and Jabbok, the sites of Jacob's experiences. Nathanael is thus a symbol of the pious Israelite for whom Christ came. His response typifies what the fourth Evangelist understands as the appropriate response of the true Israelite to Jesus—from initial skepticism to faith (cf. Rom 9:6).

NATHAN-MELECH

Official during King Josiah's reign. Horses for sun worship were kept near his quarters but were removed by Josiah (2 Kgs 23:11).

NEARIAH

1. One of Shemaiah's six sons and a descendant of David (1 Chr 3:22-23).

2. Captain of 500 men of Simeon's tribe who went to Mt Seir, where they destroyed the remnant of the Amalekites and settled their own people in Hezekiah's time (1 Chr 4:42).

NEBAI

Political leader who signed Ezra's covenant of faithfulness to God with Nehemiah and others after the Exile (Neh 10:19).

NEBAIOTH

Firstborn of Ishmael's 12 sons (Gn 25:13; 1 Chr 1:29) whose sister, Mahalath (also called Basemath, cf. Gn 36:3) later married Esau (Gn 28:9). The identification of Nebaioth's descendants is uncertain, though possibly they are the ancestors of the Nabatean Arabian tribe who possessed the land of Edom and parts of the Transjordan as far north as Palmyra (ancient Tadmor). The descendants of both Nebaioth and Kedar are noted for their superb flocks of sheep (Is 60:7) and are mentioned in the inscriptions of the Assyrian king Ashurbanipal (seventh century BC).

NEBAT

Ephraimite of Zeredah in the Jordan Valley, a servant to Solomon, and the father of King Jeroboam (1 Kgs 11:26).

NEBO

Forefather of 52 descendants who returned with Zerubbabel to Judah following the Exile (Ezr 2:29; Neh 7:33), 7 of whom were encouraged by Ezra to divorce their foreign wives (Ezr 10:43). Some suggest that Nebo refers to a town in Benjamin's tribe from which some inhabitants went into exile to Babylon.

NEBO-SARSEKIM

Personal name or title of an official who participated with Nebuchadnezzar and the Chaldean army in conquering Jerusalem (Jer 39:3).

NEBUCHADNEZZAR

Babylonian king (605–562 BC) who captured and destroyed Jerusalem in 586 BC. He was the son of Nabopolassar and the foremost ruler of the Neo-Babylonian Empire (612–539 BC); his name is alternately spelled Nebuchadrezzar in Jeremiah and Ezekiel (see NLT mg).

Nebuchadnezzar states that he conquered all of "Hatti-country," which is a term used for all of Palestine and Syria, including Judah. Jehoiakim had been made king of Judah by Pharaoh Neco (2 Kgs 23:34) and initially submitted to Nebuchadnezzar (24:2; cf. Dn 1:1-2), but three years later rebelled. Jehoiakim died and his son Jehoiachin succeeded to the throne (2 Kgs 24:6); however, he reigned for only three months. Nebuchadnezzar came to Jerusalem in 598 BC and took Jehoiachin captive to Babylon (vv 10-17). He replaced Jehoiachin with his Uncle Mattaniah, whom he renamed Zedekiah (2 Kgs 24:17; 2 Chr 36:10).

QUICKTAKE

NEBUCHADNEZZAR

STRENGTHS AND ACCOMPLISHMENTS
• Greatest of the Babylonian kings
• Known as a builder of cities
• Described in the Bible as one of the foreign rulers God used for his purposes

WEAKNESSES AND MISTAKES
• Thought of himself as a god and was persuaded to build a gold statue that all were to worship
• Became extremely proud, which led to a bout of insanity
• Tended to forget the demonstrations of God's power he had witnessed

LESSONS FROM HIS LIFE
• History records the actions of God's willing servants and those who were his unwitting tools
• A leader's greatness is affected by the quality of his advisers
• Uncontrolled pride is self-destructive

VITAL STATISTICS
Where: Babylon
Occupation: King
Relatives: Father: Nabopolassar. Son: Evil-merodach. Grandson: Belshazzar
Contemporaries: Jeremiah, Ezekiel, Daniel, Jehoiakim, Jehoiachin, Zedekiah

KEY VERSE
"Now I, Nebuchadnezzar, praise and glorify and honor the King of heaven. All his acts are just and true, and he is able to humble the proud" (Daniel 4:37).

Nebuchadnezzar's story is told in 2 Kings 24–25; 2 Chronicles 36; Jeremiah 21–52; Daniel 1–4.

Zedekiah also rebelled against the king of Babylon (2 Kgs 24:20). Nebuchadnezzar's armies besieged the city of Jerusalem and captured Zedekiah. He was brought to Nebuchadnezzar at Riblah, where Zedekiah's sons were slain before his eyes. He was then blinded, bound, and taken captive to Babylon (25:6-7). The Temple was looted and burned, the city walls were dismantled, and the city was plundered and razed (vv 9-17). The leading people of the nation were either killed or taken into captivity.

The remnant of the people in Judah were put under the charge of Gedaliah, the appointed governor. After his treacherous murder, the Jews fled to Egypt. Both Jeremiah (Jer 43:8-13; 46:13-24) and Ezekiel (Ez 29–32) prophesied that Nebuchadnezzar would invade Egypt. Josephus gives the date as the 23rd year of Nebuchadnezzar (582/581 BC), but a fragmentary historical inscription dating to the 37th year of Nebuchadnezzar (568/567 BC) indicates that the defeat of Egypt occurred during the reign of Amasis.

Nebuchadnezzar's military successes were in many respects overshadowed by his building activities in Babylon. The king voiced his pride when he declared, "Is not this great Babylon, which I have built by my mighty power as a royal residence and for the glory of my majesty?" (Dn 4:30, RSV). The hanging gardens were acclaimed as one of the seven wonders of the ancient world. They were built on terraces in an effort to cure his Median queen of her homesickness for the mountains of her homeland.

The events of the book of Daniel center on Babylon and Nebuchadnezzar. Daniel was among the captives taken to Babylon in 605 BC. Nebuchadnezzar became aware of Daniel when the king had a dream that none of his occult experts could interpret (ch 2). The Lord gave to Daniel the interpretation of the dream; the human image that the king saw in his dream represented the various governments from the New Babylonian Empire to the reign of the Messiah.

Nebuchadnezzar set up a large human statue that was 90 feet (27.4 meters) high and 9 feet (2.7 meters) wide. Failure to worship the image would incur death by fire. The three compatriots of Daniel refused and were thrown into a furnace from which the Lord delivered them unhurt (ch 3).

The king had another dream about a great tree that was cut down but later sprouted from the stump (4:4-27). Again the "wise men of Babylon" could not give the interpretation, but Daniel informed the king that the dream prophesied a humbling experience lasting seven years as a consequence of the king's pride (vv 28-33).

NEBUSHAZBAN

Babylonian officer among those ordered to provide safety for Jeremiah after the Babylonians conquered Jerusalem (Jer 39:13).

NEBUZARADAN

Chief Babylonian official and captain of the bodyguard during Nebuchadnezzar's reign (605–562 BC). Nebuzaradan was one of the officials whom Nebuchadnezzar authorized to oversee Jerusalem and Judah and the deportations of Jewish exiles to Babylon (2 Kgs 25:8-20; Jer 39:9-10; 52:12-30). On the king's orders, he appointed Gedaliah governor of Judah and Jeremiah's guardian (Jer 39:11-13; 41:10; 43:6).

NECO

Pharaoh of the 26th dynasty of the Saite kings, who succeeded his father, Psammetichus, in 610 BC. Psammetichus had ruled 54 years over Egypt and was instrumental in the renewal of archaic art forms and in the revival of religious fervor. In addition to this, Psammetichus had fortified the borders with garrisons and driven the Assyrians beyond the northeast border into Canaan. The alliance of the Babylonians and Medes made Psammetichus realize the potential threat to Egypt's independence, and he allied himself with Assyria, his former enemy. Neco fell heir to the accomplishments of his father and to an international political scene out of which he could not easily withdraw. He was allied with a losing power, as Nineveh, Assyria's capital, fell in 612 BC. Neco was called upon to assist the king of Assyria, who had retreated to Harran from the Babylonian forces under Nebuchadnezzar. Neco moved his troops through Judah on his way to Carchemish to engage in battle with the Babylonians. As the troops moved through the Megiddo pass, they were ambushed by Judean troops under King Josiah. Neco had requested safe passage, but Josiah foolhardily refused. Josiah was killed in the field (2 Kgs 23:29-30; cf. 2 Chr 35:20-25). Neco continued onward to Carchemish. The battle (605 BC) turned out to be a great victory for the young Nebuchadnezzar. Nebuchadnezzar recorded it in glowing terms: "As for the rest of the Egyptian army which had escaped from the defeat . . . the Babylonian troops overtook and defeated them; so that not a single man escaped to that country." The OT briefly observes: "The king of Egypt did not venture out of his country after that" (2 Kgs 24:7, NLT).

Neco strengthened Egypt by a policy of isolation. He made Judah a buffer zone and fortified the borders successfully in order to keep the Babylonians from penetrating into Egypt. He had deposed Jehoahaz, the newly enthroned king of three months, brought him to Riblah in Syria, and later to Egypt (2 Kgs 23:33-34). Jehoiakim succeeded to the Davidic throne in Jerusalem, and Judah was forced to pay a tribute of 100 talents of silver and a talent of gold (vv 33-36). When Judah fell to Babylon, the Judeans considered the Egyptian interest in their survival as vital to Egypt's independence and requested help against Babylonia. The prophet Jeremiah strongly spoke against this dependence on Egypt (Jer 46:17-24). Whether Neco risked his forces to penetrate into Judah, a Babylonian province, is not certain. Nebuchadnezzar quickly moved his forces to Judah, exiled Jehoiakim to Babylon, and enthroned Zedekiah (597 BC). Shortly thereafter, Neco died (595 BC). His son, Psammetichus II, succeeded him.

See also Josiah #1.

NEDABIAH

Son of Jeconiah (NLT "Jehoiachin"), king of Judah (1 Chr 3:18).

NEHEMIAH

Name of three men mentioned in the OT after the period of the Exile. The name means "the Lord comforts" and was appropriate for this time of hope and fulfillment.

1. Governor of Judah during the restoration. Originally cupbearer to the Persian king Artaxerxes I (464–424 BC), Nehemiah pleaded to be sent to Judah to aid his fellow Jews in their difficulties and in particular to rebuild Jerusalem (Neh 1:1–2:8). He was appointed governor of Judah for 12 years.

After inspecting the walls upon his arrival, he realized that their repair was to be his prime task. This repair would guarantee the security of the city and could provide a focal point for the Jewish community scattered throughout Judah. That he was able to marshal support for this project and to complete it attests to his skills in management and administration. He also had a strong personal faith, as his prayers (Neh 1:4-11; 2:4) and conviction of divine guidance and help (2:8, 18, 20) attest. He had to overcome hostility and intimidation from powerful neighboring authorities in Samaria, Ammon, and Arabia (4:1-9; 6:1-14). He also required economic justice (ch 5). A few rich Jews were exploiting a food shortage by exacting high interest

QUICKTAKE

NEHEMIAH

STRENGTHS AND ACCOMPLISHMENTS
- A man of character, persistence, and prayer
- Brilliant planner, organizer, and motivator
- Under his leadership, the wall around Jerusalem was rebuilt in 52 days
- As political leader, led the nation to religious reform and spiritual awakening
- Was calm in the face of opposition
- Was capable of being bluntly honest with his people when they were sinning

LESSONS FROM HIS LIFE
- The first step in any venture is to pray
- People under God's direction can accomplish "impossible" tasks
- There are two parts to real service for God: talking with him and walking with him

VITAL STATISTICS
Where: Persia, Jerusalem
Occupations: King's cup-bearer, city builder, governor of Judah
Relative: Father: Hacaliah
Contemporaries: Ezra, Artaxerxes, Tobiah, Sanballat

KEY VERSE
"Then I told them about how the gracious hand of God had been on me, and about my conversation with the king.

"They replied at once, 'Yes, let's rebuild the wall!' So they began the good work" (Nehemiah 2:18).

Nehemiah's story is told in the book of Nehemiah.

from their poorer brothers. Included in Nehemiah's concern for Jerusalem was a strong interest in the maintenance of Temple worship. He was involved in the production of a document in which the Jewish community pledged themselves to support the Temple personnel and to provide offerings (Neh 10:1, 32-39). Clearly, he realized that Judah needed at its heart a religious emphasis as well as political stability. These particular religious reforms are linked with those of his

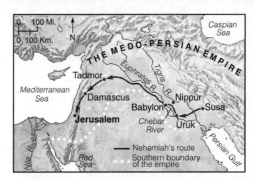

Nehemiah's Journey to Jerusalem: When Nehemiah heard that the rebuilding projects in Jerusalem were progressing slowly, he asked the king of the Medo-Persian Empire, for whom he worked, for permission to go there to help his people complete the task of rebuilding their city's walls. The king agreed to let him go; so he left as soon as possible, traveling along much the same route Ezra had taken seven years earlier.

second period as governor (ch 13). Other reforms of that period concerned the observance of the Sabbath (13:15-22) and the problem of marriages to non-Jews (13:23-27). Nehemiah was a forceful leader (v 25) who used his imperial powers to restore to the settlers a national and religious identity in a period of political and economic weakness. *See also* Ezra #1.

2. Leader mentioned in a list of Jewish exiles who returned from Babylon with Zerubbabel sometime after 538 BC (Ezr 2:2; Neh 7:7).

3. Ruler of half the district of Beth-zur who helped rebuild the Jerusalem wall in 444 BC (Neh 3:16).

NEHUSHTA
Mother of Jehoiachin, king of Judah, who was deported with her son to Babylon (2 Kgs 24:8-15).

NEHUSHTAN
Name given to the bronze serpent that Moses made during the wilderness wanderings. At the time of King Hezekiah's reforms, it was destroyed (2 Kgs 18:4).

NEKODA
1. Father of a family of Temple servants who returned to Jerusalem following the Exile (Ezr 2:48; Neh 7:50).

2. Father of a family of returned exiles who could not prove their Israelite descent (Ezr 2:60; Neh 7:62).

NEMUEL

1. Reubenite and the son of Eliab (Nm 26:9).
2. One of Simeon's sons (Nm 26:12; 1 Chr 4:24), also called Jemuel (Gn 46:10). *See* Jemuel.

NEPHEG

1. Levite of the family of Kohath and the second of Izhar's three sons (Ex 6:21).
2. David's son born to him during his reign in Jerusalem (2 Sm 5:15; 1 Chr 3:7; 14:6).

NER

Benjaminite, father of Abner and brother of Kish; he was probably the uncle of Saul (1 Sm 14:51; 26:5; 2 Sm 2:8; 1 Kgs 2:32; 1 Chr 26:28). Although Ner's father's name was given as Abiel (1 Sm 14:51), disputed readings put Ner among the sons of Jeiel (1 Chr 8:29-30; 9:35-36). Elsewhere he is listed as the father of Kish, the father of Saul (8:33; 9:39). Ner was, then, the grandfather or the uncle of Saul, probably the latter. One suggestion is that there were two men called Kish, one of whom was Ner's brother, the other his son. Another is that there were two men called Ner. These speculations demonstrate that genealogical tables were sometimes incomplete or ambiguous.

NEREUS

Roman Christian to whom Paul sent greetings in the salutation of his letter to Rome (Rom 16:15).

NERGAL

Heathen deity worshiped by the men of Cuth after the fall of Israel in 722 BC (2 Kgs 17:30). Nergal, lord of the netherworld and associated with the sun god, was the city god of the northern Babylonian city of Cuthah (cf. v 24).

NERGAL-SHAREZER

Babylonian prince who held the title "Rabmag." Nergal-sharezer participated with Nebuchadnezzar and the Chaldean army in conquering Jerusalem after a three-year siege from 588 to 586 BC (Jer 39:3) and later entrusted Jeremiah to Gedaliah's care (v 13).

NERI

Ancestor of Jesus in Luke's genealogy (Lk 3:27).

NERIAH

Father of Baruch the scribe (Jer 32:12, 16; 36:4, 8) and Seraiah the quartermaster (51:59), both of whom served Jeremiah the prophet.

NETHANEL

Common OT name spelled Nethaneel in the KJV.

1. Zuar's son and the prince of Issachar's tribe at the start of Israel's wilderness wanderings (Nm 1:8; 2:5; 10:15), who represented his kinsmen at the altar's dedication (7:18, 23).

2. Judahite, the fourth son of Jesse and David's brother (1 Chr 2:14).

3. One of the priests assigned to blow a trumpet before the Ark in the procession led by David when the Ark was moved to Jerusalem (1 Chr 15:24).

4. Levite and the father of Shemaiah, the scribe who recorded the 24 divisions of priests founded during David's reign (1 Chr 24:6).

5. Korahite Levite and Obed-edom's fifth son in David's reign (1 Chr 26:4).

6. One of the princes sent by King Jehoshaphat to teach the law in the cities of Judah (2 Chr 17:7).

7. One of the Levitical chiefs who generously gave animals to the Levites for the celebration of the Passover feast during King Josiah's reign (2 Chr 35:9).

8. Priest and one of Pashhur's six sons who was encouraged by Ezra to divorce his foreign wife during the postexilic era (Ezr 10:22).

9. Head of Jedaiah's priestly family during the days of Joiakim, the high priest, in postexilic Jerusalem (Neh 12:21).

10. One of the priestly musicians who performed at the dedication of the Jerusalem wall during Nehemiah's day (Neh 12:36).

NETHANIAH

1. Elishama's son, father of Ishmael and a member of the royal family of Judah (2 Kgs 25:23-25; Jer 40:8-15; 41:1-18).

2. One of Asaph's four sons and the leader of the fifth of 24 divisions of musicians trained for service in the sanctuary during David's reign (1 Chr 25:2, 12).

3. One of the Levites sent by King Jehoshaphat of Judah to teach the law in the cities of Judah (2 Chr 17:8).

4. Shelemiah's son and the father of Jehudi. Jehudi served in the court of King Jehoiakim of Judah (Jer 36:14).

NEZIAH

Forefather of a family of Temple servants who returned to Jerusalem with Zerubbabel following the Babylonian captivity (Ezr 2:54; Neh 7:56).

NEZIB

One of the cities in the lowland allotted to Judah for an inheritance (Jos 15:43). Its site is identified with modern Khirbet Beit Nesib, east of Lachish.

NIBHAZ

The name of a god worshiped by displaced Avvites after they were forcibly resettled in Samaria by the Assyrians in 722 BC. They brought the worship of this idol, as well as that of Tartak, with them at that time (2 Kgs 17:31). Although purported to be of Mesopotamian origin, this is not likely because the worshipers were Syrian. The word Nibhaz may be a Hebrew corruption of "altar" and hence a reference to a deified altar that was the object of worship.

NICANOR

One of the seven chosen by the early church to supervise the daily distribution to the poor saints in Jerusalem (Acts 6:5).

NICODEMUS

Pharisee and member of the Sanhedrin mentioned only in John's Gospel (Jn 3:1-15; 7:50-52; 19:39-41). According to John 3, Nicodemus came to Jesus at night and acknowledged him as a teacher sent by God. He was convinced that Jesus could not perform such things if God were not with him. Following an exchange concerning the need to be born again, Jesus asked how Nicodemus, a member of the Jewish religious court, could fail to understand such things. At that time he evidently made no profession of faith, but later he did defend Jesus before the Sanhedrin (7:50-52). After Jesus' death, Nicodemus openly assisted Joseph of Arimathea with the burial of his body (19:39-42).

Some scholars suggest that Nicodemus was one of the Jewish leaders who believed in Jesus but did not confess him openly for fear of excommunication (12:42). Tradition subsequently held that he belonged to the household of faith, as one persuaded to believe through the message and deeds of Jesus, but remained intimidated by the religious establishment.

NICOLAS

One of the seven men named in Acts 6:5, who was enlisted for service in the Jerusalem church in its early days. His duty as specified in Acts 6:1-4 was to direct the fair and equal distribution of food. Due to the use of terms in Acts 6:1 ("daily distribution" or "service") and 6:2 ("to distribute at tables" or "to serve"), these seven men traditionally have been called "deacons" (or "servers").

Nicolas, the last named in the list, is identified as a proselyte. Thus, he was a Gentile convert to Judaism before he became a Christian. His name is Greek, and the city of Antioch is mentioned as his home. The NT writings provide no further information about him.

NIMROD

Cush's son and grandson of Ham the son of Noah (Gn 10:8; 1 Chr 1:10). He is described as "the first man of might on earth" and "a mighty hunter" (Gn 10:8-9). Nimrod was the first to establish a great empire and was a well-known hunter. Tradition makes him ruler over

Babylon and Akkad in southern Mesopotamia, and over Nineveh in Assyria. The phrase "land of Nimrod" seems to be synonymous with Assyria (Mi 5:6).

The OT references to Nimrod indicate that in ancient tradition he was a man of indomitable personality, possessing extraordinary talents and powers. Some scholars identify him with a Mesopotamian king who united Assyria and Babylon in the 13th century BC. This conflicts with the statement connecting him with Cush the son of Ham and pointing to an association with the south of Egypt where Cush was located (Gn 10:8).

The name and fame of Nimrod have a secure place in Talmudic Judaism and in Islamic tradition. In the former he personifies both rebellion against God and military might in the earth. In rabbinic tradition, the Tower of Babel (Gn 11:1-9) is "the house of Nimrod" where idolatry was practiced and divine homage offered to Nimrod. In Islam, Nimrod persecutes Abraham and has him thrown into a fiery furnace.

NIMSHI

Father of Jehoshaphat and grandfather of Jehu, who was king of Israel (1 Kgs 19:16; 2 Kgs 9:2-20; 2 Chr 22:7).

NOADIAH

1. Binnui's son and one of the two Levites present when the Temple treasure that was brought back to Jerusalem by Ezra was weighed and recorded (Ezr 8:33).

2. Prophetess who, along with Tobiah, Sanballat, and some false prophets, attempted to intimidate Nehemiah when he was engaged in rebuilding Jerusalem's walls after the Exile (Neh 6:14).

NOAH

1. Son of Lamech and the grandson of Methuselah, a descendant of Seth, third son of Adam (Gn 5:3-20). Lamech named his son Noah, a name that sounds like a Hebrew term that can mean "relief" or "comfort." When Lamech gave him this name, he said, "May he bring us relief from our work and the painful labor of farming this ground that the LORD has cursed" (v 29, NLT).

Determined to destroy creation because of rampant wickedness (cf. Mt 24:37-39; Lk 17:26-27), God made an exception with Noah, a man righteous in God's sight and blameless before people (Gn 6:3-9). Following God's precise instructions, Noah constructed an ark into which went only eight people—Noah and his wife and his three sons and their wives—and all kinds of creatures in pairs. They were thus protected from the ensuing deluge in which all other living things perished (6:14–8:19). When they emerged from the ark, Noah built an altar and sacrificed burnt offerings that pleased God, who promised that the Flood would never be repeated or the sequence of the seasons disrupted, despite man's sin (8:20–9:17).

Noah had withstood mighty temptations, but, whether through carelessness or old

QUICKTAKE

NOAH

STRENGTHS AND ACCOMPLISHMENTS
- Only follower of God left in his generation
- Second father of the human race
- Man of patience, consistency, and obedience
- First major shipbuilder

WEAKNESS AND MISTAKE
- Got drunk and embarrassed himself in front of his sons

LESSONS FROM HIS LIFE
- God is faithful to those who obey him
- God does not always protect us from trouble, but cares for us in spite of trouble
- Obedience is a long-term commitment
- A man may be faithful, but his sinful nature always travels with him

VITAL STATISTICS
Where: We're not told how far from the Garden of Eden people had settled
Occupation: Farmer, shipbuilder, preacher
Relatives: Grandfather: Methuselah. Father: Lamech. Sons: Ham, Shem, and Japheth

KEY VERSE
"So Noah did everything exactly as God had commanded him" (Genesis 6:22).

Noah's story is told in Genesis 5:28–10:32. He is also mentioned in 1 Chronicles 1:3, 4; Isaiah 54:9; Ezekiel 14:14, 20; Matthew 24:37, 38; Luke 3:36; 17:26, 27; Hebrews 11:7; 1 Peter 3:20; 2 Peter 2:5.

age, he became drunk. Family members reacted differently and were judged accordingly. Shem and Japheth received blessing. Ham received no blessing, but his son Canaan was cursed (9:20-27). Noah was 950 years old when he died, 350 years after the Flood.

Noah, Daniel, and Job are specifically cited for "their righteousness" in Ezekiel 14:12-14, 19-20. The Letter to the Hebrews commends Noah, who by faith, holy fear, and rejection of the world became the heir of righteousness (11:7), and 2 Peter 2:5 calls him "a preacher of righteousness."

2. Daughter of Zelophehad of Manasseh's tribe (Nm 26:33). When their father died

without a son, she and her four sisters successfully petitioned for a change in the law that would protect their inheritance rights (Nm 27:1-11; cf. Jos 17:3-6). They were, however, restricted to marrying within their own tribe (Nm 36:1-12).

NOBAH
Manassite who conquered and settled the town of Kenath, east of the Jordan, and subsequently renamed it after himself (Nm 32:42).

NOGAH
One of 13 sons of David born in Jerusalem after David established his kingdom (1 Chr 3:7; 14:6).

NOHAH
Fourth son of Benjamin (1 Chr 8:2).

NOT MY PEOPLE
Symbolic name given by the prophet Hosea to his third son (Hos 1:9) as a warning of the coming judgment of God upon Israel. *See* Lo-Ammi.

NUN
Ephraimite, Elishama's son, and the father of Joshua, the great leader of Israel (Ex 33:11; Nm 11:28; Dt 1:38; Jos 1:1; Jgs 2:8).

NYMPHA
Christian woman living in Laodicea (or perhaps Colossae), in whose house believers gathered for worship. Paul sent greetings to her and the church (Col 4:15, KJV uses the masculine form "Nymphas").

OBADIAH

1. Governor of Ahab's house (1 Kgs 18:3-16). Elijah met him after the years of drought, and requested Obadiah to bring Ahab to him, while both Ahab and Obadiah were looking for water and grass (v 5). Obadiah was an important officer in charge of Ahab's house. Unlike his master, Obadiah was faithful to the Lord, as he hid 100 prophets in caves and provided them with food and drink.

2. Descendant of David (1 Chr 3:21).

3. Descendant of Izrahiah from Issachar's tribe (1 Chr 7:3).

4. Azel's son and a descendant of King Saul from Benjamin's tribe (1 Chr 8:38; 9:44).

5. Son of Shemaiah, who was among the first Levites returning from the Exile to Jerusalem. He lived in one of the villages of the Netophathites (1 Chr 9:16). He is called Abda in Nehemiah 11:17. *See* Abda #2.

6. Gadite who joined David at his stronghold in the wilderness. He was a mighty warrior, able to handle shield and spear, and was extremely fast (1 Chr 12:8-9).

7. Father of Ishmaiah, commander over the forces of Zebulun (1 Chr 27:19).

8. Prince of Judah in Jehoshaphat's time (2 Chr 17:7). He joined four other officers and the Levites in teaching the law throughout the cities of Judah.

9. Levite overseer in Josiah's time (2 Chr 34:12), in charge of the repair of the Temple.

10. Son of Jehiel (Ezr 8:9), who joined Ezra in his journey from Babylon to Jerusalem, leading 218 men with him.

11. Priest who signed Ezra's covenant (Neh 10:5).

12. Gatekeeper and Levite charged with the oversight of the storehouses by the gates in the days of Joiakim, son of Jeshua (Neh 12:25-26).

13. Prophet who prophesied against Edom, which had rejoiced at the Babylonian victories in Jerusalem in 597 BC. Obadiah described the behavior of the Edomites (Ob 1:11-14) in his prophecy, the shortest book in the OT, and predicted God's judgment on Edom (vv 2-10, 15).

OBAL

Alternate spelling of Ebal, Joktan's descendant, in Genesis 10:28. *See* Ebal #2.

OBED

1. Ruth and Boaz's first child, listed among the ancestors of Jesus (Ru 4:17, 21-22; 1 Chr 2:12; Mt 1:5; Lk 3:32).

2. Jerahmeelite and Ephlal's son (1 Chr 2:37-38).

3. One of David's mighty men (1 Chr 11:47).

4. Shemaiah's son and an able leader who ruled his father's house (1 Chr 26:6-7).

5. Father of Azariah, a captain of Jehoiada (2 Chr 23:1).

OBED-EDOM

1. Man under whose care David placed the Ark of the Covenant when he was transferring it from Gibeah to Jerusalem (2 Sm 6:10-12; 1 Chr 13:5-14). He is called a Gittite, which indicates that his birthplace was Gath. This was not the Philistine city of Gath but the Levitical town in the territory of Dan known as Gath-rimmon (Jos 19:45). It is likely that Obed-edom was a Levite and therefore qualified to care for the Ark of the Covenant. Uzzah's rash action in steadying the Ark when the oxen stumbled brought upon him immediate death. David's consternation and fear at this turn of events led him to reconsider his intention of bringing the Ark to Jerusalem. Apparently Obed-edom's home was nearby and it was convenient to leave the Ark in his care. When David was informed after three months that the Lord had greatly blessed Obed-edom, he realized that the judgment that fell on Uzzah was incurred because the Ark was carried contrary to the method prescribed in the Law (Nm 4:15; 7:9) and not because the Lord was angry with Uzzah. He ordered that the Ark be taken from Obed-edom's home and carried to Jerusalem in the proper manner (1 Chr 15:25-28). Apparently Obed-edom was rewarded for his faithful service by being appointed a gatekeeper for the Ark in Jerusalem (15:24; 26:4, 8, 15). But some scholars believe that Obed-edom the gatekeeper was a man other than the one referred to above.

2. Levitical musician who ministered before the Ark (1 Chr 15:21; 16:5, 38). He was the son of Jeduthun, one of David's chief singers. Some scholars think that the musician and singer were different men.

3. Levitical guardian of the sacred vessels of the Temple taken hostage by Joash (2 Chr 25:24).

OBIL
Ishmaelite steward of King David's camels (1 Chr 27:30).

OCRAN
Father of Pagiel, the leader of Asher's tribe during the wilderness journeys (Nm 1:13; 2:27; 7:72, 77; 10:26).

OG
King whose fame partly came from his being a giant. "King Og of Bashan was the last survivor of the giant Rephaites. His bed made of iron and was was more than thirteen feet [4.1 meters] long and six feet [1.8 meters] wide" (Dt 3:11, NLT).

Og, king of Bashan, fell before Moses' assault immediately after the defeat of King Sihon the Amorite (Nm 21:33-35). Bashan lay along the northern part of the Transjordan. Og's land stretched northeastward from the lower course of the Jarmuk (Yarmuk) River, and lofty mountain ranges protected him on the east from scorching desert winds.

Og and his people had several settlements, primarily Ashtaroth and Edrei (Jos 13:12). Og had fortified his land with 60 walled cities and was probably overconfident before Moses' army. Moses completely destroyed the populace of those cities; he spared only the livestock and the spoils of war (Dt 3:5-6).

Three tribes of Israel found the Transjordan particularly suitable for grazing their herds. So at the defeat of Sihon and Og, Moses assigned the newly won lands to the tribes of Gad, Reuben, and half of Manasseh (Nm 32:33; Jos 12:4-6).

OHAD

Simeon's son (Gn 46:10; Ex 6:15), whose name does not appear in the list of Numbers 26:12-14.

OHEL

Descendant of Jehoiakim and King David (1 Chr 3:20).

OHOLAH AND OHOLIBAH

Names given to the northern kingdom (KJV "Aholah"), with its capital at Samaria, and to the southern kingdom (KJV "Aholibah"), with its capital at Jerusalem, respectively, by Ezekiel in his allegory depicting the unfaithfulness of God's people (Ez 23). The names characterized the basic attitude of each of the twin kingdoms toward God and his worship. Samaria (Oholah) had "her own tent" (the literal meaning of the name) and had invented her own centers of worship; Jerusalem (Oholibah, literally "my tent is in her") prided herself in being the custodian of the Temple.

Rather than being true to the Lord, Samaria had committed spiritual adultery. Not being content with her spiritual infidelity in wooing the gods of Egypt, she had lusted after the idols of Assyria and the worldly attractions that the Neo-Assyrian culture held out before her. Both courses of action are adequately documented by archaeological discoveries from the ancient Near East, such as Jehu's act of homage as portrayed on the Black Obelisk of King Shalmaneser III of Assyria (859–824 BC). Samaria's conduct had been judged by God; her newfound desire had proved to be her destruction, God giving her over into the hands of the Assyrian conqueror.

Far from learning from Israel's example, Judah had not only courted Assyria and its idolatry (e.g., 2 Kgs 16:10-18) but also had added to her affections the Neo-Babylonian Empire (e.g., 20:14-18) and then had turned once again to Egypt (e.g., Jer 37; 46), her earlier lover (Ez 23:11-21). Therefore, God would sorely punish her at the hands of the Babylonians, and she would know the just judgment of God.

Ezekiel closes his allegory with a rehearsal of God's charges against the two kingdoms. God's people were doubly guilty. Not being content with their apostasy, they had gone so far as to profane the sanctuary of God and his Sabbath by entering the Temple with hands bloodied in the sacrifice of their own children in pagan rites.

OHOLIAB

Man assigned by Moses to assist Bezalel, the master craftsman, in the construction and ornamentation of the Tabernacle. Son of Ahisamach and member of Dan's tribe, Oholiab was specifically noted as a designer and embroiderer. Along with Bezalel, he taught the skills necessary for the construction of the Tabernacle (Ex 31:6; 35:34; 36:1-2; 38:23; KJV "Aholiab").

OHOLIBAMAH

1. Esau's wife, the daughter of Anah the Hivite (Gn 36:2, 5, 14, 18, 25, KJV "Aholibamah"), who bore to him Jeush, Jalam, and Korah before Esau left Canaan for Seir.

    The absence of her name from the other lists of Esau's wives (see Gn 26:34; 28:9) has occasioned a great deal of discussion. The considerable variation in these lists may indicate either a confusion in the scribal transmission or may point to the use of alternate names, gained either at marriage or as a result of some memorable event in the women's lives. Whether or not she is identified with Judith, as some have suggested, the scriptural observation that she was "a source of grief to Isaac and Rebekah" is true (26:35).

2. Edomite clan chieftain descended from Esau (Gn 36:41; 1 Chr 1:52, KJV "Aholibamah").

OLYMPAS

Member of the church in Rome to whom Paul sent personal greetings (Rom 16:15).

OMAR

Second son of Eliphaz, grandson of Esau and the great-grandson of Abraham (Gn 36:11, 15; 1 Chr 1:36); an Edomite clan chief.

OMRI

1. King of Israel who first appears in Scripture as general of the army during the reign of Elah, king of Israel. In 885 BC Elah sent Omri to besiege the Philistine fortress of Gibbethon. During the siege, Zimri, another military leader, launched a coup against Elah, killed him, and immediately wiped out all of Elah's male relatives. When Omri heard of the assassination, he had the army declare him king and marched to the capital at Tirzah to deal with Zimri. When Zimri saw that the siege of Tirzah was going to be successful, he set fire to the king's palace and died in the flames after only seven days on the throne.

    But Omri's rule over Israel was not yet established. Tibni seized control of part of the state and held it for about four years. Finally, Omri was able to crush Tibni and extend his power over all Israel. He established Israel's fourth ruling dynasty, which was destined to continue through three more generations after his own. His reign lasted a total of 12 years (885–874 BC), including the years of sovereignty disputed with Tibni.

    International Developments To the northeast of Israel, the Arameans of Syria were building a strong state with its capital at Damascus. A few years before Omri took the throne, Asa of Judah had sought the help of Syria against Baasha of Israel. Soon Syria would become a threat to both Hebrew kingdoms.

Farther east, Assyria was growing in strength under the leadership of Ashurnasirpal II (883–859 BC), the founder of the empire. He marched into Phoenicia, but Israel was spared Assyrian attack until the days of Omri's son Ahab.

Omri's Reign Since the purpose of Scripture is not to provide a political, military, or even social history of Israel or the countries surrounding it, administrations of the kings of Israel and Judah are often very briefly treated. For a fuller picture, it is necessary to turn to nonbiblical sources. From Assyrian records, it is evident that Omri must have been an impressive ruler. Generations later, Assyrians still spoke of Israel as the "land of Omri."

Perceptive leader that he was, Omri recognized that the nations needed a capital that was centrally located and militarily defensible. He settled on the site of Samaria, the third and most significant capital of the realm (Shechem and Tirzah had previously served as capitals). Located seven miles (11.3 kilometers) northwest of Shechem on the main road leading to Galilee and Phoenicia, it perched on a free-standing hill that rose some 300 to 400 feet (91.4–121.9 meters) above the surrounding plain. Thus it could be quite easily defended; it had a prosperous hinterland to supply it with food and taxes; and it was conveniently located on a main road. Omri bought the hill from Shemer and named the city after its owner. Then he leveled the top of the hill and built the palace compound. He also built a 33-foot-(10.1-meter-) thick wall around the summit of the hill.

Omri's expansionist activities are not mentioned in 1 Kings, but Scripture is supplemented by discovery of the Moabite Stone in 1868 at Dibon, east of the Jordan River. On this stela, Mesha, king of Moab, tells that Omri conquered Moab. Israel had continued to subjugate the land in the days of Ahab, but during his days, Mesha successfully rebelled against Israel (2 Kgs 3:4). That Omri could mount a successful war against Moab soon after becoming king shows that he was a capable ruler, because previously the kingdom of Israel had been greatly weakened by insurrection and political instability.

Omri also reestablished the friendly relations with Phoenicia that had been initiated in the days of David and Solomon. Presumably, he made a full alliance with King Ethbaal of Tyre and then sealed it with the marriage of his son Ahab to the Phoenician princess Jezebel. Such an alliance would have been mutually beneficial, for it would have brought cedar, beautifully crafted goods, and Phoenician architectural and technical expertise to Israel, and it would have provided Israelite grain and olive oil to Phoenicia. Moreover, it would have linked their forces against the threat of the rising power of Assyria.

This pact was destined to corrupt Israel, however, for it brought Baal worship into the land. Probably this is what the writer of Kings had in mind when he said that Omri "did worse" than the other kings of Israel before him (1 Kgs 16:25) because he practiced the idolatrous ways of Jeroboam. Baal worship was regarded as more degrading than the calf worship Jeroboam had introduced. Omri, and his son Ahab after him, subscribed to both.

Omri was one of the most powerful kings of Israel, building its new capital, winning for the state a reputation for prowess, and setting a course for future kings to follow. But unfortunately that course was morally corrupt; the introduction of Baal worship was one of the terrible results of Omri's alliance with Tyre.

2. One of Beker's sons from Benjamin's tribe (1 Chr 7:8).

3. Descendant of Perez, son of Judah (1 Chr 9:4).

4. Son of Michael, prince of the tribe of Issachar during David's reign (1 Chr 27:18).

ON

Reubenite, Peleth's son who joined Korah's rebellion against Moses and Aaron in the wilderness (Nm 16:1).

ONAM

1. Grandson of Seir and Shobal's fifth son (Gn 36:23; 1 Chr 1:40).

2. Son of Jerahmeel and Atarah, the father of a clan in Judah (1 Chr 2:26-28).

ONAN

Second son of Judah and a Canaanitess named Shua (Gn 38:4-10; 46:12; Nm 26:19; 1 Chr 2:3). Judah forced him to enter into a levirate marriage with Tamar, the wife of his deceased brother, Er. Er and Tamar had no children. Onan refused to have children by Tamar, knowing that they would be heirs to his brother's estate. As a result of Onan's refusal to raise up descendants for his brother, the Lord punished him with death (Gn 38:8-10).

ONESIMUS

Slave on whose behalf Paul wrote the Letter to Philemon. A slave of Philemon, he had robbed his master and run away from him. He is also mentioned with Tychicus as a bearer of the Letter to the Colossians (Col 4:9), indicating that he came from that region. Paul became acquainted with him, converted him, and developed a close friendship with him (Phlm 1:10). Paul wanted to keep Onesimus with him during his imprisonment because he had been helpful to him (in Greek, Onesimus means "useful"). However, Paul returned the slave to his master, confident that the runaway slave would be received by his former owner as a Christian brother and that Philemon would charge any wrong that Onesimus had done to Paul's account.

See also Philemon.

ONESIPHORUS

Christian who took care of Paul during his confinement in Ephesus. After Paul's transfer to Rome, Onesiphorus eagerly sought him out and ministered to him there (2 Tm 1:16). In the salutation of his Second Letter to Timothy, Paul sent greetings to Onesiphorus and his household (4:19).

OPHIR

Joktan's son and a descendant of Shem through Arphaxad's line (Gn 10:29; 1 Chr 1:23).

OPHRAH

Meonothai's son from Judah's tribe (1 Chr 4:14).

OREB

One of two Midianite chieftains (the other being Zeeb) put to death by men from Ephraim's tribe (Jgs 7:25). The occasion for this execution was Gideon's surprise attack on the Midianite encampment at the hill of Moreh in the valley of Jezreel. The Midianites' line of retreat eastward required them to recross the Jordan River. Gideon sent word to the Ephraimites to seize the fording places on the river to prevent the Midianites from escaping. The Ephraimites, following the orders, intercepted a contingent of fleeing Midianites, including the prominent leaders Oreb and Zeeb. They beheaded these two leaders and sent their heads as a war prize to Gideon, who was then pursuing the Midianites on the east side of the Jordan (8:3).

During Israel's later history, the deaths of Oreb and Zeeb were recognized as a great triumph of God over the enemies of his people. The psalmist implores God to overthrow the nobles among Israel's current enemies just as he did the Midianite chieftains (Ps 83:11). The Lord, speaking through his prophet Isaiah, pledged that the Assyrians would be overthrown like the slaughter of Midian at the rock of Oreb (Is 9:4; 10:26), implying that the earlier victory amounted to more than the capture of two leaders; it was an important and strategic defeat of the Midianite invasion force.

OREN

Descendant of Judah and the third son of Jerahmeel (1 Chr 2:25).

ORPAH

Woman of Moab who married Chilion (Ru 1:1-14), son of Elimelech and Naomi. After her husband and sons died, Naomi decided to return to Judah. Both Orpah and Ruth resolved to go with Naomi, but at Naomi's urging Orpah remained in her homeland.

See also Ruth.

OTHNI

Levite; Shemaiah's son and a gatekeeper in Solomon's Temple (1 Chr 26:7).

OTHNIEL

Judge of Israel, mentioned as the son of Kenaz and Caleb's nephew (or perhaps brother), who delivered Israel from the tyranny of Cushan-rishathaim, and who earlier distinguished himself by capturing Debir (Jos 15:15-17; Jgs 1:11-13; 3:8-11).

At Caleb's prompting (promising his daughter Achsah to anyone who could conquer Debir), Othniel took Kiriath-sepher (Debir) and received Achsah for his wife. When Caleb gave her and her land as a present, Achsah asked for a water source and was given the upper springs and the lower springs (Jos 15:19; Jgs 1:15).

Later, Othniel delivered the Israelites from the oppressive Cushan-rishathaim, king of Mesopotamia (Aram-naharaim), whom the Israelites had served for eight years on account of their sin (Jgs 3:7). When the people cried for relief, the Lord raised up Othniel. Delivering them, he was described as someone that the "Spirit of the Lord came upon" (v 10). The effects of his work as judge lasted for a generation (vv 9-11).

OZEM

1. Sixth son of Jesse and a descendant of Hezron (1 Chr 2:15).

2. Fourth son of Jerahmeel by his first wife (1 Chr 2:25).

OZNI

Alternate name for Ezbon and his descendants (Nm 26:16). *See* Ezbon #1.

PAARAI

One of David's mighty men, said to be from Arba, in Judah (2 Sm 23:35); perhaps the same as Naarai the son of Ezbai (1 Chr 11:37).

PADON

Forefather of a family of Temple servants who returned with Zerubbabel to Palestine following the Babylonian captivity (Ezr 2:44; Neh 7:47).

PAGIEL

Ocran's son from Asher's tribe, who was appointed by Moses to help number the people in the wilderness. He also served as leader of his tribe during that time (Nm 1:13; 2:27; 7:72, 77; 10:26).

PAHATH-MOAB

Head of a family of Israelites who returned with Zerubbabel to Palestine after the Babylonian captivity (Ezr 2:6; Neh 7:11). Other members of his family, about 200 men, came with Ezra (Ezr 8:4). After the return, certain of his sons were included among the Israelites who vowed to sever their relationships with foreign wives (10:30). Hasshub, Pahath-moab's son, helped rebuild the Jerusalem wall and the tower of furnaces in Nehemiah's day (Neh 3:11). Pahath-moab, called a chief of the people, set his seal on Ezra's covenant (10:14).

PALAL

Uzai's son, who helped rebuild the Jerusalem wall in Nehemiah's day (Neh 3:25).

PALLU

Reuben's son, father of Eliab (Gn 46:9; Ex 6:14; Nm 26:8; 1 Chr 5:3) and the founder of the Palluite family (Nm 26:5).

PALTI

1. One of the 12 spies Moses sent to explore the land of Canaan before the Israelite conquest. Palti represented Benjamin's tribe (Nm 13:9).
2. Laish's son, to whom King Saul gave Michal, his daughter and David's wife, after the break between Saul and David (1 Sm 25:44). Michal was recovered from him and returned to David (2 Sm 3:15); in that reference he is called Paltiel.

PALTIEL

1. Son of Azzan and a leader of Issachar's tribe (Nm 34:26). He was appointed by Eleazar and Joshua to assist in the distribution of the land west of the Jordan River among the ten tribes to whom it was given.
2. Alternate rendering of Palti, Laish's son, in 2 Samuel 3:15. *See* Palti #2.

PARMASHTA
One of the 10 sons of Haman killed by the Jews (Est 9:9).

PARMENAS
One of the seven men full of the Spirit and of wisdom chosen by the Jerusalem church to minister to the widows (Acts 6:5).

PARNACH
Elizaphan's father from Zebulun's tribe (Nm 34:25).

PAROSH
Head of a family who returned to Jerusalem with Zerubbabel after the Babylonian exile (Ezr 2:3; Neh 7:8). One of his descendants, Pedaiah, participated in rebuilding the Jerusalem wall (Neh 3:25); other descendants are mentioned as having taken foreign wives (Ezr 10:25).

PARSHANDATHA
One of the 10 sons of Haman slain by the Jews (Est 9:7).

PARUAH
Father of Jehoshaphat from Issachar's tribe. Jehoshaphat was appointed to provide food for King Solomon and his household one month out of the year (1 Kgs 4:7, 17).

PASACH
Japhlet's son from Asher's tribe (1 Chr 7:33).

PASEAH
1. Eshton's son, the brother of Beth-rapha and a descendant of Kelub from Judah's tribe. Paseah was mentioned as one of the men of Recah (1 Chr 4:12).

2. Ancestor of a family of Temple servants who returned to Palestine with Zerubbabel after the Babylonian captivity (Ezr 2:49; Neh 7:51).

3. Joiada's father. Joiada, along with Meshullam, repaired the Old Gate of Jerusalem under Nehemiah's direction during the postexilic period (Neh 3:6).

PASHHUR
1. Forefather of a family of priests who returned to Jerusalem with Zerubbabel after the exile (Ezr 2:38; Neh 7:41). He was perhaps also the son of Malkijah and the grandfather of Adaiah the priest. Adaiah served in the sanctuary during the postexilic period (1 Chr 9:12). Six of Pashhur's sons were encouraged by Ezra to divorce their foreign wives (Ezr 10:22).

2. One of the priests who with Nehemiah set his seal on the covenant of Ezra (Neh 10:3).

3. Immer's son and the priest and chief officer of the sanctuary during the reign of King Zedekiah of Judah (597–586 BC). Frustrated with Jeremiah's predictions of doom for Jerusalem, Pashhur beat him and had him put in stocks at the Temple's Benjamin Gate. Upon his release, Jeremiah exposed Pashhur's false prophecies and foretold his exile and death in Babylon (Jer 20:1-6). Jeremiah also gave Pashhur the name "Magor-Missabib." The name Pashhur means "prosperity round about"; the new name means "terror on every side" (20:3) because Pashhur was to see the horrors of the Babylonian invasion.

4. Son of Malkijah and perhaps the grandson of King Zedekiah of Judah (597–586 BC; Jer 21:1; 38:1; cf. 38:6). The king sent Pashhur, with Zephaniah the priest, to Jeremiah, requesting that he ask the Lord to deal favorably with Judah. It was in his father's cistern that Jeremiah was imprisoned (Jer 38:6).

5. Father of Gedaliah. Gedaliah—with Shephatiah, Jucal, and Pashhur—opposed Jeremiah and attempted to kill him by imprisoning him in Malkijah's cistern (Jer 38:1).

PATROBAS
One of the Christians in Rome to whom Paul sent greetings (Rom 16:14).

PAUL, THE APOSTLE
Prominent leader of the first-century church; apostle to the Gentiles; author of 13 NT epistles.

Preview
- Family and Cultural Background
- Education
- Saul the Persecutor
- Conversion and Calling
- Preparation for Ministry
- Sent Out from Antioch
- Traveling with Barnabas
- The Council of Jerusalem
- Further Travel
- Labor in the Gospel
- The Arrest in Jerusalem
- Voyage and Stay in Rome
- Final Years and Martyrdom

Family and Cultural Background
Paul was born around AD 10, a Jew in a family of Pharisees (Acts 23:6) of the tribe of Benjamin (Phil 3:5) in Tarsus of Cilicia (Acts 9:11; 21:39; 22:3), a center of commerce and

QUICKTAKE

PAUL

STRENGTHS AND ACCOMPLISHMENTS
- Transformed by God from a persecutor of Christians to a preacher for Christ
- Preached for Christ throughout the Roman Empire on three missionary journeys
- Wrote letters to various churches, which became part of the New Testament
- Was never afraid to face an issue head-on and deal with it
- Was sensitive to God's leading and, despite his strong personality, always did as God directed
- Is often called the apostle to the Gentiles

WEAKNESSES AND MISTAKES
- Witnessed and approved of Stephen's stoning
- Set out to destroy Christianity by persecuting Christians

LESSONS FROM HIS LIFE
- The Good News is that forgiveness and eternal life are available to all people and are gifts of God's grace through faith in Christ
- Obedience results from a relationship with God, but obedience will never create or earn that relationship
- Real freedom doesn't come until we no longer have to prove our freedom
- God does not waste our time; he will use our past and present so we may serve him with our future

VITAL STATISTICS
Where: Born in Tarsus but became a world traveler for Christ
Occupations: Trained as a Pharisee, learned the tentmaking trade, served as a missionary
Contemporaries: Gamaliel, Stephen, the apostles, Luke, Barnabas, Timothy

KEY VERSES
"For to me, living means living for Christ, and dying is even better. But if I live, I can do more fruitful work for Christ. So I really don't know which is better. I'm torn between two desires: I long to go and be with Christ, which would be far better for me. But for your sakes, it is better that I continue to live" (Philippians 1:21-24).

Paul's story is told in Acts 7:58–28:31 and throughout his New Testament letters.

learning that embraced the Hellenistic spirit and Roman politics. It was a city of which he could be proud (21:39). His parents named him Saul, perhaps after the first king of Israel, who was also a Benjaminite (1 Sm 11:15; Acts 13:21), but Acts 13:9 notes that he "was also called Paul." He uses the Roman name Paul throughout his letters.

From religious parents Paul received knowledge of the Law and Prophets and the Hebrew and Aramaic languages (Acts 21:40; 22:2-3; 23:6; Gal 1:14; Phil 3:5-6). Tarsus, however, was not a Jewish city. Rather, it had a Greek character, being a place where the Greek language was spoken and Greek literature was cultivated. This accounts for Paul's familiarity with Greek (Acts 21:37), the language of the streets and shops of Tarsus.

Jews were brought to Tarsus, the capital of the Roman province of Cilicia, in 171 BC to promote business in the region. At that time Paul's ancestors were probably given Roman citizenship. Paul inherited from his father both Tarsisian and Roman citizenship, which would prove to be of great value to Paul in his later life as he traveled with the gospel throughout the Roman Empire (Acts 16:37; 22:25-29; 23:27). Paul may have had several brothers and sisters, but Acts 23:16 mentions only one sister, whose son performed a lifesaving act for his uncle.

Paul was a tent maker (Acts 18:3). He may have learned this trade from his father, or he may have selected it as a means of self-support, as was the custom of those in rabbinical training. Tarsus was well known for the goat's-hair cloth called cilicium. It was the weaving of this cloth and the fashioning of it into tents, sails, awnings, and cloaks that gave Paul his economic independence during his apostolic ministry (Acts 18:3; 20:34; 28:30; 2 Cor 11:9; 1 Thes 2:9; 2 Thes 3:8).

Education

Although born in Tarsus, Paul testified to the Jews in Jerusalem that he had been brought up in Jerusalem and studied under Gamaliel (Acts 22:3). It is not clear when Paul was first brought to Jerusalem, but it is likely that sometime between the ages of 13 and 20 he began his formal rabbinical studies. This is the same Gamaliel whose wisdom persuaded the Sanhedrin to spare the lives of Peter and the apostles (5:33-40). No doubt, it was while studying under Gamaliel in Hillel's school that Paul began to advance in Judaism beyond many Jews of his own age and became extremely zealous for the traditions of his fathers (Gal 1:14). Perhaps then also Paul began to experience the struggles with the law he would later describe in Romans 7.

While Paul was studying the Jewish law in Jerusalem, Jesus was working as a carpenter in Nazareth. Then Jesus gathered the disciples who would one day be Paul's coworkers in the gospel, fulfilled his ministry, and accomplished redemption on the cross of Calvary (AD 30). Christ's resurrection gave birth to the church, which was baptized in the Holy Spirit at the Feast of Pentecost in Jerusalem.

Saul the Persecutor

Shortly after these world-changing events, the members of certain synagogues in Jerusalem, including the Cilician synagogue, that of Paul's native land, tried and executed a disciple named Stephen (Acts 6:9–7:53). He became the first Christian martyr. Though the record does not fully reveal the role Paul played in these proceedings, we know that he was present and prominent because the witnesses against Stephen, who were required to throw the first stones in the execution, "laid their clothes at the feet of a young man called Saul [Paul]" (v 58, NIV).

At Stephen's trial, Paul heard Stephen's historical method of defense, and he later used it himself at Antioch of Pisidia (Acts 13:16-41). Stephen's testimony and death initiated the events that would culminate in Paul's conversion and commission as the apostle to the Gentiles. But at that time Paul was a leader of the oppressors of the church. He breathed threats and murder against the disciples of the Lord (9:1); he persecuted the church of God and tried to destroy it (Gal 1:13) by imprisoning Christians, both male and female (Acts 22:4), in many cities.

Conversion and Calling

Paul had obtained letters from the high priest in Jerusalem to the synagogues in Damascus authorizing him to arrest the believers there and bring them to Jerusalem for trial (Acts 9:1-2). Paul traveled to Damascus for this purpose. Then, on the outskirts of the city, came the event that was to transform this law-keeping persecutor of Jesus Christ and blasphemous destroyer of the infant church into the chief propagator of the gospel of grace and master builder of the church (1 Cor 3:10; 1 Tm 1:13). This was the occasion of Paul's conversion (c. AD 31–33). It was of such revolutionary and lasting importance that three detailed accounts of it are given in the book of Acts (Acts 9:1-19; 22:1-21; 26:1-23), and many references are given to it in Paul's own writings (1 Cor 9:1; 15:8; Gal 1:15-16; Eph 3:3; Phil 3:12).

At that time a light from heaven, brighter than the midday sun, shone around Paul and his traveling companions, and they fell to the ground (Acts 26:13-14). Only Paul, however, heard the voice of Jesus instruct him in his commission as a minister and witness to the Gentiles (vv 14-18). Temporarily blinded, Paul was led into Damascus (9:8). There, the disciple Ananias and the Christian community forgave Paul, baptized him, and helped him through the bewildering event of his conversion (vv 10-22). After a short time with the church there, Paul was threatened with death by the Jews to whom he preached Jesus (vv 20-22), but he was protected by the believers and ingeniously delivered from his persecutors (vv 23-25).

Preparation for Ministry

Then began a period of preparation, which lasted about 13 years. During this time, Paul first was in the desert of Arabia for three years. Here was his opportunity to pray and reflect on Stephen's defense to the Sanhedrin, the momentous significance of his conversion, the vision he received of Jesus Christ, and the meaning of all this in the light of Jewish theology. Following this, Paul returned to Damascus and then visited Peter in Jerusalem for 15 days (Gal 1:17-18).

At first, the disciples in Jerusalem were afraid of him because they did not believe he was a disciple of Jesus (Acts 9:26), but he was championed by Barnabas and thus accepted by the believers in Jerusalem (vv 27-28). While there, Paul may have heard the oral gospel, a summary of the words and deeds of Jesus, handed down to all converts. This would have included the institution of the Lord's Supper (1 Cor 11:23-25), specific words of the Lord (Acts 20:35; 1 Cor 7:10; 9:14), the appearances of the resurrected Christ (1 Cor 15:3-8), and the spirit and character of Jesus (2 Cor 10:1; Phil 2:5-8). Paul also preached in Jerusalem, perhaps in the same synagogues in which he had heard Stephen. However, when his life was again threatened by the Jews, the believers sent him away to Tarsus (Acts 9:29-30; Gal 1:21).

The end of Paul's preparation came when Barnabas went to Tarsus to look for him and bring him to Antioch. By this time Paul had lived for 10 years in Cilicia. Since his conversion, before being sent to Tarsus, he had proclaimed Jesus (Acts 9:20), speaking boldly in the name of the Lord (v 27). There is no reason to think he did otherwise while living among the Gentiles in Cilicia. In fact, his work may have been so effective that he began to attract attention in Antioch. During these years, Paul probably underwent many of the sufferings mentioned in 2 Corinthians 11:24-26. Several scholars think that the ecstatic experience mentioned in 2 Corinthians 12:1-9, with its accompanying thorn in the flesh, also took place before he came to Antioch.

Sent Out from Antioch

The church in Antioch had its origins in the persecution fomented by Paul after the death of Stephen. Until they arrived in Antioch, the scattered believers had only spoken the word to Jews (Acts 11:19). It was here that the Gentiles first heard the Good News (v 20), and many became believers (v 21). It is fitting that Paul, the apostle to the Gentiles (Acts 22:21; Rom 11:13), who was as yet unknown by sight to the churches of Judea (Gal 1:22), should appear in Antioch to formally begin the ministry to which he was called (Acts 26:17-18).

Barnabas and Paul stayed with the church in Antioch for a year. Their work there was so blessed that a new name, Christian, was coined to distinguish the believers in Antioch from Gentiles and Jews (Acts 11:26). Hearing of a famine in Judea, the disciples in Antioch determined to send relief to the believers in Judea and did so by Barnabas and Paul (v 30). Such a gift displayed to the Jewish churches the potency of the gospel among the Gentiles. Their mission complete, Barnabas and Paul returned to Antioch with John Mark (12:25), Barnabas's cousin (Col 4:10).

Beginning from the Day of Pentecost, the work in the gospel had been casual and incidental. Contacts were made in the homes, the marketplace, the streets, synagogues, highways, etc. (Acts 3:1; 5:12, 42; 8:26-29; 10:22). But in Antioch the Holy Spirit initiated a determined effort to evangelize a section of the Roman Empire (13:1-3). By the Holy Spirit's instructions, the church separated Barnabas and Paul for this work. With the prayers and encouragement of this church, and with John Mark as their assistant, Barnabas and Paul, sent out by the Holy Spirit, sailed for Cyprus (v 4).

Traveling with Barnabas

Arriving in Salamis, they preached in the synagogues as they traveled the length of the island to Paphos (Acts 13:5-6). There the Roman proconsul, Sergius Paulus, wanted to hear the word of God (v 7). A magician named Elymas Bar-Jesus tried to prevent the proconsul from believing in Jesus but was stricken with temporary blindness by Paul's command (vv 8-11). This was the first manifestation in Paul of the signs of an apostle (2 Cor 12:12). From then on, the name Paul, not Saul, is used in Luke's record of the Acts of the Apostles (Acts 13:9), and Paul replaced Barnabas as the leader of the party. So "Paul and his company" set sail from Paphos and arrived in Perga of Pamphylia (v 13). John Mark deserted them at Perga and returned to his home in Jerusalem (v 13). This caused discord (15:39), but Paul and Mark were later reconciled (Col 4:10; 2 Tm 4:11).

Paul's travels with the gospel now continued through the Roman province of Asia, specifically in the southern portion of Galatia, the areas of Pamphylia, Pisidia, and Lycaonia. The coastal area where the party landed is a hot, malarial region. It is thought that Paul contracted malaria there and so traveled inland through the mountains to the 4,000-foot-(1,219.2-meter-) high tablelands. Such a journey would have been full of dangerous rivers and bandits (2 Cor 11:26), but Paul was well cared for by the Galatian highlanders when he arrived (Gal 4:13-15) and was rewarded with a warm reception to his message (Acts 13:48-49).

Paul and Barnabas were asked to speak at the synagogue of Antioch in Pisidia (Acts 13:15), and Paul delivered a discourse full of the characteristics of the gospel he would later record in his letters to the churches (vv 16-41). He was invited to speak the next week (v 42); nearly the whole city gathered together to hear the word of God (v 44). This stirred up jealousy in the Jews who opposed Paul's words (v 45), causing the apostles' dramatic turn to the Gentiles (vv 46-47). Many Gentiles in Antioch believed and spread the word throughout the region, but Paul and Barnabas were forced out and went to Iconium in Lycaonia (vv 48-51).

The success in Antioch was duplicated in Iconium as was the Jews' opposition (Acts 14:1), and the apostles fled from the threat of a stoning to Lystra and Derbe in Lycaonia (vv 5-6). In Lystra the signs of an apostle were again seen when Paul healed a man who had been crippled since birth (vv 8-10). The idolatrous citizens of the town, however, primed by the popular belief that Jupiter, accompanied by Mercury, had once visited their region, worshiped Paul and Barnabas as these deities (vv 11-13). Even the convincing words of Paul, whom they mistook for Mercury, hardly restrained the crowds from offering a sacrifice (vv 14-18).

It was in Lystra that Paul was first given a taste of the same medicine he had once administered to Christians. The Jews stoned him, dragged him out of the city, and left him for dead (Acts 14:19). Timothy (16:1-3) may have been among the new disciples surrounding Paul as he lay outside the gate (14:20). Timothy was Paul's son in the faith (1 Cor 4:17; 1 Tm 1:2), eyewitness to his suffering (2 Tm 3:10-11), faithful companion, and fellow worker (Acts 19:22; 20:4; Rom 16:21; 1 Thes 3:2). The next day Barnabas and Paul went on to Derbe (Acts 14:20).

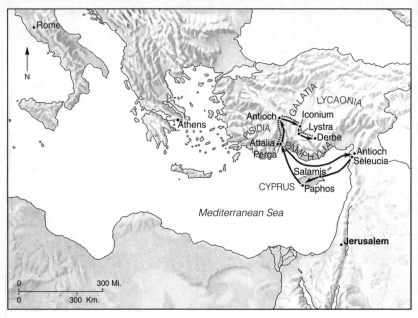

Paul's First Missionary Journey (Acts 13:1–14:28)

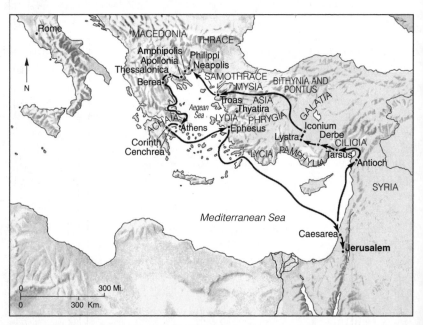

Paul's Third Missionary Journey (Acts 18:12–21:16)

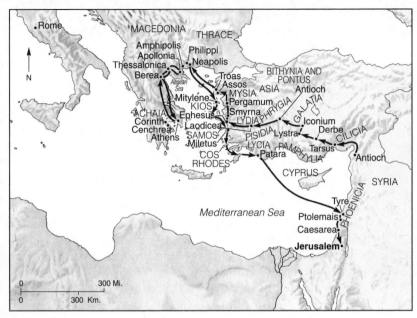

Paul's Second Missionary Journey (Acts 15:36–18:22)

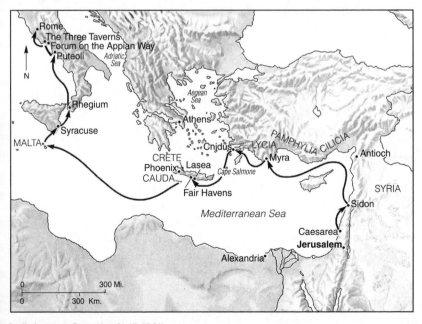

Paul's Journey to Rome (Acts 21:17–28:31)

After making many disciples in Derbe, the apostles retraced their steps through Lystra, Iconium, and Antioch of Pisidia, strengthening and encouraging the new believers and appointing elders in each church (Acts 14:21-23). Arriving again in Perga, they sailed back to Antioch of Syria, where they reported to the church the wonderful news that God had opened a door of faith for the Gentiles (vv 25-27).

The Council of Jerusalem

The Jews, who had dogged the steps of Paul and Barnabas throughout Galatia, followed on their heels to bewitch the Gentiles there, convincing them to desert the grace of Christ and submit to the Jewish law (Gal 1:6; 3:1). Shortly after the apostles' return to Antioch, Judaizers came from Judea to Antioch, teaching salvation by the law (Acts 15:1). This began the war against the gospel of grace, which Paul preached.

The church in Antioch sent Paul, Barnabas, and others to Jerusalem to settle the controversy of the law versus grace with the apostles and elders there (AD 49, Acts 15:2). Along the way to Jerusalem they spread the news of the conversion of the Gentiles. This brought great joy to the believers (v 3). Such joy was not shared by some in Jerusalem, who in the first meeting of the council said that the Gentiles should be ordered to keep the law of Moses (v 5).

After this meeting, Paul and Barnabas met privately with Peter, John, and James (Gal 2:1-10) and explained the gospel they had been preaching to the Gentiles. These three leaders of the church in Jerusalem saw the grace that had been given to Paul to bring the gospel to the Gentiles and extended to him the "right hand of fellowship." This private meeting seems to have decided the question of compliance to the Jewish law because in the next general meeting Peter said, "We believe that we shall be saved through the grace of the Lord Jesus" (Acts 15:11, RSV), and James reached the decision that "we should not trouble those of the Gentiles who turn to God" (Acts 15:19, RSV). This was a great victory for Paul and Barnabas, and the news was received with rejoicing by the church in Antioch (vv 30-35).

Later, Peter visited Antioch and freely associated with the Gentile believers as he had timidly done in Cornelius's house (Acts 10:28). This continued until "certain men came from James." Their presence brought fear to Peter, clouding the light of the gospel of grace, and causing him to separate himself from the Gentiles. Peter's action influenced others, including Barnabas, to do the same (Gal 2:12-13). Paul rose to the challenge of this serious crisis, confronted Peter publicly, and charged him with Judaizing and hypocrisy (v 14). Paul won the battle and rescued Peter and Barnabas with eloquent words on justification by faith (vv 15-21), but the Judaizers had resumed their war. From this time on, they did not rest; rather, they tormented and persecuted Paul all over the world. But the apostle did not submit to them for a moment. He was engaged in the fight of his life, so that the truth of the gospel might remain with the Gentile believers (v 5).

Further Travel

Paul wanted to visit the new believers and see how they were doing. So he proposed to Barnabas that they return to the cities where they had previously preached about Jesus

(Acts 15:36). Barnabas wanted to take John Mark with them, but Paul would not take him since he had deserted them during their earlier journey (13:13). This sharp disagreement ended Barnabas's association with Paul (15:37-39). Silas, a leader among the brothers in Jerusalem (v 22), accompanied Paul as he set out by land through Syria and Cilicia, strengthening the churches (vv 40-41).

Beginning from Derbe in Galatia, Paul and Silas revisited the churches Paul had established with Barnabas. While in Lystra, they were joined by Timothy (Acts 16:1-3). The apostles delivered to these young churches the letter drafted by the elders and apostles in Jerusalem concerning the observance of the law (15:23-29), thus strengthening and increasing them (16:4-5).

It is likely that Ephesus, a major city in the Roman province of Asia, was the party's main objective for the advancement of the gospel, but they were "forbidden by the Holy Spirit to speak the word in Asia" (Acts 16:6). Then they attempted to turn north and enter the region of Bithynia, "but the Spirit of Jesus did not allow them" (v 7). In this way they were forced by God to continue straight westward to Troas on the Aegean Sea, where Luke joined them ("we" in v 10), and Paul had a vision in which he was called out of Asia into Macedonia (vv 8-9). Paul and his party immediately crossed by boat into Europe (v 11) where they carried the gospel to Philippi, Thessalonica, Berea, Athens, and Corinth.

Philippi was a Roman colony and military outpost where there were few Jews, so Paul went to a place by the river where the local Jews prayed. He spoke to some women there, notably Lydia, who believed and with her household was baptized (Acts 16:12-15), beginning the first church in Europe. Paul cast a spirit of divination out of a girl in Philippi, and as a result he and Silas were jailed (vv 16-24). The events of their night in jail made the jailer a believer in God (vv 25-34), and he and his family were added to the church in Philippi, which met in Lydia's home (v 40). When Paul disclosed his Roman citizenship, he was released and was asked to leave the city (vv 35-39).

At Thessalonica the Jews, aroused to jealousy by the success of Paul's gospel message, raised a mob to search for the apostles. They complained to the city authorities that the people "who have turned the world upside down have come here also" and accused the apostles of "saying that there is another king [besides Caesar], Jesus" (Acts 17:5-7).

Paul and Silas quickly left Thessalonica by night and arrived in Berea, a city thereafter distinguished by its citizens who eagerly and thoughtfully received the gospel (Acts 17:10-12). The Thessalonian Jews did not rest but trailed Paul to Berea to incite the crowds. The believers then sent Paul away to Athens, while Silas and Timothy stayed behind (vv 13-15).

The Athenians called Paul a babbler but let him air his views before the Areopagus. Paul's speech there was alive with his broad knowledge. He alluded to Greco-Roman philosophy (Acts 17:27), poetry (v 28), sculpture (vv 25, 29), architecture (v 24), and religion while proclaiming the existence of an "unknown god" (v 23). But he was rudely cut short by scoffing and indifference when he mentioned the resurrection (v 32). Paul's words delighted the minds of many but influenced the wills of few, so when he arrived in Corinth, he determined not to proclaim the mystery of God in lofty words of wisdom so that the believers' faith would not rest on human wisdom but on the power of God (1 Cor 2:1-5).

In Corinth Paul met Aquila and Priscilla (Acts 18:2-3), Roman Jews with whom he lived and worked as a tent maker and who would become prominent among the churches (Acts 18:26; Rom 16:3; 1 Cor 16:19; 2 Tm 4:19). He stayed in Corinth 18 months from AD 50 to 51, raising up a church (Acts 18:11) on the strength of a vision from God (vv 9-10) and in spite of the attacks of the Jews (vv 12-17). Paul wrote the first and second letters to the Thessalonians from Corinth to establish the believers in a holy, industrious life (1 Thes 3:13; 5:23; 2 Thes 3:7-12) in hope of the second coming of Jesus Christ (1 Thes 4:15-18; 2 Thes 2:1ff.).

Accompanied by Priscilla and Aquila, Paul sailed from Corinth for Syria. He left his fellow workers in Ephesus, sailed to Caesarea, briefly visited Jerusalem, and returned to Antioch (Acts 18:18-22). Paul stayed in Antioch for awhile but did not remain absent from the field of his labors for long. Alone, he departed from Antioch, went from place to place in Galatia and Phrygia strengthening all the disciples, and eventually arrived in Ephesus (18:23; 19:1).

Labor in the Gospel

A Jew named Apollos had ministered in Ephesus prior to Paul's arrival and had recently gone over to Corinth (Acts 18:24-28). There Apollos innocently became the cause of such discord (1 Cor 3:3-9) that he left and refused to return even at Paul's request (16:12). Paul's earlier visit to Ephesus (Acts 18:19-20), Apollos's ministry, and the presence of Priscilla and Aquila had prepared Ephesus for the apostle's preaching of the gospel of Christ.

Paul began his work in Ephesus by setting straight some ill-informed disciples of John the Baptist (Acts 19:1-7). He then spent three months preaching at the local synagogue until members of the congregation "spoke evil of the Way" (v 9). Paul then took the disciples and continued his arguments on the neutral ground of Tyrannus's school (vv 8-9), where Jews and Greeks were free to come. He continued there for two years and "all the residents of Asia, both Jews and Greeks, heard the word of the Lord" (v 10).

The work in Ephesus was a great success (Acts 19:10, 20, 26). Paul enjoyed an open door for effective work (1 Cor 16:9), bolstered by extraordinary miracles (Acts 19:11-17), a public burning of valuable books of sorcery (vv 18-19), and the assistance of friendly officials from the province of Asia (v 31). There were also many adversaries (1 Cor 15:32; 16:9), especially among the artisans associated with the Temple of Diana. Paul's ministry had hurt their trade to the extent that they were incited to riot (Acts 19:23-41). Paul had intended to stay in Ephesus until Pentecost (1 Cor 16:8), but this tumult seems to have hastened his departure (Acts 20:1).

During his stay in Ephesus, the household of Chloe sent word to Paul from Corinth that there were divisions in the church there (1 Cor 1:10-13). This report generated a flurry of letters and travels. Paul wrote a letter, which is now lost, to this church (5:9). The church in Corinth wrote a letter (7:1) and sent messengers to Paul (16:17), and Paul sent Timothy to them (4:17; 16:10). Paul then wrote 1 Corinthians (AD 53) and sent it by Titus, who was to meet him in Troas to report the results (2 Cor 2:12-13).

After his hasty exit from Ephesus, Paul found an open door for the gospel in Troas, but he so longed to hear from Corinth that he pushed on into Macedonia (2 Cor 2:12-13). There he was finally comforted by Titus (7:5-7) and rejoiced at the news of the Corinthians' repentance, earnestness, longing, and zeal (vv 8-16). From Macedonia Paul wrote 2 Corinthians (AD 54), toured northwest to proclaim the good news of Christ in Illyricum (Rom 15:19), and then turned south for Achaia and his third visit to Corinth (Acts 19:21; 20:1-3; 2 Cor 13:1).

The time and place from which Paul wrote his letter to the Galatians is a topic of controversy. Some date it before the council at Jerusalem, about AD 45. Others say he wrote it from Corinth at this stage in his history. The latter opinion is the choice of this narrative.

A three-month winter stay in Corinth (AD 55–56) produced the Letter to the Romans, which firmly set the benchmark of the gospel for all the ages. Paul had many personal friends in Rome (Rom 16) and had long intended to visit there (1:10-15). His plans were to deliver a collection from the Gentile churches to Jerusalem (Acts 20:35; Rom 15:25-26; 1 Cor 16:1) and then visit Rome (Acts 19:21) on his way to Spain (Rom 15:23-24).

The Arrest in Jerusalem

Paul's trip from Corinth to Jerusalem was marked by abundant warnings of the danger awaiting him in Jerusalem. The Judaizers' acrimony toward Paul was common talk everywhere, but all alarms went unheeded (Acts 20:22-24, 38; 21:4, 10-15). However, the request for prayer in Romans 15:30-32 shows that Paul knew he might soon need a divine rescue from the unbelievers in Judea.

The travelers, carrying the collection for Jerusalem, journeyed swiftly in order to reach Jerusalem by Pentecost (Acts 20:16). They proceeded by land from Achaia, through Macedonia, to Philippi in time for the Passover (spring AD 56, v 6). Crossing by sea to Troas, they visited the believers there (vv 7-12) and then sailed through the archipelago of the eastern Aegean Sea to Miletus (vv 13-16). From Miletus, Paul sent for the elders of Ephesus, to whom he delivered an impassioned speech containing his own dire warnings for them (vv 17-38).

Parting from them, Paul and his companions set sail to Cos, to Rhodes, and then to Patara, where they changed ships for Phoenicia (Acts 21:1-2). A straight course to Tyre brought them within sight of Cyprus, with its memories of Barnabas and Sergius Paulus (v 3). "Through the Spirit" the disciples in Tyre "told Paul not to go on to Jerusalem" (v 4), but he pressed on to Caesarea, where he and his company stayed with Philip, who had formerly served with the martyred Stephen (21:8; cf. 6:5). In Caesarea, Paul would not be persuaded by an especially dramatic prophecy of his coming arrest (21:10-14).

In Jerusalem the apostolic band stayed with Mnason, an early disciple, and were warmly welcomed by the brothers there (Acts 21:15-17). James and the elders of the church praised God when they heard of the things he had done through Paul among the Gentiles (vv 18-20), and when they received the collection from the churches (24:17). They told Paul of his bad reputation among the thousands of Jewish believers in Jerusalem and urged him to set right the Judaizers' misrepresentation that he encouraged Jewish Christians to forsake the Mosaic customs (21:21-24). Acts 21:25 shows the Jerusalem elders understood that the Gentiles were under no obligation to Moses; their concern was for Paul to demonstrate that Jewish believers were free to continue their traditional observances.

Paul had kept the Jewish feasts (Acts 20:6), as had Jesus and the early disciples in Jerusalem. He had also cut his hair in a vow at Cenchreae (18:18), so it was a small matter for him, a Jew, to ceremonially purify himself after becoming a Christian, especially if it would undermine the arguments of the Judaizers. To have refused the elders' request would have lent credence to the Judaizers' charge. The success of this plan is seen in that it was the Jews from Asia, visiting Jerusalem for the Pentecost feast of AD 57, who stirred up trouble for Paul (21:27-29)—not the Judaizers from Jerusalem.

The whole city was aroused by Paul's persistent persecutors. A violent crowd dragged him out of the Temple just as Stephen had once been hauled to his martyrdom. They tried to kill him, but he was rescued by Roman soldiers as the mob cried, "Away with him!"— just as they had done to Jesus (Acts 21:30-36). At this juncture the educational and cultural diversity of Paul's life came to his rescue. As he was carried for safety to the Roman barracks, he spoke in Greek to the tribune, who had mistaken him for an Egyptian assassin (vv 37-38). Given permission to speak to the crowd, he did so in the Aramaic language then common in Israel (vv 39-40). The hushed crowd eagerly heard Paul's defense until he uttered the word "Gentiles." At this, the crowd resumed its threatening and violence, and Paul was brought into the barracks (22:1-24). There the Romans prepared to flog him, until Paul revealed that he was not only a Jew from Tarsus but also a freeborn Roman citizen. The tribune was afraid, since he had bound a Roman citizen. Wanting to know the charges against Paul, he brought him to the Sanhedrin (vv 25-30).

This meeting of the Jewish judiciary was shortly reduced to dissension and violence. Paul resorted to tactics justifiable in such a war and hopelessly divided the Sanhedrin on the subject of the resurrection (Acts 23:1-9). Paul again was rescued, this time from the contending factions of the Jewish leadership, and taken to the barracks, where the Lord encouraged him, promising that he would go to Rome (AD 56, vv 10-11).

In the meantime 40 Jews entered into a murderous plot against Paul. They vowed not to eat or drink until they had killed the apostle (Acts 23:12-15). They almost succeeded, but with the help of the son of Paul's sister (v 16), the conspiracy was exposed. For safety, Paul was taken from Jerusalem to Caesarea under guard of 470 soldiers and handed over to the custody of Felix the governor (vv 16-35). Inconclusive hearings before Felix (Acts 24), his successor, Festus (25:1-12), and King Agrippa (25:23–26:32) occupied Paul in his two years of imprisonment in Caesarea. Festus, wanting to please the Jews, suggested that Paul be returned to Jerusalem for trial, but Paul knew the murderous intent of his accusers and again utilized his Roman citizenship by making a dramatic appeal to Caesar (25:9-12).

Voyage and Stay in Rome

To plead his case at Caesar's court, Paul and his companions, Aristarchus and Luke, were taken on a perilous voyage (AD 58, Acts 27:1–28:16). Their passage by ship from Caesarea to Rome is one of the most remarkable on record. Luke's detailed account is a treasure of information on ancient ships, navigation, and seamanship. It is also a beautiful portrait of a heroic and dignified apostle Paul, the gospel's ambassador in chains (Eph 6:20), who with the guidance and assurance of his God (Acts 27:23-26), led the 276 people on board to safety (v 37).

Luke traces the voyage stage by stage through every crisis, with a change of ship at Myra, delay at Fair Havens on Crete, and the shipwreck on Malta. Finally, in the spring of AD 59, they arrived at Puteoli, Italy, and made their way to Rome, welcomed by the believers along the Appian Way (Acts 28:13-16).

Luke provided a peaceful denouement to the Acts, notwithstanding the fact that the apostle was an imperial prisoner of Caesar Nero. Paul lived by himself in his own house, chained to a Roman guard (Acts 28:16, 30). There he received the local Jewish leaders—to calm any misgivings they may have had about him and, at the same time, to convince them about Jesus. His efforts had mixed success (vv 17-28). During Paul's two or more years in Rome, the Judaizers seem to have withdrawn, only to be replaced by the peril of Eastern Gnosticism. This is seen in Paul's letters to the Philippians, Colossians, and Ephesians, and to Philemon, all written at this time. It is unlikely that Paul's accusers appeared in Rome to bring formal charges before Caesar, so Paul was probably released in AD 61.

Final Years and Martyrdom

It is here assumed that the Pastoral Letters (1 Timothy, 2 Timothy, and Titus) are truly Paul's work. Only through them can the probable course of events in Paul's final years be traced. Romans 15:28 shows that Paul intended to deliver the collection to Jerusalem and then to "set out by way of you [Rome] to Spain." The arrest and imprisonment in Jerusalem not only destroyed these plans but also extracted five precious years from the prime of a most

PAUL
The Times of Paul

AD 5/10?
Paul was born in Tarsus, Asia Minor and gained Roman citizenship from his father (Acts 22:3).

AD 20/30?
Paul begins rabbinical training in Jerusalem under Gamaliel (Acts 22:3).

AD 33?
Paul witnesses the stoning of Stephen and begins arresting Christians (Acts 8:1).

AD 35
Paul is knocked to the ground while traveling to Damascus and is converted to Christ (Acts 9).

AD 35–38?
Paul is alone in the Arabian desert (Galatians 1:17-18).

AD 38?
Paul meets with Peter and other disciples in Jerusalem (Acts 9:26-30; Galatians 1:18).

AD 38–46?
Paul lives in his hometown of Tarsus (Acts 9:30).

AD 46
The Antioch church sends Paul and Barnabas on first missionary journey (Acts 13–14).

AD 49–51
Paul takes a second missionary journey with Silas and adds Timothy to their number (Acts 15:39–18:23).

AD 53–57
Paul takes his third missionary journey (Acts 18:23–21:17).

AD 57
Paul writes to the Romans and is imprisoned in Caesarea, where he appeals to Caesar (Acts 23–26).

AD 59
Paul is taken to Rome, where he writes epistles under house arrest and is released in AD 61/62 (Acts 27–28).

AD 67?
Paul is martyred in Rome (tradition says he was beheaded).

productive life. Although Clement of Rome implied that Paul did fulfill his desire to go to Spain (*Clement to the Corinthians* 5), it is certain that the daily pressure of Paul's anxious care for all the churches (2 Cor 11:28) did not abate.

If Paul went to Spain, he may have been there when Rome was burned on July 19, AD 64. Tradition says that Paul traveled as far as Britain, but there is no evidence to confirm this. Returning east, he left Titus in Crete (Ti 1:5) and traveled through Miletus, south of Ephesus, where he left Trophimus sick (2 Tm 4:20). Traveling toward Macedonia, Paul visited Timothy in Ephesus (1 Tm 1:3). On the way, Paul left his cloak and books with Carpus in Troas (2 Tm 4:13). This indicates that he intended to return there for his possessions. From Macedonia Paul wrote his loving yet apprehensive first letter to Timothy (AD 62–64). He had decided to spend the winter in Nicopolis (Ti 3:12), northwest of Corinth on the Adriatic Sea, but was still in Macedonia when he wrote his letter to Titus. This letter is similar to 1 Timothy, yet with a somewhat harsher tone. In it is a final glimpse of the eloquent and zealous Apollos (Ti 3:13), who is still in association with Paul 10 or more years after his first appearance in Ephesus (Acts 18:24).

From here Paul's path is obscure. He may have wintered in Nicopolis, but he did not return to Troas for his winter cloak (2 Tm 4:13). At some point he was arrested by the Romans, because he spent a winter in Rome's Mamertine Prison, suffering from the cold in that rock cell before he wrote his second letter to Timothy (AD 66–67). He may have been anticipating the coming winter when he requested that Timothy bring his cloak (vv 13, 21). It is possible that the charges against Paul were related to the burning of Rome; this is unknown. It was, however, now "illegal" to be a Christian since the "new religion" was no longer protected by Roman law as being part of Judaism (which was a legalized, recognized religion by Roman law).

It was dangerous to be associated with Paul at this time. Many deserted him (2 Tm 4:16), including all his coworkers in Asia (1:15) and Demas, who loved the world (4:10). Only Luke, the physician and author of Luke and Acts, was with him when he wrote his second letter to Timothy (v 11). Faithful believers still in hiding in Rome were also in contact with the apostle (1:16; 4:19, 21). He told Timothy to come to him in Rome and bring Mark also (4:11). Apparently Timothy did come and was imprisoned (Heb 13:23). Paul's request for the books and parchments (2 Tm 4:13) discloses that he was reading and studying the Scripture to the end.

The apostle Paul had two hearings before Caesar Nero. At his first defense only the Lord stood by him (2 Tm 4:16). There he not only pleaded his own cause but also that of the gospel, still longing that all the Gentiles would hear its message. Perhaps no decision was made, and thus he was "rescued from the lion's mouth" (v 17). Though he knew he would soon die, he was not afraid, but was assured that the Lord would give him a crown of righteousness on the last day (v 8). Finally, the apostle himself recorded his seminal encouragement to all believers: "The Lord be with your spirit. Grace be with you" (v 22, RSV). After this, the Scripture is silent regarding Paul.

Nothing is known of Paul's second hearing but that it resulted in the sentence of capital punishment. History does not record Paul's end. Nero died in the summer of AD 68, so Paul was executed before that date. As a Roman citizen, he must have been spared the lingering torture that had recently been suffered by his fellow martyrs. Tradition says that he was decapitated by the sword of an imperial headsman on the Ostian Road just outside of Rome, and buried nearby. This fulfilled Paul's desire "to depart and be with Christ, for that is far better" (Phil 1:23, RSV).

PAULUS, SERGIUS
See Sergius Paulus.

PEDAHEL
Ammihud's son from Naphtali's tribe, appointed to work with Joshua and Eleazar in distributing Canaanite territory west of the Jordan River among the Israelites (Nm 34:28).

PEDAHZUR
Gamaliel's father from Manasseh's tribe (Nm 1:10; 2:20; 7:54, 59; 10:23).

PEDAIAH
1. Maternal grandfather of Judah's King Jehoiakim. Pedaiah was from Rumah (2 Kgs 23:36).

2. Jeconiah's third son (1 Chr 3:18-19).

3. Joel's father from the half-tribe of Manasseh (1 Chr 27:20).

4. Parosh's son, who worked with the Temple servants in repairing the Jerusalem wall opposite the Water Gate (Neh 3:25).

5. One who stood beside Ezra during the public reading of the Law (Neh 8:4).

6. Kolaiah's son and Joed's father (Neh 11:7). He was a member of Benjamin's tribe and lived in Jerusalem after the return from exile.

7. Levite appointed by Nehemiah as treasurer of the storehouse to distribute grain, wine, and oil to the priests who served in the Temple (Neh 13:13).

PEKAH
Son of Remaliah and 18th king of Israel. His name means "he has opened [the eyes]." It is an abbreviated form of the name of his predecessor, Pekahiah, "Yahweh has opened [the eyes]." The name has been found on a fragment of an eighth-century-BC wine jar from Hazor stratum V, the level destroyed by Tiglath-pileser in 734 BC. It is thought that this is a reference to Pekah and to a kind of wine. It is likely that the usurper Pekah was so eager to ensure his position as king that he deliberately assumed the name of his predecessor. Moreover, Isaiah refers to him as the "son of Remaliah," almost scornfully, to indicate his nonroyal descent. But when Isaiah refers to his heathen ally, he uses the specific name "Rezin, the king of Syria" (Is 7:4-9; 8:6).

Accession to the Throne

Pekah, an officer of Pekahiah, was the third man in a chariot, apart from the driver and the warrior. He was the shield and armor bearer of the warrior. In time the term came to signify a royal aide-de-camp.

The account of Pekah's murder of Pekahiah has been somewhat obscured because of the difficulty in understanding the terms Argob and Arieh (2 Kgs 15:25). Some translators and commentators have thought these referred to persons, whereas others have held these are place-names. Some scholars radically alter the text here and eliminate the troublesome words by claiming they were a scribal mistake or emendation. A key seems to have been found by comparing them with the Ugaritic. The terms mean "eagle" and "lion," respectively. Thus, Pekah was murdered "near the eagle and the lion." It is suggested that this means he was put to death near the guardian sphinxes of his palace. Such sphinxes were a common motif in ancient eastern palaces and were duplicated on ivory plaques erected in the gateway. This interpretation seems very plausible, since it avoids critical emendation and solves the major problems in the text.

Political Significance

The brilliant Tiglath-pileser III, leading the kingdom of Assyria to prominence, appeared on Israel's border. Menahem deemed it wise to become tributary to him. Apparently Pekahiah, Menahem's successor, could not appease the Assyrians during his short reign. The conciliatory efforts of Menahem and Pekahiah may well have prompted the Syrians to conspire with Pekah, the army officer, to gain control of the throne of Samaria in order to present a united military front against Assyrian encroachment. Once Samaria was under control, the Syrians led by Rezin, Israel ruled by Pekah, and several Transjordanian kingdoms formed a powerful alliance.

In time Pekah and Rezin began to pressure the kingdom of Judah in order to induce it to join their alliance against the impending Assyrian attack. Jotham resisted their invitations and fortified the Judean hill country. Jotham's son, Ahaz, continued his father's policy of noncooperation with the Samaria-Damascus coalition. Pekah and Rezin invaded Judah with the intent of taking Jerusalem and placing "the son of Tabeel" on the throne of Judah in Ahaz's place (Is 7:1-6). He presumably was a son of Uzziah or Jotham by a princess of Tabeel. Although the actual siege of Jerusalem was unsuccessful, Pekah and Rezin inflicted severe casualties upon Ahaz's army. In one day of battle they killed 120,000 men of Judah and carried away 200,000 captives, including women and children. However, the prophet Oded prophesied in Samaria before the army. He urged the leaders of Samaria to return the captives. The leaders heeded the prophetic word and sent the captives back to Jericho (2 Chr 28:8-15).

Rezin's revolt against Assyria brought a quick response from Tiglath-pileser, who laid siege to Damascus in 734 BC. The city fell in 732 BC. Another detachment of the Assyrian army descended on the upper districts of Syria and Samaria. Second Kings 15:29 lists the districts and cities that were overrun. They included Gilead (regions beyond Jordan), Naphtali (regions lying to the west of the lakes of Galilee and Merom), and all Galilee as far south as the plain of Esdraelon and the valley of Jezreel. Isaiah refers to this lost tribal territory (Is 9:1-7). From this Assyrian-controlled region the messianic ruler would arise and give light to those who lived in a land of darkness (v 2). Thus Pekah's kingdom was reduced to a third of its original size by the Assyrian campaign of 734–732 BC. In 732 a palace conspiracy led by Hoshea plotted the assassination of Pekah. He was put to death in the coup d'État and the throne was usurped by Hoshea.

The author of Kings evaluates the reign of Pekah as follows: "But Pekah did what was evil in the LORD's sight. He refused to turn from the sins of idolatry that Jeroboam son of Nebat had led Israel to commit" (2 Kgs 15:28, NLT). It is likely that he continued the calf worship at the shrines at Dan and Bethel. The continuation of the apostasy during successive regencies was the cause for the judgment that befell the northern kingdom. Pekah is the last king of Israel given such an evaluation.

PEKAHIAH

Son of Menahem, king of Israel. Pekahiah (whose name means "Yahweh has opened [his eyes]") was among the 20 kings who ruled Israel from Samaria following its decline consequent to the fracture of the Solomonic monarchy in the tenth century BC. The brief account in the Bible concerning him (2 Kgs 15:22-26) points to the godlessness of his life (v 24). His sin, like that of his father (Menahem), was linked to the false worship of Jeroboam, who built shrines at Dan and Bethel to rival worship in the Temple at Jerusalem. Such religious activity threatened the true worship of God by attempting to fuse biblical concepts with the fertility cult of Baal, a movement sharply denounced by the Word of God (1 Kgs 13:1-5). Like many of Israel's kings, Pekahiah ruled briefly, being assassinated in the second year of his reign. The chief instigator of the plot against him, a captain named Pekah, took 50 men of Gilead and killed the king, along with two aides, in the citadel of the royal palace at Samaria. His successor, Pekah, was regrettably as evil as Pekahiah and received the condemnation of Scripture typical of virtually all the Israelite kings: he "did what was evil in the LORD's sight" (2 Kgs 15:28, NLT).

See also Pekah.

PELAIAH

1. Elioenai's son and a remote descendant of David (1 Chr 3:24).

2. Levite who helped Ezra explain (or translate) the Law to the people after it was read to them (Neh 8:7; 10:10).

PELALIAH

Forefather of Adaiah, a priest living in Jerusalem during Ezra's day (Neh 11:12).

PELATIAH

1. Hananiah's son, in a list of King Solomon's descendants (1 Chr 3:21).

2. Military leader among the Simeonites who helped destroy an Amalekite remnant at Mt Seir during Hezekiah's reign (1 Chr 4:42).

3. Political leader who signed Ezra's covenant of faithfulness to God with Nehemiah and others after the Exile (Neh 10:22).

4. Benaiah's son and one of the two princes seen by Ezekiel in a vision of judgment, identified by the Spirit of the Lord as one who devises wickedness and gives wicked counsel in the city (Ez 11:1-2, 13).

PELEG

Son of Eber and father of Reu (Gn 10:25; 11:16-19; 1 Chr 1:19, 25; Lk 3:35). During his lifetime, the earth was divided (Peleg means "division" or "watercourse"). Precisely what the division refers to is still debated. Suggestions include (1) the geographical and linguistic dispersion following the Tower of Babel fiasco (Gn 11:1-9); (2) dispersion of Noah's descendants; (3) separation of the people of Arphaxad from Joktanide Arabs (Gn 10:24-29); and (4) the division of land by irrigation canals (the term is so used in Jb 29:6; 38:25; Is 30:25; 32:2). The origin of the name is usually traced to the city of Phalga, north of the junction of the Euphrates and Khabur rivers.

PELET

1. Jahdai's son from Judah's tribe (1 Chr 2:47).

2. Warrior from Benjamin's tribe who joined David at Ziklag in his struggle against King Saul. Pelet was one of David's ambidextrous archers and slingers (1 Chr 12:2-3).

PELETH

1. On's father from Reuben's tribe (Nm 16:1).

2. Jonathan's son and a Jerahmeelite from Judah's tribe (1 Chr 2:33).

PENINNAH

One of Elkanah's two wives, the other and more favored being Hannah (1 Sm 1:2-6). Peninnah's fortune in bearing children was the source of much domestic friction for the childless Hannah, especially at the time of the annual sacrifice at Shiloh. Rabbinic tradition explains Peninnah's taunts as attempts to provoke Hannah into pregnancy, but the biblical record portrays the women as rivals.

PENUEL

1. Descendant (possibly son) of Hur and father (in the sense of progenitor) of Gedor from Judah's tribe (1 Chr 4:4).

2. Shashak's son from Benjamin's tribe (1 Chr 8:25).

PEOR

Contraction for the Canaanite god of Baal-peor, or for the place itself (Nm 23:28; 25:3, 5).

PERESH

Son of Maachah and Makir from Manasseh's tribe, and the grandson of Manasseh (1 Chr 7:16).

PEREZ

Son of Judah whose name is derived from a Hebrew word meaning "he who bursts forth"; his name refers to the manner in which he unexpectedly came first from Tamar's womb before his twin brother, Zerah (Gn 38:29). He fathered two sons, Hezron and Hamul, and became the ancestral head of the Perezite family (Gn 46:12; Nm 26:20-21; 1 Chr 2:4-5; 4:1). The KJV and the Apocrypha translate the name variously as Pharez, Phares, and Pharzite.

Through the descent of his son Hezron, he became the ancestor of David and Jesus Christ (Ru 4:18-22; Mt 1:3; Lk 3:33). The esteem this clan enjoyed in the tribe of Judah is evidenced by the blessing pronounced upon it by the men of Bethlehem (Ru 4:12). A descendant named Jashobeam commanded David's captains for the first month of each year (1 Chr 27:2-3). Upon the return from captivity in Babylon, 468 Perezites were chosen to live in Jerusalem (1 Chr 9:4; Neh 11:4-6).

PERSIS

Christian woman in Rome to whom Paul sent greetings (Rom 16:12).

PERUDA

Head of a family of Solomon's servants (Ezr 2:55); alternately called Perida in Nehemiah 7:57. His descendants formed part of the remnant of Israel that returned to Jerusalem after the Exile (1 Esd 5:33).

PETER, THE APOSTLE

One of the 12 disciples; rose to prominence both among the disciples during Jesus' ministry and among the apostles afterwards.

There are actually four forms of Peter's name in the New Testament: the Hebrew translated into Greek, "Simeon" to "Simon," and the Aramaic translated into Greek, "Cephas" to "Petros" (meaning "rock"). His given name was Simeon bar-Jonah (Mt 16:17; cf. Jn 1:42), "Simon the son of John," which was common Semitic nomenclature. It is most likely that "Simon" was not merely the Greek equivalent of "Simeon" but that, having his home in bilingual Galilee, "Simon" was the alternate form he used in dealings with Gentiles. In fact, it was quite common for a cosmopolitan Jew to employ three forms of his name depending on the occasion: Aramaic, Latin, and Greek. The double name "Simon Peter" (or "Simon called Peter") demonstrates that the second name was a later addition, similar to "Jesus, the Christ." The number of times that the Aramaic equivalent "Cephas" is used (once in John, four times each in Galatians and 1 Corinthians), as well as its translation into the Greek (not common with proper names), indicates the importance of the secondary name. Both Aramaic and Greek forms mean "the rock," an obvious indication of Peter's stature in the early church (see "Peter the Rock" below). It is obvious that he was called "Simon" throughout Jesus' ministry but came to be known as "Peter" more and more in the apostolic age.

Preview
- Peter's Background
- Peter's Conversion and Call
- Peter's Place among the Twelve
- Peter the Rock
- Peter the Apostle
- Peter's Future Ministry

Peter's Background

Peter was raised in bilingual Galilee. John 1:44 says that the home of Andrew (his brother) and Peter was Bethsaida, the whereabouts of which is difficult to place archaeologically. The only site about which we know is east of the Jordan in the district called Gaulanitis. Yet John 12:21 places Bethsaida in Galilee; however, it is possible that John is reflecting the popular use of the term "Galilee" rather than the legally correct one. Peter and Andrew had a fishing business centered in Capernaum (Mk 1:21, 29) and perhaps were partners with James and John (Lk 5:10). It is also likely that they intermittently continued in their business while disciples, as indicated in the fishing scene in John 21:1-8.

One difficulty with this is the series of statements saying, "We have left all and followed You" (Mt 19:27; Mk 10:28; Lk 18:28, NKJV). The majority of interpreters have given this an absolute sense of "sold" or "left" their business. However, Luke 18:28 occurs in the context of leaving their homes but obviously is not meant in an absolute sense. It seems most likely that the disciples did leave the practice of their fishing businesses to follow Christ, but kept the tools of their trade and returned to their trades when necessary.

They certainly did not abandon their families, as evidenced by Peter, who returned to his home at the end of each tour. The New Testament tells us that Peter was married. In Mark 1:29-31 Jesus heals his mother-in-law, who perhaps was living with Peter. In fact, it is possible that his home became Jesus' headquarters in Galilee. (Matthew 8:14 may indicate that Jesus dwelt there.) First Corinthians 9:5 says that Peter, along with the other married apostles, often took his wife with him on his missionary journeys. Later tradition speaks of his children (Clement of Alexandria's *Stromateis* 2.6.52) and says that Peter was present at the martyrdom of his wife (Eusebius's *Ecclesiastical History* 3.30.2).

Peter's Conversion and Call

Peter's brother, Andrew, was a disciple of John the Baptist, according to John 1:35-40. This follows the witness of John in 1:29-34 and is the second stage of John's discipleship drama in chapter one—i.e., after bearing witness he now sends his own followers to Jesus. Andrew and the unnamed disciple (perhaps Philip as in Jn 1:43 or the "beloved

QUICKTAKE

PETER

STRENGTHS AND ACCOMPLISHMENTS
- Became the recognized leader among Jesus' disciples—one of the inner group of three
- Was the first great voice of the gospel during and after Pentecost
- Probably knew Mark and gave him information for the Gospel of Mark
- Wrote 1 and 2 Peter

WEAKNESSES AND MISTAKES
- Often spoke without thinking; was brash and impulsive
- During Jesus' trial, denied three times that he even knew Jesus
- Later found it hard to treat Gentile Christians as equals

LESSONS FROM HIS LIFE
- Enthusiasm has to be backed up by faith and understanding, or it fails
- God's faithfulness can compensate for our greatest unfaithfulness
- It is better to be a follower who sometimes fails than one who fails to follow

VITAL STATISTICS
Occupations: Fisherman, disciple
Relatives: Father: John. Brother: Andrew
Contemporaries: Jesus, Pilate, Herod

KEY VERSE
"Now I say to you that you are Peter (which means 'rock'), and upon this rock I will build my church, and all the powers of hell will not conquer it" (Matthew 16:18).

Peter's story is told in the Gospels and the book of Acts. He is mentioned in Galatians 1:18 and 2:7-14; and he wrote the books of 1 and 2 Peter.

disciple," whom many identify with John himself) then "follow" Jesus (a term used often in John for discipleship). The next day Andrew follows the Baptist's example and finds his brother Simon, saying, "We have found the Messiah" (Jn 1:41, NKJV). Peter's conversion is presupposed in John 1:42, where Simon is brought to Jesus by Andrew and there given a new name.

There are three separate episodes in the Gospels in which Simon is called, and these overlap with three episodes in which he is given the name "Cephas" ("Peter," which means "rock") by Jesus. John locates the event in Judea where John the Baptist was baptizing. The synoptic Gospels have two different scenes. The first call takes place at the Sea of Galilee (Mk 1:16-20; Mt 4:18-22). Jesus is walking along the shore and sees Peter and Andrew along with James and John casting their nets into the sea. At this time he calls them to become "fishers of men." Luke then expands this into a fishing scene (Lk 5:1-11), in which the disciples have fished all night and caught nothing but at the command of Jesus lower their nets and catch an amount of fish so great that the boat starts to sink. The episode concludes exactly like the Markan abbreviated form: Jesus says that from now on they will "catch men," and as a result they leave everything and follow him.

The second synoptic episode involving Peter's call (and his new name) is the official choice of the Twelve upon the mountain (Mk 3:13-19 and parallels); in the list of the names we have "Simon he surnamed Peter." The final occurrence dealing with Peter's new name is found in Matthew 16:17-19, in connection with Peter's confession at Caesarea Philippi.

It is somewhat difficult to harmonize these episodes properly. Were there three different episodes in which Simon was called (Jn 1:42; Mk 1:20; 3:16) and three separate incidents in which he was given the name Cephas/Peter (Jn 1:42; Mk 3:16; Mt 16:18)? It is attractive to a broad spectrum of academia to assume that one single event, which happened at some indeterminate time toward the beginning of Jesus' ministry, was later expanded into these diverse traditions. However, a closer examination of the Gospel data does not necessitate such a conclusion. John 1:35-42 is not an institutional scene that connotes an official call. Rather, it describes the first encounter with Jesus and realization regarding his significance. The "renaming" is in the future tense and looks to a later event. Moreover, John deliberately omits most of the crisis events in Jesus' life (the baptism, the choice of the Twelve, the Transfiguration, the words of institution at the Last Supper, Gethsemane) and replaces them with highly theological scenes that teach the spiritual significance of the events. This is what he has done here.

The same is true of the first synoptic call, i.e., the fishing scene. Again, there is no hint of official ordination to office here but rather a proleptic or prophetic hint of future ministry. This is especially true of the highly theological scene in Luke, which promises abundant results. Again in all three accounts the future tense is employed: "I will make you fishers of men" (Matthew and Mark), "You will catch men" (Luke, NKJV). The call in Mark 1:20 and Matthew 4:21 and their reaction (leaving all behind and following Jesus) is the opening gambit that is finalized in the actual institutional scene in Mark 3:13-19 and parallels. The wording does not indicate that these two episodes are doublets, for the actual appointment of the disciples occurs in the second passage. We must differentiate between the original call to one segment (who became the so-called "inner circle" of the Twelve) and the final choice of all the disciples.

Peter's Place among the Twelve

The prominence of Simon Peter in the Gospels and Acts cannot be disputed. While some have attempted to attribute this to his leadership role in the later church, there is no basis for that in the text of the NT. From the very beginning Simon attained preeminence above the others. In the lists of the Twelve just mentioned, Simon's name always appears first, and in Matthew 10:2 it introduces his name as "the first." Moreover, the Twelve are often designated "Peter and those with him" (Mk 1:36; Lk 9:32; 8:45, NKJV).

Throughout the accounts Peter acted and spoke on behalf of the other disciples. At the Transfiguration it is Peter who wanted to erect tents (Mk 9:5), and he alone had sufficient faith to attempt walking on the water (Mt 14:28-31). It is Peter who asks the Lord to explain his teaching on forgiveness (Mt 18:21) and parables (Mt 15:15; Lk 12:41) and who speaks the disciples' minds in Matthew 19:27, "Behold, we have left everything and followed you; what's in it for us?" (paraphrased). The collectors of the Temple tax come to Peter as leader of the group (Mt 17:24). As a member of the inner circle (with James and John, possibly Andrew in Mk 13:3) he was often alone with Jesus (at the raising of Jairus's daughter, Mk 5:37 and parallels; at the Transfiguration, Mk 9:2 and parallels; at Gethsemane, Mk 14:33 and Mt 26:37). Jesus asks Peter and John to prepare the Passover meal in Luke 22:8, and in Mark 14:37 (and Mt 26:40) he directs his rebuke to Peter as representing the others ("Could ye not watch with me one hour?"). Finally, the message of the angel at the tomb as recorded in Mark 16:7 said, "Go your way, tell his disciples and Peter." Certainly Peter held a very special place among the Twelve.

This was especially evident in the Caesarea Philippi episode (Mk 8:27-33 and parallels). It was Peter whose confession became the high point of the Gospel accounts, "Thou art the Christ" (Luke adds "of God"; Matthew, "the Son of the living God"). After Jesus then spoke of the suffering of the Son of Man, Peter rebuked him, and in Mark's description Jesus then turned, gazed at all the disciples, and said to Peter, "Get thee behind me, Satan: for thou savourest not the things that be of God, but the things that be of men" (v 33, KJV). This was obviously directed at them all through Peter.

The portrait of Peter that comes through all four accounts pictures him as impulsive, often rash; he is the first to act and speak his mind and was typified by his enthusiasm for everything in which he had a part. At the sight of Jesus walking on the water, Peter asked that the Lord command him to do the same and then immediately leaped out of the boat and began doing just that. At the Transfiguration, while the others were awed into silence by the appearance of Moses and Elijah, Peter the man of action said, "If thou wilt, let us make here three tabernacles" (Mt 17:4, KJV). Mark and Luke both add here that Peter did not know what he was saying. Peter's unguarded and unthinking tendency to protest Jesus' statements is seen not only at Caesarea Philippi but also at the foot-washing scene in John 13:4-11 when he said first, "You shall never ever wash my feet"; and then after Jesus' strong retort, "If I do not wash you, you have no part with Me," he reversed himself completely, stating, "Lord, not my feet only, but also my hands and head" (13:8-9, NKJV). Finally, in the account of the race to the tomb (Jn 20:2-10), the beloved disciple, reaching the tomb first, paused while Peter immediately and impulsively entered it. Peter was certainly one who "rushed in where angels fear to tread." However, this very trait aligns him with all of us and may be one of the major reasons why he becomes the representative disciple throughout the Gospels.

Peter the Rock

The key to the significance of Simon Peter is obviously the controversial addendum to the Caesarea Philippi episode, found only in Matthew 16:17-19, Jesus' testimonial to Peter. There are several crucial aspects of this saying. The most important for this study is verse 18, "And I say also unto thee, That thou art Peter, and upon this rock I will build my church" (KJV). There have been many interpretations of this down through history: (1) It refers to Peter as the "rock" or first bishop of the church. This was the Roman Catholic interpretation from the third century on and was employed as a prooftext for apostolic succession, but it is not hinted at anywhere in the context or even in the epistles: it was not a first-century concept. (2) The majority of Protestants since the Reformation have taken this to be a reference to Peter's statement of faith rather than to Peter himself; but this neglects the wordplay, which is even more pronounced in Aramaic, which has only one form for "Cephas" (rock). (3) An alternative has been to take "this rock" as a reference to Jesus himself, but that is fanciful and is hardly in the context. In conclusion, "this rock" is almost certainly a reference to Peter, but it must be understood in two ways. First, Peter was to become the foundation upon which Christ would build his church, a position clearly attested to in Acts. This does not mean that Peter had an authority above the other apostles. Paul's rebuke of Peter in Galatians 2:11-14 demonstrates that he was not above them, and at the Jerusalem council in Acts 15 it is James who has the position of leadership. Second, Peter is seen here not merely as an individual but as the representative of the disciples. This view is coming to increasing prominence today. It recognized the Jewish concept of "corporate identity" in which the leader was identified with the corporate body (e.g., the king or high priest representing the nation before God). This concept is also in keeping with Matthew 18:18-20, which passes on the same authority to the church as is here given to Peter. In this view Peter as the rock becomes the first of the building blocks upon which Christ, the chief cornerstone (to continue the metaphor), will build his church (see Eph 2:19-20).

Two other aspects are worth noting here. First, verse 18 says, "the gates of hell shall not prevail against it." The "gates of hell" is a common Jewish euphemism for death's inevitable and irrevocable power. Jesus is saying that Satan will not be triumphant over the church, and his sphere of operations, death, will be defeated (cf. 1 Cor 15:26, 54-55). The church would undergo persecution and martyrdom, but the church would be triumphant.

Second, verse 19 promises, "I will give unto thee [singular] the keys of the kingdom," another statement used of apostolic succession by the medieval church. Again, this must be understood in light of corporate identity; Peter, as the preeminent figure in the early church, here embodies the community in his leadership. The "keys of the kingdom" are in direct contrast to the "gates of hell" (cf. Rev 1:18, "the keys of hell and death" and Rev 3:7, the "key of David"), and this follows the imagery of the building seen in the rock upon which Christ will build his church. Here Peter is given the keys that will unlock the power of the kingdom in building God's community, the church. The future tense ("will give") undoubtedly points to the postresurrection period, when that power was unleashed and the church erected.

Peter the Apostle

Two events led to the new Peter who fills the pages of Acts: his reinstatement described in John 21:15-17 and the resurrection appearance of the Lord, which is never described but alluded to in Luke 24:34 and 1 Corinthians 15:5. His denial was certainly proof that he was not yet able to assume his predicted position as the rock of the church. Both Luke and Paul seem to state that the risen Lord appeared to Simon Peter before the others, which would be fitting in light of his preeminence in the early church. During the Palestinian era, the fifteen-year period prior to the Gentile mission, Peter was the leading figure. The others mentioned in Acts 1–12 are all secondary to Peter, the dominant director of church policy. These include John, who is with Peter in the Temple (3:1), the prison (4:13), and Samaria (8:14); Stephen, who was one of the Seven and whose revolutionary preaching led to his martyrdom (chs 6–7); Philip, another of the Seven who proclaimed the gospel in Samaria and to the Ethiopian eunuch (ch 8); Barnabas, who set an example of communal sharing (4:36-37) and was an official delegate to Antioch (11:20-30); Paul, a miraculous convert and witness (9:1-30; 11:25-30; 12:25); and James, who became the first apostolic martyr (12:2). It is Peter who proposes the choice of the 12th disciple (1:15-17), who proclaims the gospel at Pentecost (2:14-40), who utters the healing word (3:6), and who defends the gospel before the Sanhedrin (4:8-12, 19-20; 5:29-32). The episode regarding Ananias and Sapphira is particularly poignant, for here Peter functions as the avenging messenger of God; nowhere is his authority more evident. We would also note his authority in the scene at Samaria concerning the attempt of Simon the Sorcerer to buy the charismatic power (8:18-24). Again, it is Peter whose influence commands the situation. In these two incidents we certainly see the "binding and loosing" jurisdiction (cf. Mt 16:19) exhibited in Peter.

Yet Peter and the church still came under the strictures of their Jewish heritage. The evidence points to a Jewish proselyte self-consciousness on the part of the early church. They viewed themselves as the righteous remnant, living in the age of Messianic fulfillment, but still interpreted themselves in a Jewish sense and conducted their evangelism in the proselyte form of Jewish particularism (i.e., Gentiles could only be converted through Judaism). Two events altered this. First, the Hellenistic Jewish branch of the church rebelled against the Hebrew Christians, which resulted in the appointment of the seven deacons and a change in the orthodox policy of the Palestinian church. Second, this then led to a new preaching ministry, first by Stephen, whose insights ended in his martyrdom and the dispersal of the Hellenistic branch in chapter 8; then by Philip and others, who extended the gospel even further, to the Samaritans and God-fearers. As a further result, Peter and John came to Samaria (8:14), the next significant step toward the Gentile mission. Thus ended the centrality of Jerusalem in the unfolding story.

The two miracles of Peter, at Lydda (the paralytic) and Joppa (raising the dead woman) in Acts 9:32-42, are probably intended to parallel similar miracles of Jesus in Luke's first work (Lk 5:18-26; 8:49-56). This is part of a major theme in Acts whereby Jesus' life and ministry are paralleled and continued in the work of the Spirit through the church. Again Peter is seen in a representative role.

The new relationships are extended in two further scenes. First, Peter stays with "Simon, a tanner," in Joppa, an unclean trade; no pious Jew would knowingly have social contact with such a one. Even more important, God teaches Peter through a dream (10:10-16) that the old dichotomy between clean and unclean has been broken. This then leads Peter to the home of an uncircumcised Gentile, the most serious social taboo for the Jew, and subsequent events force Peter to admit Gentiles into the church without the necessity of Jewish proselyte requirements. The serious consequences of this are seen in the debate that ensued in Jerusalem (Acts 11:2-3) and later at the council (Acts 15:1-21). The centrality of this event is demonstrated in the extent to which Luke reproduces Peter's speech, which seems to be a repetition of chapter 10 but is meant to highlight this crucial episode. Often forgotten in the significance of this for the early church is the fact that for Luke the Gentile mission begins with Peter, not Paul. He is the one upon whom the salvific act of God descends; and as the leader of the church, he was the first important witness to it.

The persecution of Herod Agrippa (Acts 12:1-4) was likely due to the furor caused by this free intercourse with Gentiles; and it ended the period of Peter's leadership in Jerusalem. The Jewish people were greatly offended by the new Christian push; and according to Luke in Acts, the idyllic period of popularity, in which the common people supported the church, effectively ceased at this time. Peter's miraculous release and the dramatic scene at Mary's house typified the special place of Peter, but the momentum shifts. Peter is forced to flee Jerusalem, and in the interim James arises to leadership (Acts 12:17); at the Jerusalem council it is the latter who has the chair and presents the council's decision (Acts 15:6-29).

The exact relationship between Peter and the other disciples, especially with the so-called pillars—James and John—and the apostle Paul, cannot be ascertained. The evidence is too vague. Many have thought that indeed there were no truly universal leaders, for the early church was too diverse. However, that is unlikely, and Luke's portrayal in Acts parallels Paul's statement in Galatians 2:8 that Peter was the apostle par excellence to the "circumcised" and Paul to the "Gentiles." They were the universal leaders, while James became the local leader of the Jerusalem eldership. However, neither Peter nor Paul had dominical status similar to that of later popes (i.e., neither was the absolute spokesman of the church and above criticism). So-called emissaries from James could have such an influence on Peter that he would hypocritically change his behavior before Gentiles (Gal 2:12), and Paul could rebuke Peter publicly for doing so (Gal 2:11-14). Paul never claimed authority over the other disciples and even sought their approval and "the right hands of fellowship" for his ministry to the Gentiles (Gal 2:1-10).

Peter's Future Ministry

We have very little hard evidence for Peter's other movements. It seems as though Peter gradually turned from leadership to missionary work. However, this is an oversimplification. It is most likely that, following the similar pattern of Paul, he combined the two. The presence of a "Cephas party" at Corinth (1 Cor 1:12; 3:22) may indicate that Peter had spent some time there. This is made even more likely when Paul uses Peter as the main example for taking one's wife on missionary expeditions (1 Cor 9:5). The "Cephas party" probably consisted of those who were converted under his ministry; it is probable that they were Jewish Christians and opposed the "Paul party" on Jewish-Gentile debates reflected elsewhere in 1 Corinthians.

The First Epistle of Peter was sent to churches in northern Asia Minor—the provinces of Pontus, Galatia, Cappadocia, Asia, and Bithynia. The problem here is that there is no hint that Peter had been there and no personal notations in the epistle to demonstrate his acquaintance with these churches. However, it does show that he was very interested in them. In fact, some believe that the reason why Paul was not allowed into this district according to Acts 16:7-8 was that Peter was already ministering there. In short, the question of Peter's involvement in Asia Minor must remain an open one.

There is no final NT evidence that Peter went to Rome. First Peter 5:13 says that the epistle was sent from "Babylon," and it is doubtful that this was the literal Babylon, because there is no tradition that Peter ever went there, and Babylon was sparsely populated back then. It is probably a cryptic symbol for Rome, the "Babylon of the West." It is most likely that the "Babylon" of Revelation 14:8 and 16:19 is also a symbol of Rome. This would fit the strong tradition in the early church that indeed Peter did minister there.

There are four early external witnesses concerning Peter's death. John 21:18 mentions only the martyrdom of Peter but does not give any hint as to the place. First Clement was written at the end of the first century and reports the martyrdom of Peter and Paul among others. While 1 Clement 5:4 testifies only to the fact and not the place of Peter's martyrdom, a study of two aspects favors Rome—the reference to a "great multitude" of martyrdoms, which best fits the Neronian persecution, and the phrase "glorious example among us," which shows that the people of Clement's own church (Rome) were involved. Ignatius's letter to the Romans (4:3) also testifies generally to the martyrdom of Peter and Paul, and again the context favors Rome as the place. He says, "I did not command you as did Peter and Paul," which shows that they had ministries in Rome. The Ascension of Isaiah 4:2-3, a Jewish Christian

PETER
The Times of Peter

AD 27
Peter is called to be a disciple of Jesus (Matthew 4:18).

AD 29
Peter declares that Jesus is the Messiah (Matthew 16:16).

APRIL, AD 30
At Jesus' crucifixion, Peter denies knowing Jesus (Matthew 26:69-75).

MAY, AD 30
Peter is forgiven and restored by Jesus after the resurrection (John 21).

JUNE, AD 30
At Pentecost, Peter serves as chief speaker for the disciples (Acts 2).

AD 30–43
Peter leads the church, preaches, heals, and is often in trouble with Jerusalem authorities (Acts 2–12).

AD 41?
Peter helps Cornelius, a Roman officer, find Christ (Acts 10).

AD 43
Peter is imprisoned and then miraculously escapes (Acts 12).

AD 46?
Peter is challenged by Paul about not eating with Gentiles (Galatians 2:11-14).

AD 48
In a council of apostles, Peter supports Paul on the issue of Gentile conversion (Acts 15:7-11).

AD 48–64
Peter ministers in Corinth, possibly Asia Minor, and eventually Rome.

AD 64–67
In Rome, Peter is imprisoned for some period of time and writes his epistles (1 Peter, 2 Peter).

AD 67
Peter is martyred by Emperor Nero (tradition says he was crucified upside down).

work of the same period, speaks of Beliar (probably Nero) who martyrs "one of the Twelve," almost certainly Peter. Therefore the earliest evidence does not explicitly point to Rome as the place of Peter's death, but that is the most likely hypothesis.

Definite statements to that effect appear toward the end of the second century. Dionysius, bishop of Corinth, in a letter dated c. 170 (preserved in Eusebius's *Ecclesiastical History* 2.25.8) says that Peter and Paul taught together in Italy. At the end of that century Irenaeus says (in *Against Heresies* 2.1-3) that Peter and Paul preached in Rome, and Tertullian in the same general period adds that Peter was martyred "like . . . the Lord" (*Scorpiace* 15). Clement of Alexandria and Origen both allude to Peter's presence in Rome, and the latter adds the belief that he was "crucified head-downwards" (Eusebius's *Ecclesiastical History* 2.15.2; 3.1.2). The tradition that Peter was crucified may be supported in John 21:18: "when thou shalt be old, thou shalt stretch forth thy hands, and another shall . . . carry thee wither thou wouldest not" (KJV).

The fact that Paul's Epistle to the Romans (c. 55–57) does not mention Peter tells us that he could not have gone there earlier than that. If 1 Peter was written during the Neronian persecution, as those who hold to Petrine authorship believe, he must have gone there sometime in the late 50s or early 60s. Of course, the extent of his ministry in Rome also cannot be known. Some indeed have posited that he had little or no extensive stay in Rome. The facts, as they can be recovered, point to certain tentative conclusions. Peter did have some type of ministry in Rome, though the extent of it cannot be known. However, it is doubtful, in light of the early testimony to his preaching ministry there, that he was merely passing through Rome when caught in Nero's pogrom. Therefore he most likely spent the last years of his ministry in Rome and there suffered martyrdom under Nero, perhaps by crucifixion.

Simon Peter, along with Paul, was the leading figure in the early church. His impact has been tragically dimmed by the acrimonious debates of Roman Catholic–Protestant circles, but the biblical evidence is clear. He was the leading disciple of Jesus and indeed the "rock" who provided the foundation for the church. As the representative disciple, his enthusiasm and even his weaknesses have made him the supreme example of the developing disciple, one who, through the power of the risen Lord, rose above his faults to become a towering figure on the church scene.

PETHAHIAH

1. Levite and ancestor of one of the postexilic priestly families (1 Chr 24:16).

2. Levite who obeyed Ezra's exhortation to divorce his pagan wife after the Exile (Ezr 10:23).

3. Levite who assisted Ezra at the Feast of Tabernacles (Neh 9:5).

4. Meshezabel's son from Judah's tribe, who served as an adviser to the Persian king (Neh 11:24).

PETHUEL

Father of the prophet Joel (Jl 1:1).

PEULLETHAI

Obed-edom's son, who was a Levite gatekeeper in the sanctuary during David's reign (1 Chr 26:5).

PHANUEL

Father of Anna the prophetess. Anna prophesied in connection with the presentation of the infant Jesus at the Temple (Lk 2:36).

PHARAOH

Ruler over Egypt also known as "the King of Upper and Lower Egypt." He lived in a palace known as the "great house," which was the symbol of his authority. The Egyptian word for the palace was applied to the kings themselves during the New Kingdom (c. 1550–1070 BC). As king, the pharaoh personified the rule of the gods over Egypt. The 18th and 19th dynasties frequently employed the term "pharaoh" without giving the actual name of the pharaoh.

The title was not used officially. Rather, it was a popular designation for the king. In the OT the title was used to refer to men who lived in different historical periods. They were representatives of various dynasties. The use of the royal designation without the name was sufficient for the period in which the pharaoh ruled or for people who were acquainted with the pharaoh. For us today it is often difficult to ascertain who the pharaoh was at any given period and what dynastic period he ruled in.

In the OT the title pharaoh appears by itself (Gn 12:15), as well as with the additional description "king of Egypt" (Dt 7:8), and the name of the pharaoh, such as Neco (2 Kgs 23:29). The pharaoh was considered to be a representative of the gods Ra and Amon on earth. They upheld the divine order in Egypt and were supportive of the Temples. The position of the pharaoh as civil and religious head of state gave him unique authority. Unlike his counterparts in the surrounding nations, the authority of the Egyptian king was not easily upset by insurrection.

It remains difficult to identify the pharaohs during the period of the patriarchs. Abraham and Joseph had dealings with the pharaohs of the Middle Kingdom and the second intermediate period. Also, the identity of the pharaoh of the oppression of the Israelites and of the Exodus is not satisfactorily resolved. Those who hold to the early date of the Exodus see Thutmose III as the pharaoh who began the oppression of the Israelites in Egypt (Ex 1:8). In this view Amenhotep II (c. 1440 BC), who succeeded Thutmose upon his death (2:23), is the pharaoh of the Exodus. Another view is that the oppression began under the 18th dynasty and continued until the 19th dynasty. In this view Ramses II is the pharaoh of the Exodus (c. 1290 BC).

During the united monarchy, Israel's position as an international power grew. David subdued the nations on Israel's border zones. When Joab took Edom, an Edomite prince, Hadad, fled to Egypt to find protection at pharaoh's court. The 21st dynasty ruled in Egypt during David's time, and it may be that Pharaoh Siamun welcomed Hadad as a political weapon to be used against the growing strength of Israel (1 Kgs 11:14-22). Pharaoh Siamun is possibly also to be identified with the pharaoh who made an incursion into the Philistine coastland, conquering Gezer to be given as dowry to Solomon at the marriage of his daughter to Solomon (3:1-2). At the collapse of Israel's unity, Pharaoh Shishak (Shishong I) of the 22nd dynasty made a campaign against Judah and Israel and took much booty with him (14:25-26).

Pharaoh Neco defeated the Judean forces at Megiddo, killing King Josiah in action (2 Kgs 23:29). The last king of Judah (Zedekiah) hoped in vain for help from Egypt, where Pharaoh Hophra of the 26th dynasty ruled. The prophet Ezekiel spoke harshly against the king of Egypt: "Thus says the Lord GOD: 'Behold, I am against you, Pharaoh king of Egypt.... It [Egypt] shall be the most lowly of the kingdoms, and never again exalt itself above the nations; and I will make them so small that they will never again rule over the nations'" (Ez 29:3, 15, RSV). Under the Persian regime, the power of the pharaohs dwindled, in fulfillment of the prophetic word.

PHARAOH HOPHRA
Fourth king of the 26th dynasty (Egypt), he ruled 589–570 BC (Jer 44:30). *See* Hophra.

PHARAOH NECO
See Neco.

PHICOL
Commander of Abimelech's army, mentioned in connection with his ruler's treaty negotiations with Abraham and Isaac (Gn 21:22, 32; 26:26). The presence of an army commander should have indicated Abraham's vulnerability, but the adversaries acknowledged the superior power of Abraham's God and thus sought peaceful coexistence with him.

PHILEMON
Christian known only from the letter addressed to him by the apostle Paul. He is mentioned nowhere else in the NT. From Colossians 4:17 it is clear that Archippus, mentioned along with Philemon in Philemon 1:2 (and perhaps his son), was a man of Colosse. Although Paul had never visited that city (Col 2:1), he obviously knew Philemon well. He addressed him as "our beloved co-worker" (Phlm 1:1); perhaps Philemon had been a colleague during Paul's three-year mission in Ephesus (Acts 19:8-10; 20:31), and Paul knew that he could appeal to him on behalf of his runaway slave, Onesimus.

PHILETUS
False teacher who, along with his companion Hymenaeus, held an erroneous view of the resurrection of believers—that the resurrection had already happened (2 Tm 2:17; cf. v 11).

QUICKTAKE

PHILIP

STRENGTHS AND ACCOMPLISHMENTS
• One of the seven organizers of food distribution in the early church
• Became an evangelist, one of the first traveling missionaries
• One of the first to obey Jesus' command to take the gospel to all people
• A careful student of the Bible who could explain its meaning clearly

LESSONS FROM HIS LIFE
• God finds great and various uses for those willing to obey wholeheartedly
• The gospel is universal Good News
• The whole Bible, not just the New Testament, helps us understand more about Jesus
• Both mass response (the Samaritans) and individual response (the man from Ethiopia) to the gospel are valuable

VITAL STATISTICS
Occupations: Deacon, evangelist
Relatives: Four daughters
Contemporaries: Paul, Stephen, the apostles

KEY VERSE
"So beginning with this same Scripture, Philip told him the Good News about Jesus" (Acts 8:35).

Philip's story is told in Acts 6:1-7; 8:5-40; 21:8-10.

PHILIP

1. Hellenistic Jew and one of the seven men appointed by the church in Jerusalem to supervise the daily ministry of assistance to the impoverished widows of the Christian community. They all, including Philip, had Greek names, and one of them, Nicolaus, was a proselyte (i.e., not a Jew by birth). Whether or not they were regarded as deacons in the technical sense is not absolutely clear from the account; this occasion has, however, been generally accepted as the origin of the order of the diaconate (Acts 6:1-7). Of the seven, Stephen and Philip are the only ones of whom we have any further record in the NT. They are described as men of good repute, full of the Spirit and of wisdom (v 3).

   That Philip became known as "the evangelist" is apparent from Acts 21:8. The designation was well deserved, for when the Jerusalem Christians were scattered by the persecution led by Saul of Tarsus, Philip went to a city of Samaria and proclaimed the gospel with such power there that a great number of people joyfully turned to Christ (Acts 8:1-8). In the midst of this spectacular work, Philip was divinely instructed to leave Samaria and go down to the desert area in the southern part of the country. Humanly speaking, for him to turn away from the multitudes, who were so eagerly responding to his preaching and to go to the uninhabited territory in the south, must have seemed foolish. Yet Philip showed himself not only sensitive but also obedient to the will of God and followed this guidance without question. In the desert he found not a crowd but a single person, an important Ethiopian court official who had visited Jerusalem and was now returning to Africa. The wisdom of God in directing Philip to this place was fully vindicated, for the Ethiopian was reading Isaiah 53, the great gospel chapter of the OT. Philip gave him the good news that this prophecy pointed to Jesus Christ. The Ethiopian subsequently believed and was baptized and went on his way rejoicing (vv 25-40). The conversion of this one person meant not only that Philip was the first to proclaim the gospel to a Gentile but also that the gospel was taken by this Ethiopian courtier to the continent of Africa.

The prevailing nationalistic pride of the Jews was such that they despised the Samaritans and regarded the Gentiles as ceremonially unclean. But Philip, by his eager preaching of Christ first to the Samaritans and then to the Ethiopian, reflected the way in which the gospel penetrated social barriers and dissolved racial prejudices and demonstrated that the grace of God in Christ Jesus is freely available to all. Subsequently, Philip made his home in the coastal town of Caesarea. There he hospitably entertained Paul and Luke when they were en route to Jerusalem at the conclusion of the apostle's third missionary journey. Luke tells us that Philip had four unmarried daughters who were prophetesses (Acts 21:8-9). Not long after this, when Paul was in custody in Caesarea for two years, the kindness and friendship of Philip must have meant much to him (23:31-35; 24:23, 27).

2. Apostle whose name is placed fifth in each of the lists of the twelve after the two pairs of brothers, Simon Peter and Andrew, and James and John (Mt 10:3; Mk 3:18; Lk 6:14). John says that when John the Baptist bore witness to Jesus with the words, "Behold, the Lamb of God!" two of his disciples began to follow Jesus, and that one of these two was Andrew, who then declared to his brother Simon Peter, "We have found the Messiah," and brought him to Jesus. (The other unnamed disciple was quite probably John himself, the writer of this account.) On the next day Jesus went to Galilee and there found Philip and addressed the call to him: "Follow me." John adds that Philip was from Bethsaida. Philip in turn found Nathanael and told him, "We have found him of whom Moses in the law and also the prophets wrote," and invited Nathanael, who was skeptical that any good could come out of Nazareth, to come and see for himself (Jn 1:35-51,

RSV). From this is concluded that Philip was one of the first to follow Jesus and that he lost no time in persuading others to do the same.

Like the other apostles, however, he still had much to learn about the person and the power of Christ. Hence, the testing question of Jesus to him on the occasion of the feeding of the 5,000, "How are we to buy bread, so that these people may eat?" and Philip's puzzled response that even if they had 200 denarii (i.e., a large sum, roughly a person's wages for half a year), it would not buy enough bread for each one to be given just a little to eat (Jn 6:5-7). The miracle that followed taught him that the feeding of this multitude presented no problem to the one who is the Lord of all creation. Philip's next appearance is in Jerusalem after Christ's triumphal entry into the city, when "some Greeks" (i.e., Greek-speaking non-Jews) approached him with the request "Sir, we wish to see Jesus." Philip informs Andrew, and together they bring them to Jesus (12:20-22). This perhaps indicates that Philip was a person whom others found readily approachable, and also that he spoke Greek. In the upper room, prior to his arrest and trial, Jesus took the opportunity to impart further instruction to Philip, who had said, "Lord, show us the Father, and we shall be satisfied." Philip hoped perhaps, in all devoutness, for the privilege of some special revelation (reminiscent of the request of Moses, Ex 33:18). But Jesus taught him that he himself, the incarnate Son, is the all-sufficient revelation of the Father to humanity (Jn 14:8-10).

There is a tendency to confuse the apostle with the evangelist (see below) of the same name. It seems probable, however, that after preaching in various parts, the apostle settled in Hierapolis, a city of the Roman province of Asia, and died there. Whether his was a natural or a martyr's death is uncertain.

3. Son of Herod the Great and Cleopatra and half brother of Antipas, whose mother was Malthace. He is called Herod in Luke 3:1. The latter was tetrarch of Perea and Galilee from 4 BC to AD 39; Philip was tetrarch of Iturea and Trachonitis (plus certain other territories) to the northeast of Galilee for 37 years (4 BC to AD 33). His wife was his niece Salome, who danced for Herod in exchange for the head of John the Baptist (Mt 14:3-12; Mk 6:17-29). *See also* Herod.

4. Son of Herod the Great and Mariamne and husband of Salome's mother, Herodias, who left him to become the mistress of his half brother Herod Antipas. It was for this immoral relationship that John the Baptist rebuked Herod and was later imprisoned and beheaded (Mt 14:3-12; Mk 6:17-29; Lk 3:19-20).

PHILOLOGUS

Early Christian acquaintance or friend of the apostle Paul to whom he sent greetings (Rom 16:15). In the series of greetings, he seems to be paired with a woman named Julia.

PHINEHAS

1. Eleazer's son, grandson of Aaron (Ex 6:25), and Abishua's father (1 Chr 6:4, 50). During the high priesthood of Eleazer, Phinehas had charge over the gatekeepers

of the Tabernacle (9:20), as did Eleazer his father, when Aaron served as chief priest (cf. Nm 3:32). Phinehas, grieved by Israel's sin with Baal of Peor at Shittim, killed an Israelite man and a Midianite woman for their licentious behavior (25:7). Following this act, the Lord turned away his anger toward Israel and made a covenant of peace with Phinehas, which was a covenant of a perpetual priesthood for him and his descendants (vv 11-13); his deed was reckoned to him as righteousness from generation to generation forever (Ps 106:30). Except for the brief interval when Eli acted as high priest (cf 1 Sm 1–3; 14:3), Phinehas and his posterity officiated at the high priestly position until the destruction of the Jerusalem Temple by the Romans in AD 70.

Following the Baal of Peor incident, Phinehas joined Israel in defeating the Midianites in war (Nm 31:6). After Israel took possession of the land of Canaan, Phinehas was given the town of Gibeah in the hill country of Ephraim for an inheritance (Jos 24:33). He was sent with a small delegation of Israelite leaders to question the building of an altar on the west bank of the Jordan River by the tribes of Israel living east of the Jordan (Jos 22:13, 30-32). Later, at Bethel, Phinehas promised Israel victory over Benjamin's tribe in battle (Jgs 20:28). His descendants Ezra the scribe (Ezr 7:5) and Gershom (8:2) returned with their families to Jerusalem following the Exile.

2. One of Eli's two sons, who served as a priest at Shiloh (1 Sm 1:3). According to 1 Samuel, Phinehas was a despicable priest, who, along with Hophni his brother, profaned the offered sacrifices (2:12-17) and the sanctuary (v 22), and scorned Eli (v 25). His death was foretold to his father by a man of God (v 34). In a subsequent war with the Philistines, Phinehas was killed on the same day his wife bore him a son, named Ichabod (4:11, 17-19; 14:3).

3. Eleazer's father. Eleazer helped Meremoth and the Levites, Jozabad and Noadiah, take inventory of the Temple's precious metals and vessels during the postexilic era (Ezr 8:33).

PHLEGON
Christian in Rome to whom Paul sent greetings (Rom 16:14).

PHOEBE
Christian woman of the church at Cenchrea, the eastern port for the city of Corinth. In Romans 16:1-2, Paul commended Phoebe to the recipients of the letter on the basis of her valuable service to other Christians. He asked that they give her whatever assistance she needed.

The term "deacon" is applied to Phoebe. It probably designates an official position in the church, as in Philippians 1:1, although it may mean "minister" in the same sense that Paul uses it elsewhere of himself and others (1 Cor 3:5; 2 Cor 3:6; 6:4).

PHYGELUS
Asian Christian who, along with others, abandoned Paul (2 Tm 1:15). Phygelus is mentioned with Hermogenes, also otherwise unknown.

QUICKTAKE

PILATE

STRENGTH AND ACCOMPLISHMENT
• Roman governor of Judea

WEAKNESSES AND MISTAKES
• He failed in his attempt to rule a people who were defeated militarily but never dominated by Rome
• His constant political struggles made him a cynical and uncaring compromiser, susceptible to pressure
• Although he realized Jesus was innocent, he bowed to the public demand for his execution

LESSONS FROM HIS LIFE
• Great evil can happen when truth is at the mercy of political pressures
• Resisting the truth leaves a person without purpose or direction

VITAL STATISTICS
Where: Judea
Occupation: Roman governor of Judea
Relative: Wife: unnamed
Contemporaries: Jesus, Caiaphas, Herod

KEY VERSES
"'What is truth?' Pilate asked. Then he went out again to the people and told them, 'He is not guilty of any crime. But you have a custom of asking me to release one prisoner each year at Passover. Would you like me to release this "King of the Jews"?'" (John 18:38, 39).

Pilate's story is told in the Gospels. He is also mentioned in Acts 3:13; 4:27; 13:28; 1 Timothy 6:13.

PILATE, PONTIUS

Appointed by Tiberius as the fifth prefect of Judea, Pilate served in that capacity from AD 26–36. He appears prominently in the trial narratives of the Gospels as the Roman governor who authorized Jesus' crucifixion. In addition, he appears in a variety of extra-biblical sources as a dispassionate administrator who relentlessly pursued Roman authority in Judea.

Tacitus (*Annals* 15.44) mentions Pilate in connection with the crucifixion of Jesus but adds little to the Gospel account. Josephus, on the other hand, provides three narratives. First, he describes Pilate's arrival as the new prefect (*War* 2.9.2; *Antiquities* 18.3.1; cf. Eusebius's *Histories* 2.6). Offending Jewish law, Pilate brought ensigns into Jerusalem that bore the image of Caesar. A large gathering of Jews then came to Caesarea in protest, fasting there for five days. Pilate called in troops to dismiss them, but he learned his first lesson about Jewish intransigence. The Jews were ready to die rather than tolerate the ensigns. Soon thereafter Pilate relented.

A second incident occurred when Pilate appropriated Temple funds in order to construct a 35-mile (56.3-kilometer) aqueduct for Jerusalem (*War* 2.9.4; *Antiquities* 18.3.2). Again, there was a major protest. Pilate ordered his soldiers to dress in tunics and infiltrate the crowds in disguise. At his command, the troops used clubs to beat the offenders. Many Jews were killed. Josephus records the horror with which Jerusalem perceived the affair.

Finally, Josephus records the story of Pilate's dismissal (*Antiquities* 18.4.1-2). In AD 36 a Samaritan false prophet (pretending to be the *Taheb*, or Samaritan messiah) promised to show his followers sacred vessels hidden by Moses on Mt Gerizim. Pilate sent a heavily armed contingent of footmen and cavalry who intercepted the pilgrims and slaughtered most of them. The Samaritans complained to Vitellius, the prefect of Syria, whereupon Pilate was ordered to report to the emperor Tiberius. Another prefect, Marcellus, was then sent by Rome as Pilate's replacement.

Philo records yet another event (*Leg. to Caius* 299-305). While extolling the liberal policies of Tiberius toward Judaism, he cites a negative example in Pontius Pilate. The prefect had erected gilded shields in Herod's former palace in Jerusalem that bore the name of the emperor. Refusing to hear Jewish complaints, the sons of Herod appealed to Tiberius, who ordered Pilate to transfer the shields to the Temple of Augustus in Caesarea. The similarities with the parallel story in Josephus have led many scholars to believe that Philo is merely recounting another version of the same event.

Luke mentions a minor incident that contributes to this same portrait. In Luke 13:1 some Jews tell Jesus about the Galileans whose blood Pilate had mixed with their sacrifices. While this story is not corroborated by any other witness, it conforms to the impressions of Pilate's character given by Philo and Josephus. In fact, Luke adds another detail of interest in his trial narrative. In Luke 23:12 he says that prior to the crucifixion of Jesus, Herod Antipas (in Galilee) and Pilate had been at enmity with each other. This may have stemmed not simply from Pilate's usual antagonism but particularly from the Galilean incident.

Pilate's role in the death of Jesus is recorded in each Gospel (Mt 27:2; Mk 15:1; Lk 23:1; Jn 18:29) and was remembered as a historical datum in the preaching of the apostles (Acts 3:13; 4:27; 13:28; 1 Tm 6:13). In order to secure the conviction and death of Jesus, Caiaphas and the Sanhedrin brought their charges to Pilate. While the accusations took on a political flavor to evoke the governor's interest, he still could find no grounds for condemnation. In the end, Pilate unexpectedly accommodates the Jewish leaders and has Jesus crucified.

All of the Gospels and particularly John show Pilate's repeated verdict of Jesus' innocence. According to Matthew 27:19, Pilate's wife had an ominous dream about Jesus' conviction, and she warned her husband. Pilate tried to have Jesus released, but the crowd cried for Barabbas. Matthew even records that Pilate washed his hands (27:24-25), declaring his own innocence in this. And finally, John says that Pilate refused to alter the title over the cross (Jn 19:19-22). These accounts, therefore, take the full blame for Jesus' death from Pilate and place it on the Jewish leaders of the Sanhedrin. They are ultimately responsible.

But why would Pilate act in behalf of the Sanhedrin? Two answers are possible. First, there may have been collusion between Caiaphas and Pilate that stemmed from a long-standing relationship and coterminous reign. Ten of Caiaphas's eighteen years in power were under Pilate, and when the prefect was dismissed in AD 36, Caiaphas was simultaneously removed. Second, if Jesus' trial occurred in AD 33, Pilate may have been concerned about his impeachment. He had originally been appointed by Sejanus (prefect of the praetorians in Rome who had appointed men to colonial office under Tiberius), but in the autumn of AD 31 Sejanus died. This explains why a Jewish delegation could report directly to Tiberius during the votive shield incident. Hence, the charge recorded in John 19:12 ("If you release this man, you are not Caesar's friend") would have had genuine power over Pilate. Pilate perceived his jeopardy and was anxious to pacify the Jews and please the emperor.

The history of Pilate after his dismissal in AD 36 is unknown. Eusebius reports that Pilate ultimately committed suicide during the reign of the emperor Caligula, AD 37–41 (*History* 2.7).

PILDASH
Sixth son of Nahor and Milcah; nephew of Abraham (Gn 22:22).

PILHA
Political leader who set his seal on Ezra's covenant during the postexilic era (Neh 10:24).

PILTAI
Priest and head of Modiah's house during the days of Joiakim the high priest in the postexilic period (Neh 12:17).

PINON
One of the "chiefs" (NLT "leaders") descended from Esau (Gn 36:41; 1 Chr 1:52).

PIRAM
King of Jarmuth, a Canaanite city located southwest of Jerusalem. After joining an alliance with four Amorite kings against Joshua, Piram—along with other kings—was defeated and killed (Jos 10:3).

PISPAH
Jether's son from Asher's tribe (1 Chr 7:38).

PITHON
Benjaminite, Micah's son and a descendant of Jonathan (1 Chr 8:35; 9:41).

POKERETH-HAZZEBAIM
Head of a family of Solomon's servants who returned from the Exile with Zerubbabel (Ezr 2:57; Neh 7:59). The KJV renders the name Pochereth of Zebaim, making the latter part a place-name.

PONTIUS PILATE
See Pilate, Pontius.

PORATHA
One of the ten sons of Haman killed by the Jews (Est 9:8).

PORCIUS FESTUS
See Festus, Porcius.

POTIPHAR
Officer who purchased Joseph when he arrived in Egypt after being sold by his brothers to the Ishmaelites or Midianites (Gn 37:36; 39:1). The word translated "officer" is derived from an Akkadian word for a court official. By the first millennium, the meaning "eunuch" was attached to the term; hence, the NEB, following the Septuagint tradition, has "eunuch" in Genesis 37:36. But most English versions are correct in rendering it "officer" or "official." Little, if anything, is known of eunuchs in Egypt, and certainly they played no role in Pharaoh's court in the second millennium BC.

A second title held by Potiphar was "captain of the guard," which seems to be a Semitic expression for an Egyptian title rather than a transliteration of an Egyptian phrase. This same title is applied to Nebuzaradan, Nebuchadnezzar's general (see 2 Kgs 25:8, 11, 20; Jer 39:9-11). The Egyptian counterpart to this title suggests that this officer was an instructor for retainers who were attached to the king. The titles indicate that Potiphar was a man of some importance and status. His purchase of a Semitic slave to serve in domestic affairs is in keeping with the practice of Egyptians from 1800 BC onward.

The name Potiphar seems to be a transliteration of the Egyptian name, meaning "he whom Re [the sun god] has given." This name formula is known in Egypt beginning around the 13th century BC.

When falsely accused of trying to seduce Potiphar's wife, Joseph was placed in prison (Gn 39:20). Some think that Potiphar as "captain of the guard" would have been the warden. But Genesis 39:21 tells us that the "keeper of the prison" was impressed with Joseph's abilities (something Potiphar had already learned—cf. vv 2-6), and so gave him special responsibilities. The warden's discovery of Joseph's talents while in prison suggests that he was a different man.

See also Joseph #1.

QUICKTAKE

PRISCILLA and AQUILA

STRENGTHS AND ACCOMPLISHMENTS
- Outstanding husband/wife team who ministered in the early church
- Supported themselves by tentmaking while serving Christ
- Close friends of Paul
- Explained to Apollos the full message of Christ

LESSONS FROM THEIR LIVES
- Couples can have an effective ministry together
- The home is a valuable tool for evangelism
- Every believer needs to be well educated in the faith, whatever his or her role in the church

VITAL STATISTICS
Where: Originally from Rome, moved to Corinth, then Ephesus
Occupation: Tentmakers
Contemporaries: Emperor Claudius, Paul, Timothy, Apollos

KEY VERSES
"Give my greetings to Priscilla and Aquila, my co-workers in the ministry of Christ Jesus. In fact, they once risked their lives for me. I am thankful to them, and so are all the Gentile churches" (Romans 16:3-4).

Their story is told in Acts 18. They are also mentioned in Romans 16:3-5; 1 Corinthians 16:19; 2 Timothy 4:19.

POTIPHERA
Priest of On whose daughter, Asenath, was given to Joseph as his wife by Pharaoh (Gn 41:45, 50; 46:20). On (or Heliopolis) was the center of the sun-god cult, and Potiphera was likely a high-ranking priest in the cult. His name, which means "he whom Re [the son god] has given," does not appear in Egyptian records until the tenth century BC, a fact employed by those who prefer a late date for the book of Genesis. Yet the name is known from the 15th century (the time of Moses), and its full form may be a modernization of a name common in Joseph's era (20th century BC).
See also Joseph #1.

PRISCILLA AND AQUILA
Christian couple who were friends and possibly converts of the apostle Paul during his ministry at Corinth (Acts 18:1-3). They are always mentioned together in the NT. Priscilla's

personal character or her leadership role in the church may account for her name coming before her husband's in four out of six references (Acts 18:18, 26; Rom 16:3; 2 Tm 4:19).

Aquila was a Jew and a native of Pontus in Asia Minor. He had been expelled from Rome by the AD 49 edict of Claudius (Acts 18:2). Suetonius records that the emperor "banished from Rome all the Jews, who were continually making disturbances at the instigation of one Chrestus." From Rome, Aquila and Priscilla went to Corinth, where Paul (on his second missionary journey) met them. There they lived together and worked at the same trade of making tents. After such close association with Paul, they were able to instruct even the learned Apollos, a Jewish teacher who then became a Christian (vv 24-28).

Both Priscilla and Aquila were Paul's loyal friends and trusted coworkers (Rom 16:3-4). When he left Corinth, they accompanied him and remained at Ephesus after he returned to Syria (Acts 18:18-19). When Paul wrote the First Letter to Corinth, they were still at Ephesus, where their home was used as a place for Christians to gather (1 Cor 16:19). Since the decree of Claudius was temporary, Priscilla and Aquila were again in Rome when Paul wrote to the Roman Christians (Rom 16:3). When the Second Letter to Timothy was written, they were again in Ephesus (2 Tm 4:19).

PROCORUS

One of the seven men appointed by the apostles in Jerusalem for service in the early days of the church (Acts 6:5). They were to oversee the fair distribution of food in the Christian community.

PUAH

1. One of two Hebrew midwives ordered by Pharaoh to kill Hebrew males at birth. However, she feared God and did not carry out the order (Ex 1:15).

2. Father of Tola, a judge of Israel (Jgs 10:1).

3. Issachar's son, who went with Jacob and his household to Egypt, where they sought refuge from the severe famine in Palestine (Gn 46:13; NLT "Puah"). Puvah founded the Punite family (Nm 26:23).

PUBLIUS

Name of a resident of the island of Malta, mentioned in Acts 28:7-8. He hosted Paul and others briefly after a shipwreck had stranded them on the island as they journeyed to Rome. Publius bore a title that indicated he was an important official on Malta at the time. His ailing father was healed by Paul during the visit.

PUDENS

Companion of Paul mentioned in 2 Timothy 4:21. At the close of the letter his personal greetings are communicated to the recipient. Three other companions, who also send greetings, are named: Eubulus, Linus, and Claudia.

PUL

1. Name given to Tiglath-pileser, the Assyrian ruler (745–727 BC), when he became king of Babylon (729–727 BC; 2 Kgs 15:19; 1 Chr 5:26). The meaning of the name is unknown, and Assyrian manuscripts do not mention it, suggesting to some scholars that Pul was Tiglath-pileser's original name. *See* Tiglath-pileser.

2. African people mentioned only in Isaiah 66:19 (KJV). Their connection with Tarshish and Lud has strongly suggested that Pul is a copyist's error for Put (as in various Greek manuscripts), a people related to the Egyptians and possibly a subculture of Libyans.

PURAH

Gideon's servant, who accompanied his master on a secret night visit to the Midianite camp, where they were encouraged by the Lord (Jgs 7:10-11).

PUT

Third of Ham's four sons, who most likely settled in northern Africa and is perhaps the forefather of the peoples of Egypt and Libya (Gn 10:6; 1 Chr 1:8).

PUTIEL

Father of Eleazer's wife and the grandfather of Phinehas (Ex 6:25).

PYRRHUS

Father of Sopater of Berea, who, with others, accompanied Paul on his return trip through Macedonia (Acts 20:4).

Q,R

QUARTUS

Christian who joined the apostle Paul in sending greetings to the church in Rome (Rom 16:23).

QUEEN OF SHEBA

Female member of royalty from the territory located in southwestern Arabia known also as the kingdom of Saba (Hebrew *Seba*'). During the Solomonic era (970–930 BC), the queen of Sheba traveled to Jerusalem to see Solomon's riches and to test his wisdom with riddles. Solomon exceeded her expectations on both counts (1 Kgs 10:1-13; 2 Chr 9:1-12).

QUIRINIUS

Roman governor of Syria at the time of Jesus' birth (Lk 2:2). According to the Roman historian Tacitus (*Annals* 3.48), Publius Sulpicius Quirinius was elected consul of Syria in 12 BC. He was appointed around 7 BC, along with Varus, legatus (or governor) of Syria. His duties concentrated on military and foreign affairs, while Varus concerned himself with civil matters. Quirinius's first administration as governor lasted several years, during which time he led a successful expedition against the Homonadenses, an unruly group of rebel mountaineers who lived in the Cilician province of Asia Minor, and superintended in his region the empire-wide census decreed by Caesar Augustus. Luke records that Jesus' birth took place at the time of this first enrollment "when Quirinius was governor of Syria" (Lk 2:2), and according to Matthew, during the days of King Herod the Great (Mt 2:1)—presumably in 4 BC.

Quirinius became rector to Gaius Caesar in 1 BC and married Aemilia Ledipa in AD 2, whom he subsequently divorced. In AD 6, he was reappointed legatus of Syria, perhaps serving in this position for a couple of years. In this second administration Quirinius again supervised a census of Judea. However, the second census was not administered according to Jewish custom, as was the first. The second census taxed the Jews as a subservient people to the Roman state, thus causing Jewish opposition and rebellion toward Rome. This is probably the census referred to by the Jewish historian Josephus (*Antiquities* 17.13.5) and Gamaliel (Acts 5:37). The remainder of Quirinius's career was probably spent in Rome, where he died at an advanced age (c. AD 21).

R

RAAMAH

One of Cush's five sons and a descendant of Ham's line. He was the father of Sheba and Dedan (Gn 10:7; 1 Chr 1:9). Ezekiel 27:22 mentions the people of Sheba and Raamah trading spices and precious stones with the merchants of Tyre. Raamah's name was later given to a town perhaps identifiable with Ma'in in southwest Arabia.

QUICKTAKE

RACHEL

STRENGTHS AND ACCOMPLISHMENTS
• She showed great loyalty to her family
• She gave birth to Joseph and Benjamin after being barren for many years

WEAKNESSES AND MISTAKES
• Her envy and competitiveness marred her relationship with her sister, Leah
• She was capable of dishonesty when she took her loyalty too far
• She failed to recognize that Jacob's devotion was not dependent on her ability
  to have children

LESSONS FROM HER LIFE
• Loyalty must be controlled by what is true and right
• Love is accepted, not earned

VITAL STATISTICS
Where: Haran
Occupation: Shepherdess, wife, mother, household manager
Relatives: Father: Laban. Aunt: Rebekah. Sister: Leah. Husband: Jacob. Sons: Joseph
    and Benjamin

KEY VERSE
"So Jacob worked seven years to pay for Rachel. But his love for her was so strong that it
seemed to him but a few days" (Genesis 29:20).

Rachel's story is told in Genesis 29–35:20. She is also mentioned in Ruth 4:11.

RACHEL

Beautiful younger daughter of Laban; she was the favorite wife of Jacob. He first met her
as he arrived at Haran in Paddan-aram. There he assisted her by attending to the needs
of Rachel's father's sheep, removing a stone from the mouth of a well in order to water
them (Gn 29:10). Jacob loved Rachel exceedingly and agreed to work seven years for Laban
in return for her hand in marriage. His seven years' service seemed like only a few days
because of his great love for her. Laban deceptively reneged on his bargain and required
Jacob to marry Leah, his older, less attractive daughter, before finally giving him Rachel for
his wife. Unlike Leah, Rachel was barren in the early years of her marriage to Jacob (30:1).
Consequently, she gave her servant, Bilhah, to Jacob in order to have children. Thus, through

this commonly accepted ancient custom, Dan and Naphtali were born. In time, Rachel herself conceived and bore Joseph (vv 22-25). After this, Jacob took his wives, children, and possessions away from Haran.

Somewhere between Bethel and Bethlehem, Rachel died while giving birth to Benjamin (Gn 35:16, 19). Jacob set up a pillar over her tomb there, a landmark known even in the days of Saul (1 Sm 10:2). Rachel and Leah are highly regarded as those who built up the house of Israel (Ru 4:11). In Jeremiah 31:15, Rachel is pictured as crying for her children being carried off into captivity. Later, Matthew recalls Jeremiah's words in Herod's slaughter of the male infants (Mt 2:18).

See also Jacob #1.

QUICKTAKE

RAHAB

STRENGTHS AND ACCOMPLISHMENTS
- Relative of Boaz, and thus an ancestor of David and Jesus
- One of only two women listed in the Hall of Faith in Hebrews 11
- Resourceful, willing to help others at great cost to herself

WEAKNESS AND MISTAKE
- She was a prostitute

LESSON FROM HER LIFE
- She did not let fear affect her faith in God's ability to deliver

VITAL STATISTICS
Where: Jericho
Occupations: Prostitute/innkeeper, later became a wife
Relatives: Ancestor of David and Jesus (Matthew 1:5)
Contemporary: Joshua

KEY VERSE
"It was by faith that Rahab the prostitute was not destroyed with the people in her city who refused to obey God. For she had given a friendly welcome to the spies" (Hebrews 11:31).

Rahab's story is told in Joshua 2 and 6:22, 23. She is also mentioned in Matthew 1:5; Hebrews 11:31; and James 2:25.

RADDAI

Fifth of Jesse's seven sons and the brother of David from Judah's tribe (1 Chr 2:14).

RAHAB

Heroine of the battle of Jericho (Jos 2–6). Soon after Moses' death, God told Joshua that he and the people were to cross the Jordan and occupy the land of promise. Before the crossing, however, Joshua sent two spies into the land to reconnoiter the opposition, in particular the fortified city of Jericho. Upon entering the city, the spies found their way quickly to Rahab's house, which was perhaps an inn and/or a brothel. She apparently was a prostitute.

News of the arrival of spies was not long in reaching the king of Jericho, who quite naturally demanded that Rahab divulge their whereabouts. She cleverly admitted seeing them but insisted that they had left the city at nightfall. Actually, the spies were hiding under the stalks of flax on the roof of her house. When the king's search party left Jericho to hunt the spies, Rahab confessed to the spies the reason for her complicity with the Israelites' cause. She feared the God of the Jews, believing that he would surely give them victory (Jos 2:11).

For her help, the spies agreed to save Rahab and her family. The sign was to be a cord of scarlet thread hanging from her window, the same avenue the spies used to escape the city. Rahab and her family were indeed the only survivors of the subsequent battle. They were led to safety, on Joshua's command, by the very men Rahab had saved.

Rahab became the wife of Salmon and mother of Boaz, and thus an ancestor of Jesus (Mt 1:5). Rahab is listed, along with Moses, David, Samson, and Samuel, as an example of faith (Heb 11:31). Her deed is an example of good works and justification (Jas 2:25).

RAHAM

Son of Shema, and father of Jorkeam (1 Chr 2:44). He was a descendant of Judah.

RAKEM

Manasseh's grandson (1 Chr 7:16).

RAM

1. Ancestor of King David (Ru 4:19; 1 Chr 2:9-10), listed in Matthew's genealogy of Christ (Mt 1:3-4; called Arni in Lk 3:33).

2. Jerahmeel's eldest son (1 Chr 2:25-27), and perhaps the nephew of #1 above.

3. Head of the family of Elihu, one of Job's friends (Jb 32:2).

RAMIAH

Parosh's son, who obeyed Ezra's exhortation to divorce his foreign wife after the Exile (Ezr 10:25).

RAPHA

1. Benjamin's fifth son (1 Chr 8:2). His name is omitted in the earlier list of Genesis 46:21.

2. KJV spelling of Raphah, an alternate name for Rephaiah, Binea's son, in 1 Chronicles 8:37. *See* Rephaiah #4.

RAPHU

Benjaminite and the father of Palti, one of the 12 spies sent to search out the land of Canaan (Nm 13:9).

REAIAH

1. Shobal's son and the father of Jahath from the tribe of Judah (1 Chr 4:2), perhaps identifiable with Haroeh (2:52).

2. Reubenite, Micah's son and the father of Baal (1 Chr 5:5).

3. Head or founder of a family of Temple servants who returned with Zerubbabel from captivity in Babylon (Ezr 2:47; Neh 7:50).

REBA

One of the five Midianite kings killed by Moses at the Lord's command for seducing the Israelite settlers to idol worship (Nm 31:8; Jos 13:21).

REBEKAH

Daughter of Bethuel and the wife of the patriarch Isaac. Her name, which means "well fed" or "choice," appears 31 times in Genesis (primarily in chs 24–27) and once in Romans 9:10.

Rebekah's father was Bethuel, who in turn was the son of Milcah and Nahor, Abraham's brother (Gn 22:20-23). Abraham was her great-uncle and eventually, of course, her father-in-law. Laban, the father of Leah and Rachel, was her brother. Thus her son Jacob married his two cousins, who were sisters.

Genesis 24 is the account of the successful search by Abraham's servant for a wife for Isaac. He went to Aram-naharaim (northwest Mesopotamia) in obedience to Abraham, who did not want his son to marry a local Canaanite. In answer to the servant's prayer, Rebekah not only gave a drink to the man but also watered his camels. After a certain amount of hospitality was extended and payment was made, Rebekah willingly went to meet her new husband.

Rebekah bore twins, Esau and Jacob (25:20-27). She preferred Jacob, the younger, over Esau and was a party to the deception of her husband in securing the right of the firstborn for Jacob. Disguising Jacob to feel, look, and smell like Esau the outdoorsman was her idea. She also prepared Isaac's favorite dish in order to facilitate the event (27:5-17).

Scripture records little more of her life but does report that she was buried next to her husband in the cave of Machpelah near Mamre (49:31).

See also Isaac.

RECAB

1. Rimmon's son who, with his brother Baanah, commanded bands of raiders under Saul's son Ishbosheth. Hoping to please David, they killed Ishbosheth. David, however, angered with this killing, had the two put to death (2 Sm 4:1-3, 5-12).

2. Father of Jehonadab (or Jonadab), the violent supporter of Jehu who killed Ahab's supporters in Samaria (2 Kgs 10:15-27). Jeremiah refers to the followers and descendants of Recab as Recabites. These were nomadic people who lived by Jonadab's command that his descendants not drink wine, live in houses, sow seed, or plant vineyards. Jeremiah applauded the Recabites' loyalty to their forebear, contrasting them with Judah and Jerusalem's unfaithfulness to God. Jeremiah predicted doom for Judah and Jerusalem but promised that Recabites would be preserved (Jer 35:1-19).

REELAIAH

Head of a family who returned to Jerusalem with Zerubbabel after the Exile (Ezr 2:2); alternately called Raamiah (Neh 7:7).

REGEM

Jahdai's son and a descendant of Caleb (1 Chr 2:47).

REGEMMELECH

One of the delegation sent to inquire whether fasting to commemorate the Temple destruction should continue (Zec 7:2). The name may refer to a person or could be a title meaning "friend of the king."

REHABIAH

Levite, son of Eliezer the priest and Moses' grandson (1 Chr 23:17; 24:21; 26:25).

REHOB

1. King of Zobah whose son, Hadadezer, was defeated by David at the Euphrates River (2 Sm 8:3, 12).

2. One of the Levites who set his seal on Ezra's covenant (Neh 10:11).

REHOBOAM

King (930–913 BC) especially remembered for his part in perpetuating the split of the Hebrew kingdom and for being the first king of the separate kingdom of Judah.

Split of the Kingdom

When Solomon died (930 BC), his son Rehoboam ascended to the throne. Perhaps as a concession to the Ephraimites, who often seemed to have been piqued at their inferior status, Rehoboam agreed to hold his coronation in their town of Shechem instead of in Jerusalem, a traditional place of meeting on which "all Israel" could agree (1 Kgs 12:1).

At the conclave, leaders of the northern tribes, accompanied by Jeroboam, approached the new king for concessions. Jeroboam—an official under Solomon's administration who had fled to Egypt when Solomon suspected him of treason—had returned to Israel to assume a position of leadership. Jeroboam was destined to be the ruler of Israel because of Solomon's apostasy (1 Kgs 11). Solomon's numerous building projects and his ostentation seem to have bankrupted the kingdom, resulting in an intolerable tax burden. Especially objectionable was forced labor on various projects (see 1 Kgs 12:4; 2 Chr 10:4). The populace sought relief from high taxes.

QUICKTAKE

REHOBOAM

STRENGTHS AND ACCOMPLISHMENTS
- Fourth and last king of the united nation of Israel, but only for a short time
- Fortified his kingdom and achieved a measure of popularity

WEAKNESSES AND MISTAKES
- Followed unwise advice and divided his kingdom
- Married foreign women, as his father, Solomon, had done
- Abandoned the worship of God and allowed idolatry to flourish

LESSONS FROM HIS LIFE
- Thoughtless decisions often lead to exchanging what is most valuable for something of far less value
- Every choice we make has real and long-lasting consequences

VITAL STATISTICS
Where: Jerusalem
Occupation: King of the united kingdom of Israel and later of the southern kingdom of Judah
Relatives: Father: Solomon. Mother: Naamah. Son: Abijah. Wife: Maacah
Contemporaries: Jeroboam, Shishak, Shemaiah

KEY VERSE
"But when Rehoboam was firmly established and strong, he abandoned the Law of the LORD, and all Israel followed him in this sin" (2 Chronicles 12:1).

Rehoboam's story is told in 1 Kings 11:43–14:31 and 2 Chronicles 9:31–13:7. He is also mentioned in Matthew 1:7.

The new king asked for a three-day grace period in which to study the request. Advisers from Solomon's administration counseled concessions; the younger men urged no moderation but an even greater tax burden. Following the advice of his peers, Rehoboam arrogantly threatened even higher taxes. The restless northern tribes broke away to establish a separate kingdom under the leadership of Jeroboam. Judah and Benjamin were the only tribes loyal to Rehoboam.

The separate existence of the northern kingdom was not a new development. After Saul's death, the north had gone its own way while David ruled in Hebron. Some 30 years later, it had briefly supported Sheba in a revolt against David. Now under the leadership of Jeroboam, the rupture was to become permanent.

Not accepting the apparent success of the secession, Rehoboam sent his tribute master or treasurer, Adoram (Adoniram), to try to heal the division. North Israelite partisans stoned him to death, and Rehoboam and his party fled to Jerusalem. Rehoboam immediately tried to subjugate the rebellious tribes. Raising a force of 180,000 men from Judah and Benjamin, he prepared to march north, but the prophet Shemaiah brought word from God to abandon the project since the breakup of the kingdom was part of the judgment of God on Israel for the sinfulness of the nation during Solomon's reign. Rehoboam promptly abandoned his military efforts, but intermittent military skirmishes plagued the relations of Rehoboam and Jeroboam throughout their reigns.

Reign of Rehoboam

In the face of constant threat of attack, Rehoboam set about to fortify his kingdom. He built extensive fortifications with adequate supplies of weapons and food at Bethlehem, Etam, Tekoa, Beth-zur, Soco, Adullam, Gath, Maresha, Ziph, Adoraim, Lachish, Azekah, Zorah, Aijalon, and Hebron.

Military preparedness was supplemented by spiritual underpinning. As a result of the establishment of a new apostate religion in the northern kingdom, priests and Levites streamed to the south, where they greatly strengthened the spiritual fiber of the realm. Apparently, they helped to maintain the stability of Judah for three years.

However, the people built high places and pagan

REHOBOAM
The Kings of Judah (South)

930–913 BC
Rehoboam (1 Kings 12:1-24; 14:21-31)

913–910 BC
Abijah (1 Kings 15:1-8)

910–869 BC
Asa (1 Kings 15:9-24)

872–848 BC
Jehoshaphat (1 Kings 22:41-50)

853–841 BC
Jehoram (2 Kings 8:16-24)

841 BC
Ahaziah (2 Kings 8:25-29)

841–835 BC
Athaliah (queen) (2 Kings 11)

835–796 BC
Joash (2 Kings 12)

796–768 BC
Amaziah (2 Kings 14:1-22)

792–740 BC
Azariah (Uzziah) (2 Kings 15:1-7)

750–735 BC
Jotham (2 Kings 15:32-38)

735–715 BC
Ahaz (2 Kings 16)

715–686 BC
Hezekiah (2 Kings 18:1-20:21)

697–642 BC
Manasseh (2 Kings 21:1-18)

642–640 BC
Amon (2 Kings 21:19-26)

640–609 BC
Josiah (2 Kings 22:1-23:30)

609 BC
Jehoahaz (2 Kings 23:31-33)

609–598 BC
Jehoiakim (2 Kings 23:34–24:7)

598 BC
Jehoiachin (2 Kings 24:8-17)

597–586 BC
Zedekiah (2 Kings 24:18–25:26)

sanctuaries throughout the land. They began to engage in the corrupt religious practices of the heathen nations around them, including homosexuality (1 Kgs 14:22-24).

Soon Rehoboam forsook the law of the Lord, and all Israel followed him (2 Chr 12:1). Rehoboam was the son of Solomon, a preoccupied father who himself grew increasingly lax about spiritual things. Rehoboam's mother was Naamah, a pagan Ammonite princess who presumably lacked any spiritual perception (1 Kgs 14:21). His father's example of keeping a harem and having numerous children likewise had an impact on him. Rehoboam had 18 wives, 60 concubines, 28 sons, and 60 daughters. He spent a considerable amount of time providing living arrangements for them in the fortified cities of Judah (2 Chr 11:21-23).

At length, the apostasy of Judah became so great that God brought judgment on the nation in the form of a foreign invasion. In the fifth year of Rehoboam (c. 926 BC), Shishak I (Sheshonk I) of Egypt invaded Palestine with 1,200 chariots and 60,000 men (1 Kgs 14:25; 2 Chr 12:2-3).

After Shishak's initial successes, the prophet Shemaiah made it clear to the king and the nobility that the invasion was direct punishment for their sinful ways. When they repented of their waywardness, God promised to moderate their punishment. They were subjected to either heavy tribute or a plundering of their cities. The national treasury and the Temple treasury were emptied to satisfy the demands of the Egyptians.

Shishak's invasion continued into the northern kingdom, for his inscription in the Temple of Karnak at Luxor tells of his conquest of 156 towns in the two kingdoms. Only a fraction of the names listed can be identified.

Rehoboam's repentance was only temporary. Scripture indicates that his latter years were characterized by evil (2 Chr 12:14), and that his son and successor, Abijam, "walked in all the sins which his father did before him" (1 Kgs 15:3). Probably the sins of his father would not have been condemned if Rehoboam's last 12 years had been a good example to his maturing son.

Rehoboam was 41 when he ascended the throne, and he reigned for 17 years.

REHUM

1. One of the 12 Jewish leaders who returned from captivity with Zerubbabel (Ezr 2:2; Neh 7:7, where "Nehum" is apparently a copyist's error).

2. Persian commander who, with Shimshai the scribe, wrote to Artaxerxes I, complaining of the Jews' Temple-rebuilding project and promising dire consequences should the project be completed. The king's response halted construction until the second year of Darius's reign (Ezr 4:8-23).

3. Levite identified as Bani's son, who helped repair the Jerusalem wall under Nehemiah's direction (Neh 3:17).

4. Leader who set his seal on Ezra's covenant (Neh 10:25).

5. Priest who accompanied Zerubbabel (Neh 12:3); elsewhere he was called Harim (see NLT mg). *See* Harim #5.

REI
Officer who supported Solomon when Adonijah attempted to become king near the end of David's reign (1 Kgs 1:8).

REKEM
1. Prince or king of Midian killed with his four accomplices in a battle waged by Moses at the Lord's command (Nm 31:8, Jos 13:21). Israelites living in the vicinity of Rekem's dominion had been seduced to the worship of Baal-peor.
2. Son of Hebron, a descendant of Caleb, and Shammai's father (1 Chr 2:43-44).

REMALIAH
Father of King Pekah of Israel (737–732 BC). Pekah, through treachery, claimed Israel's throne (2 Kgs 15:25-37) and later terrorized Jerusalem (Is 7:1-9).

REPHAEL
Shemaiah's son and a Temple gatekeeper in David's time (1 Chr 26:7-8).

REPHAH
Resheph's father from Ephraim's tribe (1 Chr 7:25).

REPHAIAH
1. Jeshaiah's son and a descendant of Solomon (1 Chr 3:21).
2. Ishi's son and a captain from Simeon's tribe who led 500 Israelites to destroy the Amalekites at Mt Seir (1 Chr 4:42-43).
3. Tola's son and a warrior from Issachar's tribe in the days of David (1 Chr 7:1-2).
4. Son of Binea and father of Eleasah, a descendant of Saul (1 Chr 9:43); also called Raphah in 1 Chronicles 8:37 (KJV "Rapha").
5. Hur's son, who worked on the Jerusalem wall during the days of Nehemiah (Neh 3:9).

RESHEPH
Rephah's son, a descendant of Ephraim and an ancestor of Joshua, son of Nun (1 Chr 7:25).

REU
Peleg's son, the father of Serug, and a descendant of Shem (Gn 11:18-21; 1 Chr 1:25), listed in Luke's genealogy of Christ (Lk 3:35).

REUBEN
Eldest son of Jacob and Leah (Gn 29:32; 46:8) and forefather of one of the 12 tribes of Israel. Reuben was involved in the mandrake incident (30:14) and had sexual relations with Bilhah, his father's concubine (35:22). But he emerges into full adulthood as one of the

QUICKTAKE

REUBEN

STRENGTHS AND ACCOMPLISHMENTS
• Saved Joseph's life by talking the other brothers out of murder
• Showed intense love for his father by offering his own sons as a guarantee that Benjamin's life would be safe

WEAKNESSES AND MISTAKES
• Gave in quickly to group pressure
• Did not directly protect Joseph from his brothers, although as oldest son he had the authority to do so
• Slept with one of his father's wives

LESSONS FROM HIS LIFE
• Public and private integrity must be the same, or one will destroy the other
• Punishment for sin may not be immediate, but it is certain

VITAL STATISTICS
Where: Canaan, Egypt
Occupation: Shepherd
Relatives: Parents: Jacob and Leah. Eleven brothers, one sister

KEY VERSES
"'Reuben, you are my firstborn, my strength, the child of my vigorous youth. You are first in rank and first in power. But you are as unruly as a flood, and you will be first no longer. For you went to bed with my wife; you defiled my marriage couch'" (Genesis 49:3, 4).

Reuben's story is told in Genesis 29–50.

more honorable of Jacob's sons. Reuben objected to the plot to kill Joseph and planned to rescue him from the pit (37:22-35). He moralized about the brothers' imprisonment in Egypt (42:22) and guaranteed the safety of Benjamin at immense risk to his own family. Yet at Jacob's pronouncement of blessing, Reuben is declared unstable and his birthright forfeited (49:3-4). He fathered four sons (1 Chr 5:3).

REUEL

1. Son of Esau by his wife Basemath, and the father of four sons: Nahath, Zerah, Shammah, and Mizzah (Gn 36:4, 10-17).

2. Priest of Midian who gave his daughter to Moses for a wife. He is perhaps the same person as #1 above, and identical to Jethro (Ex 2:18; cf. 3:1). He is also called Raguel in Numbers 10:29 (KJV). *See* Jethro.

3. Alternate spelling of Deuel, Eliasaph's father, in Numbers 2:14. *See* Deuel.

4. Ancestor of Meshullam in Benjamin's tribe (1 Chr 9:8).

REUMAH

Nahor's concubine (Gn 22:24). Her four sons became the ancestors of the Aramean tribes living north of Damascus.

REZIN

1. Syrian monarch who ruled in Damascus during the earlier part of Isaiah's prophetic ministry and during the last years that the northern 10 tribes existed as a nation. Rezin was used by God to humble both Israel and Judah because they had forsaken him and rejected his covenant (2 Chr 28:5-6).

    Rezin was born in the town of Bit-hadara near Damascus in the land of Syria (also called Aram). Upon his accession to the throne, the Syrian people (also called Arameans) reasserted their independence from Israel's domination. During this period, Assyria was strengthening itself and expanding its empire throughout the Near East. Along with King Menahem of Israel, Rezin was forced to pay tribute to the Assyrian monarch Tiglath-pileser III in 738 BC. The heavy burden of vassalage to the Assyrians generated anti-Assyrian sentiment among the Syrian and neighboring people. During this time, Rezin seems to have helped Pekah in his successful coup to seize the throne of Israel. Immediately upon his accession to the throne, Pekah formed an anti-Assyrian coalition with Rezin. They soon realized that successful resistance against Assyria required a larger alliance. They invited King Ahaz of Judah to join their coalition, but Ahaz adamantly refused. With the intention of placing an Aramean of Davidic lineage upon the throne of Judah in order to effect a broader Syrian-Israelite alliance, Rezin and Pekah joined in an attack on Judah. In spite of winning most battles, Rezin and Pekah were unsuccessful in their attempt to take Jerusalem and replace Ahaz (2 Chr 28:5-15; Is 7:1-9). During these dark days for Judah, Isaiah brought an encouraging word to the people. He prophesied the imminent destruction of Israel (Ephraim) and Damascus by Assyria (Is 7:1-9; 8:1-8). So certain was the destruction of these kingdoms that he referred to their two kings as "stubs of smoldering firebrands" about to be extinguished (7:4). Disregarding Isaiah's prophecy, Ahaz sent a large sum of money to Tiglath-pileser III, hoping to induce him to come to Judah's aid.

    Rezin and Pekah moved their forces to the north to prepare for the impending Assyrian invasion. Tiglath-pileser attacked in 733 BC and captured much of the area of Galilee. He then turned his attention to Damascus, to which Rezin had fled. Assyrian records refer to Rezin as a "caged bird" in besieged Damascus. When Damascus fell in 732 BC, Rezin was executed and many citizens of Damascus were exiled. Samaria, the capital city of Israel, fell to the Assyrians in 722 BC. Damascus and the nation of Syria became an Assyrian province. Rezin thus was the last Syrian king to reign in Damascus.

2. Father of some of the Temple servants who served in postexilic times (Ezr 2:48; Neh 7:50).

REZON

Son of Eliada, who set himself up as ruler of Damascus and Syria following David's killing of Hadadezer, king of Zobah. Rezon was a God-appointed adversary who despised Israel and was a constant problem to Solomon during his reign (1 Kgs 11:23-25).

RHESA

Descendant of Zerubbabel and an ancestor of Jesus Christ (Lk 3:27).

RHODA

Maid in the home of Mary the mother of John Mark in Jerusalem. Rhoda reported to those in the house that Peter was standing outside the door. Since they were unaware of his release from prison, the others at first did not believe her report (Acts 12:13-15).

RIBAI

Benjaminite of Gibeah and the father of Ittai, one of David's mighty men (2 Sm 23:29; 1 Chr 11:31).

RIMMON

1. Benjaminite of Beeroth, whose two sons, Baanah and Recab, assassinated Ishbosheth (2 Sm 4:2, 5, 9).

2. Deity revered by the Syrians of Damascus, whose temple was frequented by Naaman, captain of the Syrian army, and his master (2 Kgs 5:18). *See* Hadad-rimmon.

RINNAH

Shimon's son from Judah's tribe (1 Chr 4:20).

RIPHATH

Gomer's son and the brother of Ashkenaz and Togarmah, non-Semitic descendants of Noah through Japheth's line (Gn 10:3). First Chronicles 1:6, a parallel passage, reads Diphath instead of Riphath, undoubtedly a latter copyist's misspelling that was never corrected.

RIZIA

Capable leader and mighty warrior, Ulla's son from Asher's tribe (1 Chr 7:39).

RIZPAH

Daughter of Aiah and a concubine of Saul. She bore two sons, Armoni and Mephibosheth, to Saul. In a dispute between Ishbosheth and Abner, Ishbosheth accused Abner of having relations with Rizpah, suggesting an attempt to become a royal claimant to Saul's throne. Infuriated at this apparent false accusation, Abner vowed to assist David in defeating Saul and to make David king of Israel (2 Sm 3:7-10). During the reign of David, Rizpah's two sons, along with five other sons of Saul, were killed by the Gibeonites as reparation for Saul's unwarranted slaughter of the sons of Gibeon. Rizpah courageously protected her son's exposed bodies from natural predators until they were buried by David (2 Sm 21:8-11).

RODANIM

Fourth son of Javan and a descendant of Noah through Japheth's line (1 Chr 1:7). An alternate spelling in Genesis 10:4 reads Dodanim, possibly a copyist's error. Both words probably refer to the Greek peoples of Rhodes and its neighboring islands in the Aegean Sea.

ROHGAH

Shemer's son from Asher's tribe (1 Chr 7:34).

ROMAMTI-EZER

Heman's son and a musician appointed by King David to serve in the sanctuary (1 Chr 25:4, 31).

ROSH

Seventh of Benjamin's ten sons (Gn 46:21).

RUFUS

1. One of the sons of Simon of Cyrene (Mk 15:21).

2. Christian to whom Paul sent greetings, adding a special endearing comment about his mother (Rom 16:13). He is perhaps the same as #1 above.

RUHAMAH

One of two symbolic names showing God's altered perspective toward Israel from one of hostility to one of mercy. God's attitude of displeasure was symbolized by the name Lo-ruhamah (meaning "Not pitied"), which Hosea named his daughter. God had withdrawn his compassion from Israel because of their great sin (Hos 1:6, 8). His new attitude of mercy was portrayed by the name Ruhamah (meaning "She has obtained pity"), revealing God's revived spirit of compassion that was to be poured out on Israel (2:1, 23).

RUTH

Moabitess and the widow of Mahlon, the son of Naomi and Elimelech, who were Ephrathites from Bethlehem living in Moab because of a severe famine in Judah. After the death of

QUICKTAKE

RUTH

STRENGTHS AND ACCOMPLISHMENTS
- A willingness to forsake her home and family to follow God
- A strong relationship with her mother-in-law
- A place in the ancestry of Jesus

LESSON FROM HER LIFE
- God's living presence in a relationship overcomes differences that might otherwise create division and disharmony

VITAL STATISTICS
Where: Moab, Bethlehem
Occupation: Wife, widow, daughter-in-law, grain-gatherer
Relatives: Elimelech, Mahlon, Kilion, Orpah, Boaz

KEY VERSES
"But Ruth replied, 'Don't ask me to leave you and turn back. Wherever you go, I will go; wherever you live, I will live. Your people will be my people, and your God will be my God. Wherever you die, I will die, and there I will be buried. May the LORD punish me severely if I allow anything but death to separate us!'" (Ruth 1:16-17).

Her story is told in the book of Ruth. Ruth is also mentioned in Matthew 1:5.

Elimelech and Naomi's two sons, Naomi returned to Bethlehem with her daughter-in-law Ruth during the time of the barley harvest (Ru 1:4-22). While gleaning in the barley fields of Boaz, Ruth found favor in his eyes (2:2-22). She later married Boaz, when he, serving as nearest kin to the childless Naomi, purchased Naomi's estate to keep it within the family (4:5-13). Ruth is mentioned in Matthew's genealogy of Christ as the mother of Obed and the great-grandmother of David (Mt 1:5).

SABTAH

One of Cush's five sons and a descendant of Noah through Ham's line (Gn 10:7; 1 Chr 1:9). Sabtah presumably settled along the southern coast of Arabia, where several cities bear his name.

SABTECA

One of Cush's five sons and a descendant of Noah through Ham's line (Gn 10:7; 1 Chr 1:9). Sabteca settled in Arabia.

SACAR

1. Hararite and Ahiam's father. Sacar was one of David's mighty men (1 Chr 11:35). In a parallel account he is alternately called Sharar the Hararite (2 Sm 23:33).

2. Korahite and one of Obed-edom's eight sons. Sacar and his brothers were listed among the families of gatekeepers (1 Chr 26:4).

SAKIA

Son of Shaharaim and Hodesh from Benjamin's tribe (1 Chr 8:10).

SALLAI

1. One of 928 Benjaminites who lived in the city of Jerusalem during the postexilic period (Neh 11:8).

2. Levitical household in the postexilic period during the days of Joiakim, the high priest (Neh 12:20; NLT "Sallu"); perhaps the same as Sallu in Nehemiah 12:7. *See* Sallu #2.

SALLU

1. Son of Meshullam and a Benjaminite, who resided in the city of Jerusalem during the postexilic period (1 Chr 9:7; Neh 11:7).

2. Levitical priest who returned to Jerusalem with Zerubbabel following the Babylonian captivity (Neh 12:7). The Sallai mentioned in some translations of Nehemiah 12:20 is thought to be a variant spelling of Sallu.

SALMA

1. Hur's son of Caleb's family. He is considered the founding father of Bethlehem (1 Chr 2:51, 54).

2. An alternate spelling for "Salmon" in 1 Chronicles 2:11. *See* Salmon.

SALMON

Nahshon's son and an ancestor of David from Judah's tribe (1 Chr 2:11). Salmon fathered Boaz by Rahab (Ru 4:20-21) and is listed in Matthew's genealogy as a forefather of Jesus Christ (Mt 1:4-5); in the Greek his name is spelled Sala in Luke's genealogy (Lk 3:32).

SALOME

Name deriving from the Hebrew greeting *shalom* (peace), with the additional letter being a Greek suffix.

1. Woman who followed Jesus and was perhaps Mary's sister and the mother of James and John. In Mark 15:40, the evangelist describes the women who stood at the foot of the cross, and names three of them: Mary Magdalene, Mary the mother of James the lesser and of Joses, and Salome. Similarly, when describing the women who arrived at the tomb at dawn, Mark recounts that Mary Magdalene, Mary the mother of James, and Salome had brought spices to anoint the body (Mk 16:1). Matthew speaks of two women named Mary, and the mother of the sons of Zebedee, who could have been Salome (Mt 27:56). John speaks of four women: (1) Mary the mother of Jesus; (2) Mary the wife of Clopas; (3) Mary Magdalene; and (4) Mary's sister—unnamed (Jn 19:25). If Mary's sister was Salome, and she and the mother of the sons of Zebedee were one and the same, then James and John, the sons of Zebedee, were cousins of Jesus.

2. Daughter of Herodias, from her first marriage to Herod Philip. Although not specifically named in Matthew 14:6 or Mark 6:22, she is traditionally believed to be the girl whose dancing so pleased Herod that he promised her on oath anything she asked for up to half his kingdom. Prompted by her mother, she demanded the head of John the Baptist.

SALU

Zimri's father from Simeon's tribe. Zimri, head of his father's household, was killed by Phinehas (Nm 25:14).

SAMLAH

King of the Edomites from the town of Masrekah. Samlah came to power before any king ruled in Israel (Gn 36:36-37; 1 Chr 1:47-48).

SAMSON

Manoah's son, from Dan's tribe. His mother, whose name is not given in the Bible, had been barren. The angel of the Lord announced to her that she would have a son, who was to be a Nazirite all of his life (i.e., he was not to drink wine or strong drink, not to eat anything ceremonially unclean, and not to allow a razor to touch his head, Nm 6:1-6). She was also told that he would begin to deliver Israel from the Philistines, who had subjugated them for 40 years (Jgs 13:1-5). She reported this to her husband, Manoah, and Manoah prayed concerning this angelic visit (v 8). The angel of the Lord appeared again and gave instructions about the child who was to be born. Manoah made a burnt offering, and the angel of the Lord ascended to heaven in the smoke. Manoah feared that they would die, for he now realized that they had seen God (v 22). The child was born and the Lord blessed him as he grew. The Spirit of the Lord moved upon him in Mahaneh-dan (v 25).

Samson went to Timnah and saw a Philistine woman whom he wished to marry. The

Lord was seeking an opportunity against the Philistines, and in Samson's case these occasions came through Philistine women. When he and his parents went to Timnah to arrange the marriage, a lion came out of the vineyards, and Samson, upon whom the Spirit of the Lord came mightily, tore the lion in half. Later he found that a swarm of bees had made honey in the carcass of the lion (Jgs 14:2-9).

Samson made a feast at Timnah, as was the custom, and told the Philistine men a riddle that involved the lion and the honey. A wager was made on the riddle and the Philistines

QUICKTAKE

SAMSON

STRENGTHS AND ACCOMPLISHMENTS
- Dedicated to God from birth as a Nazirite
- Known for his feats of strength
- Listed in the Hall of Faith in Hebrews 11
- Began to free Israel from Philistine oppression

WEAKNESSES AND MISTAKES
- Violated his vow and God's laws on many occasions
- Was controlled by sensuality
- Confided in the wrong people
- Used his gifts and abilities unwisely

LESSONS FROM HIS LIFE
- Great strength in one area of life does not make up for great weaknesses in other areas
- God's presence does not overwhelm a person's will
- God can use a person of faith in spite of his or her mistakes

VITAL STATISTICS
Where: Zorah, Timnah, Ashkelon, Gaza, valley of Sorek
Occupation: Judge
Relative: Father: Manoah
Contemporaries: Delilah, Samuel (who might have been born while Samson was a judge)

KEY VERSE
"You will become pregnant and give birth to a son, and his hair must never be cut. For he will be dedicated to God as a Nazirite from birth. He will begin to rescue Israel from the Philistines" (Judges 13:5).

His story is told in Judges 13–16. He is also mentioned in Hebrews 11:32.

prevailed upon his wife to learn the answer and disclose it to them. When they came up with the answer, Samson knew what had happened, so he went out and killed 30 Philistine men to pay for his bet (Jgs 14:19). Samson went home, and his father-in-law gave Samson's wife to Samson's best man.

When Samson returned to see his wife, he was not allowed to visit her, so he took 300 foxes, tied them in pairs tail to tail, fixed a torch to each pair, and turned them loose in the grainfields of the Philistines, so that the shocks and standing grain were burned. Consequently, the Philistines came and burned his wife and her father. In revenge, Samson went out and slaughtered many of them (Jgs 15:1-8).

During these days, the Philistines came against Judah, and the people of Judah bound Samson with new ropes to turn him over to the Philistines. When they came to Lehi, where the Philistines were camped, the Spirit of the Lord came on him mightily. He snapped the ropes, seized the jawbone of a donkey, and killed 1,000 Philistines. Being very thirsty, he cried to the Lord, so God opened a spring of water at Lehi (Jgs 15:9-20).

Samson's weakness for Philistine women continued to create trouble for both him and the Philistines. He went down to Gaza, where he became involved with a prostitute (Jgs 16:1). The men of the city learned that he was there and plotted to kill him at dawn, but he arose at midnight and walked off with the doors, posts, and bar of the city gate and put them on top of the hill before Hebron.

Then he found Delilah, from the valley of Sorek. The Philistines enlisted her by bribery to find out the source of his strength (Jgs 16:4-5). She kept pestering him, so he told her that if they bound him with seven fresh bowstrings he would be as weak as other men. So she bound him and cried, "The Philistines are upon you." He easily broke the bowstrings. In response to her continued questions, he kept lying to her about the secret of his strength. In succession, she bound him with new ropes and seven locks of his hair woven together and attached to a loom. Finally, she wore him down and he told her the truth. If someone shaved his head and broke his Nazirite vow, his strength would be gone. While Samson slept with his head on her knees, she called a barber, who shaved off his hair. This time when she cried, "The Philistines are upon you," the Philistines seized him, gouged out his eyes, and took him to Gaza (v 21).

At Gaza, Samson was bound with bronze fetters and forced to grind at a mill, during which time his hair began to grow again. At a time when the Philistines were having a great festival at the Temple of their god, Dagon, they celebrated their victory over Samson and asked that he be brought so they could mock him. Some 3,000 people watched while Samson entertained them. At his request, Samson was placed between the two pillars supporting the Temple. He asked the Lord for strength and pushed against the pillars, so that the entire building collapsed. Samson died with the Philistines as he had requested, but he killed more Philistines in this final act than he had previously (Jgs 16:1-30).

Samson's family came to retrieve his body, and they buried him between Zorah and Eshtaol in the tomb of his father, Manoah. He had served as "judge," or leader, of Israel for 20 years (Jgs 16:31).

SAMUEL

Last of the judges, his name means "name of God" or "his name is El" (El is the name of the God of strength and power). The play on words in 1 Samuel 1:20 (cf. Ex 2:10) is not intended to be an explanation of the meaning of Samuel's name; Hannah's words recall only her prayer and the circumstances surrounding her son's birth.

Personal History

Samuel's parents were a devout couple who went annually to the sanctuary at Shiloh (1 Sm 1:3). His father, Elkanah, was a Levite (1 Chr 6:26) and a resident in Ramah, territory

QUICKTAKE

SAMUEL

STRENGTHS AND ACCOMPLISHMENTS
- Used by God to assist Israel's transition from a loosely governed tribal people to a monarchy
- Anointed the first two kings of Israel
- Was the last and most effective of Israel's judges
- Is listed in the Hall of Faith in Hebrews 11

WEAKNESS AND MISTAKE
- Was unable to lead his sons into a close relationship with God

LESSONS FROM HIS LIFE
- The significance of what people accomplish is directly related to their relationship with God
- The kind of person we are is more important than anything we might do

VITAL STATISTICS
Where: Ephraim
Occupations: Judge, prophet, priest
Relatives: Mother: Hannah. Father: Elkanah. Sons: Joel and Abijah
Contemporaries: Eli, Saul, David

KEY VERSES
"As Samuel grew up, the LORD was with him, and everything Samuel said was proved to be reliable. And all Israel, from Dan in the north to Beersheba in the south, knew that Samuel was confirmed as a prophet of the LORD" (1 Samuel 3:19, 20).

His story is told in 1 Samuel 1–28. He is also mentioned in Psalm 99:6; Jeremiah 15:1; Acts 3:24; 13:20; Hebrews 11:32.

of Ephraim. His mother, Hannah, was unable to bear children early in their marriage. Elkanah had a second wife, Peninnah.

On a visit to Shiloh, Hannah prayed in the sanctuary (1 Sm 1:6-11), vowing that, if the Lord would give her a son, she would dedicate him as a Nazirite (Nm 6:1-21) to God's service for life. The Lord heard Hannah's prayer and granted her request. She had no other children until after Samuel's dedication.

When Samuel was presented to Eli and began his service in the sanctuary, he bowed before the Lord and "worshiped the Lord there" (1 Sm 1:28). Three ingredients—a feeling of worth, a knowledge of his parents' love (cf. 2:19), and a sense of purpose—laid the foundation of his personality and his future accomplishments.

Further proof of Samuel's valuable early training is evidenced in 1 Samuel 2. Eli's sons had followed the licentious practices of the pagan religions about them. Eli was old, indulgent, and powerless to restrain them. Samuel neither developed irreverence for Eli nor followed his sons in the path of evil. God determined to judge Eli and his house for their sins. When God announced his purpose to Samuel, Samuel responded with reverence and respect. His personal and spiritual growth indicated that he had been marked out as a future prophet of the Lord.

When everyone did what was right in his or her own eyes (cf. Jgs 17:6; 21:25), God allowed an adjacent nation to serve as his instrument to chasten his people, until a judge arose to deliver them. When the Philistines again invaded the land (1 Sm 4–6), the Israelites mustered their army at Ebenezer, only to be defeated. Believing that the Ark of the Covenant would guarantee success, they sent to Shiloh for it. The next day the Israelites were again defeated and the Ark captured. When this news reached Eli, he fell from his stool and died.

Twenty years elapsed before Samuel's name is mentioned again (1 Sm 7:2-3). Evidently, following the destruction of Shiloh (cf. Jer 7:12-14; 26:6, 9; Ps 78:60), he lived in Ramah and went on annual preaching missions that included Bethel, Gilgal, and Mizpah, "judging" the people in these places (cf. Dt 16:18-22; 17:8-13). Samuel probably also founded "schools of the prophets" during this period. Schools were

SAMUEL
The Times of Samuel

1105 BC
Samuel is born
(1 Samuel 1:20).

1102? BC
Samuel's parents leave
him with Eli the priest
(1 Samuel 1–2).

1093? BC
Samuel is called by God
in the middle of the night
(1 Samuel 3).

1055? BC
Samuel begins ruling Israel
as priest and judge
(1 Samuel 3:21–4:1).

1050 BC
Samuel anoints Saul as
Israel's first king
(1 Samuel 10:1).

1050–1015? BC
Samuel has ongoing
conflicts with King Saul
(1 Samuel 13–15).

1025 BC
Samuel anoints David as
Israel's second king, but Saul
still rules (1 Samuel 16).

1015? BC
Samuel dies (1 Samuel 25:1).

established at Bethel (1 Sm 10:5; 2 Kgs 2:3), Gilgal (2 Kgs 4:38), Ramah (1 Sm 19:20), and elsewhere (2 Kgs 2:5), perhaps as a natural outgrowth of Samuel's ministry.

After a 20-year ministry, Samuel thought it timely to move toward spiritual and national unification. He convened a meeting at Mizpah (1 Sm 7). There, with a symbolic rite expressive of deep humiliation and in keeping with the libations of a treaty, the Israelites poured out water on the ground, fasted, and prayed.

The Philistines mistook the nature of the convocation and decided to attack the defenseless worshipers, who entreated Samuel to pray for them. He offered a sacrifice and the Lord sent a violent thunderstorm, causing the invaders to flee in panic. The pursuing Israelites won a significant victory at Ebenezer (1 Sm 7:12).

In Samuel's declining years, the elders rejected his leadership in favor of a king (1 Sm 8). Following earnest prayer, he received new direction from the Lord, acceded to their request, and later anointed Saul prince over God's people. Samuel then summoned the Israelites to Mizpah, where God's choice was made official, and Saul was hailed as king. Following Saul's victory over Nahash (ch 11), Samuel at Gilgal confirmed Saul's kingship. Thereafter, Samuel retired to Ramah to train men to carry on his ministry.

Samuel twice had to reprove Saul, first for impatience and disobedience (1 Sm 13:5-14), and then for disobeying the express command of the Lord (15:20-23), who rejected him as king. Samuel was then sent to the home of Jesse in Bethlehem, where he anointed David as the chosen one of the Lord (16:1-13).

In 1 Samuel 25:1 is a brief account of Samuel's passing, when all Israel gathered together and mourned for him. He was buried in Ramah. The only subsequent mention of Samuel is in 1 Samuel 28. Summoned by the witch of Endor at Saul's request, Samuel announced that on the following day Saul and his sons would die in battle (vv 4-19).

Character

Samuel overcame many problems through piety, perseverance, and dedication to the service of the Lord. His overriding concern was for the good of his people. Wise and courageous, he boldly rebuked king, elders, and people when necessary, always from the sure ground of the revealed will of God.

While Samuel served as judge and priest, he was preeminently a prophet. Through his ministry the spiritual life of the Israelites improved. In inaugurating the monarchy, he led the people from tribal disunity to national solidarity. He appointed gatekeepers to the tent of meeting (1 Chr 9:17-26), organized observance of the Passover so memorably that it was still spoken about in Josiah's day (2 Chr 35:18), put into writing how a king and his kingdom should be (1 Sm 10:25), and penned "The Chronicles of Samuel the Seer" (1 Chr 29:29).

Samuel well deserves a place among the great men of faith (Heb 11:32). He was the last of the judges (1 Sm 7:6, 15-17) and the first of the prophets (1 Sm 3:20; Acts 3:24; 13:20).

SANBALLAT

Leading political official of Samaria residing at Beth-horon in Ephraim. In a letter from Elephantine of Egypt, Sanballat was named as the governor of Samaria in 407 BC. Sanballat, along with Tobiah the Ammonite and Geshem the Arab, were adversaries of Nehemiah. They tried to prevent him from rebuilding the walls of Jerusalem during the postexilic period (Neh 2:10, 19; 4:1, 7; 6:1-14; 13:28). The Judean province probably had been included under Samaritan rule since its defeat by Babylon under Nebuchadnezzar in 586 BC. Nehemiah's determination to rebuild the walls of Jerusalem was in essence an assertion of Judean independence from Sanballat and Samaritan control.

SAPH
Descendant of the giants, killed by Sibbecai the Hushathite (one of David's warriors) at Gad in a battle between Israel and Philistia (2 Sm 21:18); alternately called Sippai (1 Chr 20:4).

SAPPHIRA
Member of the Jerusalem church and wife of Ananias (Acts 5:1). *See* Ananias #1.

SARAH
1. Wife of Abraham whose name was originally Sarai (Gn 11:29). Her name was changed to Sarah ("princess") when she was promised that she would bear a son and become the mother of nations and kings (17:15-16). Sarah was both the wife and the half sister of Abraham (20:12).

   Sarah accompanied Abraham in his journey from Ur of the Chaldees to Haran and eventually into the land of Canaan (Gn 11:31; 12:5). She remained barren for much of her marriage. When God promised Abraham that he would make of him a great nation (12:2) and that the land of Canaan would be given to his seed (v 7), Sarah was still barren.

   After 10 years had passed (cf. Gn 12:4; 16:16) and Sarah continued without children, she gave her Egyptian slave, Hagar, to Abraham as a concubine. Hagar conceived and bore a son, Ishmael (16:3-4). God promised that a nation would come from Ishmael (17:20) but indicated that he was not to be the child of the promise. Sarah herself was to be the mother of this child, even though she laughed when the birth was predicted. The fulfillment of this prediction took place with the birth of Isaac (21:2-3), when Sarah was 90 years old, 25 years after the original promise of a son to Abraham (17:17; 21:5).

   When famine forced Abraham and Sarah to journey down into Egypt shortly after their entrance into Canaan, Sarah was represented to the Egyptians as Abraham's sister. This resulted in Sarah's being taken into the harem of Pharaoh because of her great beauty (Gn 12:11-15), and Abraham's being well treated and rewarded by the Egyptians instead of being killed. God intervened to protect the marriage of Abraham and Sarah by plaguing the house of Pharaoh to force Sarah's release. A similar tactic was followed by Abraham and Sarah on another occasion in Gerar (ch 20), where she was taken into the household of Abimelech the king of Gerar. Again God protected Sarah, preserved her as the mother of the promised seed, and prevented any suspicion or doubt concerning who was the father of Isaac. Significantly, Isaac was born not long

QUICKTAKE

SARAH

STRENGTHS AND ACCOMPLISHMENTS
• Was intensely loyal to her own child
• Became the mother of a nation and an ancestor of Jesus
• Was a woman of faith, the first woman listed in the Hall of Faith in Hebrews 11

WEAKNESSES AND MISTAKES
• Had trouble believing God's promises to her
• Attempted to work problems out on her own, without consulting God
• Tried to cover her faults by blaming others

LESSONS FROM HER LIFE
• God responds to faith even in the midst of failure
• God is not bound by what usually happens; he can stretch the limits and cause unheard-
  of events to occur

VITAL STATISTICS
Where: Married Abram in Ur of the Chaldeans, then moved with him to Canaan
Occupation: Wife, mother, household manager
Relatives: Father: Terah. Husband: Abraham. Half brothers: Nahor and Haran. Nephew:
  Lot. Son: Isaac

KEY VERSE
"It was by faith that even Sarah was able to have a child, though she was barren and was
too old. She believed that God would keep his promise" (Hebrews 11:11).

Sarah's story is told in Genesis 11–25. She is also mentioned in Isaiah 51:2; Romans 4:19; 9:9;
Hebrews 11:11; 1 Peter 3:6.

after this incident (21:1-5), his birth having been promised about a year earlier (17:21;
18:10-14). Sarah died at the age of 127 and was buried in the cave at Machpelah, which
Abraham had purchased from Ephron the Hittite (ch 23).

Apart from the book of Genesis, Sarah is referred to in the OT only in Isaiah 51:2.
Reference is made to her in the NT in Romans 4:19, 9:9, Hebrews 11:11, 1 Peter 3:6, and
Galatians 4:21-31, although in the Galatians text she is not mentioned by name.
See also Abraham.

2. KJV spelling of Serah, Asher's daughter, in Numbers 26:46. *See* Serah.

SARAI

Original name of Sarah, Abraham's wife (Gn 11:29). *See* Sarah.

SARAPH

Shelah's son from Judah's tribe. Saraph ruled in Moab and later returned to Lehem. "Lehem" may refer either to his own countrymen or to a geographical location. The reading of the Hebrew text is unclear (1 Chr 4:22).

SARGON

Assyrian monarch from 722–705 BC, whose military campaigns are historically well documented. Excavations have revealed his palace at what was probably Nineveh as well as an incomplete palace at Khorsabad. Sargon II bore the name of an illustrious conqueror who lived and fought some 1,500 years earlier (Sargon I of Agade). His true identity has not been easily discerned. Previous generations, thinking that his name was an "alias," incorrectly identified him as Shalmaneser V (727–722 BC), Sennacherib (705–681 BC), or Esarhaddon (699–681 BC).

The only place in the Bible where Sargon is specifically mentioned is Isaiah 20:1. Despite warnings of the prophet Isaiah against placing any trust in Egypt (Is 10:9), Judah was moving contrary to her best interests by considering just such an alliance. But in 713 BC the Philistine city of Ashdod rebelled against Assyria, thereby instigating a campaign by the forces of Sargon against this strategically important metropolis. A man named Yamani sought to secure support from Egypt, Ethiopia, and even Judah in mounting an effective coalition against the might of Sargon. However, in 711 BC Ashdod was subjugated by Sargon's army under his delegated official, "the Tartan" (Is 20:1, KJV).

Sargon finished the task of conquering Samaria, begun by his predecessor, Shalmaneser V. Apparently, Shalmaneser V had besieged the northern kingdom of Israel for three years (2 Kgs 17:5-6) and had virtually completed that campaign when he died. While other military victories earmark the public life of Sargon, many of his battles were indecisive. A large part of his reign was spent suppressing rebellions and handling major domestic problems. He was finally killed on the battlefield in a remote area known as Tabal. Sargon's son, Sennacherib, succeeded him in 705 BC.

SAUL

Name meaning "asked," with the implication being "asked *of God*." A name with a usage extending far back into prebiblical times, it is attested in third-millennium texts from Tell Mardikh in Syria (ancient Ebla) and appears also to have been used in the second millennium in the city of Ugarit on the coast of Syria.

In addition to the conventional spelling, it is sometimes spelled Shaul in older English versions. Apart from King Saul, the most famous bearer of the name, one other person called Saul (Shaul) is referred to in the OT, though little is known about him (*see* Shaul).

1. Saul, king of Edom, is mentioned in an ancient list of kings who ruled Edom (in

Transjordan) in pre-Israelite times (Gn 36:37-38; 1 Chr 1:48-49). He is described as coming from "Rehoboth on the river," the "river" perhaps referring to a small river in the vicinity of Edom.

2. Saul, the first king of Israel, is the best known and documented person with his name in the OT. He was a member of the tribe of Benjamin, one of the smallest of the Israelite tribes, whose territory was located just north of the Canaanite city of Jerusalem. His father was Kish, son of Abiel. Saul was born in Gibeah, a small town just a few miles north of Jerusalem in the hill country, and apart from his travels and military expeditions, Gibeah was Saul's hometown for his entire life. He was a married man with one wife, Ahinoam, and five children—three sons and two daughters (1 Sm 14:49-50). His best-known son, Jonathan, later served him in a senior military capacity; three of Saul's sons died with him in battle (31:2). Of his two daughters, the best-known is Michal, the younger daughter, who married David.

Saul the Soldier Saul lived during a critical period in the history of the Israelite tribes. Though the dates cannot be determined with any certainty, he lived during the latter half of the 11th century BC and probably ruled as king from about 1020 to 1000 BC. Before he became king, the Israelite tribes were on the verge of military collapse. The Philistines, a powerful military people, had settled along the Mediterranean coast; they were well established on the coast and planned to move eastward and take control of Palestine as a whole. In order to do this, they first had to eliminate the Israelites, who were settled in the hill country on the west of the Jordan and also in Transjordan. The absence of any strong and permanent military authority among the Israelites meant that the Philistines were a grave military threat to the continued existence of Israel.

The immediate crisis, which was to contribute to Saul's rise to power, was a crushing defeat of the Israelite army by the Philistines at Ebenezer, in the vicinity of Aphek (1 Sm 4:1ff.). The victory gave the Philistines more or less complete control of Israelite territories lying to the west of the Jordan; they attempted to maintain that control by establishing military garrisons throughout the country they had captured. Israel, weakened by the Philistine defeat, became vulnerable to enemies on other borders. The nation of Ammon, situated to the east of the Israelites' land in Transjordan, attacked and laid siege to the town of Jabesh (11:1). Saul, summoning an army of volunteers, delivered the inhabitants of Jabesh and defeated the Ammonites (v 11). It was after this event that Saul became king. He had already been anointed a prince or leader among the people by Samuel; after his military success at Jabesh, he assumed the office formally at the sanctuary in Gilgal (v 15).

The defeat of the Ammonites provided a significant boost to Israelite morale, but it did not change the military crisis and threat posed by the Philistines. Indeed, the location of Saul's appointment to kingship is significant. Gilgal, in the Jordan Valley near Jericho, was chosen partly because the earlier shrine of Shiloh was held by the

QUICKTAKE

SAUL

STRENGTHS AND ACCOMPLISHMENTS
- First God-appointed king of Israel
- Known for his personal courage and generosity
- Stood tall, with a striking appearance

WEAKNESSES AND MISTAKES
- His leadership abilities did not match the expectations created by his appearance
- Impulsive by nature, he tended to overstep his bounds
- Jealous of David, he tried to kill him
- He specifically disobeyed God on several occasions

LESSONS FROM HIS LIFE
- God wants obedience from the heart, not mere acts of religious ritual
- Obedience always involves sacrifice, but sacrifice is not always obedience
- God wants to make use of our strengths and weaknesses
- Weaknesses should help us remember our need for God's guidance and help

VITAL STATISTICS
Where: The land of Benjamin
Occupation: King of Israel
Relatives: Father: Kish. Sons: Jonathan and Ishbosheth. Wife: Ahinoam. Daughters: Merab and Michal

KEY VERSES
"But Samuel replied, 'What is more pleasing to the LORD: your burnt offerings and sacrifices or your obedience to his voice? Listen! Obedience is better than sacrifice, and submission is better than offering the fat of rams. Rebellion is as sinful as witchcraft, and stubbornness as bad as worshiping idols. So because you have rejected the command of the LORD, he has rejected you as king'" (1 Samuel 15:22, 23).

His story is told in 1 Samuel 9–31. He is also mentioned in Acts 13:21

Philistines. Gilgal was in one of the few areas remaining outside Philistine control. Hence, if Saul's kingship was to mean anything, he had to address the Philistine problem immediately; if he did not, there would be no Israel to rule.

Saul acted promptly. Although the precise historical details are difficult to reconstruct, a general view of Saul's anti-Philistine campaign is provided in the biblical text.

He attacked garrisons at Gibeah and, later, at Micmash, about four miles (6.4 kilometers) northeast of Gibeah (1 Sm 13:16ff.). He had great success at Micmash, thanks in part to the military aid of his son Jonathan. The Philistines were routed and retreated from that portion of the hill country (14:15-23). Saul established his military base in his hometown, Gibeah, and built a citadel there.

In the years that followed this initial campaign against the Philistines, Saul was constantly engaged in other military activities. He continued to fight with enemies on his eastern borders, particularly Ammon and Moab, to the east of the Dead Sea (1 Sm 14:47). He engaged in a major campaign on the southern border with the old enemies of the Israelites, the Amalekites (15:7); in this, too, he was successful. And throughout all this, he had to keep constant watch on Philistine activity on his western border.

Saul was faced with an extraordinarily difficult task as military commander. His home ground had the advantage of being reasonably easy to protect, for most of it was mountainous countryside. But he was surrounded on all four sides by enemies who wanted his land, he had inadequate weapons (Philistines controlled the supply of iron), he had no large standing army, he had inadequate communication systems, and he did not have the wholehearted support of all the Israelites. For several years he was relatively successful against almost impossible odds, but eventually his military genius failed.

The Philistines assembled a large army in the vicinity of Aphek (1 Sm 29:1), but instead of attacking Saul's mountain territory directly, the army moved northward and then began to penetrate Israelite territory at a weak point in the vicinity of Jezreel (v 11). Saul attempted to gather an adequate military force to meet the Philistine threat, but he was unable to do so. With inadequate preparation and insufficient forces, he prepared for battle at Mt Gilboa (31:1); he should never have entered that battle, for it could not have been won. His sons were killed on the battlefield, and Saul, rather than fall into the hands of the Philistines, committed suicide (vv 2-6).

From a military perspective, Saul had become king at a time of crisis; he had averted disaster and gained some respite for his country. But the battle in which he died was a disaster for Israel; the country he left behind after his death was in worse straits than it had been on his assumption of power.

Saul the King If Saul had a difficult task as Israel's military commander, he had an even more difficult task as Israel's king. Before Saul's time, there had been no king in Israel. The absence of any form of monarchy in Israel was largely a religious matter. God was the one and only true King of Israel; he was the one who reigned (Ex 15:18). Consequently, although there had been single, powerful rulers in Israel's earlier history (Moses, Joshua, and certain judges), nobody had assumed the title or office of king, for it was thought that that would undermine the central position of God as King. However, provision had been made for the rise of kingship in the law (Dt 19:14-20).

It was sheer necessity that brought a monarchy to Israel, a necessity created by the constant military threat of the Philistines. A brief external threat could have been met by a temporary ruler, a judge. But a permanent and serious threat to Israel's existence could not be thwarted by such temporary measures. If Israel was to survive as a nation (and it very nearly did not), it needed a central military government with recognized authority over the various tribes that constituted the nation of Israel. Thus the kingdom was established and Saul became the first king, facing incredible difficulties.

Since there had never been a kingdom before in Israel, there were no precedents. What were his responsibilities? Primarily, they were military, for that was why the monarchy had been established. In this area, Saul was successful in the early years of his reign. But apart from his military responsibilities, King Saul faced an enormously difficult task. Given the nature of Hebrew theology, it was inevitable that many Israelites were opposed to the idea of kingship from the beginning. Indeed, Samuel, who was instrumental in the initial anointing of Saul and then in the formal coronation, appears to have been ambiguous in his attitudes toward the kingship (1 Sm 8:6), and later toward Saul himself (15:23). Furthermore, nobody had specified precisely what it was that the leader could do. He was a soldier—that much was clear. But did he also have religious responsibilities? Though the judgment of history upon Saul is often harsh, it is wise to recall the difficulty of the task he undertook. The military problems alone would have been more than sufficient for most great men; Saul also had to fashion the new role as king. In practical matters, Saul's leadership was modest and praiseworthy. He sought none of the pomp and splendor of many Eastern kings. He had a small court, located in his military stronghold of Gibeah; there is little evidence that it was characterized by great wealth. For practical purposes, he had no standing army; he had only a few men close to him, in particular his son Jonathan and his general Abner. He also sought out young men of promise, like David. Saul's court was rustic and feudal in comparison to the later splendor of David and Solomon. But Saul, as national leader, ran into difficulties with Samuel, who had appointed him and had influenced Israel prior to his kingship. While the responsibility for the trouble may lie primarily with Saul, Samuel himself does not appear to have been particularly supportive and helpful. On one occasion, Saul was roundly criticized and condemned by Samuel for assuming the priestly role of offering sacrifices in the absence of Samuel at Gilgal (1 Sm 13:8-15). The judgment was no doubt deserved, though one can perceive Saul's dilemma. Did the king have a priestly role or not? This issue had not been made clear. Furthermore, Saul was at the time in a state of crisis; he had waited seven days for Samuel to turn up, and as each day passed, his army was reduced by deserters. So Saul acted. Perhaps he may not be excused, but his actions may easily be understood, and the incident itself is indicative of the difficulty of being a nation's first king. Again, after the Amalekite war, Saul was subject to divine condemnation through Samuel.

Saul was Israel's first king but not its greatest. Yet no criticism of Saul's leadership should be so harsh as to ignore his strengths. He faced extraordinary difficulties and for a while was successful. Few other men could have done what he did. Ultimately, he died in failure, yet his achievements might have been better remembered if he had been succeeded by any other leader than David. David's gifts and competence were so magnificent and unusual that Saul's modest achievements paled and only his failures are remembered.

Saul the Man The writers of the OT have presented the story of Saul in a fascinating manner. While some OT characters remain shadowy figures, Saul stands out, with all his strengths and weaknesses, as a fully human figure. He was, in many ways, a great man, but there were also flaws in his personality that emerged more and more in the later years of his life. Born of a wealthy father, Saul is described as being tall and handsome (1 Sm 9:1-2). He was a man of immense courage, and part of his military success was rooted in his fearlessness. In his early years as king, Saul is portrayed as a man whose basic instincts were generous; he was kind and loyal to his friends and did not easily carry a grudge or hatred toward those who opposed him (11:12-13). But the real strength of Saul, in his early days, was in his relationship to God. For all his natural gifts and abilities, Saul became king as a result of divine appointment (10:1) and because the "Spirit of the Lord" came upon him (v 6).

In his later life, a change came over Saul that transformed him into a tragic, pitiable person. The many incidents in Saul's relationship to the young David provide insight into the transformation. Once a friend, then perceived as an enemy, David became the object of Saul's unfounded suspicions and irrational jealousy. Saul's periods of sanity became punctuated by periods of depression and paranoia. The paranoia affected his rational thought. Instead of warring against the invading Philistines, his energy was diverted toward the pursuit of David. The biblical writers describe this change as "the departure of the Spirit of God from Saul" and "an evil spirit from the LORD tormenting him" (1 Sm 16:14). Many modern writers have interpreted this as the onset of a form of mental illness, perhaps manic-depression, the alternation between active and lucid periods, followed by intense depression and paranoia. But there is a certain danger in psychoanalyzing the figures of ancient history, principally because the literary sources are rarely adequate to the task. The biblical writers indicated a theological basis for the change in Saul: the Spirit of God had departed from him. From a simple human perspective, the man was not equal to the enormity of the task before him. Overcome by its complexity, and lagging in the faith of the one who appointed him to such awesome responsibility, Saul ended his days in tragedy.

See also David.

3. Saul, mentioned in the NT, whose name was changed to Paul (Acts 13:9). *See* Paul, The Apostle.

SCEVA

Father of seven sons and a Jewish chief priest in Ephesus at the time of Paul's visit on his third missionary journey. Sceva's sons attempted to imitate Paul's exorcism of evil spirits in the name of Jesus. The exorcisms failed, and their authority was not recognized. Consequently, they were attacked and harmed by the evil spirits they tried to rebuke (Acts 19:14).

SECUNDUS

A Thessalonian believer; traveling companion of Aristarchus. Secundus accompanied Paul on his third missionary journey through Macedonia and Greece and awaited him at Troas in Asia Minor (Acts 20:4). It is not known whether Secundus remained at Troas or went with Paul on his final trip to Jerusalem.

SEGUB

1. Youngest son of Hiel the Bethelite. Hiel rebuilt Jericho during the reign of King Ahab of Israel. His violation of Joshua's curse against anyone rebuilding the city (Jos 6:26) cost him his oldest and youngest sons. Segub was killed as a result of the rebuilding of the city gates (1 Kgs 16:34).

2. Son borne to Hezron by the daughter of Makir, the father of Gilead. Segub was the father of Jair (1 Chr 2:21-22).

SEIR

Father of seven sons and a descendant of Abraham through Esau's line. Originally a Horite tribe dwelling in the land of Edom, the nation descended from Seir was first dispossessed by, but later intermarried with, Esau's descendants. Perhaps for this reason Seir and his offspring were included in the genealogies of Abraham (Gn 36:20-21; 1 Chr 1:38).

SELED

Nadab's son from Judah's tribe (1 Chr 2:30).

SEMAKIAH

Korahite Levite, Shemaiah's son and a gatekeeper in the Temple (1 Chr 26:7).

SEMEIN

Descendant of Josech and an ancestor of Jesus Christ (Lk 3:26).

SENAAH

Father of a family of Israelites who returned with Zerubbabel to Palestine following the Exile (Ezr 2:35; Neh 7:38). They helped Nehemiah rebuild part of the Jerusalem wall (Neh 3:3; Hassenaah is an alternate spelling for Senaah). Hassenuah is a possible variant for Senaah (1 Chr 9:7; Neh 11:9, where KJV reads "Senuah").

See also Hassenuah.

SENNACHERIB

King of the Assyrian Empire from 705 to 681 BC. His name, meaning "son has replaced brothers," may refer to a specific family situation by means of which he, a younger son of Sargon II, came to succeed his father. Before the death of his father, Sennacherib acted as military governor of the northern provinces of the Assyrian Empire. He was successful in quelling unrest in those areas. When Sargon II was assassinated in 705 BC, Sennacherib lost no time in claiming the throne.

As king of Assyria, he was a bold administrator. He was soon known to be a just and tolerant man, for thus the biblical account speaks of him. Extrabiblical sources indicate that, while he was conducting military campaigns, he also developed a strong rule at home and, employing slave labor acquired through his military victories, he did much building in Nineveh, his capital city. Many of the decorations of his palace, as well as inscriptions he prepared, are housed in museums today.

Shortly after Sennacherib became king, he was confronted by rebellion in the eastern and western provinces. It is at this point that the biblical record refers to Sennacherib. Judah was a vassal state of Assyria. It is likely that Merodach-baladan in Babylon and Hezekiah, king of Judah, joined in this insurrection (2 Kgs 18:7-8).

Sennacherib was ready for the challenge from Babylon and Palestine. In 703 BC he first led his forces to Kish near Babylon, where he defeated Merodach-baladan's army and then captured the city of Babylon itself. Turning west in 701 BC, Sennacherib led his armies against the Palestinian alliance headed by Hezekiah. He captured the cities of Tyre and Sidon and then continued his campaign southward. Several of the Philistine cities submitted before the Assyrian onslaught, but Ashkelon, Beth-dagon, and Joppa resisted and were captured and plundered. The leaders of the city of Ekron were put to death by being skinned alive because they had delivered up their pro-Assyrian king to Hezekiah. Sennacherib then turned to Judah. He besieged the Judean city of Lachish and captured 46 other towns, taking 200,150 Jewish captives. Hezekiah began to realize his desperate situation as Sennacherib's military victories came one after the other, so he sent tribute to Sennacherib at Lachish. The tribute amounted to 300 talents of silver and 30 talents of gold (2 Kgs 18:13-16). From his camp at Lachish, Sennacherib sent envoys to Jerusalem to demoralize the city inhabitants. In their effort to convince Jerusalem that it should surrender, the Assyrians referred to Hezekiah's removal of altars and places of worship. This act was considered an affront to the God the Judeans worshiped and on whom they relied for victory; he would not aid a people led by an idol-breaking king such as Hezekiah.

While Sennacherib was threatening Jerusalem, Tirhakah, the Ethiopian king of Egypt, led his army to Libnah. Sennacherib was able to defeat this Egyptian force. He then turned his full attention to Jerusalem again (2 Kgs 19:15-19). Isaiah was sent by God to inform Hezekiah that the mocking Sennacherib would be humbled and Jerusalem would be spared for David's sake. The Lord's word was fulfilled. Sennacherib's plans to take Jerusalem by siege had to be abandoned when 185,000 of his troops died of a miraculous plague.

Sennacherib returned to Nineveh, the capital city of Assyria. He was murdered in the

Temple of Nisroch by Adrammelech and Sharezer, two of his sons. A third son, Esarhaddon, succeeded him upon the throne of Assyria.

SEORIM
Levite and head of the fourth of 24 divisions of priests formed during David's reign (1 Chr 24:8).

SERAH
Asher's daughter (Gn 46:17; Nm 26:46; 1 Chr 7:30).

SERAIAH
1. Royal secretary of King David (2 Sm 8:17); alternately called Sheva in 2 Samuel 20:25, Shisha in 1 Kings 4:3, and Shavsha in 1 Chronicles 18:16.

2. Chief priest in Jerusalem at the time of its destruction by the Babylonians in 586 BC. He was taken by Nebuzaradan, the captain of the guard, to Nebuchadnezzar at Riblah, where he was put to death (2 Kgs 25:18; Jer 52:24). First Chronicles 6:14 records Seraiah as the son of Azariah, the father of Jehozadak and a descendant of Levi through Aaron's line.

3. Son of Tanhumeth the Netophathite and one of the captains of the Judean forces who sought clemency from Nebuchadnezzar under Gedaliah (2 Kgs 25:23; Jer 40:8).

4. Judahite, the son of Kenaz, the brother of Othniel and Joab's father (1 Chr 4:13-14).

5. Simeonite, the son of Asiel and Joshibiah's father (1 Chr 4:35).

6. One of the men who returned with Zerubbabel to Judah following the Exile (Ezr 2:2); called Azariah in Nehemiah 7:7. See Azariah #23.

7. Father of Ezra the scribe. Ezra returned to Jerusalem during the reign of King Artaxerxes I of Persia (464–424 BC; Ezr 7:1). He is perhaps identical with #2 above, in which case Jehozadak would be Ezra's brother.

8. One of the priests who set his seal on the covenant of Ezra (Neh 10:2).

9. Son of Hilkiah and a priest living in Jerusalem during the postexilic era (Neh 11:11); called Azariah in 1 Chronicles 9:11. See Azariah #10.

10. One of the leaders of the priests who returned with Zerubbabel and Jeshua to Judah after the Exile (Neh 12:1). His house in the next generation was headed by Meraiah. He is perhaps identical with #6 above.

11. Son of Azriel who, with Jerahmeel and Shelemiah, was ordered by King Jehoiakim of Judah (609–598 BC) to capture Baruch and Jeremiah (Jer 36:26).

12. Son of Neriah and the official who accompanied King Zedekiah of Judah (597–586 BC) to Babylon. Seraiah was to relay Jeremiah's message against Babylon (Jer 51:59-61).

SERED

One of Zebulun's sons (Gn 46:14) and the father of the Seredite family (Nm 26:26).

SERGIUS PAULUS

Proconsul of Cyprus, described as a "man of intelligence" (Acts 13:7). Paul and Barnabas, on their first missionary journey, evangelized the Cyprian city of Paphos, Sergius Paulus's residence. Here they met the Jewish false prophet and sorcerer named Bar-Jesus (or Elymas), who strongly opposed their gospel message before the proconsul. Paul, however, rebuked Elymas and cursed him with blindness. When Sergius Paulus witnessed what had happened, he believed. Thus, he became the first recorded convert on Paul's first missionary journey.

It is here that we find the transition from the name Saul to that of Paul. Origen and many since his time have believed that Paul made the change at this point in honor of his famous convert.

SERUG

Reu's son from Shem's line (Gn 11:20-23), Abraham's forefather and an ancestor of Jesus Christ (Lk 3:35; KJV "Saruch").

SETH

Third son of Adam and Eve, replacing Abel, whom Cain murdered (Gn 4:25). He appears as the firstborn son of Adam in the genealogies of Genesis 5:3-8, 1 Chronicles 1:1 (KJV "Sheth"), and Luke 3:38. It was through Seth's line that Jesus was born. Seth was the father of Enosh and lived 912 years.

SETHUR

Asherite, Michael's son and one of the 12 spies sent by Moses to search out the land of Canaan (Nm 13:13).

SHAAPH

1. Jahdai's sixth son, included in the genealogy of Caleb, Jerahmeel's brother (1 Chr 2:47).

2. Son of Caleb by his concubine; the brother of Jerahmeel; the father of Madmannah (1 Chr 2:49).

SHAASHGAZ

Eunuch of King Ahasuerus, in charge of the concubines (Est 2:14).

SHABBETHAI

1. Levite who opposed Ezra's suggestion that the sons of Israel should divorce the foreign women they had married upon returning to Palestine from exile (Ezr 10:15). He explained the law to the people at Ezra's reading (Neh 8:7).

2. One of the chiefs of the Levites who oversaw the outside work of the sanctuary during the postexilic period (Neh 11:16). He is perhaps identical with #1 above.

SHADRACH, MESHACH, AND ABEDNEGO

Babylonian names of three Hebrew youths, Hananiah, Mishael, and Azariah, who along with Daniel and others were taken to Babylon as hostages by Nebuchadnezzar in 605 BC (2 Kgs 24:1; Dn 1:1-4). They may have been of royal descent (2 Kgs 20:18; Is 39:7), and thus their presence in Babylon would be thought to guarantee the good behavior of the Judean king Jehoiakim. Nebuchadnezzar, desiring to grace his court with intelligent and handsome men and provide able administrators for his kingdom, directed that certain of the Judean hostages be selected for special training. Among those chosen were Daniel and his three friends. Their Hebrew names, each of which exalted Yahweh, were changed to Babylonian names whose meanings are not clear but may have been intended to honor a Babylonian god. Thus, Hananiah ("The Lord is gracious") was changed to Shadrach ("Command of Aku"—the Sumerian moon god), Mishael ("Who is what God is") was changed to Meshach ("Who is what Aku is"), and Azariah ("The Lord has helped") was changed to Abednego ("Servant of Nabu"—the Babylonian god of wisdom). Also Daniel ("My judge is God") was changed to Belteshazzar ("Bel protects"—the chief Babylonian god). These young men underwent a three-year course of instruction in the languages and literature of the Chaldeans, the learned men of Babylon. This instruction no doubt included the Aramaic, Akkadian, and Sumerian languages; cuneiform writing; and perhaps also astronomy, mathematics, history, and agriculture.

Nebuchadnezzar provided food for this academy. The four Hebrew youths refused to defile themselves with it because it likely had been sacrificed to one or more of the pagan gods. It had not been properly prepared, therefore, and was unfit for Jewish consumption (cf. Ex 34:15; Lv 17:10-14). Fearing the king's displeasure should the young scholars appear undernourished, the chief eunuch expressed his concern to Daniel. Daniel proposed a substitute diet of vegetables to be tested for ten days. At the end of that period, the four Hebrew youths appeared healthier than their colleagues and were allowed to continue their diet. When the course of their instruction was completed, the four stood out from the rest because of their academic excellence and superior competence in every area of knowledge. Their intellectual superiority had been bestowed upon them by God.

Apparently, these four young men joined the ranks of the "wise men of Babylon" (Dn 2:12-49). When the others (the enchanters, sorcerers, and wise men) were unable to tell Nebuchadnezzar the nature and interpretation of a dream, he lashed out at them in a fitful rage and ordered them all put to death. Daniel appealed to the king, and their lives were spared when the dream and its interpretation were made known to him in a vision. Later, Shadrach, Meshach, and Abednego refused to comply with the king's command to prostrate themselves before an enormous golden image that Nebuchadnezzar had erected (ch 3). Confronted by Nebuchadnezzar and threatened with terrible punishment for their intransigence, they replied that their trust was fully in the Lord. A blazing furnace was stoked for the immediate execution of the faithful Hebrews. The Lord was with his faithful servants and preserved their lives by sending his angel to protect them in the furnace. In the end it was Nebuchadnezzar who had to acknowledge that his own kingdom and power could not compare to that of the true God.

See also Daniel.

SHAGEE
Hararite and Jonathan's father (2 Sm 23:33; 1 Chr 11:34). Jonathan was one of David's mighty men.

SHAHARAIM
Benjaminite living in Moab, father of nine sons, who divorced two of his three wives (1 Chr 8:8).

SHALLUM
1. Son of Jabesh and Israel's 16th king (752 BC). In a conspiracy against King Zechariah, Shallum murdered the monarch at Ibleam and declared himself ruler of Israel during the 39th year of King Uzziah's (Azariah's) reign in Judah (792–740 BC). However, in like manner, he was killed at the hands of Gadi after ruling for only one month (2 Kgs 15:10-15).

2. Son of Tikvah (alternately spelled Tokhath, see 2 Chr 34:22), who was keeper of the wardrobe and the husband of Huldah the prophetess, living in Jerusalem during the days of King Josiah (640–609 BC; 2 Kgs 22:14).

3. Sismai's son and the father of Jekamiah from Judah's tribe (1 Chr 2:40-41).

4. Alternate name for Jehoahaz, the youngest of King Josiah's four sons and later Judah's 17th king, in 1 Chronicles 3:15 and Jeremiah 22:11. *See* Jehoahaz #2.

5. Shaul's son, Simeon's grandson, and the father of Mibsam (1 Chr 4:25).

6. Alternate name for Meshullam, Zadok's son and Ezra's forefather, in 1 Chronicles 6:12-13 and Ezra 7:2. *See* Meshullam #7.

7. Alternate name for Shillem, the youngest of Naphtali's four sons, in 1 Chronicles 7:13. *See* Shillem.

8. Alternate name for Meshullam, Kore's son and chief of the gatekeepers (1 Chr 9:17-19, 31; Ezr 2:42; Neh 7:45). *See* Meshullam #20.

9. Ephraimite and the father of Jehizkiah (2 Chr 28:12).

10. One of the Levitical gatekeepers who was encouraged by Ezra to divorce his foreign wife during the post-exilic era (Ezr 10:24).

11. One of the descendants of Binnui who was encouraged by Ezra to divorce his foreign wife (Ezr 10:42).

12. Hallohesh's son and a ruler of Jerusalem who, along with his daughters, repaired the section of city wall next to the Tower of the Ovens (Neh 3:12).

13. Col-hozeh's son and ruler of the Mizpah district, who rebuilt the Fountain Gate and the wall of the pool of Shelah of the king's garden (Neh 3:15).

14. Uncle of Hanamel and Jeremiah, who sold to the latter his field at Anathoth during King Zedekiah's reign (597–586 BC; Jer 32:7). He is perhaps identifiable with #2 above.

15. Maaseiah's father. Maaseiah, keeper of the threshold, owned a chamber in the sanctuary during Jehoiakim's reign (609–598 BC; Jer 35:4, KJV; cf. 52:24).

SHALMAI
Father of a family of Temple servants returning to the land of Canaan with Zerubbabel after the Babylonian captivity.

SHALMAN
Unknown conqueror whose brutal destruction of Beth-arbel was descriptive of Israel's approaching judgment (Hos 10:14). Several suggestions as to the identification of Shalman are the following: Salamanu, the king of Moab who paid tribute to Tiglath-pileser of Assyria; one of the Shalmaneser kings of Assyria; and Shalmah, a north Arabian tribe that invaded the Negev.

SHALMANESER
Name of several Assyrian rulers, two of whom had direct contact with the people of Israel. However, only Shalmaneser V (727–722 BC) is known by name in the Bible. He was able to bring Hoshea, the last king of Israel (732–723 BC), under his control (2 Kgs 17:3).

Hoshea failed to pay his annual tribute in his seventh regnal year and was visited by Shalmaneser V, who placed Samaria, the capital of Israel, under siege. The king of Egypt was implicated in this treachery in some way, for he gave encouragement to Hoshea in his rebellious intentions. The siege of Samaria lasted for three years, and in Hoshea's ninth year the city fell. The biblical record seems to attribute the fall of the city to Shalmaneser. Unfortunately, there are no extant records for the reign of Shalmaneser V, and the capture of Samaria was claimed by Shalmaneser's son Sargon II (721–705 BC) in his own annals as an important event in his accession year.

SHAMA
One of the mighty men of David's army, son of Hotham the Aroerite and the brother of Jeiel (1 Chr 11:44).

SHAMGAR
Son of Anath from Beth-anath; a judge of Israel. Two brief references in the OT (Jgs 3:31; 5:6) tell us little of the man except for his one major exploit: the killing of 600 Philistines with an oxgoad. How such a feat was performed is not recorded. The oxgoad could have

had a sharpened metal tip and may have been used as a spear. The timing of the reference indicates that his deeds took place early in the period of Philistine settlement in Canaan. Judges 5:6 would place him prior to the battle of Kishon (c. 1125 BC).

SHAMIR

Micah's son from Levi's tribe (1 Chr 24:24).

SHAMMA

Zophah's son from Asher's tribe (1 Chr 7:37).

SHAMMAH

1. One of Reuel's four sons, the grandson of Esau and a chief in the land of Edom (Gn 36:13; 17; 1 Chr 1:37).

2. Third of Jesse's eight sons, the brother of David (1 Sm 16:9; 17:13) and the father of Jonathan (2 Sm 21:20-21) and Jonadab (2 Sm 13:3 ff.). Shammah is alternately called Shimea in 1 Chronicles 2:13 and 20:7, Shimeah in 2 Samuel 13:3, and Shimei in 21:21.

3. Son of Agee the Hararite and one of the elite among David's mighty men. He was renowned for his valiant stand against the Philistines at Lehi (2 Sm 23:11-12).

4. Harodite and one of David's 30 valiant warriors. He was listed between Elhanan and Elika (2 Sm 23:24-25). The parallel passage of 1 Chronicles 11:27 reads "Shammoth," the plural form of Shammah. In 27:8 Shamhuth the Irahite, the commander of a division of David's soldiers, is no doubt the same man.

5. Hararite and one of David's mighty men, listed between Jonathan and Ahiam (2 Sm 23:33).

SHAMMAI

1. Onam's son, brother of Jada and the father of Nadab and Abishur from Judah's tribe (1 Chr 2:28, 32).

2. Rekem's son and the father of Maon from Caleb's house (1 Chr 2:44-45).

3. Mered's son by Bithiah, Pharaoh's daughter, and a descendant of Caleb (1 Chr 4:17-18).

SHAMMUA

1. Reubenite, Zaccur's son and one of the 12 spies sent by Moses to search out the land of Canaan (Nm 13:4).

2. Alternate name for Shimea, David's son, in 2 Samuel 5:14 and 1 Chronicles 14:4. See Shimea #2.

3. Alternate name for Shemaiah, Galal's son, in Nehemiah 11:17. See Shemaiah #6.

4. Head of a family who returned to Jerusalem with Zerubbabel after the Babylonian exile (Neh 12:18).

SHAMSHERAI
Jeroham's son and a chief in Benjamin's tribe (1 Chr 8:26).

SHAPHAM
Leader in Gad's tribe (1 Chr 5:12). He is believed to have lived in Bashan and served during the days of Jotham, king of Judah (v 17).

SHAPHAN
1. Son of Azaliah and the father of Ahikam, Elasah, and Gemariah. He and his household favored Josiah's reforms, supported the prophet Jeremiah, and complied with Babylonian hegemony.

   Shaphan served as the royal secretary to Josiah, king of Judah (640–609 BC). He read the Book of the Law to the king after it was found by the high priest Hilkiah in the sanctuary of Jerusalem. Later, Josiah sent him with a small delegation to hear the words of the prophetess Huldah (2 Kgs 22:3-14; 2 Chr 34:8-28).

   Shaphan's sons were mentioned among the political leaders of Judah during the days of its desolation by Nebuchadnezzar of Babylon (605–586 BC). Ahikam assisted with the repair of the sanctuary and protected Jeremiah from the men who sought his death during the reign of King Jehoiakim (609–598 BC; 2 Kgs 22:12; Jer 26:24). Elasah delivered a message from King Zedekiah of Judah (597–586 BC) to Nebuchadnezzar in Babylon (Jer 29:3). Gemariah was the prince of Judah from whose chamber Baruch read the scroll of Jeremiah to the people (36:10-12).

   Shaphan was the grandfather of Micaiah (Jer 36:11-13) and Gedaliah. Gedaliah was appointed governor of Judah by Nebuchadnezzar (2 Kgs 25:22; Jer 40:5-11) and ordered to protect Jeremiah (Jer 39:14). Gedaliah was later murdered by a mob led by Ishmael (41:2).

2. Father of Jaazaniah and, in Ezekiel's vision, a leader of idolatrous practices in Israel (Ez 8:11).

SHAPHAT
1. Simeonite, Hori's son and one of the 12 spies sent by Moses to search out the land of Canaan (Nm 13:5).

2. Father of the prophet Elisha from the town of Abel-meholah (1 Kgs 19:16, 19; 2 Kgs 3:11; 6:31).

3. Youngest of Shemaiah's six sons from Judah's tribe and a descendant of David (1 Chr 3:22).

4. Gadite chief in Bashan, a region west of the Jordan River (1 Chr 5:12).

5. Adlai's son and a member of King David's staff. Shaphat had charge of David's cattle in the valleys (1 Chr 27:29).

SHARAI

One of Binnui's sons who was encouraged by Ezra to divorce his foreign wife during the postexilic era (Ezr 10:40).

SHARAR

Alternate name for Sacar, Ahiam's father, in 2 Samuel 23:33. *See* Sacar #1.

SHAREZER

1. One of the sons of Sennacherib, the king of Assyria. In 681 BC he, along with his brother Adrammelech, killed Sennacherib while he was praying in the house of Nisroch (2 Kgs 19:37; Is 37:38).

2. One who was sent from Bethel to inquire of the priests and prophets as to whether or not the mourning and feasting in commemoration of the destruction of the Temple should be confined to the fifth month of that year. Since the Temple was nearing its restoration, there was some question about the commemoration on the part of the populace at Bethel (Zec 7:2-3).

SHASHAI

Binnui's son, who was encouraged by Ezra to divorce his foreign wife during the postexilic era (Ezr 10:40).

SHASHAK

Benjaminite, Elpaal's son and the father of 11 sons (1 Chr 8:14, 25).

SHAUL

1. Alternate name for Saul, an Edomite king, in Genesis 36:37-38 and 1 Chronicles 1:48-49. *See* Saul #1.

2. Son of Simeon by a Canaanite woman (Gn 46:10; Ex 6:15; 1 Chr 4:24) and head of the Shaulite family (Nm 26:13).

3. Levite and Uzziah's son from the house of Kohath (1 Chr 6:24).

SHEAL

One of Bani's sons who was told by Ezra to divorce his foreign wife (Ezr 10:29).

SHEALTIEL

Son of King Jeconiah (Jehoiachin) of Judah (598–597 BC) and the father of Zerubbabel. Zerubbabel led the Jews back to Palestine and there ruled as governor of Judah during the postexilic period (Ezr 3:2; 5:2; Neh 12:1; Hg 1:1, 12-14). In the genealogies of Jesus Christ, Shealtiel is variously mentioned as the son of Jeconiah (Mt 1:12) and as the son of Neri

(Lk 3:27). In 1 Chronicles 3:17-19, Shealtiel appears to be the grandfather or perhaps the uncle of Zerubbabel. One probable solution is that Shealtiel was the son of Neri and the heir apparent to the throne of Jeconiah and that, at Shealtiel's death, Zerubbabel was next in succession.

SHEARIAH
One of Azel's six sons, a descendant of Jonathan, son of King Saul, from Benjamin's tribe (1 Chr 8:38; 9:44).

SHEAR-JASHUB
Isaiah's son whose name, meaning "a remnant shall return," symbolized the prophecy that, although Israel and Judah would be destroyed, a remnant would be saved and later return (Is 7:3).

SHEBA
1. Son of Raamah, the brother of Dedan and a descendant of Noah through Ham's line (Gn 10:7; 1 Chr 1:9).

2. One of the 13 sons of Joktan and a descendant of Noah through Shem's line (Gn 10:28; 1 Chr 1:22).

3. Son of Jokshan, the brother of Dedan and the grandson of Abraham and Keturah (Gn 25:3; 1 Chr 1:32).

4. Benjaminite and the son of Bicri. After the death of Absalom, Sheba incited Israel to rebel against David. Under the command of Joab, the revolt was subdued and Sheba was beheaded at Abel-beth-maacah (2 Sm 20:1-22).

5. One of the Gadite leaders ruling in Bashan, registered during the reigns of Jotham king of Judah (750–732 BC) and Jeroboam II king of Israel (793–753 BC); see 1 Chr 5:13, 16-17.

SHEBANIAH
1. One of the seven priests assigned to blow a trumpet before the Ark of God in the procession led by David, when the Ark was moved to Jerusalem (1 Chr 15:24).

2. One of the Levites who led the people in worship when Ezra read the law (Neh 9:4-5).

3. Head of a priestly family who set his seal on the covenant of Ezra (Neh 10:4; 12:14) and perhaps the same person as Shecaniah in Nehemiah 12:3. See Shechaniah #9.

4. Another Levite who set his seal on the covenant of Ezra (Neh 10:12).

SHEBER
Caleb's son by his concubine Maacah (1 Chr 2:48).

SHEBNA

Eighth-century official of the kingdom of Judah. The name Shebna is Aramaic in form and has been interpreted to mean "return, please [O Lord]," relating it to either a fuller spelling (Shebaniah) or to a Semitic root meaning "youthful." Because of the Aramaic spelling, some have argued that Shebna was of foreign birth. The appearance of the name, however, on several contemporary Palestinian inscriptions (e.g., from Lachish) may make such a view unnecessary.

Two major passages mention Shebna by name: Isaiah 22:15-25 and 2 Kings 18:17–19:7. The unlikelihood of two men with the same name, both holding high-ranking positions in the Judahite government in the same general time period, has caused most scholars to argue that the two passages in Isaiah and 2 Kings refer to a single individual.

Because of his arrogance in building an ostentatious tomb for himself, and because of excessive pride in his position and importance, Shebna was denounced by the prophet Isaiah. In fact, the prophet even predicted that Shebna would go into exile and die in a foreign country (Is 22:18). The events described in 2 Kings 18:17–19:7 (cf. the parallel account in Is 37) are clearly traceable to the year 701 BC and the invasion of Sennacherib. If the Shebna described in this story is the same person denounced by Isaiah in the passage just discussed, as seems likely, the date of the prophetic denouncement must be placed sometime earlier than 701.

In 701 the Assyrian ruler Sennacherib captured virtually all of the cities of Judah and clearly had his heart set on the capture of Jerusalem. King Hezekiah of Judah sent three official representatives to negotiate with the invading Assyrians. At this time, Eliakim was titled "the one who is in charge of the [king's] household" (2 Kgs 18:18) and Shebna held the rank of *sopher,* an important position, probably equal to that of a secretary of state.

SHEBUEL

1. Gershon's son and Moses' grandson from Levi's tribe (1 Chr 23:15-16); father of Jehdeiah (24:20, "Shubael"). He was the chief officer in charge of the treasuries (26:24).

2. Levite, Heman's son and a musician in the Tabernacle (1 Chr 25:4, 20, "Shubael").

SHECANIAH

1. Descendant of David through the line of Zerubbabel living in postexilic Palestine (1 Chr 3:21-22).

2. Levite and the head of the 10th of 24 divisions of priests formed during the reign of David (1 Chr 24:11).

3. One of six priests serving under Kore during the reign of King Hezekiah of Judah (715–686 BC). Shecaniah assisted with the distribution of the Temple offerings among his fellow priests living in the priestly cities (2 Chr 31:15).

4. Father of Hattush, who returned with Ezra to Judah following the Babylonian captivity during the reign of King Artaxerxes I of Persia (464–424 BC; Ezr 8:3).

5. Son of Jahaziel who returned with Ezra to Judah during the reign of King Artaxerxes I of Persia (Ezr 8:5).

6. Son of Jehiel in the house of Elam, who urged Ezra to command the sons of Israel to divorce the foreign women they had married (Ezr 10:2).

7. Father of Shemaiah. Shemaiah, the keeper of the East Gate, helped Nehemiah rebuild a section of the Jerusalem wall (Neh 3:29).

8. Father-in-law of Tobiah the Ammonite and the son of Arah (Neh 6:18).

9. Head of a priestly family who returned to Judah with Zerubbabel following the Exile (Neh 12:3). Shecaniah is perhaps identical with Shebaniah in verse 14. *See* Shebaniah #3.

SHECHEM

1. Son of Hamor the Hivite. He raped Dinah, the daughter of Jacob, and was later killed along with his father and all the males of his town by Simeon and Levi (Gn 34; Jos 24:32).

2. One of Gilead's six sons, a descendant of Joseph through Manasseh's line, and the founder of the Shechemite family (Nm 26:31; Jos 17:2).

3. One of Shemida's four sons from Manasseh's tribe (1 Chr 7:19).

SHEDEUR

Elizur's father. Elizur represented Reuben's tribe in Moses' census of the men capable of bearing arms (Nm 1:5; 2:10; 10:18), and in the dedication of the altar (7:30-35).

SHEERAH

Daughter or granddaughter of Ephraim. Her offspring built lower and upper Beth-horon and Uzzen-sheerah, named after her (1 Chr 7:24).

SHEHARIAH

Jehoram's son and a chief of Benjamin's tribe in Jerusalem after the Exile (1 Chr 8:26).

SHELAH

1. Arphaxad's son and the father of Eber (Gn 10:24; 11:12-15; 1 Chr 1:18). Shelah is listed in Luke's genealogy of Christ as the son of Cainan the son of Arphaxad (Lk 3:35).

2. Judah's third son by Bathshua the Canaanitess. He was born at Kezib, a small town in Judah (Gn 38:5; 1 Chr 2:3). Shelah founded the Shelanite family

(Nm 26:20), which should possibly be read instead of "Shilonite" in Nehemiah 11:5; 1 Chronicles 9:5.

SHELEMIAH

1. Korahite from the tribe of Levi and a gatekeeper who was chosen by lot to guard the east gate of the sanctuary during David's reign (1 Chr 26:14); also named Meshelemiah (vv 1-2). *See* Meshelemiah.

2, 3. Two of Binnui's sons, who were encouraged to divorce their foreign wives during Ezra's postexilic reforms in Israel (Ezr 10:39-41).

4. Father of Hananiah. Hananiah repaired a section of the Jerusalem wall under Nehemiah (Neh 3:30).

5. Priest and one of the three men appointed by Nehemiah as the treasurers of the Temple in Jerusalem. Their task was to oversee the distribution of the tithes among their fellow priests (Neh 13:13).

6. Son of Cushi, the father of Nethaniah, and a forefather of Jehudi (Jer 36:14).

7. Son of Abdeel who, with Jerahmeel and Seraiah, was commanded by King Jehoiakim of Judah (609–598 BC) to seize Baruch and Jeremiah (Jer 36:26).

8. Father of Jehucal (Jer 37:3), alternately spelled Jucal in 38:1 (NLT mg).

9. Son of Hananiah and the father of Irijah. Irijah arrested Jeremiah for apparently deserting to the Babylonians (Jer 37:13).

SHELEPH

Joktan's son and the founder of an Arabian tribe living in Yemen (Gn 10:26; 1 Chr 1:20).

SHELESH

Helem's son and a chief of Asher's tribe (1 Chr 7:35).

SHELOMI

Ahihud's father. Ahihud represented Asher's tribe in the division of the land of Canaan among Israel's ten tribes west of the Jordan (Nm 34:27).

SHELOMITH

1. Dibri's daughter and the mother of a man from Dan's tribe who blasphemed the Lord's name, for which he was subsequently stoned to death (Lv 24:11-16).

2. Sister of Meshullam and Hananiah, all of whom were descendants of David (1 Chr 3:19).

3. KJV spelling of Shelomoth, Shimei's son, in 1 Chronicles 23:9. *See* Shelomoth #1.

4. Alternate spelling of Shelomoth, Izhar's son, in 1 Chronicles 23:18. *See* Shelomoth #2.

5. KJV spelling of Shelomoth, Zicri's son, in 1 Chronicles 26:25-28. *See* Shelomoth #3.

6. Son of Rehoboam and Maachah (2 Chr 11:20).

7. One of Ezra's companions (Ezr 8:10).

SHELOMOTH

1. Gershonite Levite and one of Shimei's sons serving in the sanctuary during David's reign (1 Chr 23:9).

2. Levite and priest from the family of Izhar during David's reign (1 Chr 23:18, "Shelomith"; 24:22).

3. Zicri's son, who was in charge of the royal treasuries during David's reign (1 Chr 26:25-28).

SHELUMIEL

Simeonite, Zurishaddai's son and one of the leaders who assisted Moses in taking a census of Israel in the wilderness (Nm 1:6; 2:12; 7:36, 41; 10:19). He is the forefather of the apocryphal Judith (Jdt 8:1, where his name is Salamiel and his father's Sarasadai).

SHEM

Eldest son of Noah (Gn 5:32; 6:10; 7:13; 9:18, 23, 26-27; 11:10; 1 Chr 1:4, 17-27; Lk 3:36) and the ancestor of the Semitic peoples (Gn 10:1, 21-31). Shem lived 600 years (11:10-11). In Hebrew, Shem means "name," perhaps implying that Noah expected this son's name to become great.

After their deliverance from the great Flood, Shem and Japheth acted with respect and dignity toward their drunken father Noah on an occasion when their brother Ham dishonored him (Gn 9:20-29). Because of this act, Noah later pronounced a curse on Canaan, the son of Ham, and a blessing on both Shem and Japheth.

In Genesis 11:10-27, the line of descent for the promised seed, which was to crush Satan (Gn 3:15; 5:1-32), is traced through Shem to Abraham, and ultimately through Judah and David to Christ (cf. Lk 3:36). The blessing of Noah on Shem is thus to be taken as an indication that the line of Shem will be the line through which the seed of Genesis 3:15 will come. This is the first time in the Bible that God is called the God of some particular individual or group of people. The statement that Canaan would be a servant to Shem was fulfilled centuries later when the Israelites, who descended from Shem, entered the land of Canaan and subdued the inhabitants of the land (cf. 1 Kgs 9:20-21).

Noah also said that Japheth would be enlarged and dwell in the tents of Shem (Gn 9:27), the latter of which would seem to imply sustenance and protection. After Japheth would be greatly increased in numbers, the Japhethites would be brought into contact with Shem and would share in the blessings and promises of the Semitic faith. Many scholars see fulfillment of this prophecy in the opening of the gospel to the Gentiles during the NT era of the establishment of the church.

In the "table of nations" recorded in Genesis 10, five descendants of Shem are mentioned (Elam, Asshur, Arphaxad, Lud, and Aram). Receiving particular emphasis among these descendants is Eber from the line of Arphaxad, whose line is traced to Abraham in Genesis 11:16-27.

See also Abraham; Noah #1.

SHEMA

1. Judahite, Hebron's son and a descendant of Caleb (1 Chr 2:43-44).

2. Reubenite and Joel's son (1 Chr 5:8). He is perhaps identifiable with Shemaiah or Shimei in 1 Chronicles 5:4.

3. Benjaminite and head of a family in Aijalon, who helped defeat the inhabitants of Gath (1 Chr 8:13).

4. Levite who explained to the people passages from the law read by Ezra (Neh 8:4).

SHEMAAH

Father of Ahiezer and Joash, two bowmen who joined David at Ziklag (1 Chr 12:3).

SHEMAIAH

1. Prophet during the reign of Rehoboam, king of Judah (930–913 BC). He warned the king not to go to war against Jeroboam and the ten northern tribes of Israel (1 Kgs 12:22-24; 2 Chr 11:2-4). Five years later he spoke words of comfort to a repentant Rehoboam and people of Judah (2 Chr 12:5-7). Shemaiah chronicled the life of Rehoboam in a book that has since been lost.

2. Son of Shecaniah, the father of six sons and a descendant of David through Rehoboam's line (1 Chr 3:22).

3. Simeonite, father of Shimri and an ancestor of Jehu (1 Chr 4:37).

4. Reubenite and a son of Joel (1 Chr 5:4).

5. Levite and the son of Hasshub, who returned to Jerusalem after the Exile (1 Chr 9:14). He was made a leader in the work of the Temple during the days of Nehemiah (Neh 11:15).

6. Son of Galal and the father of Obadiah, a Levite who returned to Jerusalem following the Babylonian captivity (1 Chr 9:16); called Shammua in Nehemiah 11:17.

7. Levite and the leader of his father's house. Shemaiah was summoned by David to help carry the Ark from Obed-edom's house to Jerusalem (1 Chr 15:8-11).

8. Son of Nethanel and the Levitical scribe who recorded the 24 divisions of the priests during David's reign in Israel (1000–961 BC; 1 Chr 24:6).

9. Oldest of Obed-edom's eight sons and the father of sons who served as the

gatekeepers of the south gate and storehouse of the sanctuary during David's reign (1 Chr 26:4-7).

10. One of the Levites sent by King Jehoshaphat of Judah (872–848 BC) to teach the law in the cities of Judah (2 Chr 17:8-9).

11. Son of Jeduthun and Uzziel's brother, who was among the Levites chosen by King Hezekiah of Judah (715–686 BC) to cleanse the house of the Lord (2 Chr 29:14-15).

12. One of the Levites assisting Kore with the distribution of the offerings among his fellow priests living in the priestly cities of Judah during the days of King Hezekiah (2 Chr 31:15).

13. One of the Levitical leaders who generously gave animals to the Levites for the celebration of the Passover feast during King Josiah's reign (640–609 BC; 2 Chr 35:9).

14. Son of Adonikam, who returned with Ezra to Judah after the Exile during the reign of King Artaxerxes I of Persia (464–424 BC; Ezr 8:13).

15. One of the Jewish leaders whom Ezra sent to Iddo at Casiphia to gather Levites and Temple servants for the caravan of Jews returning to Palestine from Babylon (Ezr 8:16-17).

16. Priest and one of Harim's five sons who was encouraged by Ezra to divorce his foreign wife during the postexilic era (Ezr 10:21).

17. Son of another Harim who was encouraged by Ezra to divorce his foreign wife (Ezr 10:31).

18. Son of Shecaniah and the keeper of the East Gate who repaired a section of the Jerusalem wall under Nehemiah's direction (Neh 3:29).

19. Son of Delaiah and a false prophet hired by Tobiah and Sanballat to frighten Nehemiah and hinder him from rebuilding the Jerusalem wall (Neh 6:10-13).

20. One of the priests who set his seal on the covenant of Ezra (Neh 10:8).

21. One of the leaders of the priests who returned with Zerubbabel and Jeshua to Judah after the Exile (Neh 12:6).

22. One of the princes of Judah who participated in the dedication of the Jerusalem wall during the postexilic period (Neh 12:34).

23. Son of Mattaniah, grandfather of Zechariah, and a descendant of Asaph. Zechariah was one of the priests who played a trumpet at the dedication of the Jerusalem wall (Neh 12:35).

24–25. Two priestly musicians who performed at the dedication of the Jerusalem wall (Neh 12:36, 42).

26. Father of Uriah the prophet from Kiriath-jearim. Like Jeremiah, his contemporary, Uriah spoke words of doom against Jerusalem and Judah during the reign of King

Jehoiakim of Judah (609–598 BC), who deplored Uriah's message and eventually had him killed (Jer 26:20-21).

27. Nehelamite and a Jew deported to Babylon by Nebuchadnezzar, from where he opposed Jeremiah. He sent letters to the priests in Jerusalem that criticized Jeremiah for predicting a long captivity for Judah. Jeremiah exposed Shemaiah as a false prophet and foretold that he and his descendants would not live to see the return to Palestine (Jer 29:24-32).

28. Father of Delaiah, a prince of Judah during the reign of King Jehoiakim (Jer 36:12).

SHEMARIAH

1. Warrior from the tribe of Benjamin who joined David at Ziklag in his struggle against King Saul. Shemariah was one of David's ambidextrous archers and slingers (1 Chr 12:5).

2. One of Rehoboam's sons (2 Chr 11:19; KJV "Shamariah").

3. Harim's son, who obeyed Ezra's exhortation to divorce his foreign wife after the Exile (Ezr 10:32).

4. Binnui's son, who obeyed Ezra's exhortation to divorce his foreign wife (Ezr 10:41).

SHEMEBER

King of Zeboiim, who joined a confederacy with four other kings in rebellion against Kedorlaomer and his allies. Abraham rescued Lot from captivity after Shemeber, along with Sodom and Gomorrah, was defeated (Gn 14:2).

SHEMED

Elpaal's son and a descendant of Benjamin through Shaharaim's line. Shemed rebuilt the towns of Ono and Lod after the Babylonian exile (1 Chr 8:12).

SHEMER

1. Owner of the hill of Samaria, which Omri, king of Israel, bought as the site of his new capital city and named after Shemer (1 Kgs 16:24).

2. Merarite Levite, Mahli's son and the father of Bani; he was a Temple singer during David's reign (1 Chr 6:46).

3. Asherite, Heber's son and a leader among his people (1 Chr 7:34).

SHEMIDA

Father of the family of Shemidaites (Nm 26:32) in Manasseh's tribe (Jos 17:2; 1 Chr 7:19).

SHEMIRAMOTH

1. One of the Levites whom David commanded to play the harp when the Ark of God

was brought from the house of Obed-edom to Jerusalem (1 Chr 15:18-22), and who retained a permanent position under Asaph as one of the ministers of the Ark (16:4-5).

2. Levite commissioned by Jehoshaphat to teach the law "through all the cities of Judah" (2 Chr 17:8).

SHEMUEL

1. Ammihud's son and the representative of Simeon's tribe in the division of the land of Canaan among Israel's 10 tribes west of the Jordan (Nm 34:20).

2. KJV rendering of Samuel, Elkanah's son, in 1 Chronicles 6:33-34. *See* Samuel.

3. Tola's son and chief in Issachar's tribe (1 Chr 7:2).

SHENAZZAR

Fourth son of Jeconiah (Jehoiachin), captive king of Judah (1 Chr 3:18).

SHEPHATIAH

1. One of six sons born to David during his seven-year reign at Hebron. Shephatiah's mother was Abital, one of David's wives (2 Sm 3:4; 1 Chr 3:3).

2. Benjaminite and the father of Meshullam, a returnee to Jerusalem after the Babylonian captivity (1 Chr 9:8).

3. Haruphite from Benjamin's tribe and one of the men of military prowess who came to David's support at Ziklag (1 Chr 12:5).

4. Son of Maacah and chief official of the Simeonites during David's reign (1 Chr 27:16).

5. One of the seven sons of King Jehoshaphat of Judah (872–848 BC) and the brother of Jehoram who became sole regent (853–841 BC) after his father's death (2 Chr 21:1-2).

6. Forefather of 372 descendants who returned with Zerubbabel to Judah following the Exile (Ezr 2:4; Neh 7:9). Later, 81 members of Shephatiah's house accompanied Ezra back to Palestine during the reign of King Artaxerxes I of Persia (464–424 BC; Ezr 8:8).

7. Founder of a household of Solomon's servants that returned with Zerubbabel to Judah after the Babylonian captivity (Ezr 2:57; Neh 7:59).

8. Descendant of Perez and an ancestor of a Judahite family living in Jerusalem during the postexilic period (Neh 11:4).

9. Son of Mattan and a prince of Judah during the reign of King Zedekiah (597–586 BC). Annoyed with Jeremiah's prophecies of doom for Jerusalem, Shephatiah (with Gedaliah, Jucal, and Pashhur) tried to put him to death. With Zedekiah's permission, they hoped to achieve their ends by imprisoning Jeremiah in a cistern (Jer 38:1).

SHEPHO

One of Shobal's five sons and a descendant of Seir the Horite. Shepho is listed in the genealogy of Abraham through Esau's contact with the nation (Gn 36:23); his name is alternately spelled Shephi (1 Chr 1:40; see NLT mg).

SHEPHUPHAN

Bela's son from Benjamin's tribe. Bela was the firstborn of Benjamin's sons (1 Chr 8:5). The exact position of Shephuphan in Benjamin's genealogy is unclear, and he is perhaps identifiable with Shupham (1 Chr 7:12).

SHEREBIAH

1. Levite, a descendant of Mahli. Sherebiah, described as a man of understanding, was sent as a priest for the Temple at Jerusalem following the Exile (Ezr 8:18; Neh 12:8). During the return journey, he was one of 12 chief priests appointed to guard the silver, gold, and vessels presented for Temple use (Ezr 8:24).
2. One who helped the people understand the law read by Ezra (Neh 8:7), and among the Levites who stood on the stairs leading the praise service (9:4-5).
3. One of the leaders of the Levites who led the songs of praise and thanksgiving (Neh 12:24).

It is possible that the above references refer to the same person.

SHERESH

Makir's son and the brother of Peresh from Manasseh's tribe (1 Chr 7:16).

SHESHAI

Descendant of Anak who was at Hebron when the 12 spies searched out the land of Canaan (Nm 13:22); he was defeated and displaced by Israel (Jos 15:14; Jgs 1:10).

SHESHAN

Descendant of Judah through Jerahmeel, whose family line is traced in 1 Chronicles 2:25-41 to Elishama, evidently a contemporary of the writer. In verse 31 Sheshan's son Ahlai is named, but verse 34 says that Sheshan had no sons. Perhaps two men of the same name are denoted here, or Ahlai may be identical with Attai, Sheshan's grandson.

SHESHBAZZAR

Jewish leader who found favor with Cyrus the Great, king of Persia. In the first year of his reign, Cyrus issued a decree that the Temple in Jerusalem should be rebuilt (Ezr 1:1-4; cf. 6:1-5). He appointed Sheshbazzar governor of Judah (Ezr 5:14) and handed over to him the gold and silver vessels that Nebuchadnezzar had carried off when he took Jerusalem (1:7-9). Sheshbazzar fulfilled this commission by taking the vessels to Jerusalem with the returning exiles (v 9) and beginning the restoration of the Temple (5:16).

Sheshbazzar is mentioned in the Bible only four times, all in the book of Ezra (1:8-9; 5:14-16). For many years it was commonly held that Sheshbazzar was another name for Zerubbabel. Both were of the royal line; Sheshbazzar is called "the prince of Judah," which may mean that he was heir apparent to the throne. Since his genealogy is not given, he may be represented in that listing by some other name, either Zerubbabel or Shenazzar (1 Chr 3:18-19). In the record of people who returned to Jerusalem, Sheshbazzar's name does not appear. The name of Zerubbabel is at the head of this list, where one would expect Sheshbazzar's to be; both were governors of the province of Judah. Zerubbabel is associated with the laying of the foundation of the Temple (Ezr 3:8-11), but that work is attributed to Sheshbazzar in 5:16, in accordance with chapter 1. It is evident that the name Sheshbazzar is found only in connection with the Persians, for chapter 1 relates his dealings with Cyrus, and in chapter 5 the two occurrences of his name are in a letter written by the Persian official, Tattenai. One may conclude that the Persians knew him as Sheshbazzar, but the Jews called him Zerubbabel. Both names are Akkadian, so there is no parallel here to the renaming of Jewish captives in Babylon (Dn 1:7).

SHETH

1. Reference to the sons of Moab, who were the cause of tumult and war to Israel (Nm 24:17).

2. KJV spelling of Seth, Adam's son, in 1 Chronicles 1:1. *See* Seth.

SHETHAR

One of Ahasuerus's seven counselors who, when Queen Vashti defied the king's command, advised him to deprive her of her title and to seek a new queen, as an example of domestic discipline (Est 1:14).

SHETHAR-BOZENAI

Persian official in a province west of the Euphrates River, who joined with Tattenai and his colleagues in writing a letter to Darius Hystaspeis, king of Persia, protesting the rebuilding of the Temple and walls of Jerusalem under Zerubbabel (Ezr 5:3, 6). Darius warned them not to interfere with Zerubbabel's work, and they obeyed him (Ezr 6:6, 13).

SHEVA

1. Scribe or personal secretary of David (2 Sm 20:25). He is called by various names elsewhere. *See* Seraiah #1.

2. Caleb's son in the family of Hezron from Judah's tribe and the father of Macbena and Gibea (1 Chr 2:49).

SHILHI

Grandfather of King Jehoshaphat of Judah (1 Kgs 22:42; 2 Chr 20:31).

SHILLEM

Fourth son of Naphtali (Gn 46:24), and father of the Shillemites (Nm 26:49); alternately called Shallum in 1 Chronicles 7:13.

SHILSHAH

Zophah's son and a chief of Asher's tribe (1 Chr 7:37).

SHIMEA

1. Alternate name for Shammah, Jesse's third son, in 1 Chronicles 2:13 and 20:7. *See* Shammah #2.

2. David's son borne to him by Bathsheba during his reign in Jerusalem (1 Chr 3:5). He is called Shammua in 2 Samuel 5:14 and 1 Chronicles 14:4.

3. Uzzah's son, the father of Haggiah and a descendant of Levi through Merari's line (1 Chr 6:30).

4. Gershonite Levite, Michael's son, the father of Berekiah, and the grandfather of Asaph. Asaph, with Heman and Ethan, was appointed by David to lead the musicians before the sanctuary (1 Chr 6:39).

SHIMEAM

Mikloth's son and the grandson of Jeiel from Benjamin's tribe (1 Chr 8:32; 1 Chr 9:38).

SHIMEATH

Ammonitess mother (2 Chr 24:26) or perhaps father (2 Kgs 12:21) of one of the royal servants who conspired against and murdered King Jehoash of Judah (835–796 BC).

SHIMEI

1. Son of Gershon, the grandson of Levi, and the brother of Libni (Ex 6:17; Nm 3:18; 1 Chr 6:17). He was the father of four sons and the founder of the Shimeite family (Nm 3:21; 1 Chr 23:7, 10; Zech 12:13).

2. Benjaminite, and the son of Gera from the house of Saul. He met King David at the village of Bahurim during the king's journey from Jerusalem to Mahanaim. Here Shimei bitterly opposed David, cursing him for the ruin of Saul's house (2 Sm 16:5-13). Later, Shimei repented of his shameful behavior, entreated David's forgiveness, and received the king's pardon (19:16-23). After David's death, King Solomon ordered Shimei to settle in Jerusalem and never to leave the city for any reason. Shimei disobeyed the decree and was killed (1 Kgs 2:8, 36-44).

3. Brother of David and the father of Jonathan (2 Sm 21:21); alternately called Shammah in 1 Samuel 16:9. *See* Shammah #2.

4. One of David's court officials who did not support Adonijah's attempt to set himself up as king (1 Kgs 1:8).

5. Benjaminite, the son of Ela and one of King Solomon's officials who oversaw the royal household (1 Kgs 4:18); perhaps identical with #4 above.

6. Judahite, the son of Pedaiah, the brother of Zerubbabel, and a descendant of David through Solomon's line (1 Chr 3:19).

7. Simeonite, the son of Zaccur and the father of 16 sons and 6 daughters (1 Chr 4:26-27).

8. Reubenite, the son of Gog and the father of Micah (1 Chr 5:4).

9. Son of Libni, the father of Uzzah, and a descendant of Levi through Merari's line (1 Chr 6:29).

10. Gershonite Levite, the son of Jahath, the father of Zimmah, and an ancestor of Asaph who served as a leader of the musicians in the sanctuary during David's reign (1 Chr 6:42).

11. Benjaminite, the father of nine sons and a head of his father's house (1 Chr 8:21); alternately called Shema in verse 13. *See* Shema #3.

12. Gershonite Levite, and the father of three sons in the house of Ladan (1 Chr 23:9).

13. Son of Jeduthun and the leader of the 10th of 24 divisions of musicians trained for service in the sanctuary during David's reign (1 Chr 25:3, 17).

14. Ramathite, and a member of King David's staff who had charge of David's vineyards (1 Chr 27:27).

15. Son of Heman, the brother of Jehuel, and one of the Levites selected to cleanse the house of the Lord during King Hezekiah's reign (715–686 BC; 2 Chr 29:14).

16. Levite, and the brother of Conaniah appointed by King Hezekiah of Judah to oversee the administration of the Temple contributions in Jerusalem (2 Chr 31:12-13).

17–19. Three men, a Levite, Hashum's son, and Binnui's son, who were encouraged by Ezra to divorce their foreign wives during the postexilic era (Ezr 10:23, 33, 38)

20. Son of Kish and grandfather of Mordecai (Est 2:5).

SHIMEON
Harim's fifth son, who was encouraged by Ezra to divorce his foreign wife whom he had married during the postexilic era (Ezr 10:31).

SHIMON
Head of a Judahite family (1 Chr 4:20).

SHIMRATH
Shimei's son from Benjamin's tribe (1 Chr 8:21).

SHIMRI

1. Simeonite, Shemaiah's son and the father of Jedaiah (1 Chr 4:37).
2. Father of Jediael (and perhaps Joha), two of David's mighty men (1 Chr 11:45).
3. Merarite Levite, Hosah's son and a Temple gatekeeper during David's reign (1 Chr 26:10).
4. Levite, of the family of Elizaphan, who assisted in Hezekiah's Temple reforms (2 Chr 29:13).

SHIMRON

Issachar's fourth son (Gn 46:13; 1 Chr 7:1) and the founder of the Shimronite family (Nm 26:24).

SHIMSHAI

Persian government official whose territory included Palestine. With another official (Rehum), he wrote a letter to Artaxerxes opposing the rebuilding of the Temple by the Jews returned from exile (Ezr 4:8-9). He succeeded in halting the rebuilding project.

SHINAB

King of Admah, who joined an alliance with four neighboring rulers against King Kedorlaomer. Kedorlaomer defeated this confederation of kings in the valley of Siddim— the southern region of the Dead Sea (Gn 14:2).

SHIPHI

Ziza's father and a prince in Simeon's tribe (1 Chr 4:37).

SHIPHRAH

One of two Hebrew midwives who refused to kill Hebrew male infants at Pharaoh's command (Ex 1:15).

SHIPHTAN

Father of Kemuel, a prince of Ephraim appointed by Moses to help divide the land among Israel's 10 tribes west of the Jordan (Nm 34:24).

SHISHA

Alternate name for Seraiah, King David's scribe, in 1 Kings 4:3. *See* Seraiah #1.

SHISHAK

Egyptian pharaoh, descendant of a powerful family of Libyan chieftains, and founder of Egypt's 22nd dynasty. His Egyptian name was Sheshonk. He was a contemporary of

Solomon, Jeroboam, and Rehoboam. His years as ruler are variously given as 940–915 BC or 935–914 BC.

During Solomon's reign, he afforded asylum to Jeroboam, Solomon's servant and subsequent adversary, who escaped to Egypt to avoid being killed by his lord, against whom he had rebelled (1 Kgs 11:40). Since Jeroboam was to set up the northern kingdom after Solomon's death—an event used by God to punish his people for Solomon's sin—Shishak's readiness to harbor the fugitive rebel played a part in God's design to bring about his purposes.

God used Shishak a second time to further his plans. When Judah under Rehoboam became sinful and engaged in idolatrous practices, allowing male shrine prostitutes to operate in the land (a practice not to be equated with the phenomenon of homosexuality as presently known), God used Shishak's invasion of Palestine to punish his people. This invasion took place in the fifth year of Rehoboam's reign (1 Kgs 14:25; cf. 2 Chr 12:2-9). A great number of Judean towns were taken, but God spared Jerusalem from being captured, when the princes and the king showed repentance and humbled themselves (2 Chr 12:7). However, Shishak showed his mastery by plundering both the Temple and royal palace in Jerusalem and by carrying off the gold shields that Solomon had made. Although the biblical account focuses on Shishak's invasion of the Judean area only, extrabiblical data indicate that he also invaded the territory of Jeroboam, to whom he had previously given refuge.

See also Rehoboam; Solomon.

SHITRAI
David's chief shepherd in charge of his flocks in Sharon (1 Chr 27:29).

SHIZA
Reubenite and the father of Adina, one of David's select warriors (1 Chr 11:42).

SHOA
Assyrian people listed with the Babylonians, Chaldeans, and other Assyrian tribes, who were used by the Lord to punish Judah (Ez 23:23).

SHOBAB
1. Second of David's four sons by Bathsheba (2 Sm 5:14; 1 Chr 3:5; 14:4).

2. Caleb's son by his wife Azubah (1 Chr 2:18).

SHOBACH
Commander of the army of Hadadezer, king of Zobah, who led the Ammonite-Syrian campaign against Israel. David's army killed Shobach and so completely destroyed his forces that the Ammonite-Syrian alliance was broken, and the kingdoms that were tributary to Hadadezer became subject to David (2 Sm 10:16-18). He is also called Shophach in 1 Chronicles 19:16-18.

SHOBAI
Ancestor of a group of people who returned to Jerusalem with Zerubbabel after the Babylonian exile (Ezr 2:42; Neh 7:45).

SHOBAL
1. One of the seven sons of Seir the Horite in Edom (Gn 36:20; 1 Chr 1:38). Shobal became the father of five sons (Gn 36:23; 1 Chr 1:40) and a chief among the Horites (Gn 36:29).
2. Hur's son, the father of Haroeh, and the founder of the families of Kiriath-jearim (1 Chr 2:50-52).
3. One of Judah's five sons and the father of Reiah (1 Chr 4:1-2); perhaps the same as #2 above.

SHOBEK
Leader who signed Ezra's covenant of faithfulness to God during the postexilic era (Neh 10:24).

SHOBI
Ammonite prince, son of King Nahash, who, along with Makir of Lo-debar and Barzillai of Rogelim, generously supplied David with food and equipment at Mahanaim during Absalom's rebellion (2 Sm 17:27).

SHOHAM
Merarite Levite, and Jaaziah's son in David's reign (1 Chr 24:27).

SHOMER
1. Father (2 Kgs 12:21), or perhaps the Moabite mother (2 Chr 24:26), of Jehozabad, a royal servant, who, with Jozacar, conspired against and murdered Joash, king of Judah. Shimrith is the feminine form of Shomer.
2. Alternate name for Shemer, Heber's son, in 1 Chronicles 7:34. See Shemer #3.

SHUA
1. Canaanite whose daughter Judah married. She bore Judah three sons: Er, Onan, and Shelah (Gn 38:2-5, 12). See Bathshua #1.
2. Asherite, Heber's daughter and the sister of Japhlet, Shomer, and Hotham (1 Chr 7:32).

SHUAH
1. One of six sons borne to Abraham by Keturah (Gn 25:2; 1 Chr 1:32). He was perhaps the forefather of the Shuhite Arab tribe that dwelt near the land of Uz (Jb 2:11).

2. KJV spelling of Shua, Judah's father-in-law, in Genesis 38:2, 12. *See* Shua #1.

3. KJV spelling of Shuhah, Kelub's brother, in 1 Chronicles 4:11. *See* Shuhah.

SHUAL
Zophah's son and a leader in Asher's tribe (1 Chr 7:36).

SHUBAEL
1. Alternate form of Shebuel, Gershon's son, in 1 Chronicles 24:20. *See* Shebuel #1.

2. Alternate form of Shebuel, Heman's son, in 1 Chronicles 25:20. *See* Shebuel #2.

SHUHAH
Kelub's brother from Judah's tribe (1 Chr 4:11).

SHUHAM
Alternate name for Hushim, Dan's son in Numbers 26:42-43. *See* Hushim #1.

SHUNI
Third of Gad's seven sons (Gn 46:16; Nm 26:15).

SHUPHAM
Benjamin's fourth son (called "Muppim" in Gen 46:21) and the father of the Shuphamite family (Nm 26:39; see NLT mg). In the corresponding genealogy of Benjamin (1 Chr 7:12) he is called Shuppim, appearing as Benjamin's great-grandson. *See* Shuppim #1. *See also* Shephuphan.

SHUPPIM
1. Son of Ir and a great-grandson of Benjamin (1 Chr 7:12). Shuppim is perhaps a shortened form of Shephupham (Shupham), mentioned in Numbers 26:39 as the son of Benjamin. It could also be an alternate spelling for Muppim (Gen 46:21). *See* Shephupham.

2. Levite gatekeeper, who, with Hosah, watched the gate of Shallecheth on the western side of Jerusalem (1 Chr 26:16).

SHUTHELAH
1. Ephraim's son, the brother of Beker and Tahan, and the father of Eran and Bered. He founded the Shuthelahite family and was an ancestor of Joshua the son of Nun (Nm 26:35; 1 Chr 7:20, 27).

2. Zabad's son from Ephraim's tribe (1 Chr 7:21).

SIAHA

Ancestor of a group of Temple assistants who returned to Jerusalem with Zerubbabel following the Exile (Neh 7:47, NLT mg; Ezra 2:44).

SIBBECAI

Zerahite from the town of Hushah and one of David's "mighty men" (1 Chr 11:29; 20:4; 27:11). He is credited with killing the giant Saph when Israel fought Philistia at Gob (2 Sm 21:18). In 2 Samuel 23:27 he is called Mebunnai, probably a later erroneous reading of the original.

SIDON

Canaan's firstborn son; Canaan was the son of Ham and grandson of Noah (Gn 10:15, 19; 1 Chr 1:13). Sidon founded a city (bearing his name) that set the northern boundary of the land of Canaan and later played a dominant role in Palestinian history.

SIHON

King of the Amorites who ruled in Heshbon, about 14 miles (22.5 kilometers) east of the north end of the Dead Sea. His defeat by Israel under Moses, together with that of Og, king of Bashan, is frequently mentioned in OT prose and poetry, in narrative and song (Dt 1:4; 2:26-37; 4:46; 29:7; 31:4; Jos 2:10; 9:10; 12:2-6; 13:10-12). In the eyes of the sacred writers, this dual defeat is so significant that it can be ranked with the Exodus as one of the singular manifestations of God's saving intervention on behalf of his people (Pss 135:11; 136:19-20), and as evidence of his everlasting love for them. In the postexilic period this event is recalled in prayer as a pleading ground for God's continuing mercy to the returned exiles (Neh 9:22).

Before Israel's arrival in Transjordan, Sihon had conquered Moab's territory as far south as the Arnon River (Nm 21:26). This conquest gives rise to a piece of ancient poetry that is incorporated into sacred Scripture (vv 27-30). Sihon's realm extends from the Arnon on the south to the Jabbok on the north, with the Jordan as its western boundary. It also includes the Jordan Valley as far as the Sea of Kinnereth (Jos 12:2-3), comprising part of the region known as Gilead. On the east it extends toward the desert and touches on Ammonite land.

Sihon's refusal to grant Israel passage through his domain is similar to that of Edom (cf. Nm 21:23 with 20:20). However, Sihon exhibits overt hostility toward Israel. Sihon was defeated and killed at Jahaz; his country was occupied by Israel. Subsequently, it was distributed to the tribes of Gad and Reuben (cf. Nm 32:33-38; Jos 13:10).

SILAS

Respected leader in the Jerusalem church, also called Silvanus (2 Cor 1:19; 1 Thes 1:1; 2 Thes 1:1; 1 Pt 5:12). "Silas" is most likely the Aramaic form of the Hebrew name "Saul," which, when given a Latin form, became *Silouanos* (Silvanus). Silas thus carried two names—a

QUICKTAKE

SILAS

STRENGTHS AND ACCOMPLISHMENTS
- A leader in the Jerusalem church
- Represented the church in carrying the "acceptance letter" prepared by the Jerusalem council to the Gentile believers in Antioch
- Was closely associated with Paul from the second missionary journey on
- Sang songs of praise to God while in jail with Paul in Philippi,
- Worked as a writing secretary for both Paul and Peter

LESSONS FROM HIS LIFE
- Partnership is a significant part of effective ministry
- God never guarantees that his servants will not suffer
- Obedience to God will often mean giving up what makes us feel secure

VITAL STATISTICS
Where: Roman citizen living in Jerusalem
Occupation: One of the first career missionaries
Contemporaries: Paul, Timothy, Peter, Mark, Barnabas

KEY VERSES
"So we decided, having come to complete agreement, to send you official representatives, along with our beloved Barnabas and Paul, who have risked their lives for the name of our Lord Jesus Christ. We are sending Judas and Silas to confirm what we have decided concerning your question" (Acts 15:25-27).

Silas's story is told in Acts 15:22–19:10. He is also mentioned in 2 Corinthians 1:19; 1 Thessalonians 1:1; 2 Thessalonians 1:1; 1 Peter 5:12.

Latin and a shorter, Semitic name. The name was known in the Hellenistic era and appears in various inscriptions. Luke used the name Silas when he narrated the history of the Jerusalem church in Acts. Paul and Peter used the Roman name in their epistles.

Silas is introduced in Acts 15:22 as a distinguished delegate who conveyed to Antioch the decree of the Jerusalem Council. Several manuscripts (of lesser quality than the best-attested ones) include 15:34; this added verse indicates that Silas remained in Antioch, because shortly thereafter he joined Paul on his second missionary tour (Acts 15:40). His service as a prophet may be evident in Acts 16:6, when the Spirit redirected the company through Asia. Silas's name appears eight times within the second tour (Acts 16:19, 25, 29; 17:4, 10, 14-15;

18:5), as he accompanied Paul through the hardships suffered at Philippi, Thessalonica, and Berea. When Paul was safely ushered out of Macedonia by the Berean Christians (17:14), Silas remained behind with Timothy to oversee the work already begun in the region. Later in Corinth (18:5), Silas and Timothy rejoined Paul. Their report prompted Paul to correspond with the church at Thessalonica. This explains Silas's name in the prescript of both 1 and 2 Thessalonians.

It seems clear that Silas was well known to the Corinthians. Not only does he stay in the city with Paul for a year and a half (Acts 18:11), but it may be conjectured that he stayed behind in Corinth after the dispute before Gallio. Paul, on his final tour, wrote to Corinth from Ephesus and mentioned Silas again (2 Cor 1:19), reminding the Corinthians of the earlier ministry among them.

The subsequent history of Silas is obscure. Some believe Silas was a respected Christian scribe. Silas's involvement in 1 and 2 Thessalonians is often mentioned, pointing to Paul's sustained use of the first person plural. Some scholars find resemblances among 1 and 2 Thessalonians, the decree of Acts 15, and 1 Peter, where Silas is mentioned as a scribe (1 Pt 5:12). This latter association with Peter is intriguing and has led to the speculation that Silas ultimately joined Peter and ministered in north Asia.

SIMEON

1. Second of the 12 sons of Jacob (Gn 35:23; 1 Chr 2:1) and the second son borne to him by Leah (Gn 29:33). Simeon fathered six sons (Ex 6:15) and settled his family in Egypt with Jacob and his brothers (1:2). He was the founder of the Simeonites (Nm 26:12-14) and one of the 12 tribes of Israel (1:23). He is remembered most for his vengeance on the men of Shechem because of Dinah's rape (Gn 34:25).

2. Pious Jew living in Jerusalem who was assured that he would not die before he saw the promised Messiah. Led by the Holy Spirit to the Temple, Simeon met Mary and Joseph there, held Jesus in his arms, and prophesied about the Messiah's coming mission (Lk 2:25-35).

3. Ancestor of Jesus in Luke's genealogy (Lk 3:30).

4. One of five prophets and teachers mentioned in Acts 13:1 who was serving in the church of Antioch. Simeon was surnamed Niger and was perhaps from Africa. Symeon is a better reading of the Greek in this text.

5. Reference to Simon Peter in Acts 15:14. *See* Peter, The Apostle.

SIMON

Greek form of a Hebrew/Aramaic name meaning "God has heard." Nine men in the NT had this name:

1. Son of Jona (Mt 16:17) or John (Jn 1:42), Andrew's brother (v 40), and surnamed Cephas and Peter (respectively Aramaic and Greek, for "rock," v 42) by Jesus. A

fisherman of Bethsaida (Mk 1:16; Jn 1:44), he became an apostle of Jesus and author of two NT letters bearing his name. *See* Peter, The Apostle.

2. Brother of Jesus, named with other brothers, James, Joses or Joseph, and Judas (Mt 13:55; Mk 6:3).

3. Leper, perhaps cured by Jesus, in whose house at Bethany Jesus and his disciples were eating when a woman poured an alabaster flask of costly ointment on the Lord's head. Over the disciples' objections against the waste of what could have been sold to support the poor, Jesus commended the act as a wonderful thing (Mt 26:6-13; Mk 14:3-9). From John 12:1-8 it appears that Simon's house was also the house of Mary, Martha, and Lazarus, but their relationship to Simon is uncertain.

4. Man of Cyrene, a district of North Africa, whom the Romans forced to carry Jesus' cross (Mt 27:32; Mk 15:21; Lk 23:26). He was the father of Alexander and Rufus (Mk 15:21; cf. Rom 16:13).

5. Apostle of Jesus called a Zealot (Lk 6:15), presumably because of prior association either with the party of political extremists by that name, who adopted terrorism to oppose the Roman occupation of Palestine, or with one of a number of Jewish groups noted for their zeal for the law. In Matthew 10:4 and Mark 3:18 he is designated the "Cananaean" (RSV)—from the Aramaic word for "zealot." He is mentioned again in Acts 1:13 as one of the 11 apostles in Jerusalem after Jesus' ascension. Otherwise, the NT is silent about him.

6. Pharisee whose treatment of Jesus evoked the parable of the two debtors (Lk 7:36-50). He invited Jesus to eat at his house but withheld courtesies customary for guests and disapproved of Jesus' acceptance of a "sinner" woman who wet the Lord's feet with her tears, dried them with her hair, and anointed them with ointment from an alabaster flask. Jesus' parable contrasted the woman's act of loving and repentant faith with Simon's unloving and self-righteous skepticism.

7. Father of Judas Iscariot, the disciple who betrayed Jesus in Gethsemane (Jn 6:71; 13:2, 26).

8. Magician (often called Simon Magus) of great repute in Samaria. Impressed by the signs and miracles performed by Philip the deacon-become-evangelist, he joined the crowd of baptized believers. He offered Peter and John money in exchange for the gift of the Holy Spirit, provoking Peter's emphatic rebuke (Acts 8:9-24). From the association of this incident with his name, the English word "simony" is derived; it denotes the sale or purchase of church positions, or any profiteering from sacred things.

9. Tanner of Joppa. Peter lodged at his house for many days (Acts 9:43; 10:6, 17, 32). On Simon's housetop, Peter experienced the vision of a great sheet let down from heaven, containing animals and birds prohibited as food in Jewish law (10:15). Peter later recognized this vision as his preparation for consenting to preach the gospel to the Gentiles (vv 28-29).

SIMON PETER

See Peter, The Apostle.

SIMON THE ZEALOT

One of Jesus' disciples (Mt 10:4; Mk 3:18; Lk 6:15; Acts 1:13). *See* Simon #5.

SISERA

1. Commander of the army of Jabin, king of Canaan. Sisera resided in Harosheth-haggoyim, from where he attacked northern Israel for 20 years. His army, strengthened by 900 iron chariots, was routed at the swollen river of Kishon near Megiddo under the leadership of Barak and Deborah. Having fled the battlefield, Sisera was killed by the hand of Jael, the wife of Heber the Kenite, in the hill country overlooking the Jordan Valley (Jgs 4; 1 Sm 12:9). The events of this battle were remembered in the Song of Deborah (Jgs 5:19-30) and Psalm 83:9.

2. Forefather of a family of Temple servants who returned with Zerubbabel to Palestine following the Babylonian captivity (Ezr 2:53; Neh 7:55).

SISMAI

Eleasah's son and the father of Shallum; a Judahite from the house of Hezron and Jerahmeel's line (1 Chr 2:40).

SITHRI

Kohathite Levite and Uzziel's third son. Sithri was the cousin of Aaron and Moses (Ex 6:22).

SO

A king of Egypt, mentioned once in Scripture (2 Kgs 17:4), with whom Hoshea, king of Israel, sought an alliance. This rebellious move, in part, prompted Shalmaneser V of Assyria to imprison Hoshea (2 Kgs 17:3-5). It is difficult to identify So with any of the rulers of Egypt who are named in extrabiblical sources.

SOCO

Son of Heber, listed in the genealogy of Caleb (1 Chr 4:18). Since the Calebites were located in the southern hill country of Judah, Soco may be identified with the city in Joshua 15:48.

SODI

Father of Gaddiel, one of the 12 spies sent by Moses to search out the land of Canaan (Nm 13:10).

SOLOMON

Third king over Israel, the second son of David and Bathsheba, who reigned 40 years (970–930 BC). His alternative name was Jedidiah, "beloved of the Lord."

QUICKTAKE

SOLOMON

STRENGTHS AND ACCOMPLISHMENTS
• Third king of Israel, David's chosen heir
• The wisest man who ever lived
• Author of Ecclesiastes and Song of Songs, as well as many of the proverbs and a couple of the psalms
• Built God's Temple in Jerusalem
• Diplomat, trader, collector, patron of the arts

WEAKNESSES AND MISTAKES
• Sealed many foreign agreements by marrying pagan women
• Allowed his wives to affect his loyalty to God
• Excessively taxed his people and drafted them into a labor and military force

LESSONS FROM HIS LIFE
• Effective leadership can be nullified by an ineffective personal life
• Solomon failed to obey God, but did not learn the lesson of repentance until late in life
• Knowing what actions are required of us means little without the will to do those actions

VITAL STATISTICS
Where: Jerusalem
Occupation: King of Israel
Relatives: Father: David. Mother: Bathsheba. Brothers: Absalom, Adonijah. Sister: Tamar. Son: Rehoboam

KEY VERSE
"Wasn't this exactly what led King Solomon of Israel into sin?" I demanded. "There was no king from any nation who could compare to him, and God loved him and made him king over all Israel. But even he was led into sin by his foreign wives" (Nehemiah 13:26).

Solomon's story is told in 2 Samuel 12:24–1 Kings 11:43. He is also mentioned in 1 Chronicles 28–29; 2 Chronicles 1–10; Nehemiah 13:26; Psalm 72; and Matthew 6:29; 12:42.

Appointed to the Throne

Once Amnon and Absalom were no longer in competition for the throne, the two most likely remaining candidates were Solomon and Adonijah, although the kingship had been assured to the former (1 Chr 22:9-10). Near the end of David's life, Adonijah contested the choice of Solomon and took steps to become king. With the help of Joab, general of the army, and Abiathar the priest, he was proclaimed the monarch. Solomon was not invited and neither were Nathan the prophet or Benaiah. Nathan brought word of this plot to Bathsheba, who in turn quizzed David as to his intentions. David then ordered Solomon to be proclaimed king over Israel; he was anointed by Zadok amidst the blowing of the trumpets and the shout of the people: "Long live King Solomon" (1 Kgs 1:34). Adonijah realized his claim had collapsed and asked for mercy, promising to be faithful to the new king.

Solomon moved swiftly to establish his hold on the government (1 Kgs 1–2). When Adonijah asked to marry Abishag, David's companion in his old age (1:1-4), Solomon refused and ordered his death because of possible claims to the throne (2:22-25). In addition, because Abiathar had joined with Adonijah, he was removed from his service as priest and sent back to Anathoth. Joab fled to the altar and there took hold of its horns and refused to let go. The king ordered his death at the hand of Benaiah, who then became commander-in-chief of the armies. Another contender, Shimei, of the house of Saul, was also executed.

One of Solomon's earliest recorded acts as king was to go to the high place at Gibeon and sacrifice 1,000 burnt offerings. On the following night, the Lord appeared to the king in a dream, asking as to his fondest wish. Solomon asked for wisdom to judge Israel, and God was pleased with the request (1 Kgs 3). Israel's king was given his wish, along with the gifts of long life, riches, and fame.

Solomon's Accomplishments

His Government

David's efforts had brought about a union of the 12 tribes, but Solomon established an organized state with many officials to help him (1 Kgs 4). The entire country was divided into 12 major districts; each district was to ensure the provisions of the king's court for one month each year. The system was equitable and designed to distribute the tax burden over the entire country.

His Buildings

One of Solomon's earliest building attempts was to construct the Temple. David had wanted to build the Temple, but this task was left to Solomon, the man of peace. Hiram, king of Tyre, provided cedar trees from Mt Lebanon for the Temple (1 Kgs 5:1-12), and in return he was given an appropriate amount of food. In order to provide the necessary labor for these building projects, the Canaanites became slaves (9:20-21). Israelites likewise were compelled to work in groups of 10,000, every third month (5:13-18; 2 Chr 2:17-18). The workers for the Temple alone comprised 80,000 stonecutters, 70,000 common laborers, and 3,600 foremen.

It took seven years to finish the Temple, which by modern standards was a rather small building: 90 feet (27.4 meters) long, 30 feet (9.1 meters) wide, and 45 feet (13.7 meters) high. Nevertheless, the gold covering for both walls and furniture made it quite expensive.

In the 11th year of Solomon's reign, the dedication of the Temple was celebrated in a great convocation (1 Kgs 6:38; 8:1-5). The presence of the Lord filled the Temple, and Solomon then offered his great dedicatory prayer (8:23-53), marking it as one of the great peaks of his devotion to the Lord. Afterward, he offered up 22,000 oxen and 120,000 sheep as well as other offerings. The people were full of joy because David had so great a successor.

Solomon built other buildings: the House of the Forest of Lebanon, the Hall of Pillars, a hall for his throne, and a house for the daughter of Pharaoh (1 Kgs 7:2-8). Thirteen years were involved in the building of his own house, large enough to take care of his wives and concubines as well as the servants. A great fortress was also built, Millo, which was used to protect the Temple (9:24), as well as other store and fortified cities.

His Trade with Other Nations

The king had an agreement with Hiram, king of Tyre, to pay yearly for cedar trees, stone-cutters, and other buildings; for 125,000 bushels (4.4 million liters) of wheat; and for 115,000 gallons (435,275 liters) of olive oil (1 Kgs 5:11). In addition, Hiram received 20 cities in Galilee to cover all indebtedness. Contrary to the instruction not to trade in horses (Dt 17:16), Solomon bought horses and chariots from the Egyptians, and some of these in turn were sold to the Hittites and Arameans at a profit (1 Kgs 10:28-29).

Furthermore, Solomon engaged in sea trade. Ships built at shipyards at Ezion-geber sailed to ports on the Red Sea and Indian Ocean. The mariners collected gold, ivory, and peacocks. From Ophir, the traders brought back 420 talents of gold, a considerable fortune.

His Wisdom

Solomon wrote 3,000 proverbs and 1,005 songs (1 Kgs 4:32). Most of the book of Proverbs is attributed to him (Prv 25:1), as well as Ecclesiastes, Song of Solomon, and Psalms 72 and 127. His obituary notice mentions his literary accomplishments in the book of the acts of Solomon (1 Kgs 11:41).

The queen of Sheba came to see and hear if the reports of Solomon's fame and wisdom were correct. After viewing all he had in Jerusalem and hearing his wisdom, her final response was to bless the Lord God of Israel, who raised up such a wise person to sit upon such a magnificent throne (1 Kgs 10).

His Fall

Solomon made many misjudgments during his reign, and one of them was his excessive taxation of the people. His worst blunder was adding more and more wives to his harem, accommodating their religious preferences with pagan shrines (1 Kgs 11:1-8). The Lord plagued Solomon, permitting Israel to be attacked on all sides. Although the kingdom was not damaged during Solomon's day, his son experienced its division. There is no record that Solomon repented, but it is quite possible that the book of Ecclesiastes does reveal his realization of his wrong decisions.

SOPATER

Man from the church at Berea who, with others, accompanied Paul to Jerusalem to deliver the offering collected by the gentile churches for the Jewish Christians who were suffering from the effects of a famine (Acts 20:4). Sopater is perhaps identical to Sosipater, the kinsman of Paul who sent greetings to the church at Rome (Rom 16:21).

SOSIPATER

Jewish Christian who joined Paul, Timothy, Lucius, and Jason in sending greetings to the church at Rome (Rom 16:21).

SOSTHENES

1. Leader of the synagogue in Corinth who brought legal action against Paul before Gallio, proconsul of Achaia. Upon hearing Gallio's dismissal of the Jewish accusations against Paul, a mob, possibly of Greeks, seized Sosthenes and beat him (Acts 18:17).

2. Christian brother and companion of Paul, known to the Christians at Corinth and mentioned by Paul in 1 Corinthians 1:1.

SOTAI

Head of a family of Temple servants who returned to Jerusalem with Zerubbabel following the Exile (Ezr 2:55; Neh 7:57).

STACHYS

Christian in Rome to whom Paul sent greetings, calling him "my beloved" (Rom 16:9).

STEPHANAS

Christian believer at Corinth. He and his household were evidently Paul's first converts in Achaia. The members of Stephanas's family were some of the few Corinthian believers personally baptized by Paul. Stephanas and his kin were praised for their devotion and service to the Corinthian church. Stephanas, with Fortunatus and Achaicus, visited Paul at Ephesus in Asia Minor. Their mission probably included bringing aid for Paul's personal needs and seeking his advice for resolving the problems in the Corinthian church. Undoubtedly, Paul wrote and sent his first letter to the Corinthian church with this small delegation when they returned to Corinth (1 Cor 1:16; 16:15-17).

STEPHEN

One of the first deacons and the first martyr of the apostolic church. For Luke, Stephen represents the growing Hellenistic interest of certain members in the early Jerusalem church. In addition, Stephen's major speech (Acts 7:1-53) serves as a critique of traditional Judaism and suggests evangelization beyond Judea.

QUICKTAKE

STEPHEN

STRENGTHS AND ACCOMPLISHMENTS
- One of seven leaders chosen to supervise food distribution to the needy in the early church
- Known for his spiritual qualities of faith, wisdom, grace, and power, and for the Spirit's presence in his life
- Outstanding leader, teacher, and debater
- First to give his life for the gospel

LESSONS FROM HIS LIFE
- Striving for excellence in small assignments prepares one for greater responsibilities
- Real understanding of God always leads to practical and compassionate actions toward people

VITAL STATISTICS
Church responsibilities: Deacon—distributing food to the needy
Contemporaries: Paul, Caiaphas, Gamaliel, the apostles

KEY VERSES
"And as they stoned him, Stephen prayed, 'Lord Jesus, receive my spirit.' He fell to his knees, shouting, 'Lord, don't charge them with this sin!' And with that, he died" (Acts 7:59, 60).

Stephen's story is told in Acts 6:3–8:2. He is also mentioned in Acts 11:19; 22:20.

In Acts 6, Luke tells us of the first division in the early church. The community consisted of two Jewish groups described as "Hebrews" and "Hellenists." These terms no doubt indicate cultural and linguistic divisions: Jews who had emerged from either Aramaic- or Greek-speaking synagogues. Stephen was one of seven deacons nominated to serve the needs of the Hellenists. Yet even in his introduction it is evident that his importance stands out; he alone is described as "full of faith and of the Holy Spirit" (v 5). After their commission Stephen is mentioned again as "full of grace and power," and as doing "great wonders and signs among the people" (v 8).

Stephen's preaching put him in contention with the Hellenistic synagogues of Jerusalem (Acts 6:9). As his subsequent speech before the Sanhedrin indicates, Stephen propounded a radical abrogation of the ancestral customs of Judaism and the Temple cult. Luke's account of his arrest and interrogation (6:10–7:60) is intended to evoke memories of Jesus' trial. While capital punishment was reserved for the Roman governor once Judea had become a province, offenses against the Temple still could be prosecuted by the Sanhedrin. In the end, Stephen's execution by stoning is pursued with a vengeance (7:54-60). As the first martyr of the church, Stephen models Jesus even in death. He commits his spirit to Jesus (as Christ had done to the Father, Lk 23:46) and dies asking forgiveness for his prosecutors (Acts 7:59-60).

The speech in Acts 7 not only provides us with Stephen's defense but in addition serves Luke's broader interests in the spread of the gospel abroad (Acts 1:8). It is the longest speech in Acts and appears at a pivotal place in apostolic history. Stephen provides a critical recital of biblical history and argues that the major pillars upon which Judaism rested were in jeopardy. The Temple, in which the Jews took pride, was not a divine invention—Solomon's Temple was contrary to the earlier Tabernacle in the wilderness. The Torah, in which religious security was sought, was used by Stephen to chronicle Israel's consistent disobedience. These same scriptures announced the coming of "the righteous one," whom Israel crucified.

The implications of the speech are vital. God is free to move beyond the national/religious boundaries of Judaism. The exclusivistic outlook of Judaism is artificial. God's work is dynamic. And if Stephen's conclusions are correct, the Jewish church ought to be free to take the gospel beyond Judea. Stephen's martyrdom introduced a major persecution in Jerusalem (Acts 8:1-3), which was followed by the proclamation of the gospel to the Samaritans and then the Greeks.

SUAH
Zophah's son, who was a leader in his father's household and a mighty warrior in Asher's tribe (1 Chr 7:36).

SUSANNA
One of the women who ministered to Jesus out of her own resources (Lk 8:3).

SUSI
Gaddi's father from Manasseh's tribe. Gaddi was one of the 12 spies sent to search out the land of Canaan (Nm 13:11).

SYNTYCHE
Woman encouraged by Paul to reconcile her differences with Euodia. Syntyche worked with Paul in proclaiming the gospel and evidently held a position of leadership in the Philippian church (Phil 4:2).

TABBAOTH

Ancestor of a family of Temple servants who returned to Jerusalem with Zerubbabel after the Exile (Ezr 2:43; Neh 7:46).

TABEEL

1. Ruler in Samaria who, with his associates, wrote a letter to King Artaxerxes I of Persia (464–424 BC) protesting Zerubbabel's rebuilding of the Jerusalem wall (Ezr 4:7).
2. Father of the man whom King Pekah of Israel and King Rezin of Syria wanted to put on the throne of Jerusalem after they conquered it and subdued Ahaz, king of Judah (735–715 BC; Is 7:6).

TABITHA

Aramaic name meaning "gazelle"; the name in Greek is Dorcas (Acts 9:36, 40). *See* Dorcas.

TABRIMMON

Hezion's son and the father of Ben-hadad I, king of Syria (1 Kgs 15:18).

TAHAN

1. Ephraim's son and the father of the Tahanite family (Nm 26:35).
2. Telah's son and a descendant of Ephraim (1 Chr 7:25).

TAHASH

Son of Nahor and Reumah his concubine; Abraham's brother (Gn 22:24).

TAHATH

1. Son of Assir and a descendant of Levi through Kohath's line. He was an ancestor of Heman, one of David's musicians, and the father of Uriel and Zephaniah (1 Chr 6:24, 37).
2. Ephraimite, the son of Bered and the father of Eleadah (1 Chr 7:20).
3. Ephraimite, the son of Eleadah and the father of Zabad (1 Chr 7:20).

TAHPENES

Egyptian queen who lived during the reigns of David (1010–970 BC) and Solomon (970–930 BC). Pharaoh gave her sister to Hadad the Edomite in marriage. Tahpenes's sister bore to Hadad a son named Genubath (1 Kgs 11:19-20).

TAHREA

A descendant of King Saul, in 1 Chronicles 8:35 and 9:41. An alternate spelling is Tarea.

TALMAI

1. Son of Anak and brother of Ahiman and Sheshai. Talmai and his people were observed by the 12 Israelite spies when they searched out the land (Nm 13:22). Later, Caleb successfully defeated Talmai and his brothers, who were living in Hebron (Jos 15:14; Jgs 1:10).

2. Son of Ammihud and father of Maacah. Maacah gave birth to Absalom, David's third son (2 Sm 3:3; 1 Chr 3:2). Absalom eventually sought refuge in Talmai's small kingdom of Geshur after murdering Amnon (2 Sm 13:37).

TALMON

Head of a Levite family who served as Temple gatekeepers (1 Chr 9:17). His descendants returned from the Exile with Zerubbabel and served as gatekeepers in the rebuilt Temple (Ezr 2:42; Neh 7:45; 11:19; 12:25).

TAMAR

1. Wife of Er, the firstborn son of Judah by a Canaanitess. Later, as a widow, Tamar bore two sons to Judah named Perez and Zerah (Gn 38:6-24; 1 Chr 2:4). Tamar preserved the line of Judah through Perez (Ru 4:12), and her name is recorded in the genealogy of Christ (Mt 1:3).

2. Sister of Absalom and the daughter of David by his wife Maacah, the Geshurite. Through deceit, Tamar was seduced by Amnon, her half brother. In vengeance, Absalom, her full brother, had Amnon murdered at Baal-hazor (2 Sm 13; 1 Chr 3:9).

3. Daughter of Absalom who was noted for her beauty (2 Sm 14:27). She perhaps married Uriel of Gibeah and became the mother of Maacah. See Maacah #4.

TANHUMETH

Seraiah's father from the town of Netophah in Judah. Seraiah was the captain of an army of Netophathite men, who served under Gedaliah during the Babylonian suzerainty (2 Kgs 25:23; Jer 40:8).

TAPHATH

Solomon's daughter and the wife of Ben-abinadab, Solomon's officer in Naphoth-dor (1 Kgs 4:11).

TAPPUAH

Hebron's son and a descendant of Caleb from Judah's tribe (1 Chr 2:43).

TARSHISH

1. One of Javan's four sons and a descendant of Noah through Japheth's line (1 Chr 1:7).

2. Sixth of Bilhan's seven sons. He was a capable leader in Benjamin's tribe and numbered among those able to go to war (1 Chr 7:10).

3. One of the seven princes of Persia and Media. These men had personal access to King Ahasuerus's presence and positions of honor second only to the king himself (Est 1:14).

TATTENAI
Persian governor of a province west of the Euphrates River who opposed the rebuilding of the Jerusalem Temple and walls under Zerubbabel during the postexilic period (Ezr 5:3, 6; 6:6, 13).

TEBAH
Son of Abraham's brother Nahor (Gn 22:24). His mother was Reumah, Nahor's concubine.

TEBALIAH
Son of Hosah, a Merarite Levite and a Temple gatekeeper who served during the postexilic period (1 Chr 26:11).

TEHINNAH
Forefather of the people of Ir-nahash in Judah's tribe (1 Chr 4:12).

TELAH
Resheph's son, father of Tahan, and an ancestor of Joshua the son of Nun from Ephraim's tribe (1 Chr 7:25).

TELEM
One of the gatekeepers who was encouraged by Ezra to divorce his foreign wife (Ezr 10:24).

TEMA
Ninth son of Ishmael who became chief of a powerful nomadic tribe in the north Arabian wilderness (Gn 25:15; 1 Chr 1:30; Jer 25:23). The descendants of Tema were primarily caravan traders who controlled access to important routes across the desert (Jb 6:19). Tema was also associated with the territory and a town.

TEMAH
Forefather of a family of Temple servants who returned with Zerubbabel to Jerusalem following the Exile (Ezr 2:53; Neh 7:55).

TEMAN
One of the chiefs of the Edomites and Eliphaz's firstborn son (Gn 36:11, 15, 42; 1 Chr 1:36, 53). He was likely either the founder or a chief of the Edomite city of Teman.

TEMENI
Ashhur's son by his wife Naarah, and a descendant of Judah (1 Chr 4:6).

TERAH

Father of Abram (Abraham), Nahor, and Haran (Gn 11:26, 1 Chr 1:26; Lk 3:34). Though Abram is listed first among his sons, it is likely that Abram was not the oldest. After Terah lived 70 years, he fathered Abram, Nahor, and Haran (Gn 11:26). Stephen reports in the NT, however, that Abram left Haran after the death of his father, at which time Abram was 75 years old (Gn 12:4; Act 7:4). Terah died at the age of 205 (v 32), which suggests that Terah was at least 130 when Abram was born. Terah initiated the trip to Canaan, though he failed to go beyond Haran (Gn 11:31-32). Abram was commanded there to leave his family and proceed to Canaan (12:1).

See also Abraham.

TERESH

One of two chamberlains who guarded the chambers of King Ahasuerus (Xerxes). When the two planned to kill the king, Mordecai discovered their plot and informed Esther, who in turn told the king. The guards were hanged (Est 2:21-23; 6:2).

TERTIUS

Paul's amanuensis (secretary) for the book of Romans (Rom 16:22). Since his name is a common Roman name, he was probably Roman and known by the recipients of the letter. The supposition that Tertius is the same person as Silas because their names had similar meanings in Latin and Hebrew lacks any biblical or traditional evidence.

TERTULLUS

Prosecuting attorney chosen by the Sanhedrin to lead in the trial of Paul before Felix, Roman procurator of Judea (Acts 24:1-2). It is not clear whether Tertullus was a Roman, Greek, or Jew. The chief arguments that he was a Jew come from references to "our law" and to the mention that Lysias had taken Paul from "our hands." However, these words are part of two verses (vv 6b-7) that are not included in the most ancient manuscripts.

From the speed with which the Jews were able to bring him forward, he was probably a professional attorney who practiced law regularly in the Roman court. His speech (Acts 24:2-8) begins with a word of flattery for Felix. Then he proceeds to charge Paul with being a public nuisance, a disturber of the peace, and a leader of the sect of the Nazarenes. All of these were serious charges in Roman law.

THADDAEUS, THE APOSTLE

One of the 12 original apostles according to the lists in Mark 3:18 and Matthew 10:3 (KJV "Lebbaeus, whose surname was Thaddaeus"). It is quite likely that this is the same person as Judas son of James (not Iscariot) in Luke 6:16 and Acts 1:13.

THEOPHILUS

Person to whom the books of Luke and Acts are addressed (Lk 1:3; Acts 1:1). Since Theophilus can be translated "lover of God" or "loved of God," many have suggested that Theophilus is a title rather than a proper name and that it designates the general audience of the books. However, the use of such generic titles is contrary to ordinary NT practice. Furthermore, the adjective "most excellent" generally designates an individual, particularly one of high rank. Paul addressed Festus as "most excellent," and Claudius Lysias and Tertullus addressed Felix in the same manner (Acts 23:26; 24:2-3; 26:25). Though Theophilus may well have had some noble standing, it is difficult to speculate what his position might have been.

THEUDAS

Rebel referred to by Gamaliel in his speech before the Sanhedrin as an example of the fact that false messiahs would fall without anyone's intervention (Acts 5:36). Theudas evidently led an unsuccessful rebellion against Rome in which he and 400 others were killed. A chronological difficulty is created by the fact that Josephus reports a rebellion led by Theudas during the reign of Claudius as occurring around AD 44, which is seven to ten years *after* Gamaliel's speech. While critics have offered this apparent anachronism as evidence that Luke (or some later editor) was in error, several other solutions are possible. Possibly the error is in Josephus's report rather than Luke's, or two different individuals named Theudas are intended. During the final years of Herod the Great, several rebellions occurred, one of which may have been instigated by Theudas. It has been suggested (without any direct evidence) that Herod's slave Simon may have adopted the name Theudas when he gained freedom and subsequently rebelled against Herod. While the identity of Theudas remains unknown, this fact does not necessarily discredit the historical accuracy of Luke's narrative.

THOMAS, THE APOSTLE

One of the 12 apostles whose name appears in all four Gospels. The name is a transliteration of an Aramaic word meaning "twin" and appears in the NT as Thomas. Among Greek Christians, there was a tendency to use his Hellenistic name, Didymus (*didumos*, "twin"); this name appears three times in John (Jn 11:16; 20:24; 21:2). There is ample evidence from koine papyri that the name Didymus was well known in the NT era.

Thomas appears in each synoptic list of apostles (Mt 10:3; Mk 3:18; Lk 6:15; cf. Acts 1:13) but plays no further role. His celebrated appearance in the fourth Gospel is interesting. Here Thomas expresses the despair of the final approach to Jerusalem (Jn 11:16) and presses Jesus to explain his words of departure in the upper room (14:5). In the Gospel's closing scenes is the familiar episode in which Thomas doubts the Lord's resurrection (20:24) and then is given compelling proof (vv 26-28), after which Thomas called Jesus "my Lord and my God." Thomas is also named in John's epilogue (21:2).

Two apocryphal, pseudepigraphical works bear Thomas's name: the Gospel of Thomas (from Nag Hammadi), which records 114 "secret sayings which the living Jesus spoke" and which Thomas is said to have preserved; and the Acts of Thomas (extant in both Greek and Syriac), which says that Jesus and Thomas were twins (sharing similar appearances and destinies) and that the apostle obtained secret teachings. This

QUICKTAKE

THOMAS

STRENGTHS AND ACCOMPLISHMENTS
- One of Jesus' 12 disciples
- Intense both in doubt and belief
- Was a loyal and honest man

WEAKNESSES AND MISTAKES
- Along with the others, abandoned Jesus at his arrest
- Refused to believe the others' claims to have seen Christ and demanded proof
- Struggled with a pessimistic outlook

LESSONS FROM HIS LIFE
- Jesus does not reject doubts that are honest and directed toward belief
- Better to doubt out loud than to disbelieve in silence

VITAL STATISTICS
Where: Galilee, Judea, Samaria
Occupation: Disciple of Jesus
Contemporaries: Jesus, other disciples, Herod, Pilate

KEY VERSES
"Then he said to Thomas, 'Put your finger here, and look at my hands. Put your hand into the wound in my side. Don't be faithless any longer. Believe!'
'My Lord and my God!' Thomas exclaimed" (John 20:27, 28).

Thomas's story is told in the Gospels. He is also mentioned in Acts 1:13.

apocryphal account even explains Thomas's fate. Against his wishes, Thomas traveled to India under the command of the Lord. There he was martyred with spears by the hand of an Indian king. He was raised up and his empty tomb took on magical properties. Today in St. Thomas, India, Christians assert that they are the spiritual descendants of the apostle.

TIBERIUS
Roman emperor (AD 14–37) during Jesus' earthly ministry (Lk 3:1). *See* Caesars, The.

TIBNI

Ginath's son, who competed with Omri to be king of Israel after Zimri's suicide (1 Kgs 16:21-22). Tibni ruled over half of Israel from 884–880 BC before Omri defeated him in a civil war.

TIDAL

King of Goiim who fought with Kedorlaomer's confederation against Sodom (Gn 14:1-9).

TIGLATH-PILESER

Name of three Assyrian kings, the most important of whom was Tiglath-pileser III (745–727 BC). The name means "my trust is in the son of the Temple Esharra," and appears in various forms (cf. 2 Kgs 15:29; also called Tilgath-pilneser in 1 Chr 5:6; 2 Chr 28:20).

Tiglath-pileser I (1115–1077 BC) was the son of Ashur-resh-ishi. Having gained independence from Babylonian overlordship, Tiglath-pileser consolidated his hold over the territory newly acquired in his father's reign, maintaining control and guarding against counterattacks from the former occupiers. Security brought increased trade and prosperity, and a large temple-building program was undertaken.

Tiglath-pileser II (c. 967–935 BC) was a weak king who ruled Assyria during a period of decline. Although he was able to maintain some degree of internal control, he was powerless to prevent outside peoples from encroaching upon Assyrian territory. In particular, the Arameans took advantage of Assyrian weakness to occupy large areas of land, and an Aramean ruler named Kapara built a palace at Guzana (the Gozan of 2 Kgs 17:6). Some of the Arameans who occupied the area have been identified from inscriptions found at the site. This period was of particular importance for the emergence of the Aramean Empire.

Tiglath-pileser III (745–727 BC) ascended to the throne at a time when he could stem and reverse another decline in Assyrian fortunes. Although not directly in line for the throne, he was probably of royal descent. On occasion, he used the name Pul (2 Kgs 15:19; 1 Chr 5:26), which may have been his real name as opposed to his throne name.

Tiglath-pileser III was a strong, able, resourceful king whose reign is remarkable for the rapid extension of Assyrian boundaries and for the peaceful administration of the newly acquired territories. He assisted Babylon by defeating the Arameans, and by his diplomacy retained Babylonian support while he concentrated his military efforts elsewhere. On the death of the vassal king Nabu-nasir of Babylon in 734 BC, Tiglath-pileser gained the support of some of the tribes and finally forced the submission of Marduk-apla-iddina (the Merodach-baladan of Is 39:1). According to the Babylonian Chronicle, he used the name Pul when acceding to the throne of Babylon himself in 729 BC. He was the first Assyrian king on the throne of Babylon in 500 years.

His reign, which was marked by a vast increase in territory coupled with a firm and able administration, also had long-term effects far beyond Assyria's immediate borders. The expansion into Syria and Palestine was bound to lead eventually to conflict with Egypt when that country wished once again to mount a more aggressive foreign policy. Tiglath-pileser was the father of Shalmaneser V (727–722 BC).

TIKVAH

1. Harhas's son, father of Shallum, and the father-in-law of Huldah the prophetess (2 Kgs 22:14); alternately called Tokhath (KJV "Tikvath") in 2 Chronicles 34:22.
2. Father of Jahzeiah, who was one of the four individuals on record who opposed Ezra's command to divorce foreign wives (Ezr 10:15).

TILON

Shimon's son from Judah's tribe (1 Chr 4:20).

TIMAEUS

Father of Bartimaeus, the blind beggar whose sight Jesus restored near the gateway leading from Jericho (Mk 10:46).

TIMNA

1. Daughter of Seir, sister of Lotan, and a native Horite inhabitant of Edom (Gn 36:22; 1 Chr 1:39). She was a concubine to Eliphaz, Esau's son, and the mother of Amalek (Gn 36:12).
2. Edomite chief (Gn 36:40; 1 Chr 1:36, 51). This name may refer either to the name of the ancestor of the Edomite clan or to the geographical area occupied by the clan.

TIMON

One of the seven men of the Jerusalem church of good repute, full of the Spirit and of wisdom, appointed to minister to the widows (Acts 6:5).

TIMOTHY

Paul's convert and companion, whose name means "one who honors God."

Timothy first appears in Acts 16:1-3 as Paul's disciple whose mother "was a believer; but his father was a Greek" (v 1). He was a third-generation Christian after his mother, Eunice, and grandmother, Lois (2 Tm 1:5). The apostle Paul, undoubtedly Timothy's spiritual father, refers to him as "my true child in the faith" (1 Tm 1:2); he perhaps converted Timothy on his first or second missionary journey. The son of a Greek (or Gentile) father, Timothy was yet uncircumcised; however, when Paul decided to take Timothy with him on the second journey, he had him circumcised so as not to hinder their missionary endeavors among the Jews.

Timothy, who was well spoken of by the believers at Lystra and Iconium (Acts 16:2), became Paul's companion and assistant on his second missionary journey at Lystra. He traveled with Paul into Europe following the Macedonian vision. When Paul decided to go to Athens, he left Silas and Timothy at Berea to establish the church there (17:14). Timothy and Silas eventually joined Paul in Corinth (18:5). He next appears with Paul in Ephesus on his third journey (19:22), from where Paul sends him into Macedonia ahead of himself. In

QUICKTAKE

TIMOTHY

STRENGTHS AND ACCOMPLISHMENTS
- Became a believer during Paul's first missionary journey and joined him for his other two journeys
- Was a respected Christian in his hometown
- Was Paul's special representative on several occasions
- Received two personal letters from Paul
- Probably knew Paul better than any other person, becoming like a son to Paul

WEAKNESSES AND MISTAKES
- Struggled with a timid and reserved nature
- Allowed others to look down on his youthfulness
- Was apparently unable to correct some of the problems in the church at Corinth when Paul sent him there

LESSONS FROM HIS LIFE
- Youthfulness should not be an excuse for ineffectiveness
- Our inadequacies and inabilities should not keep us from being available to God

VITAL STATISTICS
Where: Lystra
Occupations: Missionary, pastor
Relatives: Mother: Eunice. Grandmother: Lois. Greek father
Contemporaries: Paul, Silas, Luke, Mark, Peter, Barnabas

KEY VERSES
"I have no one else like Timothy, who genuinely cares about your welfare. All the others care only for themselves and not for what matters to Jesus Christ. But you know how Timothy has proved himself. Like a son with his father, he has served with me in preaching the Good News" (Philippians 2:20-22).

Timothy's story is told in Acts, starting in chapter 16. He is also mentioned in Romans 16:21; 1 Corinthians 4:17; 16:10-11; 2 Corinthians 1:1, 19; Philippians 1:1; 2:19-23; Colossians 1:1; 1 Thessalonians 1:1-10; 2:3-4; 3:2-6; 1 and 2 Timothy; Philemon; Hebrews 13:23.

the last mention of Timothy in Acts 20:4, he was included in the list of goodwill ambassadors who were to accompany Paul to Jerusalem with the offering for the Christian Jews.

Timothy is often mentioned in the Pauline letters. His name is included in the introductory salutations of 2 Corinthians, Philippians, Colossians, 1 and 2 Thessalonians, and Philemon. Timothy's presence with Paul when he wrote these letters confirms the accuracy of the references to him in Acts. He was in Corinth on the second journey when Paul wrote 1 and 2 Thessalonians, at Ephesus on the third journey when Paul wrote 2 Corinthians, and in Rome during Paul's first Roman imprisonment, when he wrote Philippians, Colossians, and Philemon. He is mentioned in the introductions of 1 and 2 Timothy as the recipient of those two letters.

In the closing salutations of Romans 16:21, Timothy is listed along with others who send their good wishes to the believers in Rome. In 1 Corinthians 4:17 and 16:10, Paul speaks words of praise for Timothy as he sends him with a message to Corinth (see also Phil 2:19-23; 1 Thes 3:2-6). In 2 Corinthians 1:19 Timothy is named, along with Paul and Silas, as men who were proclaiming the good news about Jesus Christ. Paul put Timothy in charge of the church at Ephesus and wrote him two pastoral letters to help him perform that responsible task.

In Hebrews 13:23 the author (probably not Paul) tells his readers that Timothy had been released from prison, and that he hoped to come with Timothy to visit the readers of that letter. By this note, we know that Timothy experienced imprisonment.

TIRAS
Japheth's seventh son listed in the "table of nations" (Gn 10:2; 1 Chr 1:5). His descendants have been alternately linked to the Thracians, the Agathyrsi, the tribes of the Taurus mountain region, and the maritime Tyrrheni, but all of these identifications are purely speculative.

TIRHAKAH
Ethiopian king who marched north to fight against the Assyrian army, thus diverting Sennacherib's siege of Jerusalem (2 Kgs 19:9; Is 37:9). The report of Tirhakah's intended invasion prompted the Rabshakeh's second threat against Jerusalem, Hezekiah's prayer for deliverance, and the subsequent divine destruction of the Assyrian army (2 Kgs 19:8-37). Tirhakah is almost certainly the Egyptian king Taharqa, who ruled from 689–664 BC during the 25th (Ethiopian) dynasty. Tirhakah probably served as commander of the army while he was crown prince, so that the reference to him as "king" refers to his then-future position.

TIRHANAH
Hezronite and the second of Caleb's four sons by Maacah, his concubine (1 Chr 2:48).

TIRIA
Jahallelel's son and a descendant of Judah through Caleb (1 Chr 4:16).

TIRZAH

One of the daughters of Zelophehad of Manasseh's tribe (Nm 26:33). Since her father had no sons, she and her sisters asked for and received their father's inheritance (Nm 27:1; Jos 17:3). This prompted the making of a new law concerning inheritance rights with the stipulation that daughters who obtained their families' inheritance must marry within the tribe (Nm 36:11).

TITIUS JUSTUS

Believer in Corinth with whom Paul stayed (Acts 18:7). *See* Justus #2.

TITUS

1. One of Paul's converts—"my true child in a common faith" (Ti 1:4, NASB)—who became an intimate and trusted associate of the apostle in his mission of planting Christianity throughout the Mediterranean world (2 Cor 8:23; 2 Tm 4:10; Ti 1:4-5). Mentioned frequently in Paul's letters (eight times in 2 Corinthians, twice in Galatians, once each in 2 Timothy and Titus), his name occurs nowhere in Acts. This is a puzzling silence that some scholars have sought to explain with the fascinating, but uncertain, suggestion that he was a brother of Luke, the author of Acts.

   Unlike Timothy, who was half Jewish, Titus was born of gentile parents. Nothing is recorded of the circumstances surrounding his conversion and initial encounter with Paul. He is first introduced as a companion of Paul and Barnabas on a visit to Jerusalem (Gal 2:3). The occasion appears to have been the Jerusalem Council, about AD 50, which Paul and Barnabas attended as official delegates from the church at Antioch not long after the apostle's first missionary journey (Acts 15).

   With the hotly contested issue of compulsory circumcision of gentile converts to Christianity before the council, Paul decided to make a test case of Titus. The council decided in Paul's favor against the Judaizing party, and Titus was accepted by the other apostles and leaders of the Jerusalem church without submitting to the rite of circumcision. Thus, Titus became a key figure in the liberation of the infant church from the Judaizing party.

   Titus probably accompanied Paul from that time on, but he does not appear again until Paul's crisis with the church at Corinth during his third missionary journey. According to 2 Corinthians, while Paul was conducting an extended ministry in Ephesus, he received word that the Corinthian church had turned hostile toward him and renounced his apostolic authority. Other attempts at reconciliation having failed, he sent Titus to Corinth to try to repair the breach. When Titus rejoined Paul somewhere in Macedonia, where the apostle had traveled from Ephesus to meet him, Titus brought the good news that the attitude of the Corinthians had changed and their former love and friendship were now restored (2 Cor 7:6-7). In view of this development Paul sent Titus back to Corinth, carrying 2 Corinthians, which included instructions to complete the collection of the relief offering for the Jewish Christians of Judea (8:6, 16). In this venture also Titus was apparently successful (Rom 15:25-26).

Assuming that Paul was released after his first Roman imprisonment, it appears that Titus accompanied him on a mission to the island of Crete. On departing from Crete, Paul left Titus behind to consolidate the new Christian movement there (Ti 1:5). The assignment was difficult, for the Cretans were unruly and the struggling church was already invaded by false teachers (vv 10-16). His handling of the Corinthian problem some years before, however, demonstrated that Titus possessed the spiritual earnestness, skillful diplomacy, and loving concern required to meet the present challenge, and Paul was confident that this new commission was therefore safe in his hands.

Paul's letter to Titus, one of his three Pastoral Letters, was written somewhat later to encourage Titus in his Cretan ministry. The letter closes with the apostle's request that Titus join him at Nicopolis, a town on the west coast of Greece, where he planned to spend the winter (Ti 3:12). Most likely it was from Nicopolis, or else later from Rome (where the apostle was imprisoned again and eventually martyred), that Paul sent Titus on the mission to Dalmatia, a Roman province in what is now Yugoslavia (see 2 Tm 4:10). If later tradition is correct, Titus returned to Crete, where he served as bishop until he was an old man.

2. Variant spelling of a gentile proselyte in Corinth, to whose house Paul went after the Jewish community in general rejected his message (Acts 18:7). Better manuscript evidence names him as Titius Justus. *See* Justus #2.

TOAH
Kohathite Levite and Samuel's ancestor (1 Chr 6:34).

TOB-ADONIJAH
One of the Levites under Jehoshaphat who went out into the cities of Judah to teach the law (2 Chr 17:8).

TOBIAH
1. Forefather of a family of people who returned with Zerubbabel to Jerusalem following the Exile. This family was not able to prove their Jewish descent (Ezr 2:60; Neh 7:62).

2. Ammonite who opposed Nehemiah when he arrived in Jerusalem about 445 BC. Tobiah was known as "the Ammonite official" (Neh 2:10, 19), a designation associated with a person of high office, such as a governor. He, together with Sanballat and Geshem, the other leading opponents of the reconstruction of the walls, were high-ranking officers in the Persian Empire. He was connected by marriage with the Jews in two ways. He married the daughter of Shecaniah, the son of Arah, and his son Jehohanan married the daughter of Meshullam son of Berekiah (6:18). These marriage relations to a prominent Jerusalem family gave him strong ties with the Jerusalem aristocracy (v 17).

Nehemiah had to face the threat posed by Tobiah and his influential allies. Nehemiah was charged with the intent of leading the Jerusalem population in a revolt against King Artaxerxes (Neh 2:19). As the work of rebuilding the wall progressed, Tobiah joined in the conspiracy of besieging Jerusalem (4:8). Nehemiah ordered the Jews to defend themselves. They continued their labors of repairing the wall with the protection of armed guards, and when the enemy forces came closer, every worker held a weapon in addition to his trowel (vv 17-19). They were encouraged by the belief that "our God will fight for us" (v 20). Tobiah also joined in the plot to assassinate Nehemiah after the walls were rebuilt (6:2-4). Nehemiah was further tested by libelous reports of insurrection and by a Jerusalemite hired by the allies to tempt Nehemiah into entering the Temple proper and thereby discredit his standing among the faithful (vv 5-13).

After Nehemiah left Jerusalem in order to report to Artaxerxes, Tobiah succeeded in reestablishing himself with those who had remained faithful to him. The priest Eliashib was also related to Tobiah and gave in to Tobiah by preparing a large room previously used for offerings in the Temple (Neh 13:4-5). Tobiah used these quarters when visiting Jerusalem. One of Nehemiah's first actions, upon his return, was to evict Tobiah from the Temple (vv 8-9) and then restore the room for its proper use.

TOBIJAH

1. Levite sent by King Jehoshaphat to teach the law in the cities of Judah (2 Chr 17:8).
2. One of four men who returned from Babylon to Jerusalem with gold and silver used to make a crown for the high priest Joshua (NLT "Jeshua," Zec 6:10, 14).

TOGARMAH

Third son of Gomer, a descendant of Japheth (Gn 10:3; 1 Chr 1:6). Beth-togarmah ("house of Togarmah") appears in Ezekiel's prophecy against the nations that opposed Israel (Ez 27:14; 38:6). Beth-togarmah was one of the principal trading partners of Tyre, providing war horses and mules. Since Togarmah is consistently linked with Javan, Tubal, Meshech, Dedan, and Tarshish, Ezekiel probably had the ethnographic lists of Genesis 10 in mind. As an ethnographic term, most have identified Togarmah with Armenia. The Armenians identify Togarmah (Thorgon) as the founder of their race.

TOHU

Kohathite Levite and Samuel's ancestor (1 Sm 1:1).

TOI

King of Hamath at the time David defeated the armies of Hadadezer (2 Sm 8:9-10; alternately called Tou in 1 Chr 18:9-10). He sent his son Joram to congratulate and give gifts to David.

TOLA

1. One of the four sons of Issachar named among the 66 descendants of Jacob who accompanied him in the migration to Egypt to join Joseph (Gn 46:13); and the

ancestor of the first of four families of the tribe of Issachar, as identified in the census of Israel undertaken by Moses and Eleazar (Nm 26:23). Tola's sons were Uzzi, Rephaiah, Jeriel, Jahmai, Ibsam, and Shemuel (1 Chr 7:2). The Israelite clan of the Tolaites took its name from him (Nm 26:23), and during the time of David the warriors of his family numbered 22,600 men (1 Chr 7:1-2).

2. One of the judges of Israel, the son of Puah and the grandson of Dodo (Jgs 10:1), of Issachar's tribe. Shamir, his home and burial place, was in the hill country of Ephraim. There he judged Israel for 23 years.

Although he "delivered" Israel after the debacle of Abimelech's abortive attempt to establish a monarchy at Shechem, his accomplishment is covered in just two verses (Jgs 10:1-2). Like other "minor judges," mentioned only briefly (e.g., 12:8-15), he actually functioned in the judicial role—some more prominent "judges" (e.g., Gideon and Jephthah) were first, and perhaps solely, military heroes.

TROPHIMUS
One of the Asians who accompanied Paul on his final trip to Jerusalem (Acts 20:4). Because the Jews had seen Trophimus the Ephesian with Paul in Jerusalem, they incorrectly assumed that he had accompanied Paul into the Temple (21:29). Since Trophimus was not a Jew, his alleged act of profaning the Temple served as the pretense for Paul's arrest and subsequent imprisonment. Trophimus was traveling with Paul as one of the representatives of the Asian church who had been selected to superintend the collection for the Jerusalem church. Trophimus was probably one of the two brothers who accompanied Titus in the delivery of 2 Corinthians to Corinth (2 Cor 8:16-24). According to 2 Timothy 4:20, Trophimus had been accompanying Paul (prior to his final imprisonment) but then stayed behind in Miletus due to illness. Legend suggests that Trophimus was ultimately beheaded by the order of Nero.

TRYPHENA
Christian woman of Rome. Along with Tryphosa, Paul called her one of the "Lord's workers" (Rom 16:12). They may have been sisters or codeaconesses.

TRYPHOSA
Christian woman of Rome. Along with Tryphena, Paul called her one of the "Lord's workers" (Rom 16:12). They may have been sisters or codeaconesses.

TUBAL
Fifth of the listed sons of Japheth in the table of nations (Gn 10:2; 1 Chr 1:5). Tubal later gained significance in the prophetic writings of Isaiah and Ezekiel as one of the nations that would be judged for threatening God's people (Is 66:19; Ez 27:13; 32:26; 38:2-3; 39:1). Tubal is typically mentioned with Javan and Meshech as either nations of the north or nations of the coastlands (Is 66:19; Ez 38:2). The fact that Tubal traded with Tyre (Ez 27:13) supports

the premise that Tubal was located in a coastland region. Beyond this sketchy evidence, it is difficult to determine Tubal's precise ethnic identification or location. It has been identified with the Scythians, the Iberians, the region between the Black and the Caspian Seas, Thessaly, and various Hittite tribes.

TUBAL-CAIN

Son of Lamech by his wife Zillah (Gn 4:22). He was "a forger of all instruments of bronze and iron." Though the text does not claim that he was the first or the "father" of all ironworkers, many scholars think that the text originally paralleled verses 20 and 21 to imply that he was the first.

TYCHICUS

One of the believers who accompanied Paul in his trip to collect and deliver the offering for the Jerusalem church (Acts 20:4). Since he is often mentioned with Trophimus of Ephesus, Tychicus was likely also a native of that city. He served as the courier for Paul's letter to Ephesus (Eph 6:21) as well as Paul's letters to Philemon and the Colossians (Col 4:7). Most believe that he was also one of the two Christians (with Trophimus) who accompanied Titus in the delivery of 2 Corinthians (2 Cor 8:16-24). Paul mentioned Tychicus twice in his later letters, first sending him to Crete to be with Titus (Ti 3:12), and later mentioning to Timothy that he had sent Tychicus to Ephesus (2 Tm 4:12). Evidently, Tychicus and Paul were close friends as well as coworkers, since Paul frequently referred to Tychicus as a "beloved brother."

UEL

Bani's descendant and a priest who was encouraged by Ezra to divorce his foreign wife during the postexilic era (Ezr 10:34).

ULAM

1. Clan in Manasseh's tribe (1 Chr 7:16-17).

2. Eshek's firstborn son and a mighty warrior in Benjamin's tribe (1 Chr 8:39-40).

ULLA

Family in Asher's tribe (1 Chr 7:39).

UNNI

1. One of the musicians appointed by the chief of the Levites to sing and play the harp as part of the Temple service during David's reign (1 Chr 15:18-20).

2. One of the Levites who participated in the Temple service during the postexilic era (Neh 12:9).

UR

Father of Eliphal, one of David's mighty men (1 Chr 11:35); probably the same as Ahasbai in the parallel passage (2 Sm 23:34).

URBANUS

Believer greeted as one of Paul's coworkers in Christ (Rom 16:9).

URI

1. Father of Bezalel from Judah's tribe, and a builder of the Tabernacle (Ex 31:2; 35:30; 38:22; 1 Chr 2:20; 2 Chr 1:5).

2. Father of Geber, one of Solomon's officers in Gilead (1 Kgs 4:19).

3. One of the Temple gatekeepers who put away his foreign wife at Ezra's request (Ezr 10:24).

URIAH

1. Hittite who joined the people of Israel, became a leader in David's army, and was listed among the king's mighty men (2 Sm 23:39; 1 Chr 11:41). Uriah's wife was Bathsheba, with whom David committed adultery while Uriah was fighting the Ammonites. Upon learning that she was pregnant, David summoned Uriah to Jerusalem, hoping that Uriah would sleep with his wife and consider himself the child's father. However, Uriah slept in the servants' quarters because he was unwilling to enjoy the comforts of home while his companions were at war. The second night David again tried to entice him to sleep with his wife. Even after falling

into a drunken stupor, Uriah still could not be persuaded to go home; instead, he spent the night at the palace. To deepen the intrigue, David sent Uriah back to the battle, ordering him positioned at a vulnerable place, where he was killed (2 Sm 11; Mt 1:6). *See also* David.

2. Priest who built an altar at Jerusalem in imitation of an Assyrian model at King Ahaz of Judah's request (2 Kgs 16:10-16).

3. Priest who was the father of Meremoth. Meremoth weighed the silver, gold, and vessels for the Temple (Ezr 8:33) and built portions of the Jerusalem wall during the days of Nehemiah (Neh 3:4, 21).

4. One of the men who stood to Ezra's right when Ezra read the law to the people (Neh 8:4). He is perhaps the same man as #3 above.

5. Priest whom Isaiah took as a witness (Is 8:2). He is perhaps the same man as #2 above.

6. Prophet and Shemaiah's son from Kiriath-jearim. Uriah enraged King Jehoiakim by prophesying against Judah and Jerusalem. Fearing for his life, Uriah fled to Egypt but was eventually abducted and brought back to King Jehoiakim, who subsequently put him to death (Jer 26:20-23).

URIEL

1. Levite of the Kohathite branch who is listed as the son of Tahath and the father of Uzziah (1 Chr 6:24).

2. Levite who officiated over the moving of the Ark from the house of Obed-edom to Jerusalem (1 Chr 15:5-11). He was a Kohathite clan chief in charge of 120 men who participated in the ceremony, and he was personally sanctified for the purpose of carrying the Ark.

3. Grandfather of King Abijah of Judah, and the father of the queen mother, Maacah (Hebrew *Micaiah*), the favored wife of Rehoboam (2 Chr 13:2). There is potential difficulty in that Absalom is also called the father of Micaiah (Maacah) in 2 Chronicles 11:20. Josephus explained this discrepancy by suggesting that Maacah's mother may have been Absalom's daughter Tamar, so that Uriel would be the father of Maacah and Absalom the maternal grandfather. While many adopt this suggestion, others have posited that Absalom was known by two different names, particularly after he had been disgraced.

UTHAI

1. One who returned to Israel following the Exile. He is listed as the son of Ammihud from the Perez branch of Judah's tribe (1 Chr 9:4).

2. One of Bigvai's sons who returned to Jerusalem with Ezra (Ezr 8:14).

UZ

1. Aram's firstborn son and a descendant of Shem (Gn 10:23). In the parallel passage in 1 Chronicles 1:17, Uz is linked directly to Shem without mention of Aram. He is perhaps the forefather of the Aramean nation situated in the Syrian desert regions.
2. Firstborn son of Abraham's brother Nahor by his concubine, Milcah (Gn 22:21).
3. Son of Dishan and the grandson of Seir the Horite (Gn 36:28; 1 Chr 1:42).

UZAI

Father of Palal, a repairer of the Jerusalem wall during Nehemiah's day (Neh 3:25).

UZAL

Son of Joktan, a descendant of Eber through Shem's line (Gn 10:27; 1 Chr 1:21).

UZZA

1. Owner or initial planter of a garden that served as the burial place for kings Manasseh and Amon of Judah (2 Kgs 21:18, 26). The "garden of Uzza" was apparently adjacent to Manasseh's royal residence.
2. KJV spelling for Uzzah, Shimei's son, in 1 Chronicles 6:29. See Uzzah #2.
3. Son or descendant of Ehud from Benjamin's tribe (1 Chr 8:7), listed as an ancestor of Mordecai in extrabiblical texts.
4. KJV spelling for Uzzah, Abinadab's son, in 1 Chronicles 13:7-11. See Uzzah #1.
5. Forefather of a family of Temple servants who returned to Jerusalem with Zerubbabel following the Exile (Ezr 2:49; Neh 7:51).

UZZAH

1. Son of Abinadab who was killed while accompanying the cart that carried the Ark of the Covenant when it was returned from the Philistines (2 Sm 6:1-8; 1 Chr 13:7-11). He was struck dead by the Lord because he took hold of the Ark while trying to steady it, thereby violating the instructions of Numbers 4:15. Uzzah's brother, Ahio, was apparently leading the oxen while Uzzah walked alongside. As a result of the incident, David renamed the site Perez-uzzah ("the breaking forth against Uzzah") and left the Ark at the home of Obed-edom.
2. Levite from the clan of Merari who is listed as the son of Shimei and the father of Shimea (1 Chr 6:29).

UZZI

1. Descendant of Eliezer who was in the direct ancestral line of high priests, though he apparently never served in that capacity (1 Chr 6:5-6, 51). He is listed as the son of Bukki and the father of Zerahiah; he was a lineal ancestor of Zadok and later Ezra (Ezr 7:4).

2. Clan chief and mighty warrior of the tribe of Issachar. He was one of the six sons of Tola and the father of Izrahiah, his successor as clan chief (1 Chr 7:2-3).

3. Clan chief and mighty warrior of Benjamin's tribe, listed as one of the sons of Bela (1 Chr 7:7).

4. Head of one of the Benjaminite clans that returned from Babylon, listed as the son of Micri and the father of Elah (1 Chr 9:8).

5. One of the overseers of the Levites in Jerusalem, listed as the son of Bani from the clan of Asaph (Neh 11:22).

6. Head of the priestly house of Jedaiah during the days of Joiakim the high priest (Neh 12:19).

7. One of the priests (or Levites) who participated in the dedication of the rebuilt Temple (Neh 12:42). He may be the same as #5 or #6 above.

UZZIA
One of David's mighty men (1 Chr 11:44). He was described as an Ashterathite, which probably means that he was from Ashtaroth, a town on the east side of the Jordan.

UZZIAH
1. Judah's king from around 792 to 740 BC (cf. 2 Kgs 14:21-22; 15:1-7; 2 Chr 26:1-23), the son of King Amaziah and Jecoliah of Jerusalem. Uzziah is the name he is called in Chronicles, but in Kings he is known as Azariah. Azariah means "the Lord has helped"; the meaning of Uzziah is "my strength is the Lord." Azariah may have been his given name and Uzziah a throne name taken upon his accession. He came to the throne at the age of 16, after the death of his father, who was assassinated in Lachish as a result of a conspiracy arising from his apostasy.

Uzziah was a capable, energetic, and well-organized person, with many diverse interests. The Lord blessed him in all of his undertakings, so that he prospered. He is characterized as one who "did what was right in the eyes of the Lord" (2 Kgs 15:3; 2 Chr 26:4). He determined to seek God and went to Zechariah (not the postexilic prophet) for spiritual instruction. Consequently, "as long as he sought the LORD, God made him prosper" (2 Chr 26:5).

The prophets of the Lord were active during his reign. Isaiah, Hosea, and Amos began their prophetic work in the time of Uzziah (Is 1:1; Hos 1:1; Am 1:1). Uzziah was also active with military campaigns. His primary success was against Israel's strong historical enemy, the Philistines. He broke down the walls of Gath, Jabneh, and Ashdod and built his own cities in Philistia. He also built many fortifications, such as fortified towers in Jerusalem and in the wilderness. He defeated some Arabs and also the Meunites, and he brought the Ammonites under tribute (2 Chr 27:5-8). Uzziah had an army "fit for war," which was drafted according to census and organized into divisions.

QUICKTAKE

UZZIAH

STRENGTHS AND ACCOMPLISHMENTS
- Pleased God during his early years as king
- Successful warrior and city builder
- Skillful in organizing and delegating
- Reigned for 52 years

WEAKNESSES AND MISTAKES
- Developed a prideful attitude due to his great success
- Tried to perform the priests' duties, in direct disobedience to God
- Failed to remove many of the symbols of idolatry in the land

LESSONS FROM HIS LIFE
- Lack of thankfulness to God can lead to pride
- Even successful people must acknowledge the role God has for others in their lives

VITAL STATISTICS
Where: Jerusalem
Occupation: King of Judah
Relatives: Father: Amaziah. Mother: Jecoliah. Son: Jotham
Contemporaries: Isaiah, Amos, Hosea, Jeroboam, Zechariah, Azariah

KEY VERSES
"And he produced machines mounted on the walls of Jerusalem, designed by experts to shoot arrows and hurl stones from the towers and the corners of the wall. His fame spread far and wide, for the LORD gave him marvelous help, and he became very powerful.

"But when he had become powerful, he also became proud, which led to his downfall. He sinned against the LORD his God by entering the sanctuary of the LORD's Temple and personally burning incense on the incense altar" (2 Chronicles 26:15, 16).

Uzziah's story is told in 2 Kings 15:1-7 (where he is called Azariah) and in 2 Chronicles 26:1-23. He is also mentioned in Isaiah 1:1; 6:1; 7:1; Hosea 1:1; Amos 1:1; Zechariah 14:5.

There were 2,600 officers and 307,500 fighting men who could wage war with mighty power. The army was well outfitted, with weapons, such as spears, bows, and sling stones, and with defensive equipment, including shields, helmets, and coats of armor (2 Chr 26:14). Second Chronicles 26:15 describes a kind of catapult, which was to be stationed on the towers and at the corners of walls for defensive purposes. This type of weapon could hurl arrows or large stones. Through his achievements and especially his military power, he became famous.

But Uzziah had a sad downfall. As Proverbs 16:18 says, pride goes before a fall. His pride became clearly evident when he presumed the function of a priest. When he entered the Temple to offer incense on the altar of incense, he was confronted for his presumptuous behavior by Azariah the priest and 80 other priests. When Uzziah became angry, the Lord struck him with leprosy, so that he was forced to live in isolation and could not enter the Temple. His son, Jotham, became acting head of state and then succeeded to the kingship at the time of Uzziah's death.

2. Kohathite Levite and forefather of Samuel (1 Chr 6:24).

3. Father of Jonathan, David's treasurer (1 Chr 27:25).

4. One of Harim's five sons who was encouraged by Ezra to divorce his foreign wife during the postexilic period (Ezr 10:21; 1 Esd 9:21).

5. Descendant of Perez from Judah's tribe (Neh 11:4).

UZZIEL

1. Youngest of the sons of Kohath of Levi's tribe, who became the head of the Uzzielite division of the Kohathites (Ex 6:18; Nm 3:19, 27, 30; 1 Chr 26:23). He was Aaron's uncle, and his sons, Mishael and Elzaphan, carried Nadab and Abihu out of the camp when they rebelled against Aaron's authority (Ex 6:22; Lv 10:4). Several of his descendants were significant during Israel's history, including Amminadab, who officiated over David's transfer of the Ark to Jerusalem, and Micah and Isshiah, who were chiefs among the Levites during the reign of Solomon (1 Chr 15:10; 23:20).

2. Son of Ishi who was one of the leaders of the Simeonite warriors who defeated the Ammonites at Seir during the reign of Hezekiah (1 Chr 4:42). As a result of defeating the Amalekites, who had not been defeated earlier by Saul or David, the Simeonites inherited the land.

3. Benjaminite clan chief who is listed as the son of Bela, the son of Benjamin (1 Chr 7:7).

4. Son of Heman of the Levite clan of Asaph (1 Chr 25:4). A variant name is Azarel (v 18, NLT mg).

5. Levite who participated in the reconsecration of the Temple under Hezekiah (2 Chr 29:14), listed as the son of Jeduthun.

6. Goldsmith who worked on rebuilding the gates of Jerusalem (Neh 3:8). His name indicates that he was likely a priest who had the responsibility of making and repairing the Temple instruments and vessels (cf. 1 Chr 9:29).

VAIZATHA

One of Haman's ten sons, who was killed during the Jews' retaliation when Haman plotted to kill them (Est 9:9).

VANIAH

Bani's son and one of the priests who divorced his foreign wife at Ezra's command (Ezr 10:36).

VASHTI

Queen during the reign of Ahasuerus (Xerxes I) who was deposed for refusing to show herself to the guests at a royal banquet (Est 1:9-19). Since neither she nor Esther is otherwise known in secular history, many have suggested that they were inferior wives or concubines who were simply dignified with the title "queen." According to Plutarch, Persian custom dictated that the kings would ordinarily eat with their legitimate wives, but when they wanted to "riot and drink," they would send their wives away and call in their concubines. While this citation is often used to support the judgment that Vashti was called because she was only a concubine, the opposite conclusion better explains Vashti's refusal to come. Vashti's position as queen is indicated by the fact that she was supposed to appear with her "royal crown," that she was always called "queen" until the time of her dismissal, and that her behavior should serve as an example for all the women in the kingdom.

VOPHSI

Man appointed by Moses from Naphtali's tribe to spy out the land of Canaan (Nm 13:14).

W, X, Y, Z

XERXES

NIV and NLT rendering of Ahasuerus in Ezra 4:6 and the book of Esther. *See* Ahasuerus #1.

YAHWEH (YHWH)

Most holy name for God in the OT, usually translated "LORD" (Ex 34:5-8). *See* God.

ZAAVAN

Second son of Ezer, a Horite clan chief (Gn 36:27; 1 Chr 1:42).

ZABAD

1. Son of Nathan (1 Chr 2:36) and a descendant of Ahlai the daughter of Sheshan (vv 30, 34-36).

2. Tahath's son and the father of Shuthelah from Ephraim's tribe (1 Chr 7:21).

3. One of David's mighty men, listed as a son of Ahlai (1 Chr 11:41); he is perhaps the same as #1 above.

4. One of the assassins of King Joash, listed as the son of Shimeath the Ammonitess (2 Chr 24:26). He is identical to Jozacar (alternately "Jozabad") in 2 Kings 12:21. Zabad was a palace official who was likely the agent of a powerful conspiracy against Joash. *See also* Jozacar.

5–7. Three priests variously descended from Zattu, Hashum, and Nebo, who renounced their foreign wives at Ezra's request during the postexilic period (Ezr 10:27, 33, 43).

ZABBAI

1. Bebai's son and one of the priests who divorced his foreign wife at Ezra's command (Ezr 10:28).

2. Father of Baruch. Baruch repaired a section of the Jerusalem wall during Nehemiah's day (Neh 3:20).

ZABDI

1. Zerah's descendant from Judah's tribe (Jos 7:1). Achan was a Zerahite of the family of Zabdi (Jos 7:17-18); alternately called Zimri (NLT mg, 1 Chr 2:6).

2. Shimei's son and a descendant of Ehud from Benjamin's tribe (1 Chr 8:19).

3. David's officer over the produce of the vineyards for the wine cellars (1 Chr 27:27). He is called a Shiphmite, which likely means that he was a native of Shepham.

4. One of the Temple musicians of the order of Asaph (Neh 11:17); alternately called Zicri (1 Chr 9:15).

ZABDIEL

1. Father of Jashobeam, the commander of the first division of David's army (1 Chr 27:2).

2. Priest and overseer of 128 "mighty men of valor" (RSV, Neh 11:14). The notation that he was a "son of Haggedolim" might indicate that he was a "son of the mighty men."

ZABUD

Priest in Solomon's court and the "king's friend" (1 Kgs 4:5). The phrase "king's friend" may be an official title given to one of the king's advisers. Hushai the Archite had a similar title in David's court (2 Sm 15:37; 16:16).

ZACCAI

Forefather of a family who returned with Zerubbabel to Judah following the Exile (Ezr 2:9; Neh 7:14).

ZACCHAEUS

Jewish tax collector who collected taxes for the Romans at Jericho. He probably secured this position by purchasing the exclusive right to collect revenue in that region or by working as a subcontractor for another affluent official. In either case, Zacchaeus himself accrued great wealth (largely by illegitimate means) from his customs enterprise. Jericho, a significant center of commerce, was situated along a major trade route connecting Jerusalem and its environs with the lands east of the Jordan.

In his Gospel, Luke records Zacchaeus's encounter with Jesus (Lk 19:2-8). Seeking Jesus, but unable to see him over the crowd because of his small stature, Zacchaeus climbed a sycamore tree to get a better view when Jesus passed by. To his astonishment, Jesus stopped under the tree and after calling him down, invited himself to the publican's house for the night. Subsequently, Zacchaeus repented and followed Jesus, promising to restore fourfold to those whom he had wrongfully exploited and give to the poor. According to Clement of Alexandria, Zacchaeus later became the bishop of Caesarea (*Homily* 3.63).

ZACCUR

1. Reubenite and father of Shammua, one of the 12 spies in the reconnaissance of Canaan (Nm 13:4).

2. Simeonite who was the son of Hammuel and the father of Shimei (1 Chr 4:26).

3. One of the descendants of Merari in the record of the divisions of the priests (1 Chr 24:27).

4. One of the sons of Asaph who was assigned responsibility for the Temple service (1 Chr 25:2). Zaccur and his sons and brothers were assigned the third lot among the various duties for the Temple musicians (1 Chr 25:10). Descendants of Zaccur were present at the dedication of the city wall following the Exile (Neh 12:35).

5. One of the descendants of Bigvai who returned to Jerusalem with Ezra (Ezr 8:14).

6. Son of Imri who worked on repairing Jerusalem's wall in the vicinity of the Sheep Gate (Neh 3:2).

7. One of the Levites who signed Nehemiah's covenant to obey the law of God (Neh 10:12).

8. Son of Mattaniah and father of Hanan, the assistant to the storehouse treasurers during Nehemiah's time (Neh 13:13). Some have suggested that he is the same as #7 above.

ZADOK
Common OT name meaning "righteous one."

1. David's priest, probably the most famous and influential of Israel's high priests apart from Aaron. He first appeared at the time of Absalom's revolt, when he and his fellow priest Abiathar showed their loyalty to David by coming to him with the Ark, fully prepared to share his exile (2 Sm 15:24-29). David refused their offer and sent them back to Jerusalem to act in his interests.

   In 2 Samuel 8:17, Zadok is listed as the son of Ahitub, who is noted in 1 Samuel 14:3 as the grandson of Eli. In the genealogies of Chronicles, Zadok's descent through Ahitub is traced back to Eleazar, the eldest son of Aaron (1 Chr 6:1-8, 50-53; Ezr 7:2-5), but with no reference to Eli. A slight problem emerges in that Zadok replaces the banished Abiathar, a descendant of Eli. This is regarded as the fulfillment of an earlier prophecy that the tenure of the high priestly office by Eli's family would be broken in favor of a different branch of Aaron's family (1 Sm 2:30-36; 1 Kgs 2:26-27).

   In both summaries of David's court officials (2 Sm 8:17; 20:25), Zadok is listed as one of David's two principal priests, an office held throughout the latter part of David's reign. When David was near death, a power struggle over the throne was precipitated by Adonijah, David's oldest surviving son. With the support of Joab, the commander of the army, and the priest Abiathar, David's long-standing friend, Adonijah declared himself king (1 Kgs 1:5-10). Nathan the prophet promptly intervened with Bathsheba as Solomon's advocate. Zadok and Benaiah, the captain of the mercenary troops, supported Solomon. Adonijah's cause was hopeless once David had indicated his approval of Nathan's plans. Consequently, the discredited Abiathar was banished (2:26-27), leaving the loyal Zadok as Solomon's chief priest (2:35; 4:4).

In the centuries that followed, the descendants of Zadok preserved this dominance, and as Jerusalem's prestige increased, so did their status. Azariah, the chief priest in Hezekiah's reign, was a Zadokite (2 Chr 31:10). Ezekiel restricted the main priestly functions to the "sons of Zadok," demoting the Levites generally to the rank of "Temple caretakers" because of their apostasy during the monarchy (Ez 44:10-16). When the Jews came under Seleucid domination in the early second century BC, the high priesthood, regarded as a political appointment, was taken away from the Zadokites. Conservative elements, however, like the Qumran covenanters, continued to look for its restoration. *See also* David.

2. Father-in-law of Uzziah and grandfather of Jotham, kings of Judah (2 Kgs 15:32-33; 2 Chr 27:1).

3. Descendant of Zadok, David's priest (1 Chr 6:12; 9:11; Neh 11:11).

4. Young man of exceptional courage, the leader of a contingent that joined David at Hebron against Saul (1 Chr 12:28).

5. Son of Baana, who helped to repair the wall of Jerusalem in Nehemiah's time (Neh 3:4).

6. Son of Immer, who also shared in Nehemiah's rebuilding operations (Neh 3:29).

7. Signatory to Nehemiah's covenant (Neh 10:21) and perhaps identifiable with #5 or #6 above.

8. One of three treasurers appointed by Nehemiah during his second term of office, called the scribe (Neh 13:13).

9. Ancestor of Christ (Mt 1:14).

ZAHAM
One of Rehoboam's sons by his wife Mahalath (2 Chr 11:19).

ZALAPH
Hanun's father. Hanun repaired a section of the Jerusalem wall during Nehemiah's day (Neh 3:30).

ZALMON
One of David's mighty men (2 Sm 23:28); alternately called Ilai the Ahohite in 1 Chronicles 11:29.

ZALMUNNA
See Zebah and Zalmunna.

ZANOAH
Descendant of Caleb from Judah's tribe (1 Chr 4:18). Zanoah was the son of Jekuthiel and, depending on the translation of the Hebrew text, may have been related to Bithiah, the

daughter of Pharaoh. Some have interpreted the text as indicating that Jekuthiel was the founder or principal settler of the city named Zanoah. In any case, Zanoah's descendants may well have been connected with the city of that name.

ZAPHENATH-PANEAH
Name given to Joseph by Pharaoh when Joseph assumed his governmental responsibilities in Egypt (Gn 41:45). The name most likely means "says the god, he will live." *See* Joseph #1.

ZATTU
1. Clan chief with whom 945 people returned with Zerubbabel (Ezr 2:8; Neh 7:13 cites 845 returnees). Of the priests who renounced their foreign wives, six are listed as "sons" of Zattu (Ezr 10:27).
2. One of the chiefs of the people who signed Nehemiah's covenant (Neh 10:14); perhaps the same person as #1 above.

ZAZA
Jonathan's son, in the family of Jerahmeel, a member of Judah's tribe (1 Chr 2:33).

ZEBADIAH
1. One of the sons of Beriah from Benjamin's tribe (1 Chr 8:15).
2. One of the sons of Elpaal from Benjamin's tribe (1 Chr 8:17).
3. One of the sons of Jeroham of Gedor, who came to David's support at Ziklag (1 Chr 12:7).
4. Korahite Levite descended from Asaph, third of Meshelemiah's seven sons and a Temple gatekeeper (1 Chr 26:2).
5. Son of Asahel, Joab's brother, who was the commander of the fourth division of David's army (1 Chr 27:7).
6. One of the Levites sent by Jehoshaphat into the cities of Judah to teach the law (2 Chr 17:8).
7. Ishmael's son and one of the leaders of the Levites whom Jehoshaphat appointed as governor of civil affairs for the house of Judah (2 Chr 19:11).
8. Michael's son from Shephatiah's house, who returned with Ezra to Jerusalem following the Exile (Ezr 8:8).
9. One of the sons of Immer who renounced his foreign wife at Ezra's command (Ezr 10:20).

ZEBAH AND ZALMUNNA
Two Midianite kings who slaughtered Gideon's brothers at Tabor. Gideon subsequently killed them in order to avenge his brothers' deaths (Jgs 8:18-21).

During Gideon's day, Midianite camel raiders annually made forays into Israelite territory at harvesttime, stealing crops and livestock (Jgs 6:3). So complete were their raids that nothing was left in Israel, including crops, sheep, oxen, or donkeys.

In this state of affairs God called Gideon to deliver Israel (Jgs 6:16). His well-known victory over Midian near Mt Moreh was an important step toward realization of this divine commission (7:1-23). In the operations following the battle, Ephraimite warriors captured and assassinated two Midianite leaders named Zeeb and Oreb (7:24–8:3).

Gideon determined to capture Zebah and Zalmunna, the kings of the Midianite forces. In tracking them down, he crossed the Jordan River and traveled more than 100 miles (160.9 kilometers) from the site of the original battle. Along the way, two successive towns, Succoth and Penuel, refused to help Gideon and his men, doubtless fearing reprisal from the Midianite raiders should Gideon fail to defeat them.

Gideon routed the remaining Midianite warriors and captured Zebah and Zalmunna (Jgs 8:12). Because Zebah and Zalmunna had killed his brothers, Gideon killed the two Midianite kings (vv 19-21). Psalm 83:11 indicates that Zebah, Zalmunna, and the Midianites were the enemies not merely of Israel but also of God.

ZEBEDEE
Father of the disciples James and John (Mt 26:37; Mk 3:17; 10:35). Zebedee was in the fishing business and may have been wealthy, considering that he had servants and apparent connections with the high priest (Jn 18:15). Although he personally appears only once in the narrative (Mt 4:21; Mk 1:19-20), his wife, Salome, appears frequently as one of the pious women who followed Christ.

ZEBIDAH
Mother of Jehoiakim, king of Judah, Josiah's wife and the daughter of Pedaiah (2 Kgs 23:36).

ZEBINA
Nebo's son, who obeyed Ezra's exhortation to divorce his foreign wife after the Exile (Ezr 10:43).

ZEBUL
Ruler of Shechem who served as an officer of Abimelech (Jgs 9:28-30). Zebul apparently obtained his position when Abimelech was crowned king at Shechem. When Gaal the son of Ebed incited the Shechemites to rebel against Abimelech, Zebul played an instrumental role in Abimelech's victory. After he goaded Gaal into attacking Abimelech outside of the city, Zebul shut Gaal out of the city, preventing retreat into its confines. It is difficult to determine Zebul's fate when Abimelech later attacked and destroyed the city, but it is possible that he too met a treacherous fate.

ZEBULUN

One of Jacob's 12 sons (Gn 35:23; 1 Chr 2:1). He was the sixth and last son borne to Jacob by Leah, who named the boy Zebulun, meaning "abode, dwelling," for she said, "Now my husband will *dwell with* me, because I have borne him six sons" (Gn 30:20, NASB, emphasis added). Later, he settled his family in Egypt with Jacob and his brothers (Ex 1:3). Jacob foretold that Zebulun's descendants would become a maritime people with their border touching Sidon (Gn 49:13). Though Zebulun's tribe was separated from the Mediterranean by Asher's tribe and from the Sea of Galilee by Naphtali, it prospered greatly in trade with the Canaanite cities of the coastal plains. Zebulun fathered three sons (Gn 46:14) and founded one of Israel's 12 tribes (Nm 1:30-31).

ZECHARIAH

Extremely popular name in the Bible; it means "the Lord remembers."

1. Son of King Jeroboam II; the 15th king of Israel and the last of Jehu's dynasty. Beginning his rule in 753 BC, the 38th year of Azariah's reign in Judah (792–740 BC), Zechariah ruled in Samaria for only six months before he was murdered at Ibleam in a conspiracy masterminded by Shallum, his successor (2 Kgs 14:29; 15:8-11). The Lord's promise to Jehu, that his descendants would rule to the fourth generation (10:30), was fulfilled with Zechariah's reign.

2. Father of Abi (or Abijah, 2 Chr 29:1). Abi was the mother of Hezekiah, who later ruled Judah for 29 years (2 Kgs 18:2).

3. Reubenite and leader of his tribe (1 Chr 5:7).

4. Korahite Levite, firstborn of Meshelemiah's seven sons and a wise counselor, selected by lot to oversee the gatekeepers of the sanctuary's northern entrance during David's reign (1 Chr 9:21; 26:2, 14).

5. Benjaminite and descendant of Jeiel (1 Chr 9:37). He is alternately called Zeker, perhaps an abbreviation of Zechariah, in 1 Chronicles 8:31.

6. One of the eight Levites assigned to play a harp before the Ark of God in the procession led by David when the Ark was brought from Obed-edom's house to Jerusalem (1 Chr 15:18, 20; 16:5).

7. One of the priests assigned to blow a trumpet in the procession led by David when the Ark was brought to Jerusalem (1 Chr 15:24).

8. Levite and a descendant of Isshiah, who served in the sanctuary during David's reign (1 Chr 24:25).

9. Merarite Levite and Hosah's son, who served as one of the gatekeepers of the sanctuary's western entrance, at the gate of Halleketh, during David's reign (1 Chr 26:11-12, 16).

10. Father of Iddo. Iddo was the chief officer of the half-tribe of Manasseh in Gilead during David's reign (1 Chr 27:21).

11. One of the officials sent by King Jehoshaphat (872–848 BC) to teach the law in the cities of Judah (2 Chr 17:7).

12. Gershonite Levite and Jahaziel's father (2 Chr 20:14).

13. One of King Jehoshaphat's seven sons and the brother of Jehoram. Jehoram became sole regent of Judah (848–841 BC) at his father's death (2 Chr 21:2).

14. Son of Jehoiada the priest, who rebuked the princes of Judah for turning against the Lord and worshiping false gods. Enraged by Zechariah's rebuff, they conspired against him, and at King Joash's command, stoned him to death in the court of the sanctuary (2 Chr 24:20-22). The Lord, however, avenged Zechariah's death by allowing the Syrians to defeat Judah, kill the princes, and severely wound Joash, who was subsequently killed by two of his own servants. In his castigation of his own generation of Jewish leaders, Jesus alluded to Zechariah's shameful murder in the Temple's sacred precincts: "You will be held responsible for the murder of all godly people of all time—from the murder of righteous Abel to the murder of Zechariah son of Barachiah, whom you killed in the Temple between the sanctuary and the altar" (Mt 23:35, NLT). Abel was the first and Zechariah the last of the recorded prophets of God who were unjustly slain, according to the OT.

15. Man who counseled King Uzziah of Judah to walk in the fear of God (2 Chr 26:5).

16. Abijah's father. Abijah was the mother of King Hezekiah of Judah (2 Chr 29:1).

17. Gershonite Levite descended from Asaph, who along with Mattaniah his kinsman was chosen by King Hezekiah to help cleanse the house of the Lord (2 Chr 29:13).

18. Kohathite Levite who was appointed to oversee the repair of the Temple during King Josiah's reign (2 Chr 34:12).

19. One of the chief officers of the house of God who generously gave animals to the priests for the celebration of the Passover feast during King Josiah's reign (2 Chr 35:8).

20. Prophet, Berechiah's son and the grandson of Iddo, who began prophesying as a young man in 520 BC during the reign of King Darius I of Persia (Zec 1:1; cf. 2:4). Little is known about the prophet. He ministered with Haggai, his contemporary, in postexilic Jerusalem during the days of Zerubbabel, the governor, and Jeshua, the high priest (Ezr 5:1). He exhorted the Jews to finish building the second Temple (6:14) and headed Iddo's priestly family during Joiakim's term as high priest (Neh 12:16). Like Jeremiah and Ezekiel, Zechariah served as both priest and prophet (Zec 1:1, 7; 7:1, 8). Numerous suggestions have been offered to resolve the discrepancy of Zechariah's pedigree. In the Ezra and Nehemiah passages, Iddo is listed as his father, whereas in Zechariah, Berechiah is the father. Some conclude that Berechiah and Iddo were different names for the same person, or that Berechiah's name (Zec 1:1, 7) was a later scribal emendation that

confused Jeberechiah's son with Iddo's son (cf. Is 8:2). A more plausible theory identifies Iddo as Zechariah's grandfather, the renowned head of his family, who returned to
Jerusalem from exile in 538 BC. Either by Berechiah's early death or by the precedence
of his grandfather's name, Zechariah was considered Iddo's successor.

21. Parosh's descendant and the head of his father's household. He returned with Ezra
    to Judah following the Exile during the reign of King Artaxerxes I of Persia (Ezr 8:3).

22. Bebai's son and the head of a household. He returned with Ezra to Judah following the
    Exile during the reign of King Artaxerxes I of Persia (Ezr 8:11).

23. One of the Jewish leaders whom Ezra sent to Iddo, the man in charge at Casiphia,
    to gather Levites and Temple servants for the caravan of Jews returning to Palestine
    from Babylon (Ezr 8:15-17).

24. One of the six descendants of Elam who was encouraged by Ezra to divorce his foreign
    wife during the postexilic period (Ezr 10:26).

25. One of the men who stood to Ezra's left when Ezra read the law to the people (Neh 8:4).

26. Descendant of Perez and an ancestor of a Judahite family headed by Athaiah living
    in Jerusalem during the postexilic period (Neh 11:4).

27. Descendant of Shelah and an ancestor of a Judahite family headed by Maaseiah living
    in Jerusalem during the postexilic era (Neh 11:5).

28. Priest, descendant of Malkijah and an ancestor of a family of priests headed by Adaiah
    living in Jerusalem during the postexilic period (Neh 11:12).

29. Jonathan's son, a descendant of Asaph. He led a group of the priestly musicians
    who played trumpets at the dedication of the Jerusalem wall in Nehemiah's day
    (Neh 12:35).

30. Priest who played a trumpet at the Jerusalem wall's dedication (Neh 12:41).

31. Jeberechiah's son and undoubtedly a man of distinction who, along with Uriah the
    priest, publicly witnessed Isaiah's writing of the puzzling expression "Maher-shalal-
    hash-baz," which later prophetically revealed God's intended judgment on Damascus
    and Samaria (Is 8:2).

32. John the Baptist's father, priest of Abijah's division, and the husband of Elizabeth, a
    woman of priestly descent. His story is recounted in Luke 1. They lived in the Judean hill
    country during King Herod the Great's reign (37–4 BC; Lk 1:5). Zechariah and Elizabeth
    both lived righteous and pious lives; however, they were advanced in years and still had
    no children. As priest, Zechariah was one of the men chosen to represent his division in
    its yearly appointed session of service in the Jerusalem Temple (the priests of Israel were
    divided into 24 orders, each being assigned an annual two-week period of service in
    the Temple). One day while serving in Jerusalem, Zechariah was selected by lot to burn
    incense in the Temple's Holy Place, a privilege granted to a priest only once in his lifetime.
    While performing this Temple duty, the angel Gabriel appeared to him, telling him that

Elizabeth his wife, though barren, would bear him a son, whose name would be called John and who would prepare the way for the Messiah. As a sign confirming the angel's report, Zechariah was made mute for his disbelief that, in their old age, he and Elizabeth would produce a child. When Zechariah returned to the Temple court, the gathered multitude perceived that the gesturing priest had seen a vision. Elizabeth became pregnant as promised and in her sixth month was visited by her relative Mary, who was also with child. Later, shortly after the baby's birth, Zechariah affirmed that his son's name would be John, at which time his speech was restored and he was filled with the Holy Spirit, prophesying and praising God for the work that he was about to do in Israel.

33. Original name proposed for John the Baptist after his father's name (Lk 1:59). *See* John the Baptist.

ZEDEKIAH

1. Judah's last king and a key political figure in the fateful final decade of the southern kingdom. His reign (597–586 BC) spanned Nebuchadnezzar's two attacks on Jerusalem, in 597 and 586. The first attack was in reprisal for the rebellion of Josiah's son, Jehoiakim (609–598 BC), against Nebuchadnezzar; however, by the time his forces captured Jerusalem, Jehoiakim was dead and had been succeeded by his 18-year-old son Jehoiachin. Nebuchadnezzar deposed the young king and deported him to Babylon, along with the elite of the nation: government officials, army officers, and craftsmen. As Jehoiachin's replacement, Nebuchadnezzar appointed his uncle Mattaniah, a younger brother of Jehoiakim and of the earlier, short-lived King Jehoahaz (609 BC). Mattaniah was thus the third son of Josiah to occupy the throne of Judah. The Babylonian king named him Zedekiah, which means "the Lord is my righteousness."

Zedekiah found himself in a difficult position as Judah's king. Many evidently still regarded Jehoiachin as the real king (cf. Jer 28:1-4). Certainly the Judeans deported to Babylonia dated events by reference to Jehoiachin (2 Kgs 25:27; Ez 1:2). Though the Babylonians exacted from Zedekiah an oath of loyalty (2 Chr 36:13; Ez 17:13-18), evidence suggests that they too viewed Zedekiah's predecessor as the legitimate king and Zedekiah as regent. They may have been holding him in reserve for possible restoration to power, should events require it.

Judah was filled with a false optimism that could hardly have helped the new king. It was confidently expected that the deportation of the leading citizens would be only temporary; prophets were guaranteeing that Babylon's power would be broken within two years (Jer 28:2-4). They were opposed by a few prophets led by Jeremiah, whose message found little support.

Pressure both from within the nation and from without was put on Zedekiah to change his political allegiance. In the fourth year of his reign (593 BC), the neighboring states of Ammon, Moab, Tyre, and Sidon formed a coalition to fight for independence from Babylon. Envoys were sent to Zedekiah (Jer 27:1-3). However, Jeremiah advised the king not to get involved. In the same year, according to Jeremiah 51:59, Zedekiah visited Babylon. He may have been summoned to affirm his loyalty and to explain his role in the political situation. The planned rebellion did not occur, perhaps because aid from Egypt failed to materialize.

Within the Judean court a strong pro-Egyptian party existed. This party saw Egypt as an ally for breaking away from their eastern master, just like the advisers of King Hezekiah a century before (cf. Is 31:1-3; 36:6). Zedekiah, finding it difficult to resist this political pressure, eventually transferred his allegiance to Egypt.

Hophra (589–570 BC), Psammetichus's heir to the Egyptian throne, organized a joint rebellion in the west against Babylon. According to Ezekiel 21:18-32 and 25:12-17, Judah and Ammon supported him, while Edom and Philistia shrewdly abstained. Zedekiah was rebuked by the prophet Ezekiel (Ez 17:13-18) for breaking his oath to Nebuchadnezzar (cf. 2 Chr 36:13) and rebelling against him by sending envoys to Egypt to negotiate for military support.

In the face of this western uprising engineered by his Egyptian rival, Nebuchadnezzar was forced to march westward. Setting up headquarters at Riblah in northern Syria, he decided to make Jerusalem his prime target (Ez 21:18-23). The ensuing siege of Jerusalem was temporarily lifted due to an Egyptian attack but afterward was resumed until the city fell. Zedekiah, fleeing eastward with his troops, was caught near Jericho and taken north to Nebuchadnezzar at Riblah. There he was put on trial for breaking his promises of vassalage. By way of punishment, his sons were killed before his eyes. This tragic sight was the last he ever saw, since his eyes were then put out. He was taken in chains to Babylon, where he eventually died in prison (2 Kgs 25:5-7; Jer 39:7; 52:8-11; cf. Ez 12:13).

2. Kenaanah's son and one of the prophets who spoke falsely to kings Ahab of Israel and Jehoshaphat of Judah, telling them that the Lord would give Ahab victory over the Syrians at Ramoth-gilead (1 Kgs 22:11). After hearing Micaiah's contrary prediction that Ahab would in fact be killed in the battle, Zedekiah, in anger, struck Micaiah (v 24).

3. Jeconiah's son and a descendant of David through Solomon's line (1 Chr 3:16).

4. Leading priest who affirmed Nehemiah's covenant during the postexilic era (Neh 10:1).

5. Maaseiah's son, who, according to Jeremiah, King Nebuchadnezzar of Babylon would kill by roasting in fire for his adultery and lying words (Jer 29:21-23).

6. Hananiah's son and a prince in Judah during King Jehoiakim's reign (Jer 36:12).

ZEEB
One of two Midianite princes executed by Gideon's army (Jgs 7:25).

ZELEK
Ammonite warrior among David's mighty men (2 Sm 23:37; 1 Chr 11:39).

ZELOPHEHAD
Hepher's son from Manasseh's tribe. He fathered five daughters but no sons (Nm 26:33). Because Zelophehad had no sons, his daughters petitioned Moses to give them their father's inheritance (27:1). Moses' subsequent ruling provided that daughters should receive the inheritance in such cases, providing that they marry within their tribe so that the tribal allotments would remain constant (Nm 27:7; 36:2; Jos 17:3).

ZEMIRAH
Beker's firstborn son, from Benjamin's tribe (1 Chr 7:8).

ZENAS
Lawyer whom Paul requested Titus to help with his travels in Crete (Ti 3:13).

ZEPHANIAH
1. Priest during the reign of Zedekiah who was executed at Riblah by the king of Babylon (2 Kgs 25:18; Jer 52:24). He was the second priest under Seraiah the chief priest and served as Zedekiah's envoy to Jeremiah during the period prior to the fall of Jerusalem (Jer 21:1; 29:25-29; 37:3).
2. Ancestor of Heman who was among the Kohathite Levites whom David placed in charge of the service of music in the house of the Lord (1 Chr 6:33-36). Zephaniah is listed as the father of Azariah and the son of Tahath.
3. Author of the book of Zephaniah (Zep 1:1). Though little is known about Zephaniah, it is possible that his ancestor Hezekiah is the same as the king by that name.
4. Father of Josiah in whose house Joshua was crowned as high priest (Zec 6:10-14).

ZEPHO
Eliphaz's son and a descendant of Esau (Gn 36:11, 15; 1 Chr 1:36).

ZEPHON
Firstborn son of Gad and the father of the Zephonite family (Gn 46:16; Nm 26:15).

ZERAH
1. One of the chiefs of the Edomites (Gn 36:17; 1 Chr 1:37), listed as the son of Reuel, Esau's son by his wife Basemath, and likely the ancestor of Jobab, who later assumed the position of king of the Edomites (Gn 36:13, 33).
2. One of the twin sons of Judah by his daughter-in-law Tamar (Gn 38:30; 46:12; Mt 1:3). Although Zerah thrust out his hand first, he retracted it, allowing his brother, Perez, to be born first. The descendants of Zerah (the Zerahites) became one of the most

influential clans of Judah (Nm 26:20; Jos 7:1, 18; 22:20; 1 Chr 2:4-6; 9:6). Because Ethan and Heman are listed as sons of Zerah in 1 Chronicles 2:6, the Ezrahites mentioned in 1 Kings 4:31 and the titles to Psalms 88 and 89 are also considered to be Zerahites. However, Ethan and Heman are listed as Levites in 1 Chronicles 15:17, thus making it more likely that the Ezrahites were a Levite clan.

3. One of the sons of Simeon from whom the Zerahite clan descended (Nm 26:13; 1 Chr 4:24); alternately called Zohar in Genesis 46:10 and Exodus 6:15.

4. One of the sons of Iddo, from the Gershonite branch of Levi's tribe (1 Chr 6:21).

5. One of the ancestors of Asaph from Levi's tribe, listed as the son of Adaiah and the father of Ethni (1 Chr 6:41). Several believe him to be the same individual as #4 above.

6. Commander of the Ethiopians (Cushites) who fought against Asa, king of Judah (2 Chr 14:9). It is difficult to identify this individual or the historical event with any certainty. The most common identification has been with Usarkon II of Egypt. The account of the battle agrees with the chronology of Usarkon's reign in Egypt, as do the number and nationalities of the troops involved in the conflict.

ZERAHIAH

1. Uzzi's son and ancestor of Ezra from the priestly line of Eleazar (1 Chr 6:6, 51; Ezr 7:4).

2. Father of Eliehoenai, who was head of a family who returned to Jerusalem with Ezra (Ezr 8:4).

ZERESH

Wife of Haman the Agagite who advised him to build the gallows for hanging Mordecai (Est 5:10, 14).

ZERETH

Asshur's son by his wife Helah from Judah's tribe (1 Chr 4:7).

ZERI

One of the sons of Jeduthun who prophesied with the lyre in thanksgiving to the Lord (1 Chr 25:3). He is likely the same person as Izri (v 11, NLT mg), a Temple musician and head of the 4th of the 24 divisions of priests for service as musicians in the sanctuary.

ZEROR

Benjaminite, Becorath's son, the father of Abiel, and an ancestor of King Saul (1 Sm 9:1).

ZERUAH

Mother of Israel's King Jeroboam I (1 Kgs 11:26).

QUICKTAKE

ZERUBBABEL

STRENGTHS AND ACCOMPLISHMENTS
- Led the first group of Jewish exiles back to Jerusalem from Babylon
- Completed the rebuilding of God's Temple
- Demonstrated wisdom in the help he accepted and refused
- Started his building project with worship as the focal point

WEAKNESSES AND MISTAKES
- Needed constant encouragement
- Allowed problems and resistance to stop the rebuilding work

LESSONS FROM HIS LIFE
- A leader needs to provide not only the initial motivation for a project but the continued encouragement necessary to keep the project going
- A leader must find his/her own dependable source of encouragement
- God's faithfulness is shown in the way he preserved David's line

VITAL STATISTICS
Where: Babylon, Jerusalem
Occupation: Recognized leader of the Exiles
Relatives: Father: Shealtiel. Grandfather: Jehoiachin
Contemporaries: Cyrus, Darius, Zechariah, Haggai

KEY VERSES
"Then he said to me, 'This is what the LORD says to Zerubbabel: It is not by force nor by strength, but by my Spirit, says the LORD of Heaven's Armies. Nothing, not even a mighty mountain, will stand in Zerubbabel's way; it will become a level plain before him! And when Zerubbabel sets the final stone of the Temple in place, the people will shout: "May God bless it! May God bless it!"'" (Zechariah 4:6, 7).

Zerubbabel's story is told in Ezra 2:2–5:2. He is also mentioned in 1 Chronicles 3:19; Nehemiah 7:7; 12:1, 47; Haggai 1:1, 12, 14; 2:4, 21, 23; Zechariah 4:6-10; Matthew 1:12, 13; Luke 3:27.

ZERUBBABEL
Babylonian-born Jew who returned to Palestine in 538 BC to serve as governor of Jerusalem under Persian rule. The name presumably means "seed [offspring] of Babylon," referring to someone born in Babylon.

The exact identity of Zerubbabel's biological father is uncertain. All biblical references except one mention Shealtiel as his father (Ezr 3:2, 8; 5:2; Neh 12:1; Hg 1:1, 12-14; 2:2, 23; Mt 1:12-13; Lk 3:27). This would make Zerubbabel the grandson of the Davidic king Jehoiachin. However, 1 Chronicles 3:19 identifies Pedaiah, the brother of Shealtiel, as Zerubbabel's father.

Two solutions have been proposed. Many scholars have assumed that Shealtiel died before fathering an heir. His brother, Pedaiah, would then have fathered Zerubbabel by Shealtiel's widow. Hence, Zerubbabel would have retained the name of Shealtiel rather than Pedaiah in accordance with the law of levirate marriage (Dt 25:5-10). This solution is weakened by its lack of textual support; similarly, the Chronicler would hardly have failed to state such an important piece of information if he had been desirous of "correcting" an error pertaining to Zerubbabel's parentage.

A simpler solution is obtained by reading the Septuagint text of 1 Chronicles 3:19, which lists Salathiel (Shealtiel) as the father of Zerubbabel. In this way, the single reference to 1 Chronicles may be harmonized with the other verses cited above.

In either case, whether Shealtiel or Pedaiah was Zerubbabel's biological father, it is clear that Zerubbabel was of Davidic lineage and was viewed by members of the Israelite community as a viable candidate for leading them back to a position of power.

Following the edict of Cyrus in 538 BC, Jews were permitted to return to Palestine and reclaim their former homeland. Zerubbabel was appointed governor, and probably by the decade of 529–520 had started work on the reconstruction of the Jerusalem Temple. However, because of several discouraging events, little was accomplished until the year 520 BC.

The writings of Haggai and Zechariah reveal much information about Zerubbabel's standing in the community. These two prophets evidently viewed Jeshua and Zerubbabel as the two men chosen by God for the task. Accordingly, in many of their oracles, support for one or both men is openly stated (e.g., Hg 2:21-23; Zec 3:8; 4:6-7; 6:12). The prophets viewed Jeshua and Zerubbabel's work as being messianic. This is most clearly seen in the vision of Zechariah (Zec 4:11-14). In the vision, two olive branches, one on either side of the lampstand, are identified as "the two anointed who stand by the Lord of the whole earth." As the context clearly shows, none other than Jeshua (or Joshua; named in 3:1-9) and Zerubbabel (named in 4:6-10) are meant. Because of his association with the rebuilding of the Temple in Jerusalem, Zerubbabel had been accorded a place of great honor in Jewish tradition.

Some hold that Zerubbabel was known to the Persians as Sheshbazzar. *See* Shesh-bazzar.

ZERUIAH

Nahash's daughter and the sister of Abigail (2 Sm 17:25). Zeruiah eventually bore three sons: Joab, Abishai, and Asahel, all of whom were David's friends during his reign (2 Sm 2:18; 3:39; 8:16; 18:2).

ZETHAM
One of Ladan's descendants, a Gershonite, in charge of the Temple treasuries (1 Chr 23:8; 26:22).

ZETHAN
Bilhan's son from Benjamin's tribe (1 Chr 7:10).

ZETHAR
One of King Ahasuerus's seven chamberlains, who was commanded to bring Queen Vashti before the king for public display of her beauty (Est 1:10).

ZIA
One of the clan leaders of Gad's tribe dwelling in Bashan (1 Chr 5:13).

ZIBA
Former servant of Saul whom David commissioned to find survivors of the house of Saul so that he might "show them kindness" (2 Sm 9:2-12). In the period following Saul's death, Ziba apparently had not only gained his freedom but had also become a successful landowner. This status was lost as a result of the discovery of Mephibosheth, Jonathan's crippled son. Ziba later became involved in a controversy with Mephibosheth concerning Mephibosheth's failure to accompany David when he fled during Absalom's rebellion (2 Sm 16:1-4; 19:17, 24-29). Most commentators have blamed Ziba with duplicity and slander in the affair, but the text allows no certain conclusion as to who was guilty. On Mephibosheth's behalf, it is unlikely that he would have believed that he could inherit the throne, as Ziba had claimed (2 Sm 16:3). Mephibosheth also seems to have been loyal to David (though it is possible that David brought him to Jerusalem to ensure that he would be under protective surveillance). In Ziba's defense, it is notable that David did believe without question that Mephibosheth might have had aspirations for the throne. Ziba also appears consistently as a loyal supporter of David in spite of the fact that David's decision had cost him his independent status (2 Sm 16:1; 19:17). Of course, Ziba's displeasure at his loss of independence might have motivated him to defame Mephibosheth. In any case, David appears to have had reason to doubt both versions of the truth. Rather than supporting either claim, he chose to divide the land between them (2 Sm 19:29).

ZIBEON
Ancestor of Oholibamah, the Canaanite wife of Esau (Gn 36:2, 14). He is listed as a Hivite in Genesis 36:2 but is probably the same as Zibeon the son of Seir the Horite (Gn 36:20, 29; 1 Chr 1:38). Possibly "Hivite" designated his tribal affiliation, while "Horite" indicated the fact that he dwelt in caves. It is also possible that "Hivite" is a transmission error in Genesis 36:2.

ZIBIA
One of the seven sons borne to Shaharaim by his wife Hodesh (1 Chr 8:9).

ZIBIAH

Mother of King Jehoash of Judah, from the town of Beersheba (2 Kgs 12:1; 2 Chr 24:1).

ZICRI

1. Kohathite Levite and a descendant of Izhar (Ex 6:21).

2. One of Shimei's sons from Benjamin's tribe (1 Chr 8:19).

3. One of Shashak's sons from Benjamin's tribe (1 Chr 8:23).

4. One of Jeroham's sons from Benjamin's tribe (1 Chr 8:27).

5. Ancestor of Mattaniah. Mattaniah returned with Zerubbabel to Israel following the Exile (1 Chr 9:15); Zicri is probably identifiable with Zabdi in Nehemiah 11:17.

6. Descendant of Eliezer, the son of Moses. His son, Shelomoth, was in charge of the treasuries of the dedicated gifts (1 Chr 26:25).

7. Father of Eliezer, the chief officer of the Reubenites during David's reign (1 Chr 27:16).

8. Father of Amasiah, a volunteer in charge of 200,000 men during Jehoshaphat's reign (2 Chr 17:16).

9. Father of Elishaphat, a participant in the conspiracy against Athaliah led by Jehoiada (2 Chr 23:1).

10. Mighty man of Ephraim who participated in Pekah's subjugation of Judah. Zicri killed Ahaz's son Maaseiah, Azrikam the commander of the palace, and Elkanah the king's deputy (2 Chr 28:7).

11. Father of Joel, overseer of the Benjaminites who returned to Jerusalem following the Exile (Neh 11:9).

12. Levite who served as a priest and the head of the clan of Abijah during the days of Joiakim the high priest (Neh 12:17).

ZIHA

1. Ancestor of a family of Temple servants who returned to Jerusalem with Zerubbabel after the Exile (Ezr 2:43; Neh 7:46).

2. Overseer of the Temple servants living at Ophel during the postexilic era (Neh 11:21). If Ziha is simply a family name, then this person is likely the same as #1 above.

ZILLAH

Second wife of Lamech and mother of Tubal-cain and Naamah (Gn 4:19-23).

ZILLETHAI

1. One of Shimei's sons from Benjamin's tribe (1 Chr 8:20).

2. One of the "chiefs of thousands" who deserted Saul and came to David at Ziklag (1 Chr 12:20).

ZILPAH

Mother of Jacob's sons Gad and Asher. Laban had given her to his daughter Leah as a hand-maid (Gn 29:24; 46:18). Later, at Leah's insistence, she became Jacob's concubine for the purpose of bearing sons (30:9; 37:2).

ZIMMAH

Gershonite Levite and ancestor of Joah (1 Chr 6:20); possibly the same Joah who assisted Hezekiah (2 Chr 29:12).

ZIMRAN

One of the sons of Abraham by Keturah (Gn 25:2; 1 Chr 1:32). Unlike the other sons of Abraham by Keturah, there is little evidence that Zimran is associated with a later tribal group.

ZIMRI

1. Clan chief of Simeon's tribe who was killed by Phinehas for consorting with a Midianite woman at Peor (Nm 25:14). Zimri's sin was magnified by the fact that he did it openly, that he was a leader within his tribe, and that the woman was the daughter of an important Midianite prince.

2. King of Israel for seven days (885 BC) following his assassination of Elah and the rest of the family of Baasha (1 Kgs 16:9-12). Zimri, commander of half of the chariot forces, failed to gain the support of the people, who supported Omri, the commander of the army. When Omri marched against Zimri at Tirzah, Zimri committed suicide by burning his palace down (16:15-18). The cruelty of Zimri's coup is reflected in Jezebel's later taunt against Jehu, when she compared his duplicity to that of Zimri (2 Kgs 9:31).

3. One of the sons of Zerah, the son of Judah by Tamar (1 Chr 2:6); alternately called Zabdi in the parallel passage in Joshua 7:1, 17. See Zabdi #1.

4. Descendant of Saul from Benjamin's tribe, listed as the son of Jehoaddah and the father of Moza (1 Chr 8:36). He is likely the same as Zimri the son of Jadah (9:42).

ZIPH

1. Descendant of Caleb from Judah's tribe (1 Chr 2:42).

2. One of the sons of Jehallelel from Judah's tribe (1 Chr 4:16).

ZIPHAH

Jehallelel's second son (or possibly daughter, since the form is feminine), listed in 1 Chronicles 4:16.

ZIPPOR

Father of the Moabite king Balak. Balak called on Balaam to curse Israel (Nm 22:2, 10, 16; 23:18; Jos 24:9; Jgs 11:25).

ZIPPORAH

Wife of Moses and mother of his sons Gershom and Eliezer (Ex 2:21). Though she is listed as the daughter of Reuel (v 18), Reuel was probably the father of Hobab (Nm 10:29; also called Jethro, Ex 3:1; 4:18), who in turn was the father of Zipporah. Zipporah circumcised Gershom to prevent Moses' death prior to his return to Egypt (Ex 4:25). Apparently at that point Zipporah and the children left Moses and went back to live with her father, returning later during the wilderness wanderings (18:2).

ZIZA

1. Chief of Simeon's tribe descending from Shemaiah (1 Chr 4:37).

2. Son of Rehoboam and Maacah (2 Chr 11:20).

3. Second of Shimei's sons and a clan chief within the Gershonite branch of Levi's tribe (1 Chr 23:11); perhaps the same as Zina in 1 Chronicles 23:10.

ZOBEBAH

One of the sons of Koz (or possibly a daughter, since the noun is feminine) from Judah's tribe (1 Chr 4:8). The genealogy is obscure.

ZOHAR

1. Father of Ephron the Hittite. Abraham bought the cave of Machpelah from Ephron (Gn 23:7-9; 25:9).

2. Alternate spelling of Zerah, Simeon's son, in Genesis 46:10 and Exodus 6:15. *See* Zerah #3.

3. Alternate spelling of Izhar in 1 Chronicles 4:7.

ZOHETH

Ishi's son from Judah's tribe (1 Chr 4:20).

ZOPHAH

Helem's son from Asher's tribe (1 Chr 7:35-36).

ZOPHAI

Alternate form of Zuph, one of Samuel's ancestors, in 1 Chronicles 6:26. *See* Zuph.

ZOPHAR

One of the "counselors" of Job who is listed as a Naamathite (Jb 2:11; 11:1; 20:1). He offers the most direct accusations against Job but later offers sacrifice for Job as commanded by the Lord (42:9).

ZUAR

Father of Nethanel, the leader of Issachar's tribe at the start of Israel's wilderness wanderings (Nm 1:8; 2:5; 7:18, 23; 10:15).

ZUPH

Ancestor of Elkanah, the father of the prophet Samuel (1 Sm 1:1). Zuph was a member of the Kohathite branch of Levites and is listed as the son of Elkanah (different than above) and the father of Toah (1 Chr 6:35). He is the same as Zophai listed in 1 Chronicles 6:26. It is evident that Zuph was a Levite, even though he is listed as an Ephraimite in the 1 Samuel passage.

ZUR

1. Midianite prince who was the father of Cozbi, the Midianite woman who was killed by Phinehas for consorting with Zimri after the incident at Baal-peor (Nm 25:15). He was one of the five "kings" of Midian who (with Balaam) were later killed by the Israelites (31:8). Apparently, he was a vassal of the Amorite king Sihon, since he is listed as one of his "princes" (Jos 13:21).

2. Son of Jeiel, the founder of Gibeon (1 Chr 8:30; 9:36). He was a Benjaminite and a distant relative of Saul.

ZURIEL

Son of Abihail and the head of the Merari family of Levites during the wilderness wanderings (Nm 3:35).

ZURISHADDAI

Father of Shelumiel, the leader of Simeon's tribe at the start of Israel's wilderness wanderings (Nm 1:6; 2:12; 7:36, 41; 10:19).

ALTERNATE SPELLINGS

Abi
See Abijah #4.

Abia
See Abijam; Abijah #6.

Abiah
See Abijah #1, #5.

Abigal
See Abigail #2.

Abishalom
See Absalom.

Achar
See Achan.

Achaz
See Ahaz #1.

Achbor
See Acbor.

Achim
See Akim.

Achsa, Achsah
See Acsah.

Ader
See Eder #1.

Adino
See Jashobeam #1.

Adoram
See Adoniram.

Ahasai
See Ahzai.

Ahohi
See Ahoah.

Aholah
See Oholah and Oholibah.

Aholiab
See Oholiab.

Aholibah
See Oholah and Oholibah.

Aholibamah
See Oholibamah #1, #2.

Ahuzam
See Ahuzzam.

Ajah
See Aiah #1.

Alameth
See Alemeth #1.

Aliah
See Alvah.

Alian
See Alvan.

Amashai
See Amashsai.

Aminadab
See Amminadab #1.

Amminadib
Recent translators have not regarded this term as a proper name and have translated along the lines of "the royal chariots of my people" (Song 6:12, NIV).

Amplias
See Ampliatus.

Antothijah
See Anthothijah.

Aphses
See Happizzez.

Arod
See Arodi.

Arpachshad
See Arphaxad.

Asahiah
See Asaiah #1.

Asareel
See Asarel.

Asharelah
See Asarelah.

Ashchenaz
See Ashkenaz.

Ashriel
See Asriel.

Ashur
See Ashhur.

Asnapper
See Ashurbanipal.

Assurbanipal
See Ashurbanipal.

Azarael
See Azarel #6.

Azareel
See Azarel #1–5.

Azur
See Azzur #2, #3.

Balac
See Balak.

Barachel
See Barakel.

Barachias
See Barachiah.

Bar-jona
See Simon Peter.

Barsabas
See Barsabbas.

Barsabas, Barsabbas
See Joseph #12; Judas #6.

Bashemath
See Basemath #1; Mahalath #1.

Basmath
See Basemath #3.

Bavvai
See Binnui #4.

Bazlith
See Bazluth.

Becher
See Beker.

Beeliada
See Eliada #1.

Belah
See Bela #2.

Ben
Levite musician (1 Chr 15:18, KJV). Modern versions omit this name based on textual evidence.

Berachiah
See Berekiah #2.

Berechiah
See Berekiah.

Berodach-baladan
See Merodach-baladan.

Bezaleel
See Bezalel.

Bichri
See Bicri.

Bigthan
See Bigthana.

Birzavith
See Birzaith.

Bocheru
See Bokeru.

Booz
See Boaz.

Bosor
See Beor #2.

Candace
See Kandake.

Careah
See Kareah.

Chalcol
See Calcol.

Chedorlaomer
See Kedorlaomer.

Chelal
See Kelal.

Chelluh
See Keluhi.

Chelub
See Kelub.

Chelubai
See Caleb #2.

Chemarim,
Chemarims
In the KJV this word
appears in Zephaniah
1:4 as a proper name.
The exact meaning of the
word is uncertain and
modern translations
render it "idolatrous
priests" (2 Kgs 23:5; Hos
10:5;
Zep 1:4).

Chenaanah
See Kenaanah.

Chenani
See Kenani.

Chenaniah
See Kenaniah.

Cheran
See Keran.

Chesed
See Kesed.

Chileab
See Kileab.

Chilion
See Kilion.

Chimham
See Kimham.

Chislon
See Kislon.

Chushan-rishathaim
See Cushan-rishathaim.

Cis
See Kish #1.

Cleophas
See Clopas.

Cononiah
See Conaniah #1.

Core
See Korah #3.

Coz
See Koz #1.

Cyrenius
See Quirinius.

Dalaiah
See Delaiah #1.

Dara
See Darda.

Dekar
See Ben-deker.

Diphath
See Riphath.

Dodavah
See Dodavahu.

Ebiasaph
See Abiasaph.

Eladah
See Eleadah.

Eliadah
See Eliada #2.

Eliah
See Elijah #2, #4.

Elias
See Elijah #1.

Elihoenai
See Eliehoenai #2.

Eliphalet
See Eliphelet #1.

Elisabeth
See Elizabeth.

Elmodam
See Elmadam.

Elpalet
See Eliphelet #3.

Emmanuel
See Immanuel.

Emmor
See Hamor.

Esaias
See Isaiah.

Esrom
See Hezron #2.

Euodias
See Euodia.

Ezar
See Ezer #1.

Ezekias
See Hezekiah #1.

Gashmu
See Geshem.

Gedeon
See Gideon.

Gispa
See Gishpa.

Habaiah
See Hobaiah.

Hadar
See Hadad #1, #3.

Hadarezer
See Hadadezer.

Hagaba
See Hagabah.

Haggeri
See Hagri.

Halohesh
See Hallohesh.

Hammelech
Hebrew word meaning
"the king," taken to be
a personal name by the
KJV (Jer 36:26; 38:6).

Hammolecheth
See Hammoleketh.

Hamran
See Hemdan.

Hamuel
See Hammuel.

Haniel
See Hanniel #2.

Hasenuah
See Hassenuah.

Hashabniah
See Hashabneiah.

Hashem
See Jashen.

Hashub
See Hasshub.

Hashupha
See Hasupha.

Hasrah
See Harhas.

Hatach
See Hathach.

Hazelelponi
See Hazzelelponi.

Hegai, Hege
Chamberlain of
Ahasuerus and keeper
of his harem when Esther
was chosen as queen
(Est 2:3).

Heglam
See Gera #4.

Heleb
See Heldai #1.

Hemam
See Heman #1.

Hen
See Josiah #2.

Henoch
See Enoch #2;
Hanoch #1.

Heth
Progenitor of the Hittite
people, name omitted
in favor of "Hittites"
in some versions (Gn
10:15; 1 Chr 1:13, NIV,
NLT).

Hezeki
See Hizki.

Hezrai
See Hezro.

Hiddai
See Hurai.

Hizkijah
See Hezekiah #3.

Hodaiah
See Hodaviah #1.

Hodevah
See Hodaviah #4.

Hodijah
See Hodiah.

Homam
See Heman #1.

Hothan
See Hotham #2.

Hozai
Term translated as "seers" rather than as a proper name in the NLT and other translations (2 Chr 33:18-19).

Huz
See Uz #2.

Huzzab
Obscure Hebrew word found only in Nahum 2:7 (KJV). Modern translations render it as "it is decreed," or as a reference to either Nineveh or an Assyrian queen rather than as a proper noun.

Igeal
See Igal #3.

Ilai
See Zalmon.

Iob
See Jashub #1.

Ishiah
See Isshiah #1.

Ishod
See Ishhod.

Ishuah
See Ishvah.

Ishuai
See Ishvi #1.

Ishui
See Ishvi #2.

Ismaiah
See Ishmaiah #1.

Ispah
See Ishpah.

Isshijah
See Ishijah.

Isuah
See Ishvah.

Isui
See Ishvi #1.

Ithra
See Jether #2.

Izehar
See Izhar #1.

Izri
See Zeri.

Jaalam
See Jalam.

Jaanai
See Janai.

Jaare-oregim
See Jair #3.

Jaasau
See Jaasu.

Jachan
See Jacan.

Jachin
See Jakin.

Jade
See Jada.

Jahaziah
See Jahzeiah.

Jahziel
See Jahzeel.

Jakan
See Jaakan.

Janohah
See Janoah #1.

Janum
See Janim.

Jarah
See Jadah.

Jareb
Term used by Hosea to designate an Assyrian king (Hos 5:13; 10:6). Many modern translations take the word as an adjective

rather than a proper name and render it "the great king."

Jaresiah
See Jaareshiah.

Jasiel
See Jaasiel #1.

Jeaterai
See Jeatherai.

Jeberechiah, Jeberekiah
See Jeberekiah.

Jecamiah
See Jekamiah #2.

Jecholiah
See Jecoliah.

Jechoniah
See Jehoiachin.

Jechonias
See Jehoiachin.

Jeconiah
See Jehoiachin.

Jeezer
See Abiezer #1.

Jehieli
See Jehiel #4.

Jehoadah, Jehoaddah
See Jadah.

Jehoaddan
See Jehoaddin.

Jehoshabeath
See Jehosheba.

Jehoshua, Jehoshuah
See Joshua #1.

Jehubbah
See Hubbah.

Jehudijah
Not a proper name; KJV mistranslation for "Jewish" (1 Chr 4:18).

Jehush
See Jeush #3.

Jeremias
See Jeremiah #1.

Jeremy
See Jeremiah #1.

Jerijah
See Jeriah.

Jerubbesheth
See Gideon.

Jerushah
See Jerusha.

Jesharelah
See Asarelah.

Jeshuah
See Jeshua #1.

Jesiah
See Isshiah #2, #3.

Jesui
See Ishvi #1.

Jeziah
See Izziah.

Jezliah
See Izliah.

Jezoar
See Izhar #2.

Jibsam
See Ibsam.

Jimna, Jimnah
See Imnah #1.

Joatham
See Jotham #2.

Jona
See John #1.

Jonan
See Jonam.

Jonas
See Jonah; John #1.

Jorkoam
See Jorkeam.

Josabad
See Jozabad #1.

Josaphat
See Jehoshaphat #1.

Jose
See Joshua #5.

Josedech
See Jehozadak.

Joses
See Barnabas; Joseph #7.

Josheb-basshebeth
See Jashobeam #1.

Josias
See Josiah #1.

Josibiah
See Joshibiah.

Jozachar
See Jozacar.

Jozadak
See Jehozadak.

Jucal
See Jehucal.

Juda
See Jude; Joda;
Judah #1, #8.

Kelubai
See Caleb #2.

Koheleth
*Hebrew title meaning
"the Preacher" or "the
Teacher"; not rendered
as a proper name in
the NLT.*

Laadan
See Ladan #1; Libni #1.

Lebana
See Lebanah.

Lebbaeus
See Thaddaeus, The
Apostle.

Lucas
See Luke.

Ludim
*Translated as a people
group ("Ludites")
rather than a proper
name in some modern
translations.*

Maachah
See Maacah.

Maadiah
See Moadiah.

Maasiai
See Maasai.

**Machbanai,
Machbannai**
See Macbannai.

Machi
See Maki.

Machir
See Makir.

Machnadebai
See Macnadebai.

Madian
See Midian.

Magor-missabib
See Pashhur #3.

Magus, Simon
See Simon #8.

Mahalah
See Mahlah #2.

Mahalaleel
See Mahalalel.

Mahali
See Mahli #1.

Malcham
See Malcam.

Malchiah
See Malkijah #1,
#2, #4, #6, #7, #8,
#9, #12.

Malchiel
See Malkiel.

Malchijah
See Malkijah.

Malchiram
See Malkiram.

Malchi-shua
See Malkishua.

Maleleel
See Mahalalel #1.

Malluchi
See Malluch.

Manasses
See Manasseh #1, #3.

Marcus
See Mark, John.

Mathusala
See Methuselah.

Mattathah
See Mattattah.

Mebunnai
See Sibbecai.

Melchi
See Melki.

Melchiah
See Malkijah #12.

Melchisedec
See Melchizedek.

Melchi-shua
See Malkishua.

Melicu
See Malluch #6.

Melzar
*Most modern trans-
lations render this
as a title rather than
a proper name (Dn
1:11, 16).*

Menan
See Menna.

Menuhoth
See Manahath.

Mesech
See Meshech #1.

Meshezabeel
See Meshezabel.

Methusael
See Methushael.

Miamin
See Mijamin #2, #4.

Micha
See Mica #1, #2, #3;
Micah #5.

Michah
See Micah #5.

Michaiah
See Maacah #4;
Mica #2; Micaiah #2,
#4, #6, #7.

Michri
See Micri.

Mirma
See Mirmah.

Mispereth
See Mispar.

Mizpar
See Mispar.

Naarai
See Paarai.

Naashon
See Nahshon.

Naasson
See Nahshon.

Nachor
See Nahor #1.

Nagge
See Naggai.

Naum
See Nahum #2.

Nebuchadrezzar
See Nebuchadnezzar.

Nebushasban
See Nebusha-ban.

Necho, Nechoh, Necoh
See Neco.

Nehum
See Rehum #1.

Nephish
See Naphish.

Nethaneel
See Nethanel.

Nicolaus
See Nicolas.

Niger
See Simeon #4.

Noe
See Noah #1.

Non
See Nun.

Ochran
See Ocran.

Ornan
See Araunah.

Oshea
See Joshua #1.

Osnapper
See Ashurbanipal.

Ozias
See Uzziah #1.

Pashur
See Pashhur.

Perida
See Peruda.

Peullathai
See Peullethai.

Phalec
See Peleg.

Phallu
See Pallu.

Phalti
See Palti #2.

Phaltiel
See Palti #2.

**Pharaoh Necho,
Pharaoh Nechoh,
Pharaoh Necoh**
See Neco.

Phares, Pharez
See Perez.

Pharosh
See Parosh.

Phaseah
See Paseah #2.

Phebe
See Phoebe.

Phichol
See Phicol.

Phurah
See Purah.

Phut
See Put.

Phuvah
See Puah.

Phygellus
See Phygelus.

Pileha
See Pilha.

Pispa
See Pispah.

Pochereth of Zebaim
See Pokereth-hazzebaim.

Pochereth-hazzebaim
See Pokereth-
hazzebaim.

Prisca
See Priscilla and Aquila.

Prochorus
See Procorus.

Pua
See Puah.

Puvah
See Puah #3.

Qoheleth
*Hebrew title meaning
"the Preacher" or "the
Teacher"; not rendered
as a proper name in
the NLT.*

Raama
See Raamah.

Raamiah
See Reelaiah.

Rabshakeh
*Name or title designat-
ing a high Assyrian
official and translated
as field commander"
in some modern
versions (2 Kgs 18:17-37;
19:4, 8; Is 36:2-22;
37:4, 8).*

Rachab
See Rahab.

Ragau
See Reu.

Raguel
See Jethro.

Rahel
See Rachel.

Ramoth
See Jeremoth #8.

Raphah
See Rephaiah #4.

Reaia
See Reaiah #2.

Rebecca
See Rebekah.

Rezia
See Rizia.

Roboam
See Rehoboam.

Sabta
See Sabtah.

Sachar
See Sacar.

Sachia, Sachiah
See Sakia.

Sadoc
See Zadok #9.

Sala
See Salmon; Shelah #1.

Salah
See Shelah #1.

Salathiel
See Shealtiel.

Samgar-nebo
*Rendered some modern
versions as a location
("Samgar") rather
than a proper name
(Jer 39:3).*

Sara
See Sarah #1.

Sarsechim, Sarsekim
See Nebo-sarsekim.

Saruch
See Serug.

Sem
See Shem.

Semachiah
See Semakiah.

Semei
See Semein.

Senuah
See Hassenuah.

Shachia
See Sakia.

Shallun
See Shallum #13.

Shamariah
See Shemariah #2.

Shamed
See Shemed.

Shamer
See Shemer #2, #3.

Shamhuth
See Shammah #4.

Shamlai
See Shalmai.

Shammoth
See Shammah #4.

Shavsha
See Seraiah #1.

Shechaniah
See Shecaniah.

Shemidah
See Shemida.

Shenazar
See Shenazzar.

Shephathiah
See Shephatiah #2.

Shephi
See Shepho.

Shephupham
See Shupham.

Sherah
See Sheerah.

Shethar-boznai
See Shether-bozenai.

Shimeah
See Shammah #2;
Shimeam.

Shimhi
See Shema #3.

Shimi
See Shimei #1.

Shimma
See Shammah #2.

Shimrith
See Shomer #1.

Shophach
See Shobach.

Sia
See Siaha.

Sibbechai
See Sibbecai.

Silvanus
See Silas.

Simon magus
See Simon #8.

Simon of Cyrene
See Simon #4.

Simon the Canaanite
See Simon #5.

Simon the Cananaean
See Simon #5.

Simon Zelotes
See Simon #5.

Simri
See Shimri #3.

Sippai
See Saph.

Sisamai
See Sismai.

Socho
See Soco.

Sophereth
See Hassophereth.

Symeon
See Simeon #4.

Tabaliah
See Tebaliah.

Tabeal
See Tabeel.

Tabrimon
See Tabrimmon.

Tamah
See Temah.

Tarea
See Tahrea.

Thahash
See Tahash.

Thamah
See Temah.

Thamar
See Tamar #1.

Thara
See Terah.

Tikvath
See Tikvah #1.

Tilgath-pilneser
See Tiglath-pileser.

Timeus
See Timaeus.

Timotheus
See Timothy.

Tokhath
See Tikvah #1.

Tryphaena
See Tryphena.

Tou
See Toi.

Ucal
Possibly a disciple of Agur (cf. Prv 30:1; see NLT mg), but also translated as "worn out."

Unno
See Unni.

Urias
See Uriah #1.

Urijah
See Uriah #2–4, 6.

Vajezatha
See Vaizatha.

Vashni
See Joel #2.

Zabbud
See Zaccur #5.

Zacchur
See Zaccur #2.

Zachariah
See Zechariah #1, #2.

Zacharias
See Zechariah #14, #31, #32.

Zacher
See Zechariah #5.

Zara, Zarah
See Zerah #2.

Zatthu
See Zattu #2.

Zavan
See Zaavan.

Zebudah
See Zebidah.

Zecher, Zeker
See Zechariah #5.

Zelotes
See Simon #5.

Zichri
See Zicri.

Zidkijah
See Zedekiah #4.

Zilthai
See Zillethai #1, #2.

Zina
See Ziza.

Zithri
See Sithri.

Zorobabel
See Zerubbabel.

Books in The Complete Book Popular Reference Series

The Complete Book of Bible Trivia contains more than 4,500 questions and answers about the Bible.

The Complete Book of Christian Heroes is an in-depth popular reference about those who have suffered for the cause of Christ throughout the world.

The Complete Book of When and Where in the Bible and throughout History focuses on more than 1,000 dates that illustrate how God has worked throughout history to do extraordinary things through ordinary people.

The Complete Book of Zingers is an alphabetized collection of one-sentence sermons.

The Complete Book of Who's Who in the Bible is your ultimate resource for learning about the people of the Bible.

The Complete Book of Bible Basics identifies and defines the names, phrases, events, stories, and terms from the Bible and church history that are familiar to most Christians.

In **The Complete Book of Bible Secrets and Mysteries** Stephen Lang, an expert on the Bible, serves up secrets and mysteries of the Bible in a fun, entertaining way.

The Complete Book of Bible Trivia: Bad Guys Edition, an extension of Stephen Lang's best-selling book *The Complete Book of Bible Trivia,* focuses on facts about the "bad guys" in the Bible.

The Complete Book of Hymns is the largest collection of behind-the-scenes stories about the most popular hymns and praise songs.

The Complete Book of Wacky Wit is filled with more than 1,500 humorous sayings to live by.